KV-423-752

INDUSTRIAL LAW IN SCOTLAND

by

ISAAC P. MILLER

B.L., Ph.D. (Glas.), LL.B. (Lond.)

*Solicitor in the Supreme Courts of Scotland, Professor of Law in the
University of Strathclyde*

Labor omnia vincit

Published under the auspices of
THE SCOTTISH UNIVERSITIES LAW INSTITUTE

EDINBURGH
W. GREEN & SON LTD.
1970

First published in 1970

© 1970. The Scottish Universities Law Institute

SBN 414 00511 2

Printed in Great Britain by
The Eastern Press Ltd., London and Reading

INDUSTRIAL LAW IN SCOTLAND

To My Parents
DAVID and AGNES MILLER

PREFACE

No textbook dealing with the law of employment has appeared in Scotland within a period of approximately seventy years. Since the days of Lord Fraser and Francis Umpherston the subject has grown enormously. No longer is it just another branch of contract, labelled "master and servant" (with that fine Victorian appreciation of the importance of the class structure in Great Britain). Industrial law is now a subject in its own right, spanning the subjects of contract, delict, trusts, property, criminal law, trade union law and industrial relations.

I have attempted, therefore, in this book to present the subject from the standpoint of Scots law and in a composite fashion. Essentially, I have drawn upon Scottish cases and materials, including applications before the Industrial Tribunals in Scotland, but where there has proved to be a paucity of Scottish authority I have relied upon any helpful English authority. However, I have not attempted to adopt a comparative approach—which I consider to be outwith my terms of reference. Where good specialised books on particular topics of law are readily available I have made appropriate references to these (e.g., factory law, merchant shipping, contract, delict, etc.) rather than throw the text out of balance by making long excursions into well-defined areas. I have tried to select cases with care so as to illustrate important points of principle, but, at the same time, I have felt it necessary in dealing with statutory law on particular topics to illustrate the court's interpretation of words and phrases and, in applications before the Industrial Tribunals, to illustrate the approach taken by a particular tribunal. It must be accepted that the jurisdiction of administrative tribunals is more likely to be extended than restricted. I have certainly not attempted to produce an exhaustive league table of cases—an exercise which I regard as meaningless.

I am indebted to Professor D. M. Walker of Glasgow University, who read the completed typescript and who made some useful suggestions for improvement, and to Professor D. J. Robertson, also of Glasgow University, for a most useful discussion on wages councils. I am also indebted to Professor T. B. Smith, Director of the Scottish Universities Law Institute, for his constant help and encouragement and to Dr. G. R. Thomson of W. Green & Son Ltd., for his expert guidance on all matters of publication. My thanks are also due to my former secretary Miss Erica M. Wilde, M.A., who typed a large proportion of the manuscript, and to the Carnegie Trust for the Universities of

Scotland whose generosity to the Law Institute enabled the remainder of the manuscript to be typed elsewhere. My special thanks are due to my colleague Ian S. Dickinson, M.A., LL.B., who undertook the laborious and exacting task of preparing the Tables of Cases and of Statutes, and to the staff of The Eastern Press Ltd. for their skill and craftsmanship in printing this volume. Lastly, but by no means least in importance, I must mention the tolerance, patience and infinite understanding of my wife during those years when this book was progressing along the assembly line.

I have tried to state the law, as I understood it to be, as at June 1, 1969, but the opportunity has been taken to note, in the text where possible or in appendices to the volume, changes in case law and new legislation reaching the Statute Book down to the end of October 1969.

ISAAC P. MILLER.

Department of Law,
University of Strathclyde,
Glasgow.

TABLE OF CONTENTS

PART III

DISSOLUTION OF THE RELATIONSHIP OF EMPLOYER AND EMPLOYEE

PART IV

TABLE OF CASES

TABLE OF STATUTES

xli

FORMATION OF THE RELATIONSHIP OF EMPLOYER AND EMPLOYEE

Part 1

FORMATION OF THE RELATIONSHIP OF
EMPLOYER AND EMPLOYEE

CHAPTER 1

DEFINITIONS

IT would seem that the term " Industrial Law " is peculiar to the United Kingdom. This term is, of course, relatively modern in its usage and dates approximately from the end of the First World War. The old Scottish textbooks—Fraser and Umpherston—used the nomenclature " Master and Servant " for the employment relationship. Even the bench today—in both Scotland and England—tend to prefer the older phraseology. Throughout this work the terms " employer " and " employee " will be used when discussing the contract of employment and the rights, duties, obligations and remedies arising therefrom. The term " Industrial Law " is used throughout this book to mean the whole field of employment. It is noticeable that recent writers in this field have preferred to use the phrase " The Law of Employment." The most notable example is, of course, G. H. L. Fridman.[1] So far as Scotland is concerned there is a solitary chapter[2] on the " law of employment " in Professor J. J. Gow's major textbook published in 1964[3] which is somewhat grandiosely titled *The Mercantile and Industrial Law of Scotland.* The mercantile law section (some 700 pages) is excellent. The balance, amounting to some 57 pages or so, is well written but could not possibly do justice to the whole field of employment.

The subject-matter, as has been indicated above, is basically the law of employer and employee, *i.e.,* the whole field of the law of employment. The term has a wider meaning which may also include industrial property —such as patents, trademarks and copyright, as well as agreements relating to " know-how " and property in inventions. Monopolies and restrictive practices also fall within the ambit of mercantile law but they also have an important part to play within the field of industrial law, particularly in relation to the trade unions.

In the United States of America and in certain continental countries what we understand by the term " Industrial Law " is generally called " Labour Law." It may be more accurate to say that the latter terminology is in a sense restricted to the field of " industrial relations," *i.e.,* to collective bargaining and collective agreements and the legal functions and powers of trade unions together with private and governmental machinery for the settlement of industrial or labour disputes. This latter interpretation of the subject is taken by the legal profession and by labour relations experts in the United States of America. Unfortunately

---

[1] *The Modern Law of Employment* (Stevens, 1963).
[2] Number 15.
[3] By W. Green & Son Ltd., Edinburgh (1964).

the appellation " labour " has a strong political connotation peculiar to the British way of life and it would probably take some years before the term " labour law " would be generally acceptable in Britain. Some of the British universities—unashamedly borrowing from America—are already adopting the term " labour law " for certain of their courses of study or for special study groups.[4]

If the American view, mentioned in the previous paragraph, is generally adopted, it will be appreciated that the common law and statutory law relating to the contract of employment and to the employment relationship in general may have to be dealt with in two ways, *viz.*: (a) under the heading of " contract " as regards the formation, termination and rights and remedies arising out of the contractual agreement and the breach thereof; and (b) under the heading of " delict," so far as regards the employer's liability to his own employees and to third parties, the employee's own liability and the rights and remedies of both employer and employee against third parties. This disjointed treatment or fragmentation of the whole field of industrial law would be unsatisfactory, and would indeed be a retrograde step—a turning-back of the time-clock. For that reason, the writer has attempted to deal with the whole relevant field under the main heading of Industrial Law, although he willingly admits that " industrial law " is not fully accepted by practitioners, even at this stage, as an independent and definitive branch of Scottish law. The subject overlaps contract, delict, property law (including trusts) and criminal law; and its true sources are in common law and statute law, with custom (on occasion) playing quite an important part. Nevertheless, it is submitted that the field of study is so clearly identifiable and so important and far-reaching—indeed affecting millions of persons within the United Kingdom—in its modern legislative developments that it is perfectly proper to study it as a separate subject, which is gradually attracting its own specialised literature.[5]

The principal stages in the historical development of the present employer and employee relationship seem to be as follows: (a) the early period of slavery, or a relationship akin to slavery [6]; (b) the period of serfdom or vassalage, most significant during the Middle Ages; (c) the Gild System of the later Middle Ages; and (d) finally, the " laissez-faire " or freedom of contract approach of the eighteenth century, moving into the early restrictions of the later Industrial Revolution period and eventually into the statutory controls of the twentieth century.[7]

---

4 See, for example, " Workshop on Labour Law," held under the auspices of the Institute of Advanced Legal Studies (London University) at L.S.E. from July 10–15, 1967; and the recent Casebook by Professor K. W. Wedderburn, published in the Cambridge University Press casebook series.

5 See, in particular, the *Biographical Guide to United Kingdom Law* (Institute of Advanced Legal Studies); London (1956), especially at Chap. IX.

6 See the interesting article " Early Labour Law in Scotland " by the late Sheriff J. R. Philip in (1934) 46 *Juridical Review* 121 *et seq.*

7 See the survey " Industrial Law (1885–1935) " by Professor W. A. Robson in 51 L.Q.R. 195 *et seq.*

Some writers have taken the view that the relationship of employer and employee was fundamentally changed during the last quarter of the nineteenth century. It is said that, since then, the employee can no longer generally exercise a free will by entering into an individual contract of service with an employer; and perhaps this freedom to bargain personally is nowadays only truly existent in the exceptional case of the very highly skilled technical or scientific senior employee. All ordinary employees are really to be regarded as members of a group—and the terms and conditions of employment of that group have largely superseded the old common law individual bargaining between employer and employee. This fundamental change has been brought about mainly by: (a) the rise of the trade unions and the growth of collective bargaining as a means of negotiating terms and conditions of employment; the power of the organisation behind the employees has become one of the most important factors of modern industrial life; and (b) the use of legislation to improve the economic and social position of employees generally— for example, in relation to safety, health, welfare, hours of work, wages, industrial injury benefits, health insurance and others. Statutory terms and conditions may be and often are mandatory, so that any purported variation of these terms and conditions by an ordinary contract of service would be quite ineffectual and invalid.

The term " employer," when used throughout this volume, will be applied to the person who is engaging or wishes to engage or has engaged labour to assist him in the efficient running and conduct of his business. The labour so engaged may be employees whose employment is regulated by a contract of service with the employer (*i.e.*, the true employer and employee relationship is in being) or independent contractors or agents. These two latter classes are not " employees " in the true sense of being persons employed under a contract of service.

The term " employee " will be applied accordingly to a person who is taken on under a contract of service (irrespective of whether a written contract exists or not) and who is part of his employer's business and organisation. The employer will have the right to " hire and fire " such employees (as indeed he can do with other persons engaged by him, whether true employees or not), but most importantly, he (the employer) will have the right to control the employees in the manner in which they perform their duties. The old concepts and definitions of " workmen," in the sense of manual labourers, are changing with the modern developments of industrial law and, therefore, unless specifically meant or explained otherwise, the term " employee " will relate to the blue-collar workers and the white-collar workers. It will be necessary, however, to keep in mind that certain of the older statutes, and other more recent ones, will apply only to " workmen " in the sense of those engaged in manual labour.

Difficulties very often arise in distinguishing the employer and employee relationship from other relationships which closely resemble it. Some of these comparable relationships are examined and distinguished in a later chapter.[8] The doctrine or concept of "control," mentioned above, has also given rise to considerable debate, discussion and argument. This matter is again separately dealt with hereafter.[9]

[8] *Infra*, Chap. 4.
[9] *Infra*, Chap. 3.

CHAPTER 2

THE RELATIONSHIP OF EMPLOYER AND EMPLOYEE

THE contract of service is a species of the contract of *locatio conductio* of Civil (or Roman) Law, in its two well-known forms, *viz.*: (a) *locatio operis faciendi*, *i.e.*, the hiring of a person to do a particular task or piece of work; and (b) *locatio operarum*, *i.e.*, the hiring of a person's services, to act in a particular capacity without reference to any specific business.[1] It is mainly with the second form that we are concerned throughout the whole of this volume.

The distinction between the modern employee and the old-fashioned slave cannot be defined easily or explained satisfactorily. A most important point might arise, for example, upon the legality or otherwise of a contract for a long term of years, particularly if harsh or intolerable conditions were sought to be imposed therein. Old Scottish legal opinion took the view that " the state of slavery is not recognised by the laws of this Kingdom, and is inconsistent with the principles thereof " and " perpetual service, without wages, is slavery." [2] On the latter point, it seems to be mostly agreed that the mere obligation of perpetual service is not slavery.

Lord Stair says [3] " servants (slaves) being wholly their master's, they could have nothing of their own, so that their peculium, which their masters committed to them to negotiate with, was wholly in their master's power, and might be taken away at his pleasure; neither could they be liable to any obligation; neither could there be any civil action for or against them; . . . they were accounted as nobody, or as dead men." Accordingly, the master not only acquired a right to the fruits of the labour of his slave, but he became the legal owner, body and soul, of a human being whom the law counted as a chattel. An example of this continuing attitude in early Scots law may be found in the position of workmen in the coal and salt mines.[4]

According to modern law, however, the definition of an employee (or servant) is a person who ultroneously agrees to give his services to another

[1] See Fraser, *Master and Servant*, 3rd ed. (1882), p. 1; *Brenan* v. *Campbell's Trs.* (1898) 25 R. 423; *Scottish Insurance Commissioners* v. *Church of Scotland*, 1914 S.C. 16; *Stagecraft Ltd.* v. *Minister of National Insurance*, 1952 S.C. 288 (*per* Lord Patrick at p. 302; also opinions of the Lord Justice-Clerk and Lord Jamieson). As for English law, see *Yewens* v. *Noakes* (1880) 6 Q.B.D. 530, C.A., *per* Lord Bramwell at pp. 532–533; and *A.E.U.* v. *Minister of Pensions and National Insurance* [1963] 1 W.L.R. 441.
[2] See *Knight* v. *Wedderburn* (1778) M. 14545.
[3] *Institutions*, I, 2, 9.
[4] The restriction on workmen in coal and salt mines (colliers and salters), who were transferable to a purchaser of the mine, and subject to prosecution if they quitted their employment, was finally abolished in 1799 (39 Geo. 3, c. 56). See T. B. Smith in *Stair Society Series*, Vol. 20, Chap. XII; also " Early Labour Law in Scotland " by the late J. R. Philip in (1934) 46 *Juridical Review* 121–132.

person for a determinate time and for an ascertained hire [5] and who may get rid of the contract by paying damages.

To a certain limited extent, a contract of service could, in older Scots law, be specifically enforced. A workman refusing to enter upon his service, or deserting it after entry, could be sentenced to imprisonment, but this statutory enforcement was repealed by subsequent legislation.[6] Nowadays no contract of service would ever be enforced specifically; the correct remedy is to seek an award of damages.

It is arguable that the law still allows a person to enter into a contract of service for a long term of years, say twenty or thirty, or even for life. This theory is doubted by some writers. The question of whether a contract to serve for life is a *pactum illicitum* is unsettled in Scotland— see *Mulcahy* v. *Herbert*.[7] Bankton says [8] that slavery is so much discountenanced that, even by agreement, one cannot become bound to serve another for life. He bases his opinion upon the old authority of *Allan and Mearns* v. *Skene*.[9] Later writers have not agreed with him, particularly Erskine.[10] In England,[11] and as late as 1837, the court held that a contract to serve for life was not illegal. The modern view would tend to favour freedom of movement, so that the court would be against the imposition of restrictions which were too rigid and dictatorial. Such purported restrictions might be regarded today as being against equity and reasonable conduct. Each case would require to be looked at carefully upon its own facts and circumstances. In the recent case of *Cook* v. *Grubb* [12] the phrase " permanent employment " was considered by the Second Division of the Court of Session (upon a reclaiming motion from an interlocutor of Lord President Clyde) and, in view of an amendment made prior to the hearing, it was held that a sufficiently specific meaning could be attached to the phrase quoted above so as to give the contract a *terminus ad quem*. The legal interpretation of the said phrase which arose for consideration in *Cook's* case is not quite the same thing as the contract to " serve for life," upon the legality (or otherwise) of which there is no firm decision in Scotland.

The essential components of the employer and employee relationship are as follows: (i) services given by the employee to his employer; (ii) a period of service during which the contractual relationship is to exist; and (iii) remuneration, given by the employer to his employee in return for the services rendered by the latter. Each of these components may be considered briefly at this stage.

(i) *Services.* The particular capacity in which the employee is engaged

[5] Erskine, I, 7, 62.
[6] See Fraser, *op. cit.*, Part III, Chap. i.
[7] (1898) 25 R. 1136.
[8] Bankton, 1, 2, 83.
[9] (1728) M. 9454.
[10] *Loc. cit.*
[11] *Wallis* v. *Day* (1837) 2 M. & W. 272.
[12] 1963 S.L.T. 78 (*per* Grant L.J.C. at pp. 83 and 84). The earlier report in 1961 S.L.T. 405 (O.H.) is interesting as it shows that the Lord President (Clyde) took the view that the phrase " permanent employment " was too vague and indefinite.

is generally a sufficient indication of the services to be rendered by him. If a claim is made for services outwith the scope of the contract, it has been laid down [13] that there must be specification of three things: (a) of the duties of the office for which X was originally engaged; (b) of the extra duties performed by him; and (c) of the agreement to give remuneration for these extra duties or services.

(ii) *Period of service.* If this is fixed by the contract, then the parties are bound by its terms. If no period is fixed, the law will presume the period from (a) the relation of the parties, (b) the circumstances of the case and (c) the custom of the district as applied to that kind of service. There is no fixed general rule of law in Scotland, as there is in England, that a contract of " general hiring " lasts for a year.

An agreement to give regular employment does not bind the employer to keep the employee for as long as the latter is willing and able to work —see *Lawrie* v. *Brown & Co.*[14] Moreover, an arrangement that the employee shall be paid so much per week, month or year does not by itself decide that the period of engagement is a week, month or year accordingly.[15] Menial or domestic servants, especially in towns, are usually presumed to be hired for six months.[16] Farm servants are presumed to be hired for a year; gardeners also—but there seems to be no direct decision on this point. Coachmen were in the same position as other domestic servants [17]; presumably, the later modern equivalent of chauffeur is in exactly the same position as the old class of coachman, although the situation might be different where a chauffeur was also a qualified mechanic responsible for maintenance of vehicles. In such a case, the presumption as to an engagement period of six months might not apply at all, as it is now extremely doubtful where the classification of " domestic servant " or quasi-domestic servant truly applies. Gamekeepers who have been provided with a house are presumed to be engaged for a period of one year.[18]

Tutors and governesses are usually presumed to be hired during the pleasure of the employer and their contracts of service may be terminated upon reasonable notice; but special circumstances may be proved to show that the contract was for a longer term.[19] Teachers, appointed by an education authority, hold their office at the pleasure of the authority, but in dismissing a teacher the statutory procedures contained in the

---

[13] See particularly *Latham* v. *Edinburgh and Glasgow Ry.* (1886) 4 M. 1084, *per* Lord President (M'Neill) at p. 1087; see also *Money* v. *Hannan and Kerr* (1867) 5 S.L.R. 32; and *Mackison* v. *Magistrates of Dundee,* 1910 S.C.(H.L.) 27; *Mackenzie* v. *Baird's Trs.,* 1907 S.C. 838; and *Mellor* v. *Beardmore,* 1927 S.C. 597.
[14] 1908 S.C. 705.
[15] See *Baird* v. *Don* (1799) Mor. 9182; 5 Bro.Supp. 514; also *Groom* v. *Clark* (1859) 21 D. 831; *Forsyth* v. *Heathery Knowe Coal Co.* (1880) 7 R. 887; and *Todd* v. *Arrol* (1881) 18 S.L.R. 673; but see *Dowling* v. *Henderson* (1890) 17 R. 921.
[16] Bell's *Principles,* s. 174.
[17] *Scott* v. *McMurdo* (1869) 6 S.L.R. 301.
[18] See *Armstrong* v. *Bainbridge* (1846) 9 D. 29 and 1198; also *Cameron* v. *Fletcher* (1872) 10 M. 301; whilst farm grieves also are presumed to be hired for a year—see *Muir* v. *Mackenzie* (1829) 7 S. 717.
[19] Bell's *Principles,* s. 174; and *Moffat* v. *Shedden* (1839) 1 D. 468.

various Education (Scotland) Acts and other relevant legislation must be followed. Schoolmasters, employed in private schools, on the other hand, in the absence of any contrary stipulation, hold office at the pleasure of the school's managers or governors.[20]

Tacit relocation may apply to renew an agreement in all its parts from term to term.[21]

(iii) *Remuneration.* This is usually fixed at the time the contract is entered into by the parties. If nothing is said about wages, these are still due and the court will fix what, in the circumstances, is a fair remuneration.

Another test which is adopted and applied to decide whether or not the relationship of employer and employee exists is that of the so-called doctrine or principle of "control," which has been referred to in the immediately preceding chapter. In more modern times, it is becoming more fashionable to rely upon the so-called "organisation" test which is thought to be more in line with modern thinking upon the functions and techniques of management. This matter is so important that it requires more lengthy examination and accordingly the immediately following chapter has been devoted to it. The relationship of employer and employee must also be compared with certain other relationships which bear a close resemblance to it but which, nevertheless, have certain important distinguishing features about them. This comparison is accordingly attempted in a later chapter.[22]

The question as to whether the true relationship is that of employer and employee is essentially a question of fact in the particular circumstances. The intention of parties to create that relationship is the primary concern of the court and, in reaching a decision, it will look for an express agreement which is clear evidence of that intention. Failing the existence of an express agreement, the court will look at the intention of parties from their conduct towards each other, from which it may deduce the implied creation of a contract of service.[23] Where the question of delictual liability of an employer is being considered by the court—and the doctrine of vicarious liability is being applied—it will be seen that it may not even be necessary for the court to look at the intention of the parties. Instead, the court may look strictly at the factual circumstances and decide for itself, upon these facts, in what capacity the particular employee did the particular wrongful act about which the pursuer is complaining Was X acting at the time as an employee or was he doing something on his own behalf, quite independent from his employment ? The answers to these questions are, as we shall see later, most important, because upon them depends the delictual liability or non-liability of the employer.

---

[20] Bell, *op. cit.,* s. 2189.
[21] *Ibid.* s. 173; and *Baird* v. *Don, cit. supra*; also *Tait* v. *Macintosh* (1841) 16 F.C. 658; and *Morrison* v. *Allardyce* (1823) 2 S. 434.
[22] Chap. 4, *infra.*
[23] See particularly *Short* v. *J. W. Henderson Ltd.*, 1946 S.C.(H.L.) 24.

CHAPTER 3

THE ELEMENT OF CONTROL

As was indicated in the preceding chapter, the general test or rule which
has been established for some time in the common law of Scotland and
England, as proving the existence of the relationship of employer and
employee, has been that of " direction and control." Mr. Umpherston,
writing in the year 1904, states [1] that " It must now be taken as quite
settled that the decisive element in determining the question of liability
is the right of control over the servant in the performance of his duties."
In support of that view he cites [2] several of the older well-known cases, [3]
including *Cairns* v. *Clyde Navigation Trs.*[4] as well as the well-known
English case of *Donovan* v. *Laing Construction Syndicate*, [5] to which
reference is again made when the topic of vicarious liability is examined
in detail. One of the earlier leading cases in Scotland on the question of
deciding liability for independent contractors and employees was that of
Stephen v. *Thurso Police Commissioners*, [6] and particularly the opinion
of Lord Gifford who said " The test always is, had the superior personal
control or power over the acting or mode of acting of the subordinate ? ...
Was there a control or direction of the person, in opposition to a mere
right to object to the quality or description of the work done ? ... It is
sometimes said the question is, whether the relation between the immediate
wrongdoer and the defender is that of master and servant or employer and
contractor. But these words are a little ambiguous; and though they may
indicate generally the rule of law, the real question always is, I think,
Who had the control and direction of the person who did the wrong ? "

The Scottish authority most often quoted in support of the control
test is the speech of Lord Kinnear in *Scottish Insurance Commissioners* v.
Church of Scotland, [7] in the course of which he said, " The relation of
master and servant exists only between persons of whom one has the
order and control of the work done by the other ... a servant is a person
subject to the command of his master as to the manner in which he shall
do his work. ... In a contract by which one undertakes to produce a
given result, but so that in the actual execution of the work he is not

---

[1] *Master and Servant*, p. 216.
[2] *Loc. cit.*, n. 4.
[3] For example, *Connelly* v. *Clyde Navigation Trs.*, (1902) 5 F. 8.
[4] (1898) 25 R. 1021.
[5] [1893] 1 Q.B. 629.
[6] (1876) 3 R. 535 (at p. 542).
[7] 1914 S.C. 16 at p. 23. See also *Scottish Insurance Commissioners* v. *McNaughton*,
1914 S.C. 826; *Scottish Insurance Commissioners* v. *Edinburgh Infirmary*, 1913 S.C. 751;
and *Ainslie* v. *Leith Dock Commissioners*, 1919 S.C. 676; see also *Stephen* v. *Thurso
Police Commissioners*, *cit. supra*; and *Sweeney* v. *Duncan* (1892) 19 R. 870.

11

under the direction of the person for whom it is done but may use his own discretion in things which are not specifically fixed by the contract itself the relation of master and servant does not exist." The second type of contract to which his lordship was referring was generally that involving the independent contractor, although it could equally well have been the contract of agency. The agency contract is not quite so clear-cut and identifiable as that of the independent contractor because it very often happens that a person may be both agent and employee at the same time. It is true to say, however, that most agents as such are seldom, if ever, employees; whilst most employees have, at some time or another, to assume and do assume the duties and responsibilities of agents. Yet it is also fair to say that an agent (who is unaffected by an ordinary type of service contract) is very often an independent contractor, although he need not necessarily be so, if, for example, he is working exclusively for a fixed principal.

Lord Denning (Denning L.J. as he then was) said in *Stevenson, Jordan and Harrison Ltd.* v. *Macdonald* [8] " . . . under a contract of service, a man is employed as part of the business and his work is done as an integral part of the business; whereas, under a contract for services, his work, although done for the business, is not integrated into it but is only accessory to it." The " business " about which his lordship was talking is, of course, the employer's business. Older English authority upon the " control " test may be found in the cases of *R.* v. *Walker* [9] and *Yewens* v. *Noakes* [10] and, in particular, in the opinion of Bramwell B. in each case. The dictum in the latter case is a much quoted one, *viz.*: " A servant is a person subject to the command of his master as to the manner in which he shall do his work." A more recent example which has found great favour south of the Border is the opinion of McCardie J. in *Performing Right Society Ltd.* v. *Mitchel and Booker (Palais de Danse) Ltd.*[11] in the course of which his lordship said, " It seems . . . reasonably clear that the final test, if there be a final test, and certainly that the test to be generally applied, lies in the nature and the degree of detailed control over the person alleged to be a servant."

There are certain other factors which may provide guides as to whether or not the service contract relationship exists. These are payment of wages or salary; fixed times of work; and disciplinary procedures (the Americans generally refer to the employer's right to " hire and fire "). It must be stressed, however, that these additional factors are useful guides only to the situation—they are not conclusive evidence that the relationship is that of employer and employee.

---

[8] [1952] 1 T.L.R. 101 at p. 111; see also the speech of Lord Simon in *Mersey Docks and Harbour Board* v. *Coggins and Griffith (Liverpool) Ltd.* [1947] A.C. 1 at p. 12.
[9] (1858) 27 L.J.M.C. 207 at p. 208.
[10] (1880) 6 Q.B.D. 530 C.A at pp. 532–533.
[11] [1924] 1 K.B. 762, particularly at p. 767.

The old simple test of " control," based upon the eighteenth- and nineteenth-century theory that the employer was the person responsible for directing how the work should be done and was, in addition, the keystone and cornerstone of the business, bears little relation to the situation of today, looking to the advances in technology and automation.[11a] Today it is much more likely to be the skilled employee, with high technical qualifications, who is able to say how the work should be done. There is again the changing emphasis from employment in family businesses to employment in vast public corporations or large industrial concerns where personal contact with management is remote or non-existent.

Consequently, there has been an attempt by the courts to find a new test for identifying the employer and employee relationship which would replace the " control " test. No substitute test has yet been found which can lay claim to universal validity. In the important case of *Stagecraft Ltd.* v. *Minister of National Insurance*,[12] Thomson L.J.-C. said [13] that there was sufficient control to bring the employee into the category of " servant " if " the employer . . . can direct the objective to which the servant's skill is directed." This statement is so wide in its terms as to be applicable to other forms of employment and, therefore, it is not conclusive nor particularly helpful in relation to the contract of service. In *Roe* v. *Minister of Health* [14] Morris L.J. (as he then was) adopted a test which was later to become very fashionable in modern thinking upon the employment relationship, *viz.*: Is the employee an " organisation man "? That is to say, is he a part of the employer's " set-up " or business? This test may be helpful in deciding the question of the employment relationship but it is certainly not conclusive in its application or in its result. It is perfectly possible for a person to be part of a business establishment or set-up without being in the true relationship of an employee to an employer. Indeed the " organisation " test might apply equally to the partnership set-up or to the board of directors of a public or private company, although in such cases the major difficulty would be in trying to identify the employer rather than to establish who were the employees. Moreover, company directors, whilst not being themselves employees, can exercise a degree of control and direction over the ordinary employees of the company which—provided there was no *ultra vires* acting on the part of the directors either in relation to their own powers or the stated powers of the company itself—would be sufficient to bind the company in law in respect of the actings of its ordinary employees.

The " organisation " test is hardly applicable to the situation where one employee is loaned by his primary employer to a secondary employer

[11a] See " Wage-slave or entrepreneur? " by Charles D. Drake in [1968] M.L.R. 408 *et seq.*
[12] 1952 S.C. 288.
[13] *Ibid.* at p. 297.
[14] [1954] 2 Q.B. 66 at p. 91.

for the more effective carrying out of a particular skilled operation or task, nor is it strictly applicable to the situation where X comes under the authority of Y for a particular occasion only, *i.e.*, as an employee *pro hac vice*. In both of these cases the " control " test is preferable because the actual direction and control of the particular operation—generally involving the exercise of physical skill on the part of X—remains with Y who stands in the position of the responsible employer and he is liable for any negligence or fault or wrongful acting by X, as an employee. These two types of case have been considered by the Scottish and English courts from time to time. Several of these cases are examined or referred to in a later chapter of this book.[15]

To sum up, therefore, the best that can be said is that there is no precise formula which can be applied to determine the liability of one person for the actings of another, be the latter an employee or independent contractor, nor is there any precise formula by which anyone is able to say that the relationship existing between X and Y is—according to that formula—that of employer and employee. Certainly, the " control " test will be considered and doubtless applied, but it is merely one factor in the whole chain or tapestry of circumstances which will require to be looked at in an attempt to decide upon the nature of the relationship which does exist. Moreover, the attitude of the courts will vary from time to time, as social and economic policies change. This is illustrated most clearly in the application of the doctrine of vicarious liability as applied between employer and employee. Admittedly the employer takes the risk in all cases of wrongful actings by his employees within the scope of their employment but he is also the person who has most to gain from the business—that is to say the risk element must be measured against the profit margin. In practical terms the doctrine of vicarious liability for employees means very little to the employer, for he is almost always very fully covered by insurance. This risk coverage is, of course, taken into account by the politicians and other framers of social policies.

" Control " is also relevant when we come to consider[16] the question of disobedience by an employee to a lawful order given to him by or on behalf of the employer. However, in that particular instance, the form of control which has to be considered is what Lord Coleridge has called,[17] in an old case in England, the " practical control " over the employee. In modern American terminology this is the " right to fire " employees (for disobedience or other just cause).

It is symptomatic of the modern attitude to the law of employment that the primary concern is that of the delictual liability of an employer —whether to his own employees or to third parties suffering injury or loss. The litigious aspect seems to take precedence over the rights and duties and obligations owed by one party to the other. The " control "

---

[15] *Vide* Chap. 12, *infra.*
[16] *Vide* Chap. 9 *infra.*
[17] *Levering* v. *St. Katherine's Dock Co.* (1887) 3 T.L.R. 607.

test has become tied to employer's liability and the broader field of vicarious liability. It is hardly ever applied as a primary test of the relationship of employer and employee where the question at issue is simply the existence or non-existence of a contract of service. The same is virtually true of labour relations and trade union law where continued use of such terminology as " trade dispute " and the like, and the stress placed upon such, is hardly likely to improve the image of industrial relations. Perhaps the point is neatly made, regrettably but not surprisingly, in the course of a recent opinion in England by Danckwerts L.J. in which he said, " . . . it appears that it would be a good deal safer to keep lions or other wild animals in a park than to engage in a business involving the employment of labour."

CHAPTER 4

COMPARISON OF THE EMPLOYER AND EMPLOYEE RELATIONSHIP WITH OTHER RELATIONSHIPS

(1) *Distinction between Locatio operis and Sale*

There is a close resemblance between these two relationships. The criterion for distinguishing them is probably this—that where nothing but the labour or the skill of the person employed is given, the contract is one of hiring, not sale. Should the workman furnish materials as well as performing some work, the contract is, in general, *sale*. There may be exceptions, *e.g.*, a contract to build a house upon land owned by the employer is location, not sale, even although the contractor supplies the materials.[1] In England, a contract to print a book has been regarded as a contract for work and services [2] whilst a contract to make a set of false teeth has been held to be a contract of sale.[3]

(2) *Distinction between Service and Partnership*

A question may arise, where X is employed by Y as his agent or traveller or clerk and where it is agreed that X is to receive a share of profits, with or without a fixed sum in addition, as to whether this is legally a partnership or not. The position in England is explained in one of the older leading textbooks.[4] It is apparently settled, in both Scotland and England, that the whole scope and purport of the agreement must be looked at; and if it appears that the intention was to create the employer and employee relationship, and not partnership, then this is adhered to.[5] The question of profit-sharing or payment of commission is irrelevant. Lord Moncrieff (L.J.-C.) was quite clear in his opinion in *Eaglesham & Co.* v. *Grant*,[6] in which he adopted the line of reasoning employed in England, that the substance and not the form of the transaction is to be looked at.

Upon the question of profit-sharing, regard must be had to the Partnership Act 1890,[7] section 2 from which the two following rules quite clearly emerge, *viz.*:

---

[1] See *Digest*, 19, 2, 2; and Bell's *Principles*, s. 147.
[2] *Clay* v. *Yates* (1856) 25 L.J.Ex. 237.
[3] *Lee* v. *Griffin* (1861) 30 L.J.Q.B. 252.
[4] See Smith, *Master and Servant*, 6th ed., p. 44 *et seq.* and cases there cited.
[5] See *London Shipping Co.* v. *Ferguson* (1850) 13 D. 51; *Eaglesham & Co.* v. *Grant* (1875) 2 R. 960; *Stott* v. *Fender and Crombie* (1878) 5 R. 1104; *Laing Bros. & Co.'s Tr.* v. *Low* (1896) 23 R. 1105; and *Brown & Co.'s Tr.* v. *M'Cosh* (1898) 1 F. 52 and (1899) 1 F.(H.L.) 86: For the position in England see Addison, *Contracts* (7th ed.), p. 982, and for the old cases see Smith, *Master and Servant*, p. 49 *et seq.*
[6] (1875) 2 R. 960 at p. 967.
[7] 53 & 54 Vict., c. 39.

(a) the sharing of gross returns does not of itself create a partnership, whether the persons sharing such returns have or have not a joint or common right or interest in any property from which or from the use of which the returns are derived; and

(b) the receipt by a person of a share of the profits of a business is prima facie evidence that he is a partner but the receipt of such a share does not of itself make him a partner; and in particular—"A contract for the remuneration of a servant or agent of a person engaged in a business by a share of the profits of the business does not of itself make the servant or agent a partner in the business or liable as such."

The reference to a share of profits being only prima facie evidence of a partnership was explained very neatly by Jessel M.R. in the old leading English case of *Pooley* v. *Driver* [8] in which he said that where persons are carrying on business and sharing profits they are to be treated as partners in that business unless there are surrounding circumstances to show that they are not really partners. Sharing of losses would be a much more vital pointer to partnership than sharing of profits and, therefore, it would be very unusual indeed to find such an undertaking or obligation written into or implied into a contract of employment.

When a third party becomes involved with persons in business the question which must be asked and which is most important is this—is the relationship between those persons engaged in business truly a partnership or is it a relationship of employer and employee? The answer to that question will decide the legal liability in such a case and it may be based upon the factual relationship of partnership or the principle of " holding out." [9]

(3) Occupation of premises as Servant or Tenant

The legal point at issue may be as follows—is the person who occupies his employer's premises doing so as a tenant or *qua* employee? The latter situation is now generally known as the " service occupancy."

Cockburn C.J. has said [10] that if the occupation were necessary to the service then the occupation is that of the master, notwithstanding that the employee receives less remuneration on account of his advantage in residing there. But if the occupation is not necessary to the service then the occupation is *qua* tenant and the question of the occupation being part of the remuneration for the service has really no effect upon the position. There is no substance in the argument that, because the employer is the owner of the particular house which is occupied by the employee and in respect of which occupancy a sum is deducted from wages, a service occupancy exists. It may, on the other hand, be a

---

[8] (1876) 5 Ch.D. 458 at p. 474.
[9] See *Lindley on Partnership*; also the Partnership Act 1890.
[10] In *R.* v. *Spurrell* (1865) L.R. 1 Q.B. 72. See also Smith (3rd ed.), p. 63 *et seq.*; and Fraser (3rd ed.), pp. 7–8 and n. (*a*) to p. 8; also p. 10 and n. 1.

tenancy—and a protected tenancy at that. If the employer/owner provided the furniture for the house the implication would be more clearly in favour of a service occupancy alone and not a full tenancy. It is, however, most unusual indeed for any employer to provide furniture in addition to the house itself. The missives of let should be so clearly drawn as to place the matter beyond any doubt or, failing missives, a suitable clause should be inserted in the contract of employment itself which should afford all necessary protection to the employer.

In Scots law the matter is always a question of fact and it can only be decided by a consideration of all the circumstances in each particular case.[11]

When the service terminates—and the occupation had been incidental to the service—then the employer can turn the employee out of the premises, without resort to any process of law.[12] The employee has no right to remain nor to claim reasonable notice to quit.

(4) Distinction between Service and Agency

The employer and employee relationship is distinctly a more personal one than that of the principal and agent. Nevertheless, the contract of hiring regulates both types of relationship.[13] The employee acts for his employer in accordance with those duties which are undertaken by him, either expressly or impliedly, in his contract of service. The agent does not give service to his principal but acts as an independent person (though possessing a certain authority from the principal) who sets up contractual relationships between the principal and third parties with whom the principal wishes to engage in business.[14] No special set of rules or conditions exists from which one can identify or point to one particular relationship or the other. The method of payment or the use of tools may help to indicate the intention of parties, but standing by themselves, these things generally settle nothing. All the circumstances must be looked at carefully in an attempt to solve the question as to which relationship is in force.

Obviously, a vital element helping to distinguish the relationships is the legal power retained by the master of controlling the performance of the employee's duties.[15] In the employer and employee relationship, the former is always entitled to direct the manner and method in which the latter performs his duties. The employee is subject to his master's discretion. This is not so in the contract of agency where the discretion to act or not to act lies entirely with the agent, though, of course, the

---

11 *Aitchison* v. *Lothian* (1890) 18 R. 337; *Dunbar's Trs.* v. *Bruce* (1900) 3 F. 137.
12 See particularly *Rose* v. *Grant* (1868) 7 M. 309; *Scott* v. *M'Murdo* (1869) 6 S.L.R. 301; *Deans* v. *Blackwood* (1869) 8 M. 1; *Ross* v. *Pender* (1874) 1 R. 352; *Greig* v. *Robertson* (1890) 7 Sh.Ct.Rep. 56; and *Wallace* v. *Hamilton* (1893) 9 Sh.Ct.Rep. 130.
13 See *Pickin* v. *Hawkes* (1878) 5 R. 676 and *Dowling* v. *Henderson* (1890) 17 R. 921.
14 See Gloag, *Contract* (2nd ed.), Chap. VIII (Agency); Bowstead on *Agency* (13th ed.) at p. 1; and, most helpfully, Powell, *The Law of Agency* (2nd ed., 1961), pp. 4–7.
15 See *supra*, Chap. 3, on the doctrine control.

principal may place limits upon the exercise of that discretion. There-fore, if the element of control is removed or the method of performance is at the discretion of the actor, the relationship is probably agency—it is not the service relationship.

To sum up, therefore, it is never easy to distinguish between an employer and employee relationship and one involving principal and agent. Professor Walker has pointed out [15a] that, although the principal/agent relationship may be wider than the employer/employee relationship, nevertheless the application of the principle of vicarious liability is narrower in agency than it is in employment—because, in the latter case, an employer may also be liable for wrongful, unauthorised acts done in the course of employment. Sometimes the pleadings become confused, as in *Percy* v. *Glasgow Corporation*, under-noted, so that the " scope of authority " test and the " scope or course of employment " test become intermingled, although very often the decision would have been the same on either test. The court must, in all these cases, examine the facts and circumstances very carefully.

(5) *Distinction between Service and the Independent Contractor*

It may often be important to ascertain whether the contractual rela-tionship is that of employer and employee or one for the performance of work by an independent contractor. In Scots law this is the essential difference between the contract *locatio operarum* and the contract *locatio operis faciendi*. The former is the true contract of employment and the latter is the contract relating to the independent contractor who is engaged to do a particular piece of work or a particular " job." When the inde-pendent contractor has finished his task he departs and renders his account for settlement; the contractual obligation is over when the work is finished and payment completes the whole transaction. The employee, on the other hand, continues in his day-to-day tasks under the direction and control as to what work is to be done and, most importantly, the methods of doing it. Practically, the foreman may instruct the employee, but the right to direct lies with the employer by virtue of his position as such. Moreover, the employee may be taken off one task and put on to another, by his employer's order; so long as the nature and character of the new task falls within the normal ambit or scope of employment of that particular employee, then the order must be obeyed.

[15a] See *Delict* (1966), pp. 134–137, but particularly at p. 136. Professor Walker's quota-tion from Lord President Cooper (see pp. 134–135) in *Mair* v. *Wood*, 1948 S.C. 83 at p. 87, and his comments thereon (at n. 81 to p. 135) should be noted; as also his references to *Percy* v. *Glasgow Corporation*, 1922 S.C.(H.L.) 144; 1922 S.L.T. 352; [1922] 2 A.C. 299; and *Neville* v. *C. & A. Modes Ltd.*, 1945 S.C. 175; 1945 S.L.T. 189; and other cases, all of which illustrate the difficulties of distinguishing between a *locatio operarum* situation and an agency arrangement. Liability attaches more widely and firmly, under the former, to the employer than it does to a principal, under the latter.

Mr. P. S. Atiyah also deals with this matter at some length in his recent work on *Vicarious Liability* (Butterworths, 1967).

Mr. Umpherston explains [16] that the English cases [17] draw the following distinction—the contractor has a separate business or independent employment, whilst the business of the ordinary employee is that of his master. The true legal meaning of the former situation is that a contractor, who is so placed and performing his contract with the person who engages him, is prosecuting a business on his own account. A similar distinction has been recognised in Scotland.[18] Lord Fraser explains [19] that, in order to determine the difference between the independent contractor and the position of a person employed under a contract of service, one must ascertain whether the service is rendered in the course of an independent occupation, representing the will of the employer only as to the *result* of the work, as distinct from the *means* by which the work is accomplished. Should X submit himself to the direction of Y (the person who engages or employs X) as to the details of the work, fulfilling his wishes not merely as to the result, but also as to all the means by which that result is to be achieved or attained, then X becomes an employee of Y in respect of that work. These matters are, of course, vitally important when we come to consider [20] the legal liability of an employer for the wrongful or delictual actings of (a) his own employee and (b) independent contractors employed or engaged by him. The doctrine of vicarious liability generally applies to the employer/employee situation so as to render the employer liable; and it does not normally apply to the employer/independent contractor situation, although there may be circumstances in which the employer of an independent contractor will be held liable. These situations are considered later on in this book.

If the contractor is truly independent, then the person employing or engaging him has no power of control over the *modus operandi* of the work. If any control is retained, then the " service " element is present [21] and, moreover, the employer will then be liable for fault or negligence, quite irrespective of whether the performer of the work is called a contractor or a servant.

As we have indicated in the preceding chapter, even the " control " test is not an infallible one. This point is illustrated from the recent English case of *Morren* v. *Swinton and Pendlebury Borough Council* [22] concerning the contractual and control position of a resident site engineer, who was selected and controlled by the consulting engineers employed by the local authority but who was paid by the local authority with whom he had a service contract. It was held that the engineer was an employee

---

[16] *Op. cit.* p. 5.

[17] *Loc. cit.* and note 1 with cases there cited.

[18] *Stephen* v. *Thurso Police Commissioners* (1876) 3 R. 535; and *Sweeney* v. *Duncan & Co.* (1892) 19 R. 870.

[19] *Op. cit.*, p. 289.

[20] See Chaps. 11 and 12, *infra*.

[21] See particularly *Stephen's* case and *Sweeney's* case, *supra*; also *Anderson* v. *Glasgow Tramway Co.* (1893) 21 R. 318; and *Connelly* v. *Clyde Navigation Trs.* (1902) 5 F. 8.

[22] [1965] 1 W.L.R. 576; [1965] 2 All E.R. 349.

of the local authority, although they had no control over him. It is submitted that the Scottish courts would take a similar common sense view in a situation such as this.

Difficulties have arisen in the " hospital cases " in deciding whether liability exists on the part of the hospital authorities for doctors, nurses, radiographers and others working within the hospital. The courts have altered their views over the years and, by and large, the hospital authorities will be liable for all staff employed by them—the only exception being, apparently, the consulting specialist, who is not normally a member of the hospital staff. This is not the place to consider these cases in detail and it is proposed to defer consideration of them to a later chapter in which the question of employer's liability is generally examined.

(6) Police Constables

In Scotland, the police are maintained and paid by the county councils in the county areas and by the police commissioners in burghs with a certain population. In the counties, they are under the direction of the Standing Joint Committee and the sheriff, and in some towns they are placed by local Acts under a similar committee of magistrates and the sheriff.[23] But they are not employees in the ordinary sense of employment, either of the county council or of the police commissioners; nor are they employees of the magistrates and town council in any other capacity than that of police officers or commissioners [24]; nor are they employees of the Standing Joint Committee.[25] Indeed, their employment is not in any way analogous to that under a contract of service. Perhaps they are best described as quasi-civil servants.

The position of a chief constable with reference to the principle of *respondeat superior*—that is to say, making him liable for the act of a subordinate—requires special consideration. The common law position was illustrated by the case of *Adamson* v. *Martin*,[26] but the matter is now regulated by statute. In terms of the Police (Scotland) Act 1956 [27] a chief constable is liable in reparation for any wrongful act or omission of a police constable who is under his direction—that is to say, a liability which corresponds to the employer's liability for his own employee. Where the chief constable is found liable in damages,[27a] the responsibility

---

[23] See J. Bennett Miller, *Outline of Local Government and Administrative Law in Scotland* (1961), pp. 265–266.

[24] *Young* v. *Glasgow Magistrates* (1891) 18 R. 825; and *Gow* v. *Greenock Police Commissioners* (1896) 13 Sh.Ct.Rep. 25.

[25] *Girdwood* v. *Standing Joint Committee of Midlothian* (1894) 22 R. 11.

[26] 1916 S.C. 319.

[27] S. 23A added by the Police Act 1964, Sched. 7; but see now the Police (Scotland) Act 1967 (c. 77), a consolidating measure.

[27a] For a most interesting recent case upon the question of whether a common law duty of care is owed by a chief constable to his police officers—although, of course, the relationship of employer and employee does not apply to this situation—see *Robertson and Another* v. *Bell and Others* (O.H.) 1969 S.L.T. 119. Lord Fraser allowed an inquiry against the second defender (*i.e.*, the chief constable) upon this point, being clearly of

for payment thereof rests with the police authority. The 1956 Act has been brought up to date and the statute law consolidated, so far as Scotland is concerned, by the Police (Scotland) Act 1967.[28] The operative section (which will replace the old section 23A) is section 39, which is in the following terms:

" 39.—(1) The chief constable of a police force shall be liable in reparation in respect of any wrongful act or omission on the part of any constable under his general direction in the performance of his functions in like manner as a master is so liable in respect of a wrongful act or omission on the part of his servant in the course of the servant's employment.

(2) The police authority shall pay—

    (*a*)   any damages or expenses awarded against the chief constable of a police force in any proceedings brought against him by virtue of this section and any expenses incurred by him in any such proceedings so far as not recovered by him in the proceedings; and

    (*b*)   any sum required in connection with the settlement of any claim made against the chief constable of a police force by virtue of this section, if the settlement is approved by the police authority.

(3) Any proceedings in respect of a claim made by virtue of this section shall be brought against the chief constable for the time being or in the case of a vacancy in that office, against the person for the time being performing the functions of the chief constable; and references in the foregoing provisions of this section to the chief constable shall be construed accordingly.

(4) The police authority may, in such cases and to such extent as they think fit, pay any damages or expenses awarded against a constable of the police force maintained for their area, or any constable for the time being required to serve with that force by virtue of section 11 of this Act, in proceedings arising from any wrongful act or omission on the part of that constable, any expenses incurred and not recovered by him in any such proceedings, and any sum

---

opinion that " some duty of care was owed by the second defender . . . because injury . . . in the event of failure to exercise reasonable care . . . could reasonably and probably be anticipated " (*ibid.* p. 121), although the nature and content of that duty in the very special circumstances applicable to police officers may not be easy to determine. His lordship was satisfied, however, that the police committee (who had been called by the first defender as third parties to the action) had no such duty, either by statute or at common law. S. 14 of the 1956 Act was not applicable or relevant. It is understood (see the S.L.T. report at p. 122) that a reclaiming motion has been enrolled against Lord Fraser's decision. This case is also referred to in Chap. 12, *infra.*

[28] 1967, c. 77. S. 39 is derived from the 1956 Act, s. 23A (1)–(4), and the Police Act 1964, Sched. 7, para. 14: It has not been brought into operation as yet.

required in connection with the settlement of any claim that has or might have given rise to such proceedings."

(7) *Pilots*

The owner or master of a vessel which is being navigated under compulsory pilotage is responsible for any damage or loss caused by the vessel or caused by any fault in navigation of the vessel [29]—that is to say, the liability arises just as if the pilot were the employee of the shipowner or master.[30]   Indeed he is *pro hac vice* the employee of the shipowner. Prior to 1913, the pilot was generally thought of as an independent contractor and, moreover, compulsory pilotage was a good defence to the shipowner.

The pilotage authority is not liable for the defaults of its pilots,[31] although it may be if it employs an unlicensed pilot through whose fault damage or injury is caused.[32]   Section 19 of the 1913 Act specifically provides that the grant of a licence to a particular pilot does not render the issuing authority liable for the act or default of that pilot.   Furthermore, if a pilotage authority is the true employer, so that the doctrine of vicarious liability operates, the Pilotage Authorities (Limitation of Liability) Act 1936 limits the liability of the authority—provided it is not at fault or otherwise involved—to the sum of £100 × (the number of pilots) holding licences for the particular district.   The pilot remains liable for his own personal fault.[33]

However, there are occasions when pilots may be servants either of a particular shipowner or of Harbour Trustees or of some other body which provides them.[32]   In the *Irvine Harbour Trustees'* case,[32] pilotage was not compulsory and the pilots concerned were not licensed pilots in the sense of the Merchant Shipping Acts.   Accordingly, it was held that all pilots provided by the Harbour Trustees in this case were their own employees.

(8) *Company Directors*

Employees of a public company are not employees of the manager or of the directors, but of the shareholders.   The manager and secretary of the company are themselves also employees of the general body of shareholders.   The position of the directors is different—they have variously been called officers, trustees and agents [34] of the company. No matter what the correct nomenclature may be, they are basically not

---

[29] Pilotage Act 1913, s. 15 (1), which reversed the old common law rule and repealed s. 633 of the Merchant Shipping Act 1894.

[30] *The Maria* (1839) 1 W.Rob. 95; *The Eden* (1846) 2 W.Rob. 442; *Beechgrove S.S. Co.* v. *A/S Fjord*, 1916 S.C.(H.L.) 1.

[31] *Shaw, Savill and Albion* v. *Timaru Harbour Board* (1889) 15 App.Cas. 429; *Parker* v. *N.B. Ry.* (1898) 25 R. 1059; *Fowles* v. *Eastern and Australian S.S. Co.* [1916] 2 A.C. 556.

[32] *Holman* v. *Irvine Harbour Trs.* (1877) 4 R. 406.

[33] See the Pilotage Act 1913, s. 35.

[34] See *Lennards Carrying Co. Ltd.* v. *Asiatic Petroleum Co. Ltd.* [1915] A.C. 705, *per* Viscount Haldane at p. 713.

employees of the company,[35] unless it can be shown that, in addition to the office of director, some salaried appointment on the company's staff is held.[36] This is a not uncommon practice in modern companies. Even an appointment as managing director does not render the particular director an employee *qua* manager of the company.[37]

There may, however, be circumstances concerning the relationship between the company and its directors which create a vicarious liability in the company itself for the wrongful acts of its directors. This is a question which is more relevant to the general field of delict (including a special consideration of the law of agency, as necessary) rather than to the employer and employee relationship which is dealt with in this volume. The point may, however, come up again in a later chapter of this work when the general liability of employers is being considered.

---

[35] See Umpherston, *The Law of Master and Servant*, p. 14 and cases cited at n. 24 there.
[36] The Companies Act 1948, s. 54 (1) (*b*); also *Lee* v. *Lee's Air Farming Ltd.* [1960] 3 W.L.R. 758, *per* Lord Morris of Borth-y-Gest at p. 766.
[37] *Hopkinson* v. *Newspaper Proprietary Syndicate* [1900] 2 Ch. 349; and *Gibson & Son* v. *Gibson* (1899) 36 S.L.R. 522.

CHAPTER 5

CAPACITY OF PARTIES SO FAR AS PECULIAR TO THE CONTRACT OF EMPLOYMENT

ALTHOUGH the question of capacity to contract is dealt with at some length in the major texts,[1] it is nevertheless appropriate to consider here the position of pupils and minors, married women, drunkards, mentally disordered persons, partners and corporations, Crown servants, unincorporated associations and trade unions who have been or are likely to be involved in the service relationship.

(1) *Pupils*

These are, of course, males under fourteen years and females under twelve years. They possess no legal capacity to bind themselves by deed or contract, whether of service or otherwise. The question of the supply of " necessaries " to pupils under the Sale of Goods Act 1893, s. 2, must also be kept in mind: this involves, of course, payment of a reasonable price for such necessaries. Yet this statutory provision is not likely to affect the normal service relationship, except in so far as mentioned in the next paragraph. It is thought that the contract may be enforced against the other party if it is beneficial to the pupil.[2] The English courts seem to take a similar view.[3] The pupil could become bound in older Scots law (when the school leaving age was lower than at present) as an employee, where his father or tutor entered into the engagement for him. But the contract could still be reduced within the *quadriennium utile* if lesion were proved. A mother has no power to bind her son in any contractual relationship, including that of employment, during the lifetime of the father.[4] Where the father is dead, the mother generally acts as tutor, although it is perfectly possible for an uncle of the pupil to be appointed as tutor.

The pupil must, however, pay a fair and reasonable price for services rendered to him, so far as *in rem versum*, including " necessary " services suitable to his estate and station in life.

Erskine says [5] quite definitely that a pupil has no legal *persona* and, therefore, he can make no valid contract and this, of course, means that any contract of employment which a pupil purports to make by himself

---

[1] See particularly Gloag, *Contract* (2nd ed.) and Gloag and Henderson, *Introduction to the Law of Scotland* (7th ed.).

[2] See Erskine, I, 7, 33 (note that the contract will *not* be enforced against the pupil himself).

[3] See the leading English cases of *Olsen* v. *Corry & Gravesend Aviation Ltd.* [1936] 3 All E.R. 241; *Roberts* v. *Gray* [1913] 1 K.B. 520; *Doyle* v. *White City Stadium* [1935] 1 K.B 110.   [4] See *Arnot* v. *Stevenson* (1698) Mor. 6017.   [5] I, 7, 14.

is quite null and void. Mr. Umpherston points out [6] that while the service actually continued the pupil was substantially in the same position as an employee under a valid contract of service, with special reference to his position under statute law and also as to claims for reparation in compensation for injury sustained by him during the course of his employment. Moreover, an act which might disqualify a major employee from compensation or other benefit or claim might not necessarily disqualify the pupil from pressing a valid claim to such. [7]

As we have said above, where the pupil was to enter employment then his father or other tutor could bind the pupil as an employee, subject only to the rule as to the reduction of the contract at the pupil's instance during his *quadriennium utile*. Where, however, a contract of employment of another person with the pupil himself is to be made, then this must be done by the tutor as tutor and administrator of the pupil's estate, in order to be legally binding. In such a case, the tutor as such and administrator of the estate is in theory the employer of the particular employee who is engaged on behalf of the particular pupil.

So far as the party contracting with the pupil is concerned, the rule is that performance of a pupil's obligations under any contract cannot be enforced against him by an action of damages or otherwise, unless the contract in question has been made by his tutor. [8] With the proposed increase in the school-leaving age to sixteen years, the question of a pupil's contracts in relation to employment at any rate is perhaps becoming just a little academic.

(2) *Minors*

These are persons under twenty-one years of age [8a] but beyond the respective ages of pupillarity. According to Mr. Bell, they have a limited capacity—or as he puts it, " Minority is a state not of total incapacity, like pupillarity, but of limited capacity, in which the minor is held capable of consent, but of inferior judgment or discretion, requiring the protection of the law." [9] The law considers them capable of certain acts and of giving consent to certain agreements or undertakings. They may or may not have curators. During the father's lifetime he is the administrator-at-law to his minor legitimate children. If the father is dead another curator may have been nominated or may be appointed by the court.

Where there is a curator in existence, the general rule is that his consent and concurrence are necessary to bind the minor. If this consent has not been obtained, the minor's actings are *ipso jure* null and void and

---

[6] *Op. cit.*, p. 16.

[7] See *Sharp* v. *Pathhead Spinning Co. Ltd.* (1885) 12 R. 574; *Traill* v. *Small and Boase* (1873) 11 M. 888; *Carty* v. *Nicoll* (1878) 6 R. 194.

[8] Umpherston, *op. cit.*, p. 16.

[8a] See now the Age of Majority (Scotland) Act 1969 (c.39) which reduces the age of majority to eighteen years. This Act came into force on Jan. 1, 1970. The text is included in Appendix 2 to this volume.   [9] *Principles*, s. 2088; see also Erskine. I, 7, 14.

no proof of lesion is necessary. Such a claim for nullity may be maintained throughout the full prescriptive period.

Where a minor has no curator, or is in fact acting with the consent of an existing curator, then his acts and deeds are perfectly valid. The minor without curators may take upon himself the obligations either of employer or employee [10] or he may do so with the consent of his father or other curator if he has such.[11] It is still, however, possible for the minor to plead lesion within the *quadriennium utile* and therefore to have the contract reduced.[12] The minor may even be entitled to enforce against the other party any contract which is void against himself.[13]

The minor who falsely represents himself to be of full age or falsely represents that a consenting party is his curator becomes bound in the obligation. This point was decided in the old case of *Harvie* v. *McIntyre*.[14] The curatory of the father ceases also by forisfamiliation, *i.e.*, when the child moves out of the immediate family circle or family home.[15]

There are cases in which the contract of a minor made without the consent of his father or other curator, is valid and not subject to reduction during the *quadriennium utile*. When, for example, a minor is engaged in trade, all transactions and obligations entered into by him in the course of trade are valid, and his trade contracts are of as full effect as if he were a major.[16] Other cases may arise where, for example, a minor has become a merchant. The important question of law then is, whether bills or other documents granted by the minor in the course of his business are valid and binding upon him, although these are granted without the consent of the father or other curator. It seems to be accepted that a minor, engaged in business or trade, who hires employees or accepts employment from others within the ordinary course of business will be bound by these employment contracts, although no parental or curatorial consent was first obtained.[17] Moreover, minority and lesion cannot be pleaded against deeds granted by the minor in relation to any employment in profession or business undertaken by him.[18] In relation to the contract of employment the most important question which has to be answered is whether a minor can become bound as an employee or as an apprentice without the consent of his curator.

In *Heddell* v. *Duncan* [19] the majority of the court was of the opinion that the case came under the general rule of law that when a minor undertakes an employment, by which he gains a part of his livelihood, he

[10] *Cameron* v. *Murray and Hepburn* (1866) 4 M. 547.
[11] *Campbell* v. *Baird* (1827) 5 S. 311; *Paul* v. *Barclay and Curle* (1856) 2 Irv. 537.
[12] *Allan* v. *Skene* (1728) Mor. 9454.
[13] Erskine, *loc. cit.*
[14] (1829) 7 S. 561; see also Fraser, *Guardian and Ward*, p. 383 *et seq.*
[15] See *McFeetridge* v. *Stewarts & Lloyds*, 1913 S.C. 773.
[16] *Heddell* v. *Duncan*, June 5, 1810, F.C.; *Galbraith* v. *Lesly* (1676) Mor. 9027 and *Craig* v. *Grant* (1732) Mor. 8955 and 9035.
[17] *Craig* v. *Grant*, *cit. supra*; also Fraser, *Guardian and Ward*, p. 383.
[18] See Fraser, *Master and Servant* (3rd ed.), p. 10 and n. (*f*) and cases cited thereat; also *Heddell* v. *Duncan*, *cit. supra*.
[19] *Cit. supra* at note 16.

becomes responsible to his employer and the public for all acts done in that situation. To hold otherwise, thought the court, would be to the prejudice of minors as a class, because no one would employ them. The points concerning the existence of a curator and the making of an agreement without his consent were not apparently pleaded in *Heddell's* case.

But attempts have been made to extend the general principle or rule above-mentioned to the extent of holding that a contract of service or indenture entered into by a minor, who has curators but does not obtain their consent, is not *ipso jure* null and void but is only voidable upon proof of lesion.[20]

On the question of the beneficiality or prejudice of the contract of hiring to the minor, Lord Fraser cites [21] two old English cases which are illustrative of the circumstances which may affect the minor. In more recent times, the question is again perhaps more clearly illustrated by several of the comparatively recent cases in England. The best known of these cases are *Clements* v. *L. & N.W. Railway* [22]; *Bromley* v. *Smith* [23]; *Roberts* v. *Gray* [24]; *Doyle* v. *White City Stadium Ltd.*[25] and *Olsen* v. *Corry and Gravesend Aviation Ltd.*[26] In the case of *Clements*, the (infant) minor was held bound as the contract, taken as a whole, was for his benefit. Similarly in the cases of *Roberts* and *Doyle*—the former case concerning a form of educational or instructional contract and the latter, though not strictly a contract of employment, a licensing contract. The overall test of benefit was applied in each case. *Bromley's* case concerned the use of restrictive covenants (*i.e.*, restraint of trade clauses) in relation to young persons who were not of full age. The dictum of Channell J. in *Bromley* is most important—" . . . there is abundant authority that contracts for (*sic*) service may be binding on (infants) although they contain restrictive terms; a contract which contains the only terms on which an (infant) can reasonably expect to get employment must, I think, be for his benefit." In *Olsen's* case, the particular contract which had to be examined was the deed of apprenticeship between Olsen and the company. The court was satisfied, upon a consideration of the whole contract, that the deed was so wide in its terms as to be void; every advantage lay with the company and there was nothing in the deed which gave any advantage whatsoever to the plaintiff. In that case he was not bound by it.

The minor's position, during the continuance of his service contract, is not unlike that of the pupil; certainly in relation to his claims for

---

[20] See particularly *Low* v. *Henry* (1797) Hume's Decis. 422; *Campbell* v. *Baird* (1827) 5 S. 335; and the dicta of Lord Ardmillan in *Stevenson* v. *Adair* (1872) 10 M. 919; see also *McFetridgee* v. *Stewarts & Lloyds*, 1913 S.C. 773.

[21] (3rd ed.); nn. (*a*) and (*b*) to p. 14.

[22] [1894] 2 Q.B. 482.

[23] [1909] 2 K.B. 235.

[24] [1913] 1 K.B. 520; see also *Mackinlay* v. *Bathurst* (1919) 36 T.L.R. 31.

[25] [1935] 1 K.B. 110.

[6] [1936] 3 All E.R. 241.

reparation, compensation and industrial injuries. However, the minor is held by law to be more responsible than the pupil and, indeed, in relation to pleas of negligence, contributory negligence and other breaches of common law or of statutory provisions he would be equated with the adult employee in respect of liability arising from such conduct.

(3) *Married Women*

It seems that a married woman can, by virtue of her *praepositura*, hire domestic servants, and that she can also, since the emancipation of her class in 1920,[27] contract as a single woman (*feme sole*) and will, therefore, be liable on her own contracts.[27a] Questions may arise as to whether she is acting (apart from the *praepositura*) in any particular set of circumstances as an agent of her husband or purely on her own behalf. In the former case the husband will be liable on the contract in accordance with the customary principles of agency which apply to this situation, while generally, in the latter case he will not be liable. The husband may acquire a contractual liability by ratifying or adopting the particular act of his wife; for example, where he is a co-partner or an undisclosed principal. Many interesting problems arose, prior to 1920, as to whether a married woman could become, without her husband's consent, an employee under a contract of service and, also, whether in the event of her taking up employment without her husband's consent, she could be proceeded against under any statute—then particularly the Master and Servant Act 1867, regulating and affecting her position as an employee. These points are now of historical interest only.

Where the spouses are voluntarily living apart or are judicially separated, the husband may be required to include in the alimentary allowance which he makes to his wife a sum representing the cost of the services of any of her employees (for example, a personal maid), but this will depend upon her station in life. Should the wife leave her husband for the purpose of taking paid employment and no longer continue to live with him, as his wife, then prima facie there is desertion on the part of the wife and the husband is no longer obliged to aliment her. Furthermore, there may well be grounds for the husband seeking a decree of divorce after the period of three years, upon a plea of desertion.

(4) *Drunkards*

The question of incapacity caused by intoxication in relation to the valid conclusion or otherwise of a contract of service is not any different from the ordinary case. The contract may be set aside if one party was so drunk as not to understand the nature of the business into which he was entering. If he did know and appreciate the position, then, although

---

[27] The Married Women's Property (Scotland) Act 1920 (10 & 11 Geo. 5, c. 64).
[27a] Legislation is pending *re* discrimination against female labour in employment, etc.; see the Anti-Discrimination Bill [No. 92] (printed February 18, 1969).

partially intoxicated, he can only have the contract reduced upon proving fraud on the part of the other party or upon proving that the other party improperly took advantage of his condition.[28]

The rule seems, therefore, to be that any contract with a drunken person—no matter what the degree of intoxication is—is voidable and not void, so that when he returns to sobriety he may insist upon the contract being fulfilled. Again, if he should ratify, when sober, a bargain made by him when drunk, he apparently becomes contractually bound by it[29] and this seems to be so both in Scotland and England. The general question of contractual incapacity caused by intoxication is helpfully dealt with in all the major works on contract and reference should be made to them.[30] It is considered to be unnecessary to elaborate upon that general question here.

(5) *Mentally Disordered Persons*

The question of incapacity caused by mental disorder, in the case of the contract of service, is also no different from that found in other types of contract. Where the incapacity is total, the contract may be reduced. For anything else of a lesser nature or degree, the person himself will be bound, unless he is able to prove fraud or circumvention. In English law the position seems to be that an insane person is apparently bound by a contract of service unless he is able to prove that he was so incapacitated at the time as to be incapable of understanding what he was doing and that the other party had knowledge of this incapacity.[31] However, the person who is insane (even to the knowledge of the other party) is liable to pay for services rendered to him, so far as these services were actually necessary for a person in his position or so far as he benefited therefrom.

(6) *Partners*

A partner has implied authority to hire employees for the purposes of the partnership, unless the person with whom he is dealing knows that he has no authority, or does not know or believe him to be a partner.[32] So also, one partner would have power to discharge an employee, but not, however, against the will of his co-partners. Dissolution of the partnership may amount to breach of a contract of employment or of a contract of apprenticeship.[33]

(7) *Corporations*

The corporation, being an artificial legal *persona*, must conform generally to the creating charter, deed or instrument by which it is established. For example, the statutory corporation is governed by its enacting

---

28 See *Taylor* v. *Provan* (1864) 2 M. 1232, *per* L.J.-C. Inglis.
29 *Matthews* v. *Baxter* (1873) 1 R.Ex. 132.
30 See particularly Gloag, *Contract* (2nd ed.), pp. 94–96, as regards Scotland.
31 *Matthews* v. *Baxter, cit. supra*; and *Imperial Loan Co.* v. *Stone* [1892] 1 Q.B. 599.
32 Partnership Act 1890 (53 & 54 Vict. c. 39), s. 5; also s. 9.
33 See Part III, *infra*—dissolution of the relationship of employer and employee.

statute, while the incorporated company (governed by one or more of the various Companies Acts) must conform to the terms and powers envisaged in its Memorandum of Association. Should any such corporation act *ultra vires* then the contract which it purports to make is void.[34] The chartered corporation is (in England, at any rate) apparently in a different position—if it makes a contract which is outwith the terms of its charter, that contractual obligation seems to be binding upon it although the result of such actions might well be that the charter is forfeited.[35] The contractual powers of trading companies incorporated under the Companies Act 1948 are regulated mainly by section 32 of that statute.

It is perhaps interesting to note that, so far as England is concerned, the fairly recent statute known as the Corporate Bodies' Contracts Act 1960 [36] provides that where private persons can contract in writing signed by the parties or orally, then a corporate body can do so also.[37] This statute does not apply to any company formed and registered under the Companies Act 1948 nor to any existing company as defined in that particular Act. Moreover, the Act of 1960 in no way affects the law of Scotland governing the capacity of corporations.

The general position in Scotland seems to be that corporations owe their origin to a Royal Charter or to an Act of Parliament or to incorporation under the Companies Acts. Limitations of the contractual powers depend upon the origin of the corporation—the body acting under Royal Charter can enter into any contract not expressly forbidden by the Charter.[38] Any restriction upon its activities rests on the principle that certain applications of funds might amount to a breach of trust. The contention that a chartered body might do anything which an individual might lawfully do has been repelled.[39]

The corporate body created by statute or exercising statutory powers cannot enter into any contract which is not authorised by the statute or which is not reasonably incidental to the powers conferred, *e.g.*, a body established for one purpose cannot engage in a different enterprise or act beyond the geographical limits within which it is authorised to act.[40] The consent of all parties, no matter how binding or rectifying it appears to be, cannot validate an act which is *ultra vires*.[41] The company incorporated under the Companies Acts specifies its objects in its Memorandum of Association and its powers to contract are those taken in the Memorandum. Anything outside that is *ultra vires* and void.[42]

[34] *Ashbury Railway Carriage and Iron Co.* v. *Riche* (1875) L.R. 7 H.L. 653.
[35] *Jenkin* v. *Pharmaceutical Society of Great Britain* [1921] 1 Ch. 392.
[36] 8 & 9 Eliz. 2, c. 46.
[37] See ss. 1, 2 and 4 (3).
[38] *Conn* v. *Corporation of Renfrew* (1906) 8 F. 905.
[39] *Kemp* v. *Corporation of Glasgow*, 1920 S.C.(H.L.) 73.
[40] *Nicol* v. *Dundee Harbour Trs.*, 1915 S.C.(H.L.) 7; and *Grieve* v. *Edinburgh Water Trs.*, 1918 S.C. 700.
[41] *Mann* v. *Edinburgh Northern Tramways Co.* (1892) 20 R.(H.L.) 7.
[42] *Shiell's Trs.* v. *Scottish Property Investment Co.* (1884) 12 R.(H.L.) 14.

In relation to the contract of employment it is true to say that the corporation can only be an employer. It cannot be an employee. The liability of a corporation under a contract of employment—whether in the field of contract, delict or crime—is a quite separate matter which will have to be considered later on in this volume. So far as the employee is concerned, he will require to be satisfied that the contract with him is being made on behalf of the corporation by a responsible officer or agent, otherwise it goes without saying that the corporation will plead that it is not bound by it. A very nice question of law may relate to the dismissal of an employee. Can a corporation dismiss i.e., has it the legal power to do so ? If so, who exercises that power on its behalf ? Does the exercise of that power require ratification, or has the officer or agent of the corporation a suffcent authority to act independently? Can the corporation delegate its powers (if any) of dismissal to any officer or agent or must it act as a whole body corporate in carrying out these matters ? These and other questions can only be answered by a very careful study of the charter, statute or memorandum of incorporation and the practices developed by the corporation in question, over the years. Difficulties may also arise in relation to the so-called employees. Are they truly employees at all ? Or, are they in some other legal position ? For example, is a policeman, a pilot or every schoolteacher quite clearly an employee in relation to his or her employing authority or governing or licensing body ? The policeman and the pilot are not normally employees within the ordinary meaning of the service contract; most schoolteachers are, nowadays, except for those employed in what are termed " private schools " in Scotland [43] whose position might be that of ordinary employees although this is by no means certain in all cases.

(8) *The Crown*

The employment relationship between the Crown and its employees is not a contractually binding relationship of the normal pattern. Crown employees or civil servants hold their appointments at the pleasure of the Crown [44] and, therefore, in theory they may be removed from their appointments at Crown pleasure. Neither the Crown Proceedings Act 1947 [45] nor the Contracts of Employment Act 1963 [46] alters the law on these points in any way. Indeed, the latter statute does not bind the Crown in any respect—either expressly or by necessary implication.

In *Duncan* v. *The Admiralty* [47] the question was raised as to whether a Crown servant could sue for his wages or remuneration. It was held that the Crown Proceedings Act 1947 had not changed the law on this point and that the action, accordingly, must be dismissed. Much the

---

[43] Compare the " public schools " in England.
[44] *Smith* v. *Lord Advocate* (1897) 25 R. 112; and *Mackin* v. *Lord Advocate* (1898) 25 R. 769.
[45] 10 & 11 Geo. 6, c. 44.
[46] 1963, c. 49.
[47] 1950 S.L.T.(Sh.Ct.) 72.

same point arose comparatively recently in England in the case of *Riordan* v. *The War Office* [48] where the plaintiff, employed under Army Council Regulations which stipulated for a period of notice, claimed that this term or stipulation was binding upon the Crown. This plea was however rejected and the term was held to be void. The court affirmed that the Crown had an absolute and unfettered right to dismiss any Crown employee without being obliged to give prior notice of dismissal.

Certainly the Crown Proceedings Act 1947 alters the law in relation to the liability of the Crown for the delictual or wrongful acts of its employees and in relation to its own position as employer or as owner, occupier or controller of certain property, but the Act does not affect in any way the previous legal position that the Crown employee cannot raise an action of wrongful dismissal nor an action for payment of arrears of salary. The Crown's prerogative or discretion remains unaltered *re* the engagement, payment and dismissal of employees. This may be another relic of feudalism in Great Britain, but it still remains unchanged in modern times. Of course, in practical terms, there is generally no hardship permitted to arise in these cases, otherwise there would be little doubt that Parliament would very quickly change the law.

(9) *Unincorporated Associations*

The voluntary association or unincorporated body does not have, in Scots law, an existence which is distinct from its members. The corporate body has a distinct legal *persona*; the unincorporated body has none. Certainly the courts may have to consider and decide upon property and other matters concerning voluntary associations. But, in doing so, the courts are not according to such associations any legal personality. The rule of law is that an unincorporated association cannot sue or be sued at common law in its collective name alone. As a matter of court practice it is necessary to call all the members of the association or those responsible officers (*e.g.*, a committee of management) who act on its behalf.[49] An exception is allowed in sheriff court procedure, where the descriptive name may be used.[50] Voluntary associations are generally divided into two groups—(a) the social club and (b) the association formed for religious, charitable, educational, industrial, scientific and other purposes. The former group involves the concept of all members sharing in the general property of the club [51] and upon death or retirement the member forfeits his share. In the case of the second group the test is the object or purpose

[48] [1959] 1 W.L.R. 1046; [1959] 3 All E.R. 552; affirmed by the Court of Appeal at [1961] 1 W.L.R. 210; [1960] 3 All E.R. 774, C.A.
[49] See *Renton Football Club* v. *McDowall* (1891) 18 R. 670; *Pagan and Osborne* v. *Haig*, 1910 S.C. 341; *Bridge* v. *South Portland Street Synagogue*, 1907 S.C. 1351.
[50] Sheriff Courts (Scotland) Act 1907, First Schedule, r. 11, as amended by the Sheriff Courts (Scotland) Act 1913. This also means that an action may be taken in Scotland against an unregistered trade union in its descriptive name.
[51] See *Murray* v. *Johnstone* (1896) 23 R. 981 at p. 990; and the comment by Professor T. B. Smith in the *Short Commentary* at p. 270 that such property is probably more correctly described as " joint property."

for which the association exists and all subscriptions and other moneys paid by members must be applied to that object [52]; these matters are governed mainly by the law of trusts and not simply by the law of contract.

So far as the employee of a club or other municipal association is concerned, it may be extremely difficult to identify the relationship of employer and employee. This matter is vital for the employee because upon the answer to it is determined the question whether the employee has any legal redress—either for damages for breach of an alleged contract of employment or for damages in a reparation action, based upon injury or loss sustained by the employee in the course of his employment. It will be important, therefore, to determine who engaged X as employee and whether that person had the requisite authority to do so. Failing authority, then X would require to sue the person concerned, as an individual, and the general law of agency would apply. In the ordinary case the employee would normally be engaged by the secretary of the club or association as representing the committee of management, acting for the whole body of members. It would also be necessary to examine the constitution and rules of the association to determine exactly what powers the committee of management or other executive group of office-bearers possessed. If the constitution were silent on this point then the matter of proving a particular custom or practice by the association might be one of extreme difficulty. The advent of the Contracts of Employment Act 1963 may help a little in this respect by identifying the employer but it would not necessarily help at all in relation to the valid constitution of a contract of employment governed by the statute if the authority of the negotiating office-bearer were in doubt or indeed if the association flatly repudiated the alleged contract of employment upon which X was relying.

(10) Trade Unions and Friendly Societies

These two forms of association are technically unincorporated associations, but as they occupy a special position in respect of their legal capacity or personality it is more usual to see them referred to by most modern writers as " quasi-corporations." The friendly societies are virtually creatures of statute law passed in the late nineteenth and early twentieth centuries and elaborate provisions are contained in these statutes for the formulation, registration, administration and general organisation of these bodies. Generally speaking, it is not too difficult to ascertain the rights, obligations and duties of an employee of these bodies.

More peculiar still, however, is the legal position of a trade union. As has been mentioned above, the trade union is generally regarded as a quasi-corporation—and this is certainly so where it has registered in accordance with the provisions of the Trade Union Acts.[52] Trade unions

---

[52] *Ewing* v. *M'Gavin* (1831) 9 S. 622; *Connell* v. *Ferguson* (1857) 19 D. 482.

need not, however, seek registration and in that case their legal position is governed by the rules of the common law. The powers and functions of a trade union may be found by an examination of the statutes [53]—where the union is governed by such—and also, in the case of all trade unions, by an examination of the constitution and rules of the union. The well-framed rulebook will carefully set forth the powers and functions and duties and obligations of the union, its executive committees, its office-bearers and its members. The registered union may sue and be sued in its registered name,[54] and formerly the union itself was held liable in damages in delict or tort for the wrongful acts of its officers.[54] The member has certain rights against his union—for example, where the union acts against the best principles of equity and " natural justice." For example, in *Bonsor* v. *Musicians' Union*,[55] a case of wrongful expulsion, a former member of the defendant trade union was held entitled to recover damages against the trade union itself in an action based upon contract, *i.e.*, a breach of the rulebook, which is generally understood to be the basic contract between the member and his union. The " natural justice " principle is illustrated by the two comparatively recent cases of *White* v. *Kuzych* [56] and *Annamunthodo* v. *Oilfield Workers' Trade Union* [57] in which there had been clear discrimination against members by the adoption of a form of proceedings in which they were badly treated or denied the right to be heard. This, however, is not the place to consider at length the position of trade unions and their effect upon the law of employment and industrial relations. It is proposed to do this, much more comprehensively, in a later chapter.[58]

Meantime, so far as the creation of a contract of employment is concerned, the employee will be advised that the test of capacity in the case of the trade union is the constitution of the union itself, taken along with the statute law and common law, as appropriate. By and large, therefore, the employee of a trade union will be in broadly the same position as the employee of a friendly society. The authority of the office-bearer or committee who engaged him will be tested by reference to the rulebook. The law of contract and of agency will then apply. The employee will be able to sue the trade union in its registered name or he will be able to sue the executive committee of an unregistered trade union. His action, based upon contract, may be taken against the trade union or its committee, as appropriate. But if the action is based upon

---

[53] The main statutes are the Trade Union Act 1871 (34 & 35 Vict. c. 31); the Trade Union Act Amendment Act 1876 (39 & 40 Vict. c. 22); and the Trade Union Act 1913. The Trade Disputes Acts 1906 and 1965 also fall within the framework of trade union law and are separately dealt with in a later chapter, *viz.* Chap. 17.

[54] *Taff Vale Railway Co.* v. *Amalgamated Society of Railway Servants* [1901] A.C. 426; the Trade Disputes Act 1906, s. 4, removed the liability upon the trade union itself. It is still possible to sue the trade union officials in a personal action.

[55] [1956] A.C. 104; [1956] 3 W.L.R. 788; [1955] 3 All E.R. 518, H.L.

[56] [1951] A.C. 585.

[57] [1961] A.C. 945.

[58] *Infra*, Chap. 17.

delict the immunity contained in the Trade Disputes Act 1906 [59] will apply. If, of course, the employee is also a member of the trade union in question then it will be necessary to keep in mind the very special provisions of section 4 of the Trade Union Act 1871, by which certain types of contract (but not a contract of employment between an employee of a trade union and his own trade union as his employer) involving trade unions are not normally enforceable in the United Kingdom courts of law, *i.e.*, by ordinary judicial process for specific implement in Scotland or specific performance in England.

[59] s. 4.

Chapter 6

CREATION OF THE CONTRACT OF EMPLOYMENT

(1) *General*

The general principles of the law of contract apply to the service relationship as they do to other cases. There must be *consensus in idem* before a valid and binding contract of service is complete.[1] The consent itself has to be a final one, otherwise an opportunity for resiling has been created. The consensus or agreement referred to does not mean that every possible term or condition likely to affect the relationship of parties has to be written into their contract. Many things will be afterwards settled by implication or from the conduct of the parties or from the intention of the parties. What is important is a willingness on the part of each party to be bound in the relationship of employer and employee by a basic general agreement. Anything short of that intention and type of contract will not be enough to set up a contract of service.[2]

The necessary elements of a valid offer and a valid acceptance to the constitution of a legal contract are fully discussed by the Institutional Writers[3] and these matters are also fully explained in the general text-books on contract.[4] It is not proposed to repeat the basic principles of contract law in this text when these principles are readily available in the standard reference works. Suffice it to say that, so long as the offer is met exactly by the acceptance, there is a binding contract. Any variation in the terms of an acceptance may be sufficient to constitute a counter-offer, which will now require to be accepted or rejected by the other side before a binding contract is concluded.

The general rules of contract relating to vitiation by error, force and fear or fraud or illegality[5] apply equally to contracts of service. So long as the consent is a real consent, willingly given, the contract is good. Mere concealment of a fact, although a material fact, does not ordinarily affect the contract.[6] It may do so, of course, where the concealment

---

[1] *Countess of Dunmore* v. *Alexander* (1836) 9 S. 190.

[2] See *Williamson* v. *Glasgow Local Pharmaceutical Committee* (O.H.) 1951 S.L.T.(Notes) 71, where the pursuer brought an action of damages for breach of a contract of service averring that he had been appointed secretary at a meeting of the local area committee for a three years' period. Some weeks after assuming that position he had been dismissed. In fact he had been *elected* as secretary, but he founded upon the minute of meeting of the committee as an improbative writ, followed by *rei interventus*. The court had no difficulty in holding that his election as secretary did not constitute a contract of service; and in any case no written contract had been relevantly averred.

[3] See Stair, Erskine and Bell on " Offer and Acceptance."

[4] See particularly Gloag, *Contract* (2nd ed., 1929), Chap. 2.

[5] Gloag, *op. cit.*, at appropriate chapters.

[6] *Fletcher* v. *Krell* (1872) 42 L.J.Q.B. 55.

induces some error in essentials on the part of the other party or gives rise to some fraud which causes loss or injury to the other party.

Although, under civil law, the contract of *locatio* was a consensual contract which did not require writing, this rule has been departed from in developed Scots law. Now the contract of service is the actual result of a contractual relationship or it is implied from the fact of service, presumed not to be given gratuitously and therefore it is a contract which may be made in writing or orally. However, it is recognised that if the duration of the contract is to exceed the period of one year it cannot be constituted by any form other than writing and the oath of a party will not supply the deficiency of a writing.[7] As to the theory behind this rule, this seems to be based upon the analogy between a hiring of services and a hiring of land.[8] There is, of course, the special case of the hiring of services of seamen. The legal position in the last-mentioned case is that writing is not essential to the actual hiring of seamen but it is nevertheless a statutory requirement which must be fulfilled before they put to sea.[9]

Where the contract of service is for less than one year it may be constituted orally and be proved by parole evidence.[10] If it is, in fact, constituted by writing then its existence is proved by reference to the writ,[11] but this does not necessarily exclude the use of parole evidence to establish a contract, some of whose conditions and terms have been set out in written form.[12] It must be kept in mind that where notices containing terms and conditions affecting employment are exhibited in places of work or where such terms and conditions are brought to the notice of the workmen in some form other than a written and signed contract or are part of an oral agreement, then such terms and conditions become imported into the contract of service and it has to be shown that the workmen were aware of their existence before they can be enforced.[13] It is the task of the party who founds upon the contract to prove its terms.[14] An engagement " at the rate of £200 a year " has been held to imply a year's contractual engagement.[15]

It is still a matter of debate whether the oral contract for a period in excess of a year is, apart from *rei interventus*, quite ineffective and invalid or whether it is good for the usual term in the particular type of

---

[7] See *Caddell* v. *Sinclair* (1749) Mor. 12, 416; *Paterson* v. *Edingtons* (1830) 8 S. 931; *Kennedy* v. *Young* (1837) 1 Swinton 474; *Stewart and M'Donald* v. *M'Call* (1869) 7 M. 544; Bell's *Principles*, s. 173; *Dickson on Evidence*, s. 567.

[8] See Fraser, *Master and Servant, op. cit.*, p. 29.

[9] See the Merchant Shipping Act 1894, ss. 113 and 114.

[10] *Smellie* v. *Gillespie* (1833) 12 S. 125; *Caddell* v. *Sinclair, supra*; Bell's *Principles*, s. 173; *Dickson on Evidence*, s. 567.

[11] See Umpherston, p. 24 and cases cited at n. 6 thereof.

[12] *Barratt* v. *Stewart* (1893) 1 S.L.T. 284.

[13] *Wright* v. *Howard, Baker & Co.* (1893) 21 R. 25; *Cowdenbeath Coal Co.* v. *Drylie* (1886) 3 Sh.Ct.Rep. 3.

[14] *Robson* v. *Overend* (1878) 6 R. 213; *Cowan* v. *McMicking* (1846) 19 Sc.Jur. 91; and see particularly *Forbes* v. *Milne* (1827) 6 S. 75; *Thomson* v. *Izat* (1831) 9 S. 598; *cf.* *Wilkie* v. *Bethune* (1848) 11 D. 132.

[15] *Dowling* v. *Henderson & Son* (1890) 17 R. 921; 27 S.L.R. 738.

service concerned or whether it is good for one year. Bell[16] suggests that the latter view is more correct whilst Lord Fraser[17] is inclined to the former. The point has been discussed in several cases[18] particularly during the mid-nineteenth-century period and again more recently in the early twentieth century[19] where Lord Low, in the *Reuter* case, favoured validity for one year where service had been entered upon, proof being by writ or oath. The matter has again been considered in several cases of more recent date, and particularly in *Nisbet* v. *Percy and Others* and *Murray* v. *Roussel Laboratories Ltd.*[20]

Accordingly, the better view seems to be that the oral or informally executed written contract of service for a period exceeding one year is ineffective for the full term; but if an oral agreement has been acted upon to the extent that service has been entered upon thereunder, the contract is binding upon the parties for one year or for a period of time regulated by custom or usage in the particular service, but in any case, for no longer than one year. There still remains to be considered the question of the effect of entering into the service relationship under an informal written contract. The writing which is required to prove the contract of service may be either a formal document or, very often, an exchange of missive letters. Such writing must be tested or be holograph of parties or be " adopted as holograph." [21] Formal styles or precedents for such written agreements or missives may be found in the reference and style books.[22]

Any writing which is improbative is not necessarily completely invalid and ineffective, because a statutory provision[23] guards against a mere informality of execution. It is to be noted, however, that any alteration in the terms of a written contract can only be proved by writing.[24] Certain important changes in the common law have recently been made by the Contracts of Employment Act 1963[25] and these are discussed later in this chapter.

(2) *Locus Poenitentiae*

The general principle relating to the period within which any party may resile without incurring liability for breach of contract applies with

---

[16] *Principles*, s. 173.
[17] *Op. cit.*, p. 30.
[18] *Caddell* v. *Sinclair, cit. supra; Paterson* v. *Edingtons, cit. supra; Stewart and M'Donald* v. *M'Call, supra; Murray* v. *M'Gilchrist* (1864) 4 Irv. 461; and *Young* v. *Scott* (1864) 4 Irv. 541; *Currie* v. *M'Lean* (1864) 2 M. 1076; *Forbes* v. *Caird* (1877) 4 R. 1141.
[19] *Reuter* v. *Douglas* (1902) 10 S.L.T. 294; *Brown* v. *Scottish Antarctic Expedition* (1902) 10 S.L.T. 433.
[20] 1951 S.C. 350 (*per* L.P. Cooper at p. 355) and 1960 S.L.T. (Notes) 31 (O.H.) respectively.
[21] See *Stewart and M'Donald* v. *M'Call, supra; Paterson* v. *Edingtons, supra; M'Aslan* v. *Finlayson* (1877) 1 Guthrie's Sh.Ct. Cases 383; *Sproul* v. *Wilson* (1809) Hume 920.
[22] See particularly the *Encyclopaedia of Scots Legal Styles* and Burns' *Conveyancing Practice* (4th ed. edited by Professor MacRitchie).
[23] See the Conveyancing (Scotland) Act 1874, s. 39; see also Burns' *Conveyancing Practice* on the topic of " Informalities of execution."
[24] *Dumbarton Glass Co.* v. *Coatsworth* (1847) 9 D. 732.
[25] 1963, c. 49.

equal force to the negotiations which take place towards a finalisation of the parties' agreement for a contract of service. Once the consensus is *ad idem* the right to resile is lost.[26]

It may be necessary to take account of some trade custom or usage, which must be fulfilled before the bargain or agreement is regarded as being final. For example, in older law, if " earnest " (or arles) had to be given when an agreement was completed the *locus poenitentiae* was still effective until the giving of earnest.[27]

(3) *Rei Interventus*

This may operate so as to exclude the rule of *locus poenitentiae* and it is equivalent to the completion of a formal contract. The classic definition may be found in the writings of Erskine and Bell.[28] The contract is perfected by the operation of *rei interventus*[29] though it is still essential that there be *consensus ad idem* as to its terms.[30] It is essential that the acts which constitute and support *rei interventus* should follow upon the agreement. Acts prior to a written agreement could only constitute *rei interventus* if they followed upon a preceding oral agreement which was subsequently reduced to writing.[31]

Where *rei interventus* follows upon an informal contract a double proof is necessary, *viz.* (a) evidence as to the particular contract and (b) evidence as to the acts themselves which it is claimed must be regarded as forming the *rei interventus*. Mr. Umpherston points out [32] that the strict rules as to proof have not always been adhered to in the case of employer and employee. There seems to be no doubt, however, that proof of the acts constituting *rei interventus* may be adduced *prout de jure*.[33]

Rei interventus may follow upon (a) the contract which is constituted orally or (b) the contract which is constituted by a writing which is informal.

In practice and in relation specifically to the employment situation, the most common form is that where the employee enters upon the service and is paid wages by the employer under the contract.

As has been mentioned above, a most important question arises where *rei interventus* follows upon an oral contract for more than a year. This was specifically considered in *Dale* v. *Dumbarton Glasswork Company*,[34] where the contract was held to be binding for the whole term. This case is perhaps not wholly authoritative because the ground of the

---

26 See Bell's *Commentaries*, i, 345; *Principles*, s. 25; Erskine III, 2, 3.
27 See note *infra* on " earnest."
28 Bell's *Principles*, s. 26; *Commentaries*, i, 346; Erskine III, 2, 3; see also Dickson, *Evidence*, ss. 841–845.
29 *Walker* v. *Flint* (1863) 1 M. 417, *per* L.J.-C. Inglis at p. 421.
30 *Alexander* v. *Montgomery & Co.* (1773) 2 Pat.App. 300.
31 See Umpherston, *op. cit.*, p. 29 and cases cited at n. 5 thereof.
32 *Op. cit.*, pp. 29 and 30 and cases, etc., cited at n. 1 to p. 30.
33 Dickson, *Evidence*, s. 832.
34 (1829) 7 S. 369; *vide* also *Murray* v. *Roussel Laboratories Ltd., cit. supra.*

decision was based on English law (as the *lex loci contractus*), wherein an oral contract for more than a year has been held to be binding.

There have been few cases [35] of *rei interventus* following upon an informal writing. In the recent case of *Tojeiro* v. *McKettrick-Agnew and Co.*,[36] wherein an employee had claimed for two years' arrears of salary on the basis of an improbative agreement, it was held that he could not succeed in the absence of specific averments of *rei interventus*. It seems that a rule analogous to that by which possession under an informal written lease constitutes sufficient *rei interventus* to validate the lease for its whole duration [37] has been applied to service under an informal written contract. Once service has been entered into under the contract and is continued therein, this sets up the contract for the full term agreed upon.

(4) *Earnest (or Arles)*

The practice of giving " earnest " seems now to be of historical interest only and it is probably no longer used in any employment at all.[38] It is said to have been a " test of engagement." Mackenzie [39] calls it " a symbol or mark of agreement." It appears to have been only suitable to a contract founded upon an oral agreement and even then it seems to have lent nothing to the agreement itself, although the custom of the particular employment might demand that it be given.[40] To hand back a sum given as earnest did not destroy or dissolve the contract.[41] But, if a contract were not effectively concluded because *locus poenitentiae* still operated, although earnest had been given, there was an obligation upon the party who received the earnest and who was then seeking to resile to return it to the giver.[42] Where a sum was given as " an evidence of a bargain closed and perfected " this was termed " dead earnest." [43] Earnest should not be confused with part payment under a contract, which may well amount to *rei interventus*.[44]

It would be most unusual, in modern practice, to require the giving of earnest as evidence of a complete bargain. Indeed none of the modern English textbooks on Industrial Law makes any reference to it at all.

[53] See however *Napier* v. *Dick* (1805) Hume 388; it is clear from *Stewart, etc.* v. *M'Call* (1869) 7 M. 544 that where an improbative writing is not followed by *rei interventus*, the contract is not a binding contract.

[36] (O.H.) 1967 S.L.T.(Notes) 11.

[37] See Umpherston, *op. cit.*, p. 31 and cases cited at n. 2 thereof.

[38] An analogous case perhaps in relation to regular enlistment in H.M. Forces is the giving of the " Queen's Shilling " which is still, or was until recently, used as evidence of the completed act of engagement. Such an engagement does not, of course, constitute the master and servant relationship.

[39] See his *Institutes*, 3, 3, 1.

[40] See Bell's *Principles*, s. 173.

[41] *Wallace* v. *Wishart* (1800) Hume 383; *Topping* v. *Barr* (1830) 8 S. 973; *Brown* v. *Whittingham* (1629) Mor. 8468; Erskine III, 3, 5.

[42] See *Lawson* v. *Auchinleck* (1699) Mor. 8402.

[43] See Stair, i. 14, 3.

[44] *Lawson* v. *Auchinleck, supra*; *Graham* v. *Corbet* (1708) Mor. 8428; *Clerk* v. *Murchison* (1799) Mor. 9186.

(5) *Implied Contracts of Service*

Any claim for wages has to be founded upon a contract to pay wages or upon services rendered by the claimant which were not understood to be gratuitous. There is a presumption that services are given for wages [45] and not gratuitously. Should it appear from the circumstances that there is a reason—other than wages—for the giving of the services, then the presumption does not apply.[46] The test to be applied is this—did the parties act in the respective capacities of employer and employee ? [47] If so, then wages will be payable upon an implied contract of service.[48] The onus of proof lies upon the person who founds upon the services rendered. Where an implied contract appears to be in existence the onus of challenging it would then lie upon the employer who would aver (and would require to prove to the court's satisfaction) that the agreement between himself and the employee related to the giving of services gratuitously or that it merely related to the giving of food and clothing by the employer, but in any case it was not in respect of wages.[49] The mere provision of food and clothing does not displace the onus [50] upon the employer, though these things are of some importance in relation to an evaluation or assessment of the services rendered to the employer. Nor is the employee entitled to receive pay for extra work done by him where the contract of service requires him to give his whole attention to the business and the particular work done—in respect of which the claim has been made—falls within the contract of service.[51] This situation is not to be confused with overtime and agreed overtime rates of pay.

Finally, a contract of service may be implied where there is a change of circumstance in the status or legal personality of the employer.[52] The most common examples are, first, the conversion of a business, formerly owned by an individual or a partnership, into a limited company or, secondly, the liquidation of a company and the subsequent appointment

---

45 See *Peter* v. *Rennie's Reps.* (1842) 14 J. 240; *Anderson* v. *Halley* (1847) 9 D. 1222; and *Thomson* v. *Thomson's Tr.* (1889) 16 R. 333; *Miller* v. *Miller* (1898) 25 R. 9951; 6 S.L.T. 57; but *Stuart* v. *M'Leod* (1901) 9 S.L.T. 192 (O.H.); but in the case of a family relationship subsisting between the parties there is no presumption of a contract to pay wages—see *Urquhart* v. *Urquhart's Tr.* (1905) 8 F. 42, etc. (in which a child assisted in his father's business and was provided with his keep, etc.) where the pursuer or claimant receives his keep, etc. (*i.e.*, an equivalent to wages); see also *Macnaughton* v. *Finlayson's Trustees* (1902) 40 S.L.R. 645; 10 S.L.T. 322; and *Russel* v. *M'Clymont* (1906) 8 F. 821; (1906) 14 S.L.T. 59.
46 *Ritchie* v. *Ferguson* (1849) 12 D. 119; *Fyffe* v. *Lawson* (1891) 8 Sh.Ct.Rep. 220; *Pratt* v. *Rankine* (1898) 6 S.L.T. 126.
47 *M'Naughton* v. *M'Naughton* (1813) Hume 396; *Shepherd* v. *Meldrum* (1812) Hume 394 and the trilogy of cases in which pursuer was the same person, *viz. Smellie* v. *Gillespie* (1833) 12 S. 125; (1834) 13 S. 700; *Smellie* v. *Cochrane* (1835) 13 S. 544; and *Smellie* v. *Miller* (1835) 14 S. 12.
48 *Ritchie* v. *Ferguson* (1849) 12 D. 119 *supra*; *Dawson* v. *Thorburn* (1888) 15 R. 891; *M'Naughton* v. *Ross* (1902) 10 S.L.T. 322.
49 See *M'Naughton* v. *M'Naughton*, *cit. supra*; and *Anderson* v. *Halley*, *cit. supra*.
50 *Shepherd* v. *Meldrum*, *cit. supra*; *Smellie* v. *Gillespie*, *cit. supra*; and *Anderson* v. *Halley*, *cit. supra*.
51 See *Money* v. *Hannan and Kerr* (1867) 5 S.L.R. 32.
52 *Adam* v. *Peter* (1842) 4 D. 599.

of a liquidator to undertake the formal liquidation or winding up thereof.[53] The employees will usually continue to serve the new company (*i.e.*, their new employer) in the former case or the liquidator in the latter case, without the preparation of fresh contracts of service or formal consents; and in each case their old contractual relationship is continued by implication to form the new contractual basis which governs their relationship with the substituted employer.[54] The provisions of the Contracts of Employment Act 1963 must now be kept in mind with special reference to section 4 and the supplemental provisions of section 5. It may or may not be necessary to give to the employees the information required by section 4, but this is a question of circumstances. Moreover, special attention must be paid to Schedule 1, paragraph 10, to the 1963 Act, as amended by section 48 (7) of the Redundancy Payments Act 1965, which deals broadly with the computation of the period of employment, so far as the Schedule is concerned, and specifically with the situation involving a change of employer, so far as the paragraph itself is concerned.

(6) *Commencement of the Employment*

The employee's duty is to enter upon the service at the time agreed, unless illness [55] or other cause, over which he has no control or for which he is not responsible, should prevent him from so doing. It is, of course, equally a breach of contract by the employer should he refuse to accept the employee into his service. Mr. Umpherston points out [56] that the date of commencing service may not be expressly stated, and, accordingly, resort must be had to the custom of the particular occupation or trade in order to ascertain the position. This difficulty is unlikely to arise in modern industrial practice where " hiring and firing " will often be done by a foreman, who will usually specify dates and times.

(7) *The Service itself*

It is most unusual to find that the total duties of any employee are carefully and expressly set forth in a contract of employment. Usually the employee is engaged in a particular character or type of employment and this is simply stated as, for example, chauffeur, housekeeper, qualified clerk or otherwise, as the case may be. The minimum requirements specified in section 4 of the Contracts of Employment Act 1963 now operate since this Act came into force and every employee must have, within a period of thirteen weeks of commencing his employment, a written statement containing the information stipulated by the section (except, as appropriate, where there are no particulars to be given under

---

[53] See *Cowan* v. *M'Micking* (1846) 19 Sc.J. 91.
[54] *Day* v. *Tait* (1900) 8 S.L.T. 40; *Taylor* v. *R. H. Thomson & Co. Ltd.* (1901) 9 S.L.T. 373; (1902) 10 S.L.T. 195; *Houston* v. *Calico Printers Association* (1903) 10 S.L.T. 532; *Berlitz School of Languages* v. *Duchêne* (1903) 6 F. 181, *per* Lord McLaren at p. 185.
[55] See *Comasky* v. *Jeffrey* (1887) 2 Guthrie's Sh.Ct. Cases 353; *Boast* v. *Firth* (1868) L.R. 4 C.P. 1.
[56] *Op. cit.*, pp. 43 and 44.

any of the headings in subsection (1) of section 4. As an alternative to the provision of a written statement an employee may, by subsection (5) of section 4, be referred to some document which he has reasonable opportunities of reading in the course of his employment or which is made readily accessible to him in some other way. Any change in the terms of employment is allowed for by subsection (4) of section 4 and the employee must be notified, within a period of one month from the date of change, of the nature of the change. This information must again be given in a written statement, of which the employee may receive a copy, or otherwise by reference to the written statement which, although retained by the employer, the employee has reasonable opportunities of reading in the course of his employment or which is made readily accessible to him in some other way.

The employee undertakes to give his time exclusively to the business of his employer [57] and to perform all the services which pertain to the particular type or character of employment, as well as to obey all lawful orders which the employer is entitled to give an employee of the particular capacity concerned.[58] The undertaking to give his time exclusively to the employer's business does not mean that the employee cannot engage in business himself or take paid work elsewhere on a part-time basis. What is meant is that the employee cannot undertake any other employment which conflicts with or is in competition with the business of his employer. He may, for example, be a cost accountant for the Scotia Shipbuilding Company during the day and be a barman in the local public-house at night, but he cannot do part-time work as a cost accountant for the Anglia Shipbuilding Company, which is in competition with his main employers.[59]

The ordinary employee must obey all lawful orders, but the personal employee or domestic servant must conform to the regulations of his master's household. The latter is not permitted to have quite the same freedom as the ordinary employee; e.g., to keep late hours, be drunk, disobey a lawful instruction or leave the house against his employer's wishes may constitute, in any one of these cases, a failure by the employee in his household duties.[60] The employer is, of course, the judge as to what is reasonable for the administration of his household. Failure to obey may be due to mere neglect; but an isolated act of neglect or forgetfulness does not usually justify instant dismissal; see, for example, Baster v.

[57] Cameron & Co. v. Gibb (1867) 3 S.L.R. 282; but cf. Currie v. Glasgow Central Stores Ltd. (1905) 13 S.L.T. 88 (no such implied term in the particular circumstances).

[58] Selby v. Baldry (1867) 5 S.L.R. 64.

[59] The following English cases are most helpful on this point: Pearce v. Foster (1886) 17 Q.B.D. 536 (dismissal of a confidential clerk advising on securities, who was himself dealing in Stock Exchange speculations). Boston Deep Sea Fishing & Ice Co. v. Ansell (1888) 39 Ch.D. 339. Hivac Ltd. v. Park Royal Scientific Instruments Ltd. [1946] Ch. 169; [1946] 1 All E.R. 350, C.A.

[60] Hamilton v. McLean (1824) 3 S. 268; A v. B (1853) 16 D. 269; Turner v. Mason (1845) 14 M. & W 112; Elder v. Bennett (1802) Hume 386; (1845) L.J.Ex. 311; Edwards v. Mackie (1848) 11 D. 67; Silvie v. Stewart (1830) 8 S. 1010.

London & County Printing Works,[61] where the Divisional Court stated that " what constitutes conduct justifying instant dismissal is always one of degree." If the neglect relates to an important matter, then instant dismissal would very probably be justified.

Nevertheless, where an employee is hired in one capacity, he cannot be held bound to perform work which is outside of the normal scope of his duties.[62] He may have to perform certain extraordinary duties if the contract provides for these expressly or if there is a local custom indicating such an obligation. But, an employee of higher grade or level is not bound to perform the tasks of a lower-grade employee, even although he is paid the same wages.[63] For example, a qualified cook cannot be compelled to run shopping errands for the household.[64] The courts today are reluctant to regard a single isolated act of disobedience as justifying dismissal.[65] Although this last reference is to an English case it is not at all unreasonable to assume that the Scottish courts would take a similar view in another case in which the facts were broadly the same.

A most interesting case of legitimate refusal to carry out an instruction from his employer is permitted to the employee when the actual doing of the particular task, though otherwise normally within the scope of his duties, would expose him to undue personal danger or risk [66]—for example, death or physical injury, or where the act would be illegal.[67] The question of risk, or threatened risk, of personal danger has arisen in England, mainly in the 1930s, in two rather interesting cases—first, in *Ottoman Bank* v. *Chakarian* [68] where the employee was successful in an action for wrongful dismissal based upon proof of danger to his life; and, secondly, in *Bouzourou* v. *Ottoman Bank* [69] where the employee was unsuccessful, since he was unable to discharge the onus of proof relating to danger to his life.

As the contract of service is personal by its nature the law requires that the employee should himself perform the obligations and duties laid upon him. Delegation is not permitted,[70] unless of course this is specifically provided for and authorised in the contract, or, alternatively,

---

[61] [1899] 1 Q.B. 901.
[62] See particularly *Stuart* v. *Richardson* (1806) Hume 390; *Thomson* v. *Douglas* (1807) Hume 392; *Kirkcaldy* v. *Landale* (1889) 5 Sh.Ct.Rep. 251; *Moffat* v. *Boothby* (1884) 11 R. 501; and *Wilson* v. *Simson* (1844) 6 D. 1256, this last case involving a special duty which the court supported on the evidence and gave judgment favourable to the employer (the servant had claimed damages for wrongous dismissal); also *Cobban* v. *Lawson* (1868) 6 S.L.R. 60 where the decision again proved favourable to the employer.
[63] *Ross* v. *Pender* (1874) 1 R. 352 (head gamekeeper cannot be forced to work as an under-keeper).
[64] *Gunn* v. *Ramsay* (1801) Hume 384.
[65] See *Laws* v. *London Chronicle (Indicator Newspapers) Ltd.* [1959] 1 W.L.R. 698.
[66] *Sutherland* v. *Monkland Railways* (1857) 19 D. 1004; and *Mackay* v. *Crawford* (1892) Sh.Ct.Rep. 52.
[67] *Phillips* v. *Innes* (1835) 13 S. 778.
[68] [1930] A.C. 277.
[69] [1930] A.C. 271.
[70] *Campbell* v. *Price* (1831) 9 S. 264.

the nature of the particular employment itself implies a right by the employee to delegate. Any performance by a third party could not, in the general case, be relied upon as a proper performance of the contract.[71] There may be circumstances in which an employee would purport to delegate his duties (*e.g.*, the driving of a vehicle) and his employer would escape liability because there would be no proper relationship of employer and employee. If, however, the employee retained some control over the delegate, then the employer is normally liable *qua* employer.[72] The matter could only be dealt with satisfactorily by the substitution of one person for another, and the substitute must be duly accepted by the employer or the provision of a particular substitute must have been previously authorised by the employer.

(8) *Place of Service*

The rule is that where the contract of service stipulates for a particular place as the place where the service is to be performed, the employer cannot have that service performed elsewhere.[73] But this rule must be interpreted reasonably, as illustrated in the *Anderson* v. *Moon*[74] case, where a female worker, directed to move her place of work from one spinning mill to another in the middle of a hiring term, was held entitled to refuse to go. Her objections to the transfer were not capricious or imaginary. The personal employee is, however, bound to attend his employer wherever he goes. This has been interpreted by the textwriters as meaning that he should accompany his employer within the United Kingdom. If, however, the employer is going abroad permanently then the employee need not go with him. Should the employer be going abroad for a short term only the personal servant is probably bound to accompany him, for a reasonable period. It is suggested by Mr. Umpherston[75] that the domestic servant cannot be moved permanently.

In these modern times there are instances of the creation of new industrial estates or the centralisation of large industrial concerns in particular areas of Scotland or England (mainly in the latter country) which involve the transfer of large numbers of employees from place to place. Unless there is a specific clause in the service contract which provides against this eventuality of transfer, it is considered that no employee could be compelled by management to move. Nevertheless the employee who does not go may forfeit valuable pension rights and other

---

[71] *British Waggon Co.* v. *Lea* (1880) 5 Q.B.D. 149; 49 L.J.Q.B. 321; *Tolhurst* v. *Associated Portland Cement Manufacturers* [1902] 2 K.B. 660; *Cooper* v. *Micklefield Coal Co* (1912) 107 L.T. 457.

[72] See the opinion of the Lord Ordinary (Fleming) in *Fulton's Tutor* v. *Mason and Sons Ltd.* (O.H.) 1927 S.L.T. 428, following *Ricketts* v. *Thomas Tilling Ltd.* [1915] 1 K.B. 644, C.A.

[73] *Anderson* v. *Moon* (1837) 15 S. 412; *Stuart* v. *Richardson* (1806) Hume 390; *Annett* v. *Glenburn Hydropathic Co.* (1893) 9 Sh.Ct.Rep. 66; see also the English case of *Eaton* v. *Western* (1882) 9 Q.B.D. 636.

[74] *Cit. supra.*

[75] *Op. cit.*, pp. 48–49.

benefits. The real hardship in cases of this type lies with the older employee, who is nearing retirement. Apart from any private arrangement which his company employers make for him, there is now in force the Redundancy Payments Act 1965,[76] which alleviates the position to some extent, in the case of declared redundancy. No private arrangement or redundancy payment can truly compensate a skilled employee when he feels that he is " being thrown on the scrap heap." The 1965 Act mentioned above is a step—but only a step—in the right direction. What is needed is an enlightened approach to the whole problem of industrial re-training and the absorption into other industries of employees who become unemployed because of redundancies in a particular establishment or because of the substantial movement of employing concerns.

(9) Days and Hours of Service

Generally, the days and hours of service depend upon three things— (a) the nature of the service, (b) the custom of the locality and (c) the regulations which are applicable within the employer's establishment. If the contract stipulates expressly the hours and days which the employee has to work, then the terms of the contract will be binding upon him.[77] Before the employee could absent himself from the employment during the stipulated period he would require to obtain permission from the employer (illness, of course, being always excusable). The question of periods of employment is generally a matter of agreement in each particular trade, between the trade union concerned on the one side and the particular employer or federation of employers on the other side. There is today a fairly general acceptance of the principle of the forty-hour week, spread over five working days (normally Monday to Friday inclusive). Daily starting times and finishing times tend to vary from industry to industry or from place to place.

It is also essential to bear in mind that statute law [78] may lay down special provisions regarding periods of employment or, more particularly, restrict periods and places of employment for special classes of persons, e.g., young persons and female employees generally. It must be said, however, that statute law has tended to leave a maximum amount of freedom of contract between the adult male employee and his employer. To restrict this freedom would draw the following valid criticisms, viz.: (a) first, that the earning capacity of adult male employees was being curtailed and (b) that the productive capacity and output of British industry generally was being prejudiced. However, government economic policies may, from time to time, be such that some ceiling or limitation upon wages has to be imposed. This has been illustrated in present times

---

[76] 1965, c. 62; considered in a later chapter, viz., Chap. 8.
[77] Cowdenbeath Coal Co. v. Drylie (1886) 3 Sh.Ct.Rep. 3.
[78] For example, in factories, mines, shops and offices by the following statutes: Factories Act 1961 (see ss. 86 to 119 inclusive); Mines and Quarries Act 1954 (see ss. 124 to 132 inclusive); and Offices, Shops and Railway Premises Act 1963.

by the Prices and Incomes Act 1966,[79] which gives the government very important compulsory powers in an attempt to combat inflation and maintain what the economic experts are pleased to call a " balanced economy." Government interference in wage negotiations is discussed in a later chapter dealing with wages generally. It is an exaggeration, in the general case, to say that every individual adult employee has a free bargaining power in the matter of fixing his wages. This is achieved nowadays by " group pressure," that is to say by a trade union or other national association or other body negotiating with a confederation of employers or with a department of state or with H.M. Treasury. Examples can be found here in relation to local government officers (negotiating through N.A.L.G.O.), schoolteachers in Scotland (negotiating through the Scottish Education Department) and university teachers (negotiating formerly through National Incomes Commission, U.G.C. and, of course, H.M. Treasury, and now through U.G.C., A.U.T. and the Ministry of Education). Alternatively, a statutory provision or wages council order—applicable to a particular trade or industry—may specify a minimum wage rate. It would therefore be exceptional in modern industrial practice to find an individual employee who could truthfully claim that his wage or salary was the subject of free and unrestricted negotiation between his employer and himself.

As regards overtime working, the common law rules applicable to this topic heading would seem to be that, where no express stipulation is made as to hours or days, the employee does not require to work overtime [80] if he does not wish to do so; if he does, then he might be able to do so upon conditions more favourable to him.[81] Furthermore, the law will not interfere in the ordinary case unless the employer is trying to impose unduly harsh and injurious conditions upon the employee. Should an emergency arise within a particular employment, the employer is entitled to the labour of his employees for a much longer period than normal.[82] The reason for this is doubtless that the interest of the employer is the interest of the employees and the latter must have regard at all times to the business of their employer.

The common law position in England seems to be that the hours to be worked by an employee are a matter for regulation by the express terms of the contract. Some term or terms as to hours of work may be implied into the contract by custom or from agreements made between the employer (or a confederation of employers) and the union to which the employee belongs. Whether such a term can be implied depends upon the circumstances surrounding the contract of employment. The

---

[79] 1966, c. 33; followed by the Prices and Incomes Act 1967 (1967, c. 53) and the Prices and Incomes Act 1968 (1968, c. 42). See Chap. 8, *infra*.
[80] *Oliver* v. *Macfarlane* (1903) 19 Sh.Ct.Rep. 204.
[81] See *Mackenzie* v. *Baird's Trs.*, 1907 S.C. 838; (1907) 14 S.L.T. 909; and *Mackison's Tr.* v. *Magistrate of Dundee*, 1909 S.C. 971; 1909, 1 S.L.T. 383, affirmed 1910 S.C.(H.L.) 27 and 1910, 1 S.L.T. 221, regarding extra services rendered by employees.
[82] *Greig* v. *Moir* (1893) 9 Sh.Ct.Rep. 341.

legal point of importance is whether the agreement or arrangement in question has been accepted as forming part of the contract.[83]

Apart from such implied terms there may be duties upon the employer in respect of hours of work, arising from statutory provisions applicable to the particular employment. For example, much legislation has been passed, particularly during the last century—mainly as a result of social reform—on the subject of the restriction of hours of work of women and young persons.

(10) *Sunday Work*

By the Act 1579, c. 70, all " handy lauboring or wirking " was prohibited in Scotland on a Sunday. That Act was confirmed by a further Act of 1690, c. 5, which now, however, excepted works of necessity and mercy.[84] These statutes are still in force.[84a] However, the Statute Law Revision (Scotland) Act 1964, under-noted,[84a] by Schedule 2, renamed the Act of 1579, c. 70, as " The Sunday Act 1579 " and also renamed the Act of 1690, c. 5, as " The Confession of Faith Ratification Act 1690." Moreover, Schedule 1 to the 1964 Act substantially pruned the text of the 1579 Act which now prohibits only markets and fairs on Sundays. All references to " handy lauboring or wirking " have been repealed. No changes were made to the text of the 1690 Act, and Chapter XXI, paragraph 8, of the Confession of Faith still refers to the Sabbath as a holy day of rest from " works, words and thoughts about worldly employments and recreations " but continues to allow works of necessity and mercy. It seems, therefore, that an employee cannot be forced to work on a Sunday, unless the service required is classified as being either one of necessity or of mercy. These exceptions will arise mainly in the industries relating to the supply of water, gas and electricity and again in the ambulance services. Interpretation of works of necessity in particular will tend to be reasonably wide and dependent upon the circumstances of the instant case. It should also be noted that any particular statute governing employment in certain places may itself enforce and confirm an absolute prohibition against Sunday work so far as certain classes of persons are concerned.[85] It has also been held that the Act of 1579, c. 70, does not apply to such an employment as that of a watchman—see *Smith* v. *William Beardmore & Co.*[86] The logic of this decision cannot be questioned, because the watchman is neither working nor labouring—he is merely keeping a watch on otherwise unoccupied premises.

[83] *National Coal Board* v. *Galley* [1958] 1 All E.R. 91 (see particularly pp. 96–97).
[84] See *Phillips* v. *Innes* (1837) 2 S. & McL. 465 (*per* L.C. Cottenham at p. 486)—a contract to work on Sunday in contravention of the 1579 and 1690 Acts was illegal. See also: the cases of *Wilson* v. *Simson* (1844) 6 D. 1256; and *Middleton* v. *Paterson* (1904) 11 S.L.T. 610; (1904) 6 F.(J.) 27.
[84a] See the Statute Law Revision (Scotland) Act 1964 (c. 80).
[85] *e.g.*, the Factories Act 1961, s. 93; and the Mines and Quarries Act 1954, ss. 126 (5) and 127 (1) and (4).
[86] 1922 S.C. 131; 1922 S.L.T. 58.

(11) *Holidays*

Before an employer comes under a duty to allow holidays to his employees the common law position seems to be that provision therefor must be expressed in the contract between them or be implied by custom of the trade or locality.[87] Accordingly, if an employee undertook to work on holidays he would be bound by his obligations; unless the fact of his so working constituted a breach of a particular statute.[88] Great care must be taken by employers to ascertain whether any particular statute applicable to their industry or trade requires certain holidays to be given to their employees. If so, then the terms of the statute must be obeyed.[89]

Bank holidays were introduced in 1871 to allow for some holidays being granted to the working classes. This measure was of specific value to shop assistants and others who were providing a daily service to the consumer public. Holidays with pay were introduced, as a principle, by the Holidays with Pay Act 1938 (which applied to road haulage and agriculture). The normal effects of this particular statute could not be made the subject of careful study because of the advent of the Second World War in 1939. There has to be kept in mind also the powers and functions of Wages Councils, in terms of the Wages Councils Act of 1959. Their tasks also include the fixing of holiday periods and holiday pay in the particular industry for which the Council is established.[90] This matter is dealt with in more detail in a later chapter of this book, when the subject of wages is more fully considered.[91]

The older common law accepted the position that when the period of service was drawing to a close, the employee was to be allowed sufficient freedom to look for other employment. This was certainly so in the case of agricultural employees who could take time off to attend a hiring fair, though they could not advance this claim so as to convert a whole working day into a holiday.[92]

(12) *Duration of the Service*

Where the period of service is not specified, this may be inferred from the nature of the service or from other terms of the contract. There was (and may still be) a presumption that a gardener[93] is hired for a year, an agricultural servant[94] and a gamekeeper[95] for a similar period, whilst

---

[87] *R.* v. *Inhabitants of Stoke-on-Trent* (1843) 5 Q.B. 303.
[88] *Learmouth* v. *Blackie* (1828) 6 S. 533; *Phillips* v. *Innes* (1837) 2 S. & McL. 465.
[89] See, for example, the Factories Act 1961, s. 94, relating to the holidays to be allowed to women and young persons employed in factories.
[90] For other examples, see the Catering Wages Act 1943; and the Agricultural Wages (Scotland) Act 1949.
[91] *Infra,* Chap. 8.
[92] See *Alexander* v. *Gardner* (1863) 1 Guthrie's Sh.Ct. Cases 369.
[93] *Mabon* v. *Elliot* (1808) Hume 393; *Scott* v. *McMurdo* (1869) 6 S.L.R. 301 (see Lord Ardmillan); *Groom* v. *Clark* (1859) 21 D. 831.
[94] See *Muir* v. *McKenzie* (1829) 7 S. 717 as well as *Mabon* and *Scott, cit. supra.*
[95] *Bentinck* v. *Macpherson* (1869) 6 S.L.R. 376; *Cameron* v. *Fletcher* (1872) 10 M. 301; *Armstrong* v. *Bainbridge* (1846) 9 D. 29, 1198; *Ross* v. *Pender* (1874) 1 R. 352.

a domestic servant [96] in an urban area is presumed to be hired for six months. These presumptions are a helpful guide only—they have no weight of absolute legal authority behind them—and will be so applied in an attempt to reach a fair decision. It may be, however, that in a particular type of service the duration thereof was fixed by custom. This may be for a year or six months as appropriate and this fact may be indicated when the service commences. It was possible to do this under older practice when hiring was related to either the Whitsunday or Martinmas term.

Failing an express or implied term in the contract, or an established local custom, it seems that the service should continue at the pleasure of both parties.[97] The duration of the contract may also be indicated by the circumstances of each particular case; by parties' intentions and so on, so that all of these things would have to be looked at carefully. Payment of wages or salary at so much per annum or per month or per week, whilst certainly not by itself conclusive in fixing the duration of the contract, may raise an understandable inference that the period of hire is on a yearly, monthly or weekly basis.[98] But all circumstances must be examined. For example, schoolteachers employed by a local authority, under the provisions of the various Education Acts, are so employed at the pleasure of the education committees of the counties (formerly the school boards)[99] and may be dismissed upon reasonable notice. Schoolteachers employed in a school which is regarded and classified as a " private " school in Scotland are so employed under the terms of their individual contracts with the governors or other managing body of the school.

There seems to be no case-law authority in Scotland on the question of the legality or otherwise of a contract of service for life or for an unlimited (but nevertheless extremely lengthy) period. The old cases [1] do not help much. The most that can be said [2] is that any contract which appears to lean towards slavery or an unreasonable restriction upon the employee will not be upheld by the courts.

(13) *Illness of the Employee*

The contractual relationship between employer and employee may be terminated by illness.[3] If not so terminated, the question to be resolved

---

[96] *Mabon* v. *Elliot, cit. supra.*
[97] *London, etc., Shipping Co.* v. *Ferguson* (1850) 13 D. 51; *Robson* v. *Overend* (1878) 6 R. 213; *Forsyth* v. *Heathery Knowe Coal Co.* (1880) 7 R. 887; *Morrison* v. *Abernethy School Board* (1876) 3 R. 945.
[98] See *Moffat* v. *Shedden* (1839) 1 D. 468 (*per* Lord MacKenzie); *Hoey* v. *M'Ewan and Auld* (1867) 5 M. 814 (*per* Lord Pres. Inglis at p. 818); *Dowling* v. *Henderson* (1890) 17 R. 921 (*per* Lord Trayner at p. 924); and, very importantly, *Campbell* v. *Fyfe* (1851) 13 D. 1041.
[99] See *Fairley* v. *Edinburgh School Board*, 1916, 1 S.L.T. 409. This case dealt, in fact, with the liability of the School Board.
[1] *Allan* v. *Skene* (1728) Mor. 9454; *Knight* v. *Wedderburn* (1778) Mor. 14, 545.
[2] See earlier note on slavery in Chap. 2 hereof.
[3] See *infra* Chap. 20.

is whether the employee can claim wages during his illness or whether the employer can reduce the wages or pay no wages at all during the period of incapacity. It is true that within the modern welfare state the incapacitated employee will receive sickness benefit, etc., under the National Insurance Acts, and it is also very often the case that an arrangement is made between an employer and an employee (the latter receiving full wages during his illness) that such state insurance benefit payments received will be handed over to the employer. But this arrangement does not affect the general legal question of liability or non-liability for payment during illness.

Stair [4] and Erskine [5] took the view that wages suffered no abatement and this seems to be supported in two older cases [6] of which the earlier one (*White* v. *Baillie*) concerned employer and employee. Here the court held that a farm servant, hired for a year, was entitled to full wages for that period although he had been incapacitated from working for eleven weeks within the year. In *McEwan* v. *Malcolm* [7] it was decided that where the disability to give the services required arose through the fault or misconduct of the employee, he had thereby disabled himself from performing his part of the contract and he could not call upon the employer to pay wages for the time of disablement. A special statutory provision applies this same principle in the case of merchant seamen.[8] Where the contract is for service for a term or terms, with wages accruing at the end of each term as a *unum quid*, then it appears that the wages payable for each term do not suffer any abatement.[9]

Where wages are payable according to the actual giving of service by the employee, he is not entitled to any wages payment for any period during which he does not serve. Should the wages be calculated on a time basis (*e.g.*, at an agreed rate per hour or per day), wages are normally payable only for the time served. Where the wages are stated to be, or are understood to be, at a certain sum per week or month (or longer) it seems that the wages will continue to accrue, unless the contract is terminated by notice or by the failure of the employee to attend at his place of employment.[10]

Custom may play an important part in this matter—for example, as Mr. Umpherston says,[11] the agricultural servant, hired for a year, is entitled to full wages if not absent from work through illness for more than six consecutive weeks during the year, disregarding the total length of time of his absences throughout the whole year. No claim can, however,

---

[4] i, 15, 2.
[5] III, 3, 16.
[6] *White* v. *Baillie* (1794) Mor. 10, 147; *McLean* v. *Fyfe*, Feb. 4, 1813, F.C., *per* Lord Meadowbank.
[7] (1867) 5 S.L.R. 62.
[8] See the Merchant Shipping Act 1894, s. 160.
[9] *Hoey* v. *M'Ewan and Auld* (1867) 5 M. 814.
[10] See Umpherston, p. 65 and n. (2) thereat.
[11] *Op. cit.*, pp. 65 and 66.

be made for wages during a period of illness which began before the date of commencement of the service and ended after that date. The reason for this is that the entering upon the service is a necessary preliminary to the earning of wages.[12] Illness, as a ground of termination of the contract of service, is more fully discussed in a later chapter.[13]

The employer is not obliged to provide medicine or medical attendance during the employee's illness, even although the injury was sustained in the former's service or the employee resided in the employer's house.[14] But if there is a duty of protection owed to an employee, then it would appear that the employer is obliged to obtain medical help or to notify the parents of the employee timeously, so that medical assistance can be obtained.[15] It must also be remembered that neglect by an employer to obtain medical assistance for an injured employee, who is subject to his control, may well be a breach of a legal obligation owed to that employee, with the result that the employer will be liable in damages.[16] It is always open to the employer, though it is most unusual and unlikely to be within modern practice, to undertake liability for medical attendance and that either expressly or by implication.[17] Where he does so the test of his liability is the extent of his undertaking.

A claim for wages is regarded as being subject to the triennial prescription, *i.e.*, it has to be pursued within the three years' period, otherwise the claimant would only be able to prove the obligation to pay by relying upon the writ or oath of the employer.[18]

(14) *Local Custom or Usage qualifying the Agreement*

Where local custom or usage is being relied upon to support an implied term in a contract of service, it is necessary that the custom averred must be " uniform and notorious " in the locality.[19]

Whilst it is accepted that custom may modify or define an obligation or term of the contract, it cannot be made use of in an attempt to create an additional or new obligation or term. If custom is excluded, either impliedly or expressly, when the contract is entered into, then it cannot be relied upon at all for a proposed or alleged modification of the contract.

---

[12] See *Comasky* v. *Jeffrey* (1887) 2 Guthrie's Sh.Ct. Cases 353.
[13] See Chap. 20 *infra*.
[14] *Sellen* v. *Norman* (1829) 4 C. & P. 80; and *Mitchell* v. *Adam* (1874) 1 Guthrie's Sh.Ct. Cases 361.
[15] *Jeffrey* v. *Donald* (1901) 9 S.L.T. 199; see also *McKeating* v. *Frame*, 1921 S.C. 382; the latter case being extremely important.
[16] See *Taylor* v. *Hill* (1900) 7 S.L.T. 318 and *McKeating* v. *Frame*, *cit. supra*.
[17] See *Montgomery* v. *North British Ry.* (1878) 5 R. 796.
[18] *Dunn* v. *Lamb* (1854) 16 D. 944; *Gobbi* v. *Lazzaroni* (1859) 21 D. 801; and on the question of defences to a claim for wages as well as possible counter-claims, see Umpherston, pp. 73–79 inclusive.
[19] See *Morrison* v. *Allardyce* (1823) 2 S. 287; and the dicta of Byles J. in *Foxall* v. *International Land Credit Co.* (1867) 16 L.T. 637 and Channell J. in *Moult* v. *Halliday* L.R. [1898] 1 Q.B. 125 at p. 129.

(15) *Recent Legislation*

Some important changes relating to the form of the service contract are contained in the Contracts of Employment Act 1963 [20] and the Redundancy Payments Act 1965.[21] The former statute now introduces into British law, for the first time, statutory minimum periods of notice by employer and employee and also provides for the giving of written particulars of the terms of employment to each employee. But the statute of 1963 also excludes from its scope certain categories of employees, of whom dockworkers, ship's masters and seamen and apprentices in the sea service are the main examples. The provisions regarding statutory minimum periods of notice are discussed in a later chapter,[22] but it is essential to look more fully, meantime, at the main provisions of both statutes so far as these relate to, or are concerned with, the formation or creation of the employment contract and the obligations upon both sides arising out of that intended relationship of employer and employee. It must be pointed out also that both of these statutes have an important part to play in the field of industrial relations and accordingly it will be necessary to refer to them again when the topic of trade union law is under consideration.[23]

The Contracts of Employment Act 1963 was hailed by certain sections of the Press as being the " workers' charter," but there is no doubt that such grandiose journalistic phraseology can be misleading. However, the statute does constitute an important landmark in British industrial law and industrial relations because, for the first time, (apart from dock workers) matters concerning the creation and termination of the contractual relationship between employer and employee are now set forth in an Act of Parliament. That statute replaces the common law in certain respects, whilst in other respects, the common law itself must be followed either as being supplementary and complementary to the statute or as providing the legal principles which are applicable in situations not governed by the statute. It will be understood immediately, therefore, that the 1963 Act does not apply to every type and kind of employment.

The first three sections of the 1963 Act deal with the question of the minimum periods of notice to be given by an employer to an employee and vice versa, the rights of the employee during the period of notice and the measure of damages in proceedings against an employer who fails to give the notice required by section 1 of the Act. These matters relate to termination of the relationship by notice or by failure to give adequate notice and accordingly their consideration is deferred until a later chapter.[24] The remaining seven sections must now be looked at,

---

[20] 1963, c. 49 (which became generally effective on July 6, 1964); see Contracts of Employment Act 1963 (Commencement) Order 1963 (No. 1916) made on November 27, 1963.
[21] 1965, c. 62.
[22] *Infra*, Chap. 18.
[23] *Infra*, Chap. 17.
[24] *Infra*, Chap. 18 particularly.

so far as these affect the creation or formation of the contract of employment.

Section 4 is the main section of the statute relating to the constitution of the contract. By this section, an employer is obliged, not later than thirteen weeks after the beginning of an employee's period of employment with him, to give to the employee a written statement identifying the parties, specifying the date when the employment began, and giving the following particulars of the terms of employment as at a specified date not more than one week before the statement is given, that is: (a) the scale or rate of remuneration, or the method of calculating remuneration; (b) the intervals at which remuneration is paid (*i.e.*, whether weekly or monthly, or by some other period); (c) any terms and conditions relating to hours of work (including any terms and conditions relating to normal working hours); (d) any terms and conditions relating to—(i) holidays and holiday pay, (ii) incapacity for work due to sickness or injury, including any provisions for sick pay, (iii) pensions and pension schemes; and (e) the length of notice which the employee is obliged to give and entitled to receive to determine his contract of employment.

It is also provided that information concerning pensions and pension schemes (paragraph (d) (iii) above) need not be given to the employees of any authority or body where the pension rights are determined by an Act of Parliament, which itself obliges the authority or body to give information regarding pension rights or the determination of questions affecting such to new employees. Should there be no information to be given under paragraph (d) above, or under any of the other paragraphs (a), (b), (c) and (e) then this fact has to be stated.[25] Where the contract is for a fixed term, the date of expiry must be stated.[26]

Where any change in the terms of employment to be included or referred to in the statement occurs after the date to which the statement under section 4 (1) relates, the employer is allowed a period of one month within which the employee must be notified of the nature of the change, by a written statement. If a copy of that statement is not given to the employee, the written statement itself must be preserved and reasonable opportunities of reading it must be given to the employee in the course of his employment, or alternatively the statement must be made reasonably accessible to him in some other way.[27] Section 4 (5) explains that a statement under section 4 (1) or section 4 (4) may, for all or any of the particulars to be given by the statement, refer the employee to some document which he has reasonable opportunities of reading in the course of his employment (*e.g.*, in a collective agreement) or which is made reasonably accessible to him in some other way (*e.g.*, by display on a works notice-board). Amendments may be made to the document itself, if it is made clear *ab initio* that the document will be used in this fashion.

[25] s. 4 (2).
[26] s. 4 (3).
[27] s. 4 (4).

This obviates the need for further, additional, separate statements each time a change is made. Moreover, if a new period of employment with the same employer is begun within six months of the date of termination of the first period of employment, then no statement under section 4 (1) need be given, provided of course that the terms and conditions remain the same.[28] If any change in terms is to be made, then section 4 (4) would operate.

Section 4 (8) makes it quite clear that the provisions of that main section 4 do not apply to an employee whose contract of employment has already been reduced to writing in one or more documents and that contract contains express terms affording the particulars to be given under each of the paragraphs in section 4 (1) and under each head of paragraph (d) of section 4 (1); but, of course, a copy of the contract (and any variations thereof) must have been given to the employee or he must have reasonable opportunities of reading such a copy in the course of his employment, or such a copy must be made reasonably accessible to him in some other way. Should this exception cease to operate at any time after the commencement of an employee's period of employment, the employer is obliged to give the employee a written statement under section 4 (1), not more than one month after the time in question.

Section 4 (9) is most important, although at first sight it seems to be relatively unimportant because of its actual placing. Subsection (9) very clearly lays down that employment during any period when the hours of employment are normally less than twenty-one hours weekly is not to be taken into account. It is also provided by the subsection that the whole of section 4 shall apply to an employee who, at any time, comes within the exception contained in the subsection or ceases to come within it, as if a period of employment terminated or began at that time.

The four opening subsections of section 5, which formerly contained the penal provisions applicable to any employer who failed to obey the provisions of section 4, have been replaced [29] by a new section 4A, which substitutes a reference to the Industrial Tribunal. This new section became operative on December 6, 1965, the date upon which the Redundancy Payments Act 1965 became law. The Industrial Tribunals in question are those created by the Industrial Training Act 1964. Initially, the task of these tribunals was to hear appeals against the training levies imposed by the Industrial Training Board. What the 1965 Act does is to utilise the tribunals [30] to deal with disputes arising under that Act and, of

---

[28] s. 4 (7).

[29] In terms of the Redundancy Payments Act 1965, s. 38.

[30] See particularly s. 51 (1) of the 1965 Act. The Minister of Labour (now the Secretary of State for Employment and Productivity) has powers under s. 46 of the 1965 Act to make procedural regulations. The Industrial Training Act 1964 had itself allowed for the issue of regulations, which in fact became the Industrial Tribunals Regulations 1965 (S.I. 1965 Nos. 1101 and 1157) effective on May 31, 1965. Moreover, the Tribunals and Inquiries (Industrial Tribunals) Order 1965 (S.I 1965 No. 1403) applied Parts I and II of Sched. 1 to the Tribunal and Inquiries Act 1958 to the Industrial Tribunals as from July 21, 1965.

course, under the new section 4A to the Contracts of Employment Act 1963. The Industrial Tribunals (England and Wales on the one hand and Scotland separately on the other) are each presided over by a legally qualified chairman and the members consist of one representative each on behalf of employers and employees. An appeal lies on a point of law to the Court of Session in Scotland and to the High Court in England. The legal position created by the new section 4A is accordingly this: where an employer is required by section 4 to give a written statement in terms of subsections (1) and (4) thereof, but fails to do so within the time limit imposed, the employee may require a reference to be made to the Industrial Tribunal to determine what particulars ought to have been included or referred to in a statement given so as to comply with the requirements of section 4.

Where a question arises between the parties upon the particulars which ought to have been included or referred to in a statement, purporting to be a statement under section 4 (1) and section 4 (4) of the 1963 Act given by an employer to an employee, so as to comply with the section 4 requirements, then the employer or the employee may require that particular question to be referred to a tribunal [31] (now the Industrial Tribunal).

Section 4A (3) refers back to section 4 (6), which permits indicated future changes in a document to which reference is made by the employer when he issues a section 4 statement to his employee, and enables an employer or employee to have referred to the Industrial Tribunal any question which arises as to the particulars which ought to have been so entered up or recorded. The tribunal may confirm the particulars or amend them or substitute other particulars as it may deem to be appropriate and the statement or particulars of change to which the reference relates under section 4A (2) and (3) shall be deemed to have been given by the employer or have been entered up or recorded in accordance with the decision of the tribunal.

Not only does the 1963 Act relate to employment particulars (section 4) in certain cases and dismissal procedures (section 1), but it also specifies the excluded categories.[32] These are registered dock workers as defined by any scheme in force under the Dock Workers (Regulation of Employment) Act 1946 (except when engaged on work which is not dock work); the master or a seaman on a seagoing British ship having a gross registered tonnage of 80 tons or more; an apprentice to the sea service (in accordance with section 108 of the Merchant Shipping Act 1894); and the skipper or a seaman on a fishing boat when registered under the Merchant Shipping Act 1894, s. 373. Section 4 does not apply where the employee is the father, mother, husband, wife, son or daughter of the employer. The section does however apply to an employee who, at any time, comes or ceases to come within the exceptions provided for by or under section 6 as if a period of employment terminated or began at that time.

[31] See s. 4A (2).
[32] 1963 Act, s. 6.

The Minister of Labour (now the Secretary of State) is given power to vary the number of weekly hours of employment (*i.e.*, twenty-one hours) specified in section 4 (9) and Schedules 1 and 2 to the 1963 Act. This can only be done by a statutory instrument giving effect to the Minister's order, but a draft of the order must be laid before Parliament and be approved by a resolution of each House.

An " employee " is defined by the interpretation section [33] as " an individual who has entered into or works under a contract with an employer, whether the contract be for manual labour, clerical work or otherwise, be expressed or implied, oral or in writing, and whether it be a contract of service or of apprenticeship. . . ." The Act does not relate to Crown employees. The reason for this is that the Act does not bind the Crown, either expressly or by implication, nor is it manifestly referable to or intended to include the Crown. Sections 1 and 2 (on dismissal procedures) are made retrospective.

The 1963 Act does not apply to employment during any period when the employee is engaged in work wholly or mainly outside Great Britain, unless where the employee ordinarily works in Great Britain and the work outside Great Britain is for the same employer.[34] The Act is to apply—apart from what is said in the immediately preceding sentence— no matter what law governs the contract of employment. The two Schedules to the Act deal respectively with computation of the period of employment and the rights of the employee in the period of notice.

So far as Scotland is concerned, all references made under section 4A of the 1963 Act are in regard to procedural matters now governed by the Industrial Tribunals (Employment and Compensation) (Scotland) Regulations 1967 [35] which replace earlier regulations of 1965.

To sum up, the position in relation to formation and creation of the contract of employment is that it is generally governed by the common law except in so far as the Contracts of Employment Act 1963 (as amended and extended by the Redundancy Payments Act 1965) has modified it, particularly in relation to dismissal procedures and certain written particulars to be made available to employees. It seems that the main effect of the Act of 1963 has been to provide many employees with a form of written contract (no matter how short that form of contract may be) which they would not otherwise have had. Nevertheless, the information which must be given under the Act is minimal. It is a complete exaggeration to regard the statute as an " employees' charter." The statute is undoubtedly a limited, protective and remedial measure, but it is a primary effort to superimpose legislative provisions upon the former " freedom of contract " relationship between employer and employee.

The recent Age Level of Employment Bill [36] is also relevant here, as it is designed to prevent employers from refusing employment to persons on the sole ground that they are aged forty-five years or over.

[33] s. 8.   [34] 1963 Act, s. 9.   [35] S.I. 1967 No. 362.
[36] [Bill 124] (printed March 26, 1969).

CHAPTER 7

AGREEMENTS IN RESTRAINT OF TRADE

CERTAIN contracts are regarded as null and void because they are either plainly illegal or are *contra bonos mores, i.e.,* immoral and unenforceable. Closely related to this group are those contracts which are void and unenforceable because they are contrary to public policy. The brocard which is applied to all of these contracts is *pacta illicita.* Agreements in restraint of trade, or restrictive covenants as they are now more commonly called, fall into the last mentioned category and are unenforceable in the general case,[1] although, of course, by applying the principle of severability the court may regard part of the contract as enforceable [2] and the remainder (including any restrictive clause) as unenforceable for the main reason which has been stated. However, in earlier times, the Scottish courts did not wholly subscribe to the general denial of restrictive covenants on the ground of public policy which was imposed in England. This is evident from the old Scottish case of *Stalker* v. *Carmichael.*[3] Times have changed and it is difficult, if not impossible, to detect any distinction between judicial decision and judicial policy north and south of the Tweed.

It is generally accepted that there are four types of agreements or covenants in restraint of trade, *viz.:*

(1) where an employer imposes a restraint upon his employees thereby preventing them (or endeavouring to prevent them) from competing with him, either during the subsistence of the contract [4] or after they leave his employment;

(2) where the main transaction between the parties is that of the sale of a business and the seller undertakes, by a restrictive covenant in the agreement governing the sale, that he will not carry on another business which is in competition with the buyer;

(3) where merchants (or manufacturers) act together in combination in order to regulate their trading relations. A good example of this in modern commercial practice is resale price maintenance or, again, the formation of a federation of small shopkeepers, *e.g.,* in the grocery trade, with the object of protecting themselves against the cut-price supermarkets. By so acting they are able to buy supplies in bulk which can then be sold in individual retail shops at a price equivalent to—or perhaps

---

[1] *Mogul S.S. Co.* v. *M'Gregor, Gow & Co.* (1889) 23 Q.B.D. 593; [1892] A.C. 25.
[2] *Stewart* v. *Stewart* (1899) 1 F. 1158, *per* Lord Moncreiff at p. 1172.
[3] 1735 M. 9455.
[4] *Watson* v. *Neuffert* (1863) 1 M. 1110; *Cameron & Co.* v. *Gibb* (1867) 3 S.L.R. 282.

sometimes slightly above or below—that offered in the supermarkets, and still leave them a reasonable margin of profit.

(4) The final type relates to the trade unions. Some writers would prefer to include the reference to trade unions under category (3) above, but with respect to them it seems preferable to identify trade union restraints or restrictive practices in these modern times as forming a special class or type of agreement which must be looked at very carefully within the framework of the law concerning and affecting trade unions. This we shall proceed to do in a later chapter.[5] As the types of agreement specified in paragraphs (2) and (3) above relate mainly if not exclusively to the world of business [6] it is not proposed to examine them in detail, but merely to refer upon occasion to certain cases decided by the courts which give valuable guidance upon the general law of restraint of trade which affects all four types.

The main concern of this chapter is the restrictive agreement or covenant between employer and employee mentioned in paragraph (1) above, and to identify the legal principles which apply to it one must examine all relevant cases, no matter whether these cases fall clearly within paragraph (1) or any of the other paragraphs or whether they overlap any two or more of the specified paragraphs. Most importantly, the laws of Scotland and of England are very close together on this topic and indeed many of the more famous cases are English cases which went to the Court of Appeal and the House of Lords. All of these leading cases have a most persuasively authoritative effect upon Scots law.

The primary requirement for an agreement in restraint of trade to be recognised by the court as being enforceable is that it must be in the public interest.[7] This requirement is a logical corollary of the statement of first principles which was made above in relation to any contract or agreement which is against public policy (including the public interest)—namely, that it is void and unenforceable, i.e., *pactum illicitum*. Public policy is a variable factor and, generally speaking, it will change as economic policy and conditions change.[8] In the first Elizabethan era all restraints of trade were, at any rate in England and Wales, regarded as being wholly void because they tended to establish monopolies. In this second Elizabethan era the position in Great Britain is that they may be acceptable and enforceable upon certain conditions, whilst the matter of monopoly will be investigated by the Monopolies Commission. The English legal historians [9] consider that the relaxation of the rigid doctrine of nullity began in 1711 with the case of *Mitchel* v. *Reynolds* [10] and from that time

---

[5] *Vide* Chap. 17 *infra.*
[6] And may be dealt with by the Monopolies Commission or by the Restrictive Practices Court.
[7] See *Nordenfelt* v. *Maxim Nordenfelt Guns and Ammunition Co.* [1894] A.C. 535.
[8] Speech of Lord Macmillan in *Vancouver Malt and Sake Brewing Co. Ltd.* v. *Vancouver Breweries Ltd.* [1934] A.C. 181 at p. 189; [1934] All E.R. 38 at p. 41.
[9] See Professor G. C. Cheshire and Mr. C. H. S. Fifoot in their *Law of Contract* (6th ed.) at pp. 324–325; and the new 7th ed. at p. 338 *et seq.*
[10] (1711) 1 P.Wms. 181.

onwards a distinction came to be drawn between agreements in general restraint and those in partial restraint, the former being void and the latter being prima facie valid. The question of the general restraint (*i.e.*, the clause in the agreement which was drawn in wide general terms) came up for consideration and decision in the outstanding case of *Nordenfelt* v. *Maxim Nordenfelt Guns and Ammunition Co.*[11] in which Nordenfelt (a manufacturer of machine-guns and other weapons of war) sold his business for £287,500 and signed a restraint of trade agreement. Some two years later the purchasing company was merged with another company which engaged Nordenfelt as managing director at a salary of £2,000 per annum. His contract of employment contained a similar but expanded restrictive covenant by which he bound and obliged himself " not for twenty-five years, if the company so long continued to carry on business, engage, except on behalf of the company, either directly or indirectly, in the trade or business of a manufacturer of guns, gun mountings or carriages, gunpowder explosives or ammunition, or in *any business competing or liable to compete in any way with that for the time being carried on by the company.*"[12] The restraint imposed was therefore a general restraint as the business was world-wide. The House of Lords upheld the general restraint in the circumstances of this case but could not accept that final part of the restrictive covenant which is shown above in italics. The decision of the House of Lords is so important because of the following four tests or propositions which emerged from it: (a) the court must have regard to all the circumstances of the case; (b) the covenant or agreement is enforceable if it is reasonable in the interests of the parties (and the party seeking to enforce it has the heavy onus of proof in this connection); (c) the covenant or agreement is enforceable if it is reasonable in the interests of the public; and (d) where part of an agreement or covenant is reasonable and conforms to the above-mentioned requirements of public interests and parties' interests then that part is valid and enforceable, but if part is unreasonable (see the italicised portion of the clause quoted above), then it is void and quite unenforceable. Lord Macnaghten took the view[13] that general and partial restraints were not distinct categories but fell to be considered by the same criteria— namely, both are restraints and both are prima facie void, but valid if reasonable looking to the circumstances and the interests of the parties and the public. His lordship put it this way: " All interferences with individual liberty of action in trading, and all restraints of trade of themselves, if there is nothing more, are contrary to public policy and therefore void. That is the general rule. But there are exceptions: restraints of trade . . . may be justified by the special circumstances of a particular case. It is a sufficient justification, and indeed it is the only justification, if the restriction is reasonable—reasonable, that is, in reference to the

[11] [1894] A.C. 535.
[12] Author's italics.
[13] [1894] A.C. 535 at p. 565

interests of the parties concerned and reasonable in reference to the interests of the public, so framed and so guarded as to afford adequate protection to the party in whose favour it is imposed, while at the same time it is in no way injurious to the public." [14] This part of the speech was, of course, *obiter* and the view expressed did not receive the blessing of all the other judges. Indeed the matter did not come up again in the House of Lords until the well-known case of *Mason* v. *Provident Clothing and Supply Co. Ltd.*[15] when the House of Lords accepted Lord Macnaghten's view and laid it down quite unequivocally that all covenants or agreements in restraint of trade are prima facie void and must be considered in relation to the test of reasonableness. The House also examined the restrictive covenant as used in contracts of service and in agreements for the sale of businesses and stressed that it could be enforced more readily in the latter situation. Obviously a strong measure of protection must be afforded to the purchaser who is paying a large sum of money for the assets and goodwill of a business. This is not so in the case of an employment contract where the employer, though acquiring the skill and technical knowledge of the employee for the duration of the contract, cannot restrict the employee in the disposing of his labour, skill and knowledge as he wishes.[16] The employer would be able to protect himself in relation to his business connections, secret processes or other trade secrets known to and acquired by the employee during his period of service,[17] by application to the court for interdict (or injunction) but this is not quite the same thing as that of a restrictive covenant sought to be imposed upon an employee which directly attempts to restrict his right to seek employment locally or in a specific kind of employment. The House considered the restrictive covenant in contracts of employment in the case of *Herbert Morris Ltd.* v. *Saxelby* [18] and stressed that it was void as being unreasonable unless the employer could point to some exceptional proprietary interest which needed to be protected. The following excerpt from Lord Parker's speech is instructive: " The reason, and the only reason, for upholding such a restraint on the part of an employee is that the employer has some proprietary right, whether in the nature of trade connection or in the nature of trade secrets, for the protection of which such a restraint is—having regard to the duties of the employee—reasonably necessary. Such a restraint has, so far as I know, never been upheld, if directed only to the prevention of competition or against the use of the personal skill and knowledge acquired by the employee in his employer's business." [19] The quotation also points to the trade secrets and business connections which have been referred to above, as protection of these may

---

14 *Ibid.* at p. 574.
15 [1913] A.C. 724.
16 *Attwood* v. *Lamont* [1920] 3 K.B. 571 at p. 589; and *Leather Cloth Co.* v. *Lorsont* (1869) L.R. 9 Eq. 345, *per* James L.J. at p. 353.
17 See particularly *Hivac Ltd.* v. *Park Royal Scientific Instruments Ltd.* [1946] Ch. 169; 62 T.L.R. 231; [1946] 2 All E.R. 350.
18 [1916] 1 A.C. 688.
19 *Ibid.* p. 710.

be perfectly justifiable. The question of the proprietary interest which allegedly needs protection was raised in the comparatively recent case of *Eastham* v. *Newcastle United Football Club* [20] where the retention and transfer rules of the Football Association and Football League governing professional footballers were considered by the court and it was held that these did not establish any proprietary interest capable of protection.

Protection of business connections is clearly recognised [21] but the onus is upon the employer to show that such protection is necessary: then the court will accept such restraint only if it is sufficient to enforce the protection—it will not accept a restraint which goes beyond the realm of adequate and legitimate protection. The employer must satisfy the court that the nature of his trade or business and the character or type of employment undertaken by the employee (who is accepting the imposition of the obligation) justifies his plea for the restraint to be upheld.[22] Moreover, it must be shown that the restriction is in the interests of both parties concerned.

Two factors are of the utmost importance in relation to all restrictive agreements or covenants—and these are the limitations upon area (or space) and time (or duration) sought to be imposed. In the English case of *Attwood* v. *Lamont*, Younger L.J. said[23]: "As the time of restriction lengthens or the space of its operation grows, the weight of the onus on the covenantee to justify it grows too." The point as to limitation upon area was markedly illustrated in *Mason* v. *Provident Clothing and Supply Co. Ltd.*[24] where a limitation upon trading within twenty-five miles of London was sought to be imposed upon a canvassing and collecting agent in Islington. The House of Lords held that the restriction was wider than was reasonably necessary for the company's protection. The court must look at all the circumstances of the case before deciding whether or not the limitation upon area is too wide.

The limitation as to time or duration is more often a more difficult matter to decide. If the time limit is excessive, such as to amount perhaps to an almost unlimited duration, it will not be acceptable to the court.[25] Of course, this does not mean that a lengthy period of restriction—even for a lifetime—is never justified; it may be justified when read along with an area limitation, as happened in *Fitch* v. *Dewes* [26] where a limitation upon a solicitor's clerk in Tamworth preventing him from ever practising

---

[20] [1963] 3 All E.R. 139. Many of the recent "petroleum agreement" cases are not relevant to industrial law.
[21] *Dewes* v. *Fitch* [1920] 2 Ch. 159, *per* Warrington L.J. at pp. 181–182 and *Fitch* v. *Dewes* [1921] 2 A.C. 158.
[22] See speech of Lord Parker in *Herbert Morris Ltd.* v. *Saxelby, cit. supra* at p. 709.
[23] [1920] 3 K.B. 571 at p. 589.
[24] [1913] A.C. 724; see also *Empire Meat Co. Ltd.* v. *Patrick* [1939] 2 All E.R. 85.
[25] *Eastes* v. *Russ* [1914] 1 Ch. 468 (an attempt to impose a restriction for life upon an assistant pathologist).
[26] [1921] 2 A.C. 158.

within seven miles of the town hall was upheld and enforced as being reasonable in all the circumstances.[27]

A most interesting case arose in England comparatively recently where the agreement in restraint was undertaken between two employers. This was the case of *Kores Manufacturing Co. Ltd.* v. *Kolok Manufacturing Co. Ltd.*[28] where two manufacturing companies in competition with each other each agreed not to employ any person who had been employed by the other during the previous five years. This was an obvious attempt to get round an individual employer/employee restriction which the courts would have rejected. The Court of Appeal did not address itself to the question as to whether the rules applicable to the employer/employee situation applied equally to restrictive practices in the employer/employer situation, but nevertheless it held that this particular agreement was void and unenforceable for the following very good reason, *viz.*: the reciprocal restraints imposed were excessive and unreasonable in the interests of the parties to the agreement, having regard to the fact that there was no discrimination between employees having access to trade secrets and those who did not have such access and also to the fact that, although the real reason for the agreement was the proximity of the factories, there was no provision in it for limiting its duration to the period while the proximity continued. The Court of Appeal applied the law as contained in *Herbert Morris* v. *Saxelby, supra.*

An examination of the older Scottish cases reveals quite distinctly that the test of the legality of an agreement in restraint of trade is virtually the same as that adopted by the English courts, *viz.*: is it reasonable in all the circumstances, having regard to the interests of the employee and of the public, for the protection of the employer's business? [29] No effect will be given to any clause which is drawn in vague terms. The restrictive clause is not to be read in isolation; it must be read as a part of, and with reference to, the whole contract. Moreover, the restrictive clause is not apparently assignable apart from the contract of which it forms part, but any restriction imposed in a contract of service cannot be assigned.[30] The Scottish courts do not, however, require that the reasonableness of the restriction should have any reference to the type or nature of the

---

[27] See also *Hepworth Manufacturing Co.* v. *Ryott* [1920] 1 Ch. 1 where the restriction sought to be imposed was not for the genuine protection of business interests but to impose an intimidating embargo upon the employment of the respondent; it was held that the covenant could be disregarded.

[28] [1959] Ch. 108; [1958] 2 All E.R. 65 (C.A.).

[29] See particularly *Stalker* v. *Carmichael*, 1735 Mor. 9455; *Curtis* v. *Sandison* (1831) 10 S. 72; *Watson* v. *Neuffert* (1863) 1 M. 1110; *Stewart* v. *Stewart* (1899) 1 F. 1158; *Williams & Son* v. *Fairbairn* (1899) 1 F. 944; *Dumbarton Steamboat Co.* v. *M'Farlane* (1899) 1 F. 993; *Ballachulish Slate Quarries Co.* v. *Grant* (1903) 5 F. 1105 and *Scottish Farmers' Dairy Co. (Glasgow) Ltd.* v. *M'Ghee*, 1933 S.C. 148; 1933 S.L.T. 142.

[30] *Berlitz School of Languages* v. *Duchêne* (1903) 6 F. 181; 11 S.L.T. 491; but see the view of the late Professor W. M. Gloag in *Contract* (2nd ed.), p. 425 and explanatory n. (1) thereto. See also Lord Cave's opinion in *Fitch* v. *Dewes*, *cit. supra* at p. 168. Nor will a restrictive covenant be enforced if the person claiming enforcement is himself guilty of a breach of that contract—see *General Billposting Co.* v. *Atkinson* [1909] A.C. 118.

particular contract in which it appears,[31] nor would they inquire into the adequacy or otherwise of the consideration involved in the contract [32] (as the English courts would).

The Scottish courts will certainly look at the possibility of dividing or separating the enforceable part of the restriction from the unenforceable part and will give effect to the former.[33] It is not the court's function, however, to rewrite or redraft the restrictive clause so that it will meet the test of reasonableness,[34] although the decision as to whether or not the restraint is reasonable is one for the court itself to make, and it will do so after a proper consideration of the true construction and legal effect of the restrictive clause itself, read along with the whole contract and as an integral part of it.

Restraint of trade in relation to the right to work and the law of trade unions and associations is, as has been indicated at the beginning of this chapter, quite a different matter from that which has been considered herein and accordingly has been reserved for examination in a later chapter.[35]

[31] *Stewart* v. *Stewart, supra; Ballachulish Slate Quarries* v. *Grant, supra.*
[32] *Stewart* v. *Stewart, supra.*
[33] *Meikle* v. *Meikle* (1895) 3 S.L.T. 204 *per* Lord Kyllachy; and *Mulvein* v. *Murray,* 1908 S.C. 528.
[34] *Dumbarton Steamboat Co.* v. *M'Farlane* (1899) 1 F. 993.
[35] *Infra,* Chap. 17.

PART II

MATTERS ARISING DURING THE SUBSISTENCE OF THE RELATIONSHIP OF EMPLOYER AND EMPLOYEE

CHAPTER 8

WAGES AND REMUNERATION IN RELATION TO THE
CONTRACT OF EMPLOYMENT; COLLECTIVE BARGAINING
AND JOINT NEGOTIATION; WAGES COUNCILS; TRUCK
ACTS; ASCERTAINMENT AND REGULATION OF WAGES IN
CERTAIN INDUSTRIES; NATIONAL INSURANCE; AND
REDUNDANCY PAYMENTS

(1) *Wages* (*generally*)

The return (or consideration [1]) for the service given is wages. Generally, wages are payable in money but may be combined with the provision of board, occupation of a dwelling-house, a clothing allowance or other benefits or perquisites.

The ordinary rule seems to be that service is performed for payment, which means wages payable in money and the obligation to pay money wages can be inferred from a contract of employment which is itself silent on the point of remuneration.[2] Otherwise, the onus would be upon the employee who is claiming money wages to prove that the agreement did in fact relate to the payment or settlement of the remuneration by money wages.[3] Proof (*prout de jure*) that an agreement to pay wages was concluded would be good enough.[4] The ordinary rule suffers an exception in the case of employment of members of the family—for example in *Urquhart* v. *Urquhart's Tr.*,[5] where a daughter of the house assisted in her father's business and in return got her keep, clothing and pocket money it was held that there was no presumption that her father had entered into a contract to pay wages to her.

Where a dwelling-house is occupied as part of the remuneration allowed to an employee it is necessary for the employee to remove himself and his goods, gear and effects therefrom [6] when his contract of employment comes to an end (by lapse of time, notice or dismissal or mutual agreement). But agreements made on the subject of rent deduction can cause difficulties in relation to the Truck Acts (hereinafter

---

[1] As the English lawyers would prefer to call it.

[2] See *Thomson* v. *Thomson's Trustee* (1889) 16 R. 333; 26 S.L.R. 217.

[3] See particularly *Watson* v. *Rose* (1741) Elchies ii, 348; *Smellie* v. *Gillespie* (1833) 12 S. 125; *Cowan* v. *McMicking* (1846) 19 Sc.Jur. 91.

[4] *Stuart* v. *Richardson* (1806) Hume 390; *Stewart* v. *Clyne* (1831) 9 S. 382; (1833) 11 S. 727; (1835) 2 S. & McL. 45; *Sinclair* v. *Erskine* (1831) 9 S. 487; *Robertson* v. *Annandale* (1749) 1 Pat.App. 293.

[5] (1905) 8 F. 42; 43 S.L.R. 7; 13 S.L.T. 430; and *cf. Russel* v. *M'Clymont* (1906) 8 F. 821; 43 S.L.R. 601; 14 S.L.T. 59.

[6] *Sinclair* v. *Tod*, 1907 S.C. 1038; 44 S.L.R. 771; 15 S.L.T. 113.

explained) and these agreements may be illegal, both in form and in relation to the deductions purported to be made by mutual agreement.[7] Care must be taken to distinguish between a free service occupancy [8] and a service tenancy (with rental deducted from wages), particularly with relevance to the Contracts of Employment Act 1963 (the new section 4A written in by the Redundancy Payments Act 1965) and the Truck Acts. It may be that during wartime also an employer would be able to remove and eject an employee who had been called up for national service,[9] particularly where the employer required the " free house " (occupied as part remuneration, and therefore not technically a " free house " at all) for a substitute employee who had to be engaged urgently. The purpose in mentioning this matter is merely to draw attention to the application of special rules and regulations during times of national emergency.

If the contract is silent as to the means of calculating the amount of wages due or if the contract is an implied contract, then the employee will be entitled to receive what is the customary amount in the particular locality for the type of employment which he has rendered; otherwise, it seems that he is entitled to a *quantum meruit*.[10]

Many industries are, of course, regulated by statute [11] and it will be necessary and appropriate to consider certain statutory provisions relating to wages in the course of this chapter.

Wages are normally calculated (a) in relation to either the actual amount of work done (*i.e.*, piecework) or (b) in relation to the period of time served by the employee. The obligation to pay wages raises, of course, the important question as to whether or not an employer must provide work. In the former case (*i.e.*, piecework) it seems that the employer is bound to provide constant employment whilst the contractual relationship is in force.[12] In the latter case, he is under no such obligation to provide work,[13] and, furthermore, he cannot make any deduction for idle time. If an employee is merely " standing by " a machine for a proportion of his working shift this makes no difference in relation to wages—he is entitled to his full rate of wages for the whole period of the working shift.

---

[7] See *Summerlee Iron Co. Ltd.* v. *Thomson*, 1913 S.C.(J.) 34; 1913, 1 S.L.T. 43. (Note that the cases of *Williams* v. *North's Navigation Collieries* (*1889*) *Limited* [1906] A.C. 136, and *M'Farlane* v. *Birrell* (1888) 16 R. (J.) 28; 2 White 126, were both followed in the *Summerlee* case.)

[8] *Gould* v. *Balliol College, Oxford* (1966) 1 I.T.R. 534.

[9] See *Cairns* v. *Innes*, 1942 S.C. 164; 1942 S.L.T. 129; 1941 S.N. 79 and the National Service (Armed Forces) (Adjustment of Contracts) Regulations 1939 (reg. 2, in particular).

[10] See *Stewart* v. *Clyne* and *Sinclair* v. *Erskine*, *cit. supra*; also *Stuart* v. *M'Cleod* (1901) 9 S.L.T. 192; Bell's *Principles*, s. 184.

[11] *e.g.*, Hosiery (1845); Silk Weaving (1845); Factories (1961); Mines and Quarries (1954) and others hereinafter considered. See also G. H. L. Fridman, *The Modern Law of Employment* (1963 with cumulative supplement), pp. 390–405 for a useful collection of examples of statutory control.

[12] Bell's *Principles*, s. 192; *Cowdenbeath Coal Co.* v. *Drylie* (1886) 3 Sh.Ct. 3 at p. 11.

[13] *Lagerwall* v. *Wilkinson* (1899) 80 L.T. 55; *Turner* v. *Sawdon* [1901] 2 K.B. 653.

It is accepted, however, that there may be circumstances in which there is an implied obligation upon the employer to provide work, (*e.g.*, if the employee is an actor or other paid public-performer then his interests (*i.e.*, the employee's) require that he be given the appropriate opportunities of appearing before the public: this is essential to the build-up of his reputation). The English cases[14] are most helpful on this particular point, although it may not always be easy to identify the contract in question as a contract of employment of the ordinary type. In *Turner* v. *Sawdon*[15] the court held that an employer had committed no breach of contract in refusing to give his employee any work to do, so long as he paid the agreed wages. The problem of an implied term in " piecework " contracts was mentioned but not decided in the English case of *Davies* v. *Richard Johnson*, etc.,[16] where Luxmoore J. was, however, prepared to assume its existence.

The question as to when wages are payable is a most important one. Do they accrue *de die in diem* or as a *unum quid* payable at stated intervals ? Where the contract is for a period of some duration with wages agreed at a fixed sum of money per year, month or half-year, then it seems that the *unum quid* theory is to be preferred.[17] This rule certainly seems to be applied in the case of domestic employees and agricultural employees who are engaged for a term or terms. Here the wages are looked upon as a *unum quid* and the right to demand payment thereof does not arise until the completion of the full term.[18] Payments to account may, of course, be made at intervals throughout the term. In other cases (and certainly in the contract of service at pleasure), wages accrue from day to day and fall to be paid at intervals, whether in terms of the agreement itself or in accordance with the custom applicable in the establishment. Usage between the parties may help to show what their agreement really meant.[19]

There may be a custom applicable in a particular trade whereby the employer is able to retain at credit or in hand an agreed portion of the wages. For example, one week's wages is not unusual in the shipbuilding industry, during the subsistence of the contract of service. This is known as " wages of lying time " or, more often, simply as " lying time." The

---

[14] See particularly *Clayton* v. *Oliver* [1930] A.C. 209; 99 L.J.K.B. 165; 142 L.T. 585; 46 T.L.R. 230; *Marbe* v. *George Edwardes Ltd.* [1928] 1 K.B. 269; 96 L.J.K.B. 980; 138 L.T. 51; 43 T.L.R. 809; *Bunning* v. *Lyric Theatre*, 71 L.T. 396; *Collier* v. *Sunday Referee Publishing Co.* [1940] 2 K.B. 647; 164 L.T. 10; 109 L.J.K.B. 974; 57 T.L.R. 2; *Turner* v. *Goldsmith* [1891] 1 Q.B. 544; 60 L.J.Q.B. 247.

[15] [1901] 2 K.B. 653 applying *Emmens* v. *Elderton* (1853) 13 C.B. 495. The use of the word " employ " does not involve an obligation upon the employer to find employment or work but merely to keep the employee in his employ in the sense of paying him wages.

[16] (1934) 51 T.L.R. 115.

[17] See *Hoey* v. *M'Ewan and Auld* (1867) 5 M. 814; *Boston Fishing Co.* v. *Ansell* (1888) 39 Ch.D. 339; *Button* v. *Thompson* (1869) L.R. 4 C.P. 330.

[18] See *Douglas* v. *Argyle* (1736) Mor. 11,102.

[19] *Macgill* v. *Park* (1899) 2 F. 272 (particularly *per* the Lord President at p. 275 who, in referring to the principle of apportionment *de die in diem*, points out that in order to apply the principle it would be necessary to have a *terminus a quo*—a date from which the contract must be taken to have run).

purpose is to enable an employer to protect himself against sudden desertion by his employees. This custom, after proof to the court, will receive effect. As regards " piecework," it seems that wages vest on the completion of each piece of work although actually payable at stated intervals.[20]

As regards the possible application of the Apportionment Act 1870 to an employee's wages, it will be recalled from the case of *Macgill* v. *Park* [21] that although the point of applicability was argued on behalf of the defenders, the court ignored this completely. The English common law rule of non-apportionment of wages is illustrated in the old case of *Cutter* v. *Powell*,[22] where a seaman died on a voyage from Jamaica to England and it was held in the circumstances, and as revealed in and stipulated by the agreement itself, that payment was only due if Cutter had duly served and completed the voyage. As payment here depended upon completion this type of contract might be regarded as a special one. The matter was again very fully discussed in England in the case of *Moriarty* v. *Regents Garage Co.*[23] Whether an employee is entitled to a proportion of his wages under English law depends upon the terms of his contract of employment; otherwise it appears that no apportionment is possible, until the superior English courts support the dicta of McCardie J. in the *Moriarty* case, equating the position south of the Border with the more equitable rule which seems to be accepted at Scottish common law.

Interest accrues upon wages from the date upon which payment is due.[24] Should the amount be unspecified, then interest will run from the date upon which the debt is validly constituted.[25] The triennial prescription applies to wages payments,[26] but in the event of a delay in demanding wages being due to any fault on the part of the employer, the employee is permitted a proof to endeavour to establish his claim.[27] The time factor for payment is also important and every employer should discharge his obligation by paying timeously. The circumstances will be considered; for example, in *Sime* v. *J. & D. Grimond*,[28] it was held that wages for the week ending on a Thursday were timeously paid on the Saturday following. Although receipts for wages and salary payments are not normally taken from employees in modern industrial and commercial practice, it has been held that where a contract of service was based upon an oral agreement between the parties and unqualified receipts had been given by the employee over a lengthy period of years,

---

[20] *Warburton* v. *Heyworth* (1880) 6 Q.B.D. 1.
[21] (1899) 2 F. 272.
[22] (1795) 6 T.R. 320.
[23] [1921] 1 K.B. 423.
[24] *Mansfield* v. *Scott* (1831) 9 S. 780; (1833) 6 W.S. 277.
[25] *Wallace* v. *Geddes* (1821) 1 Sh.Ap. 42.
[26] See *Scott* v. *Kyle*, 1966 S.L.T.(Sh.Ct.) 50.
[27] See *Inglis* v. *Smith*, 1916 S.C. 581; 1916, 1 S.L.T. 289; 53 S.L.R. 443 (proof *habili modo* allowed).
[28] (O.H.) 1920, 1 S.L.T. 270.

he (the employee) could be met by a plea of personal bar where he alleged that he had been underpaid (the evidence here being, of course, parole evidence).[29] If an employee can, however, point to a clear implied " agreement " to pay " trade union rates " then his position may be stronger and much will depend upon the circumstances, e.g., whether he has accepted a lower rate for a long number of years.[30]

Casual work offered to persons—for example, by a local authority to recipients of public assistance in order to give them something to do to occupy their minds and exercise their bodies [31] is not work provided under a contract of employment and it is not governed by the general rule to which reference has been made at the beginning of this chapter.

The employee of the Crown cannot sue for salary or wages and the Crown Proceedings Act 1947 made no change in the law on this point.[32]

It is always competent—and the practice has been recognised in certain trades for many years—for an employer and employee to make an arrangement about (either themselves or through trade union negotiation) a higher rate of pay where a greater degree of risk of injury is involved.[33] This extra payment is usually termed " danger money."

The liability for payment of wages rests squarely upon the employer. Any works manager or foreman or other person with power to hire or engage employees incurs no personal liability vis-a-vis wages,[34] unless of course he acts in an individual capacity, e.g., as an agent who assumes the role of principal. In the special case of merchant shipping, the master of the ship is always responsible for the payment of the wages of seamen who are signed on by him; and the maritime lien for wages may be utilised whenever necessary to protect master and seamen.[35]

Where an industrial or blue-collar employee does extra work, outwith his ordinary service or normal scope of duties, the question arises as to whether or not he is entitled to payment therefor. From the opinions expressed in two older cases [26] there has been evolved a general rule that where the employee was bound to give his whole time to his employer's business and the particular work done by him was suitable to the particular type or character of employee and the nature of the employment, no extra wages would be due to him. This meant that an employee could only succeed in his claim if he could prove some agreement or stipulation

---

[29] *Davies* v. *City of Glasgow Friendly Society*, 1935 S C. 224.
[30] *Eunson* v. *Johnson & Greig*, 1940 S.C. 49; 1940 S.L.T. 68; 1939 S.N. 98.
[31] *M'Geachy* v. *Dept. of Health for Scotland*, 1938 S.C. 282; 1938 S.L.T. 247; 1938 S.N. 19.
[32] *Duncan* v. *The Admiralty*, 1950 S.L.T.(Sh.Ct.) 72. The Crown employee's salary or wages is now liable to arrestment (except if he is a member of H.M. Forces) in execution, but not on the dependence of an action—see the Law Reform (Miscellaneous Provisions) (Scotland) Act 1966 (c. 19), ss. 1 and 2.
[33] See *Wieloch* v. *Balfour Beatty & Co.* (O.H.) 1951 S.L.T.(Notes) 71.
[34] *Nabonie* v. *Scott* (1815) Hume 353; *Cullen* v. *Thomson's Trustees* (1862) 24 D.(H.L.) 10; 4 Macq. 424.
[35] See *Inter-Islands Exporters Ltd.* v. *Berna S.S. Co.* (O.H.) 1959 S.L.T.(Notes) 77.
[36] *Money* v. *Hannan and Kerr* (1867) 5 S.L.R. 32; *Latham* v. *Edinburgh and Glasgow Ry.* (1866) 4 M. 1084 (see Lord President M'Neill's opinion, in particular).

governing extra pay for extra work. Nevertheless the general rule mentioned must not be overstressed—it is merely a guide for the court in reaching a decision. Where " overtime " is worked, the position in modern industrial relations is that the days, etc., allocated for working overtime and the rates of pay applicable therefor are generally a matter of agreement between the trade unions concerned in the particular industry and the employers. An " overtime " agreement is a matter of some importance to employees as it may, in some cases, mean the doubling of a basic wage rate. Otherwise, the matter is settled by the custom of the particular trade or by the custom of the particular industrial establishment. Productivity agreements and bonus schemes are also new features in modern industrial life. These are, to a greater degree, replacing the older agreements on overtime.

The " white-collar " clerical worker or professional employee will usually find that there is no remuneration for extra work upon the same footing as the ordinary industrial worker receives " overtime " payments, but that he or she will receive a payment of a fixed amount (e.g., five shillings or upwards) to meet the cost of a meal and expenses incidental to the performance of the extra work. However, this is not to say that all " white-collar " workers are deprived from earning overtime payments. This is certainly not so today where many establishments provide for such an arrangement in the employment contract or by custom. Yet, employers often complain that " overtime " arrangements do not necessarily increase productivity and resulting profit margins. More often, in their view, productivity improves slightly but profit margins may perhaps weaken.

It may be, of course, that the relationship of employer and employee does not apply to the situation—for example, the relationship in question may be either one of partnership or some form of joint venture [37] in which the parties have agreed to share the earnings, the latter being not uncommon among the fishing communities in West Scotland and East Scotland. The agreement between and among the parties will require the most careful examination to determine their true intentions and the relationship which has been established. Another situation, not uncommon in the building trade, is where a gang or squad of men agree to work together on a piecework job or " on contract work " with another party who treats them as independent contractors, exercising no control over them. The gang or squad inter se are probably partners or participants in a joint venture and again it is not an easy question to advise, say, a junior member of the squad whose services have been dispensed with and who is claiming remuneration.[38] The relationship of that junior member to the senior members may well be that of employer and employee.

[37] See Clark v. Jamieson, 1909 S.C. 132; 16 S.L.T. 450; 46 S.L.R. 73.
[38] See Littlejohn v. Brown & Co. Ltd., 1909 S.C. 169; 16 S.L.T. 446; 46 S.L.R. 42.

Wages payable during the illness of an employee. The contractual relationship between an employer and his employee may be terminated by illness, as elsewhere discussed in this work.[39] If not so terminated, the question to be resolved is whether the employee can claim wages during his illness or whether the employer can reduce the wages or pay no wages at all during the period of incapacity. It is true that under the modern welfare state the incapacitated employee will receive sickness benefit, etc., under the National Insurance Acts and it is also very often the case that an arrangement is made between an employer and an employee whereby the employee may receive full wages during temporary illness, provided that sickness benefit payments received from the state are handed over to the employer. But this arrangement does not affect the legal question of liability or non-liability for payment during illness.

Stair[40] and Erskine[41] took the view that wages suffered no abatement and this seems to be supported in two older cases[42] of which the earlier one, *viz.*, *White* v. *Baillie*, concerned employer and employee. Here the court held that a farm employee, hired for a year, was entitled to full wages for that period although he had been incapacitated from working for eleven weeks within the year. In *M'Ewan* v. *Malcolm*[43] it was decided that where the disability to give the services required arose through the fault or misconduct of the employee, he had thereby disabled himself from performing his part of the contract and accordingly he could not call upon the employer to pay wages for the time of disablement. A special statutory provision applies this same principle in the case of merchant seamen.[44] Where the contract is for employment for a term or terms, with wages accruing at the end of each term as a *unum quid*, then it appears that the wages payable for each term do not suffer any abatement.[45]

Where the wages are payable according to the actual giving of service by the employee, he is not entitled to any wages payment for any period during which he does not serve. Should the wages be calculated on a time basis (*e.g.*, at an agreed rate per hour or per day), wages are normally only payable for the time served. Where the wages are stated to be, or are understood to be, at a certain sum per week or month (or longer) it seems that the wages will continue to accrue, unless the contract is terminated by notice or by the failure of the employee to attend at his place of employment.[46] Custom may play an important part in this matter—for example, as Mr. Umpherston says,[47] in parts of Scotland the agricultural

[39] *Infra*, Chap. 20.
[40] i. 15, 2.
[41] III. 3, 16.
[42] *White* v. *Baillie* (1794) Mor. 10,147; *Thompson* v. *Millie* (1806) Mor. (*voce* Mutual Contract) App. 4; See also *M'Lean* v. *Fyfe*, Feb. 4, 1813, F.C., *per* Lord Meadowbank.
[43] (1867) 5 S.L.R. 62.
[44] See the Merchant Shipping Act 1894, s. 160.
[45] *Hoey* v. *McEwan and Auld* (1867) 5 M. 814.
[46] See Umpherston, *op. cit.*, p. 65 and n. (2) thereat.
[47] pp. 65 and 66.

employee, hired for a year, is entitled to full wages if not absent from work because of illness for more than *six consecutive weeks* during the year, disregarding the total accumulated length of time of his absences throughout the whole year. No claim can be made for wages during a period of illness which began before the date of commencement of the employment and ended after that date. The reason for this is that the entering upon the employment is a necessary preliminary to the earning of wages.[48]

An interesting point (amongst others) arose in *Doonan* v. *S.M.T. Co.*[49] where a housekeeper incapacitated in a collision whilst a passenger in an omnibus which belonged to defenders was paid £2 per week (a sum equivalent to her weekly money wage; her keep was equivalent to an additional £1 per week). Defenders argued that she had suffered no loss of wages and moved for a new trial. There was an agreement between pursuer and her employer that if she succeeded in her damages action against defenders the £2 per week for the period of incapacity would be repaid by her to her employer. The evidence indicated that the " arrangement " was a form of contribution or advance made by the employer. The court refused defenders' motion but pointed out that arrangements of this kind ought to be averred on the record to give defenders fair notice of the position.[50]

As has been pointed out earlier herein, any claim for wages, being subject to the triennial prescription, must be pursued within the three-year period, otherwise the claimant would only be able to prove the obligation to pay by relying upon the writ or oath of the employer.[51]

(2) *The Truck Acts*

The common law relating to wages was modified from time to time by the Truck Acts 1831–1940, which were designed to strike at the system of " trucking." There were earlier statutes dating from the fifteenth century dealing with " truck " but these have all been superseded by the range of statutes mentioned, which must be read along with other statutes which deal with particular industries—such as hosiery manufacturing and stannaries. This system of trucking enabled unscrupulous employers to take advantage of their employees by forcing them to buy at shops owned by the employers or at shops in which employers had an interest.[52] It would be quite unfair to suggest that all employers were, prior to 1831 or even 1896, unscrupulous but nevertheless it became obvious that

---

48 See *Comasky* v. *Jeffrey* (1887) 2 Guthrie's Sh.Ct. Cases 353.
49 1950 S.C. 136; 1950 S.L.T. 100.
50 See the L.J.-C. (Thomson) at p. 142; and the outspoken view of Lord Mackay at pp. 142 and 143.
51 *Dunn* v. *Lamb* (1854) 16 D. 944; *Gobbi* v. *Lazzaroni* (1859) 21 D. 801; and on the question of defences to a claim for wages, as well as possible counterclaims, see *Umpherston* pp. 73–79 inclusive.
52 For an interesting historical survey of the system of " trucking " see the recent work by George W. Hilton, *The Truck System* (1960).

certain employers were acting unreasonably towards their employees and the possibility of this practice becoming more widespread had to be stopped. Legislation was the only effective method by which this could be done.[53]

The Truck Act 1831 made it an offence for an employer to contract that wages payable to his employee should be paid otherwise than in coin of the realm and should he purport to do so the contract is illegal and void.[54] Some changes in the actual methods of payment have been made by the Payment of Wages Act 1960 [55] and these are discussed later. The 1831 statute also says that there must be no provision, direct or indirect, concerning the place where, or the manner in which, or the person or persons with whom the whole or any part of the wages shall be laid out or expended.[56] The entire amount due as wages must be paid in current coin.[57]

The 1831 Act applies to any " workman," as defined by the Employers and Workmen Act 1875, s. 10,[58] and this was effectively done by section 2 of the Truck Amendment Act 1887.[59] This last-mentioned section also says that the expression " artificer " as used in the principal Act is to be construed to include every workman to whom the principal Act is extended and applied by the 1887 Act. Any provision or enactment in the 1831 Act which was inconsistent with this new definition was repealed. The omnibus driver, who is also responsible for repairs to the vehicle under his service contract, comes within the Truck Acts.[60] The omnibus conductor [61] and the grocery store assistant [62] do not.

The English courts took the view in *Hart* v. *Riversdale Mill Co.*[63] that it was not a contravention of the Acts to pay a sum less than list wages to a weaver who wove badly and negligently, because this deduction was part of a method of ascertaining the true wages. This ruling was followed in *Sagar* v. *Ridehalgh & Sons Ltd.*[64]

Where wages have not been paid in current coin, in defiance of the Act, the workman is entitled to recover the whole or any such part of

[53] For a summary of the legislation see the Report of the Committee on the Truck Acts (1961)—a Ministry of Labour Departmental Committee under the Chairmanship of D. Karmel Q.C., pp. 3 to 5.
[54] See s. 1.
[55] 8 & 9 Eliz. 2, c. 37.
[56] s. 2. See also *Summerlee Iron Co. Ltd.* v. *Thomson*, 1913 S.C.(J.) 34; 1913, 1 S.L.T. 43 (including a reference to s. 23).
[57] s. 3.
[58] The s. 10 definition is:
   ' The expression ' workman ' does not include a domestic or menial servant, but save as aforesaid, means any person who, being a labourer, servant in husbandry, journeyman, artificer, handcraftsman, miner or otherwise engaged in manual labour, whether under the age of twenty-one years or above that age, has entered into or works under a contract with an employer . . . and be a contract of service or a contract personally to execute any work or labour."
[59] 50 & 51 Vict. c. 46.
[60] *Smith* v. *Associated Omnibus Co.* [1907] 1 K.B. 916.
[61] *Morgan* v. *London General Omnibus Co.* (1884) 13 Q.B.D. 832.
[62] *Bound* v. *Lawrence* (1892) 1 Q.B. 226.
[63] [1928] 1 K.B. 176.
[64] [1931] 1 Ch. 310.

the wages not so correctly paid.[65]   Deductions made by an employer are lawfully made where the employee agrees by a contract [66]; a formal writing is not necessary; it may be some note, memorandum or notice so long as the matter is brought to the attention of the employee.   The penalties for breach are contained in section 9 of the 1831 Act, as amended by or modified by section 12 of the 1887 Act.

The employer may supply (i) medicine or medical attendance, (ii) fuel,[67] (iii) materials, tools or implements to be used by workmen employed in mines, (iv) hay, corn or provender for a beast of burden, or (v) food prepared and consumed on the employer's premises and he (*i.e.*, the employer) may recover the true value of the goods or services so supplied, by deduction from wages, provided always that the employee enters into some contract or agreement signifying his consent to the deduction being made.[68]

An employer may, by an agreement or contract between his employee and himself, deduct from his employee's wages any sum owed to a third party by his employee, but he cannot deduct as of right any sum owed by the employee to him.[69]   The well-known trilogy of cases which must be mentioned upon the points raised in this paragraph are *Hewlett* v. *Allen* [69]; *Williams* v. *North's Navigation Collieries (1889) Ltd* [69]; and *Penman* v. *Fife Coal Co. Ltd.*[69]   In *Hewlett's* case, the employee was obliged by a term of his contract of employment to join a social and accident club, for which a weekly subscription was exigible.   The employers subtracted this subscription each week from the employee's wages.   These deductions were held to be lawfully made and not to be in contravention of the Truck Acts.   The application of the moneys for the employee in this case was tantamount to a payment to the employee himself.   In *Williams*, the question raised was that of the legality of deductions from an employee's wages made by an employer who held a court decree or judgment against the employee and who was proceeding to recover the sum in the decree (or judgment) by subtraction from wages.   Such deduction or subtraction was held to be illegal.   It did not matter whether the employee consented to the arrangement.

Penman's case is perhaps the most interesting one, particularly as it is basically a Scottish case.   Here the employer deducted from the pursuer's wages the rent due by the pursuer's father in respect of a dwelling-house owned by the employer and tenanted by the father.   The pursuer had signed an agreement in respect of the deductions, to prevent his father from being evicted.   Nevertheless, it was held that such deductions were

---

[65] See the 1831 Act, s. 4; and *Pratt* v. *Cook, Son & Co. (St. Paul's) Ltd.* [1940] A.C. 437; [1940] 1 All E.R. 410.

[66] 1831 Act, s. 23; and see also the Truck Act 1940 in respect of transactions occurring before July 10, 1940.

[67] See *M'Lucas* v. *Campbell* (O.H.) (1892) 30 S.L.R. 226.

[68] 1831 Act, s. 23.

[69] *Hewlett* v. *Allen* [1894] A.C. 383; *Williams* v. *North's Navigation Collieries* (1889) Ltd. [1906] A.C. 136; and *Penman* v. *Fife Coal Co. Ltd.*, 1935 S.C.(H.L.) 39; 1935 S.L.T. 401; [1936] A.C. 15.

illegal under the Truck Acts. The outstanding arrears of rent constituted a debt due by a third party (Penman's father) to the employer in respect of a transaction which was quite independent of Penman's service contractual relationship with the employer. Moreover, the House of Lords was concerned to point out that the scope of permitted deductions must not be carried too far. As the deductions were illegal the purported consent of the employee was quite ineffective and could not provide a shield of legality to a transaction which was essentially illegal.

It is not, however, an offence for an employer to advance money to his employee which is subsequently contributed to a friendly society or bank or for some sickness relief or for the education of his children. These advances may be deducted from subsequent earnings.

A comparatively recent case of some interest on the 1831 Act is *Duncan* v. *Motherwell Bridge and Engineering Co. Ltd.*[70] Here the contract of service was made between a Scottish workman and a Scottish company, although performance of the contract was to take place in a foreign country. It was agreed that certain deductions would be made from wages, payable each month, and would be deposited in a Scottish bank; these moneys to be used by the company to be offset against any claims by the company against the employee. The question of the extra-territorial application of the Truck Acts was immediately raised and it was decided that the Truck Acts do not, in principle, apply outside of the United Kingdom where the contract is to be wholly performed abroad. If performance is partly abroad and partly in the United Kingdom, then the Acts will apply. However, the deductions, in this case, were made within the Scottish jurisdiction; therefore the Truck Acts applied. These deductions were, however, contrary to the 1831 Act, s. 2, and the whole contract was void *ab initio*. Moreover, the workman could recover the sums deducted, plus interest thereon.[71] It was also held that the company were, on the principle of recompense, entitled to recover the sums counter-claimed by them (*i.e.*, for the homeward fare and the amount of the employee's debts paid by them).

The overall result of the 1831 Act is difficult to identify and explain. It appears that in some districts the " trucking " system declined substantially whilst in other districts, most notably in the West of Scotland, the employers found devious ways round the statute. The main offenders here seem to have been the colliery owners and the masters in the iron foundries. They either imposed " poundage," which was a levy of a fixed amount (normally one shilling per pound) for each pound advanced in cash to the workman or, more usually, they made an advance (or a " sub " as it was, and still is, called) to a workman and attached a condition to it that he must spend the advance or the balance of his wages when paid in the company's store. Pressure from the trade unions (notably

---

[70] 1952 S.L.T. 433; 1952 S.C. 131 (see particularly Lord Jamieson's view that the important test is the place where the employer is to perform his part by paying the wages due).
[71] 1831 Act, s. 4.

the miners) and certain sections of the press led to the appointment of
two Truck Commissioners in 1870 to investigate the system and they
reported in 1871. By the time the recommendations of the Commissioners
were effected by the Truck Amendment Act 1887, the system was substantially in decline and the impact of the statute was virtually negligible,
principally because public opinion and the trade union movement had
been outspokenly against the system for years and, very importantly,
because of the growth of the Co-operative stores.

Summing up briefly the main provisions of the 1887 Act, one sees
them to be the following: (i) it refers to and adopts the definition section
of the Employers and Workmen Act 1875 [72]; (ii) it makes it illegal for an
employer to withhold from his workman any sum which might, by custom
or agreement or otherwise, be paid in anticipation of wages (*i.e.*, an
advance or " sub "), as also to deduct any sum by way of poundage,
discount, interest or similar charge in respect of such advance [73]; (iii) it
prohibits an employer (and his agent) from making it a condition of the
employment as to the place at which, or the manner in which, or the
person with whom, his workman is to spend his wages; nor can an
employer (or his agent) dismiss a workman for doing, or failing to do,
any of these things (*i.e.*, on account of the place, manner or person at or
in which or with whom the wages or part thereof are spent or not spent) [74];
(iv) section 9 also provides for the audit of deductions made from wages
in respect of education of children, medicine, medical attendance or tools
—this audit to be carried out by two auditors appointed by the workmen,
who must have books, vouchers, documents and other facilities needed to
conduct the audit; and (v) the duty of enforcing compliance with the
principal Act and the 1887 Act rests, so far as factories, workshops and
mines are concerned, upon H.M. Inspectors of Factories and H.M.
Inspectors of Mines.

The Truck Act 1896 [75] is chiefly concerned with the following things—
(i) fines for disciplinary offences, (ii) deductions for spoiled work and
(iii) deductions for materials, etc.

In the case of (i) fines, any contract between the employer and workman which deals with or provides for the deduction of fines from wages
or the recovery of fines must comply with the following conditions—
(a) the terms must either be contained in a notice affixed constantly at a
place where the workman can enter freely and in such a position that it
may be seen, read and copied by any person whom it affects *or* the contract must be in writing and signed by the workman; (b) the contract
must specify the acts or omissions in respect of which the fine may be
imposed and the amount of the fine or certain particulars from which the
amount can be calculated; (c) the fine must be imposed in respect of some

[72] s. 10 of the 1875 Act; and s. 2 of the 1887 Act.
[73] s. 3.
[74] s. 6.
[75] 59 & 60 Vict. c. 44.

act or omission which has caused or is likely to cause damage or loss to the employer or interruption or hindrance to his business; (d) the fine must be fair and reasonable having regard to all the circumstances; and (e) the employer must not deduct the fine or receive the payments by way of recovery unless particulars in writing, showing the acts or omissions in respect of which the fine is imposed and the actual amount of the fine, are supplied to the workman.[76] This has to be done each time a deduction or payment is made.

It must be remembered that any arrangement by which an employer reserves the right to suspend a workman from employment where that workman has been guilty of some misconduct and thus suffers a loss of wages does not fall within the ambit of the Truck Acts. The reason is that this arrangement does not make any deduction from wages—because an employer does not contract to pay wages during a period of suspension.[77]

In the case of (ii) deductions for spoiled work, a similar type of contract may be made and again the conditions applicable are as follows: (a) the same as for (i) above as regards publication or writing; (b) the deduction or payment must not exceed the actual or estimated damage or loss occasioned to the employer by the act or omission of the workman, or of some person over whom he has control or for whom he is responsible by the contract; (c) the amount of the deduction or payment must be fair and reasonable, having regard to all the circumstances; whilst (d) and (e) above apply, *mutatis mutandis*, to this case also.

As regards (iii) deductions for materials, etc., again a form of contract is required in relation to materials, tools, machines and so on and once more certain conditions apply. These are: (a) as in (i) above so far as publication or writing is concerned; (b) the sum to be paid or deducted must not exceed—in respect of materials or tools supplied to the workman —the actual or estimated cost to the employer; or—in respect of the use of machinery, light and heat—a fair and reasonable rent or charge, having regard to all the circumstances; and (c) the same provision as in (i) (e) above as regards written particulars to be supplied to the workman, together with a stipulation of the actual sum to be paid or being deducted.

The Minister of Labour has power under the 1896 Act [78] to make an order dispensing with the operation of the Act, if he is satisfied that its application is not necessary for the protection of workmen of any trade or industry. It is understood that he has, in fact, exercised this power in relation to the cotton-weaving industry (notably in Lancashire and Yorkshire) and also in relation to the iron-ore mining and limestone quarrying industries (notably, again, in Lancashire and Yorkshire).

The Truck Act 1940 [79] is the next statutory development which must be noted. It is a very minor piece of legislation so far as its actual content

[76] 1896 Act, s. 1.
[77] *Bird* v. *British Celanese Ltd.* [1945] 1 All E.R. 488.
[78] This power is now exercisable by the Secretary of State for Employment and Productivity (this Department having replaced the Ministry of Labour since 1968).
[79] 3 & 4 Geo. 6, c. 38.

is concerned, although it is a " remedial " or " corrective " enactment. It was passed as a result of the case of *Pratt* v. *Cook, Son & Co.* (*St. Paul's*) *Ltd.*[80] in which the plaintiff was employed as a packer at the actual weekly wage of fifty-three shillings. Defendants supplied meals (dinner and tea) valued at ten shillings per week. Plaintiff claimed that this sum of ten shillings per week represented a wages deduction which defendants were not entitled to make—the matter was not governed by any written contract signed by him. The House of Lords upheld the plaintiff's contention. As this case would have sparked off a tremendous volume of litigation, based upon an irregularity in the form of contract required by section 23 of the 1831 Act, and at a time when the country was engaged in other matters of much greater importance, the 1940 Act was promptly passed. This statute remedied the position of past irregularities by providing a protection to employers in respect of transactions prior to July 10, 1940. No court actions could be brought in respect thereof. However, the 1940 Act made no changes in respect of agreements made after July 10, 1940. These had to comply with the section 23 requirements. If they did not do so the transaction was unlawful and could be attacked immediately by the workman.

The economic historians take the view that the Truck Acts really achieved very little and only serve to remind all of us, in modern times, first, of an outmoded social environment in which the trade union movement was powerless; secondly, of a distinction—no longer acceptable today—between manual and non-manual workers; and lastly, of an insistence (up to 1960, at any rate) upon methods of payment which were administratively undesirable.[81]

The Payment of Wages in Public Houses Prohibition Act 1883.[82] In terms of this statute no wages are to be paid to any workman at or within a public-house, beer shop or similar place or in any office, garden or place thereto belonging. The obvious exception is the employee of the owner or licensee himself. The rule applies equally to payment by an employer's agent or servant (*e.g.*, by a foreman or cashier)—for whose contravention of the statute the employer is liable. The employer may escape liability if he can prove to the satisfaction of the court that he took all reasonable means in his power to prevent the contravention.[83]

The statute applies to " workmen "—a term which includes a labourer, farm servant, journeyman, artificer, handicraftsman, or other person engaged in manual labour and irrespective of whether he is under or above the age of twenty-one years. The Act does not apply to domestic or other menial persons. Previously, the statute did not apply to miners,[84] but

[80] [1940] A.C. 437; [1940] 1 All E.R. 410.
[81] See Roy H. Campbell's article in the *Glasgow Herald* of July 21, 1961.
[82] For this and other legislation related to the Truck Acts see the Report of the Committee on the Truck Acts (the Karmel Committee Report) (1961), pp. 22–30.
[83] See s. 3.
[84] See the Coal Mines Act 1911, s. 96, which dealt specifically with miners.

the Mines and Quarries Act 1954 [85] removed the limiting words, so that miners are now brought within the framework of the 1883 Act.

The Shop Clubs Act 1902.[86] This statute is also quite closely allied to the Truck Acts. It becomes an offence thereunder, punishable by a fine, for an employer to make it a condition of employment that (i) any workman shall discontinue his membership of any friendly society or (ii) any workman shall not become a member of any friendly society other than the shop club or thrift fund.[87] The " friendly society " is, of course, one which is registered under the Friendly Societies Act 1896, whilst the " shop club " or " thrift fund " is any club or society for providing benefits to workmen in connection with a workshop, factory, dock or warehouse.[88] It is also an offence, subject to a fine, for any employer to make it a condition of employment that any workman shall join a shop club or thrift club unless it is duly registered under the Friendly Societies Act and is duly certified by the Registrar. The registration provisions are set forth in section 2. The Act exempts railways and the superannuation or insurance benefit funds thereof.[89] Section 6 contains certain provisions relating to employees who leave the particular employment and it permits them to draw their share of the club or alternatively to remain members but without rights or certain management privileges whilst out of the employment.

(3) *The Payment of Wages Act 1960*

No major change in the methods of paying wages occurred until the Payment of Wages Act 1960 [90] went on the Statute Book. The preamble indicates an intention to remove certain restrictions imposed by the Truck Acts 1831 to 1940 and other enactments. It is unarguable that with the close of the Second World War, more people, in the middle class and working class groups, were able to save and invest in certain funds— notably savings certificates, defence or development bonds, trustee savings banks, building societies and the like, which are all broadly referred to as " national savings." The bank account and the cheque book were increasing in popularity. Administratively, it was of considerable advantage to an employer to pay wages by bank transfer, cheque or other similar form. The new methods proposed also lessened the likelihood of theft and of injury to employees who were responsible for carrying large sums of cash. The Act became law on December 2, 1960 (six months after it was passed), except for section 4 (hereinafter explained) which came into effect on July 2, 1960. Section 8 became operative in Northern Ireland on June 2, 1960.

---

[85] See particularly Sched. V.
[86] 2 Edw. 7, c. 21.
[87] s. 1.
[88] s. 2.
[89] See s. 5.
[90] 8 & 9 Eliz. 2, c. 37.

The statute itself consists of nine principal sections, of which the last three comprise: the interpretation section (s. 7); a statement regarding the power of the Parliament of Northern Ireland to make laws for purposes similar to the purposes of this particular statute (s. 8); and the short title, commencement and extent (s. 9). It is clear from the interpretation section that the term " employed person," as used in the Act, means any person who is an artificer within the meaning of the Truck Acts 1831 to 1940, or of the Hosiery Manufacture (Wages) Act 1874, or is a miner within the meaning of the Stannaries Act 1887, and includes "outworkers" not directly employed, in terms of section 10 of the Truck Amendment Act 1887. The Schedule attached to the statute deals with " pay statements " and the information regarding fixed deductions to be presented in such statements, not only in the straightforward case of payment by one method but also where an instalment of wages is paid in different ways as permitted by the statute itself.

The main provisions concerning the modern methods of payment of wages to industrial workers generally are contained in the first six sections of the 1960 Act and it is accordingly necessary to examine these sections in some detail:

Section 1 deals with the position where an employed person makes a request to his employer for payment of his wages, or of part of his wages, in one of the ways authorised by the Act and the employer agrees with that request. Such a request and agreement are perfectly lawful and valid and do not constitute a breach of the Truck Act 1831, the Hosiery Manufacture (Wages) Act 1874 and the Stannaries Act 1887. The request must be made by notice in writing to the employer [91] and the employer himself may agree by an equivalent notice to the employee or, alternatively, by actually paying the wages in the method specified in the request.[92] A period of fourteen days, counting from the date of the giving of the request, is allowed for consideration and operation.[93] The request falls (i) if the employer refuses it within the stipulated period by notice in writing and (ii) generally after the fourteen days' period, unless—within that time—the employer has signified his agreement by notice or by payment. It will be appreciated that the arrangement is one which must be mutually acceptable to the parties.

The methods of payment authorised by the Act are [94]—(i) payment to a bank account (either a single account or a joint account), (ii) payment by postal order, (iii) payment by money order and (iv) payment by cheque. The first-mentioned method is thought to be the most popular of the four.

Section 2 deals with the mechanics of the operation and sets out the various requirements to be met when one of the methods of payment

[91] s. 1 (4).
[92] s. 1 (5).
[93] s. 1 (6).
[94] s. 1 (3).

authorised by the Act is adopted. Most importantly, the employee must receive a written statement [95] which sets forth the following particulars [96] —(a) the gross amount of the wages, (b) the amount of each deduction and what each deduction represents, (c) the net amount payable and (d) where payment is a " part " payment under the Act, the net amount payable by this method and the net amount of the balance (usually a normal cash payment). Errors and omissions made in good faith do not in any way invalidate the statement furnished.[97]

Notice of cancellation of the request may be given at any time by the employee and similarly for cancellation of the agreement by the employer.[98] These notices must be in writing and do not take effect until after the lapse of four weeks from the date upon which such notices are given,[99] although the parties may otherwise mutually agree upon an effective cancellation date under their written cancellation agreement.[1]

Section 4 contains the provisions which apply where an employee is absent from work (the section says absent from " the proper or usual place for payment ") because of duties to be performed elsewhere or illness or personal injury. Payment may be made by money order or postal order, in the absence of any request and agreement specifying any other method. Again the payment may relate to the whole of the wages or part of the wages.

Section 5 deals generally with the giving of requests and notices and acknowledges the existence of the authorised agent, as well as providing for service of notices either personally or by post.

Section 6 contains a number of supplemental provisions which are necessary upon the passing of the statute and which mainly refer specifically to the Truck Act 1831, s. 9; the Hosiery Manufacture (Wages) Act 1874, s. 5, and the Wages Councils Act 1959, s. 14 (1). However, subsection (5) sets forth certain provisions relating to payment by post— for example, where payment by cheque is requested, this does not imply that cheques be sent by post; whilst if payment by postal order or money order is requested it does so imply. Of course the employee may change the implication by an express provision or authorisation.

The wages position in relation to the dismissal of an employee is dealt with in a later chapter,[2] whilst the position in relation to redundancy payments is dealt with in a subsequent part of this chapter. It was considered to be more logical to treat redundancy pay along with wages in this chapter than to examine redundancy pay as an adjunct to a chapter dealing specifically with dismissal of employees.

---

[95] s. 2 (4)
[96] See s. 2 (5).
[97] s. 2 (6).
[98] s. 3 (1).
[99] s. 3 (2).
[1] s. 3 (3).
[2] See particularly Chap. 18, *infra* (termination by notice) and Chap. 19, *infra* (termination without notice).

(4) *Wages Councils*

Although voluntary negotiation upon wages and other matters is the more common method in British industrial relations, there have been occasions when statute law and statutory machinery have both been used for the fixing of minimum wages. The first Trade Boards Act 1909 [3] was the primary example of such legislation. The purpose behind the Act was to remove the evils of sweated labour in certain trades which were poorly organised and in which very low wages were paid and bad working conditions existed. The first four trades to which the 1909 Act applied were ready-made tailoring, chain-making, paper box manufacture and lace and net finishing (by machine). These Boards consisted of an equal number of employers' representatives and workers' representatives with three independent members and their main purpose was to fix statutory minimum time rates of wages. Following upon the Whitley Committee Report of 1917, which recommended that the machinery of the Trade Boards Act should be applied in those industries wherein little or no organisation existed, " pending the development of such degree of organisation as would render possible the establishment of a National Joint Industrial Council or District Councils "[4] the second Trade Boards Act 1918 was passed—and this enabled the Minister of Labour to set up a Trade Board if he was " of opinion that no adequate machinery exists for the regulation of wages throughout the trade, and that accordingly, having regard to the rates of wages prevailing in the trade, or any part of the trade, it is expedient that the principal Act should apply to that trade." From then on the number of Trade Boards began to grow, in 1938, to fifty in number covering about one and one-half million workers.[5] The next step was the Wages Councils Act 1945,[6] which was amended by two statutes of 1948 and 1959 respectively.[7] The final stage was the Wages Councils Act 1959.[8] Almost contemporaneously with the statutes above-mentioned the Road Haulage Wages Act 1938 and the Catering Wages Act 1943 were passed together with certain other statutes applicable to agriculture and affecting Scotland particularly—notably the Agricultural Wages (Regulation) (Scotland) Act 1940, the Agricultural Wages (Regulation) Act 1947 and the Agricultural Wages (Scotland) Act 1949.

With the passing of the Wages Councils Act 1959 [9] the number of workers governed by statute—and this Act is the current operative

---

[3] The Trade Boards were modelled upon an Australian pattern which had been developed in Victoria *circa* 1896.

[4] See the *Industrial Relations Handbook* (H.M.S.O.) (1961).

[5] See C. W. Guillebaud, " The Wages Councils System in Great Britain " (1958) excerpted from *Industrial Labour in India* (Asia Publishing House, Bombay).

[6] 8 & 9 Geo. 6, c. 17.

[7] The Wages Councils Act 1948 (12, 13 & 14 Geo. 6, c. 7) and the Terms and Conditions of Employment Act 1959 (7 & 8 Eliz. 2, c. 26). The Wages Councils Act 1959 (7 & 8 Eliz. 2, c. 69) repealed the Terms and Conditions of Employment Act 1959, *except* s. 8.

[8] 7 & 8 Eliz. 2, c. 69.

[9] 7 & 8 Eliz. 2, c. 69.

statute [10] upon Wages Councils—had risen to almost three and one-half millions. The Act has three main parts of which the last one (ss. 22–27) is supplementary. Part I (ss. 1–10) deals with the establishment of Wages Councils and Part II (ss. 11–21) deals with Wages Regulation Orders. This particular topic of industrial law is dealt with in several books [11] and it is not proposed to devote a large amount of space to it. It will be necessary, however, to examine some of the main points in broad outline and thereafter to consider the views of the recent Royal Commission on Trade Unions and Employers' Associations as expressed in their Report [12] (referred to hereafter, for brevity's sake, as the " Donovan Report.")

The Act enables the Minister of Labour [13] to make an order establishing a Wages Council, subject to certain provisions as to prior publicity and inquiry, by any one of the following three methods:

(a) The Minister may, on his own initiative, make such an order if he is of opinion that there is no adequate machinery for the effective regulation of the remuneration of any workers and that, having regard to the remuneration existing among those workers, it is expedient that a council should be established.[14]

(b) An application can be made to the Minister by a Joint Industrial Council (or similar body) or jointly by employers' organisations and workers' organisations for the establishment of a Wages Council on the ground that the existing machinery is likely to cease to exist or be adequate. The Minister is required to refer this application to a Commission of Inquiry, provided he is satisfied that there are sufficient grounds for doing so.[15]

(c) The Minister may, again on his own initiative, ask a Commission of Inquiry to consider whether a Wages Council should be established if he considers that adequate machinery for the effective regulation of the remuneration of any workers does not exist or is likely to cease to exist or be adequate and that a reasonable standard of remuneration will not be maintained.[16]

It is understood that those Wages Councils which have been established since 1945 have come within the operation of methods (b) and (c) above.[17] A Commission of Inquiry is governed by section 9 of the Act

---

[10] Amended, in certain respects, by the Prices and Incomes Legislation—see the Prices and Incomes Acts 1966, 1967 and 1968 (1966, c. 35, 1967, c. 53 and 1968, c. 42, respectively).

[11] Notably in the *Industrial Relations Handbook* (H.M.S.O.) (1961), Chap. X, pp. 153–167; and also G. H. L. Fridman, *The Modern Law of Employment* (1963) and Supplement, pp. 705–716; and Sir Wm. Mansfield Cooper and John C. Wood, *Outlines of Industrial Law* (5th ed.; Butterworths, 1966), pp. 115–121.

[12] Cmnd. 3623 (June 1968).

[13] Now, since 1968, the Secretary of State for Employment and Productivity (the Ministry of Labour being then replaced by the Department of Employment and Productivity).

[14] 1959 Act, s. 1 (2) (a).

[15] *Ibid*. s. 1 (2) (b) and s. 2.

[16] *Ibid*. s. 1 (2) (c).

[17] *Industrial Relations Handbook*, p. 155.

and the Fourth Schedule (the Schedule dealing in effect with the constitution, officers and proceedings of the commissions).   It consists of not
more than three independent persons (of whom one is appointed chairman) plus two persons representing employers and two persons representing workers.   The chairman is appointed from among the independent
members, and if a deputy chairman is necessary he also is drawn from
that same group.   The Minister (now the Secretary of State) makes all
the appointments.   Of the employers' and workers' representatives none
should be, in the Minister's opinion, connected with or likely to be
affected by the matters into which the commission is inquiring.   Expert
assessors may be appointed.[18]   Notice of the intention to set up a Wages
Council must be published in the *Edinburgh Gazette* (or *London Gazette*
or both, as circumstances require).   The order establishing a Wages
Council, accompanied by any relevant Commission of Inquiry, must be
laid before Parliament.   It may be annulled by a resolution of either
House.

Abolition, variation and applications for abolition of Wages Councils
are dealt with in sections 4 and 5, whilst references to a commission of
inquiry anent variation or revocation of a Wages Council order can be
taken under section 6.   Part II of the 1959 Act gives the Wages Councils
power *inter alia* to make proposals for fixing remuneration and holidays
(including holiday remuneration).   Procedure, including meetings, may
be regulated by the Minister, by regulations.   An advisory committee
for any workers within the field of operation of the Council may be
appointed by the Minister at the request of the Wages Council.[19]   Central
co-ordinating committees may be established by the Minister, by order, or
they may be abolished by him or the field of operation of such a co-
ordinating committee may be varied.[20]   Matters such as enforcement of
wages regulation orders, permits for incapacitated workers, apportionment
of remuneration, records and offences and penalties are all covered in
Part II.[21]   Enforcement of the Act is the responsibility of wages inspectors
appointed by the Minister, although he may arrange with another government department that officers from that department should act instead of
wages inspectors specifically appointed.[22]   An inspector may, in England
and Wales, institute proceedings for any offence under Part II.[23]   No
mention is made of Scotland or procedure therein.   There seems to be
therefore an implication that the matter is to be dealt with by summary
procedure through the procurator-fiscal's office.   Most of the social
historians and economic historians take the view that the Wages Councils
system has been successful in abolishing the evils of sweated labour and

[18] But they have no vote, nor are they signatories to the report or any recommendation—
see 1959 Act, Sched. IV, para. 4 (1) and (2).
[19] *Ibid.* s. 8 and Sched. III.
[20] *Ibid.* s. 7.
[21] See particularly ss. 12–20.
[22] s. 19.
[23] s. 19 (4).

competitive undercutting of wages,[24] and in raising the efficiency of labour employed in those industries to which the system applies.

The Royal Commission on Trade Unions and Employers' Associations [25] (the Donovan Commission) examined the Wages Councils system.[26] The Commission was impressed by the evidence given by the trade union movement [27] to the effect that Wages Councils statutory systems and arrangements were a hindrance to trade union organisation and the development of voluntary machinery, which would be preferable and certainly more beneficial to the workers. The Commission questions whether the statutory enforcement of minimum rates of pay is necessary and whether the continuance of the Councils is justified.[28] It is indicated [29] by the Commission that the Wages Councils are doing little to fulfil the aim of extending voluntary collective bargaining, that the voluntary organisation in those industries concerned is too weak to support extensive negotiating machinery, that the statutory machinery is proving to be a hindrance to such a development and, obviously, new measures are required. The Donovan Report contains certain important proposals which the Commission feels to be essential in modern industrial relations, viz.:

(i) The 1959 Act should be amended to empower the Secretary of State for Employment and Productivity to abolish any Wages Council where satisfied (upon an application from a trade union representing a substantial proportion of the workers) that the wages and conditions of the workpeople would not be adversely affected by the abolition. This is seen as a first step towards the extension of voluntary machinery.[30]

(ii) The 1959 Act should be amended to enable the said Secretary of State to exclude from the scope of a Wages Council any undertaking which, in his opinion, possessed satisfactory voluntary collective bargaining arrangements covering a substantial majority of workers.[31]

(iii) The " inspectorate " might be used for a limited period after the abolition of a Wages Council, to ease the transition to voluntary bargaining.[32]

(iv) Section 8 of the Terms and Conditions of Employment Act 1959 should be amended by removing the provisos in subsection (1) thereof in relation to workers in Wages Councils industries.[33] This would stimulate the movement towards voluntary machinery.

[24] C. W. Guillebaud, op. cit., p. 31.
[25] Cmnd. 3623 (1968).
[26] Ibid. paras. 225–234.
[27] Ibid. para. 229, for references.
[28] Ibid. para. 230.
[29] Ibid. para. 234.
[30] Ibid. para. 262.
[31] Ibid. para. 263.
[32] Ibid. para. 264.
[33] Ibid. para. 265.

(v) Since the existing statutory machinery has no means of en-
couraging the development of collective dealings between management and shop stewards (or other workers' representatives) in
individual factories, Wages Councils should be encouraged to
establish disputes procedures for handling grievances raised by
individual workers (or groups) through their representatives.
These procedures should not be made enforceable at law. This
proposal is seen as being likely to encourage organisation and a
development towards voluntary machinery. A " committee
system "—operating, if necessary, upon a regional basis—may
be useful here rather than have every Wages Council acting
alone.[34] Given that the tone of the Donovan Report reflects
a balance of thinking in favour of an extension and development
of voluntary bargaining machinery, supported by the authority
of a new Industrial Relations Act, it is very likely that a gradual
move away from the statutory machinery of Wages Councils
will take place, along the lines proposed by the Commission. It
is unlikely that a rapid legislative change will be made.

(5) Regulation of Wages in Certain Industries

Apart from Wages Councils, to which reference has been made in
the preceding section, the most common examples of wage regulation
are:
   (a) The Holidays with Pay Act 1938.[35]
   (b) Wages in the mining industry.
   (c) Wages in the road haulage industry.
   (d) Wages in agriculture.

(a) *Holidays with Pay Act 1938.* This statute permits a wage regulating
authority to direct that workers for whom a statutory minimum rate of
wages has been fixed, or is being fixed, shall be allowed such holidays as
may be directed. The duration of the holiday must be related to the
length of the period of the worker's employment or engagement. The
direction itself will specify details of the permitted holidays but will not
prejudice any half holidays or other days which are allowed to the employees under other statutory enactments, although the direction may
take account of these additional holidays and include them in the new
arrangements. Wages Councils have regulated holiday periods, in
addition to their normal minimum wage-fixing duties under the Wages
Councils Act 1959. Provision must be made for employees to receive
pay during their holiday periods, within the terms and provisions of the
Act. Holiday pay is to accrue and be paid at such times and upon such
terms and conditions as are directed. When an employee leaves a particular employment he is entitled to receive whatever holiday pay has

[34] *Ibid.* para. 266.
[35] 1 & 2 Geo. 6, c. 70.

accrued to the leaving date, even although the time for his holiday has not yet arrived.[36]

(b) *Wages in the mining industry*.[37] It may be the case that the wages to be paid to an employee depend upon the weight of mineral which he extracts from the working face. The weighing arrangements must be carried out as near as possible to the pit mouth. These matters are regulated by various statutes [38] and irregular arrangements between management and workers are not permissible.[39]

(c) *Wages in the road haulage industry*. By the earlier statutes, namely, the Road Haulage Wages Act 1938 and the Trade Boards and Road Haulage Wages (Emergency Provisions) Act 1940, this industry was regulated by the Central Wages Board and the appropriate Area Wages Boards. The 1938 Act was repealed in part by the Wages Councils Act 1948, which replaced the Central Wages Board by a Wages Council functioning under the Wages Councils Act 1945 and the Wages Councils Act 1959,[40] which continued in force all orders made under the earlier legislation.[41] But in any question concerning the payment of fair wages in the industry which is subject to a dispute which has been referred to the Industrial Court by the Minister, the statutory provisions contained in the 1938 Act (as amended in 1948) are still applicable.

(d) *Wages in agriculture*. Minimum rates of pay and holidays applicable to agricultural workers in Scotland are dealt with in the Agricultural Wages (Scotland) Act 1949,[42] which broadly follows the pattern of a statute of 1948 governing the position in England and Wales. The 1949 Act established the Scottish Agricultural Wages Board and appropriate wages committees,[43] established for particular districts as might be specified by the Secretary of State for Scotland, by statutory instrument. The special provisions relating to wages and holidays are to be found in sections 3–11 inclusive, of which sections 3, 4 and 6 are most important indeed. Section 6 deals specifically with those persons under instruction in agriculture (subsection (5) speaks of " an apprentice or learner ") and section 4 deals with the enforcement of wages orders and holiday orders. Failure to obey such orders is an offence and, upon summary conviction, the employer is liable to the penalties stipulated in section 4 (1), para. (*c*). Complaints are investigated by officers, appointed for the purpose and

---

[36] Holidays with Pay Act 1938, s. 2.
[37] For a detailed consideration, see G. H. L. Fridman, *The Modern Law of Employment*, pp. 395–403.
[38] See the Coal Mines Regulation Act 1887; the Coal Mines (Weighing of Minerals) Act 1905; and the Mines and Quarries Act 1954, Sched. V; and the Checkweighing in Various Industries Act 1919, which extends the checkweighing procedures to industries other than mining but akin to it.
[39] See *Kearney* v. *Whitehaven Colliery Co.* [1893] 1 Q.B. 700; But see also *Dobbie* v. *Coltness Iron Co.*, 1920 S.C.(H.L.) 121; 1920, 2 S.L.T. 32; [1920] A.C. 916; 36 T.L.R. 622 (where it was to be permissible to contract for the extraction of " clean coal " and, accordingly, anything which was not " clean coal," but *e.g.*, merely " coal," fell to be disregarded).
[40] *Ibid.* s. 26, Scheds. V and VI.
[41] See now S.I. 1966 No. 554.
[42] 12 & 13 Geo. 6, c. 30.
[43] *Ibid.* ss. 1 and 2 (and Scheds. I and II respectively).

for securing observance of the Act's provisions.[44] It should be noted that where an offence is committed (for which liability arises under section 4 or section 6 (6) by an agent of the employer, that agent may be proceeded against in the same way as if he were an employer and, of course, the employer also remains liable.[45] The agent may be charged along with the employer, or before or after the employer's conviction, and he is liable to the same punishment as the employer.[45] A special defence is available to an employer [46] who is charged with an offence under section 4 or section 6 (6), *viz.*, if he proves to the satisfaction of the court that he used due diligence to secure compliance with the relevant provisions of the Act and that the offence was in fact committed by his agent or some other person, without his knowledge, consent or connivance, he shall— in the event of the conviction of the agent or other person—be exempt from any conviction in respect of the offence. It will be seen that the wording of the subsection (*i.e.*, s. 10 (2)) requires that a conviction should be obtained against the agent (or other person) before the employer escapes conviction. It is not enough that he used due diligence, etc.

The provisions relating to the constitution and proceedings of the Scottish Agricultural Wages Board are to be found in the First Schedule to the Act. The Board is to consist of (a) six persons representing employers and six persons representing workers in agriculture (one at least of the workers' representatives shall be a woman); and (b) five persons appointed by the Secretary of State (of whom one shall be designated chairman of the Board). The corresponding provisions relating to the Scottish Agricultural Wages Committees are contained in the Second Schedule to the Act. It is there provided that an agricultural wages committee shall consist of (a) not more than eight persons (and not less than five) representing employers and an equal number of persons representing workers in agriculture in the district, (b) two impartial persons appointed by the Secretary of State for Scotland and (c) a chairman, appointed annually by the representative members of the committee (and if they fail to do so, the Secretary of State may do so).

The 1949 Act makes certain changes in the Holidays with Pay Act 1938 so far as concerns agricultural workers.[47]

Methods of calculating wages are also applied to the hosiery and silk weaving industries by the Hosiery Act 1845 and the Silk Weavers Act 1845. For more detailed information, the first three sections of each statute should be consulted,[48] and be read along with section 135 of the Factories Act 1961, which section relates to textile factories and contains very extensive provisions.[49] Such provisions may be extended to factories

---

[44] *Ibid.* s. 12.
[45] *Ibid.* s. 10 (1).
[46] *Ibid.* s. 10 (2).
[47] 1949 Act, Sched. IV; ss. 1, 2, 3 and 5 are repealed in relation to agricultural workers.
[48] See also Fridman, *op. cit.*, pp. 390–391.
[49] See Fridman, pp. 391–395.

other than textile factories in terms of section 135 (5) by special regulations made by the Minister (now the Secretary of State for Employment and Productivity).

(6) Collective Bargaining and Joint Negotiation

A study of the development of the trade union movement shows that by the middle of the nineteenth century the trade unions were concentrating upon the improvement of the working conditions of their members by achieving recognition of their own position as negotiators on behalf of their members. By the beginning of the twentieth century the more important craft unions had been successful in pressing forward with voluntary bargaining and voluntary machinery for the settlement of those industrial disputes which might arise in any trade or industry. Most often the method adopted was the creation of a joint conciliation board which adopted its own procedures.[50] The preliminary negotiations or arrangements made between employers (or associations of employers) on the one side and the trade union (or trade unions) concerned on the other side are known and recognised as " bargaining " processes. This voluntary bargaining is usually directed towards the settlement of wages claims and conditions of employment generally. Once the collective bargaining process [51] is completed and an agreement has been reached this agreement is referred to as a collective agreement. Employers and their associations (the most important being the Confederation of British Industry or C.B.I.) and trade unions (in particular, the Trades Union Congress or T.U.C., to which many of the leading unions are affiliated) and their members are very jealous of their own rights and their own powers to bargain and negotiate voluntarily in the whole field of industrial relations. The concept of compulsory bargaining or compulsory arbitration by state machinery would be regarded as disastrous to industrial peace, mainly from the trade union viewpoint. Certainly the law has contributed little to the field of industrial relations. Not only did it hinder the development of the unions themselves by a strict application of the doctrine of restraint of trade on the one hand but—at the same time—it underlined the so-called " freedom of contract " theory in such a way that workers and their organisations began to lose faith in the legal machinery. Perhaps this was particularly noticeable in the mid-nineteenth century, where criminal law processes were invoked against workers and their unions, mainly in England and Wales.[52] Hence the background record of industrial relations in Great Britain seems to be based upon mutual distrust rather than mutual respect. That is a disgraceful state of affairs and it is high time that the record was altered.

[50] See *Industrial Relations Handbook* (H.M.S.O.; 1961), p. 18.
[51] For valuable chapters on collective bargaining and joint consultation see, particularly, *The System of Industrial Relations in Great Britain* (ed. Allan Flanders and H. A. Clegg; Blackwell, 1956), Chaps. V and VI; also *An Introduction to the Study of Industrial Relations* by Professor J. Henry Richardson (Allen & Unwin, 1954), Chap. 15.
[52] See Chap. 17, *infra*, regarding the legal position of trade unions.

The Report of the Royal Commission on the Trade Unions and Employers' Associations [53] (both referred to generally in this book as the Donovan Commission and the Donovan Report) recommends more close attention to the teaching of industrial law (or labour law) in the British universities. It is equally important, in the writer's opinion, that lawyers should also be taught to understand and appreciate the whole system of industrial relations. Perhaps when these studies have been fully developed the law will be able to make a valid positive contribution rather than its customary " last ditch " negative contribution.

In modern industrial practice it is virtually unknown for a skilled industrial worker to make an individual bargain or contract with his employer. It may happen in the case of a highly skilled employee in the scientific or technical fields but usually such an employee is, by virtue of his qualifications and status, able to bargain personally and probably also he is not—and does not find it necessary to become—a member of a trade union. But that situation is exceptional and most major industries in Britain accept and operate the system of collective bargaining and collective agreements. The state encourages the voluntary system and supplements it in certain ways by the creation of statutory machinery which may be used to assist in the settlement of serious disputes. [54] Valuable work has been done by the Whitley Committee and by the various National Joint Councils and Joint Industrial Councils, not only in the main private industries but also in the nationalised industries and in the public services. [55] However, it is no part of our task to consider these matters in detail, but instead it is necessary to examine the legal force or otherwise of the negotiated collective agreement.

The leading question is, of course, whether a collective agreement is a binding legal agreement. That question seems to be a simple one, but it contains two further questions within it, viz.—(i) is a collective agreement legal? and (ii) is it binding (i.e., enforceable by the courts)? The answers are not simple and straightforward positives or negatives.

Certain agreements were, mainly, it is believed, at the instance of the leading trade unionists of the time, kept out of the ambit of the law courts. These are particularised in the Trade Union Act 1871,[56] s. 4, which is in the following terms, viz.—

> " 4. Nothing in this Act shall enable any court to entertain any legal proceeding instituted with the object of directly enforcing or recovering damages for the breach of any of the following agreements, namely,
>
> (1) Any agreement between members of a trade union as such, concerning the conditions on which any members for the

---

[53] Cmnd. 3623 (1968).
[54] See Chap. 17, infra, on the " settlement of disputes."
[55] For a most informative and instructive survey of these matters, see the *Industrial Relations Handbook*, Chap. II (pp. 20–26); and Chaps. III, IV and V.
[56] 34 & 35 Vict., c. 31.

time being of such trade union shall or shall not sell their goods, transact business, employ, or be employed:

(2) Any agreement for the payment by any person of any subscription or penalty to a trade union:

(3) Any agreement for the application of the funds of a trade union,—

(a) To provide benefits to members; or,

(b) To furnish contributions to any employer or workman not a member of such trade union, in consideration of such employer or workman acting in conformity with the rules or resolutions of such trade union; or,

(c) To discharge any fine imposed upon any person by sentence of a court of justice; or,

(4) Any agreement made between one trade union and another; or

(5) Any bond to secure the performance of any of the above-mentioned agreements.

But nothing in this section shall be deemed to constitute any of the above-mentioned agreements unlawful."

It will be seen therefore that collective agreements would fall under paragraph (4) of section 4. It is clearly stated that nothing in section 4 is to make any agreement of the kinds mentioned unlawful. Accordingly a negotiated collective agreement would be perfectly legal on general grounds—but is it binding on the parties and legally enforceable? Most writers [57] in the field of industrial relations take the view that such agreements are " gentlemen's agreements " only—that is to say, binding in honour and accepted and carried into effect voluntarily by the parties concerned,[58] but not strictly enforceable as contracts by due legal process. This, it is fair to say, is the accepted view.[59] However, it must be noted immediately that the legal question as to whether a collective agreement is legally binding and enforceable has been raised very recently in the

---

[57] Notably Professor Otto Kahn-Freund, *The System of Industrial Relations in Great Britain*, *op. cit.*, Chap. II (Legal Framework), pp. 56–61, in particular. Mr. J. L. Gayler dissents from the views (or perhaps, more accurately from the reasons) given by Professor Kahn-Freund—see his textbook on *Industrial Law* (English Universities Press, 1955), pp. 172–174.

[58] For some examples and general notes see the Donovan Report, paras. 31–38.

[59] A view concurred in by the Commission in para. 470. See also the dicta by Lord Sterndale M.R. in *McLuskey* v. *Cole* [1922] 1 Ch. 7 *re* agreements falling under the Trade Union Act 1871, s. 4. The case of *Bellshill and Mossend Co-operative Society* v. *Dalziel Co-operative Society Ltd.*, 1960 S.C.(H.L.) 64; 1960 S.L.T. 165; [1960] A.C. 832; [1960] 2 W.L.R. 580; [1960] 1 All E.R. 673 (H.L.) is also interesting. Both societies who were members of a co-operative union were in dispute about their trading rights in a particular part of Lanarkshire. The union rules provided that such a dispute was to go to arbitration and the award was to be final and binding. Any member of the union could withdraw after giving notice in writing. The arbitration award was adverse to respondents, who then served notice of withdrawal and refused to comply with the award. Appellants claimed that respondents were bound by it (under the agreement)—but their appeal was refused. Lord Reid delivered the main speech in the House and his views on rule 10 of the union's rules (the reference to arbitration) are clear—in his lordship's opinion the appellants were not bound when they gave up membership of the union.

Queen's Bench Division in England in the so-called "test case" of
Ford Motor Co. Ltd. v. *Amalgamated Union of Engineering and Foundry
Workers and Others.*[59a] Mr. Justice Geoffrey Lane, in the course of his
opinion, pointed out that the parties did not intend to make the agreement enforceable at law and he went on to say, "Agreements such as
these, composed largely of optimistic aspirations, presenting grave
practical problems of enforcement and reached against a background of
opinion adverse to enforceability, are, in my judgment, not contracts in
the legal sense and are not enforceable at law. Without clear and express
provisions making them amenable to legal action, they remain in the
realm of undertakings binding in honour." The decision never went
any higher on appeal, as the injunctions were discharged, but there
is every likelihood that a higher court in England and the Court of Session
in Scotland would have taken a view exactly similar to that taken by Mr.
Justice Lane.

The Donovan Commission devotes a whole chapter [60] of its Report
to the question of the enforcement of collective agreements. It proceeds
from the basis of the development of certain legislative techniques in
order to reduce the incidence of strikes and points out that the most
important of these techniques would be the transformation of either
collective agreements in general or of procedure agreements in particular
into legally binding contracts which could be enforced in a court of
law.[61] It is the unofficial strike in breach of a procedure agreement which
causes most concern.[62] Nevertheless, says the Commission, the parties
to a so-called "collective bargain" (a term first used by Beatrice Webb)
do not intend to make a legally binding contract and without this intention there can be no contract between the parties in the strict legal sense.
This policy to keep collective bargaining outwith the scope of the law
is a most important characteristic in the British industrial relations
system. Therefore, points out the Commission,[63] if existing collective
agreements or existing procedure agreements were to be made into legal
contracts this would have to be done by a statute attaching the force of
law to the terms of a bargain contrary to the wishes of the parties—which
would be an unprecedented step contrary to the common law principles
of the law of contract. The Commission concludes by rejecting the
proposal to make collective agreements—whether substantive or procedural—enforceable at the present time.[64] Their principal reason for
so doing is that the law cannot, in Britain today, assist in the reduction

---

59a [1969] 1 W.L.R. 339 (which was an application for *ex parte* injunctions against defendants
to prevent the continuation of a long and costly strike at Fords).

60 *Ibid.* Chap. VIII, paras. 458–519. In its earlier Chap. IV the Commission recommends
the registration of certain collective agreements with the Department of Employment and
Productivity, duly authorised by a new Industrial Relations Act.

61 *Ibid.* para. 460.

62 *Ibid.* para. 462. The Commission points out in Chap. VII that 95 per cent. of all strikes
in Britain are unofficial.

63 *Ibid.* para. 474.

64 *Ibid.* para. 506.

of the number of unofficial strikes. Indeed they go further than that and say [64] that to take such steps today would not only be useless but also harmful and would undo much of the good which the Commission hopes to see develop from its own recommendations for a reform of the collective bargaining system.[65] The Commission does, however, go on to indicate how—if the need should arise in the field of industrial relations for legal sanctions to be imposed—procedure agreements could be made legally enforceable and fit into a reformed system of collective bargaining.[66] Lord Robens and Sir George Pollock, in a Note of Dissent,[67] regarding procedure agreements, take the view that where parties cannot agree the Industrial Relations Commission should, after consultation, draft a procedure agreement and the Secretary of State should have power to put it into operation by order; and also where employees take part in an " unofficial dispute," they should be regarded as having broken their contracts of service, automatically losing all title to benefits that would have accrued by reason of previous service.

This legalistic attitude taken towards a " collective bargain " is based on the premise that the " bargain " in question is a contract. In fact, it is nothing of the kind, it is an open-ended negotiating process which will be translated into a collective agreement containing certain terms and conditions. That agreement itself—having no machinery for enforcement—is very probably looked upon by both sides as pointing to a satisfactory solution to a claim from workers, agreeably settled and perhaps, by mutual consent, thought to be operative for a period of, say, two years. But it is no more than that and indeed it may sometimes be regarded as clearing the way for the next wages claim which will then come under active discussion from the trade union side. Although the collective agreement has *per se* no binding legal force, it may well be that the terms of employment or conditions of engagement contained in it become incorporated into the contracts of employment of the employees concerned. That incorporation can be done by (i) an express inclusion [68] of the terms and conditions or a direct reference to or mutual acceptance of the " union rates and conditions " applicable in the industry or shop [69]; or by (ii) custom or usage—either industry-wide or applicable to a local area—which means that there is an implied acceptance of the terms and conditions and by long established practice in the industry or area these terms and conditions become implied into the contracts of employment. Accordingly, both the express terms and the implied terms, or either of them, then become fully enforceable within the framework of the contract of employment and any breach of these terms and conditions could result

---

[65] The Commission is supremely confident that its recommendations will vastly reduce the size of the problem—see para. 509, but the problem will not vanish altogether.
[66] See paras. 510–518.
[67] para. 519.
[68] See *National Coal Board* v. *Galley* [1958] 1 All E.R. 91; [1958] 1 W.L.R. 16.
[69] See *Tomlinson* v. *L.M. & S. Ry.* [1944] 1 All E.R. 537 (C.A.); and *Rookes* v. *Barnard* [1964] A.C. 1129; [1964] 2 W.L.R. 269; [1964] 1 All E.R. 367; [1964] 1 Lloyd's Rep. 28.

in an action of damages, based in contract, or an application for specific implement, depending upon the circumstances. The incorporation may also take place under the Wages Councils Acts [70]; under the Road Haulage Wages Act 1938 [71]; or under the House of Commons Resolutions on Fair Wages. There have been in fact three resolutions of the House of Commons dealing with " fair wages "—the first in 1891 [72]; the second in 1909 [73]; and the third in 1946. [74] The important elements of the 1946 Resolution may be summarised as follows:

    (a) The contractors must observe such terms or conditions as have been established for the trade or industry by joint negotiating machinery or by arbitration; or, in the absence of these standards, terms and conditions which are not less favourable than the general level of wages and conditions observed by other employers in similar circumstances.

    (b) The contractor must observe " fair " conditions of work as well as " fair " wages and apply them to all employees engaged on the contract.

    (c) Any question whether " fair wages " are or are not being paid must be referred to the Minister of Labour (now the Secretary of State for Employment and Productivity) and if it is not then settled by negotiation or conciliation it must be referred to arbitration or to the Industrial Court. [75]

    (d) The contractor must recognise the freedom of his employees to take up trade union membership.

    (e) The contractor is responsible that sub-contractors employed by him should also observe the terms and spirit of the Resolution.

Finally, there must also be mentioned the " claims procedure " contained in section 8 of the Terms and Conditions of Employment Act 1959. [76] This procedure is considered in detail in a later chapter [77] and brief mention need only be made of it here. It is possible, by this process, for a representative organisation of employers or workers to invoke the aid of the Industrial Court, after the lodgment of a " claim " through the Minister (now the Secretary of State) that the " recognised terms and conditions " are not being observed by an employer. Certain contentions

---

[70] See *supra*, section (4) of this chapter.

[71] See *supra*, section (5) of this chapter; and the Transport Acts 1962 and 1968.

[72] Passed on February 13, 1891 (see *Industrial Relations Handbook*, Appendix III, p. 214 for the text).

[73] Passed on March 10, 1909 (see *Industrial Relations Handbook*, *loc. cit.*).

[74] Passed on October 14, 1946 (see *Industrial Relations Handbook*, Appendix III, pp. 214–215). For a list of statutes containing a " fair wages " clause in relation to certain industries or public authorities see the *Industrial Relations Handbook*, Appendix III at pp. 215–216.

[75] For two interesting examples of this procedure see *The National Association of Toolmakers against The Pressed Steel Co. Ltd., Cowley, Oxford* (Industrial Court: Case 3009); and *The National Union of Dyers against William Denby & Sons Ltd.* (Industrial Court: Case 3071); both of these are quoted and noted by Prof. K. W. Wedderburn in his valuable collection of *Cases and Materials on Labour Law* (Cambridge Univ. Press; 1967).

[76] 7 & 8 Eliz. 2, c. 26. This is in fact the only remaining and operative section of this Act. The remainder of the Act was repealed by the Wages Councils Act 1959.

[77] *Infra*, Chap. 17.

have to be made in the claim and it is the function of the Industrial Court to determine whether the claim is well-founded. If satisfied that it is, the Industrial Court will issue an award requiring the employer in question to observe the recognised terms and conditions—unless, of course, it finds that he is operating terms or conditions which are not less favourable. By section 8 (4), an award issued has the effect of an implied term of the contract of employment from such a date as may be determined by the Industrial Court, but the award in question may itself be superseded or replaced by a new award or a new agreement which varies or abrogates the particular agreement upon which the claim itself was originally based.

(7) *Prices and Incomes Legislation*

Because of difficulties in the economic field in recent years the Government had established the National Economic Development Council to maintain an oversight of the national economy, to promote industrial and commercial development and to increase exports from Great Britain, so as to keep the trading gap between exports and imports at a reasonable and manageable level, necessary for economic survival. One method of tackling the ever-present problem of inflation—with the spiralling of prices followed by the customary demands for wage and salary increases—was the establishment of the National Board for Prices and Incomes.[78] This legislation is very unpopular and there is no saying what will happen if and when a Conservative Government returns to power. It is perhaps not generally disputed that some machinery was essential in the dangerous economic situation and had the prices and incomes legislation not been passed things might well have been worse. However, there may be some validity in the argument that the Board has more recently concentrated upon wages and incomes as its priority task rather than upon prices. There is no doubt that prices can be operated upwards in a skilful manner which would not attract too much attention if carefully spread over a period. But the situation becomes explosive when the gap between income level and price level is too wide. Another criticism, in which there may be more than a grain of validity is that the Board has become a political tool—to be manoeuvred at the whim of the ruling political party. However, it is not the writer's task to explore political and economic theories—however alluring that temptation is—in relation to the Board. It is the legalities of the machinery which require examination.

The relevant legislation is meantime contained in three statutes (and certain Orders) which are the Prices and Incomes Act 1966,[79] the Prices and Incomes Act 1967 [80] and the Prices and Incomes Act 1968.[81] The

[78] The successor to the National Incomes Commission.
[79] 1966, c. 33 (which came into force on August 12, 1966, except for Part IV (October 6, 1966) and Part II (August 12, 1967).
[80] 1967, c. 53.
[81] 1968, c. 42.

National Board for Prices and Incomes was established by Part I (ss. 1–5) of the 1966 Act. Notices and standstills are governed by Part II. Section 6 is the enacting section in relation to Part II and gives the necessary power by Order in Council for the provisions [82] in that Part to be brought into force for a period of twelve months beginning with the date specified in the Order and to be extended or further extended from time to time by a further period of twelve months. The first Order became effective from August 12, 1967, and was to remain operative for twelve months.[82] Sections 7–12 deal with prices and charges and company distributions and are not particularly relevant to this volume. Sections 13–18 deal specifically with terms and conditions of employment, including notice of pay claims and other claims [83]; notice of awards and settlements [84]; the standstill for other awards and settlements [85]; and enforcement of terms and conditions of employment.[86] Section 17 defines " trade dispute " by reference to the Trade Disputes Act 1906, s. 5 (3), which is to include " any dispute between employers and workmen, or between workmen and workmen, which is connected with the restrictions imposed by this Part of this Act, and ' dispute ' shall include any difference of opinion as to the manner in which account is to be taken of the provisions of this Part of this Act." Employment under the Crown is governed by section 18. Proceedings against trade unions, a trade union organisation or an employers' organisation, being unincorporated bodies, are to be brought in the name of the body and the procedure rules are to be applied as if it were a corporation. The Scottish position with regard to proceedings on indictment is dealt with in subsection (4).

Part IV [87] allows temporary restrictions to be placed upon prices and incomes. Section 25 is the general section which sets out the administrative procedures to be followed in operating Part IV. Section 28 specifically governs restrictions on pay increases,[88] and allows the Secretary of State to apply this section, by order, to remuneration under contracts of employment for any kind of work to be performed wholly

---

[82] S. 6 (2) specifies the ways in which Part II may be brought into operation, viz., all the provisions or all except ss. 7–12 or all except ss. 13–18. See thereafter the Prices and Incomes Act 1966 (commencement of Part II) Order 1967 (No. 1142 (c. 18)). Part II effective for 12 months from August 12, 1967.

[83] Ibid. s. 13.

[84] Ibid. s. 14.

[85] Ibid. s. 15. See also the 1967 Act, s. 4 (3).

[86] Ibid. s. 16. The penalties are specified in subss. (3) and (4). Subs. (5) states categorically that s. 16 should not give rise to any criminal or tortious liability for conspiracy or any other liability in tort (in England and Wales). Subs. (6) confirms that subs. (5) does not apply to Scotland, but where any act is prohibited by s. 16 the fact of its prohibition is to be treated as irrelevant for the purposes of any civil proceedings in Scotland. S. 16 (6) and s. 16 (1) and (4) were subsequently amended by s. 4 (1) of the 1967 Act.

[87] Part IV came into force on October 6, 1966—see Prices and Incomes Act 1966 (commencement of Part IV) Order 1966 (No. 1262 (C. 14)).

[88] But it does not apply to increases to which employees are contractually entitled before the dates prescribed for operation of the 1966 Act—see *Allen* v. *Thorn Electrical Industries*; *Griffin* v. *Metropolitan Police District Receiver* [1967] 3 W.L.R. 858; [1967] 2 All E.R. 1137 (C.A.) (" rate of remuneration paid " in s. 28 (2) and s. 29 (4) means " the rate of remuneration contracted to be paid ").

or substantially within the United Kingdom or on British ships or air-craft.[89] The penalty for contravention of the section [90] is, upon summary conviction, a fine not exceeding one hundred pounds and, upon conviction on indictment, a fine (which, in the case where the offender is not a body corporate, is not to exceed five hundred pounds) which may be very substantial indeed.[91] Subsections (4), (5) and (6) of section 16 are applied within section 28 [92] as though they also related to the payments of re-muneration by an employer which would be in contravention of section 28 or the next following section. An order may be made under both of these sections in respect of persons employed by or under the Crown,[93] but Part IV does not bind the Crown nor is the Crown to be under any obligation in relation to that order. Section 28 (7) specifies the ways in which the order, made under subsection (1), may be described and applied (e.g., to employees in specified kinds of work, or in specified localities, or working in specified undertakings or for specified employers).[94] Section 29 goes on to deal with restrictions on pay by reference to levels at July 20, 1966.[95] Employers are given a certain authority to disregard pay increases in existing contracts.[96] Sections 31 and 32 [97] tie in with wages regulation orders made under the Wages Councils Act 1959 and orders made under the Agricultural Wages (Scotland) Act 1949. Section 34 is the " inter-pretation " section. Full explanations of " freezes " or " standstills " on prices and incomes until December 1966 and " severe restraint " thereafter for six months (i.e., until the end of June 1967) are given in Schedule 2 [98] to the Act.

The Prices and Incomes Act 1967 [99] supplements and amends the 1966 Act. Section 1 gives certain powers to extend the standstill period under Part II of the 1966 Act on an increase of prices and charges or on implementation of an award or settlement relating to terms and conditions of employment. Section 2 deals with the imposition of a standstill after an increase of prices or implementation of an award, but before publica-tion of the Board's report. The imposition of a standstill after publication of the Board's report is covered by the subsequent section.[1] Section 4 makes certain modifications and clarifications to the 1966 Act—mainly

---

[89] Ss. 28 and 29 are amended by the 1967 Act, s. 4 (2).
[90] The specific mandatory restriction upon the employer is contained in s. 28 (2).
[91] s. 28 (3).
[92] Vide s. 28 (4).
[93] " employment by or under the Crown " is to be construed in accordance with s. 18 (3) and (4).
[94] See s. 28 (7), para. (b), contains certain additional guidelines as regards employees working in specified undertakings or for specified employers.
[95] For examples of such—see [1967] C.L.Y. 1439.
[96] Vide s. 30.
[97] See s. 32 (4) as regards the application of s. 32 to Scotland.
[98] The original Sched. 2 considerations were amended and replaced by a memorandum contained in the Schedule to the Prices and Incomes (General Considerations) Order 1966 (S.I. 1966 No. 1021). See now the Prices and Incomes (General Considerations) Order 1968 (No. 616).
[99] 1967, c. 53.
[1] Ibid. s. 3.

to sections 16 and 28.   Sections 16 (1) and (4) are amended by section 4 (1) (paras. (*a*) and (*b*)) of the 1967 Act and section 16 (6) (which relates specifically to Scotland) is amended by section 4 (1) of the 1967 Act so that the reference back in subsection (6) is to subsection (4) and not to the whole of section 16.   Contracts providing for increased remuneration are no longer to be invalid—it is only that part of the contract which relates to the excess which will be and will remain invalid.[2]   The excess is not automatically revived when the restriction or standstill ends. Employers who have withheld pay increases before July 1967 are protected by the 1967 Act.[3]   Section 6 is the supplementary section.   The 1967 Act received the Royal Assent on July 14, 1967, and generally came into force on that date.   However sections 1, 2 and 3 of the 1967 Act did not come into force until August 12, 1967,[4] and no order or direction made under these sections for the application or continuation of any provision of the 1966 Act (or the Part II provisions) was to be effective after August 11, 1968.   The Schedule to the 1967 Act contains six clauses of provisions relating to the operation of sections 1 and 3 of that Act.

The Prices and Incomes Act 1968 [5] continues in force Part II of the 1966 Act [6] and sections 1–3 of the 1967 Act.[7]   It also enables a standstill imposed under section 1 or 3 of the 1967 Act to be extended in time.[8] Prices or charges may be reduced in accordance with the provision of section 4.   Moreover, certain wages regulation orders and agricultural wages orders may be deferred.[9]   Part II of the 1968 Act deals at some length with restriction on ordinary dividends and other related restrictions (ss. 6–8 inclusive).   Part III provides for the regulation or restriction of rent increases (ss. 9–12), under regulated tenancies and local authority rents in four extensive sections.   However, both Parts II and III are not particularly relevant to this work.   The 1968 Act received the Royal Assent on July 10, 1968, and came into force on that day.   It is provided by section 13 (4) that the various sections (other than sections 2 and 12) are to cease to be effective at the end of the year 1969.[10]   Section 2 of the 1968 Act substitutes for section 6 (3) of the 1967 Act a new subsection (3) which reads as follows:

" (3) Sections 1 to 3 above shall cease to have effect at the end of the year 1969, but the expiration of those sections shall not affect any

---

2 *Ibid.* s. 4 (2) of the 1967 Act.
3 *Ibid.* s. 5.   This is a very lengthy and difficult section which requires the closest examination.
4 *Ibid.* s. 6 (3).   This subsection was replaced by a new subsection contained in s. 2 of the 1968 Act.   The new subsection is quoted *infra* in the text hereof.   Broadly ss. 1 and 3 are continued until the end of 1969.
5 1968, c. 42.   Part I (ss. 1–5) is particularly relevant to this volume.
6 *Ibid.* s. 1.
7 *Ibid.* s. 2.
8 *Ibid.* ss. 3 (2) and 3 (3) in particular.
9 *Vide* s. 5 and the provisions of Sched. 2.
10 Subject always to the operation of s. 38 (2) of the Interpretation Act 1889, read along with Sched. 3 to the 1968 Act itself.

order or direction previously made or given under or by virtue of them for the application of any provision of the Prices and Incomes Act 1966, nor the operation of those sections for purposes of any such order or direction and matters arising therefrom."

Section 3 of the 1968 Act contains very important provisions indeed relating to the extension and amendment of (i) orders made under section 1 (2) (*b*) of the 1967 Act or directions given under section 2 (2) (*c*) of that Act [11]; and (ii) orders made under section 3 (1) of the 1967 Act.[12] Further extensions—within the statutory limits now provided in both the 1967 Act [13] and the 1968 Act [14]—are possible by order made under subsection 3 (4) of the 1968 Act. The technique of a second reference to the Board as an excuse for a further deferment of an award or settlement is prohibited by section 3 (5).

In the field of industrial disputes, affecting the general economic life of the community, there is little doubt in anyone's mind that it is the application of the mandatory restriction of wage increases (including bonus and productivity awards) under section 28 of the 1966 Act, amended as above noted, which is likely to cause resentment and unrest. In reality this would result in a direct confrontation between the trade unions and the Government and what would be of interest to labour lawyers and industrial relations experts alike would be the possible use of penal sanctions against the workers. The recent Report [15] of the Donovan Commission does not favour the use of imprisonment and similar penal sanctions against workers. Nor can the present Labour Government afford to alienate the affections of the employed classes, although if it shows weakness in handling the situation the whole purpose of the legislation is obviously defeated and it becomes virtually useless. The ordinary British citizen (and that includes the ordinary worker) has a healthy respect for the law and for justice and it might be that a strong Secretary of State for Employment and Productivity would be prepared to put the legal machinery to the final test.

The Donovan Commission has recommended the setting up of an Industrial Relations Commission with fairly wide terms of reference in respect of industrial relations. It may be that the function of the Prices and Incomes Board in relation to wage awards and settlements will be taken over by the new Commission, leaving the Board (if it is to survive) to deal with prices, dividends and rents.

---

[11] See the 1968 Act, s. 3 (2). (Maximum period 11 months.)
[12] *Ibid.* s. 3 (3). (Maximum period 8 months.)
[13] Ss. 1 (2) (*b*) and 3 (1).
[14] The whole of s. 3.
[15] Cmnd. 3623 (1968).

(8) *Selective Employment Tax and the Selective Employment Payments Act 1966* [16]

This statute originates from the Finance Act 1966,[17] s. 44 (and Sched. 11 to the Act), which established selective employment tax.[18] This legislation proceeds on the basis that employment falls into three classes—(i) the manufacturing industries which qualify for a refund and a premium, (ii) employments qualifying for a refund only and (iii) employments which are liable to pay tax and do not qualify for any refund. In theory the intention is that service employments—and so-called " non-productive " or non-manufacturing industries—should subsidise the manufacturing industries and the policy-makers hope that there will be a movement of labour from the former grouping to the latter grouping, for the general economic welfare and survival of Britain as a trading and manufacturing country. Many criticisms have been levelled against S.E.T. but this is not the appropriate place to discuss these. The tax is collected through the medium of the national insurance stamp. The bodies which examine questions and issues arising from the legislation are the administrative tribunals (*e.g.*, the Industrial Tribunals). Section 1 of the Selective Employment Payments Act 1966 provides for the payment of selective employment premium at the rates specified [19] in subsection (1) for certain types of manufacturing employments.[20] Refund of selective employment tax is governed by section 2. Payments to public bodies [21] and local authorities [22] are also dealt with in subsequent sections. Refunds to charities [23] are governed by section 5 and special refunds to certain households by section 6. The administration of the scheme, including such matters as the compilation and maintenance of registers, the determination of claims and disputes arising, is governed by section 7. The Department of Employment and Productivity (formerly the Ministry of Labour) is responsible for payment of premiums; and as regards payment of refunds the responsible Minister for Scotland is the Secretary of State for Scotland. Section 8 specifies the penalties [24] and powers necessary to ensure compliance with the statutory provisions, much on the same lines as the powers of entry and inspection given to factory inspectors. Amending powers are given to the Minister (now the Secretary of State for Employment and Productivity) and the Treasury by section 9. The

---

[16] 1966, c. 32.
[17] 1966, c. 18.
[18] See Cmnd. 2986, which allegedly justifies the introduction of this tax as official government policy. The present Conservative Opposition have indicated that they would repeal this legislation if and when re-elected to power.
[19] 7s. 6d. per male employee over 18; 3s. 9d. per male employee under 18 and female employee over 18; and 2s. 6d. per female employee under 18. Premium payments began in February 1967 (for the quarter preceding) and are made quarterly.
[20] See s. 1 (2) for details, including the reference to the Standard Industrial Classification.
[21] 1966 Act, s. 3 (1) (and Part I of Sched. 1); and s. 3 (2) (and Parts II and III of Sched. 1).
[22] *Ibid.* s. 4.
[23] As regards Scotland see s. 5 (4); also *Income Tax Special Purposes Commissioners* v. *Pemsel* [1891] A.C. 531; and *Inland Revenue Commissioners* v. *Glasgow Police Athletic Association*, 1953 S.C.(H.L.) 13; [1953] A.C. 380.
[24] See particularly s. 8 (2).

" interpretation " section follows, whilst the matter of expenses [25] incurred by any ministerial department in relation to any provision of the Act are to be defrayed by moneys provided by Parliament.

There have been a few cases arising under this legislation, mainly concerned with questions of premium and refund of tax. A selection of the more important Scottish decisions follows and, where considered appropriate, references to English decisions have been included. The following decisions may be found to be helpful, viz.:

Reliant Tool Company v. *The Minister of Labour*.[26] Applicants are designers of machines and tools used in the manufacture of products falling within the Standard Industrial Classification (Ords. III to XVI). The tribunal held [26a] that design work forms an essential part of the manufacturing process of machine tools and therefore applicants' business satisfied the requirements of section 1 (2) of the Selective Employment Payments Act 1966. Expenses were awarded to applicants.

Martin v. *Minister of Labour*.[27]—a butcher's shop wherein employees are mainly occupied in the preparation of cuts of meat for retail sale does not satisfy the requirements of section 1 (2) of the S.E.P. Act 1966. A business concerned with the processing of vegetables for the catering trade has been held to be a business which satisfies the requirements of section 1 (2) [28]: *Drumry Testing Company Ltd.* v. *Minister of Labour* [29]— the business of testing building and road materials for local authorities, contractors, etc., in the building and civil engineering industries does not satisfy the requirements of section 1 of the S.E.P. Act 1966. In *Charles H. Julian Limited* v. *Minister of Labour* [30] a firm of " whisky blenders " were held not entitled to the S.E. premium because at least half of their employees were engaged in non-qualifying activities. *Peter McAinsh*

---

[25] s. 11.

[26] II K.I.R. 294. See also *G. C. Phillips (Coventry) Limited* v. *Minister of Labour*, II K.I.R. 293—where the tribunal held that designing of machines and machinery is not an activity within Ords. III to XVI of the S.I.C., but that it falls within Ord. XXII thereof; and *F. W. Payne & Son* v. *Minister of Labour*, III K.I.R. 348—a firm designing, arranging the manufacture of and supervising the erection of dredges for use in tin mines in Malaya was held to be engaged in an activity under Ord. VI of the S.I.C.

[26a] This decision by the tribunal was subsequently taken on appeal to the Court of Session (see 1967 I.T.R. 498) but the appeal was dismissed. Thereafter the Minister appealed to the House of Lords (1968 I.T.R. 70). Their lordships' views were that the tribunal was entitled to decide, on the evidence, that the respondents' activities formed part of the manufacture of metal-working machine-tools and fell within minimum list heading 332. Lord Guest's speech is particularly helpful.

When the tribunal's decision was under appeal to the Court of Session, another decision was being brought on appeal almost simultaneously—see *Minister of Labour* v. *Shieldness Produce Ltd.*, 1967 I.T.R. 493.

[27] II K.I.R. 179. The boning, cutting and packing of meat is not an activity within the S.I.C. (Ords. III to XVI)—see *Swift & Company Limited* v. *Minister of Labour*, III K.I.R. 82. But where a company was engaged in buying meat, cutting it up, treating it by a quick-freezing process and selling it to butchers exclusively for use in making sausages pies, etc., this has been held, in a Scottish decision, to be an activity falling within Ord. III of the S.I.C.—see *Dobson* v. *Minister of Labour*, III K.I.R. 78.

[28] *Shieldness Produce Limited* v. *Minister of Labour*, II K.I.R. 293; and on appeal to the Court of Session, 1967 I.T.R. 493.

[29] II K.I.R. 687.

[30] II K.I.R. 892. The bottling of " Guinness," ale and lager is an activity within Ord. III of the S.I.C.—see *Robert Porter & Co. Ltd.* v. *Minister of Labour*, III K.I.R. 351.

Limited v. *Minister of Labour* [31] is an interesting decision raising two points—(a) the tribunal held that the offices of applicants in Crieff did not satisfy the requirements of section 1 and (b) the tribunal had no power to review a refusal by the Minister to treat the office premises and the sawmilling premises as a single establishment.[32] A refund has been refused to a firm of " timber merchants and forwarding agents " who had failed to satisfy the section 2 (2) requirements.[33] The reference in section 2 (3) (c) of the S.E.P. Act 1966 to an " establishment such as is mentioned either in section 1 (2) of this Act or in subsection (2) of this section " has been held to mean an establishment which satisfies the *whole* of those subsections and not just a part—and, accordingly, an establishment falling within section 1 (2) (b) would not be such an establishment.[34] The position of proof-readers and type-setters was considered recently in England in *A. H. Stockwell Limited* v. *Minister of Labour*,[35] when the tribunal held that such persons were *not* engaged in non-qualifying activities. In *William Freeland & Sons (Aberdeen) Limited* v. *Minister of Labour* [36] the buying, processing and dispatch of fish to wholesalers has been held to be an activity within Order III of the Standard Industrial Classification.

The making of detailed drawings of sections of structural steelwork used in the construction of multi-storey buildings has been held to be an activity falling within Order XXII of the Standard Industrial Classification.[37] The Scottish decision in *Alexander McAslan & Company Limited* v. *Minister of Labour* [38] is interesting as it raised the point of a manufacturing parent company distributing its products through a subsidiary company. The parent company was entitled to premium; was the subsidiary company so entitled? The tribunal held that it was not so entitled. The repair of and servicing of industrial sewing machines within the factories of clothing manufacturers is an activity within the Standard Industrial Classification.[39]

Shearing of steel plate falls within Order V of the Standard Industrial Classification.[40] In *Jackson* v. *Secretary of State for Scotland (Department of Agriculture and Fisheries)*[41] the tribunal held that the erection and repair of farm fences is an activity within the S.I.C. Refund of S.E. Tax was refused in *Walton and Burgass* v. *Minister of Labour*,[42] in respect of a fishing ghillie, because the salmon fishings owned by applicants were

31 II K.I.R. 893.
32 In *Wilson* v. *Minister of Labour*, IV K.I.R. 507, the Scottish Tribunal has held that a dentist's workshop located at the end of his garden (his house containing his surgery) was a separate establishment for purposes of the S.E.P. Act 1966.
33 See *A. & W. Fullarton Limited* v. *Minister of Labour*, II K.I.R. 892.
34 *United Dairies (London) Ltd.* v. *Minister of Labour*, III K.I.R. 477.
35 III K.I.R. 80.
36 III K.I.R. 83.
37 *The Woodside Drawing Company* v. *Minister of Labour*, III K.I.R. 78.
38 III K.I.R. 79.
39 *McGuire* v. *Minister of Labour*, III K.I.R. 738.
40 *Glen Metals Limited* v. *Minister of Labour*, III K.I.R. 79.
41 III K.I.R. 195. See also *Morton* v. *Dept. of Agriculture and Fisheries for Scotland*, 1969 I.T.R. 117; VI K.I.R. 163.
42 III K.I.R. 479.

primarily for the sporting use of themselves and their guests; but an application for refund was granted recently (February 1966) under section 2 in *Holytown Building Materials Limited* v. *Minister of Labour* [43] —the applicant company being engaged in the excavation and delivery of minerals from old deposits of industrial waste.

The tribunal may exercise its discretion under section 7 (2) of the 1966 Act, where applicants have failed to register within the time limit for repayment of tax and for payment of premium, and—after taking into account all the circumstances and being satisfied that to refuse to ante-date the registration would have been too harsh—may order that the establishment be deemed to have been registered at an earlier date (specified by it.) [44]

The Chancellor of the Exchequer has just recently indicated in his Budget Speech [44a] that it is proposed to increase the weekly rates of selective employment tax with effect from July 7, 1969, and to make certain changes in classifications.

(9) *National Insurance*

The first statutory provision introducing compulsory insurance against sickness and unemployment was passed in 1911,[45] amended subsequently by various Acts and consolidated in 1936 as the National Health Insurance Act. The operative statutes prior to the year 1948 applied to manual workers and to non-manual workers earning not more than £420 per annum. At the close of the Second World War the attention of Parliament (*i.e.*, the Attlee Administration of 1945) was directed towards new schemes of nationalisation of certain industries, full employment, social services and necessary legislation, as well as the new concept of the welfare state. Much parliamentary time was taken up, during and after the war years, in debates and writings on these matters. From the " social insurance " viewpoint, the outstanding document was the Beveridge Report.[46]

With the adoption by the Government of that time of the Beveridge Plan, the national insurance legislation and workmen's compensation legislation was replaced by two major statutes, namely, the National Insurance Act 1946 [47] and the National Insurance (Industrial Injuries) Act 1946.[48] These Acts introduced respectively in Great Britain (i) a comprehensive

---

[43] IV K.I.R. 413.
[44] See *John Bryan Atkinson Limited* v. *Minister of Labour*, IV K.I.R. 67; and *Fenerty* v. *Minister of Labour*, IV K.I.R. 68.
[44a] On April 15, 1969 (H.C. Deb., Vol. 781, No. 94, col. 991). The new weekly rates will be 48s. for men, 24s. for women and boys under 18 years and 16s. for girls under 18 years.
[45] 1 & 2 Geo. 5, c. 55.
[46] The official title is the Report of the " United Kingdom Interdepartmental Committee on Social Insurance Allied Services " (Cmd. 6404) (1942). For an interesting picture of the historical background to the 1946 legislation mentioned hereafter, see Part I of the General Introduction to Potter and Stansfeld, *National Insurance* (see note 5 of this section) (2nd ed.).
[47] 9 & 10 Geo. 6, c. 67.
[48] 9 & 10 Geo. 6, c. 62.

and compulsory scheme of national insurance against unemployment, sickness, old age and death, and which provided also for certain payments of maternity benefit, widow's benefits and allowances for certain dependants [49]; and (ii) a comprehensive scheme of insurance against industrial injuries and diseases. [50] This legislation was amended on many occasions between 1948 (the year in which the two Acts of 1946 came into operation generally) and 1965, when two new consolidating statutes were introduced to replace the vast accumulation of statutory material. These new statutes are the National Insurance Act 1965 [51] and the National Insurance (Industrial Injuries) Act 1965 [52] and, in fact, other legislation has appeared on the Statute Book since then. [53]

The National Insurance Scheme applies to all persons in Great Britain who are over school age and under pensionable age. [54] Certain exceptions are permitted—notably in the case of married women, those over school age undergoing full-time education and certain persons whose incomes do not exceed a specified limit. The scheme does not necessarily apply strictly only to those persons who are resident and working in Great Britain. The Minister has power to make regulations which take account of employment or work outside of Great Britain which might qualify within the statutes. [55]

Insured persons are divided into three groups or classes, *viz.*:

(1) Those gainfully occupied, *i.e.*, employed in Great Britain under a contract of service.

(2) Those who are self-employed persons in Great Britain, *i.e.*, gainfully occupied but not under a contract of service.

(3) Those who are not employed (*i.e.*, who do not fall under categories (1) and (2)).

The differentiation between categories (1) and (2) is, of course, the basic distinction between the " contract of service " and the " contract for services." [56] The " control test " has been regarded as important in

---

[49] See Potter (D.) and Stansfeld (D. H.), *National Insurance* (2nd ed.) (Butterworths, 1949), the standard reference work on the 1946 legislation, but now becoming out of date.

[50] See Potter (D.) and Stansfeld (D. H.), *National Insurance (Industrial Injuries)* (2nd ed.) (Butterworths, 1950), the standard reference work on the 1946 legislation.

[51] 1965, c. 51 (which came into force on September 6, 1965 (see the National Insurance Act 1965 (Commencement) Order 1965 (No. 1650)); this date also applies to the National Insurance (Industrial Injuries) Act 1965).

[52] 1965, c. 52. See *infra*, Chap. 11 (s. 7), where the Industrial Injuries Scheme is considered.

[53] See also the Family Allowances Act 1965 (c. 53); the National Health Service Contributions Act 1965 (c. 54); and the Statute Law Revision (Consequential Repeals) Act 1965 (c. 55), all of which are relevant; also the National Insurance Act 1966 (c. 6); the National Insurance Act 1967 (c. 73); the Family Allowances and National Insurance Act 1967 (c. 90); the Family Allowances and National Insurance Act 1968 (c. 40); the National Insurance &c Act 1969 (c. 4); and the National Insurance Act 1969 (c. 44).

[54] *i.e.*, 65 years for men; and 60 years for women.

[55] National Insurance Act 1965, ss. 1 (3) (*a*) (ii) and 103 (2), and relevant statutory instruments (those prior to 1965 being 1948—No. 1275, amended 1950—Nos. 1264 and 1946; 1952—No. 1407; and 1954—No. 189).

[56] See Chaps. 2 and 4, *supra*.

distinguishing between categories (1) and (2), although the courts have said that it is not always beneficial to rely upon cases and statutes outwith the field of national insurance.[57] The meaning of the phrase " gainfully occupied " was examined in *Vandyk* v. *Minister of Pensions and National Insurance*.[58] The use of the word " gainfully " (as the layman understands it in its ordinary meaning) is misleading—and employment, without gain, under a contract of service falls within the scope of the statutes.

The married woman who is not gainfully employed under a contract of service or who is not self-employed benefits through the medium of her husband's contributions and is the best example of the " excepted person."

The contribution rates [59] are set forth in the First Schedule to the 1965 Act and these are liable to automatic increase at quinquennial periods after 1965, *i.e.*, in 1970, 1975 and 1980,[60] and power is given to H.M. Treasury by section 6 to increase the flat-rate contributions as necessary. The benefits which may be obtained are specified in the Third and Fourth Schedules. The most important from the point of view of the employed person are unemployment benefit and sickness benefit. The ordinary employee may get both, while the self-employed person may qualify for sickness benefit. Next in importance come retirement pension and graduated retirement benefit. Certain other benefits are obtainable.[61] Certain conditions must be fulfilled before payment of unemployment benefit can be made—namely, (i) not less than twenty-six contributions must have been paid between entry to the scheme and the days of unemployment giving rise to the claim, and (ii) a minimum of fifty contributions must have been paid or credited for the last contribution year [62] preceding the benefit year.[62] The first three days of unemployment do not count for benefit, unless within the thirteen weeks' period (commencing with the first day of unemployment) a further nine days of unemployment occur and these days form part of the same period of interruption of employment.[63] The applicant himself must have been available for and capable of employment upon every day which is being reckoned for inclusion in the claim.[64] Benefit may be drawn for the maximum period of 312 days, and thereafter thirteen contributions must be paid before applicant re-qualifies for unemployment benefit.

---

[57] *Gould* v. *Minister of National Insurance* [1951] 1 K.B. 731 at p. 734; [1951] 1 All E.R. 368 at p. 371. See also Chap. 3, *supra*, on the " element of control."

[58] [1955] 1 Q.B. 29; [1954] 2 All E.R. 723.

[59] Prima facie, an employer is liable for payment of both his own and his employees' contributions, but recovers the latter proportion by deduction from wages—see s. 11 (1). An employee has a right of action against an employer who fails to pay the contributions exigible (subject to a limitation period of one year for such action—see s. 54).

[60] 1965 Act, s. 5.

[61] Notably widow's benefit, maternity benefit, guardian's allowance, children's allowances, death grant.

[62] See s. 114 (1).

[63] s. 19 (6).

[64] s. 20 (1).

Disqualification [65] for receipt of unemployment benefit, for a period not exceeding six weeks, arises if:

(1) X loses his job through his misconduct or he quits without good cause; or

(2) X refuses a suitable job notified to him or refuses such a job which is offered to him; or

(3) X neglects to avail himself of a reasonable opportunity of suitable employment; or

(4) X refuses to carry out or fails to carry out, without good cause, any written instructions given to him by an officer of the Employment Exchange with the purpose of finding him a suitable job; or

(5) X refuses to undertake approved training, designed to equip him for entry into or return to suitable employment. [66]

An important disqualification may also arise under section 22 (1), which provides that a person who has lost his employment because of a trade dispute at his place of employment is not eligible for unemployment benefit during the stoppage of work, unless (i) he has become bona fide employed elsewhere in his usual occupation or has become regularly employed in another occupation or (ii) he is not participating in, financing or is interested directly in the dispute and (iii) he does not belong to a trade or class of worker of which, immediately before the stoppage, there were members employed at his place of employment any of whom are participating in, financing or directly interested in the dispute.

" Trade dispute," as used in the National Insurance Acts means [67] any dispute between employers and employees, or between employees, connected with the employment or non-employment or the terms or conditions of employment of any persons whether employees of the employer with whom the dispute arises or not. Inter-union disputes and sympathetic strikes would, therefore, fall within the definition. If X's union finances a strike or other dispute which results in X becoming unemployed then X is not entitled to benefit in view of the operating disqualification.

The 1965 Act establishes the National Insurance Advisory Committee, [68] which has the task of giving advice and assistance to the Minister, [69] and perhaps more importantly, the task of examining draft regulations which the Minister [69] proposes to make (subject to certain specified exceptions which need not be so submitted). [70] Certain orders and regulations (for

---

[65] See particularly s. 22 (2).
[66] As to employment which will not be deemed to be " suitable " see s. 22 (5).
[67] s. 22 (6) (a).
[68] s. 88 and Sched. 8 (composition, etc.)
[69] Now the Secretary of State. (The department is now called the Department of Social Services—formerly the Ministry of Social Security and prior to that it was termed the Ministry of Pensions and National Insurance.)
[70] See s. 108; but see the 1969 Act (c. 4), s. 3 (1), re regulations made under s. 3 (2) of that Act.

example, those varying the rates of contribution or embodying supplementary schemes and the like) must be laid before Parliament and be approved by a resolution of each House.[71] The National Advisory Committee is supplemented by local committees representing employers and insured persons.[72]

The claims procedure is relatively straightforward. Primarily, the claim is dealt with by the local officer of the Department [73] or he may refer the matter to the local tribunal. This tribunal also acts, from time to time, as an appellate tribunal upon decisions of the local insurance officer which are referred to it on appeal, in terms of regulations. Such regulations would and do also provide for appeals being taken from the tribunal to the National Insurance Commissioner or the Deputy Commissioner.[74]

Certain questions are reserved for determination by the Minister (*i.e.*, now the Secretary of State). These are as follows [75]:

(*a*) whether the contribution conditions for any benefit are satisfied, or otherwise relating to a person's contributions or payments under section 58 of this Act in lieu of contributions;

(*b*) which of two or more persons satisfying the conditions for an increase of benefit, whether of the same or a different description, shall be entitled to the increase where by virtue of some provision of this Act not more than one of them is so entitled;

(*c*) as to the class of insured persons in which a person is to be included;

(*d*) as to the person to be treated as maintaining a child, or as to the family in which a child is to be treated as included, in a case where by virtue of the Schedule to the Family Allowances Act that question falls to be decided by the Minister in his discretion.[76]

The Minister may refer any question of law [77] arising from the determination by him of any question such as is mentioned in the foregoing paragraphs (*a*) to (*c*) of section 64 to the Court of Session [78] (or in England, to the High Court). Where the Minister decides to refer any question of law, as just mentioned, he must send notice in writing of that intention to the applicant.[79] Any person aggrieved by a decision of the Minister on any question of law such as is mentioned [80] in subsection (1) of section 65 which is not referred in accordance with that subsection may appeal from that decision to the Court of Session (or

[71] See s. 107.
[72] s. 89.
[73] Formerly the Ministry of Social Security.
[74] s. 70.
[75] s. 64 (1).
[76] Any decision under this paragraph may relate to a period before the date of the decision.
[77] s. 65 (1).
[78] s. 65 (8).
[79] s. 65 (2).
[80] *i.e.*, questions arising under s. 64 (1), paras. (*a*) to (*c*).

High Court, as the case may be).[81] The Minister may appear and be
heard upon any such reference or appeal under subsections (1) and (3)
of section 65.

The 1965 Act consolidated the " graduated contributions " which
may be paid by those over eighteen years of age who are earning more than
£9 per week. The purpose behind these additional contributions is to
improve the final amount payable to the insured by way of retirement
benefit.[82] The present Government have indicated in their recent White
Paper (published at the beginning of 1969) on the social services that a
substantial review of the present scheme will be introduced in 1971 or
thereabout, which will result in a substantial increase in retirement pensions
but with a very substantial consequential rise in the weekly contribution
rates.   This publication has been criticised as being a " political
pamphlet " or an " election manifesto " and of course it is quite idle—
at this stage and for very obvious reasons—to speculate whether this
plan is likely to come into operation.

It is sometimes argued that national insurance is no longer a part of
industrial law (or labour law) but is instead a part of the new emerging
field of social insurance law. However, the insurance contribution does
figure quite prominently as a deduction from the wage-packet of every
blue-collar and white-collar employee and for that reason it has been
included in this chapter.

(10) *Redundancy Payments*

The first statutory provision in Great Britain which dealt specifically
with redundancy was the Redundancy Payments Act 1965.[83] This Act
followed upon much discussion between management and trade unions
concerning the protection of employees who had been declared redundant.
Of course, this matter of protection was also under discussion and consideration at the International Labour Organisation,[84] as well as at
C.B.I., T.U.C. and parliamentary level. The statute represents a considerable forward step in the industrial and commercial fields and it
ranks along with the Contracts of Employment Act 1963 [85] and the
Industrial Training Act 1964 and other statutes [86] as firm evidence of
the new protective legislation pattern which emerged during the first

[81] s. 65 (3).
[82] See particularly ss. 36 and 37; and the National Insurance (Assessment of Graduated
Contributions) Amendment Regulations 1966 (No. 549) (to be read along with the
1960 Regulations, as amended) and the National Insurance (Assessment of Graduated
Contributions) Regulations 1967 (No. 844).
[83] 1965, c. 62. The Act received the Royal Assent on August 5, 1965. The " appointed
day " under the Act is December 6, 1965; see the Redundancy Payments Act 1965
(Appointed Day) Order 1965 (S.I. 1965 No. 1757). If an employee left his employment before that day he is not entitled to a redundancy payment—see *Bradford* v.
Holland & Hannen & Cubitts (Scotland) Ltd., 1967 I.T.R. 251; see also *Couper* v.
Harvey, 1967 I.T.R. 79 (employee not entitled to a redundancy payment where his
employment was terminated by the employer's death prior to December 6, 1965).
[84] See Chaps. 18 and 19, *infra*, re dismissals.
[85] 1963, c. 49.
[86] For example, the Payment of Wages Act 1960.

half of the 1960–70 decade within the employment relationship itself.[87] Part II (ss. 26–36 inclusive) establishes the Redundancy Fund [88] and deals with such matters as contributions and the collection thereof,[89] their application [90] and rebates to employers,[91] as well as payments out of the Fund to employers [92] and employees [93] and references and appeals to the tribunal regarding payments out of the Fund.[94] This Part has its own interpretation section.[95]

Part III (ss. 37–59 inclusive) contains certain miscellaneous and supplementary provisions, of which the following are perhaps the most important: (a) the question of continuity of employment in case of a strike [96]; (b) the matter of particulars of the terms of employment to be supplied to employees [97]; (c) the very important matter of a strike occurring during the currency of the employer's notice of termination of the employee's contract of employment [98]; (d) the matter of procedure before tribunals,[99] in respect of which the Secretary of State for Employment and Productivity (formerly the Minister of Labour) may make regulations [1]; (e) the position of persons whose membership of or employment with statutory bodies (specified in regulations [2] made under section 50) ceases as if a dismissal by reason of redundancy had operated; (f) the interpretation provisions.[3]

It will be necessary to consider some of these matters in more detail at a later stage in this chapter.

Part I (ss. 1–25) is, understandably, the most important part of the

---

[87] The 1965 Act not only introduces the new concept of redundancy awards but it also modifies and extends the Contracts of Employment Act 1963 as well as widening the powers of the Industrial Tribunals established by the Industrial Training Act 1964.

[88] s. 26.

[89] ss. 27 and 28 respectively.

[90] s. 29.

[91] s. 30.

[92] s. 31.

[93] s. 32.

[94] s. 34.

[95] s. 36.

[96] See s. 37; which amends para. 7 (2) of Sched. 1 to the Contracts of Employment Act 1963. See also Chap. 6, *supra*, and Chap. 17, *infra*.

[97] See s. 38; which removes the penal provisions of s. 5 of the Contracts of Employment Act 1963 and adds a new s. 4A to the 1963 Act, whereby an employee who has not been given the proper written information under s. 4 can require a reference to the Industrial Tribunal under the 1965 Act. The new s. 4A sets out at length the steps which may be taken by the tribunal.

[98] See the extensive provisions contained in s. 40. By and large the section extends the employment period beyond the normal termination date of the contract as specified in the notice, allowing for the employee's participation in the strike. But his redundancy payment may be affected (see s. 40 (6)) or a reference to the tribunal may be made (s. 40 (6)).

[99] The proceedings are listed in s. 46 (1) and the particular provisions which may be incorporated into the regulations made under this section are set forth in s. 46 (2).

[1] See s. 54 as to the method of making such regulations.

[2] *i.e.*, under s. 50, but in the manner provided by s. 54.

[3] See s. 56.

statute. The right to a redundancy payment is created by section 1 (1)[4] and that right emerges from one of two situations: (a) where the employee is dismissed by reason of redundancy[5]; or (b) where the employee is laid off or kept on short time to the extent specified in subsection (1) of section 6 and complies with the requirements of that section.

"Dismissal by reason of redundancy" arises, in terms of subsection (2) of section 1, if an employee is dismissed and that dismissal is attributable wholly or mainly to[6]:

(a) the fact that the employer has ceased, or intends to cease, to carry on the business for the purposes of which the employee was employed by him or has ceased or intends to cease that business in the place where the employee was so employed, or

(b) the fact that the requirements of that business for employees to carry out work of a particular kind, or for employees to carry out work of a particular kind in the places where he was so employed, have ceased or diminished or are expected to cease or diminish.

There have been many decisions taken by the Industrial Tribunals upon the operation of section 1. The undernoted selection[7] may be helpful.

---

[4] With which must be read Sched. 1 to the Act, giving the basis of calculation of the redundancy payments. The maximum which is payable is based on a total employment period of 20 years (on a graded scale depending upon age) and the week's pay is calculated by reference to the minimum remuneration in Sched. 2 to the Contracts of Employment Act 1963, read along with the conditions contained in the 1965 Act, Sched. 1, para. 5 (2). A reduction in the payment may be made by regulations under s. 14.

[5] See, in illustration, the following decisions: *Jamieson* v. *John Finnie & Sons*, 1966 I.T.R. 277 (employee's job no longer available after his illness and return to work; claim allowed); *McKillen* v. *James R. Turner (Metals) Ltd.*, 1966 I.T.R. 303 (female employee dismissed when her job was allocated to a male employee; held to be a dismissal by reason of redundancy); *Mackenzie* v. *William Paton Ltd.*, 1966 I.T.R. 507 (an unqualified cost accountant was dismissed and subsequently the company appointed a fully qualified accountant; held this was dismissal for reasons other than redundancy; application refused); *Morrison* v. *Rowen Engineering Co. Ltd.*, 1967 I.T.R. 211 (the tribunal's finding was that the refusal to re-employ applicant was based on personal differences and consequently he was not redundant); *Clarkson* v. *Bowie-Castlebank Ltd.*, 1966 I.T.R. 334 (applicant's contract terminated at the amalgamation of two companies; she became redundant and was entitled to a redundancy payment).

[6] The phrase "attributable wholly or mainly to" is of the utmost importance—and where dismissal is not justifiable summary dismissal it is for the tribunal to say whether or not dismissal was attributable wholly or mainly to redundancy as defined in s. 1 (2). The tribunal will consider the grounds or reasons which influenced the employer in deciding to dismiss the employee—the link word in the exercise is "attributable."

[7] This selection is divided for convenience into two parts:
(a) *Decisions in which employee held to be not redundant and/or not entitled to redundancy pay*—see *Petrie* v. *Yarrow and Company*, 1966 I.T.R. 382 (change of type of employment with same employer—no termination of employment—and applicant not entitled to redundancy pay under s. 1 (1) (a)); *Gemmell* v. *Darngavil Brickworks Ltd.*, 1967 I.T.R. 20 (works closed for 13 weeks—employee dismissed—held to be dismissed for redundancy—ss. 1 (2) and 25 (3); *Brownlie* v. *Purvis*, 1968 I.T.R. 375 (employee purchasing farm upon which he worked—claim under s. 1 (2) (a) and s. 13— but held he was not entitled to a redundancy payment; s. 3 (1) was also raised but held to be inapplicable; the tribunal *dubitante* about s. 22 in this case); *Stevenson* v. *North British Steel Foundry Ltd.*, 1966 I.T.R. 450 (applicant's periods off work were not attributable to his being laid-off or put on short-time; nor did his part-time work fall under s. 5 (2)); *Burgess* v. *O'Brien*, 1966 I.T.R. 164 (where dissolution of a partnership occurs this does not constitute dismissal of a partner under s. 1, although he is paid a salary and commission); *Ferguson* v. *Telford Grier Mackay & Co. Ltd.*, 1967 I.T.R. 387

Section 2 specifies those general cases in which a redundancy payment is excluded, *viz.*—(1) the male employee attaining sixty-five years immediately before the relevant date, and the female employee similarly attaining sixty years of age [8]; (2) where an employee is dismissed, without notice,[9] by reason of his conduct and the employer is entitled to terminate the employment contract; (3) where a renewal of the existing contract is offered or a new contract is offered (and the capacity, place of employment and other terms and conditions are not different from the previous contractual provisions) on or before the relevant date, and the employee has unreasonably refused the offer made to him; (4) where an offer to renew the contract, or an offer of a new contract, has been made and so that the provisions of the renewed or substituted contract would differ (wholly or in part) from the corresponding provisions of the contract in force immediately before dismissal but the offer in question constitutes an offer of suitable employment[9a] in relation to the employee, and the renewal or re-engagement would take effect on or before the relevant date [10] or not later than four weeks after that date, and the employee has unreasonably refused that offer.[11] If an employer, who is entitled

(the commencement of a creditor's voluntary liquidation did not operate as a dismissal of employees; here applicant (secretary and a director) was held to be an employee; redundancy payment awarded).

(b) *Decisions in which employee held to be dismissed by reason of redundancy*: *Dunbar* v. *James Wyllie and Sons (Grain Merchants) Ltd.*, 1967 I.T.R. 275 (the tribunal pointing out, in addition, that it was unnecessary to have regard to the presumption in s. 9 (2) (b) except when there is no evidence or the evidence is evenly balanced); *Rosie* v. *Watt*, 1967 I.T.R. 201.

[8] s. 2 (1). See the decision of *Ross* v. *Alexander Campbell & Co. Ltd.*, 1966 I.T.R. 189 (employee dismissed because of illness and advancing age—unable to carry out his duties—held not entitled to a redundancy payment as he was not dismissed by reason of redundancy).

[9] Or on shorter notice than is required in the ordinary case; or on ordinary notice, which includes or is accompanied by a written statement that the employer was entitled to terminate the contract, by reason of the conduct. See *Clark* v. *Blairs Ltd.*, 1966 I.T.R. 545 (dismissal for misconduct—breaks the continuity of employment; see the Contracts of Employment Act 1963, Sched. 1, paras. 2, 3 and 4–6).

[9a] The question of suitability should be decided before the question of reasonable refusal—see *Carron Co.* v. *Robertson*, 1967 S.C. 273; 1967 I.T.R. 484.

[10] S. 2 (5) deals with the situation where the relevant date falls on a Friday, Saturday or Sunday.

[11] Unreasonable refusal under s. 2 has been considered in the following decisions: *Paisley* v. *Scottish Co-operative Wholesale Society Ltd.*, 1967 I.T.R. 7; and *McRoberts* v. *Costain Concrete Ltd.*, 1967 I.T.R. 58; *MacGregor* v. *William Tawse Ltd.*, 1967 I.T.R. 198. " Change of ownership . . . and an offer of suitable employment " and reasonable rejection of an employer's offer, as well as employment which is not suitable, have been considered, thus:

(a) *Change of ownership and an offer of suitable employment, viz.*—*Anderson* v. *David Winter & Sons Ltd.*, 1966 I.T.R. 326 (a vague offer of new employment at a different remuneration and in different premises and made verbally did not constitute an offer of alternative employment within s. 2 (4)).

(b) *Employment unsuitable and/or reasonably rejected, viz.*—*Collier* v. *E. Pollard (Display) Ltd.*, 1966 I.T.R. 399 (the burden of proof is upon the employee to prove that work is not suitable and his refusal is not unreasonable); *Ireland* v. *Fairfield-Rowan Ltd.*, 1966 I.T.R. 191 (refusal not unreasonable in view of the uncertainty); *Nelson* v. *George Grierson & Son*, 1966 I.T.R. 309; *Gay* v. *The Commander, U.S. Naval Activities, United Kingdom*, 1966 I.T.R. 347 (where the tribunal held that the offer was not an offer of suitable employment and was not unreasonably refused. This was a " recommendation " to the U.S. Government for payment of redundancy pay, in view of the sovereignty issue involved); *Shields* v. *James Scott & Co. Ltd.*, 1966 I.T.R. 307 (an employee who was normally employed in the Glasgow area was offered work to dismiss an employee summarily, gives him notice without an accompanying statement (as specified in s. 2 (2) (c)) he (the employer) is not thereby precluded from proving that the employee was not redundant and, accordingly, was not entitled to redundancy pay.[12] An offer of alternative employment by another employer is not an offer within the meaning of section 2 (4) of the Act and a redundancy payment will be ordered.[13]

Section 3 explains the situations and conditions in and upon which an employee shall be taken to be dismissed by his employer, for the purposes of Part I of the Act,[14] and those situations in which he shall not be taken to be so dismissed.[15] The words " relevant date " are explained in section 3 (4), subject to what is said in section 4. This section has also given rise to many decisions before the tribunals and a selection of these are undernoted for useful reference.[16]

Section 4 (1) deals with the situation where the employer gives notice of termination and the employee within that " obligatory " (notice)

in Fort William. Held that the offer was not suitable in relation to applicant and redundancy payment ordered, but the tribunal's decision describes this as " a narrow case "); *Souter* v. *Henry Balfour and Company Limited*, 1966 I.T.R. 383; contrast with *Shields*' case that of *Paisley* v. *Scottish Co-operative Wholesale Society Ltd.*, 1967 I.T.R. 7 (an employee's refusal to move from the south of Scotland to the north of Scotland was held to be unreasonable); a refusal which was not unreasonable was again upheld in *MacCallum* v. *William Tawse Ltd.*, 1967 I.T.R. 199; and *Dunn* v. *James Jack and Son*, 1967 I.T.R. 267; *McIntosh* v. *British Rail* (*Scottish Region*), 1968 I.T.R. 26 (the tribunal stating that the terms of a joint agreement between the parties does not bind the tribunal, but may preclude respondents from arguing—in certain circumstances—that the employment was suitable); see also *Anderson* v. *National Coal Board*, 1967 I.T.R. 138 (offer of lower grade unreasonable); and contrast *Graham* v. *National Coal Board*, 1967 I.T.R. 193 (refusal unreasonable looking to the prospects). But see *Murray* v. *Robt. Rome & Son* (*Rutherglen*) *Ltd.*, 1969 I.T.R. 20, where an employee refused to move to a new site to continue his work, and the tribunal held that the contract of employment did not limit the area of employment and accordingly dismissal was not due to redundancy. On appeal, the Court of Session held that the tribunal had come to the correct conclusion (the Lord President distinguishing *O'Brien and Others* v. *Associated Fire Alarms Ltd.*, 1968 I.T.R. 182; and Lord Migdale " following " *McCaffrey* v. *E. E. Jeavons & Co. Ltd.*, 1967 I.T.R. 636, as being very much in point); and *I.C.I.* v. *McCallum*; *I.C.I.* v. *Aitken*, 1969 I.T.R. 24, where the Court of Session held, in the circumstances (applicants awarded redundancy pay by tribunal after refusal to accept lower grade work and leaving employment), that the tribunal had erred in awarding redundancy payments—the tribunal had not found that either of the respondents had been dismissed by appellants—and appeals allowed. Refusal has been held to be not unreasonable in the very recent case of *McColl* v. *Norman Insurance Company Ltd.*, 1969 I.T.R. 285 (the terms of a staff application form were considered in some detail.)
    Refusals were also held to be unreasonable in the recent cases of *Gunn* v. *St. Cuthbert's Co-operative Association Ltd*; and *Johnston* v. *St. Cuthbert's Co-operative Association Ltd.*, 1969 I.T.R. 137 (the Court of Session rejecting the appeals); and *Williamson* v. *N.C.B.* (*Glasgow Herald*, July 4, 1969) (the Court of Session rejecting the appeal by a majority of two to one)—see [1969] 9 C.L. 618.
[12] *Fleming* v. *Ritchies Limited*, 1966 I.T.R. 304.
[13] *Farquharson* v. *Ross*, 1966 I.T.R. 335.
[14] See particularly s. 3 (1) (subject to what is said in s. 10 (4)).
[15] subss. (2) and (3) of s. 3.
[16] *Shedden* v. *Youth Hostels Association* (*Scottish*), 1966 I.T.R. 327 (employee informed of intended move of employer's business and that he would not be going with them— applicant secured other employment and left—held not entitled to a redundancy payment as he had not been " dismissed " within the meaning of s. 3); *McAloon* v. *Merchants Facilities* (*Glasgow*) *Ltd.*, 1966 I.T.R. 517 (if a dismissed employee is re-engaged by the employer within four weeks of dismissal s. 3 (2) (b) does not prevent the dismissal operating for purposes of Part I of the Act provided the offer to re-engage was made

period, himself gives notice of termination of his own contract of employment at a date earlier than that specified by the employer. In these circumstances the employee shall [17] be taken to be dismissed by the employer and the " relevant date " of that dismissal shall be the date of expiry of the employee's notice.[18] The employer may call for withdrawal of the employee's notice or contest the payment of a redundancy award,[19] and such a payment will not then fall to be made, unless the Industrial Tribunal determines that the employee is entitled to receive from the employer (i) the whole of the redundancy payment or (ii) such part of that redundancy payment as the tribunal thinks fit.[20] The " obligatory period " is determined in accordance with the provisions of subsection (5) of section 4. The decisions undernoted [21] are of some importance in relation to the operation of section 4.

Sections 5, 6 and 7 relate to matters of lay-off and short-time. The purpose of these sections is to prevent " sharp practice " by an employer, *i.e.*, any attempt to evade a redundancy payment by laying-off an employee or by putting him on short time for an indefinite period, in the hope that the employee will eventually depart of his own free will. Lay-off [22] and short-time [23] are both defined in section 5, as is " week " in relation to employees paid weekly and those not so paid.[24] The distinction between lay-off and dismissal is of vital importance.[25]

Section 6 specifically deals with the right to a redundancy payment because of lay-off or short-time and requires that an employee shall not be entitled to a redundancy payment because he is laid off or kept on short time unless he gives notice in writing of his intention to claim [26] such redundancy payment and he fulfils one or other of the conditions

---

after the employment ceased); *Williamson* v. *William Paton Ltd.*, 1966 I.T.R. 149 (if an offer to re-engage is too vague and in any case, made after the termination date of the employment, redundancy pay will be allowed); *Ramage* v. *Harper-Mackay Limited*, 1966 I.T.R. 503 (employer repudiating his obligations—offering a job of much lower status—resignation of employee—offer to re-engage—employee's claim upheld); *Squair* v. *Merchants Facilities (Glasgow) Ltd.*, 1966 I.T.R. 384 (the conditions of s. 3 (2) were satisfied—applicant not dismissed); *Smith* v. *Archibald* (1) *and Tay Dental Laboratories* (2), 1967 I.T.R. 195 (terms of s. 3 (2) not complied with).

[17] For the purposes of the Part I provisions.
[18] s. 4 (2).   [19] s. 4 (3).   [20] s. 4 (4).
[21] *Armit* v. *McLauchlan*, 1966 I.T.R. 280 (applicant had given notice (a) verbally and (b) before the obligatory period of notice had commenced and accordingly s. 4 did not apply; he must be treated as having left voluntarily—no redundancy payment); *Ritchie* v. *Smith's Bakery*, 1966 I.T.R. 449 (employee leaving before expiry of notice on being told to go—held he did not thereby lose his right to a redundancy payment); *Duncan* v. *Fairfield-Rowan Ltd.*, 1966 I.T.R. 153 (notice by employer—counter-notice by employee—s. 4 (3)—applicant's refusal to comply was reasonable and he was entitled to a redundancy payment); *Brown* v. *Singer Manufacturing Co. Ltd.*, 1967 I.T.R. 213 (employee omitting to give notice in writing under s. 4 (1) (*b*) and who left during the notice period—her redundancy payment application dismissed).
[22] s. 5 (1).
[23] s. 5 (2) and Sched. 2 of the Act (which itself incorporates certain provisions of Sched. 2 to the Contracts of Employment Act 1963, as amended by s. 39 of the Redundancy Payments Act 1965).
[24] s. 5 (3).
[25] See *Sneddon* v. *Ivorycrete (Builders) Ltd.*, 1966 I.T.R. 538, which illustrates the point very neatly; see also *Campbell* v. *Mecca Ltd.*, 1967 I.T.R. 394.
[26] " A notice of intention to claim." The " relevant date " in relation to this matter is defined in subs. (2) of s. 6.

contained in section 6 (1). The notice of intention to claim must be given not later than four weeks after the end of the lay-off period or short-time period. An employee cannot have a " double ", or " overlapping " claim, *i.e.*, a right to a redundancy payment plus a claim to be retained in employment for a period up to six months.[27] If there is a reasonable expectation, upon the date of service of the notice of intention to claim, that an employee would (provided he continued with the same employer), not later than four weeks after that date, enter upon a period of employment of not less than thirteen weeks and within which period he would not be laid off or kept on short-time for any week, then—subject to the provisions of subsection (5)[28]—the employee in question shall not be entitled to a redundancy payment in pursuance of the notice.[29]

Section 7 contains certain provisions which are supplementary to the two preceding sections. Subsection (1) must, for example, be read along with subsection (4) of section 6 as the former shows the operation of a conclusive presumption that the condition specified in subsection (4) was not fulfilled. Section 7 (3) provides that no account is to be taken of any week for which an employee is laid off or kept on short-time because of a strike or lock-out.[30] If an employer does not withdraw his counter-notice by a subsequent written notice the employee is not entitled to a redundancy payment except in accordance with a decision of a tribunal.[31] Section 7 (5) specifies—in three different situations—the period allowed for the purposes of section 6 (3) (*a*). *A propos* paragraph (*c*) of subsection (5), no account is to be taken of any appeal against the tribunal's decision, or of any requirement to the tribunal to state a case for the opinion of the High Court or the Court of Session, or of any proceedings or decision in consequence of such an appeal or requirement.[32]

Section 8 (1) governs or establishes the condition of continuous employment for the requisite period.[33] Subsection (2) of section 8 applies Schedule 1 to the Contracts of Employment Act 1963 in order to determine continuous employment for the requisite period, in terms of the 1965 Act.[34] However, there are three special situations which must

---

[27] See s. 6 (3) read along with s. 7 (5); and considering—but discounting—the terms of s. 21.

[28] Which provides that subs. (4) shall not apply unless the employer gives a " counter-notice " (see s. 7 of the Act) within seven days (after receiving the notice of intention to claim) that he will contest any liability to pay a redundancy payment. The case of *Taylor* v. *Dunbar (Builders) Ltd.*, 1966 I.T.R. 249 illustrates this situation of a counter-notice which brings subss. (4) and (5) into operation.   [29] subs. (4) of s. 6.

[30] The lay-off or short-time working must be wholly or mainly attributable to the strike or lock-out.   [31] s. 7 (4).   [32] s. 7 (6).

[33] Which, for purposes of s. 1 (1) of the 1965 Act, is a period of 104 weeks (after attaining 18 years) ending with the relevant date.

[34] In *Fitzgerald* v. *Hall Russell & Co. Ltd.*, 1969 I.T.R. 32; 1969 S.L.T. 169, the decision had hinged upon the phrase " temporary cessation of work " occurring in para. 5 (1) (*b*) of Sched. 1 to the Contracts of Employment Act 1963. The tribunal had disregarded a period from November 1962—January 1963 (when appellant was not engaged by employers) in awarding a redundancy payment. The Court of Session, in the subsequent appeal, held that the tribunal had not erred and the appeal must fail. The phrase " temporary cessation of work " applied to an employer's business and not to an employee. Respondents had not ceased work but had continued their business upon a

not be overlooked, *viz.*: (a) renewal or re-engagement under section 3 (2) does not break the continuity [35] of employment; (b) section 17 of the 1965 Act applies to employment abroad [36]; and (c) regard must be had to the provisions contained in section 24 [37] when continuity of employment is being calculated. Continuity of employment is not normally broken by a lapse of up to four weeks [38] between dismissal and re-engagement, but a longer period (*e.g.*, five weeks) [39] does break the continuity. If an employee is " on loan " from one employer to another this does not break continuity in calculating a redundancy payment.[40] Absences due to pregnancy have been held to break the continuity and as the applicant had not been continuously employed for the requisite period her claim failed.[41] However, absence (above 26 weeks) because of illness only interrupts the continuity of employment if there is no contract of employment between employer and employee.[42]

Section 9 (1) provides that any question arising under Part I [43] of the Act as to the right of an employee to a redundancy payment, or as to the amount thereof, shall be referred to and determined by a tribunal,[44] in accordance with regulations [45] made under Part III of the Act. When a tribunal has made a determination in an application before it, that is an end of the matter; it cannot hear a further application in relation to the same matters.[46] An appeal from a decision of a tribunal, on a point of law, may be taken to the Court of Session [47] and a further appeal, with leave of the Court of Session or the House of Lords, may be taken to the House of Lords.[48] It is important to note that, for the purposes of

---

reduced scale and accordingly the facts did not fall within para. 5 (1) (*b*) of Sched. 1. The House of Lords has now *reversed* the Court of Session holding that " cessation of work " refers to cessation of the employee's job, and has explained that the tribunal should construe the statutes from the viewpoint of the individual workman—*The Times*, October 22, 1969 and [1969] 10 C.L. (Notes of cases) 291b.

[35] Although the position is otherwise under the Contracts of Employment Act 1963.
[36] Sched. 1 to the Contracts of Employment Act 1963 does not apply here.
[37] See note *infra* in the text.
[38] *Gray* v. *Burntisland Shipbuilding Company*, 1967 I.T.R. 255 (s. 8 (3) and para. 1 (1) (*b*) of Schedule 1 to the 1965 Act).
[39] *Tervitt* v. *West Lothian Steel Foundry Ltd.*, 1967 I.T.R. 253. The meaning of " temporary cessation of work " was considered in *Houston* v. *Murdoch Mackenzie Ltd.*, 1967 I.T.R. 125.
[40] *Proctor* v. *J. & R. Anderson*, 1967 I.T.R. 334; and *Alexander* v. *McMillan and Others*, 1969 I.T.R. 171.
[41] *Whiteley* v. *The Garfield Spinning Co. Ltd.*, 1967 I.T.R. 128.
[42] *Thomson* v. *Monteiths Ltd.*, 1967 I.T.R. 205.   [43] Which covers ss. 1–25 both inclusive.
[44] The Industrial Tribunals (separate tribunals exist for Scotland). The President of the Industrial Tribunals (Scotland) is Mr. Robert Reid, Q.C.
[45] See, in illustration, Dix, *Contracts of Employment*, etc. (3rd ed., 1968), Appendix D, and—for Scotland—the Industrial Tribunals (Redundancy Payments) (Scotland) Regulations 1967 (S.I. 1967 No. 360) and the Industrial Tribunals (Employment and Compensation) (Scotland) Regulations 1967 (S.I. 1967 No. 362), in particular; the former being more important in relation to most claims arising under the 1965 Act.
[46] *Ferguson* v. *Crawford*, 1968 I.T.R. 405.
[47] See *Carron Company* v. *Robertson*, 1967 I.T.R. 484 (where the Court of Session sent the case back to the tribunal directing it to express its views on " suitability " and, if suitable, the reasonableness of the refusal). If a point of law is not taken before the tribunal, it is not arguable before the Court of Session in a subsequent appeal—see *Stewart and Others* v. *Alexander*, 1969 I.T.R. 234.
[48] See the Tribunals and Inquiries Act 1958, s. 9 (1), as applied to Scotland by s. 9 (6).

any such reference as is mentioned in subsection (1), the two presumptions contained in subsection (2) will apply, *viz.*: (a) employment during any period shall, unless the contrary is proved, be presumed to have been continuous [49]; and (b) an employee who has been dismissed by his employer shall, unless the contrary is proved, be presumed to have been dismissed by reason of redundancy.[50]   The onus of proof rests upon the employer by section 9 (2) and it is his task to rebut these presumptions.[51]   Section 9 (3) links up with section 6 (3) (a), in respect of lay-off or short time, and provides that there shall be included, within the questions arising under section 9 (1) above, any question as to whether an employee will become entitled to a redundancy payment if he is not dismissed by his employer but he terminates his contract of employment as mentioned in section 6 (3) (a).

Section 10 contains certain special provisions relating to termination of contract in cases of misconduct or industrial dispute and indeed makes certain exceptions to the provisions of section 2 of the Act (under which X is disentitled to a redundancy payment if justifiably dismissed without notice).   Subsection (1) of section 10 provides that an employee who has been given notice of termination of his employment or who has given notice to his employer under section 6 (1) and takes part in a strike, at such time as is mentioned in subsection (2) of section 10, may still be entitled to a redundancy payment, as section 2 (2) of the Act is not to apply; *i.e.*, his right to a redundancy payment is protected by subsection (1).   The tribunal has the discretionary power, under section 10 (3), to award the whole of a redundancy payment or any part thereof, where there has been dismissal for misconduct—but certainly not where there has been participation in a strike.[52]   Subsection (4) of section 10 ensures

---

[49] See *H. A. Rencoule (Joiners and Shopfitters)* v. *Thomas Hunt*, 1967 I.T.R. 475; 1967 S.C. 131 (before the Lord President and Lords Cameron, Guthrie and Migdale—their lordships holding that the tribunal (see 1967 I.T.R. 18) had been correct in awarding a redundancy payment and appeal refused: the judicial opinions are all helpful).

[50] *MacLaughlan* v. *Alexander Paterson Ltd.*, 1968 I.T.R. 251; 1968 S.L.T. 377 (a case in which the employer had failed to rebut the presumption and appeal allowed); see also *Irvine* v. *The National Fishcuring Co. Ltd.*, 1966 I.T.R. 151 (employers again had failed to discharge the onus of proof that the applicant was not redundant).

[51] See *McLeod* v. *Fisher*, 1966 I.T.R. 251; and see the references to s. 9 (2), para. (b) in *Dunbar* v. *James Wyllie & Sons (Grain Merchants) Ltd.*, 1967 I.T.R. 275; see also *Lappin* v. *Fairfield-Rowan Ltd.*, 1967 I.T.R. 8 (respondents had satisfied the onus upon them under s. 9 (2); application dismissed).

In *Douglas* v. *Provident Clothing and Supply Co. Ltd.*, 1969 I.T.R. 15; 1969 S.L.T. 57, the Court of Session (refusing the appeal) has confirmed that the rules of evidence applicable to courts of law do not apply to proceedings before tribunals.   The tribunal were justified in dismissing the application although only one witness appeared for the employers—to rebut the presumption created by s. 9 (2) (b), (*i.e.*, corroboration was not necessary).   The recent decision by the (English) Court of Appeal in *Hindle* v. *Percival Boats Ltd.*, 1969 I.T.R. 86; V K.I.R. 462 (involving ss. 1 (2) and 9 (2) (b) of the 1965 Act) is also interesting.   The court, by a majority of two to one, refused the appeal (see opinions of Sachs L.J. and Widgery L.J.), but it is the dissenting opinion of the Master of the Rolls which is very important—he was for requiring the strongest proof from the employers to rebut the presumption in s. 9 (2) (b), and he would have allowed the appeal in the circumstances.

[52] See *Cairns* v. *Burnside Shoe Repairs Ltd.*, 1967 I.T.R. 75 (an award of two-thirds of the redundancy payment).

that section 3 (1) (*c*) does not apply where X is locked out by his employer and, because of that situation, he terminates his contract without notice.

Section 11 enables the Secretary of State to make exemption orders by which he may exclude from the operation of section 1 of the Act any employments in respect of which there is in force a collective agreement providing for alternative rights to employees upon termination of their contracts. The method of reference to a tribunal under section 9 of the Act is preserved, in the event of a dispute arising out of the agreement and the Secretary of State must be satisfied about this.[53] Exemption orders are made effective by the issue of statutory instruments. The agreements referred to in subsection (1) are specifically preserved as valid by section 25 (5), although all other agreements which attempt to evade the Part I provisions are void.[54]

Section 12 takes account of the " claims procedure " under section 8 of the Terms and Conditions of Employment Act 1959 [55] and enables the Minister to refer matters of non-compliance with recognised terms and conditions, and these matters now include agreements which deal with redundancy pay. The Industrial Court's jurisdiction has therefore been extended by that extent. Subsection (2) of section 12 brings within the ambit of the Industrial Court and the 1959 Act procedure those redundancy schemes which have been exempted under section 11 of the 1965 Act.

Section 13 is a most important one indeed because it governs the redundancy payment position where there has been a change of ownership of a business and as a result of that change of ownership a termination of employment occurs, either with notice or without notice.[56] The criterion is whether X has been dismissed or not. If his original contract has not been terminated and he has not been dismissed section 13 is inapplicable. It is the dismissal which breaks the continuity of employment and gives rise to the claim for redundancy. The continuity of employment is not broken where the employee continues in employment —accepting his new employer in place of his old employer and, of course, the question of redundancy does not arise. The employee's " service " is aggregated over the employers *in toto*, no matter how many, so long as the continuity remains unbroken.[57] On the other hand, if the original contract is terminated and the new owner makes an offer of re-engagement this is equated with the provisions of sections 2 and 3 of the Act. That is to say, if the re-engagement offer is upon the same terms as with the previous owner sections 2 (3), 2 (4) and 3 (2) will apply and the employee does not then qualify for a redundancy payment if he unreasonably refuses the offer.[58] The tribunal will normally have to decide whether the

[53] s. 11 (2) and (3).
[54] s. 25 (4).
[55] 7 & 8 Eliz. 2, c. 26.
[56] See subs. (1), para. (*a*)—change of ownership of a business or part thereof; and para. (*b*)—resulting termination of employment, with or without notice.
[57] See *Tucker* v. *Cox*, 1967 I.T.R. 395.
[58] See s. 13 (3) and (4).

employee's refusal was reasonable or unreasonable. If the employee had been offered a different type of job and had refused it the tribunal's task is to consider the work offered in relation to the employee himself, *i.e.*, was it suitable alternative employment for that particular employee ? If it was and it is unreasonably refused there will be no claim or right to a redundancy payment. The employee's task, in all cases arising under section 13, is to satisfy the tribunal that his refusal was not—in the circumstances—unreasonable. Where an owner of a business dies and the ownership vests in his personal representatives section 13 has no application.[59]

Many interesting decisions have arisen upon the operation of section 13; most of these being concerned with whether or not there has been a change of ownership. The meaning of " change of ownership " was considered and defined [60] by Diplock L.J. in a recent appeal in England to the Divisional Court from a decision of the Industrial Tribunal—see *Dallow Industrial Properties Ltd.* v. *Else.*[61] Situations in which it has been held that there was no change of ownership have arisen in the under-noted decisions.[62] On the other hand, situations in which it has been held that there was a change of ownership accompanied by preservation of the continuity of employment have arisen in the selection of decisions noted hereunder.[63] Other points of interest which have arisen upon consideration of certain other aspects of section 13 must not be overlooked. These have included, for example—(a) temporary employment for a brief trial period does not constitute the renewal of applicant's previous contract of employment or re-engagement under section 13 (2) [64]; (b) an offer to re-engage made by a new owner need not be in writing,[65] but an offer by a new owner upon different terms must be in writing [66] and in accordance with the terms of section 2 (4).

---

[59] See particularly Sched. 4, Part I, para. 2.

[60] His lordship saying " . . . In order to come within section 13 (1) of the Act of 1965, there must be a change of ownership, not merely in an asset of a business as in this case, but a change of ownership in the combination of operations carried on by the trader or by the non-trading body of persons, and there can only be a change of ownership in a business or part of a business . . . if what is transferred is a separate and self-contained part of the operations of the transferor in which assets, stock-in-trade and the like are engaged, or the corresponding expression which would apply to a body of persons which was carrying on operations not for profit."

[61] [1967] 2 Q.B. 449; [1967] 2 All E.R. 30.

[62] No change of ownership: *Rowlatt* v. *Budden and Harris*, 1966 I.T.R. 269 (s. 13 does not operate where employees are engaged by a new employer who purchases only fixtures and fittings—this is not a change of ownership of a business); *Douglas* v. *Merchants Facilities (Glasgow) Ltd.*, 1966 I.T.R. 374 (sale of employer's assets to a purchaser who employed applicant—held to be a renewal of contract under s. 13 (2) and applicant not entitled to a redundancy payment); *McKinney* v. *McCaig, Paisley and Melville*, 1966 I.T.R. 240 (s. 13 only applies where there is a change of ownership of a business); *McLeod* v. *Fisher*, 1966 I.T.R. 251; *Cameron* v. *Hector Finlayson and Co. Ltd.*, 1967 I.T.R. 110.

[63] Change of ownership (and continuity maintained): *Anderson* v. *David Winter & Sons Ltd.*, 1966 I.T.R. 326 (continuity maintained and applicant entitled to a redundancy payment); *Nelson* v. *George Grierson & Son*, 1966 I.T.R. 309 (but see footnotes to s. 2); *Squair* v. *Merchants Facilities (Glasgow) Ltd.*, 1966 I.T.R. 384.

[64] *Brown* v. *Hamilton* (1) *John Waugh & Co. (Edinburgh) Ltd.* (2), 1967 I.T.R. 281.

[65] *Pilkington* v *Pickstone*, 1966 I.T.R. 363 (and s. 3 (2) also raised).

[66] *Nealon* v. *H. and L. Motors Ltd.*, 1967 I.T.R. 67.

Section 14 enables the Secretary of State to make regulations by which a redundancy payment may be excluded or reduced in the case of any employee who has a separate contractual right to a lump sum payment or periodical payment by way of pension, gratuity or superannuation allowance upon the termination of his employment. Such regulations must reserve the right to a redundancy payment, which is not to be excluded or reduced by reason of any right or claim to payment of a lump sum or periodical payment by way of compensation arising under a statutory provision as is mentioned in section 47 (1).[67]

Section 15 applies to the " fixed-term " contract. If that contract was entered into before the " appointed day " [68] for a period of two years or more—and was not a contract of apprenticeship—it does not fall within the Act's provisions. The parties may, in any contract made after the passing of the Act [69] being a fixed-term contract for two years or more (and including a contract of apprenticeship), make an agreement whereby the employee forgoes his right to a redundancy payment if he is not subsequently re-engaged.[70] If there is no such agreement, the employee has a right to a redundancy payment. Section 15 does not apply to any mariner (other than a share fisherman) to whom section 20 of the Act applies.[71]

Those classes of employees who are excluded from the operation of the Act are specified in section 16. These classes are—(i) registered dock workers and limited dock workers,[72] (ii) master and crew members of fishing vessels (if not remunerated otherwise than by a share in the profit or gross earnings of the vessel),[73] (iii) where the employer is the husband or wife of the employee,[74] (iv) certain public office holders, the civil service and employment by any such body as specified in Schedule 3 to the Act [75]; and employment by the government of an overseas territory.[76] The Secretary of State has power to vary or modify the foregoing excepted or excluded classes.[77]

Employment wholly or partly abroad is dealt with by section 17. The test is whether the employee ordinarily works in Great Britain and he is entitled to a redundancy payment at the termination of his contract of employment, even if he is outside Great Britain at that time.[78] Conversely the employee who normally works abroad is not entitled to a redundancy

---

[67] s. 14 (2).
[68] December 6, 1965.
[69] August 5, 1965.
[70] s. 15 (2).
[71] See s. 20 (2).
[72] s. 16 (1).
[73] s. 16 (2).
[74] s. 16 (3). But see *Bernstein and Another* v. *Bernstein Brothers*, 1969 I.T.R. 106, where the London tribunal held that an employee of a partnership, one of the partners of which is the spouse of the employee, is not excluded by s. 16 (3) from the benefits of the Act.
[75] s. 16 (4); see *Morrison* v. *Ministry of Aviation*, 1966 I.T.R. 502.
[76] s. 16 (5).
[77] See subss. (6), (7) and (8).
[78] s. 17 (1).

payment, unless he is in Great Britain, in accordance with his employer's instructions, at the time when the contract of employment terminates.[79] The computation of a " week of employment," continuity and the related matter of national insurance contributions (which affects the operation of section 17) are explained in subsections (3) to (8) both inclusive.

Section 18 requires an employer to give to an employee a written statement indicating how the amount of the redundancy payment is calculated.[80] This is quite separate from any case in which the Industrial Tribunal specifies in its decision the amount of the redundancy payment which is to be made. Failure to comply with this provision is an offence.[81] The employee is given a statutory right to require a written statement to be delivered to him within one week of the day when he (the employee) gave written notice requesting the statement. Failure to comply, without reasonable excuse, is an offence and a fine may be imposed.[82] In calculating the amount of redundancy pay the basis is the " normal working week " and although " overtime " is usually to be excluded from the " normal working hours," this is not so if the overtime working is a compulsory part of the normal working week.[83] If overtime is not obligatory it should be disregarded in making the computation.[84]

Domestic servants are governed by the 1965 Act, as if they were ordinary business employees,[85] except where the " family relationship " test imposed in subsection (2) of section 19 applies.

Mariners, other than share fishermen, as defined in subsection (3) of section 20, are covered by the Act and section 17 (employment abroad) does not apply to them nor do the provisions of section 15 (" fixed term " contracts) if they come within the definition in subsection (3).

Section 21 deals with the time limit for claims and provides that an employee shall not be entitled to a redundancy payment unless, before the end of the period of six months [86] beginning with the relevant date,—

  (a) the payment has been agreed and paid, or
  (b) the employee [87] has made a written claim for payment to the employer, or

---

[79] s. 17 (2).
[80] s. 18 (1); unless there is a " reasonable excuse."
[81] s. 18 (2). The maximum fine, upon summary conviction, is £20.
[82] £20 fine (maximum) for a first offence; £100 fine (maximum) for a subsequent offence.
[83] *Welsh* v. *John Thompson Water Tube Boilers Ltd.*, 1966 I.T.R. 272.
[84] See *Batchelor and Others* v. *Babcock and Wilcox (Operations) Ltd.*, 1966 I.T.R. 78; see also *Charnley* v. *Howard and Bullogh Ltd.*, 1967 I.T.R. 15; and *Pearson and Workman* v. *William Jones Ltd.*, 1967 I.T.R. 152.
[85] s. 19 (1). S. 13 (change of ownership) does not, however, apply to this situation.
[86] Where a personal representative is claiming payment, after the employee's death, the period is extended to one year—see Sched. 4, para. 20. Posting of the notice of claim within the six-month period is good enough even if it were not received within the period—*McCutcheon* v. *Sykes Macfarlane Ltd.*, 1967 I.T.R. 621; see also *McHardy* v. *The Caledon Shipbuilding and Engineering Co. Ltd.*, 1967 I.T.R. 337 (the application was out of time in relation to the time limit specified in s. 21).
[87] The notice of claim must be to the firm or company as such—see *Stoughton* v. *Bancroft Folding Machines Ltd.*, 1967 I.T.R. 32. The tribunal also held, in this case, that notification by an employee's solicitor does not meet the requirement of para. (b) of s. 21 (see above).

(c) the question as to the employee's right to the payment, or as to the amount thereof, has been referred to the Industrial Tribunal, under the Part III provisions of the Act.

The question of implied or constructive termination of contract is covered by section 22. Where, in accordance with any enactment or rule of law (a) any act on the employer's part, or (b) any event affecting an employer (including, in the case of an individual, his death) operates as a termination of contract, the act or event is to be treated as a termination of contract, although in any other case outwith the subsection,[88] this would not be so. If the employee's contract is not renewed, and he is not re-engaged under a new contract (see section 3 (2) of the Act) he is to be taken to be dismissed by reason of redundancy if the circumstances are wholly or mainly attributable to one or other of the facts specified in paragraphs (a) and (b) of section 1 (2) of the Act.

Where an employer dies, the provisions of Part I of Schedule 4 are to operate [88a]; and where an employee dies, the Part II provisions of that Schedule apply.[89]

Once a redundancy payment has been paid to an employee this operates as a break in the continuity of his employment and the new build-up of continuity is then re-calculated from the time when the employee is re-engaged or his contract is renewed, whether by his former employer or by another employer.[90]

Section 25 is the " interpretation section." Subsection (1) says that " business "—" includes a trade or profession and includes any activity carried on by a body of persons, whether corporate or unincorporate." There follows thereafter the definition of an " employee " which corresponds exactly with that which appears in the Contracts of Employment Act 1963, s. 8. Any purported contractual attempt to evade the provisions of the 1965 Act is declared to be invalid by subsection (4) of section 25, unless where section 11 (1) applies (and an order is required to give effect thereto) or section 15 applies.[91] It is obvious that the distinction between the contract of service and the contract for services is vitally important and those principles and cases which have been mentioned in earlier chapters will apply with equal force here.[92] The word " activity " was considered by Diplock L.J. in *Dallow Industrial Properties* v. *Else*,[93] in the context of " trade profession or business," and his lordship thought that it meant " the combination of operations undertaken by the corporate body whether or not amounting to a business trade or profession in the ordinary sense."

---

[88] *i.e.*, subs. (1) of s. 22.
[88a] In *Narang* v. *The Trustees of J. Hodge (decd.)*, VI K.I.R. 74, an employee who refused to continue working after his employer's death had his application for redundancy pay rejected by the tribunal.
[89] s. 23.
[90] s. 24.
[91] See subs. (5) of s. 25.
[92] See Chaps. 2 and 3, *supra*.
[93] [1967] 2 Q.B. 449 at p. 458; [1967] 2 All E.R. 30 at p. 33.

There have been many decisions of the Industrial Tribunals centred on the application of the term " employee," within the definition of that term as contained in section 25 (1). The following selection (from Scotland and England) may be found to be helpful,[94] but an exhaustive catalogue will not be attempted.

It is interesting to note that subsection (4) of section 56 (which is the general interpretation section) adopts a device similar to that in subsection (2) of section 9 of the Contracts of Employment Act 1963 by stipulating that it is immaterial whether the law which (apart from the Act) governs the person's employment is the law of Great Britain, or of a part of Great Britain, or not. It makes no difference which system of law it is—the Act will still be applicable to the contract of employment.

Certain changes in the general administration proceedings of the 1965 Act—and in particular the question of a modification of the employer's entitlement to claim rebates—are still under active consideration by Parliament, which is concerned about the solvency of the Redundancy Fund. It has also been indicated in the White Paper, " In Place of Strife," [95] that changes in the Contracts of Employment Act 1963 are to be made to give greater protection to long service employees. Consequential amendments to the 1965 Act may then be necessary.

The declared intention by the present Government to reduce the rebates payable to employers (being one of the matters referred to in the preceding paragraph) has now been brought into legal effect with the passing of the Redundancy Rebates Act 1969.[96] The general effect of this statute is to reduce the rebates payable under section 30 of the 1965 Act. Section 1 (1) of the 1969 Act substitutes new fractions for those contained in Schedule 5 to the 1965 Act, viz., the rebate will now be " one-half " in lieu of " seven-ninths " as stipulated formerly in paragraphs 3 and 12 of the Schedule. Other amendments are made to paragraphs 2 and 9 of the Schedule by section 1 (1). Certain rebates are not, however, to be reduced, namely: (first) by section 1 (2) where the " relevant date " under section 3 (4), 4 (2) or 6 (2) of the 1965 Act is earlier than March 17, 1969; and (secondly) by section 1 (3) (a) and section 1 (3) (b) in relation to such agreements as are mentioned in sections 30 (1) (b) and 30 (1) (c) of the 1965 Act, provided that the " date of termination " was prior to March 17, 1969. The 1969 Act came into operation on March 17, 1969, and obviously the amendments made by section 1 (1) are most important in relation to new cases.

---

94 See *Hill* v. *Barrie*, 1967 I.T.R. 206 (a taxicab driver is not an " employee " as defined in s. 25 (1); *Ferguson* v. *Telford, Grier Mackay & Co. Ltd.*, 1967 I.T.R. 387 (applicant, who was the secretary and a director, held to be an employee); *Burgess* v. *O'Brien*, 1966 I.T.R. 164 (the salaried partner); *Park* v. *Orr*, 1966 I.T.R. 488 (the chaplain on staff of an industrial mission was not an employee); *J. C. King Ltd.* v. *Valencia*, 1966 I.T.R. 67 (a " selling agent " paid by weekly salary plus commission was an employee).
95 Cmnd. 3888 (1969).
96 1969, c. 8 (which received the Royal Assent on March 6, 1969).

Chapter 9

EMPLOYEE'S DUTIES AND RESPONSIBILITIES GENERALLY

THERE are undoubtedly certain general duties and obligations which the common law places upon the employee, arising from the creation of the contractual relationship. It is essential to look at these duties and obligations in some detail and to consider, in the light of modern law and practice, what changes have occurred or would be beneficial.

(1) *Employee must Enter into Service and Continue in it*

The employee is obliged to enter into the service at the agreed time, otherwise he becomes liable in damages for a breach of contract. He cannot force his employer to accept a substitute for him, as the rule of *delectus personae* is implied in the contract of service.[1] After entry upon the employment, the requirement is that the employee should continue therein until such time as the contract is legally terminated[2] or until the employer himself is in breach of contract, when the employee will normally be justified in leaving. Any desertion of the service would result in a forfeiture of wages,[3] as well as enabling the employer to sue for breach of contract. The employer would have to decide whether it was prudent for him to sue, in relation to his other employees or whether it was a worthwhile exercise. If a substantial loss were indicated then the employer would be quite right to sue.

(2) *Knowledge of Work and Careful Performance*

When the employee takes on his particular employment he is held to be giving an assurance or guarantee to his employer that he is competent to perform the tasks customarily to be carried out within that type of employment. He must, therefore, exercise all reasonable care and diligence in the performance of his work.[4] The maxim applied here is *spondet peritiam artis.*[5]

---

[1] *Campbell* v. *Price* (1831) 9 S. 264.
[2] See *infra*, Termination of Contract (Chaps. 18, 19 and 20).
[3] *Supra*, Chap. 8, on wages, etc.
[4] See particularly Bell's *Principles*, ss. 148–150 and 154; Erskine 3, 3, 16; *Peddie* v. *Roger and Scott* (1798) Hume's *Decisions* 304; *Harmer* v. *Cornelius* (1858) 28 L.J.C.P. 85; dicta of Willes J. approved of by Lord Campbell in *Cuckson* v. *Stones* (1858) 28 L.J.Q.B. 25; *Searle* v. *Ridley* (1873) 28 L.T. 411; *Jackson* v. *Union Marine Insurance* (1874) L.R. 10 C.P. 125; 31 L.T. 789; *Lister* v. *Romford Ice and Cold Storage Co. Ltd.* [1957] A.C. 555, *per* Viscount Simonds at pp. 572–573 on the duty of taking care, imposed upon a lorry driver; and McNair J. in *Harvey* v. *R. G. O'Dell Ltd.* [1958] 1 All E.R. 657 at pp. 667–668, citing from Willes J. (above-mentioned) and dealing very carefully with the right of indemnity (distinguishing *Lister*).
[5] Bell, *Commentaries*, 459; *Dickson* v. *The Hygienic Institute*, 1910 S.C. 352; *Free Church of Scotland* v. *MacKnight's Trs.*, 1916 S.C. 349.

It follows from what has been said above that if one employee is required to work with valuable materials belonging to his employer whilst another employee works with inferior materials, then a greater degree of care and diligence is required from the first employee.[6] The rule is the same whether the employee is hired to discharge a particular office or to perform a particular task. Incompetency will free the employer from the contractual obligation,[7] unless there is an acquiescence in the situation by the employer himself.[8] The employer may hope that the employee will eventually learn to do his task reasonably efficiently. On the other hand, if the employee frankly discloses his incompetence but nevertheless is engaged, the employer cannot break the contract on a plea of incompetence,[9] because the new test becomes the reasonable exercise of the actual skill which the employee possesses.

An employee is not obliged to reveal his past history to a prospective employer—see *Walker* v. *Greenock and District Combination Hospital Board*.[10] The Lord Ordinary (Lord Sorn) said [11] in the course of his opinion therein, " I think it is going altogether too far to expect that an applicant, in addition to saying what he can in his own favour, should proceed also, uninvited, to say all that could be said against himself. An applicant is not a trustee for his prospective employer." The Lord President (Lord Cooper) put it this way,[12] " hiring of service is not a contract *uberrimae fidei*," and then a little later on, ". . . employers are entitled to investigate all relevant matters and to verify the facts by independent testimonials. . . . " A very interesting case has arisen comparatively recently in England, *viz.*, *Cork* v. *Kirby MacLean Ltd.*[13] on the undisclosed medical record of an employee. This particular employee had suffered from epilepsy and had been warned by his doctor not to work at any height above ground level, but he had not told his employers this fact. The court reduced the damages awarded to the employee to the extent of one-half, because of his failure to disclose his medical condition. This case must be read with reference to the concept of " fault " in reparation actions. It is not to be accepted as an authority for any general duty of disclosure on the part of an employee.

The employee is always required to exercise care in the handling of property belonging to his employer, any failure in reasonable care rendering

---

[6] See Bell's *Commentaries*, Vol. I, pp. 488–490; *Hinshaw* v. *Adam* (1870) 8 M. 933
[7] Erskine, III, 3, 16; Bell's *Principles*, s. 154.
[8] See particularly *Robertson* v. *Brown* (1876) 3 R. 652; 13 S.L.R. 436. If the employer orders a labourer to do a piece of work, out of line with his ordinary job, which could with safety only be done by a skilled workman, the employer is responsible if the workman is injured. The employer would also be responsible in the ordinary case to any third party who suffered injury.
[9] *Gunn* v. *Ramsay* (1801) Hume's *Decisions*, p. 384; Bell's *Principles, loc. cit.*
[10] 1951 S.L.T. 329; 1951 S.C. 464. The English cases in point are *Fletcher* v. *Krell* (1872) 42 L.J.K.B. 55; 28 L.T. 105; and *Bell* v. *Lever Bros.* [1932] A.C. *per* Lord Atkin at pp. 226–227.
[11] 1951 S.C. 467.
[12] *Ibid.* 470.
[13] [1952] 2 All E.R. 402.

him liable in damages for any loss suffered by the employer.[14] Nevertheless, the employee does not guarantee his employer's property against all risks. There is no liability upon him for loss caused by inevitable accident or *damnum fatale*.

(3) *Respect and Obedience*

It is the employee's duty to be respectful to his employer at all times. Insolence provides a good ground for dismissal[15]—though the test of insolence has to be related to the relationship of parties, *e.g.*, it may more easily be insolence in the case of the domestic employee than in the case of a qualified tradesman who may be questioning the opinion of his employer on a technical matter but doing so firmly and tactlessly rather than intentionally insolently.

Blatant disobedience is quite another matter, however. Any wilful refusal to obey orders or any action committed in violation of orders amounts to a major breach of contract justifying the employer in dismissing the employee (provided always, as hereafter mentioned, that the order was lawful and that the employer was entitled to give it and perhaps also, following the English view, that it was, in the circumstances, reasonable).[16]

The trend of the cases illustrates the guiding principle that each side must act reasonably and with common sense. This is an understandable guiding principle in modern industrial relations, but it may be difficult to follow in practice, particularly where there is a vociferous " hot-headed " element on one side and an arrogant and unbending element on the other side. The result could be a lengthy stoppage of work. The strict legal course may not therefore be the more sensible one to follow in these circumstances. Compromise, without loss of face, very often pays handsome dividends. The employer need not give explanations or reasons to the employee for any general or particular order. It is sufficient that the order in question is lawful and is one which would normally be expected from the employer in the particular type and scope of the employment. Nor may the employee refuse to perform the ordered task until explanations are given to him.[17]

In a well-known English case, the employer was held justified in dismissing a housemaid who absented herself from his household, against orders, for the purpose of visiting her sick and dying mother.[18] Three of the older Scottish cases illustrate a similar approach by the courts here,[19] where again there was disobedience (after due warnings) to the

---

[14] *Walker* v. *The British Guarantee Association* (1852) 18 Q.B. 277; Bankton 1, 20, 21; Erskine III, 3, 16; *Clydesdale Bank* v. *Beatson* (1882) 10 R. 88.
[15] See Fraser, p. 71; *Trotters* v. *Briggs* (1897) 5 S.L.T. 17; *Edwards* v. *Levy* (1860) 2 F. & F. 94; *Pepper* v. *Webb*, VI K.I.R. 109.
[16] *Turner* v. *Mason* (1845) 14 M. & W. 112, 116; *A.* v. *B.* (1853) 16 D. 269; *Silvie* v. *Stewart* (1830) 8 S. 1010; *McKellar* v. *Macfarlane* (1852) 15 D. 246; and *Thomson* v. *Stewart* (1888) 15 R. 806.
[17] *Thomson* v. *Douglas* (1807) Hume's *Decisions*, 392.
[18] *Turner* v. *Mason* (1845) 14 M. & W. 112.
[19] *Elder* v. *Bennet* (1802) Hume's *Decisions*, 386; *Hamilton* v. *McLean* (1824) 3 S. 268; and *A.* v. *B.* (1853) 16 D. 269.

lawful orders of the employer. It is likely that the courts today would take a more humane view of circumstances like those arising in *Turner* v. *Mason* but, nevertheless, where there was repeated absence, against the wishes and instructions of an employer, the courts would be obliged to follow that decision. The courts would not be too anxious to weaken the reasonable disciplinary authority of employers.

It does not seem to be a valid defence for the employee to say that he disobeyed his employer's instructions so as to benefit his employer or to say that his conduct was due to over-zealousness or over-anxiety.

Should the employer order the employee to do something which is morally or legally wrong, the courts would recognise immediately that the order, being unlawful or immoral, could not be forced upon the employee. Disobedience in such a case will not constitute a ground for the employee's dismissal, nor will the court impose upon the employee any penalty or other award in respect of his non-performance. Of course, any agreement by an employee to do for his employer any act which is illegal or immoral will usually result in both employee and employer being held liable under the criminal law as well as in damages under the civil law. It is not a defence to the employee to plead that he was ordered to do the particular act by his employer.[20]

(4) *Time of Employment*

Where the contract specifies the times during which the employee is to work, any question between the parties becomes a question of construction and interpretation of the contract itself. If nothing is said in the contract, the length of time of the employment falls to be decided by reference to the custom or usage of the trade or of the locality or establishment or, failing all of these tests, by reference to what is a reasonable time in the circumstances. Obviously, the determination of what time is reasonable will vary according to the nature of the work involved and the status of the employee concerned. In the fairly recent case of *National Coal Board* v. *Galley* [21] it has been held that a requirement that an employee " work such days or part days as may reasonably be required " is enforceable. As Pearce L.J. said in the Court of Appeal, " the parties have explicitly provided that reasonableness shall be the test."

It is essential that the employee should attend punctually at his place of employment and he must not be absent without just cause.[22] Any failure to do so may lead, in most circumstances, to his dismissal. It seems to be accepted that when an employee is under notice from his employer or is " working his own notice " he is entitled to some time off to look for another situation. As the legal requirement of notice is primarily designed to enable the employer to obtain a replacement and the employee to obtain alternative employment, some reasonable freedom

---

[20] *Cullen* v. *Thomson* (1862) 4 Macq. 424, 432.
[21] [1958] 1 All E.R. 91.
[22] See *infra* on termination of contract.

of movement must be allowed.[23]   The employee himself must act reasonably in the matter, so as not to cause any unnecessary inconvenience to his employer, *e.g.*, if the absence can be arranged during a slightly extended lunch-hour period, this is reasonable, rather than have the employer inconvenienced during a particularly busy morning period or afternoon period.   Where the employee is not under notice, he must ask permission from his employer before absenting himself for interview or for the purpose of seeking other employment.   While he is not bound to disclose the reason for his absence, nevertheless he must protect himself by obtaining a proper permission.

(5) *Type of Work*

The obligation upon the employee is to perform the type or kind of work for which he was engaged.   There is no obligation upon him, in the ordinary case (*i.e.*, emergency apart), to perform some other type of work or to act in some other capacity.   Obviously, this question as to what is a different type of work or what constitutes employment in a different capacity from that which was contracted upon between the parties is one which can give rise to innumerable disputes between employer and employee.   Lord Fraser says [24] that a general rule has been evolved to the effect that although the work demanded from the employee may not be within the precise line of his contract, yet if it is asked of him during an emergency, his scruples to do it will not be listened to and he will be guilty of disobedience.   Mr. Bell suggests [25] that orders inferring trifling deviations from the line of duty form no grounds of objection in favour of the employee, so long as these orders are not often repeated. But if the deviation is substantial, or takes place on numerous occasions, or if the employee is placed in some personal danger, then the court will protect the employee by upholding his refusal to perform.

Moreover, an employee cannot be obliged or compelled to work on a lower status than that at which he was engaged.   There are several older Scottish cases [26] which support this point.   It will be appreciated that if the employee is taken on for the performance of general duties (perhaps on the basis of an unskilled labourer) then he or she can be ordered to do any lawful task within the scope of that general employment.   There is no room for a demarcation dispute (between employer and employee) in such a case.

On the question of risk of personal danger or violence justifying refusal to obey an order from the employer, reference may be made to

---

[23] See particularly *R.* v. *Polesworth* (1819) 2 B. & Ald. 483, that absence by an employee to seek other employment does not justify dismissal.

[24] *Op. cit.* p. 78.   [25] *Principles*, s. 176.

[26] *Fairie* v. *McVicar* (1771) 2 Hutch. 108, note; *Peter* v. *Terrol* (1818) 2 Mur. 28; *Gunn* v, *Ramsay* (1801) Hume's *Decisions*, 384; *Stuart* v. *Richardson* (1806) Hume's *Decisions*. 390; *Thomson* v. *Douglas* (1807) Hume's *Decisions*, 392; and *Ross* v. *Pender* (1874) 1 R. 352 (where the employer improperly dismissed his head gamekeeper and offered him the same wages in a subordinate employment. *Held* that the employee was not bound to accept the offer), and *Moffat* v. *Boothby* (1884) 11 R. 501.

certain of the older cases.[27] The test seems to be that the risk involved is not fairly within the contemplation of the contract. This approach to the question has been continued in modern law and is illustrated by several notable cases, in both England and Scotland, of which the three examples quoted below [28] are perhaps the most outstanding.

(6) *Moral Conduct*

The employee must behave decently and not do anything which scandalises or brings disrepute upon the employer or his family. This is particularly so in the case of the employee who is resident in the employer's household [29] (though employees of this class are undoubtedly a rapidly diminishing group). Although the immoral act is committed outwith the employer's household, this will justify dismissal if the employer's interests, feelings or reputation are seriously prejudiced thereby.[30] The misconduct in question must occur during the employment. Prior misconduct does not—unless continued—justify dismissal.[31]

Moreover, in the absence of fraud by the employee, there is no obligation upon an employee, when he is being engaged, to disclose to his employer any material fact concerning his character. The *uberrima fides* principle has no application here, as it has in certain other contracts.[32]

Dishonesty is one of the more common types of acts of moral turpitude. If the employee steals the employer's property then he is guilty of a breach of faith and of contract, and may be dismissed.[33] Any other act of moral turpitude may justify dismissal, although a prosecution had not been or could not be taken; for example, the use of obscene language by a tutor to his master's children which justifies his instant dismissal [34] or gross misconduct in the treatment of female workers on a farm by the foreman, thereby causing quarrels, etc., with his wife and consequent interruptions of work.[35]

---

[27] See *Turner* v. *Mason* (1845) 14 M. & W. 112; *Sutherland* v. *Monkland Railways Co.* (1857) 19 D. 1004; *Priestly* v. *Fowler* (1837) 3 M. & W. 1; Fraser, Cap. X and cases cited therein.

[28] See particularly *McKeating* v. *Frame*, 1921 S.C. 382 (an order to a domestic servant to go home when she was too ill to move from her bed was quite unreasonable); *Ottoman Bank* v. *Chakarian* [1930] A.C. 277 (an order to an Armenian employee of the Bank sending him to Istanbul where his life was in danger—and on his refusal to serve there, he was dismissed. He succeeded in his action against the Bank for wrongful dismissal); but *cf. Bouzourou* v. *Ottoman Bank* [1930] A.C. 271 (here the plaintiff failed to discharge the onus of proof that his life was in danger).

[29] See *Atkin* v. *Acton* (1830) 4 C. & P. 208 (dismissal of a resident employee guilty of assaulting a maid-servant with intent to ravish her was held to be justified).

[30] *Connors* v. *Justice* (1862) 13 Irv.C.L.R. 457; *Mathieson* v. *MacKinnon* (1832) 10 S. 825; and *Greig* v. *Sanderson* (1864) 2 M. 1278.

[31] *R.* v. *Westmeon* (1781) Cald. 134.

[32] See *Fletcher* v. *Krell* (1872) 42 L.J.Q.B. 55; *Hands* v. *Simpson Fawcett and Co. Ltd.* (1928) 44 T.L.R. 295 and *Bell* v. *Lever Bros. Ltd.* [1932] A.C. 101.

[33] Bell's *Principles*, s. 178; *Turner* v. *Robinson* (1833) 6 C. & P. 15; *Baillie* v. *Kell* (1838) 4 Bing.N.C. 638; *Smith* v. *Thomson* (1849) 8 C.B. 44; 18 L.J.C.P. 314; *Blenkarn* v. *Hodges' Distillery Co.* (1867) 16 L.T.(N.S.) 608.

[34] *Matheson* v. *MacKinnon* (1832) 10 S. 825.

[35] *Greig* v. *Sanderson* (1864) 2 M. 1278. A recent publication dealing with misconduct justifying dismissal or discipline is *Employees' Misconduct* by Professor Alfred Avins (Law Book Co., Allahabad; 1968).

Intoxication is another example of improper conduct. Before dismissal is justified, the intoxication must be habitual or frequent, unless of course it can be shown that one particular instance was, of itself, of such a serious and aggravated character [36] as to justify dismissal. It is always a question of circumstances as to the extent of intoxication which justifies dismissal. Not only is the degree of intoxication and its frequency to be looked at but, in addition, the position of parties and the nature of the service should also be carefully considered.[37] The basic general test as between employer and employee would appear to be whether the state of intoxication interfered in any way (that is to say, to a substantial and material extent) with the proper function of the employee's duties. If it does, then dismissal is justified.

(7) *Revealing Secrets*

In important manufactures, processes or trades the employer may have some secret or hidden method of manufacture which may be quite unknown to rival traders. His reputation and business superiority and his success will usually depend upon that process, which he earnestly desires to keep secret and in regard to which the law will give him a measure of protection. When an employee is engaged it is not unusual in such trades to require him to maintain strict silence as to the methods or processes used by his employer. If he should break that undertaking which he has given, then he may be liable in damages to his employer, and he may well be dismissed.[38] The employer may be able to take interdict proceedings to prevent any disclosure of trade secrets by an employee or former employee [39] or he may be able to take such proceedings against another employer who is employing the first employer's skilled employees on a part-time basis. This latter situation arose in the well-known English case of *Hivac Ltd.* v. *Park Royal Scientific Instruments Ltd.*,[40] where employees of one company were making use of secret scientific and technical processes used in the production of miniature valves for hearing aids whilst they were engaged in part-time employment with a rival company. It was held that the former company was entitled to an injunction (Scottish, interdict). Of course, the employees themselves are, in this type of situation, in breach of faith or loyalty and also therefore in breach of contract, but it may or may not be politic and economic for the employer to dismiss them. The sharp " hands off " warning to rival concerns may be enough.

---

[36] *Edwards* v. *Mackie* (1848) 11 D. 67; *Speck* v. *Phillips* (1839) 5 M. & W. 279; *Wise* v. *Wilson* (1844) 1 C. & K. 662.

[37] *McKellar* v. *Macfarlane* (1852) 15 D. 246 (master of a ship dismissed for drunkenness in a foreign port; reinstated and told not to carry liquor on board; disobeyed; subsequently drunk on homeward voyage; *held* to have forfeited his wages as master).

[38] *Rutherford* v. *Boak* (Mar. 19, 1836) F.C. (Jury Sittings), Vol. xi, p. 32.

[39] *Liverpool Victoria Friendly Society* v. *Houston* (1900) 3 F. 42; 8 S.L.T. 230.

[40] [1946] Ch. 169; [1946] 1 All E.R. 350, C.A. See also the earlier case of *British Industrial Plastics* v. *Ferguson* [1938] 4 All E.R. 405; 160 L.T. 95; 56 R.P.C. 271; and the later case of *Cranleigh Precision Engineering Ltd.* v. *Bryant* [1964] 3 All E.R. 289; [1965] 1 W.L.R. 1293.

A question sometimes arises regarding the retention by an employee of certain information or materials acquired by him during the course of his employment. Is he entitled to retain such materials or information? This matter came up in *Earl of Crawford* v. *Paton* [41] where the defender, a professional searcher of records, was employed by the pursuer through an agent. The defender made certain notes (partly shorthand, partly longhand), from which he compiled certain abstracts in bound volume form upon the Lindsay family. The pursuer sought delivery of the notes. The Lord Ordinary (Lord Skerrington) assoilzied the defender, holding that the property in the notes lay with the defender. The Lord Ordinary pointed out [42] that the pursuer would be protected in the ordinary way if the defender were to make any improper use of the notes. The case was then taken, on a reclaiming motion, to the Second Division of the Court of Session, which upheld the Lord Ordinary's finding. The opinions of Lord Dundas [43] and Lord Salvesen [44] are most helpful and, indeed, Lord Dundas drew a very clear distinction between the situation in this case and certain of the English cases, particularly *ex parte Horsfall*.[45]

(8) *Earnings*

During the hours of employment, the employee's time and labour belong to his employer. By the contract itself, the employer is purchasing he skill, ingenuity and labour of the employee. Therefore, the employee comes under a legal obligation (not just a moral one) to exert these things to the maximum for the advantage and benefit of his employer.

If the employee is hired exclusively to one employer and thereafter, without that employer's consent, hires himself to a second employer, it appears that the law requires him to hand over to the first employer all those earnings which he has gained from his second employer.[46] Should the first employer give his consent to the second employment, then it is possible that the first employer might recover the employee's wages, based upon the conception of an agency contract. But if the employee takes on secondary employment without the consent of his first employer, the correct remedy in Scotland seems to be for the first employer to proceed against the second employer for loss of services or against the employee himself for breach of contract. It is inappropriate to claim wages here from the second employer because the pursuer, not being a party to the second contract, has no *locus standi* in any proposed action. If, however, the wages had been paid to the employee by the second employer, it would appear to be quite competent for the first employer (*i.e.*, the real or primary employer) to recover these wages from the employee.

[41] 1910, 1 S.L.T. 423 (Outer House case); and on reclaiming motion at 1911 S.C. 1017; 1911, 2 S.L.T. 67, distinguishing *Ex parte Horsfall* (1827) 7 B. & C. 528.
[42] *Ibid.* p. 424.
[43] 1911 S.C. 1017 at pp. 1023–1025 particularly.
[44] *Ibid.* at p. 1027.
[45] (1827) 7 B. & C. 528.
[46] *Thompson* v. *Havelock* (1808) 1 Camp. 527 *per* Lord Ellenborough.

The above rules would apply where the actings of the employee are clearly prejudicial to the first employer's interests. Theoretically, the second contract is regarded as being void because it is against public policy.

Should the actings of the employee *vis-à-vis* his second employment be in no way prejudicial to his original employer, it would seem that the second employment is perfectly lawful and the first employer cannot interfere. It is accepted nowadays that an employee may take non-prejudicial employment elsewhere during his spare time, but he cannot undertake (without the special consent of his primary employer) to work for a second employer during a period of time when he is under contract to his primary employer. Every employee is obliged to account to his employer for all moneys and property received by him on behalf of his employer from third parties. This obligation to account probably also covers bribes and other rewards which have been paid to the employee as an inducement to do certain things, but excepting always " tips " which are an accepted practice in certain types of service and may even be encouraged by certain employers, although in other cases " tips " are formally forbidden. The employer may proceed to recover these payments and also any undisclosed profit which the employee makes out of any transaction.[47]

(9) *Accompany Employer*

There is no doubt that in certain cases the employee must accompany his employer wherever he goes within the United Kingdom, particularly where the nature of the service is personal, *e.g.*, a domestic servant, chauffeur, private secretary, valet or the like. But, he is not bound to go outwith the United Kingdom, if he does not wish to do so.[48] Both Bell [49] and Tait [50] take the view that the employee in Scotland is not bound to go to either England and Wales or Ireland. It will be appreciated that, where the employee's contract is terminated whilst he is absent from home, he is entitled to his expenses for the journey home. Moreover, it is reasonable to allow him a certain time during which to seek alternative employment and, accordingly, the employer should permit him to return home a short time before his engagement ends, which might be sufficient for this purpose.

Where the work to be performed by a particular employee has reference to a place rather than to a person, it would appear that the employer cannot remove him to another place which is at an inconvenient distance for the employee. This rule is departed from during the emergencies of war-time when movement of employees becomes generally regulated by

---

[47] *Reading* v. *Att.-Gen.* [1951] A.C. 507, where an army sergeant was held accountable to the Crown for moneys paid to him for his part in a customs-evading operation.
[48] *Stuart* v. *Richardson* (1806) Hume's *Decisions* 390.
[49] *Principles*, s. 180.
[50] *Justice* (*vide* servant).

the Ministry of Labour and National Service and the actual engagement of artisan employees becomes subject to compulsory regulation by the state.

The place where the employer has his business at the time of the original engagement is (unless expressly stipulated otherwise) held to be the place where it is implied that the employee is to serve. In *Anderson v. Moon* [51] a girl had been hired to work at a certain factory and it was held that her employer could not compel her to work at another factory half-a-mile away although he offered to provide someone to take her meals to her. She would have been put to inconvenience, would have had a longer road to travel at night and would have been deprived of the company of her sisters who worked at the factory where she herself had served from the beginning.

(10) *Protection of Employer's Business*

If there is any question of the employee's conduct causing serious harm or loss to the employer's business, then dismissal is justified. The conduct here is something other than moral turpitude, disobedience or habitual negligence. [52] A case which is not unusual when considering injurious conduct of the type mentioned above is where an employee solicits business from his employer's customers knowing that he (the employee) is about to commence in business for himself. The principle which applies here would seem to be this: that if the employee is soliciting business when the service relationship is at an end, there is no justification for dismissal. However, if the service relationship is still subsisting, then the employer may justifiably dismiss him and sue for damages for the loss incurred. [53]

If the employee engages in business on his own account and that business is in competition with the business of his employer, he becomes liable to dismissal, even although he can show that he has given full time and attention to the employer's business. [54] As soon as the service relationship is over there is no restriction upon the ex-employee from commencing business on his own account. If he can persuade his former employer's customers to patronise his new business, then it seems that his old employer can do nothing about this. [55] In view of this possible

---

[51] (1837) 15 S. 412.
[52] *Turner* v. *Robinson* (1833) 5 B. & Ad. 789; 6 C. & P. 15; *Read* v. *Dunsmore* (1840) 9 C. & P. 588; and *Lacy* v. *Osbaldiston* (1837) 8 C. & P. 80; also *Amor* v. *Fearon* (1839) 9 A. & E. 548; *Malloch* v. *Duffy* (1882) 19 S.L.R. 697; and *Liverpool, etc., Friendly Society* v. *Houston* (1900) 3 F. 42.
[53] *Nichols* v. *Martin* (1799) 2 Esp. 732.
[54] See *Mercer* v. *Whall* (1845) 5 Q.B. 447; *Hobson* v. *Cowley* (1858) 27 L.J.Ex. 205; also *Cameron and Co.* v. *Gibb* (1867) 3 S.L.R. 282, where it was held to be a breach of the contract of employment for an employee (1) to take time off from his employer's business and devote that time to his own affairs and (2) to carry on a similar business in competition with his employer.
[55] See *Graham* v. *R. and S. Paton*, 1917 S.C. 203, *per* Lord Johnston at p. 207 and Lord Mackenzie at pp. 209–210 on the implied obligations of an employee, in such circumstances.

danger it is not unusual to find somewhat strict restrictive covenants being introduced into the contract of employment so as to prevent the former employee from setting up in business in opposition for a specified number of years and within a certain prescribed area. The question which then arises is whether—looking to the public interest and also to the interests of the parties themselves (and the onus of proof is upon the person claiming to enforce the restriction)—the particular restrictive covenant is wholly or partially enforceable. If it is too wide, then it will be void and unenforceable. This matter has been more fully covered in an earlier chapter.[56]

The basic rule in Scotland seems to be identical with that in England, namely—any agreement by which a man binds himself that he will not carry on a trade of any kind, though limited in space, or alternatively that he will not carry on a particular trade, if unlimited in space, are both equally bad in law.[57]

(11) *Employee's Inventions*

This topic is very often a source of great difficulty and one which causes considerable trouble in trying to reach an equitable and beneficial settlement between the parties.

It is, perhaps, not surprising that the Institutional Writers of Scotland give little or no help on the question of the employee's inventions. There is, of course, in the pages of Stair, Erskine and Bell, a statement of general principles relating to the law of employment, but in no case is this specific topic dealt with by them. Accordingly, our attention must be directed to the works of Fraser [58] and Umpherston,[59] the two leading Scottish authorities on " Master and Servant." The former work deals very briefly with the topic and cites the old English case of *Bloxam* v. *Elsee* [60] as authority for the proposition that, where a master employs a skilful person for the express purpose of inventing, then the inventions belong to the master and he may take out a patent for them. In addition to *Bloxam*, the old Scottish case of *Rollo* v. *Thomson* [61] is cited. In *Rollo's* case the question raised related to ownership of books in which Rollo, an experienced draughtsman employed by Thomsons, had made sketches of all the machinery manufactured by his employers. Finished drawings were made from these sketches, which were themselves revised by the employers. Rollo also claimed that he had purchased the books from the stationers and therefore he must be entitled to them. The First Division of the Court of Session [62] had no difficulty in holding that the books

---

[56] See Chap. 7, *supra.*
[57] See Fraser, p. 91, *op. cit.*
[58] Fraser (P.), *Master and Servant and Master and Apprentice*; first published in 1846 as part of a larger work; 2nd ed. 1872; 3rd ed. 1882.
[59] Umpherston (F. A.), *Law of Master and Servant*, 1904.
[60] 1 C. & P. 558; Abbott (1827) 6 B. & C. 169.
[61] (July 14, 1857) 19 D. 994.
[62] See particularly the opinions of the Lord President (M'Neill) at p. 995 and of Lord Deas at pp. 995–996 of the report.

belonged to Thomsons, relying principally upon the facts that the drawings were made in furtherance of their business and moreover the work in the books was a combined effort. There was no original work in the books, to which Rollo could point as being his very own. The fact that Rollo had paid the stationers for the books was immaterial, because he had the authority to buy in the firm's name in any case and to have the books charged to Thomsons.

A case, not unlike Rollo's in certain respects, was that of *Martin and Ors.* v. *Boyd*,[63] which also went to the First Division, on appeal. Here Boyd, a solicitor acting for the heritors of a parish, had prepared an elaborate scheme of rental which he had had engrossed in a book which belonged to his clients. The book also contained particulars of sums received by Boyd for his clients, accounts of his expenses and receipts. The court had no difficulty in holding that the book belonged to the heritors—because it was prepared in their service and was paid for by them—and, accordingly, when Boyd's duties were completed, the book had to be returned to the heritors. The opinion of the Lord President [64] is quite clear. Lord Shand [65] makes an interesting observation, which is of course *obiter*. He points out that Boyd would have been successful had he been able to show either that he held a position quite independent of the heritors or that the document(s) was in fact his and not theirs. This, of course, Boyd was quite unable to do in the circumstances. Mr. Umpherston [66] cites the foregoing case in support of the general proposition that as the employee engages to give services to his employer in return for wages, the property of whatever is produced by his labour in the employment is in the employer. Again, under the same proposition, if an architect is engaged to prepare plans for a house, these plans belong to the employing client, unless the architect can show by proof of custom to the contrary that he is entitled to them.[67]

The same rule would apply where the employee was taken on for the specific purpose of making inventions or discoveries, pertaining to his employer's business,[68] and also to the copyright in literary productions by a person employed to do literary work. Here it is his inventive faculty or ability which ensures his getting the appointment in the first place. In the cases of *Walter* v. *Howe* [68] and *Lamb* v. *Evans* [68] the question concerned ownership of copyright under the old Copyright Act 1842 [69] and need not detain us here.

Where, however, the servant's invention is not part of the work which he engaged to perform, then he, and not his employer, is entitled to the

---

[63] (1882) 19 S.L.Rep. 447.
[64] See p. 448 of the report.
[65] See pp. 448 and 449 of the report.
[66] *Op. cit.* p. 51.
[67] *Lindsay* v. *MacKenzie* (1883) 2 Guthrie's Sh.Ct. Cases 498.
[68] See the English cases of: *Walter* v. *Howe* (1881) L.R. 17 Ch.D. 708; and *Lamb* v. *Evans* [1893] 1 Ch. 218.
[69] 5 & 6 Vict. c. 45 (s. 18 in particular); see thereafter the Copyright Acts 1911 and 1956 respectively.

patent for the invention, even although the invention is made during the employment and while the service relationship still exists.[70] In the most recent Scottish case,[71] the defender, Michaelis, who was at all material times the employee of the I Company was appointed a part-time general manager of the pursuers. He later patented a ventilation fitting, using materials of the I Company in his researches. He was not employed by the pursuers in connection with ventilation accessories, but the pursuers claimed to be entitled to the benefit of the patent. It was held, in the sheriff court, that the defender did not hold the invention on trust for the pursuers but was himself entitled to the patent right and benefit. There is no real difficulty about this case because it is immediately obvious that the discovery by Michaelis was in no way connected with his service obligations to the pursuers. Of course, the question between Michaelis and his main employers, the I Company, as to the benefit right in the invention was quite another matter but it did not arise in the present action.

The dearth of recent Scottish decisions on this difficult question of the right to the benefit of an employee's invention necessitates our considering certain of the main English cases which are in point. It is probably right to accept that the broad legal principles governing this topic are the same in Scotland and England. The Scottish courts will consider the " persuasive influence " of the English decisions though not generally holding themselves bound by the English cases, excepting perhaps decisions of the House of Lords on points of law, where the law is the same in both countries.

Two of the earlier of the English cases [72] do not raise much difficulty. In *Moore's* case, the service contract between him and his employers contained no express covenant as to patents, and it was terminated by the dismissal of the employee. The former employers applied for, and were granted, an injunction (interdict in Scotland) against their former employee restraining him from infringing certain patents taken out in his own name during the subsistence of the agreement. Had the court permitted the employee to infringe these patents for the benefit of new employers this would have been tantamount to the condonation of an act of bad faith. The most recent case, along similar lines, is *British Syphon Co. Ltd.* v. *Homewood* [73] where the court (Roxburgh J.) again found for the plaintiff company, stressing that it would not be consistent with good faith to allow the defendant to dispose of an invention, relating specifically to the employer's business, as he (the employee) might think fit. In

---

[70] See *Mellor* v. *William Beardmore and Co.*, 1927 S.C. 597, wherein the Second Division awarded the sum of £1,075 (with interest) on the basis of recompense, not implied contract; the patent right remained with pursuer (he was not generally employed to make inventions or solve engineering problems).

[71] *Anemostat (Scotland)* v. *Michaelis* [1957] R.P.C. 167.

[72] *Workington Pumping Engine Co.* v. *Moore* (1902) 19 T.L.R. 84; and *British Reinforced Concrete Engineering Co.* v. *Lind* (1917) 86 L.J.(Ch.) 486.

[73] [1956] 2 All E.R. 897.

Lind's case the defendant, a draughtsman in the employment of the plaintiffs, was instructed to prepare designs for linings or headings in a colliery. During his inspections of the mine, in connection with his duties, the defendant made a discovery which he subsequently patented. The plaintiffs claimed the benefit of the patent on the ground that the discovery arose directly out of and during the defendant's service with them. The court declared that the defendant must hold the patent as trustee for the employers. *Lind's* case was not followed in the subsequent Scottish case of *Mellor* v. *William Beardmore and Co.*[74] but, of course, the facts and circumstances were quite different. Lind's discovery was very closely related to his daily job and arose out of it. Mellor's inventions were coincidental with but not closely related to his daily task.

But, it is to the comparatively recent English decisions of *Triplex Safety Glass Co.* v. *Scorah*[75]; *British Celanese Ltd.* v. *Moncrieff*[76]; and *Sterling Engineering Co. Ltd.* v. *Patchett*[77] that reference must be made to attempt to identify the modern view of the courts.

In the *Triplex* case, the defendant, Scorah, was an assistant chemist, and he undertook, in his service contract with the plaintiff company, to communicate to the company any processes discovered by him and to assign to the company any patents granted to him. The service contract also contained a clause, in general terms, that all available information gained by the defendant should be communicated to the company and such information should then become the exclusive property of the company. Defendant made certain discoveries in 1932 (which the company did not use) and prior to leaving plaintiff's service on April 30, 1934, had also communicated to the company certain discoveries made before that date. After leaving the plaintiff company's employment, defendant made another discovery (which was related to his earlier discoveries in that it concerned acrylic acid) which was not for the use or purpose of safety glass (plaintiff's business) but for the purpose of laboratory glass. The patent, however, would have prevented the plaintiff company from using a certain type of acid in connection with the manufacture of safety glass, which they wished to do. Negotiations with the defendant for purchase of the patent were unsuccessful, with the result that the company brought the action for declaration that they were entitled to have the patent assigned to them. The court, looking at the general clause (as mentioned above) of the agreement and the particular circumstances, *held* (1) that the general clause was too wide in its effect once the employment had ceased and therefore it was unenforceable, but (2) the defendant was a trustee of the invention for the company and was bound to assign his rights therein, subject to his being indemnified as to costs to which he might be put. Farwell J.,[78] after disposing of the question of the clause in

---

[74] 1927 S.C. 597.
[75] [1938] Ch. 211; [1937] 4 All E.R. 693.
[76] [1948] 2 All E.R. 44.
[77] [1955] A.C. 534; [1955] 1 All E.R. 369.
[78] See [1937] 4 All E.R. 693 at pp. 697–699 inclusive.

general terms, turned his attention to the question of defendant's obligation to his employers, quite apart from the express contract. His lordship explained that, where any invention or discovery was made in the course of the employment by an employee, who was doing that which he was engaged to do and instructed to do, during working hours and using his employers' materials, it was an implied term of the employment, apart altogether from express covenants, that the invention or discovery was the property of the employers. The employee then became a trustee for his employer of the invention or discovery and was bound, as trustee, to give the benefit thereof to his employer, at any rate during the employment. Only the beneficiaries could release him from that obligation—which they had not done in all the circumstances here, and accordingly the plaintiff company must succeed.

In 1948 the case of *British Celanese Ltd.* v. *Moncrieff*[79] came before the Court of Appeal. Here the defendant was employed as a research chemist under a service contract which (i) provided *inter alia* that he would treat as confidential the affairs of the (plaintiff) company and would not divulge them during his employment or for five years thereafter and (ii) contained an agreement (in clause 5 of the service contract) or undertaking by defendant that, so long as he was bound by the contract, he would communicate to the company all inventions or improvements which he might make or discover. All such inventions or discoveries were to become the sole exclusive property of the company, without payment, and defendant was to apply, if required by the company, for all letters patent or other protection in all such countries as the company might stipulate. The company agreed to pay such remuneration in respect of the inventions, etc., as it thought reasonable. Defendant made certain inventions in 1943 and patents were applied for in Great Britain for these. By a subsequent agreement (contained, in fact, in a letter) made between the parties on June 29, 1945, the original service contract was " terminated " and a new clause 3 (a) was substituted for clause 4 of the original service contract (apparently repeating it almost in its entirety[80]) but no new clause was inserted in the 1945 agreement (the " leaving " agreement) which dealt with the future of the subject-matter covered by clause 5 of the original agreement. In 1947 the company asked defendant to assist to obtain patent protection for the inventions in foreign countries, but he refused to do so, claiming that his liability under clause 5 of the original service contract was cancelled by the leaving agreement. The company then applied for a declaration that defendant was a trustee of certain inventions for them and they called for an assignment (assignation, in Scots law) of the defendant's interest in applications for letters patent in certain Dominion and foreign countries. Romer J.[81] granted the appropriate order, upholding the company's claim. Defendant appealed

[79] Cit. supra.
[80] Except for a provision extending defendant's obligation to June 30, 1950.
[81] Reported [1948] 1 All E.R. 123.

but the Court of Appeal dismissed the appeal [82] holding that the effect of the service agreement was to set up the relationship of trustee and beneficiary in respect of the inventions and that the defendant was under a continuing obligation to the company to hold the inventions as their sole exclusive property, because the leaving agreement had not terminated defendant's obligation to execute the documents necessary to enable the company to secure protection in foreign countries. The Court of Appeal took the view that reference in the leaving agreement to clause 5 of the original service contract was unnecessary (as it merely provided machinery) because the obligations in clause 5 were implied by law in defendant's undertaking that the inventions should be the sole exclusive property of the company. The opinion of Lord Greene M.R.,[83] who delivered the judgment of the Court of Appeal, is most instructive. His lordship considered the earlier case of *Vokes Ltd.* v. *Heather* [84] and then went on to explain the opinion of Farwell J. in the *Triplex* case [85] wherein the learned judge had, as explained above, found a relationship of trust arising out of the unwritten contract of employment and therefore this relationship had a contractual basis. Lord Greene M.R. went on to explain further that there was no inconsistency between *Vokes* and *Triplex Glass*, although he did point out [86] that the use of the word " trustee " was not perfectly accurate but that it was a " convenient " term to employ. His lordship was quite clear, however, that the obligation by defendant not to use the inventions for his own purposes and the obligation to hold them as the sole exclusive property of the company were continuing duties, and therefore the defendant was bound and obliged to sign the applications for the foreign patents.

There now remains the case of *Sterling Engineering Co. Ltd.* v. *Patchett*,[87] which went to the House of Lords on appeal. In this case the respondent, Patchett, had made several inventions during the course of his employment and patents had been applied for in the joint names of the respondent and the company. There was a so-called " understanding " as to payment but no express agreement. Respondent applied to the company for payment of royalty but, when they refused this, he sought a declaration of his title to a royalty or, alternatively, he claimed that the benefit of the inventions should be apportioned under section 56 (2) of the Patents Act 1949.[88] At first instance, respondent's claim was dismissed and an order was made later in favour of the company. The Court of Appeal discharged the original order on December 14, 1953, and it was against that subsequent order that the company appealed.

---

[82] [1948] 2 All E.R. 44.
[83] See pp. 45–51, inclusive, of the report.
[84] (1945) 62 R.P.C. 135.
[85] *Cit. supra.*
[86] [1948] 2 All E.R. 44, at p. 48.
[87] *Cit. supra.*
[88] 12, 13 & 14 Geo. 6, c. 87.

The House allowed the appeal [89] holding (i) that the ordinary rule governing the master and servant relationship that, if an employee's invention was patented in joint names of employer and employee, the employee held his interest as trustee for the employer, could only be excluded by an express agreement that it should be varied and some other legal relationship should be created: and here, the ordinary rule had not been displaced; and (ii) that, as the court was satisfied that the appellant company was legally entitled to the benefit of the inventions to the exclusion of the respondent, section 56 (2) of the Patents Act 1949 did not apply.

Much criticism has been made of the House's view of section 56 (2) of the Patents Act 1949. In a short but interesting article,[90] Sir Kenneth R. Swan discussed some of the difficulties which might arise in considering whether the patent rights should go to the employers or to the employee, and he gives two useful examples [91] where there might well be a case for apportionment of the benefit between both parties. However, in the *Sterling* case the House of Lords, reversing the Court of Appeal which favoured apportionment, came down on the side of the employers upon the particular facts of the case. The House did not deem it necessary to consider the question of apportionment in relation to section 56 (2) of the Patents Act 1949. The disquieting feature about the decision is the speech of Lord Reid [92] wherein he discusses, admittedly *obiter*, the application of section 56 (2). His lordship expressed the opinion that in the absence of agreement between the parties there could be no case where one party was not entitled to the whole benefit to the exclusion of the other and, accordingly, the subsection could only come into operation if there were some agreement, either express or implied, to share the benefit. The meaning of the word " entitled," occurring in the said section of the Act, said his lordship, was " legally entitled," although this would result in a very limited operation of the section. It is submitted, with respect, that his lordship is taking too restricted a view of section 56 (2). Until the Act of 1949 was passed, there was no judicial machinery by which the court could make an apportionment of benefit. The writer believes that the intention of the legislature was to remedy the deficiency in the law by permitting the court, or the Comptroller-General of Patents, to apportion the benefit in any case in which it was not immediately apparent that one party was legally entitled to the whole benefit and whether there was an agreement or not (provided always that any such agreement as did exist did not clearly and voluntarily pass the benefit to the employer, in which case apportionment was again unnecessary). Apparently in deciding this question, the court would have to have regard to all the facts and circumstances of the case and then make its

---

[89] See particularly the speeches of Viscount Simonds [1955] 1 All E.R. 370–375 inclusive and Lord Reid at 375–377 inclusive.
[90] " Patent Rights in an Employee's Invention " (1959) 75 L.Q.R. 77.
[91] *Ibid.* p. 78.
[92] [1955] A.C. 546 *et seq.*; [1955] 1 All E.R. 375–377, inclusive.

decision as to apportionment. The existence of an agreement between the parties—whether it be an express one or an implied one—will be a factor in enabling the court (or the Comptroller-General) to reach a decision on the question of the particular apportionment which is reasonable in the circumstances. If there was no agreement at all the court must surely look at the facts and surrounding circumstances of the particular case before it and then, being satisfied that no party is exclusively entitled to the whole benefit of the patent, make an apportionment between the parties upon a just and equitable basis. When the judgment has been made, there is then created in favour of each party a legal right in the benefit of the patent to the extent to which the court has decided. These rights are protected by registration.

Neither the Scottish courts nor the English courts have yet had to decide the full meaning and operation of section 56 (2) of the Patents Act 1949. It might well be that a forward-looking Division of the Court of Session would find that the difficulties envisaged by Lord Reid in Sterling's case were exaggerated and this court might well make an apportionment, within the intended operation of the section. If, in any future case brought under section 56 (2) or relying upon it, the restricted view envisaged by Lord Reid in the Sterling case is taken by the court, this may well result in the parties making separate application to the Comptroller-General or, alternatively, agreeing to refer their difficulties to arbitration for a settlement. The trade unions might have to consider (1) an adaptation of the " shop right rule " as used in the United States of America, although Professor C. Robert Morris Jr., in a fairly recent and very instructive article,[93] in which he traces the development, operation and effect of the rule, explains that this rule was designed primarily to prevent an employee from asserting a patent monopoly against his employer and it gives to these employers a right or licence to practise the invention, or (2) writing an " inventions " clause into every collective agreement and thereafter having this clause carried by implication into the service contracts.

If the true and correct view of section 56 (2) of the Patents Act 1949 is that it is no more than a piece of negative legislation then the sooner it is put right the better. Parliament will not, apparently, take the necessary amending step until it has been shown quite clearly that there is a proper case for replacement of the section. All that can be hoped for meantime is that the court (and preferably the House of Lords as the final appellate tribunal) will be called upon to decide, at a not too distant date, the true meaning of section 56 (2) and by what method it is to be applied. It will be to the advantage of both sides of industry to have this matter decided one way or the other.

A Bill was introduced in Parliament, during 1965, on the subject of employees' inventions, with the intention of adopting the apportionment

---

[93] (1959) 75 L.Q.R. 483 et seq.

method as the fairest means of settlement. It was subsequently withdrawn and has not again been re-introduced.

(12) *Copyright in Literary and Artistic Works*

The legal position in this matter seems to be broadly the same as that relating to patents and inventions. It has been held that a book prepared by a clerk to the heritors of a parish belonged to them as his employers [94]; that plans of a house prepared by an architect belonged to his employing client, unless a contrary custom could be established [95]; and that rough sketches of machinery made by a draughtsman in an engineering establishment belonged to his employers.[96] Although the foregoing cases dealt with ownership as distinct from copyright in the particular productions, the principle is the same. If the literary or artistic production is not reasonably incidental to the employment and not an essential and formal part of it, then it seems that the copyright therein remains with the employee. However, reference must be made to the Copyright Act 1956,[97] section 4 which deals specifically with ownership of copyright in literary, dramatic, musical and artistic works. Subsection (1) states that the author of a work shall—subject to the provisions of section 4—be entitled to any copyright subsisting in it. Subsection (2) deals with the preparation of a literary, dramatic or artistic work by its author in the course of his employment with the proprietor of a newspaper, magazine or similar periodical under a contract of service or apprenticeship and the work in question is intended for publication. Copyright as regards publication and any reproduction for publication purposes rests with the employer; in all other respects it remains with the employee. Subsection (3) relates to photographs, paintings and drawings and engravings commissioned by persons and paid for in money or money's worth: the copyright in such productions belongs to the persons who commissioned them. Subsection (4) specifically states that where the case in point does not fall under subsection (2) or (3) above-mentioned but nevertheless a work is made in the course of the author's employment by another person under a contract of service or apprenticeship, that other person is entitled to the copyright. Subsection (5) permits the parties themselves to make an agreement which may exclude the operation of each of the subsections (2), (3) and (4) in any particular case.

The phrase in the statute which requires special attention is " in the course of his employment " where it occurs in subsections (2) and (4). The ordinary meaning attaching to these words, when used in the field of industrial law and employers' liability, is: in the course of the work which the employee is employed to do and whatever is incidental to that work.

---

[94] *Martin* v. *Boyd* (1882) 19 S.L.R. 447.
[95] *Lindsay* v. *Mackenzie* (1883) 2 Guthrie's Sh.Ct. Cases 498.
[96] *Rollo* v. *Thomson* (1857) 19 D. 994; but see *Earl of Crawford* v. *Paton* (O.H.) 1910, 1 S.L.T. 423; and thereafter 1911 S.C. 1017; 1911 2 S.L.T. 67.
[97] 4 & 5 Eliz. 2, c. 74.

If something purely coincidental with the employee's daily job is done or made or produced, then that particular thing is not done, made or produced in the course of X's (*i.e.*, the employee in question) employment. The case of *St. Helen's Colliery Co. Ltd.* v. *Hewitson* [98] indicates that the phrase does not simply mean during the currency of a contract of employment. It should be reasonably obvious that advantage should be taken of the general import of subsection (5)—and not just of its machinery for excluding subsections (2), (3) and (4)—by having a clause inserted in the contract of employment which will deal with copyright, patents and inventions. It is not unusual to find in modern industrial practice that firms make use of bonus and other incentive awards for the inventive employee who submits his ideas for improvement in machine products, systems, output methods, production control and others, to management, whether by way of the " suggestion box " or direct to the general manager, works manager or other responsible official. Substantial money payments are very often made in this way. This is a practice which should be encouraged, particularly as it gives the employee a technical interest in the business and the employer a better opportunity of achieving improved industrial efficiency (and thereby increasing his profits).

---

[98] *St. Helen's Colliery Co. Ltd.* v. *Hewitson* [1924] A.C. 59; (1924) 40 T.L.R. 125. See the speech of Lord Wrenbury.

CHAPTER 10

EMPLOYER'S DUTIES AND RESPONSIBILITIES GENERALLY

As a corollary to the duties owed by an employee, there must now be considered the corresponding duties and obligations owed by an employer to his employees. At the same time, account must be taken of changing attitudes in modern industrial relations which may have had some impact upon the old common law obligations.

(1) *Acceptance of Employee*

The employer's primary duty is to take the employee into his employment and to allow him to continue therein.[1] The exceptions to these obligations are considered elsewhere in this volume under the headings of "termination" and "justifiable dismissal." If an agreement has no fixed term of endurance, any action by an employee wherein he alleges breach of that agreement may be held to be irrelevant, even although the contract is one which purports to give the employee regular employment.[2]

(2) *To Treat the Employee Properly*

The nature of the relationship requires a mutual respect for each other—a forbearance, lenity and reserve in using the service and a mildness in giving orders.[3] It has already been explained in the previous chapter that an employee must impliedly give obedience, submission, loyalty and respect to his employer. Equally there is implied upon the employer an obligation of protection and moderation in the treatment of his employee. The test as to whether an employee may leave his employment because the employer is not fulfilling his obligation has to be a test of reasonableness in the circumstances. The law does not, and can hardly be expected to, protect the over-sensitive employee. The employee cannot leave, with any justification, upon the ground that his employer is always gruff or bad-tempered in his manner or perhaps even just generally disagreeable. Something more is needed—perhaps personal violence or threat of such; the habitual use of intemperate language; or acts of cruelty such as destroy the relationship which, as has been said above, should be based upon mutual trust and mutual respect.[4] The court will

---

[1] Bell's *Principles*, s. 182; *Bracegirdle* v. *Heald*, 1 B. & Ald. 722; *Clarke* v. *Allatt*, 4 C.B. 335.
[2] *Lawrie* v. *Brown & Co. Ltd.*, 1908 S.C. 705; (1908) 15 S.L.T. 981.
[3] See Fraser, *Master and Servant*, p. 124, quoting from Paley's *Moral and Political Philosophy.*
[4] See particularly Bankton 1, 2, 55; and *Smart* v. *Gairns* (1794) Hume's *Decisions* 18, as to cruel treatment of an apprentice.

look at the circumstances of each case [5] and whilst the decision in any one case of this type may be a guide to a set of circumstances arising subsequently it should not necessarily be regarded as a precedent. The court will obviously prefer to look at each case upon its own facts and circumstances and it will also be concerned to see that the principle of " natural justice " is in no way transgressed by the employer.[6]

One aspect of the authority which the employer had over his employee is illustrated by the former so-called right of personal chastisement. Erskine [7] took the view that the employer had a power of moderate chastisement over his employees. Later writers have opposed that view because there was no need, they said, for an employer to have such power. In any case this so-called power could be used as an instrument of torture or oppression. It is conceded that, in earlier days, when young employees and apprentices spent their time at the employer's place of work or in his house, some quasi-parental authority was necessary and the practice of mild chastisement might have been acceptable.[8] It is submitted that this former power of chastisement (whether " mild " or not) must be completely disregarded in modern law. The same is probably true of the master and apprenticeship relationship also, in which the concept of personal chastisement had been more readily and understandably accepted. It may be that today the only person or quasi-employer with a power to chastise those who work under him is the ship's master and he is protected by the Merchant Shipping Acts. There is no doubt whatsoever that the legal position of a ship's master, so far as the law of employment is concerned, is that he is an employee. In the general case of employer and employee there is no need for personal chastisement when the law permits dismissal (justifiable) to the employer and an action in damages to the employee.

The female employee would be entitled to leave the service if her employer had attempted to seduce her.[9] In such a case the employer is due to pay her wages for the whole period of the contract of employment and perhaps also to pay for such further loss or damage as she has suffered.

Most importantly, as soon as a good reason for leaving arises, the employee should depart at once. If he does not do so he will be held to have condoned the particular act complained of and will then have debarred himself from founding upon it.[10]

---

[5] Wood, *Master and Servant*, s. 146.
[6] *Palmer* v. *Inverness Hospitals Board of Management* (O.H.) 1963 S.L.T. 124. See also Chap. 17 *infra*, *re* the trade union position.
[7] Erskine, I, 7, 62.
[8] See Blackstone 6, 1, c. 14; and *Winstone* v. *Linn*, 1 B. & C. 469; 2 D. & R. 465.
[9] See *McLean* v. *Miller* (1832) 5 Deas' Rep. 270; also *Gray* v. *Miller* (1901) 39 S.L.R. 256; and *Reid* v. *Macfarlane*, 1919 S.C. 518; 1919, 2 S.L.T. 24 (the last-mentioned case being most interesting for the observations it contains regarding the evidence necessary to prove seduction by the employer).
[10] See the opinion of Lord President Inglis in *Fraser* v. *Laing* (1878) 5 R. 596 (a catalogue of grievances cannot be brought up and founded upon as a ground for damages where a domestic servant has remained in the service for the full period).

(3) *To Provide Work*

It is accepted that wages are payable (a) in proportion to the amount of work done, *i.e.*, piecework; or (b) according to the time served. In the former case the employer appears to be bound to provide constant employment during the subsistence of the agreement.[11] In the latter case there is generally no obligation to provide work [12] and wages must be paid on the agreed basis although the employee be merely standing by doing nothing.

It may also be that there is an implied obligation to provide work, for example, where the employee is an actor, concert pianist or other person who has to maintain a reputation before the public or whose business interests require him to maintain contact with a particular market. It is, furthermore, important to note that where the contract is a written one its terms provide the basis of the agreement and the employer cannot say that he has an implied right or privilege of varying these terms. This one employer tried to do in an old case,[13] claiming that as new raw material supplied was of better quality and more easily processed in manufacture, he was entitled to reduce the piecework rate of wages. The court refused, however, to accept his contention.

The question of implied terms had also arisen in certain English cases decided not long after the above-mentioned Scottish case. For example, in one instance, there was a written agreement between employers (colliery owners) and the employee in which it was stipulated that, when the pit was idle, the employee should continue to serve and be subject to his employers' orders and directions and should perform a full day's work on every working day. The court held that the employers were not bound to employ the plaintiff on all reasonable working days or to create work for him in order that he might obtain employment.[14] There was nothing imperative in the agreement. In a later case the agreement with a collier provided that wages should be paid fortnightly and that he should not be discharged without twenty-one days' notice in writing, except in the case of misconduct. It was held that this implied an obligation to find work for the employee and to pay him wages every fortnight.[15]

The trend, where the question of an implied obligation has arisen, of the more recent decisions has been to support the general principle that there is no obligation upon an employer to provide work. It must be said that most of these decisions are from England [16] but, nevertheless,

---

[11] Bell's *Principles,* c. 192; *Cowdenbeath Coal Co.* v. *Drylie* (1886) 3 Sh.Ct.Rep. 3 at p. 11; *Turner* v. *Goldsmith* [1891] 1 Q.B. 544 (wages here were payable by commission and it was held that the employer was bound to give the opportunity of earning it).

[12] *Lagerwall* v. *Wilkinson* (1899) 80 L.T. 55; *Turner* v. *Sawdon* [1901] 2 K.B. 653.

[13] *Grieve* v. *Gordon* (1821) 1 S. 41.

[14] See *Williamson* v. *Taylor* (1843) 13 L.J.Q.B. 81; *Hartley* v. *Cummings* (1847) 17 L.J.C.P. 84; and *Pilkington* v. *Scott* (1846) 15 M. & W. 657.

[15] See *Whittle* v. *Frankland* (1862) 2 B. & S. 49; also *Cook* v. *Sherwood* (1863) 11 W.R. 595.

[16] See *Clayton* v. *Oliver* [1930] A.C. 209; 99 L.J.K.B. 165; 46 T.L.R. 230; *Turner* v. *Sawdon* [1901] 2 K.B. 653; *Marbe* v. *George Edwardes Ltd.* [1928] 1 K.B. 269; 96 L.J.K.B. 980; 43 T.L.R 809; but see *Withers* v. *General Theatre Corporation* [1933]

this is a topic upon which, it is submitted, there is no variation between the laws of Scotland and England.

(4) *To Provide Food and Lodging*

It will depend upon the terms of the agreement or upon the nature of the service whether or not an employer is bound to provide food and lodging for his employee. Most commonly, this obligation will arise towards the domestic employee [17] and any failure in performance of that obligation will allow the employee to leave the service. Before leaving, however, the employee has a duty to notify the employer of her grievance, and so give him a chance to put matters right. Once the grievance has been reported and nothing has been done about it, then it is in order for the employee to leave.[18] Lord Fraser says [19] that, so far as lodgings are concerned, the employer may compel a male domestic employee to reside out of the house upon paying board wages, but he cannot do so in the case of the female employee because it is implied in her engagement that she shall have the protection of the employer's house and family.

Mr. Umpherston explains [20] that it is not uncommon in agricultural service—and perhaps in other cases too, by agreement—for the employer to allow to the employee a specified quantity of meal, potatoes, coal, etc., although the employee has not necessarily a right to demand these particular items. It seems, however, that the agricultural employee is absolutely entitled to a certain quantity of sustenance or fuel.[21] The case just cited (*i.e., Sheills* v. *Dalyell*) supports the view that the employer may not make any change in the specific articles supplied unless the circumstances become so extraordinary and unforeseen as to make the fulfilment of the letter of the contract impracticable.

This question was perhaps important to the employee in the Victorian era, but it is of little significance today, certainly since the close of the Second World War. Oddly enough, however, it has reappeared in modern business life in the form of luncheon vouchers. These constitute an added inducement to employees to remain in a particular employment or to prospective employees to join that particular establishment. Certain tax reliefs and expenses are obtainable under this arrangement, but these are tax law and accounting matters and need not detain us. The employee is concerned to know whether or not the provision of luncheon vouchers has become a term or condition of the contract of employment. This is an important matter for him as it means the conferment of a benefit upon him which is equivalent to a rise in wages of, say, twenty shillings per week.

---

2 K.B. 536; 102 L.J.K.B. 719; also *Collier* v. *Sunday Referee Publishing Co.* [1940] 2 K.B. 647; 109 L.J.K.B. 974; 57 T.L.R. 2; and *Re Reubel Bronze Co.* [1918] 1 K.B. 315; 87 L.J.K.B. 466; 34 T.L.R. 171.

[17] Bell's *Principles*, s. 182; Bankton 1, 2, 55; 2 Hutch. 170.
[18] Fraser, *op. cit.* p. 127.
[19] Fraser, *loc. cit.* and note (*b*) thereof.
[20] *Master and Servant*, p. 72.
[21] See *Sheills* v. *Dalyell* (1825) 4 S. 136.

It is also relevant to this particular section to consider briefly whether there was or is any obligation upon an employer to provide medical aid or medical attendance for his employees. It seems to have been accepted generally at common law that there was no obligation upon an employer to provide medicine or medical attendance during illness. Nor was any exception to this rule made where the illness was caused by an injury received in the service or during residence in the employer's household.[22] Mr. Umpherston has suggested [23] that the employer's obligation of protection, in the case of female and young domestic employees, implied a quasi-parental care of and for an employee's health and morals, similar to the master and apprentice relationship of the eighteenth and early nineteenth centuries. He also thought that such an obligation might, in certain circumstances, include the provision of medical attendance. In support of this view he quoted the case of *Jeffrey* v. *Donald* [24] where a young female domestic employee was injured within the household and subsequently died without the employer having sent for a doctor or having communicated with the girl's parents until three days after the accident. Whilst agreeing that the particular decision was justified upon a failure to fulfil his duty of protection, Mr. Umpherston submits [25] that the employer's conduct in the circumstances given above was not just a moral delinquency but a failure in a legal obligation, because the employee was, at the relevant time, subject to the employer's control and being helpless, such an emergency imposed a legal duty on the employer to obtain medical assistance.[26] This is certainly a very sound argument. The question of the legal duty of care imposed upon the employer in similar circumstances came up again in certain later cases [27] and these are regarded as being very soundly decided. English law appears to take a similar view of the duty of care so imposed. A breach of that legal duty gives rise to an action in damages which is grounded in delict. Statute law may, however, impose a special duty upon an employer in respect of certain medical services.[28]

The employer could, however, undertake liability for medical attendance, whether expressly or impliedly. When he did this, the liability was limited to the extent of the undertaking.[29] He could not make any deduction from wages in respect of that medical attendance, unless he was able to point to a stipulation to that effect.[30] Where the employee calls in his own doctor, then he alone is responsible for the fees paid to that

---

[22] See *Sellen* v. *Norman* (1829) 4 C. & P. 80; *Mitchell* v. *Adam* (1874) 1 Guthrie's Sh.Ct. Cases 361.
[23] *Op. cit.* p. 66.
[24] (1901) 9 S.L.T. 199.
[25] *Op. cit.* p. 67.
[26] See *Taylor* v. *Hill* (1900) 7 S.L.T. 318.
[27] See particularly *McKeating* v. *Frame*, 1921 S.C. 382.
[28] See, for example, the Factories Act 1961, s. 11, and the Mines and Quarries Act 1954, ss. 91, 92 and 115.
[29] *Montgomery* v. *North British Railway Co.* (1878) 5 R. 796.
[30] *Mitchell* v. *Adam* (1874) 1 Guthrie's Sh.Ct. Cases 361.

doctor,[31] except that no fees may be payable if the employee is a registered patient of the particular doctor under the National Health Scheme.

In view of the developments in National Health Insurance Schemes and Industrial Injuries benefits [32] during the twentieth century, and in particular since the introduction of the state schemes in 1946, this question of an obligation in the nature of a broad, general, quasi-parental protection is not so important as formerly, although the obligation of a legal duty of care towards the employee still remains with the employer in modern law.

It is interesting to note that the Conspiracy and Protection of Property Act 1875 [33] makes it a criminal offence, punishable by fine or imprisonment and after a summary conviction, for an employer who is legally liable to provide for his employee or apprentice necessary food, clothing, medical aid or lodging, to refuse or neglect to provide such food, etc.

(5) *Employer's Common Law Obligations*

The common law imposed and continues to impose upon the employer a three-fold obligation, *videlicet*:
  (a) to provide and maintain suitable materials;
  (b) to keep premises safe and work upon a safe system; and
  (c) to exercise care in the selection of fellow-employees.

The obligation attaches to the employer *qua* employer. Accordingly, if the system of working were dangerous or if he employed young or inexperienced workers on dangerous work for which they were quite unsuited, the employer could not—before the doctrine of common employment disappeared—and still cannot today evade his liability by pleading delegation to a foreman or other manager, who is also an employee. Since the passing of the Law Reform (Personal Injuries) Act 1948 [34]—which abolished the doctrine of common employment—the common law three-fold obligation above-mentioned has become less important in certain respects, although it does remain relevant in any reparation claim which is brought at common law by an employee against his employer.

It will be necessary to consider the common law obligation in much more detail, and it is proposed to do this in the following chapter, where the liability of an employer to his employees (i) at common law and (ii) by statute, is more fully examined.

(6) *To Indemnify the Employee for Injury Sustained in Employment*

Lord Fraser considers the application of the Employers' Liability Act 1880 to this general question of indemnity by the employer and he also asks whether the statute was intended to abrogate the common law.

---

[31] *Cunningham* v. *Weir* (1868) 1 Guthrie's Sh.Ct. Cases 358.
[32] See particularly the National Health Service (Scotland) Acts; the National Insurance Act 1965 and the National Insurance (Industrial Injuries) Act 1965.
[33] 38 & 39 Vict. c. 86, s. 6.
[34] 11 & 12 Geo. 6, c. 41.

He resolves, however, that it did not do so and that the employee could still elect to sue under the Act or at common law (or perhaps both).[35] The common law position of the employer in relation to his own personal fault seems to be clear.   Every employer is bound to conduct his business so as not to endanger the lives and limbs of his workmen, either recklessly or unnecessarily.   If he acts recklessly or carelessly or neglects to take proper precautions, he becomes liable in damages for the resultant injury.

The employee, for his part, is regarded as contemplating and assuming all ordinary risks of the particular employment, even where the work is highly dangerous.   No employer is an insurer against all risks, so far as the common law is concerned.   Statute law may, however, place an absolute duty upon an employer, for example, the absolute requirement that prime-movers in factories must be fenced.

The general principle seems to be that the employer is responsible for injuries whose causes ought to have been foreseen by him and against which precautions ought to have been taken, for example, injuries resulting from defective machinery, lack of safety equipment, incompetent foremen and the like.   The employee may have as good a chance as the employer of becoming aware of the danger or of appreciating the danger.   He may indeed continue to work without objection or he may willingly assume a greater risk than is necessary for the proper performance of his task or he may act contrary to orders.   In all such cases, he will lose the right of recourse against the employer; the principle of *volenti non fit injuria* will be applicable.[36]   The obligation upon the employer is that of using "reasonable care."   One of the most important early cases on this point

---

[35] *Op. cit.* pp. 172–174.

[36] See *M'Neill* v. *Wallace* (1835) 15 D. 818; *Gray* v. *Lawson* (1860) 22 D. 710; *Cook* v. *Bell* (1857) 20 D. 137; and *O'Neill* v. *Wilson* (1858) 20 D. 427.   See also Lord Curriehill's opinion in *Cook* v. *Bell, supra,* and that of L.J.-C. Hope in *Paterson* v. *Wallace* (1855) 17 D. 623 (and remarks on this latter case by Lord Cranworth in *Bartonshill Coal Co.* v. *Reid* (1858) 3 M'Q. 286).   *Paterson's* case was reversed on appeal but the principle of knowledge of risk on the employee's part was fully accepted.   The principle was raised again in *Wallace* v. *Culter Paper Mills Co. Ltd.* (1892) 19 R. 915, where an employee was killed whilst pointing out a defect in a machine to his employer's engineer. The machine was proved to have been dangerous.   Employers were held liable.   The court took the view that, where an employee continues to work in the knowledge of existing danger, there is no implied agreement by him to relieve the employers of their responsibility.   In other words, the court said that *scientia* is insufficient; the employee must be *volens, i.e.,* willingly assume the risk and undertake to relieve the employer of liability.   Nothing less than that will do.   The opinions of Lord Adam and Lord M'Laren are helpful and both were satisfied that the leading English case of *Smith* v. *Baker and Sons* [1891] A.C. 325, decided the year before by the House of Lords, ought to be followed because the principle of law in both countries was the same on this matter.

In *Wilkinson* v. *Kinneil Cannel Coking & Coal Company Ltd.* (1897) 24 R. 1001, a court of seven judges allowed an issue on the *volenti* principle—and more importantly perhaps on the "volunteer" principle (which was later to become well known in England in such cases as *Haynes* v. *Harwood* [1935] 1 K.B. 146; [1934] All E.R. 103). Once again the *volenti* principle arose in *Robertson* v. *Primrose and Co.,* 1910 S.C. 111, when the First Division recalled an interlocutor of the Lord Ordinary and allowed an issue (and jury proof), following *Smith* v. *Baker & Sons Ltd., supra.*   L.P. Dunedin's opinion (pp. 114 and 115) is most valuable.   The plea of *volenti* has arisen regularly in reparation cases ever since.   In the recent case of *Kirkham* v. *Cementation Co.* (O.H.) 1964 S.L.T. (Notes) 33 it was repelled because the defender's averments could not support it.

is the English case of *Priestley* v. *Fowler*,[37] where the plaintiff was employed by a butcher and was carried on the butcher's van in the course of his employment. On the occasion in question, the van was overloaded, a wheel collapsed and the plaintiff was injured. He did not aver that the defendant knew about the overloading or the defect in the vehicle. Lord Abinger refused to extend the doctrine of vicarious liability, but he did indicate *obiter* that there was a general duty upon an employer to take reasonable care for the safety of his servants. This case has been accepted as an important precedent in later cases. It is more widely known as the forerunner or ancestor of the doctrine of common employment—the American courts taking a similar view some short time later in *Farwell* v. *Boston and Worcester Rail Road Corporation*.[38] Illustrating the principle that no liability attaches to the employer when full knowledge of the risks exists in the employee are several well-known old cases.[39] If the danger is concealed from the employee or if he is led to believe (or might reasonably believe) that proper precautions are to be taken, and an accident happens, the employer will be liable. Where the employee is well aware of the danger and continues in his employment or neglects to take the precautions open to him to avoid the risk, he has, in the general case, no right of recourse against the employer.[40]

A situation may arise wherein the employee might be said to have been induced by the employer to continue work which was dangerous, even although the employee knew perfectly well that it was dangerous and has complained of it. Does the law then regard him as having assumed the risk ? Apparently not.[41] The opinion of Cockburn C.J. is most instructive. He drew a clear distinction between the case where an employee knowingly enters into a contract to work upon defective machinery, and the other case where, upon a defect arising, the employee is induced by the employer, to whose notice the defect has now been brought, to continue in the employment and perform his service in the usual manner, under a promise that the defect will be remedied.

The English case of *Holmes* v. *Clarke* [41] is not too easily reconciled with the Scottish case of *Crichton* v. *Keir* [42] where defenders knowingly supplied an unfit horse, but induced the pursuer to continue his work, promising him another horse. Pursuer's averments showed that he was well aware of the risk and the court held that he had no ground of action.

37 (1837) 3 M. & W. 1. See also *Riley* v. *Baxendale* (1861) 30 L.J.Ex. 87; and *Ogden* v. *Rummens* (1863) 3 F. & F. 751.
38 (1842) 4 Metcalf 49.
39 See *Woodley* v. *Metropolitan District Railway Co.* (1877) 2 Ex.D. 384; *Assop.* v. *Yates*, 27 L.J.Ex. 156; *Saxton* v. *Hawksworth* (1872) 26 L.T. 851; *Skipp* v. *Eastern Counties Railway Co.*, 23 L.J.Ex. 23; and *Robertson* v. *Adamson* (1862) 24 D. 1231.
40 *McNeill* v. *Wallace*; *Gray* v. *Lawson*; and *O'Neill* v. *Wilson*, *cit. supra*.
41 See *Holmes* v. *Clarke* (1862) 31 L.J.Ex. 356 (where fencing had broken and the employer had promised to replace it. Accordingly, there was an element of personal negligence involved, quite apart from breach of statutory duty, as an additional ground of action); also *Holmes* v. *Worthington* (1861) 2 F. & F. 533.
42 (1863) 1 M. 407 (opinion of L.J.-C. Inglis is important on the points raised).

He ought to have refused to continue working in the face of manifest danger.

Although the employer may have been negligent, nevertheless he escaped liability under the old law if he could show that the employee's own recklessness or negligence materially contributed to the accident.[43] The Employers' Liability Act 1880 (since repealed), whilst making very important limitations upon the old common law principles of common employment (or the " fellow-servant " doctrine), made no change whatsoever in the position of the employer who could plead contributory negligence on the part of the employee such as to contribute materially to the accident. Although a modification of the strict common law rule upon contributory negligence (which excused an employer absolutely if the employee had contributed in any way to his own injury) was sought by the employed classes and by the trade unions, it was not until the year 1945 that a major change occurred. The Law Reform (Contributory Negligence) Act 1945 [44] enabled the jury or the court (if no jury was sitting) to assess the total amount of the loss arising from the accident and then to apportion the blame between the pursuer and defender. Damages would then be awarded (if appropriate) against the defender, based upon the jury's assessment of his responsibility for the accident, *i.e.*, his percentage of blameworthiness must be taken into account. If no blame could be attached to the pursuer, then he would receive the full sum arrived at by the iury.[45] Solatium and expenses of the action would also require to be taken into account, and a deduction of one-half of the amount of any industrial injury benefit received also fell to be made. This Act was a very important measure indeed and enabled actions to be brought with a reasonable measure of success,[46] though prior to that the employee was virtually without any remedy.

One very important question, which may well settle at once the question of the employer's liability in the circumstances, is whether or not the employee was acting within the scope of his employment at the time when the accident occurred.[47] Where, however, the employee clearly volunteers to do something outwith the scope of his duties, then the risk of injury lies with him alone and he cannot hold his employer responsible.[48]

Where there is a latent danger in the particular operation, and the employer knows, or ought to have known, of this and neglects to inform

---

[43] See, as a matter of historical interest, the cases of *Senior* v. *Ward* (1859) 28 L.J.Q.B. 139; *McNaughton* v. *Caledonian Railway Co.* (1858) 21 D. 160; also *McMartin* v. *Hannay* (1872) 10 M. 413; *Galloway* v. *King* (1872) 10 M. 788; *Dublin, etc., Railway Co.* v. *Slattery* (1878) 3 App.Cas. 1166; *Radley* v. *London and North-Western Railway Co.* (1876) 1 App.Cas. 754; also Fraser, *op. cit.*, Chap. 13.

[44] 8 & 9 Geo. 6, c. 28.

[45] See Professor D. M. Walker, *Law of Delict in Scotland* (1966), p. 364 *et seq.*

[46] See Professor D. M. Walker, *Law of Damages in Scotland* (1955), pp. 779–781.

[47] See *Marshall and Others* v. *Stewart* (1852) 14 D. 596; rev. (1855) 2 M'Q. 30; Paterson, Appeal Reports 447; see also remarks by Lord Cranworth upon this case in *Bartonshill Coal Co.* v. *Reid* (1858) 3 M'Q. 286; Paterson, Appeal Reports 793.

[48] See *Sutherland* v. *Monkland Railways Co.* (1857) 19 D. 1004.

the employee, then the employer will be liable for injury to the employee.[49] The rule is the same where the danger is not obvious to a person in the employee's position and where the latter might reasonably be held to have relied upon the judgment of his employer for his protection.[50] The employer may also be liable if he is guilty of negligence and the risk involved is not incidental to the service.[51]

On the subject of machinery, the position at common law is clearly that the employer must provide reliable and sufficient machinery—but it need not be the very latest, up-to-the-minute appliance produced within the particular industry [52]—which is to be kept in a proper state of repair, but he does not warrant that machinery to his employees. He is not liable *qua* insurer. Whilst an employer must exercise the caution and skill of the prudent man of business (*i.e.*, in his particular trade or business), he cannot be held responsible for latent defects quite unknown to him or of whose existence he could reasonably be supposed to be unaware.[53] The onus of proving negligence and knowledge of a defect (or the reasonable apprehension of a defect by using ordinary skill and attention) lies squarely upon the employee who avers negligence by the employer.[54]

[49] See *Davies* v. *England* (1864) 33 L.J.Q.B. 321.
[50] See *Pollock* v. *Cassidy* (1870) 8 M. 615; *Stark* v. *McLaren* (1871) 10 M. 31; *Robertson* v. *Brown* (1876) 3 R. 652.
[51] See *Mansfield* v. *Baddeley* (1876) 34 L.T. 696.
[52] Observations of the L.J.-C. in *Edwards* v. *Hutcheon* (1889) 16 R. 694; 26 S.L.R. 550; and the earlier case of *Mitchell* v. *Patullo* (1885) 23 S.L.R. 207.
[53] *Ovington* v. *McVicar* (1864) 2 M. 1066.
[54] See *Weems* v. *Mathieson* (1861) 4 M'Q. 215; Paterson, Appeal Reports 1044; also Lord MacKenzie in *Sneddon* v. *Addie* (1849) 11 D. 1159; *Gemmills* v. *Gourock Ropework Co.* (1861) 23 D. 425; *Darby* v. *Duncan & Co.* (1861) 23 D. 529; and *Murphy* v. *Phillips* (1876) 35 L.T. 477.

It has been held in the recent case of *McMillan* v. *B.P. Refinery (Grangemouth) Ltd.*, 1961 S.L.T.(Notes) 79 that, if there is a latent defect in machinery supplied to a work-man's employers, the onus is upon the workman to prove that the makers were not reputable manufacturers upon whose skill his employers were entitled to rely. This is an extremely heavy onus of proof. This case seems to be a corollary to *Sullivan* v. *Gallagher and Craig*, 1959 S.C. 243, which was being heard by the Court of Session whilst *Davie* v. *New Merton Board Mills Ltd.* [1959] A.C. 604 was before the House of Lords and, indeed, the Scottish case was adjourned to await the Lords decision in *Davie*. Although the Scottish judges were impressed by the House of Lords decision in *Davie*, the circumstances in *Sullivan* were not identical. Sullivan's employers were held not liable for a latent defect in a truck supplied by the third-named defenders in the original action. (These defenders had been held responsible to Sullivan by the Lord Ordinary who had awarded £400 damages.) L.J.-C. Thomson stressed that, after *Davie's* case, it could no longer be said that an employer who engages an outsider to provide plant which his employees will use is automatically made vicariously liable for the outsider's negligence. His lordship had previously taken that view in *Donnelly* v. *Glasgow Corporation*, 1953 S.C. 107, which was clearly overruled by *Davie*. Lord Patrick was much impressed by the decision in *Davie* and confirmed his view that the employer is not under a wide (or absolute) liability for *any* defect in plant supplied by him. The correct statement of the law—accepted by H.L. in *Davie*—seems to be that expressed by Lord Herschell in *Smith* v. *Baker & Sons* [1891] A.C. 325 at p. 362, *viz.*: "The duty of taking reasonable care to provide proper appliances and to maintain them in a proper condition, and so carry on his operations as not to subject those employed by him to unnecessary risk."

This so-called personal duty of care had been firmly established by the well-known Scottish case of *English* v. *Wilsons and Clyde Coal Co.*, 1937 S.C.(H.L.) 46, but it had tended to be interpreted—wrongly, as it now seems, in certain respects—as an "absolute" duty. Both *Davie* and *Sullivan* have now corrected that misinterpretation.

However, account must be taken of the Employer's Liability (Defective Equipment) Bill 1969, which proposes to place a particular and joint liability for negligence upon

Statute law may, however, place a very heavy obligation upon the employer to protect his workmen and any failure to fulfil that obligation may make him liable beyond question. The statutory provision will have to be carefully studied to confirm whether the particular requirement is obligatory or whether it allows the employer a measure of discretion (*e.g.*, has he to do something " so far as reasonably practicable " or is it good enough if the particular machinery is safe by position?). References to the Factories Act 1961 and the Mines and Quarries Act 1954 will illustrate the point of difficulty which is made here. Not only does the particular statute usually provide a penalty upon the employer but, in addition, the employee may well be able to bring an action in reparation founded upon the failure to carry out the statutory obligation; the employer's failure having caused or materially contributed to the accident. The employer, for his part, may still be able to plead contributory negligence on the part of the employee, although he himself is in breach of a statutory duty.[55] The question of apportionment of responsibility under the Law Reform (Contributory Negligence) Act 1945 would then be dealt with, once it had been established that there was, in fact, contributory negligence on the employer's part.

an employer in relation to personal injury caused to an employee in consequence of defective equipment (supplied by a third party) provided by the employer for use in the business, in situations which correspond to *Davie's* case and *Sullivan's* case. If the Bill becomes law, then it seems that lengthy legal debate upon onus of proof will become a matter of historical interest. Moreover, the employer is not to be permitted to contract out of his liability or to limit his liability by agreement (with the employee). The law relating to contributory negligence and to contribution is preserved. The employer will no longer be able to rely (as in *Davie*) upon a supplier, who is reputable, to evade liability to his employee. The proposed change will give an employee immediate recourse against the employer (who is now, by statute, to be made vicariously liable for the fault of a third party in respect of defective equipment supplied). Clause 1 of the Bill is most important. In its present form, it reads as follows:
" 1.—(1) Where after the commencement of this Act—
    (*a*) an employee suffers personal injury in the course of his employment in consequence of a defect in equipment provided by his employer for the purposes of the employer's business; and
    (*b*) the defect is attributable wholly or partly to the fault of a third party (whether identified or not),
the injury shall be deemed to be also attributable to negligence on the part of the employer (whether or not he is liable in respect of the injury apart from this subsection), but without prejudice to the law relating to contributory negligence and to any remedy by way of contribution or in contract or otherwise which is available to the employer in respect of the injury.
    (2) In so far as any agreement purports to exclude or limit any liability of an employer arising under subsection (1) of this section, the agreement shall be void."
The Bill passed its third reading and the House of Lords on May 20, 1969. It is to come into effect three months after it is formally passed. It should now be noted that the Employer's Liability (Defective Equipment) Act, 1969 (c. 37) received the Royal Assent on 25th July, 1969 and came into effect on 25th October, 1969. The text of the Act is contained in Appendix 1 to this volume.

5   *Casswell* v. *Worth* (1856) 25 L.J.Q.B. 121; but see also *Gibb* v. *Crombie* (1875) 2 R. **886**; and *per contra*, Lord Chelmsford in *Wilson* v. *Merry and Cunningham*, Paterson, Appeal Reports 1597; L.R. 1 Sc.App. 326; (1868) 6 M.(H.L.) 84; see also *Traill* v. *Small and Boase* (1873) 11 M. 888; *Holmes* v. *Clarke* (1862) 31 L.J.Ex. 356; *Britton* v. *Great Western Cotton Co.* (1872) L.R. 7 Ex. 130; and see particularly *Caswell* v. *Powell Duffryn Associated Collieries Ltd.* [1940] A.C. 152; [1939] 3 All E.R. 722—the employer still escaped liability (although himself in breach of a statutory duty) if there was contributory negligence by the employee. This was changed, of course, by the Law Reform (Contributory Negligence) Act 1945.

(7) *Employer's Liability for Injury Caused by a Fellow-Servant*

One of the risks—that is, the ordinary risks within the particular type of employment undertaken—is the danger of suffering injury from the negligence of fellow-servants.   Initially, this was a limitation upon the liability of employers.   It has been argued that this doctrine of " fellow-servant " or " common employment," as it was more widely called, originated in the United States, was subsequently developed in England and thereafter was imposed upon Scots law by the House of Lords.[56] Before the injured servant could have recovered damages, he would have had to show that the wrongdoing employee was not acting within the course of employment common to both of them at the time when the accident to him occurred.   In Scotland, before the *Bartonshill* case in 1858, the general rule was that the mere fact that the injury was suffered by employee X because of the negligence of Y, his fellow-employee, made no difference to the employer's liability.   The employer was still clearly liable according to the maxim " *qui facit per alium facit per se*."   In the then well-known (*i.e.*, prior to 1858) case of *Dixon* v. *Ranken*[57] the Court of Session rejected the " doctrine of common employment " on the ground that the " recent English cases," if correct, depended upon a foreign system of jurisprudence.   Lord Hope (L.J.-C.) defined the employer's responsibility for fellow-employees in that case.   But the House of Lords was to overrule the Scottish view by imposing upon Scots law[58] the " common employment " doctrine in the *Bartonshill* cases to spark off a complexity of litigation (much of it needless and illogical) which was to last for nearly a hundred years.   In *Bartonshill Coal Co.* v. *Reid*[59] the old Scottish legal opinion was swept aside.   In this case, the defenders had asked for a direction that if they had used due and reasonable care in the selection and appointment of the engineman (whose fault had caused the accident) and if he was fully qualified to perform his duties and was furnished with proper machinery and other necessary appliances, then they were not liable for his fault or negligence.   Pursuers maintained that admitting the soundness of the plea where common employment was properly present, it did not apply here as both employees were not engaged in the same task.   The Scottish Court of Session disallowed the defenders' plea but that decision was reversed on appeal.[60]   The decision drew a

---

[56] See *Farwell* v. *Boston and Worcester Railroad Corporation* (1842) 4 Metc. 49; *Hutchison* v. *York, Newcastle and Berwick Ry.* (1850) 19 L.J.Ex. 296; and *Bartonshill Coal Co.* v. *Reid* (1858) 3 M'Q. 286; Paterson, Appeal Reports 793 (see Lord Cranworth's references to the judgment of Shaw C.J. in the *Farwell* case).   See also Fraser, *Master and Servant*, 2nd ed., p. 198 *et seq.*, and 3rd ed., p. 193 *et seq.*   But Mr. Munkman (in his book on *Employer's Liability*) does *not* agree with the origins of common employment as American.   He takes the view that *Priestley* v. *Fowler* (1837) 3 M. & W. 1 is the foundation of the doctrine and that only some five years or so later did the Americans establish the doctrine in the *Farwell* case.

[57] (1852) 14 D. 420.

[58] See Emeritus Professor A. D. Gibb's *Law from over the Border* at pp. 58 and 59.

[59] *Reid* v. *Bartonshill Coal Co.*, 17 D. 1017; reversed (1858) 3 M'Q. 266; Paterson, Appeal Reports 785; *sub nom. Bartonshill Coal Co* v. *Reid*.

[60] The House of Lords judgment being delivered by Lord Cranworth.

clear distinction between the liability of the employer to a stranger suffering injury from an employee's fault or negligence and the absence of liability upon the employer where a fellow-servant suffered the injury. The House was firmly of the opinion that the law in Scotland and England should be the same on this particular point and, accordingly, what had previously been the law of England now also became the common law in Scotland.[61]

At the same time as *Reid's* case was before the courts, another case,[62] arising out of the same accident, was being decided. Here the Lord Chancellor (Chelmsford) said: " It is necessary, in each particular case, to ascertain whether the servants are fellow-labourers in the same work. . . . Where employees, therefore, are engaged in different departments of duty, an injury committed by one employee upon the other by carelessness or negligence in the course of his peculiar work is not within the exception and the employer's liability attaches in that case. . . . " Lord Brougham put the point more succinctly by saying: " To bring the case within the exemption, there must be this most material qualification, that the two employees shall be men in the same common employment." Following upon the House of Lords judgment in the *Bartonshill* cases, the Court of Session attempted to limit the immunity of the employer to cases of common employment in the most strict sense—excluding cases where one employee was the " superior " of the other and also drawing distinctions in cases where the fault was committed by a " superior " employee.[63] This view was shortly thereafter to be considered by the House of Lords and to be quite discounted by them—again restoring the strength of the doctrine in the employer's favour. Lord Fraser points out [64] that, after the dicta pronounced in *Wilson* v. *Merry and Cunningham*,[65] such distinctions resorted to by the Court of Session, and as have been referred to, were no longer sound. Accordingly, a foreman or manager or overseer is just as much a fellow-employee as the employee who is working at the next machine or bench—or, better still, the same machine or bench. He then goes on to consider, at some length, who are or are not fellow-employees.[66]

The " volunteer " employee was, in relation to the old doctrine of common employment, no better off than the injured fellow-employee. No recourse against the temporary employers was open to him or to his dependants.[67] It was important to ascertain whether or not the pursuer was a volunteer employee. If so, he might not sue [68]—but if he could

---

[61] See comments in *Law from over the Border, loc. cit.*
[62] *Bartonshill Coal Co.* v. *McGuire* (1858) 3 M'Q. 300; Paterson, Appeal Reports 785.
[63] See Fraser, *op. cit.* p. 214 *et seq.*
[64] *Op. cit.* p. 198.
[65] (1867) 5 M. 807; affirmed (1868) 6 M.(H.L.) 84; L.R. 1 Sc.App. 326; (1868) Paterson, Appeal Reports 1597.
[66] *Op. cit.* pp. 202–203.
[67] *Degg* v. *Midland Railway Co.* (1857) 1 H. & N. 733; 26 L.J.Ex. 171; *Potter* v. *Faulkener* (1861) 5 L.T. 455; 31 L.J.Q.B. 30.
[68] See *Wiggett* v. *Fox* (1856) 11 Exch. 832; 25 L.J.Ex. 188.

establish that he was not a fellow-employee (whether volunteer or ordinary) he might well be able to recover.[69]   The same test of " scope of employment " and the relationship of fellow-employees has been accepted and continues to test the liability of an employer—although the old " common employment " doctrine has gone.   This is illustrated and confirmed by the following cases, viz.: *Malley* v. *L.M.S. Railway Co.*[70]; *Kelly* v. *Spencer and Co.*[71]; and *Leckie* v. *Caledonian Glass Co.*[72]

So long as the employer took reasonable care in the selection of competent employees, he escaped liability for negligence by them which caused injury to other employees.   This was an accepted extension of the doctrine of common employment.[73]   But if the employer should interfere personally in the management of his work he may thereby incur a liability towards an injured employee.   This point is well illustrated in the English case of *Roberts* v. *Smith*,[74] where a labourer had rejected certain poles as unfit for use but the employer ordered him to use them.   One defective pole snapped, causing the collapse of a scaffold upon which plaintiff was working.   It was held that there was sufficient evidence to go to the jury, of personal interference and negligence by the employer.   The point is further illustrated by two later Scottish cases.[75]   If the employer goes further than the stage of interfering with the work and himself acts as if he were a fellow-employee, it appears that he will be answerable for his negligence to the other employees.[76]   The theory of liability is that the employee is entitled to expect from an employer that care and attention which the superior position and sense of duty of the employer ought to command.   The ordinary doctrine of common employment has no application to such a case.

An interesting point which also arises in the field of common employment is this—is the employee of a contractor a fellow-employee with the employee of the contractor's employer ?   Although the doctrine of common employment has vanished, this question may still be important in relation to the definition and ascertainment of the " scope of employment " test as well as the " control " test, when an employee appears to be under the orders of two employers.[77]   On this point, the old case of

---

[69] *Wyllie* v. *Caledonian Railway Co.* (1871) 9 M. 463; *Holmes* v. *North Eastern Railway Co.* (1869) L.R. 4 Ex. 254; *Wright* v. *London and North Western Railway Co.* (1876) 1 Q.B.D. 252; and *Woodhead* v. *Gartness Mineral Co.* (1877) 4 R. 480 *per* L.P. Inglis.
[70] 1944 S.C. 129; 1945 S.L.T. 313.
[71] 1949 S.C. 143; 1949 S.L.T. 178.
[72] 1957 S.C. 89; 1958 S.L.T. 25. See also *Alford* v. *National Coal Board*, 1952 S.L.T. 204 (the House of Lords affirming the First Division of the Court of Session).
[73] See particularly *Tarrant* v. *Webb* (1856) 25 L.J.C.P. 261; *Balleny* v. *Cree* (1873) 11 M. 626; *Sneddon* v. *Mossend Iron Co.* (1876) 3 R. 868; *Gallagher* v. *Piper*, 33 L.J.C.P. 329.
[74] (1857) 2 H. & N. 213; 26 L.J.Ex. 319.
[75] *Stark* v. *McLaren* (1871) 10 M. 31; and *Robertson* v. *Brown* (1876) 3 R. 652.
[76] *Ashworth* v. *Stanwix* (1861) 30 L.J.Q.B. 183; and *Mellors* v. *Shaw* (1861) 30 L.J.Q.B. 333.
[77] See the comments in *Malley*; *Kelly*; and *Leckie, cit. supra.* It was made quite clear in *Lindsay* v. *Charles Connell and Co.*, 1951 S.C. 281; 1951 S.L.T. 395, that, as the doctrine of common employment was no longer applicable, the law would be the same as that prior to 1858 and employers would normally be liable once again for the fault of fellow-servants.

Woodhead v. *Gartness Mineral Co.*[78] is helpful. A miner employed by contractors upon work in a mine, belonging to an owning company whose manager and underground manager were in charge of the mine, was killed because of the negligence of the underground manager, who was admittedly a competent person. Moreover, the pit complied with the rules and regulations contained in the Coal Mines Regulation Act, which was the relevant statute then in force. The court (on a majority of seven judges) held that the owning company was not liable. The Lord President (Inglis) put the matter most clearly, in the course of his opinion, " . . . the mine-owner is free from responsibility, not because the injured and injurer are both his own hired and paid employees, but because he is not personally in fault and has not warranted the injured workman against the perils of the work. On the other hand, if there was personal fault of the mine-owner in selecting for the work an incompetent person, from whose incompetency the injured workman suffered, the owner would be equally liable, whether the incompetent person selected by him were an employee or what is called an independent contractor. In all cases his liability must rest on personal fault, and where there is personal fault it will be attended by liability."

The *Woodhead* case might usefully be compared with the English case of *Rourke* v. *White Moss Colliery Co.*,[79] which went to the Court of Appeal. Although the action was taken against the defendants as colliery-owners, they were held not liable in the circumstances as the engineer whose negligence caused the injury to plaintiff was at the time of the accident under the orders and control of the contractors who were employed to do a job in the mine, although he (the engineer) remained the general employee of the defendants. Here the " control test " was applied. In *Woodhead's* case the particular contractor had no control over the underground manager whose negligence caused the accident. Again in the English case of *Turner* v. *Great Eastern Railway Co.*[80] the common employment theory was not invoked because the fellow-servant relationship did not exist; this would have prevented the contractor's employee from recovering damages from the employing company. Lord Fraser discusses [81] the position of employees of one railway company injuring employees of another railway company as illustrative of the difficult and narrow questions which can arise in applying the common employment doctrine. Historically, these cases are of interest and they were, of course, added to quite substantially right up to the year 1948. However, it must be remembered that the common employment doctrine protected the employer only in relation to the employees themselves. It did not do so where, for example, the wife of one employee had been injured by the negligence of a fellow-employee. It is submitted that liability certainly exists in this case but it does so under the ordinary principle of vicarious liability.

[78] (1877) 4 R. 469, overruling *Gregory* v. *Hill* (1869) 8 M. 282.
[79] (1877) 2 C.P.D. 205.
[80] (1875) 33 L.T. 431.
[81] *Op. cit.* pp. 212–213 and footnotes there.

In *Webb* v. *Inglis*,[82] Lord Wheatley approved a claim by the wife of an employee (driver) against his employer based upon the latter's vicarious responsibility for the employee's negligence. In this case, his lordship took account of and approved of (though he was not bound to follow) the Court of Appeal's finding in *Broom* v. *Morgan*.[83] From the procedural point of view, actions of this type have perhaps changed to this extent that, since the passing of the Law Reform (Husband and Wife) Act 1962,[84] it is also possible for a wife to sue her husband in a personal action in damages for his fault or negligence. As a practical exercise, the claim would doubtless be met by the appropriate insurance company which issued the policy protecting the driver. It may be, in certain cases, less difficult for the wife to prove liability and fault by her husband as an individual defender rather than sue the employers *qua* employers, when she has the additional task of establishing " scope of employment " in order to render the employers vicariously liable. Moreover, where a stranger was injured by the negligence or fault of the employees of another person, it was, in Scotland, no defence for that other person (*i.e.*, the employer involved in the claim for damages) to say that the pursuer's fellow-employees were guilty of contributory negligence.[85] It seemed that the English courts had taken an opposite view from this.[86]

Certain inroads into the protection afforded to employers by the common employment doctrine were made by the Employers' Liability Act 1880. To succeed in his action, based on the statute, the workman had to prove that the accident resulted from defect in " the ways, works, machinery or plant " or from the negligence of some person placed in a position of supervisor or superintendent or whose orders the workman had to obey or, in the railway cases, from the negligence of engine-driver or signalman.[87] The defence of common employment was *pro tanto* excluded in those limited categories of cases coming within the Act. The Act applied to railway employees and manual workers generally but it gave only a partial remedy. The employee had to sue under the Act or at common law.

This statute was followed by the scheme of Workmen's Compensation (contained in the statutes of 1897, 1906 and the consolidating statute of 1925) in which common employment played no part. Compensation (not damages) became automatic where there was an accident in the course of employment and incapacity for work resulted. The sum awarded was very much lower than a damages award would have been in an ordinary reparation action. The amount of litigation which arose from this legislation was voluminous and totally unexpected. The judges were also moving— slowly but nevertheless with deliberation—towards a total abolition of the

[82] 1958 S.L.T.(Notes) 8 (O.H.).
[83] [1953] 1 Q.B. 597.
[84] 10 & 11 Eliz. 2, c. 48.
[85] *Adams* v. *Glasgow and South Western Railway Co.* (1875) 3 R. 215.
[86] *Armstrong* v. *Lancashire and Yorkshire Railway Co.* (1875) L.R. 10 Ex. 47.
[87] See the opinion of Lord Watson in *Smith* v. *Baker and Sons* [1891] A.C. 325.

common employment doctrine. This becomes evident from a careful study of the cases from 1880 down to 1948.[88] Finally, some three years or so after the close of the Second World War, the doctrine of common employment was swept away by the Law Reform (Personal Injuries) Act 1948.[89]

(8) *To Pay Wages*

It is accepted that, in return for the services rendered to him, there is —in the general case—an obligation upon an employer to pay wages. This obligation has been considered at some length elsewhere in this volume [90] and it is accordingly unnecessary to repeat what has already been said.

(9) *Giving Employee a Testimonial or Character*

It seems that there is no legal obligation upon an employer to give a testimonial or " character " or certificate of service to his employee. If, however, he chooses to give one, then it must be given in bona fide and what is said therein ought to be true.[91]

Sometimes it may be made a condition prior to commencement of service that a satisfactory testimonial or certificate of character from the former employer should be exhibited. If the former employer refuses to issue one, with the result that the employee does not get the new appointment because of failure to fulfil the condition precedent of producing such, there can be no damages action taken against the former employer.[92] Nevertheless, an employer is perfectly entitled to give a character to an employee if he wishes to do so and, in that case, the testimonial should be given in good faith, having regard to the existing legal principles which apply to misrepresentation and defamation.[93] He may claim qualified

---

[88] See particularly *Calder* v. *Caledonian Railway* (1871) 9 M. 833 (a guard of one railway company and a pointsman of another were not in common employment); *Johnson* v. *Lindsay and Co.* [1891] A.C. 371, where two contractors were engaged in building the same house—employee of one dropped a bucket on to the employee of the other. Held that the injured man could recover damages from employer of the negligent man (different employers); *The Petrel* [1893] P. 320—crews of two ships owned by the same company were not in common employment, at least on the Thames or the high seas; *Radcliffe* v. *Ribble Motor Services Ltd.* [1939] A.C. 215; [1939] 1 All E.R. 637—drivers of motor coaches in convoy were not in common employment when out on streets; *Hay* v. *Central S.M.T. Co. Ltd.*, 1944 S.L.T. 196; *Kerr* v. *Glasgow Corporation*, 1945 S.C. 335; 1946 S.L.T. 41; *Glasgow Corporation* v. *Neilson* [1948] A.C. 79; [1947] 2 All E.R. 346—drivers and conductors of different motor-buses were *not* in common employment; *Miller* v. *Glasgow Corporation* [1947] A.C. 368; [1947] 1 All E.R. 1— drivers and conductors of different tramcars *were* in common employment (this case being distinguished by the House of Lords in *Neilson*); and *Lancaster* v. *London Passenger Transport Board* [1948] 2 All E.R. 796—where a trolley-bus injured a man on a tower-wagon who was repairing the overboard wires. Majority decision of the House of Lords was against common employment on the ground that the plaintiff might equally well have been injured by any other tall vehicle.

[89] 11 & 12 Geo. 6, c. 41.

[90] See Chap. 8, *supra.*

[91] *Fell* v. *Ashburton* (Dec. 12, 1809) F.C.; *Grant* v. *Ramage and Ferguson* (1897) 25 R. 35, *per* Lord Young at p. 39; *Moult* v. *Halliday* [1898] 1 Q.B. 125, *per* Hawkins J. at p. 129.

[92] *Carrol* v. *Bird* (1800) 3 Esp. 201.

[93] *Christian* v. *Kennedy* (1818) 1 Mur. 419; *Anderson* v. *Wishart* (1818) 1 Mur. 429; *Mushets Ltd.* v. *Mackenzie Bros.* (1899) 1 F 756.

privilege in doing this so long as the recipient has an interest in receiving it. The recipient may be the employee himself or a prospective employer or a person acting as intermediary or a person with whom the employee has entered into a contract of employment.[94] But there can be no publication of it without sufficient cause.[95] In the interesting English case of *Gardner* v. *Slade*,[96] the former employee was held entitled to communicate to the new employer facts which came to the former's knowledge after the grant of the certificate of character, and which were inconsistent with the tenor of the certificate.

The employer is entitled to issue a certificate of character *ex proprio motu*.[97] If he does so, there may be a suspicion that this reflects some malicious intent on his part. However, if he gives the certificate in good faith, he is probably safeguarded from any action.[98]

When an employee is dismissed for misconduct, the employer is entitled at the time of dismissal to state the reason for dismissal and he is privileged in so doing.[99] This privilege has been held to apply to statements made to the parents of a girl who had been dismissed for immorality.[1] An equal protection extends, for example, to the headmaster of a school[2] or a railway inspector[3] in making proper reports upon junior employees. Furthermore, a member of a public body may criticise the performance of duties by its employees and any accusation of incompetence, neglect, dishonesty of others is privileged.[4] The case of *Dundas* v. *Livingstone & Co.*[5] is interesting in this respect. Here, a firm—insured against defalcations—stated to the insurance company that a commercial traveller who had by this time left their employment had embezzled a considerable amount of money belonging to them. This statement was held to be privileged. Once the privilege of the employer is established (a point of law) it is for the employee to overcome the privilege by showing malice—and this is a question of fact for the jury. The general principles of the law of defamation will apply, including reliance upon innuendo, which requires a very high degree of proof (first, before the judge will allow it, and, secondly, before the jury will find that the words complained of had the particular meaning attributed to them).[6] As

---

[94] *Child* v. *Affleck* (1829) 9 B. & C. 403.
[95] *Christian* v. *Kennedy* (1818) 1 Mur. 419, *per* L.C.C. Adam at p. 427.
[96] (1849) 13 Q.B. (A. & E.) 796, particularly *per* Wightman J. at p 801.
[97] *Pattison* v. *Jones* (1828) 8 B. & C. 578.
[98] See *per* Rooke J. in *Rogers* v. *Clifton* (1803) 3 B. & P. 587.
[99] *R.* v. *Perry* (1833) 15 Cox C.C. 169; *Taylor* v. *Hawkins* (1851) 16 Q.B.(A. & E.) 308; *Manby* v. *Witt* (1856) 18 C.B. 544; *Stuart* v. *Moss* (1885) 13 R. 299.
[1] *Watson* v. *Burnet* (1862) 24 D. 494.
[2] *Milne* v. *Bauchope* (1867) 5 M. 1114.
[3] *Martin* v. *Cruickshanks* (1896) 23 R. 874.
[4] *Neilson* v. *Johnston* (1890) 17 R. 442; *Munro* v. *Mudie* (1901) 9 S.L.T. 91; *Teague* v. *Russell* (1900) 8 S.L.T. 253; *Pittard* v. *Oliver* [1891] 1 Q.B. 474; *Leitch* v. *Lyal* (1903) 11 S.L.T. 394.
[5] (1900) 3 F. 37.
[6] See *Neilson* v. *Johnston*, *cit. supra*; *Laidlaw* v. *Gunn* (1890) 17 R. 394; *Macdonald* v. *M'Coll* (1901) 3 F. 1082; *Macdonald* v. *Rupprecht* (1894) 21 R. 389; *Kennedy* v. *Henderson* (1903) 11 S.L.T. 156.

Jervis C.J. said in *Manby* v. *Witt*,[7] the circumstances " must be such as to induce the court or any reasonable person to conclude that the occasion has been taken advantage of to give utterance to an unfounded charge." The presence of a third party when the statement is made does not necessarily displace the privilege but it may be indicative of a malicious intention, as the element of bona fide now seems prima facie to be lacking.

There seems to be no doubt at all that where an employer fraudulently gives an employee a good character, with the intention of assisting him to procure employment, and a third party, relying upon this character, which is false, employs the employee and thereafter suffers loss, the aggrieved third party may take an action in damages for his loss against the first employer, basing his action upon the issue of the false character which caused him loss.[8]

Before leaving this section, there remains to be considered the Servants' Characters Act 1792.[9] Mr. Umpherston dismisses this extremely briefly by a note [10] that the Act was evidently not intended to apply to, and had not in fact been applied in, Scotland. Lord Fraser summarises the penalties upon employers and employees imposed by the Act and then goes on to quote from Tait's *Justice* to the effect that the statute applies to England. The learned editor of the third edition of Lord Fraser's work on *Master and Servant* goes somewhat further and disagrees with Mr. Tait's view that the Act applies to England only. He says [11] that the Act is quite absolute and general and that there is nothing in it to indicate that it was to be restricted to England in its operation. Mr. Tait took the view that the Scottish common law dealt quite vigorously and effectively with the types of offences mentioned in the Act as frauds. Nevertheless, the statute might have afforded a speedy and effective check, whilst the common law was somewhat vague both as to procedure and punishment.

The 1792 Act made it an offence for any person to impersonate a master (or his executor, administrator, wife, agent or servant) and personally or in writing to give a false or forged or counterfeit testimonial; or for any person to assert that a servant has been hired or retained for any period or in any capacity other than that in which the servant was in fact hired; or to assert that the servant was discharged or left the service or had not been hired, contrary to the truth.[12] A person who offers himself as a servant commits an offence if he falsely pretends that he has served in a service in which he has not actually served or if he adds, alters, effaces or erases anything contained in or referred to in a certificate given

---

[7] *Cit. supra.*
[8] *Foster* v. *Charles* (1830) 6 Bing. 396; 7 Bing. 106; *Wilkin* v. *Reed* (1854) 15 C.B. 192; and *Anderson* v. *Wishart* (1818) 1 Mur. 429, *per* L.C.C. Adam at p. 440.
[9] 32 Geo. 3, c. 56.
[10] See p. 184.
[11] See pp. 133–134.
[12] ss. 1, 2 and 3.

to him by a former master or mistress; or who falsely asserts that he has not been hired or retained in any previous service.[13]

(10) *Duty towards Disabled Employees*

This duty upon an employer rests wholly upon statute law and is regulated by the Disabled Persons (Employment) Act, 1944 [14] as amended by the Disabled Persons (Employment) Act 1958.[15] Both of these statutes must be read along with the relevant regulations governed by statutory instruments.[16] These Acts represent another example of social legislation in the field of industrial law and to that extent they illustrate an enlightened attitude to the handicapped worker. However, it is one thing to pass legislation of this type and quite another thing to ensure that it is properly enforced by the appropriate government ministerial department charged with the task. The writer remains to be convinced that the legislation is being effectively enforced for the benefit of disabled workers. Perhaps it is too easy for management—with a ruthless attitude to efficiency—to dispose of the disabled worker, even upon the basis of a reasonable notice period settlement.

The statutes adopt a twofold technique: (i) by compelling employers to employ a stipulated quota of disabled workers and (ii) by permitting the designation [17] of certain types of employment as suitable for the employment of disabled workers. The " disabled person " within the meaning [18] of the Acts is a person who, on account of injury, disease [19] or congenital deformity, is substantially handicapped in obtaining or keeping employment, or in undertaking work on his own account, of a kind which (apart from the injury, disease or deformity in question) would be suited to his age, experience and qualifications. Vocational training courses and industrial rehabilitation courses [20] are to be arranged for disabled persons over 15 years of age.[21]

A register [22] of disabled persons is to be kept by the Minister concerned. The applicant for registration (who may apply by himself or through an authorised agent) must satisfy the definition above-mentioned and must also be able to show that he is likely to be so handicapped for a period of not less than twelve months. Prior to the 1958 Act, this minimal

---

[13] ss. 4 and 5.
[14] 7 & 8 Geo. 6, c. 10.
[15] 6 & 7 Eliz. 2, c. 33.
[16] Notably S.R. & O. 1945 No. 938 (amended by S.I. 1959 No. 1510); S.R. & O. 1946 No. 262; S.R. & O. 1946 No. 1256 and No. 1257 (itself amended by the 1958 Act above cited).
[17] By Ministerial Order.
[18] 1944 Act, s. 1
[19] This term including any physical or mental condition arising from any imperfect development.
[20] 1944 Act, s. 3.
[21] *i.e.*, the present compulsory school-leaving age. The 1958 Act reduced the age limit from 16 years to 15 years.
[22] 1944 Act, s. 6.

period of incapacity was six months.[23] He must also satisfy the residence qualification required by the Acts, unless he was a member of H.M. Forces. Foreign nationals who have served mainly in H.M. Forces or the Merchant Navy may obtain the benefit of the statutes, but in the case of other foreign nationals the circumstances must be very exceptional before registration would be permitted.

The quota system operates in relation to every employer who employs a minimum of twenty persons. The calculations are based upon a standard percentage and a special percentage, both of which (provided the special percentage is relevant) are applied to the total number of employees on the staff of the establishment in order to arrive at the personal quota which is applicable.[24]

The sanction imposed by the Acts for any failure to take the appropriate quota or for any dismissal or discharge of a registered person without reasonable cause is a fine not exceeding £100 or imprisonment for a term not exceeding three months, or both [25]; whilst that imposed for any failure to keep records in proper form is a fine and, for any falsification thereof, imprisonment.[26]

(11) *Reinstatement in Civilian Employment* [27]

This obligation upon employers is a statutory one which dates from the Reinstatement in Civil Employment Act 1944,[28] which was designed as a piece of wartime emergency legislation to protect the interests of persons serving full-time in H.M. Forces and those giving similar service in the Civil Defence forces. That statute is still important but, from the historical viewpoint, it was virtually superseded by the National Service Act 1948 [29] (which was in turn amended by the Reinstatement in Civil Employment Act 1950 [30]) as the later statute referred basically to those persons who served in H.M. Forces by virtue of an enlistment notice issued after January 1, 1949. The 1948 Act made no provision for the volunteer soldier. The 1950 Act above-mentioned and the Reserve and Auxiliary Forces (Training) Act 1951 [31] both made certain changes in the 1948 Act. The Army Reserve Act 1962 [32] permitted the retention of National Service men for up to six months after completion of basic " National Service," allowed the recall of persons on the reserved list and created the Territorial

---

[23] The war veteran from 1914–18 on disability pension is deemed to be substantially handicapped without any further proof and he is entitled to registration as of right, without formal application: 1944 Act, s. 7.
[24] *Ibid.* s. 10 (1), (2), (3) and (4) in particular.
[25] *Ibid.* s. 9 (6).
[26] *Ibid.* s. 14.
[27] See G. H. L. Fridman, *Modern Law of Employment*, pp. 643–645.
[28] 7 & 8 Geo. 6, c. 15.
[29] 11 & 12 Geo. 6, c. 64 (see Part II thereof).
[30] 14 & 15 Geo. 6, c. 10, providing for the Korean situation.
[31] 14 & 15 Geo. 6, c. 23.
[32] 10 & 11 Eliz. 2, c. 10.

Army Emergency Reserve.[33] Section 5 safeguards those persons affected by the Act and authorises their reinstatement.

The application for reinstatement may be made direct to the employer or through an employment exchange and it must be in written form,[34] made normally within one month of the termination of service (except if sickness or other reasonable cause prevents this). A notice of availability for work must also be sent to the employer. If an employer alleges that an employee has failed to obey the procedural requirements as to presentation of the application or any renewal thereof, then he must specifically plead that failure and be able to substantiate it; otherwise the requirements are held to be fulfilled.[35]

The statutes are enforced by reinstatement committees, whose procedure is governed by the Reinstatement in Civil Employment (Procedure) Regulations 1944.[36] Appeal from a committee decision lies to the umpire or to a deputy-umpire (each sitting with two assessors).

The term " former employer " [37] is used throughout the statutory legislation. This phrase means primarily the employer by whom the applicant was last employed within the period of four weeks immediately preceding the beginning of the applicant's service period (i.e., service in H.M. Forces). Where the business of the employer is taken over by another employer or is merged with another business, the obligation to reinstate transmits to the new proprietor/employer or to the new undertaking, as the case may be.

But, it is with the employer's obligations that we are primarily concerned. Basically, the employer must re-employ the applicant in the occupation in which he was employed immediately prior to his call-up for service, and that upon terms and conditions not less favourable than those which would have applied had the applicant not been called up for service. If such is not reasonable and practicable, then the employer must provide the applicant with the most favourable occupation, and on the most favourable terms and conditions which are reasonable and practicable in the case of the applicant. These provisions allow for any change in the applicant's original occupation and permit the employer to offer a similar alternative employment which is not less favourable to the applicant. The employer fulfils his statutory obligation by offering reinstatement at the first reasonable opportunity—and that only where it is reasonable and practicable to re-employ. If the employee has reasonable

---

[33] *Ibid.* s. 3.
[34] 1948 Act, s. 36 (1) and (2), as amended by the 1950 Act, s. 5 (1). For the form of application, see the Civil Employment (Procedure) Regulations 1944.
[35] *Hannah* v. *Greenock Centre for Community Service* (1947) R.E. 1/68; and *Tomlin* v. *Stewarts and Lloyds Ltd.* (1960) R.E. 1/90 (No. 1672).
[36] S.R. & O. 1944 No. 880. See also the Tribunals and Inquiries Act 1958, ss. 3 and 4, as regards the creation of committees and panels. The 1958 Act was itself amended, in several respects, by the Tribunals and Inquiries Act 1966 (c. 43). The position of the Council of Tribunals should be kept in mind (1958 Act, s. 1). The 1966 Act, s. 2, relates specifically to Scotland and enables the Secretary of State for Scotland to make rules of procedure under s. 7A of the 1958 Act.
[37] See *Macpherson* v. *McVitie and Price Ltd.* (1946) R.E. 1/35.

cause for refusing reinstatement—or believes he so has—he should notify the employer. When reinstatement takes place, the employer is obliged to employ the applicant for a period of twenty-six weeks (in the original occupation or any substituted occupation, most favourable, as reasonable and practicable). If the employee's original service had been for a consecutive period of fifty-two weeks, the reinstatement period is fifty-two weeks. However, where the prior employment period is less than thirteen weeks, the reinstatement period is thirteen weeks. It must be noted that reference to reinstatement periods does not in any way guarantee that the employee shall remain in employment for the full period. The employer retains his rights of summary dismissal for any conduct by a reinstated employee which would justify the dismissal of an ordinary employee.

Any attempted evasion of the statutory provisions may result in the employer being prosecuted and he may be ordered, in the appropriate circumstances, to pay compensation to the employee in question.

(12) *National Insurance*

It is pertinent to mention briefly here the statutory obligations which arise in respect of state insurance schemes against: (i) unemployment and sickness; and (ii) industrial injuries. The former have developed from the first statutory scheme in 1911 through a plethora of legislative measures (statutory and ministerial) until the recent consolidation in the National Insurance Act 1965,[38] whilst industrial injuries originated in the first Workmen's Compensation Scheme in 1897,[39] subsequently expanded and re-enacted by the principal Act of 1925 [40] and thereafter replaced by the " Industrial Injuries " scheme commencing with a statute in 1946 [41] and now consolidated by the National Insurance (Industrial Injuries) Act 1965.[42] The administrative responsibility for carrying out the statutory obligations rests upon the employer, who is himself liable to make quite substantial contributions under both headings. The employee's contributions (and employer's) are represented by the affixing of insurance stamps to the employee's insurance card. The employee's proportion is reflected as a deduction in the wages statement which he receives from his employer although, of course, the amount in question is balanced by the appropriate credits on the insurance card.

The government department responsible for, *inter alia*, the administration of the state schemes of national insurance and national insurance

---

[38] 1965, c. 51; subsequently amended by the National Insurance Acts 1966 and 1967 (1966, c. 6, and 1967, c. 73), etc.; the National Insurance, etc., Act 1969 (c. 4) and the National Insurance Act 1969 (c. 44).
[39] 60 & 61 Vict., c. 37.
[40] 15 & 16 Geo. 5, c. 84.
[41] 9 & 10 Geo. 6, c. 62.
[42] 1965, c. 52; subsequently amended or affected by the National Insurance (Industrial Injuries) (Amendment) Act 1967 (c. 25) and the Industrial Injuries and Diseases (Old Cases) Act 1967 (c. 34), etc.; including the National Insurance, etc., Act 1969 (c. 4), ss. 2 and 3.

(industrial injuries) was formerly the Ministry of Pensions and National Insurance, thereafter known, since 1966, as the Ministry of Social Security [43] (a new terminology which is perhaps more psychedelic but less accurate than the previous one).

It is considered to be more logical to deal with these matters of national insurance and national insurance (industrial injuries) in the chapters relating to wages and statutory liabilities respectively, because of the impact which these topics have upon the law and practice concerning wages and statutory liability. Accordingly, reference is made to the appropriate sections of the relevant chapters [44] of this book, where the major provisions of the legislation are explained.

(13) *Compulsory Insurance*

The new statutory duty relating to compulsory insurance of employees against bodily injury or disease arising out of and in the course of employment in Great Britain is dealt with in the succeeding chapter.[45] This is a new duty imposed upon certain employers (others are exempted by section 3 of the new Act) by the Employers' Liability (Compulsory Insurance) Act 1969.[46] Insurance is not necessary for those employees who come within the ambit of section 2 (2).

---

[43] Ministry of Social Security Act 1966 (c. 20); and is now generally known as the Department of Social Services.
[44] See Chap. 8, *supra*, and Chap. 11, *infra*, respectively.
[45] See chapter 11 *infra*, Part B, section (8).
[46] 1969 c. 57. This new legislation is still to be made operative by statutory instrument. The text of the new Act is contained in Appendix No. 3 to this volume.

CHAPTER 11

THE SPECIFIC LIABILITY OF THE EMPLOYER TO HIS
EMPLOYEES FOR THEIR SAFETY, ETC., (A) AT COMMON
LAW; AND (B) UNDER STATUTE (INCLUDING THE FACTORIES
ACT 1961, MINES AND QUARRIES ACT 1954, OFFICES, SHOPS
AND RAILWAY PREMISES ACT 1963, AGRICULTURE (SCOT-
LAND) ACTS, THE MERCHANT SHIPPING ACTS, AND THE
NATIONAL INSURANCE (INDUSTRIAL INJURIES) ACT 1965,
ETC.)

PART A—THE EMPLOYER'S COMMON LAW OBLIGATIONS

IT is accepted today that the main duty incumbent upon an employer—
whether he is acting personally or through an agent—is to take reasonable care for the safety of his workmen and other employees, in the
course of their employment.[1] The duty certainly extends to the place
of work, the plant and machinery which is in use on the premises and the
system of work but it is not restricted to these things [2]; and the duty
exists whether there is inherent danger in the employment or not.[3] Moreover, it is a duty which is owed to each individual employee and accordingly if any one employee suffers from a physical incapacity regard must
be had by the employer to that fact and a higher degree of care must be
exercised.[4]

The older method of stating the law was that an employee should not
be exposed to any " unnecessary " or " unreasonable " risk.[5] Since the
Wilsons and Clyde case, the House of Lords has referred broadly to a
" safe system of work " and in many of the subsequent cases a general
reference has been made to the employer's duty of " taking reasonable
care for the safety of the employee." [6]

---

[1] The claim or action brought against the employer must be based upon the relationship
of employer and employee—*Keatings* v. *Secretary of State for Scotland* (1961) 77
Sh.Ct.Rep. 113; 1961 S.L.T.(Sh.Ct.) 63 (injury caused by prisoner to fellow-prisoner.
Claim irrelevant as no relationship of employer and employee existed. Moreover, no
relevant averment of fault in any case and action dismissed.).
[2] See *Wilsons and Clyde Coal Co. Ltd.* v. *English* [1938] A.C. 57; [1937] 3 All E.R. 628,
per Lord Wright at p. 84 and p. 644 respectively; and in the Scottish reports at 1937
S.C.(H.L.) 46 and 1937 S.L.T. 523 *sub nom. English* v. *Wilsons and Clyde Coal Co. Ltd.*;
also *Davie* v. *New Merton Board Mills* [1958] 1 Q.B. 210; [1958] 1 All E.R. 67, *per*
Parker L.J. (as he then was) at pp. 237–238 and p. 82 respectively: the House of Lords
decision is thereafter reported in [1959] A.C. 604; [1959] 2 W.L.R. 331; [1959] 1 All
E.R. 346, on appeal to the House of Lords.
[3] *Colfar* v. *Coggins and Griffith (Liverpool) Ltd.* [1945] A.C. 197; [1945] 1 All E.R. 326,
per Viscount Simon L.C.
[4] *Porteous* v. *National Coal Board* (O.H.) 1967 S.L.T. 117 (the employee with defective
vision).
[5] See *Bartonshill Coal Co.* v. *Reid* (1858) 3 Macq. 300 and other cases of that vintage.
[6] See Lord Keith in *Cavanagh* v. *Ulster Weaving Co. Ltd.* [1960] A.C. 145; [1959] 2 All
E.R. 745.

Formerly, the courts took the view that every employee accepted the risk of inherent dangers, relying upon his own skill and experience for his own safety, but this is no longer acceptable today. If one type of employment is more dangerous than another, a higher degree of care is required in the more dangerous case.[6a]

Should it prove impossible to eliminate the risk of danger the obligation upon the employer is to minimise that risk.[6b] Where an employer has taken all reasonable care in the circumstances but nevertheless an employee sustains injury from an inherent risk that employee will not succeed in a reparation action against the employer, because there has been no negligence on the employer's part.[7] It must not, however, be forgotten that knowledge of the existence or probability of danger on the employee's part is always relevant in two major respects, viz.: (a) in enabling the jury or the court to determine whether or not there has been contributory negligence on the part of the employee [8]; and (b) in enabling the court to decide whether an employee has himself voluntarily assumed a risk for his own purposes and has thereby agreed to relieve the employer of his primary duty or obligation in the matter of safety, thereby allowing the employer to invoke the defence of *volenti non fit injuria*.[9] No pursuer will succeed in the general case in any common law action of reparation unless he proves negligence on the defender's part. The reason for this is that an employer is not bound by law in any absolute warranty or guarantee that his machinery is safe or that any system of work adopted by him is completely free from risk. Moreover, the principle of *res ipsa loquitur* has to be applied with care in the employer/employee cases,[10] yet it may well be a perfectly valid plea.[11]

[6a] *Paris* v. *Stepney Borough Council* [1951] A.C. 367; [1951] 1 All E.R. 42, *per* Lord Morton.

[6b] *General Cleaning Contractors Ltd.* v. *Christmas* [1953] A.C. 180; [1952] 2 All E.R. 1110.

[7] *Rands* v. *McNeil* [1955] 1 Q.B. 253; [1954] 3 All E.R. 593.

[8] But the facts and circumstances must be looked at carefully—see *Graham* v. *Scott's Shipbuilding and Engineering Co.*, 1963 S.L.T.(Notes) 78 (where a vertical steel ladder was not in itself a safe access, the employee—who, it was alleged, had failed to place his feet properly on the ladder—was held not to be guilty of contributory negligence).

[9] See D. M. Walker, *The Law of Delict in Scotland* (1966), pp. 352–354 and p. 581 where the defence of *volenti non fit injuria* in relation to employment is discussed. One of the early leading cases in England on this defence was *Smith* v. *Baker & Sons* [1891] A.C. 325 (where the defence was not, in fact, accepted in the particular case). This case has a high persuasive authority in Scotland and, in fact, it was followed in Scotland in the case of *Smith* v. *Forbes & Co.* (1897) 24 R. 699; 4 S.L.T. 341. See also *Robertson* v. *Primrose & Co.*, 1910 S.C. 111; 1909, 2 S.L.T. 409; *Frost* v. *E. K. Cole Ltd.* (O.H.) 1949 S.L.T.(Notes) 41; *Keenan* v. *City Line Ltd.* (O.H.) 1953 S.L.T. 128; and *Kirkham* v. *Cementation Co.* (O.H.) 1964 S.L.T.(Notes) 33 (a plea of *volenti* must be supported by relevant averments). It should be pointed out—and indeed this is done later on in this chapter—that *Smith* v. *Baker & Sons* was preceded, in Scotland, by *Sword* v. *Cameron* (1839) 1 D. 493, which (although not raising the *volenti non fit injuria* directly) was one of the earliest common law cases dealing with a " safe system of work."

[10] See *Hook* v. *Brown* (O.H.) 1963 S.L.T.(Notes) 52 (the *res ipsa loquitur* principle could not be relied upon by a pursuer who averred failure by his employers to guard a saw blade—as regards the breaking of the blade).

[11] See *Devine* v. *Colvilles Ltd.*, 1968 S.L.T.(Notes) 43 (here defenders had not displaced the inference of negligence *re* an explosion in an oxygen plant); and, on appeal, (H.L.) 1969 S.L.T. 154; [1969] 1 W.L.R. 475; [1969] 2 All E.R. 53 (H.L.)

The duty of care depends upon the existence of the employer/employee relationship, but it may also arise where one employee is on temporary loan from one employer to another or indeed where a person is a " volunteer " employee. The basic test of liability has been accepted as arising from the right to exercise " control " over the employee.[12] The case of the " volunteer " (who comes to the aid or rescue of another person) is illustrated by several well-known Scottish cases [13] and English cases [14] and these cases are generally referred to as the " rescue " cases.

The employer is now, once again, liable for the negligence of fellow-servants acting in the course of their employment, and the *Bartonshill* cases and others following the same principle of law are now mainly of historical interest only, but he is not normally liable for the " independent contractor," over whom he has no control in the ordinary case.

The broad test of negligence on the part of an employer was referred to in *Gallagher* v. *Balfour Beatty & Co. Ltd.*[15] and the court was at some pains to point out that the formula laid down by Lord Dunedin in *Morton* v. *Dixon* [16] had not been weakened in any way by subsequent decisions. Lord Dunedin had said: " Where the negligence of the employer consists of what I may call a fault of omission, I think it is absolutely necessary that the proof of that fault of omission should be one of two kinds, either—to show that the thing which he did not do was a thing which was commonly done by other persons in like circumstances, or—to show that it was a thing which was so obviously wanted that it would be folly in anyone to neglect to provide it." The general principles of the law of delict are, of course, always applicable to the employer/employee situation and the test of foreseeability of danger,[17] causation,[18] remoteness of injury and of damage,[19] and greater precautions for dangerous work [20] are carefully applied, as well as statutory provisions relating to prescription

---

[12] *Supra* Chap. 3.
[13] See particularly, *Steel* v. *Glasgow Iron & Steel Co.*, 1944 S.C. 237 and the cases referred to therein; also *Wilkinson* v. *Kinneil Cannel & Coking Coal Co.* (1897) 24 R. 1001; 4 S.L.T. 349.
[14] See particularly *Haynes* v. *Harwood* [1935] 1 K.B. 146; *D'Urso* v. *Sanson* [1939] 4 All E.R. 26; and the fairly recent cases of *Ward* v. *T. E. Hopkins & Son Ltd.* and *Baker* v. *T. E. Hopkins & Son Ltd.* [1959] 3 All E.R. 225 (men poisoned by fumes in a well).
[15] 1951 S.C. 712.
[16] 1909 S.C. 807 (at p. 809); 1909 S.L.T. 346.
[17] *Grace* v. *Alexander Stephen & Son Ltd.*, 1952 S.C. 61; 1952 S.L.T. 117; *Harvey* v. *Singer Manufacturing Co. Ltd.*, 1960 S.C. 155; 1960 S.L.T. 178; *McColl* v. *D. Macaulay & Noble Ltd.* (O.H.) 1961 S.L.T. (Notes) 46; *Skinner* v. *Glasgow Corporation*, 1961 S.L.T. 130 (pursuer unsuccessful here as defender's alleged fault was not relevantly averred); *McGown* v. *George McLellan & Co.* (O.H.) 1962 S.L.T.(Notes) 30 (accident not reasonably foreseeable as no inherent danger in the process).
[18] See, for example, *Blaikie* v. *British Transport Commission*, 1961 S.C. 44; 1961 S.L.T. 189.
[19] *Singh* v. *Glasgow Corporation* (O.H.) 1962 S.L.T.(Notes) 6; *McKillen* v. *Barclay Curle & Co. Ltd.*, 1967 S.L.T. 41 (reversing 1965 S.L.T.(Notes) 19); and *cf. McKew* v. *Holland & Hannen & Cubitts (Scotland) Ltd.*, 1968 S.L.T. 12.
[20] *Donn* v. *Mitchell Construction Co.* (O.H.) 1957 S.L.T. (Notes) 2 (hole in a concrete foundation allegedly hidden by muddy water and creating a trap or hidden source of danger).

of claims for damages.[21]   Assessment of damages may also raise
some interesting problems—for example, injury to an employee during
his first working day in a new job [22] or an allegation that the pursuer now
had a diminished value in the labour market.[23] A detailed consideration
of these general principles is out of place here, but they are dealt with at
length in the leading reference books on delict and tort.[24]

It is convenient to regard the employer's common law obligation of
safety towards his employees as a three-part obligation requiring him to
do the following things:

(1) to provide and maintain suitable materials (*i.e.*, plant, machinery
      and equipment),

(2) to keep premises safe and work upon a safe system;

(3) to exercise care in the selection of fellow-employees (*i.e.*, com-
      petent workmen).

Mr. Umpherston points out [25] that it used to be argued that a distinction fell to be made, as regards the employer's obligations, between the
case where an employer personally superintended his works and the
other case where he did not do so but delegated this to a manager. In
the latter case, the employer's obligation was then said to be limited to
providing suitable plant and materials and to employing competent
managers. The decisions, however, show that the employer's liability is
as wide in a question with his own workmen as it is with strangers whether
personal supervision is exercised or not.[26] A selection of some of the
older cases indicates quite clearly that the obligations attach to the
employer *qua* employer and it does not matter how he chooses to carry
on his business.[27] This statement is true both of an obligation which
arises at common law or one which arises specifically under statute. If
the system of working was dangerous or if he employed young or inexperienced workers on dangerous work for which they were quite unsuited,
then the employer could not escape liability by pleading delegation to a
manager.[28]

[21] See particularly *Clark* v. *R. B. Tennent Ltd.* (O.H.) 1962 S.C. 578; *Gardner* v. *Alexander
      Finlay & Co.* (O.H.) 1963 S.L.T.(Notes) 55; and *Brown's Exrx.* v. *North British Steel
      Foundry Ltd.*, 1967 S.L.T.(Notes) 111; and the Law Reform (Limitation of Actions,
      etc.) Act 1954 (mainly ss. 6 and 7).
[22] *Sweeney* v. *Colvilles Ltd.* (O.H.) 1962 S.L.T.(Notes) 42 (earnings in previous employ-
      ment were relevant).
[23] *Odgers* v. *British Railways Board*, 1967 S.L.T.(Notes) 97.
[24] See particularly D. M. Walker, *Delict* (1966); Glegg, *Reparation* (4th ed., 1955);
      Clerk and Lindsell, *Torts* (12th ed., 1961) and cumulative supplement; and *Charlesworth
      on Negligence* (4th ed., 1962 and cumulative supplement).
[25] *Master and Servant*, pp. 156 and 157.
[26] *Sword* v. *Cameron* (1839) 1 D. 493; *Paterson* v. *Wallace* (1854) 1 Macq. 748; *Bartonshill
      Coal Co.* v. *Reid* (1858) 3 Macq. 266; *Bartonshill Coal Co.* v. *M'Guire* (1858) 3 Macq.
      300; *Wallace* v. *Culter Paper Mills Co.* (1892) 19 R. 915; *Darby* v. *Duncan & Co.*
      (1861) 23 D. 529; 33 J. 206.
[27] *Wright* v. *Dunlop & Co.* (1893) 20 R. 363; *M'Killop* v. *N.B. Railway Co.* (1896) 23 R.
      768; *Macdonald* v. *Udston Coal Co.* (1896) 23 R. 504; *Henderson* v. *John Watson Ltd.*
      (1892) 19 R. 954.
[28] *McKillop* v. *N.B.Ry.*, cit. supra; *O'Byrne* v. *Burn* (1854) 16 D. 1025; *Gibson* v. *Nimmo
      and Co.* (1895) 22 R. 491.

(1) The employer's primary duty at common law is to provide and maintain suitable and fit materials for carrying on the work. He does not —and he cannot be expected to—warrant his plant and machinery against latent defect. He does, however, undertake that, latent defect apart, the plant will be reasonably fit and suitable for the purpose for which it was supplied.[29] Initially, of course, this undertaking applies to the condition of the material or appliances originally provided—e.g., if a scaffolding were constructed of wood which was in a rotting condition, the employer would be liable if a section collapsed under stress or strain causing injury to an employee [30] (or indeed to a third party who was entitled to be on the premises). Cases involving faulty wagons, vessels or machinery have been quite common.[31] The obligation was formerly in no way affected by the employer himself trying to establish that the faulty appliances were supplied by a third party and were not manufactured by the employer himself,[32] but this view has been modified in the light of more recent cases such as *Davie* v. *New Merton Board Mills* [33] and others hereinafter examined. It is also the case that an employer is obliged, as a precautionary measure, to inspect from time to time any machinery or plant which is liable to become defective through ordinary wear and tear.[34] Accordingly, in any action against the employer in which the pursuer avers that the defect could have been discovered by inspection (the onus of proof resting in such case with the pursuer) [35] the employer may disprove the alleged negligence on his part by showing that by periodical inspection he had taken all ordinary and reasonable steps to detect any defects.[36] It is the jury's task to say what periodical inspection was reasonable and whether the measures taken to that end were also reasonable, looking to all the circumstances.[37] It will be appreciated that the duty of inspection follows on from the main obligation to provide and maintain suitable materials. Accordingly if the employer's employees are working on occasion with

[29] *Ovington* v. *M'Vicar* (1864) 2 M. 1066; *Weems* v. *Mathieson* (1861) 4 Macq. 215; and *Lindsay* v. *Saunders & Connor (Barrhead) Ltd.* (O.H.) 1957 S.L.T.(Notes) 4.

[30] See *Scott* v. *Craig* (1862) 24 D. 789; 34 J. 401 (scaffold proved to be insufficient and patently defective).

[31] See particularly the older cases of *Matthews* v. *M'Donald Grieve & Co.* (1865) 3 M. 506; *Rothwell* v. *Hutchison* (1886) 13 R. 463; *Welsh* v. *Moir* (1885) 12 R. 590; and also *White* v. *Tullis, Russell & Co.*, 1951 S.L.T.(Notes) 63.

[32] See particularly *Donnelly* v. *Glasgow Corporation*, 1953 S.C. 107.

[33] [1959] A.C. 604; [1959] 2 W.L.R. 331; [1959] 1 All E.R. 346; and, in Scotland, *Sullivan* v. *Gallagher and Craig*, 1960 S.L.T. 70 (which followed the line taken by *Davie's* case in England), a case concerning defective electric trucks in use by pursuer's employers. However, in the fairly recent case of *McMillan* v. *B.P. Refinery (Grangemouth) Ltd.*, 1961 S.L.T.(Notes) 79, the view has been expressed that where there is a latent defect in machinery supplied to a workman's employers, the onus is upon the workman to prove that the makers were not reputable manufacturers upon whose skill his employers were entitled to rely. But see Employer's Liability (Defective Equipment) Act, 1969 (c. 37) and Appendix 1 to this volume.

[34] See particularly *Szuca* v. *Balfour Beatty & Co.*, 1953 S.L.T.(Notes) 6. (observations upon intervals of inspections).

[35] *Gavin* v. *Rogers* (1889) 17 R. 206 (an example of *res ipsa loquitur*).

[36] *Sneddon* v. *Addie & Co.* (1849) 11 D. 1159; *Gavin* v. *Rogers, cit. supra*; *Fraser* v. *Fraser* (1882) 9 R. 896; *Irwin* v. *Dennystoun Forge Co.* (1885) 22 S.L.R. 379; *Tarry* v. *Ashton* (1876) 1 Q.B.D. 314; and see Cockburn C.J. in *Webb* v. *Rennie* (1865) 4 F. & F. 608.

[37] See *Murphy* v. *Phillips* (1876) 35 L.T.(N.S.) 477, *per* Pollock B.

defective plant belonging to a third party, then there is no special duty upon the employer to inspect that plant in the general case.[38] Yet the circumstances may alter the employer's responsibility in respect of inspection—for example, if plant or machinery which is on loan from another person is used by the employer in such a way as to form part of his own plant and equipment, then a duty of inspection will arise.[39] The contract for the hire or use of plant may impose a liability upon the hirer.[40]

The employer, after fulfilling his primary obligation as mentioned above, cannot be held responsible for any improper use which his own employees make of the plant and machinery,[41] or for such defects as subsequently arise and ought to have been put right by the employees themselves.[42] The employer is also liable for any bad workmanship by the employees in effecting repairs to plant and machinery, as also for any use of the wrong type of equipment by the employees or for failure to utilise equipment which is available for the particular job. If, however, an employer personally superintends the work in which use is being made of particular materials, plant or machinery, then, quite apart from his responsibility as an employer, there arises an additional and personal responsibility from the superintendence or control of the work and a liability will now accrue to him in respect of all defects which ought to have been discovered and remedied during the progress of the particular work. If the pursuer can show that the resulting defect (arising after an initial supply of plant which was then in good working order) was known to the employer or ought to have been known to him and went unremedied, liability attaches to the employer.[43] Where it is established that there is a need for certain plant or machinery, any failure to supply it will amount to negligence.[44] But before negligence can be firmly established the pursuer must show: (a) that the need for the particular plant or appliance was obvious or it was actually known to the defender; or (b) a reasonable man would

---

[38] See particularly *Robinson* v. *John Watson Ltd.* (1892) 20 R. 144; *Nelson* v. *Scott. Croall & Sons* (1892) 19 R. 425; *M'Inulty* v. *Primrose* (1897) 24 R. 442; *Simpson* v. *Paton* (1896) 23 R. 590; *M'Lachlan* v. *SS. " Peveril " Co. Ltd.* (1896) 23 R. 753; and *Oliver* v. *Saddler & Co.*, 1929 S.C.(H.L.) 94 where employees of a porterage company were held entitled to rely upon inspection by a stevedoring firm of slings supplied by that firm.

[39] See *Warwick* v. *Caledonian Railway Co.* (1897) 24 R. 429 (which was *distinguished* in *Oliver* v. *Saddler & Co., cit. supra*); and *Macdonald* v. *Wylie* (1898) 1 F. 339, followed in *Thomson* v. *Wallace* (O.H.) 1933 S.N. 15.

[40] See *McGlynn* v. *Robert Rome & Son Ltd.* (O.H.) 1968 S.L.T.(Notes) 16 (liability of sub-contractors using contractors' plant for injury to employee of the latter, *per* a condition in the contract).

[41] *Watt* v. *Neilson & Co.* (1888) 15 R. 772; 25 S.L.R. 576.

[42] *Wilson* v. *Mer.y and Cunningham* (1868) 6 M. (H.L.) 84; *Stewart* v. *Coltness Iron Co.* (1877) 4 R. 952; *Cook* v. *Bell* (1857) 20 D. 137; *Cook* v. *Duncan* (1857) 20 D. 180; *Gordon* v. *Pyper* (1892) 20 R.(H.L.) 23; *M'Laughlan* v. *Dunlop & Co.* (1882) 20 S.L.R. 271; *Mackenzie* v. *SS. " Tregenna " Co.*, 31 S.L R. 141.

[43] *Stanforth* v. *Burnbank Foundry Co.* (1887) 24 S.L.R. 722; and see also *Marney* v. *Scott* [1899] 1 Q.B. 986, *per* Bigham J. at p. 992; and *Henderson* v. *Carron Co.* (1889) 16 R. 633; 26 S.L.R. 456.

[44] See *Williams* v. *Birmingham Battery and Metal Co.* [1899] 2 Q.B. 338 (failure to supply a ladder or other proper access); *Lovell* v. *Blundells and Crompton & Co. Ltd.* [1944] K.B. 502; [1944] 2 All E.R. 53 (failure to provide planks).

recognise that it was necessary.[45] The employer is not liable in the general case, unless he knew or ought to have known of the defect or damage.[46] But, as has been indicated above, where an employer buys new equipment from a reputable supplier, or indeed direct from the manufacturer, he is entitled to rely upon the manufacturer and he is not expected to carry out independent tests or examination for latent defects.[47] The *New Merton Board Mills* case [48] is interesting because the House of Lords held that the manufacturer cannot be regarded as a person to whom the employer has delegated the performance of his duty so as to make the employer vicariously liable for latent defects due to negligence in the manufacture; and this principle also holds even if equipment is bought direct from the manufacturer to a special order (*e.g.*, the chassis of the omnibus in *Donnelly's* case [49]). In the subsequent Scottish case of *McMillan* v. *B.P. Refinery (Grangemouth) Ltd.*[50] it was held by the First Division that where there was a latent defect in machinery supplied to a workman's employers the onus was upon the workman to establish that the makers were not reputable manufacturers upon whose skill his employers were entitled to rely.[50a] Yet the employer may be liable for any negligence in his own specification or if he does entrust or delegate the performance of his duty to provide plant to some other person. The same principle applies where the employer *hires* plant from a reputable source—see *Sullivan* v. *Gallagher and Craig.*[51] Where machinery is dangerous in its ordinary working, then the employer will have a duty to instal any requisite safety device.[52]

It seems that an employer is not bound to adopt the latest improvements—yet the absence of the latest improvement or device has to be taken into account in conjunction with the other circumstances of the case, because such absence may clearly point to negligence. The employer has to do his best—*e.g.*, if his equipment is needing replacement and this cannot all be done at once, there is no necessary negligence if he retains some obsolete equipment in use pending its replacement.[53] Yet it is inadvisable for any employer to use less safe equipment where he could have obtained proper and better equipment for the job—see *Ralston* v.

---

[45] See *Bright* v. *Thames Stevedoring Co.* [1951] 1 Lloyd's Rep. 116 (where a light ought to have been provided for a bogie to be used on an uneven dock surface).
[46] See *Bowater* v. *Rowley Regis Corporation* [1944] K.B. 476; [1944] 1 All E.R. 465 (supply of horses known to be unsafe).
[47] See *Mason* v. *Williams and Williams Ltd. and Thomas Turton & Sons Ltd.* [1955] 1 All E.R. 808 (steel chisel too hard and splintered); and the leading case of *Davie* v. *New Merton Board Mills Ltd.* [1959] A.C. 604 (overruling *Donnelly* v. *Glasgow Corporation*, 1953 S.C. 107—the defective front spring; employers held liable); and *Sullivan* v. *Gallagher and Craig, cit. supra.*
[48] [1959] A.C. 604; [1959] 2 W.L.R. 331; [1959] 1 All E.R. 346.
[49] 1953 S.C. 107 (subsequently overruled).
[50] 1961 S.L.T.(Notes) 79.
[50a] See the Employer's Liability (Defective Equipment) Bill 1969. For a note thereon, see Chap. 10, *supra* (n. 54). The new Act is contained in Appendix 1 hereto.
[51] 1960 S.L.T. 70 (trucks hired by the ship which an employer was loading; held that the employer was not liable in the circumstances but that the stevedores were liable).
[52] *Jones* v. *Richard* [1955] 1 All E.R. 463 (farm machinery); *Close* v. *Steel Co. of Wales Ltd.* [1961] 2 All E.R. 953 (machinery liable to throw out fragments, not required to be fenced under the Factories Act).
[53] *O'Connor* v. *B.T.C.* [1958] 1 All E.R. 558 (C.A.).

British Railways Board.[54]   Where the employer entrusts the maintenance of his machinery to an independent contractor who is negligent, the liability falls upon the employer himself.[55]

If an accident has been caused by a defect whose existence was unknown until the accident occurred, it has to be proved that the defect could have been discovered by the exercise of reasonable care—see *Gavin* v. *Rogers.*[56]   There is always a general duty to inspect and test plant.   But it is a question of factual evidence as to how and how often this is done.   It may also be necessary to supplement inspection by requiring " defect reports " from employees.[57]   Selection of safe plant for the work in hand is now the employer's responsibility generally whether he makes the choice personally or acts through his employees. But if it can be shown that the employer specifically left the selection of the equipment to the pursuer, then so long as the pursuer (*i.e.,* employee) was a competent and experienced man, it would seem that the employer might not be liable—see *Johnson* v. *Croggon & Co. Ltd.*[58]

(2) The second common law obligation which rests upon an employer is that of keeping his premises in a safe condition (so far as consistent with the performance of his work) and of conducting his business according to a system which does not involve unusual or unnecessary danger to those whom he employs (commonly called a " safe system of work ").[59] This obligation, taken along with the former obligation already discussed, may perhaps be described comprehensively as a duty to take precautions for the safety of employees.   Understandably, the responsibility will vary with the nature and conditions of the work carried on by the employer— but the degree of precaution required is no higher than that which is reasonably and ordinarily to be expected or, more commonly, " usual and necessary " in the circumstances.[60]   The common law does not place

---

[54]   1967 S.L.T.(Notes) 105 (O.H.).

[55]   *Rodgers* v. *Dunsmuir Confectionery Co.,* 1952 S.L.T.(Notes) 9.

[56]   (1889) 17 R. 206.

[57]   *Barkway* v. *South Wales Transport Co. Ltd.* [1950] A.C. 185; [1950] 1 All E.R. 392 (accident caused by burst tyre; inspection system good but failure to keep a satisfactory report system).

[58]   [1954] 1 All E.R. 121 (faulty ladder; delegation by custom of trade of the duty of selecting equipment—plaintiff was an experienced steel erector—no negligence on the employer's part—the owners of the ladder were not liable as second defendants as they gave no guarantee about suitability of the ladder and did not press its use here).

[59]   See *English* v. *Wilsons and Clyde Coal Co.,* 1937 S.C.(H.L.) 46; 1937 S.L.T. 523 (there can be no delegation of this duty so as to avoid responsibility); *Henderson* v. *John Stuart (Farms) Ltd.,* 1963 S.L.T. 22 (O.H.); see also *Williams* v. *Grimshaw* and *Houghton* v. *Hackney Borough Council* (1967) 3 K.I.R. 610 and 615 respectively (safe system of work includes the protection of employees from unnecessary risks—one of such risks being the risk of injury from criminals).

[60]   *Murray* v. *Merry and Cunningham* (1890) 17 R. 815; *M'Culloch* v. *Clyde Navigation Trustees* (1903) 11 S.L.T. 242; and see also *Cringles* v. *Clyde Alloy Steel Co. Ltd.,* 1961 S.L.T.(Notes) 74 (O.H.) (averments—onus of proof—prima facie presumption *re* cause of disease); *Burns* v. *Dixon's Ironworks,* 1961 S.C. 102 (sufficiency of averments); *Robertson* v. *Guardbridge Paper Co.,* 1961 S.L.T.(Notes) 10 (O.H.) (action not irrelevant because normal practice or obvious necessity for precautions not averred); *Gardiner* v. *Motherwell Machinery & Scrap Co. Ltd.,* 1961 S.C.(H.L.) 1; 1962 S.L.T. 2 (the prima facie presumption test of negligence again applied); *Brander* v. *James Spencer & Co.,* 1964 S.L.T.(Notes) 14 (O.H.) (an employee basing his case

the employer in the position of a guarantor or insurer. Nor does it require him to use the very latest and safest appliances: so long as he makes use of those appliances which are reasonably safe and in general use, that is good enough.[61] Should it happen that the operation proposed is a very difficult one, which requires the taking of special precautions or unusual measures for the safety of the employees, then these special precautions must be taken.[62]

It is clear that the common law has for many years required the employer to take reasonable care to establish and enforce a proper system or method of work—see *Sword* v. *Cameron* [63] and the English case of *Smith* v. *Baker & Sons*.[64] It would appear that Scottish common law was ahead of English law on this particular point of the employer being obliged by law to conduct his business upon a safe and proper system. Indeed, it was only in the leading case of *English* v. *Wilsons & Clyde Coal Co.*[65] that the need for a proper system of work became fully and firmly established in all parts of the United Kingdom. Quite naturally, many cases followed in the wake of the *Wilsons & Clyde* case. It must be clearly understood that the question of whether or not the system adopted is safe or not is a question of fact—apparently, there is no doctrine of precedent which requires cases to be followed upon the facts themselves, even where the facts are similar.[66] Precedent by itself is, of course, a doctrine of law.

The meaning of "system of work" has been discussed in several cases.[67] No clear definition has been attempted, but certain remarks by Lord Greene M.R. in England in *Speed* v. *Swift* (*Thomas*) & *Co. Ltd.*[68] are helpful. Whilst he is planning or laying out the system of work, the employer must take into account the possibility that employees tend to

---

upon a faulty system was not bound to aver what a safe system would have been); and *Dillon* v. *Clyde Stevedoring Co.*, 1967 S.L.T.(Notes) 18 (O.H.) (statements of fact alone are not enough—there must be averments pointing to negligence by defender).

[61] *Moore* v. *Ross* (1890) 17 R. 796; *M'Gill* v. *Bowman & Co.* (1890) 17 R. 206; and *Mitchell* v. *Patullo* (1885) 23 S.L.R. 207.

[62] See *Pollock* v. *Cassidy* (1870) 8 M. 615; 42 J. 303; also *Stark* v. *M'Laren* (1871) 10 M. 31; *Henderson* v. *Carron Co.* (1889) 16 R. 633; *M'Mullan* v. *John Collins Ltd.* (O.H.), May 17, 1950 ([1950] C.L.Y. 4781); *M'Gilvray* v. *British Insulated Callender's Cables Ltd.*, 1965 S.L.T.(Notes) 61; and *Cochrane* v. *Colvilles Ltd.*, 1968 S.L.T.(Sh.Ct.) 48 (employer must not ignore the absence of a safety precaution whose benefits were obvious to him).

[63] (1839) 1 D. 493 (employees in a quarry not given enough time to get clear before an explosion).

[64] [1891] A.C. 325; the House of Lords held that swinging heavy stones overhead by crane without a proper warning system was an unsafe system of work (though this was not the main point before the House).

[65] 1937 S.C.(H.L.) 46; 1937 S.L.T. 523; and in the English reports (*sub nom. Wilsons & Clyde Coal Co.* v. *English*) at [1938] A.C. 57; [1937] 3 All E.R. 628.

[66] *Qualcast* (*Wolverhampton*) *Ltd.* v. *Haynes* [1959] A.C. 743; [1959] 2 All E.R. 38 (an experienced moulder pouring molten metal—not wearing protective spats, not urged to do so, but employers *held not* negligent in the circumstances).

[67] See *Winter* v. *Cardiff Rural District Council* [1950] 1 All E.R. 819, *per* Lord Oaksey at p. 822; and *Speed* v. *Swift* (*Thomas*) & *Co. Ltd.* [1943] K.B. 557; [1943] 1 All E.R. 539, *per* Lord Greene M.R. at pp. 563 and 542 respectively; this case was approved by the House of Lords in *Colfar* v. *Coggins and Griffith* (*Liverpool*) *Ltd.* [1945] A.C. 197; [1945] 1 All E.R. 326.

[68] [1943] K.B. 557; [1943] 1 All E.R. 539 at pp. 563 and 542 respectively.

become blasé or careless about the risks which arise in their daily tasks.[69] A most important extension of the principle is that allowance must be made for the infirmities or inexperience of individual workmen.[70] In *Nolan v. Dental Manufacturing Co. Ltd.*,[71] a case involving a serious risk of injury to the eyes in the use of grinding tools where toolsetters were not willing to wear goggles, it was held that strict orders should have been given to wear goggles and should have been enforced by supervision. Cases illustrative of the unsafe or defective system of work are numerous.[72] As the employer remains responsible for his own personal negligence and the negligence of his servants in failing to carry out routine working operations safely, what is required, therefore, is the exercise of reasonable care in the conduct of routine operations—see *Staveley Iron & Chemical Co. Ltd. v. Jones.*[73]

A good example of one of the highest precautions which an employer must take for the safety of his employees is the fencing of machinery. Quite apart from the statutory obligation imposed by the Factories Act 1961 [74] or any other statute or regulation, the common law clearly imposes such a duty upon the employer. When the fencing of machinery is an ordinary and reasonable precaution for the safety of employees, then it must be done.[75] If the machinery is to be used by young and/or inexperienced persons, then, obviously, in deciding upon the supply of fencing or no fencing, serious regard will have to be paid to the quality of the employees.[75a] Fencing is, of course, a continuing obligation so long as the machine is in use.[76] Any failure in the statutory obligation or common

---

[69] *General Cleaning Contractors Ltd. v. Christmas* [1953] A.C. 180; [1952] 2 All E.R. 1110 at pp. 189 and 1114 respectively *per* Lord Oaksey and *per* Lord Reid at pp. 194 and 1117; and see also *McWilliams v. Sir Wm. Arrol and Co. Ltd.*, 1962 S.C.(H.L.) 70; 1962 S.L.T. 121; and [1962] 1 All E.R. 623.

[70] See *Paris v. Stepney Borough Council* [1951] A.C. 367; [1951] 1 All E.R. 42 (the one-eyed workman hammering a rusty bolt on to a motor-vehicle who was blinded by a chip of metal. The trial judge held that goggles should have been provided. The House of Lords, by a majority, refused to set aside this finding of fact); *Byers v. Head Wrightson & Co. Ltd.* [1961] 2 All E.R. 538.

[71] [1958] 2 All E.R. 449.

[72] *Qualcast (Wolverhampton) Ltd. v. Haynes* [1959] A.C. 743; [1959] 2 All E.R. 38; *Brown v. Rolls Royce Ltd.* [1960] 1 All E.R. 577; *Calvert v. London Transport Executive* [1949] W.N. 341; *Kerr v. Glasgow Corporation*, 1945 S.C. 335; *Porter v. Port of Liverpool Stevedoring Co. Ltd.* [1944] 2 All E.R. 411; *Grantham v. New Zealand Shipping Co. Ltd.* [1940] 4 All E.R. 258; *Thurogood v. Van den Berghs and Jurgens Ltd.* [1951] 2 K.B. 537; [1951] 1 All E.R. 682; *Jones v. Richards* [1955] 1 All E.R. 463; *Kilgollan v. Wm. Cooke & Co. Ltd.* [1956] 2 All E.R. 294; *Lewis v. High Duty Alloys Ltd.* [1957] 1 All E.R. 740; *General Cleaning Contractors Ltd. v. Christmas* [1953] A.C. 180; [1952] 2 All E.R. 1110; *Drummond v. British Building Cleaners Ltd.* [1954] 3 All E.R. 507; *Wilson v. Tyneside Window Cleaning Co.* [1958] 1 Q.B. 110; [1958] 2 All E.R. 265; *Rands v. McNeil* [1955] 1 Q.B. 253; [1954] 3 All E.R. 265; and *McWilliams v. Sir Wm. Arrol & Co. Ltd.*, 1962 S.C.(H.L.) 70; 1962 S.L.T. 121; [1962] 1 All E.R. 623.

[73] [1956] A.C. 627; [1956] 1 All E.R. 403.

[74] See Part B, *infra.*

[75] *Edwards v. Hutcheon* (1889) 16 R. 694; *Ross v. Thomson & Co.* (1882) 20 S.L.R. 46; *Murray v. Merry and Cunningham* (1890) 17 R. 815; *Milligan v. Muir & Co.* (1891) 19 R. 18; *Cameron v. Walker* (1898) 25 R. 449.

[75a] *Gemmill v. Gourock Ropework Co.* (1861) 23 D. 425.

[76] *Traill v. Small and Boase* (1873) 11 M. 888.

law duty [77] to fence raises an immediate presumption of liability on the employer's part where injury results.[78] Unless the statutory obligation is an absolute one (and this will require to be ascertained from a careful interpretation of the particular section), the presumption mentioned may be rebutted by the employer if he can show that the accident was attributable to some cause other than lack of fencing, *e.g.*, carelessness or negligence on the part of the employee himself.[79] This plea by the defender (*i.e.*, the employer) may, of course, be incompetent in the circumstances where a statute is obviously designed to protect a certain class or classes of person (*e.g.*, young persons) against this very happening.[80]

Exactly the same principles apply to the employment of young and/or inexperienced persons at dangerous and unsuitable work. The ground of liability may be either (a) that a dangerous system of work is in operation where such persons are employed or (b) that the employees falling into this category cannot be held to have undertaken the risk of employment as ordinarily competent, qualified or experienced employees do in the general case. There seems to be no doubt that any such employment in these forms amounts to negligence on the part of the employer.[81] Again, a presumption of liability arises when an injury occurs,[82] but this presumption may also be rebutted by the employer if he can show a wilful disobedience to orders or some misconduct by the employee which caused the injury.[83]

Examples of breaches of the obligation to keep premises in a safe condition are very numerous, but perhaps the following will serve to illustrate failure therein: if pitfalls are allowed to exist in unlighted places [84]; or if nothing is done about defective gates,[85] whose unsafe condition is known or ought to have been known to the employer [86]; or, again, if an unsafe pit shaft [87] is kept in use.

Moreover, the duty to take care, in relation to premises, encompasses the premises and plant of third parties, where appropriate, and does not

---

[77] But it is irrelevant to refer to statutory provisions in an action based upon common law—see *Paterson* v. *Charles Brand & Son Ltd.*, 1964 S.L.T.(Notes) 75; and *Murray* v. *Donald MacDonald (Antartex) Ltd.* (O.H.) 1968 S.L.T. 10.

[78] *Traill* v. *Small and Boase, cit. supra*; *Kelly* v. *Glebe Sugar Refining Co.* (1893) 20 R. 833; *Shields* v. *Murdoch and Cameron* (1893) 20 R. 727.

[79] *Greer* v. *Turnbull & Co.* (1891) 19 R. 21; *Robb* v. *Bulloch, Lade & Co.* (1892) 19 R. 971; *Cameron* v. *Walker* (1898) 25 R. 449.

[80] *Pringle* v. *Grosvenor* (1894) 21 R. 532; and see the Factories Act 1961 so far as relating to women and young persons (dealt with, *inter alia*, in Part B of this chapter).

[81] *O'Byrne* v. *Burn* (1854) 16 D. 1025; *Robertson* v. *Brown* (1876) 3 R. 652.

[82] *Sharp* v. *Pathhead Spinning Co.* (1885) 12 R. 574; *Gibson* v. *Nimmo & Co.* (1895) 22 R. 491; *Gibb* v. *Crombie* (1875) 2 R. 886; *cf. Carty* v. *Nicoll* (1878) 6 R. 194; and *Walker* v. *Olsen* (1882) 9 R. 946; 19 S.L.R. 708.

[83] *Morris* v. *Boase Spinning Co.* (1895) 22 R. 336.

[84] *Jamieson* v. *Russell & Co.* (1892) 19 R. 898; *Macleod* v. *Caledonian Railway Co.* (1885) 23 S.L.R. 68.

[85] *Johnson* v. *Mitchell & Co.* (1885) 22 S.L.R. 698.

[86] *Paterson* v. *Wallace* (1854) 1 Macq. 748; *Brydon or Marshall* v. *Stewart* (1855) 2 Macq. 30.

[87] *Brydon or Marshall* v. *Stewart, cit. supra.*

just relate to the employer's own premises.[88] The duty will, however, vary according to the circumstances of each case. Custom of trade may have to be considered as it may allow an employer to rely to a certain extent upon the diligence of a third party.[89] The statutory duty owed by occupiers of land and premises is regulated by the Occupiers' Liability (Scotland) Act 1960.[90]

The allegation of carrying on work upon a dangerous or defective system means that the employer has been guilty of some failure in giving instructions or some failure in taking precautions to ensure that the workmen are reasonably safely protected whilst carrying out a dangerous operation. The cases on these failures are quite numerous as the old textbooks show and indeed much litigation occurs today in the Court of Session upon this concept of a " safe system of work." [91] A good example of a failure of this type would be the situation where a gang of railway platelayers was working on a section of main line track, without adequate look-outs being posted to warn the men of approaching trains.[92] The allegation mentioned applies equally to the adoption of a negligent method of utilising machinery which is perfectly sound in itself.[93] It will be realised

---

[88] *General Cleaning Contractors Ltd.* v. *Christmas* [1953] A.C. 180; [1952] 2 All E.R. 1110; *Thomson* v. *Cremin* [1953] 2 All E.R. 1185; *Smith* v. *Austin Lifts Ltd.* [1959] 1 All E.R. 81; See also the important Scottish case of *M'Quilter* v. *Goulandris Brothers Ltd.*, 1951 S.L.T.(Notes) 75 (employers liable for a failure to see that lighting was provided); *Jack* v. *Keiller & Son Ltd.* (O.H.) 1952 S.L.T.(Notes) 28; *Pullar* v. *Window Clean Ltd.*, 1956 S.C. 13; 1956 S.L.T. 17. But special circumstances may have to be taken into account and these might relieve an employer from liability for negligence, *e.g.*, in *Gemmill* v. *MacDonald* (O.H.) 1964 S.L.T.(Notes) 9 it was held that the employers of a watchman were under no general duty or obligation to inspect a ship, whereon his duties were to be carried out.

[89] *Thomson* v. *Cremin* [1953] 2 All E.R. 1185; approving *M'Lachlan* v. *The Peverill SS. Co. Ltd.* and *MacGregor and Ferguson* (1896) 23 R. 753 (that stevedores are in general entitled to rely upon the shipowners for safety).

[90] 8 & 9 Eliz. 2, c. 30.

[91] *Sword* v. *Cameron* (1839) 1 D. 493; *Smith* v. *Baker & Sons* [1891] A.C. 325; *M'Inally* v. *King's Trs.* (1886) 14 R. 8; *M'Guire* v. *Cairns & Co.* (1890) 17 R. 540; *Cook* v. *Stark* (1886) 14 R. 1; *Morton* v. *Edinburgh and Glasgow Railway Co.* (1864) 2 M. 589; *Edgar* v. *Law and Brand* (1871) 10 M. 236; *Murdoch* v. *MacKinnon* (1885) 12 R. 810; *Stark* v. *M'Laren* (1871) 10 M. 31; *Pollock* v. *Cassidy* (1870) 8 M. 615; *Grant* v. *Drysdale* (1883) 10 R. 1159. The following is a selection of the more modern Scottish cases on " safe system of work," *viz.*: *Kabango* v. *Renfrew Stevedoring Co.*, 1949 S.L.T.(Notes) 33; *Ramsay* v. *Wimpey & Co.* 1951 S.C. 692; 1952 S.L.T. 46 (consideration of employer's duty outwith working hours); *Bell* v. *United Turkey Red Co.*, 1952 S.L.T.(Notes) 7 (O.H.); *Gillies* v. *Bonnington Castings Ltd.*, 1956 S.L.T.(Notes) 48; *Anderson* v. *William Band & Son*, 1956 S.L.T.(Notes) 22 (employers not bound to issue special instructions to an experienced workman examining the tip-up mechanism of a lorry); *Bruce* v. *Alexander Stephen & Sons Ltd.*, 1957 S.L.T. 78 (O.H.); *Brown* v. *Rolls Royce Ltd.*, 1960 S.L.T. 9; [1960] 1 W.L.R. 210; [1960] 1 All E.R. 577 (H.L.); *Reid* v. *Colvilles Ltd.*, 1959 S.L.T.(Notes) 6 (employers guilty of negligence in failing to take reasonable steps to enforce their system of working); *Heron* v. *Scottish Spade & Shovel Works Ltd.*, 1959 S.L.T.(Notes) 13; *McLaughlin* v. *Scott's Shipbuilding & Engineering Co. Ltd.*, 1960 S.L.T.(Notes) 58 (O.H.) (undisciplined rush of employees when the " whistle " blew); and *Lydon* v. *J. & A. Smith of Maddiston Ltd.*, 1962 S.L.T.(Notes) 42 (O.H.) (an employer not negligent where there was no practical precaution to obviate a danger arising in the course of work).

[92] A somewhat similar situation occurred in *Bremner* v. *M'Alpine* (1907) 15 S.L.T. 106 (Outer House case), where a railway line was in course of construction and there was a failure to provide a " redcap " during shunting.

[93] See *Welsh* v. *Moir* (1885) 12 R. 590.

that the exceptional operation, or the casual operation,[94] does not form part of a " system of working." [95]

It may be the case that an employer has tried to prohibit the use of bad working practices amongst his own employees but has failed in his attempt to do so, and accordingly the continued use of such bad practices may—depending upon the circumstances—then have developed into what is really a defective system of work for which the employer will be clearly answerable.[96] The facts are generally ascertained more clearly in the course of a jury trial rather than a proof.[97] The basis of any claim against the employer should be a sound one and it should point to a material failure of duty by him. The allegation that there has been a failure of duty which, upon examination, is revealed as being based upon some trifling matter will simply not do.[98]

(3) The final obligation undertaken by the employer towards each individual employee is that he (the employer) will exercise reasonable skill in the selection of other employees.[99] This obligation is perhaps no longer so important today as it was prior to the passing of the Law Reform (Personal Injuries) Act 1948 when the doctrine of common employment was in force. Before 1948 any failure by an employer to select competent employees precluded him from relying upon the doctrine.[1] For example, if an employer engaged a person of intemperate habits as an employee, this would be an act of negligence in many circumstances, upon which an injured fellow-employee would be able to rely in his claim against the employer.[2] Certainly, in the general case, the common employment doctrine was—prior to 1948—a device for the protection of employers, although it must be pointed out in fairness that the Employers' Liability Act 1880 [3] had limited, fairly substantially, the freedom which the employers had enjoyed in relation to the defences of common employment and contributory negligence, but mainly the former. The old defence or shield of " contributory negligence "—which operated formerly as a complete defence in an employer's favour—finally disappeared with the passing of the Law Reform (Contributory Negligence) Act 1945.[4]

There may be also perhaps a duty to give adequate supervision, if this

---

[94] See *McMillan* v. *Barclay Curle & Co.*, 1912 S.C. 263; 1912, 1 S.L.T. 63 (casual danger emerging in the course of work; no relevant averment of negligence).

[95] See *Harper* v. *Dunlop & Co.* (1902) 5 F. 208.

[96] See *Andrews* v. *Colvilles Ltd.*, 1947 S.L.T.(Notes) 23; 1947 S.N. 10. If an employer teaches a workman a method of work which is dangerous, there seems to be no doubt that liability rests firmly upon the employer—see *Herton* v. *Blaw Knox Ltd.*, VI K.I.R. 35.

[97] *McAulay* v. *Colvilles Ltd.* (O.H.) 1967 S.L.T.(Notes) 19.

[98] See *Jamieson* v. *National Coal Board* (O.H.) 1963 S.L.T.(Notes) 76 (action of negligence based on pursuer having to climb over a rope 2 feet above ground held to be irrelevant).

[99] *Bartonshill Coal Co.* v. *Reid* (1858) 3 Macq. 266; *Bartonshill Coal Co.* v. *M'Guire* (1858) 3 Macq. 300; *Wilson* v. *Merry and Cunningham* (1868) 6 M.(H.L.) 84; *Tarrant* v. *Webb* (1856) 18 C.B. 797; *Black* v. *Fife Coal Co. Ltd.* [1912] A.C. 149.

[1] *M'Aulay* v. *Brownlie* (1860) 22 D. 975.

[2] *Donald* v. *Brand* (1862) 24 D. 295; *Morton* v. *Edinburgh and Glasgow Railway Co.* (1864) 2 M. 589.

[3] See Fraser, *Master and Servant* (3rd ed.), Chap. XI.

[4] 8 & 9 Geo. 6, c. 28.

can be distinguished from a system of work. For example, in the *Crossley Brothers* case,[5] cited below, the court was satisfied that this particular practical joke could not reasonably have been foreseen by the employers and therefore there was no failure, on the evidence, in a duty of supervision. This case was distinguished in *Hudson* v. *Ridge Manufacturing Co.*,[6] where the employers were held liable because the fellow-employee at fault here was in the habit of playing practical jokes upon other employees and no steps had been taken by the employers to stop him—accordingly, they had failed in their duty to the employees generally.

Of course, with the appearance on the Statute Book of the Law Reform (Personal Injuries) Act 1948, which abolished the doctrine of common employment, the three common law obligations previously mentioned have ceased to be quite so important as they formerly were (particularly the third obligation), although all are still perfectly relevant to any reparation claim which is taken at common law. The tendency in modern industrial law is for the legislature to impose, by statute or statutory instrument or in a code of special regulations relating to a particular industry, more and more duties and liabilities upon employers. Recent examples of this legislation relate to factories (1961), mines and quarries (1954) and offices, shops and railway premises (1963).

PART B—THE EMPLOYER'S STATUTORY OBLIGATIONS

(1) *Factories*

Before commencing to consider in some detail the modern legislation concerning factories and the position of employees therein, it might be of some relevance to look briefly at the background history of this section of the law. Whilst undeniably such historical development is of interest to the economic and social historian it ought also to be of some interest and importance to the lawyer.

Historical Introduction to Factory Legislation

The Health and Morals of Apprentices Act of 1802,[1] the first of the many statutes in this field, may be regarded in a sense as an extension of the Poor Law of Elizabeth I's time (*circa* 1601) rather than as an attempted governmental control or executive control over industrial life. It will be recalled that the 1601 Poor Law made provision for destitute children and orphans being apprenticed to some trade or other and as a consequence

---

[5] See *Smith* v. *Crossley Brothers Ltd.* (1951) 95 Sol.J. 655 where two apprentices mischievously injected compressed air into a third, but the Court of Appeal held, on the evidence, that their action could *not* reasonably have been foreseen, so that there was no failure in the duty of supervision. The act was an act of wilful misbehaviour not reasonably to be foreseen.

[6] [1957] 2 Q.B. 348; [1957] 2 W.L.R. 948; [1957] 2 All E.R. 229.

[1] 42 Geo. 3, c. 73.

of that legislation there appeared those alarming buildings known as Industrial Schools and workhouses as major landscape features of the seventeenth and eighteenth centuries.

Public attention appears to have been drawn to the conditions of working children in the factories by an outbreak of fever in 1784 at the Radcliffe Cotton Works in Lancashire. The Justices of the Peace for the county requested an immediate investigation from a team of doctors drawn from Manchester. The report subsequently issued stressed the overworking of children by the mill-owners as one of the main evils of the new industrial system. The Manchester magistrates, by a resolution issued in 1784, stated that they would refuse to allow " indentures of parish apprentices whereby they shall be bound to owners of cotton mills and other works in which children are obliged to work in the night or more than ten hours in the day "—and this seems to have been the first attempt by a public body to limit or restrict the working hours of children.[2]

By a statute of 1793 the justices of the peace were given special power to impose a fine of forty shillings upon any master or mistress who was convicted of ill-using an apprentice. Unfortunately, there is no evidence available to establish whether or not the justices themselves effectively invoked and enforced this measure.

Sir Robert Peel's " Health and Morals of Apprentices Act 1802 " above-mentioned was an important landmark, although it was not a Factory Act proper in the twentieth-century sense. Broadly, the Act provided as follows:
(a) working hours to be limited to twelve per day;
(b) night work to be discontinued and to cease by June 1804;
(c) apprentices to be instructed in reading, writing and arithmetic; and a suit of clothing to be given to each apprentice annually;
(d) factories to be whitewashed twice per annum and be properly ventilated at all times;
(e) separate sleeping apartments to be provided for the sexes and not more than two persons to share a bed; and
(f) apprentices were to attend church at least once per month.

These provisions were to be enforced by the justices of the peace, who were to appoint two inspectors (one a clergyman) from amongst themselves to visit the factories in their area. All mills and factories were to be registered annually with the Clerk of the Peace. The Justices might impose fines ranging from £2 to £5 for any failure or neglect to obey these provisions. The preamble explained that the Act was to apply, not just to apprentices but also to all cotton and woollen factories wherein twenty or more persons were employed. The statutory provisions which related to restriction of hours and to education and provision of clothing were applied only to apprentices. The Act did not distinguish between youthful

---

[2] *A History of Factory Legislation* by B. L. Hutchins and A. Harrison (1926) at p. 9 (a book to which the author is indebted for much helpful material).

apprentices and adult apprentices. It applied simply to " apprentices " (irrespective of age or sex) and imposed a uniform rule for all of them.

The next milestone is the Act of 1819,[3] which is said to have seen the light of day eventually as a watered-down version of Robert Owen's original draft. This Act did the following things:

    (i) fixed the minimum employment age at nine years;

    (ii) prohibited any young person under sixteen years of age from being employed for more than twelve hours per day, excluding meal times;

    (iii) continued the inspection duties of the justices (although such inspection became impracticable);

    (iv) applied only to cotton mills.

The substantial forces of capitalism were marshalled against the 1819 Act and two main assumptions were relied upon in the arguments against this legislation, viz.: (a) the protection of the commercial side of industry was a state responsibility and (b) regulations and restrictions imposed under the statute would only injure trade, inhibit an industrial expansion and reduce employers and workers to penury.

A subsequent statute of 1825 [4] made the following stipulations: (1) no young person under sixteen years was to work more than twelve hours per day (not counting meal times); (2) the dinner hour must be taken between 11 o'clock a.m. and 3 o'clock p.m.; and (3) not more than nine hours of work was permitted on a Saturday and this must fall within the period 5 o'clock a.m. and 4.30 p.m. If an employer employed a child who was under the legal age limit and in so doing he relied upon an assurance from the parent or guardian that the child had attained or exceeded the legal age limit no responsibility attached to the employer for a breach of the age limit stipulation. The period of complaint (i.e., complaint to the justices) was reduced to two months. By an amending statute of 1831 [5] this period of complaint was further reduced to three weeks and brothers of mill-owners were not allowed to sit as justices for the enforcement of this legislation. The 1831 Act introduced an early form of register (open to inspection by the justices) and extended the twelve-hour day to all persons under eighteen years, as well as prohibiting night work to all persons under twenty-one years; but all of these provisions related only to cotton mills.

The Factory Act 1833 [6] was of major historical and legal importance because it introduced an entirely new branch of the Administration or Civil Service, namely, H.M. Inspectorate of Factories.[7] The Act also

---

[3] The Factory Act 1819 (59 Geo. 3, c. 66), amended by the Factory Act 1820 (60 Geo. 3, c. 5).
[4] The Factory Act 1825 (6 Geo. 4, c. 63) (amended by two similar statutes in 1830).
[5] The Factory Act 1831 (1 & 2 Will. 4, c. 39).
[6] 3 & 4 Will. 4, c. 103.
[7] Credit for this is given to Mr. Edwin (later Sir Edwin) Chadwick (a member of the 1833 Commission on factory reform).

prohibited night work [8] for all persons under eighteen years in cotton, woollen, worsted, hemp, flax, tow, linen and silk mills, and no such person (*i.e.*, under eighteen years) was to be employed for more than twelve hours per day or sixty-nine per week. No child was to be employed, except in silk mills. No child under thirteen years (phased over the first three years of the Act from eleven years to thirteen years inclusive) was to be employed for more than forty-eight hours per week or nine hours per day. Initially, four government inspectors were appointed and they were required to report twice per annum. These inspectors were responsible, in large measure, for the changes made in the Factory Act 1844.[9] By that Act, the statutory provisions were extended to female employees, upon more or less the same basis as young persons. Attention was now directed to the safeguarding of dangerous machinery and to the provision of secure fencing. No child or young person or female worker was to be allowed to clean a machine whilst it was in motion. No changes were made in the hours of work or the working day, but a " half-time system " for child employees was introduced. The minimum age limit was reduced to eight years. The " public clock " to regulate working hours and meal times was introduced. The factory whistle was now heard in the land. The administrative machinery was expanded and fines and penalties were increased. Further statutes followed in 1847, 1850 and 1853, introducing *inter alia* a definite normal working day for women, young persons and children. This period is characterised by two interesting movements upon the industrial scene: first, among the working classes, who were agitating for some limitation upon the "running times" of machinery in an endeavour to compel some adherence to the legislation on working hours; and secondly, among the employers, who regarded the new legislation as an interference with their business. The employers got round that legislation by adopting the " relay system " (or " shift system " as it was later to be called). The 1850 Act [10] is important because it clearly established the normal working day (*i.e.*, the lawful working day being made to coincide with the lawful period of employment—and allowing for meal times) and this was extended to children by a statute of 1853, sponsored by Palmerston. The legal hours of work for children were now six and one-half hours per day or ten hours upon three alternate days and no child could be employed prior to 6 o'clock a.m. or later than 6 o'clock p.m. At the same time, a move was afoot to apply these early Factory Acts to all factories, including bleaching and dyeing processes and other industries. This was accomplished eventually by the Factory Acts Extension Act 1867 (amended in 1871) and the Workshops Regulation Act 1867, both of these measures being repealed and replaced by a new consolidating Act of 1878 (amended in 1883, 1891 and 1895) which was itself repealed by a further consolidating Act in 1901, *i.e.*, on the threshold of the twentieth century.

[8] *i.e.*, between 8.30 p.m. and 5.30 a.m.
[9] 7 & 8 Vict., c. 15.
[10] The Factory Act 1850 (13 & 14 Vict., c. 54).

The 1878 Act [11] had followed upon a Commission, appointed in 1876, to consider the consolidation of factory and workshop laws. The 1878 Act removed the arbitrary distinction between what was a " factory " and what was a " workshop " and substituted a new general definition of a factory as premises where articles were made, altered, repaired, ornamented, finished or adapted for sale, by means of manual labour exercised for gain; and where mechanical power was used on the premises. Those premises to which the Act applied were classified as follows—(i) textile factories, (ii) non-textile factories, (iii) workshops employing children, young persons and women, (iv) women's workshops and (v) domestic workshops. The age limit for child labour was raised to eleven years by section 18 of the 1891 statute. In more recent times employment of children is governed or controlled by the various Education Acts and the Children and Young Persons Acts, in both Scotland and England. Where an Act is intended to apply to Scotland alone then—in the examples given —it will become an Education (Scotland) Act or a Children and Young Persons (Scotland) Act, although reference to other statutes, having a general application to the United Kingdom in these fields, might also have to be made for guidance.

The 1901 Act [12] is the next vital statutory milestone which demands some consideration in this historical backcloth. One of its important provisions was that no child under the age of twelve years was to be employed in a factory or workshop. The Act also extended the control and inspection of workshops by local authorities. It did, however, make notable advances in the field of health and safety, but the pattern of legislation continued to be piecemeal and, therefore, unnecessarily complicated.[13] The Act made no attempt to limit or restrict the hours of work of adult male employees in the general case, although in the case of dangerous trades special regulations could be made,[14] which would limit these hours—taking into account the dangerous nature of the work itself or the unhealthy conditions which prevailed or were likely to prevail in a particular type of manufacturing process. Fire precautions did not figure too prominently in the 1901 legislation, but it will be seen shortly that greater attention has been paid in recent years to this very important matter. Finally, notification of accidents and diseases was formally incorporated into the 1901 Act [15] and has been retained ever since. Two minor statutes of 1907 and 1911 dealt with laundries and cotton cloth

---

[11] The Factory and Workshops (Consolidation) Act 1878 (41 Vict., c. 16), amended by the Factory and Workshop Act 1883 (46 & 47 Vict., c. 53), the Factory and Workshop Act 1891 (54 & 55 Vict., c. 75) and by the Factory and Workshop Act 1895 (58 & 59 Vict., c. 37).

[12] The Factory and Workshop Act 1901 (1 Edw. 7, c. 22) (criticised widely for the powers it gave to local authorities instead of to the Factory Inspectorate).

[13] See, for example, the criticism by Sir Frank Tillyard in *The Worker and the State* (3rd ed., 1948), at p. 121, with particular reference to periods of work, Sunday working hours, allowances for meal times, etc.

[14] See in particular section 79 of the 1901 Act and the powers given to make " special orders " thereunder.

[15] See thereafter the Notice of Accidents Act 1906.

factories respectively (the latter Act being replaced by another statute of 1929) and eventually factory legislation was consolidated and amended by the Factories Act 1937,[16] which was a comprehensive statute containing 160 sections and four Schedules. This Act dealt, in some considerable detail, with the following major topics—health, safety and welfare (both general and special provisions); notification and investigation of accidents and industrial diseases; employment of women and young persons; special applications to special premises (*e.g.*, tenement factories, electrical stations, docks, ships, etc.); homework and piecework; and the keeping of registers and records. The 1937 Act was amended first in 1948 [17] and again in 1959.[18] The 1959 statute was the more important amendment to the principal Act as it extended the statutory provisions governing dangerous fumes and dangerous substances, hoists and lifts, floors, passages and stairs, etc. (expanding the section 25 (1) requirement of the principal Act for floors, etc., and requiring these things to be kept, so far as was reasonably practicable, " free from obstruction and from any substance likely to cause persons to slip ") and, most importantly, it introduced a fairly comprehensive code of fire precautions as shown by sections 9 to 17 inclusive of the 1959 Act. However, although it will be necessary to refer from time to time to certain decided cases based upon the 1937 Act (amended as explained), the modern legislation regarding factories is really to be found mainly in the Factories Act 1961,[19] which is, of course, another consolidating statute—which attempts to bring the law up to date. The Law Commissions [20] may also require to consider from time to time the question of further reforms in the field of " factory law."

Factories—The Modern Legislation

As indicated in the preceding section, the modern legislation upon factories is to be found meantime in the Factories Act 1961.[21] The 1961 Act adopts the familiar pattern of the 1937 Act and is divided into the following fourteen parts:

Part I (ss. 1–11)—Health (General Provisions)

Part II (ss. 12–56)—Safety (General Provisions)

Part III (ss. 57–62)—Welfare (General Provisions)

Part IV (ss. 63–79)—Health, Safety and Welfare (Special Provisions and Regulations)

Part V (ss. 80–85)—Notification of Accidents and Industrial Diseases

Part VI (ss. 86–119)—Employment of Women and Young Persons

Part VII (ss. 120–132)—Special Applications and Extensions

Part VIII (ss. 133 and 134)—Homework

[16] 1 Edw. 8 & 1 Geo. 6, c. 67.
[17] 11 & 12 Geo. 6, c. 55.
[18] 7 & 8 Eliz. 2, c. 67.
[19] 9 & 10 Eliz. 2, c. 34.
[20] In both Scotland and England.
[21] 9 & 10 Eliz. 2, c. 34. The employer/occupier is also bound by the Occupiers' Liability (Scotland) Act 1960 (8 & 9 Eliz. 2, c. 30), ss. 1 and 2.

Part IX (ss. 135 and 136)—Wages

Part X (ss. 137–144)—Notices, Returns, Records, Duties of Persons employed and application of Weights and Measures Acts

Part XI (ss. 145–154)—Administration

Part XII (ss. 155–171)—Offences, Penalties and Legal Proceedings

Part XIII (ss. 172–174)—Application [22] of the Act

Part XIV (ss. 175–185)—Interpretation and General

together with seven relevant Schedules. The Act came into force on April 1, 1962. It must, of course, be read along with the statutory instruments, special regulations and orders and other subsidiary legislation issued by the Minister of Labour—under powers accorded to him by the statute—as well as being read along with special codes of regulations which apply to specific industries, e.g., shipbuilding [23] and woodworking.[24]

It is not proposed to undertake an exhaustive examination of every single section in the statute and to include in that examination detailed commentaries upon words and phrases occurring in each section, all duly vouched and fortified by copious citation of case-law and extensive footnotes. However, it is essential and it is hoped that it will be helpful to select some of the more well-known sections, which impose duties and obligations or which create certain rights, and to look at these sections a little more closely and with special attention to Scots law and Scottish cases. At the same time due cognisance will be taken of the major English cases which undoubtedly have an important persuasive authority upon the Scottish courts but, of course, an exhaustive citation of the English authorities will not be attempted. Most of these English authorities are readily available in the leading textbooks, casebooks and reference works used by practitioners and students of English law.[25]

PART I—Health (General Provisions)

This part comprises sections 1 to 11 inclusive. Section 1 (1) imposes a general provision that every factory shall be kept in a clean state and free from effluvia arising from any drain, sanitary convenience or nuisance. The remaining subsections proceed to spell out the methods by which the main requirement is to be achieved and to allow certain exemptions in those cases where mechanical power is not used and less than ten persons

---

[22] As follows: s. 172—General Applications; s. 173—Application to the Crown; and s. 174—Mines and Quarries.

[23] See the Shipbuilding and Ship-repairing Regulations 1960 (S.I. 1960 No. 1932) which replace the old 1931 Regulations.

[24] See the Woodworking Machinery Special Regulations 1922 (S.R. & O. 1922 No. 1196) as amended in 1927 (S.R. & O. 1927 No. 207) and again in 1945 (S.R. & O. 1945 No. 1227)

[25] See, for example, the Encyclopaedia of Factories, Shops and Offices (Sweet & Maxwell) which is kept up to date throughout each year; Redgrave's Factories Acts (21st ed., 1966); and Factory Law by H. Samuels (8th ed., 1969) being three of the well-known reference books in this field.

are employed or where the Minister [26] makes an order excluding any factory (or part thereof) of a particular class or description. There is no doubt that any breach of this section may give rise to an action of damages based upon breach of the statutory duty imposed [27] as well as to a criminal prosecution for non-observance of the statutory provisions. The Factories (Cleanliness of Walls and Ceilings) Order 1960 [28] should also be read along with section 1 of the 1961 Act.

Section 2 deals with overcrowding and subsection (1) thereof lays down that a factory shall not, while work is carried on, be so overcrowded as to cause risk of injury to the health of the persons employed in it. Subsection (2) specifies a minimal requirement of 400 cubic feet per person. The Minister is given power [29] to make regulations for any class or description of factory (or part thereof) or for any process increasing the minimal cubic feet specification, mentioned in the section.

Section 3 (1) stipulates that effective provision shall be made for securing and maintaining a reasonable temperature in each workroom and that no method is to be employed which results in the escape into the air of any workroom of any fume, which by its nature and extent, is likely to be injurious or offensive to the employees in that workroom. Subsection (2) fixes a minimal temperature of 60 degrees (after the first hour) where the bulk of the work is done sitting and no serious physical effect is involved. The Minister is again given power [30] to make special regulations for special cases.

Section 4 is a general section dealing with ventilation. Subsection (1) states that " effective and suitable provision shall be made for securing and maintaining by the circulation of fresh air in each workroom the adequate ventilation of the room, and for rendering harmless, so far as practicable, all such fumes, dust and other impurities generated in the course of any process or work carried on in the factory as may be injurious to health." The phrase " by the circulation of fresh air " was considered in the English case of *Ebbs* v. *James Whitson & Co. Ltd.*[31] and was construed as relating to both parts of this subsection (*i.e.*, for securing adequate ventilation and, secondly, the rendering harmless . . . of all fumes, dust, etc.) as may be injurious to health. As the section deals generally with ventilation it cannot be used or prayed in aid in support of an argument calling for specialised equipment and specialised methods, *e.g.*, it has been held that it does not impose an obligation to provide breathing equipment

[26] Formerly the Minister of Labour; now the Secretary of State for Employment and Productivity.
[27] See *Carroll* v. *N.B. Locomotive Co.*, 1957 S.L.T.(Sh.Ct.) 2; and *Nicholson* v. *Atlas Steel Foundry*, 1957 S.C.(H.L.) 44; [1957] 1 W.L.R. 613 (following *Wardlaw* v. *Bonnington Castings Ltd.*, 1956 S.C.(H.L.) 26; 1956 S.L.T. 135; and sub nom. *Bonnington Castings Ltd.* v. *Wardlaw* [1956] A.C. 613; [1956] 2 W.L.R. 707; [1956] 1 All E.R. 615 (H.L.)).
[28] S.I. 1960 No. 1794.
[29] By s. 2 (4); to be read along with s. 180.
[30] s. 3 (3).
[31] [1952] 2 Q.B. 877.

or masks [32] or exhaust appliances.[33]   In any case, protection against dust and fumes is specifically dealt with in a later section [34] of the Act.

Section 5 (1) requires the effective provision of sufficient and suitable lighting, whether natural or artificial.   Power is given to the Minister to issue regulations prescribing standards of lighting.[35]   All glazed windows and skylights used for providing lighting to workrooms, should be kept clean, so far as practicable, on both inner and outer surfaces [36]; the white-washing or shading of windows and skylights to mitigate heat or glare is not, however, affected by this subsection.

Section 6 deals with drainage of floors; section 7 with the provision, maintenance, lighting and cleanliness of sanitary conveniences; whilst section 8 is an administrative section which places the responsibility for enforcement of the section 7 provisions (together with any relevant regulations made under section 7 (2)) upon the appropriate [37] county council or town council in Scotland.   Sections 9 and 10 are extensions of the administrative provisions—the former setting forth the powers of an inspector in relation to sanitary defects remediable by the local authority responsible,[38] whilst the latter explains the powers available to the Minister, and any inspector duly authorised by him, where the responsible local authority has failed to enforce the statutory duties incumbent upon it.

Section 11 gives the Minister power to make regulations in respect of any factory or class or description of factory or, where a particular factory is concerned for a limited period only, to issue any order, requiring medical supervision where (i) cases of illness have occurred which he believes to be due to the nature of a process or other conditions of work; or (ii) changes in a process or in the substances used therein have been made or a new process or new substance has been introduced and there may, as a result, be a risk of injury to the health of the employees; or (iii) young persons are or are about to be employed in work which may cause risk of injury to their health.   The Minister may do likewise where there may be a risk of injury to the health of employees in a factory from (a) any substance or material brought to the factory for use or handling therein or (b) from any change in the conditions of work or other conditions in the factory.

The foregoing part of the 1961 statute is relatively straightforward and has not given rise to much litigation.   The same cannot be said for the immediately succeeding part, which has been and will doubtless remain (and even if re-enacted in some amending form) a fruitful source of litigation.

---

[32] See *Ashwood* v. *Steel Co. of Scotland*, 1957 S.C. 17; 1957 S.L.T. 244.
[33] *Graham* v. *C.W.S. Ltd.* [1957] 1 All E.R. 654; [1957] 1 W.L.R. 511.   See also *Nicholson* v. *Atlas Steel Foundry, cit. supra.*
[34] *Vide* s. 63.
[35] See, for example, the Factories (Standards of Lighting) Regulations 1941 (S.R. & O. 1941 No. 94) made under the 1937 Act.
[36] *Vide* s. 5 (4).
[37] The test will obviously be the geographical location of the factory site.
[38] The various Public Health (Scotland) Acts from 1897 onwards should also be consulted.

PART II—Safety (General Provisions)

This part comprises sections 12 to 56 inclusive. There is little doubt that from the point of view of litigation it provides a most fruitful and continuing source.

Section 12 deals principally with prime movers [39] and requires that every flywheel directly connected to a prime mover and every moving part of a prime mover (but excepting prime movers to which subsection (3) refers) shall be securely fenced.[40] The same provision applies to the head and tail race of every water wheel and of every water turbine. Thus secure fencing [41] is in terms of this section an absolute statutory requirement. Subsection (3) does, however, introduce a variation upon or alternative to secure fencing in the case of every part of electric generators, motors and rotary converters and every flywheel directly connected thereto. These things must be securely fenced unless they are in such a position or of such construction as to be as safe to every person employed or working on the premises as they would be if securely fenced.

An interesting question arose for consideration in *Parvin* v. *Morton Machine Co. Ltd.*[42] where an apprentice fitter was injured whilst cleaning a piece of machinery which had been manufactured in the defender's factory. Did that machine come within the Part II provisions of the 1961 Act ? It was held that it did not and that the Part II provisions applied only to machinery which was part of the factory and which was used in the manufacturing process. The same principle applies to a machine under repair at a factory.[43]

An employer does not escape liability by pleading that he did not use fencing because a dangerous part of machinery was not likely to be approached by any employee. The " secure fencing " obligation requires him (the employer) to guard against dangers which may reasonably be anticipated.[44] It has been pointed out that this obligation may involve the application of a foreseeability test to the statutory requirements upon

---

[39] Defined in s. 176 (1) as " every engine motor or other appliance which provides mechanical energy derived from steam, water, wind, electricity, the combustion of fuel or other source."

[40] The phrase " securely fenced " has given rise to much case-law. Finally, in the House of Lords decision in *John Summers & Sons Ltd.* v. *Frost* [1955] A.C. 740; [1955] 1 All E.R. 870, the following three points were made: (i) the duty was absolute or strict, (ii) an argument based on impracticability of fencing or uselessness of a machine if fenced was unsound and no defence, and (iii) fencing is not secure unless it gives complete protection against the dangers contemplated.

[41] Its purpose is to keep the worker out (*i.e.*, to prevent his coming into contact with the machine)—see *Nicholls* v. *Austin (Leyton) Ltd.* [1946] A.C. 493; [1946] 2 All E.R. 92, per Lord Simonds at p. 505 and p. 98 respectively; see also *Carroll* v. *Andrew Barclay & Sons Ltd.*, 1947 S.C. 411; 1947 S.L.T. 223; [1948] A.C. 447; [1948] 2 All E.R. 386 (following *Nicholls* and the earlier Scottish case of *Morton* v. *William Dixon Ltd.*, 1909 S.C. 807; 1909, 1 S.L.T. 346) which extended this principle to broken parts of transmission machinery (this was a case brought under s. 13); and also *Close* v. *Steel Company of Wales Ltd.* [1962] A.C. 367; [1961] 2 All E.R. 953 (this was a case brought under s. 14) where the House of Lords again stressed that machinery need only be fenced to prevent contact with it.

[42] 1952 S.C.(H.L.) 9; 1952 S.L.T. 201; [1952] A.C. 515; [1952] 1 All E.R. 670.

[43] *Thurogood* v. *Van den Berghs and Jurgens Ltd.* [1951] 2 K.B. 537; [1951] 1 All E.R. 682.

[44] *Burns* v. *Joseph Terry & Sons* [1951] 1 K.B. 454; [1950] 2 All E.R. 987 (C.A.).

secure fencing,[45] and there is no doubt that this is correct. The court will certainly be interested in hearing as a matter of evidence what steps the employer did take to obviate or minimise danger. Obviously, the prudent employer pays the strictest attention to all matters of safety; the thoughtless or callous employer does the bare minimum.

Section 13 (1) requires every part of transmission machinery [46] to be securely fenced,[47] unless it is equally safe by position or construction. Subsections (2), (3) and (4) set forth in some detail those safety devices or rules which must be used or applied in support of the section 13 (1) general provision, *e.g.*, efficient devices to cut off power; no driving belt, when not in use, to rest upon a revolving shaft; and suitable striking gear, etc., to move driving belts to and from pulleys. Subsection (5) gives the Minister power to modify any of the requirements of subsections (2) to (4) inclusive. It has been held that the test in a prosecution under section 13 (1) is not reasonable foreseeability of danger on the employer's part, nor absence of previous accidents or warning from the factory inspectorate, but whether transmission machinery (deemed by the section to be dangerous) is securely fenced.[48]

Section 14 (1) requires that every dangerous part of machinery (other than prime movers and transmission machinery, both of which are dealt with separately in sections 12 and 13 respectively) shall be securely fenced unless by position or construction it is as safe, to every employee or person working on the premises, as it would be if securely fenced. Subsection (2) introduces an alternative safety requirement where a fixed guard cannot be provided as a practical measure because of the nature of the operation— namely, the provision of some device which prevents the operator from coming into contact with the dangerous part of the machine. Subsection (3) empowers the Minister to make regulations directing the use of available and suitable safety devices in relation to any class of machinery. It is a defence [49] to any proceedings taken under subsection (3) to prove that an equally effective safety device was being used. By subsection (6) the Minister is given a general power to make regulations requiring the fencing of materials or articles which are dangerous whilst in motion in a machine.

The test of whether a machine, or part thereof, is " dangerous " is, so far as delictual liability is concerned, one of reasonable foreseeability and the court will examine all the facts and circumstances in each case to decide upon the question of danger.[50] The occupier/employer may be

---

[45] See John Munkman, *Employer's Liability at Common Law* (6th ed., 1966) at pp. 279–280.

[46] Defined in s. 176 (1).

[47] See *M'Leman* v. *Consolidated Pneumatic Tool Co.* (1950) 66 Sh.Ct.Rep. 3; and *Weir* v. *Andrew Barclay & Co. Ltd.* (O.H.) 1955 S.L.T. (Notes) 56.

[48] *Simpson* v. *Hardie & Smith Ltd.*, 1968 S.L.T. 261 (conviction substituted for acquittal in the lower court). A prosecution is proceeded with under s. 155.

[49] By s. 14 (4).

[50] See *John Summers & Sons* v. *Frost* [1955] A.C. 740; [1955] 1 All E.R. 870. In this case the House of Lords expressly approved the following passage from Lord Cooper L.J.-C. (as he then was) in *Mitchell* v. *North British Rubber Co.*, 1945 S.C.(J.) 69 at

able to plead relevantly, in a civil action upon this question of danger, that the method of working the machine must be taken into account or that a factory inspector had recently inspected the machine and was satisfied that fencing was not necessary.[51] That test of reasonable foreseeability applies equally to the " securely fenced " stipulation which appears in this section (as it does to sections 12 and 13). It will be noted immediately, however, that the duty which is imposed upon the occupier/employer in section 14—as in sections 12 and 13—is an absolute duty. What has been said above about risk of injury and about the particular machinery involved in this statutory obligation applies equally here. It is open to the occupier/employer to plead in his own defence in a civil action that the particular employee who suffered injury contributed to that injury because of his own personal negligence or carelessness.[52] The plea of contributory negligence is therefore relevant to an award of damages in a civil action but it is no defence where a prosecution is brought for a statutory breach of duty, i.e., it can never be an excuse for a breach of the statutory obligation which rests upon the occupier/employer. It is extremely doubtful whether the plea would be of any assistance to the occupier/employer even in mitigation of penalty. The principle of *volenti non fit injuria* (which many writers regard as being a doctrine or rule of evidence rather than a principle of substantive law) is never any answer to a statutory breach of duty, whether that breach results in civil or criminal proceedings. In a sense, sections 12, 13 and 14 try to impose upon employers a statutory " safe system of work " corresponding to and extending their basic common law obligation in that respect.[53] In the recent and somewhat peculiar case of *Young* v. *Caterpillar Tractor Co.*,[54] it has been

---

p. 73, *viz.*: " The question is not whether the occupiers of the factory knew that it was dangerous; nor whether the factory inspector had so reported; nor whether previous accidents had occurred; nor whether the victims of these accidents had, or had not, been contributorily negligent. The test is objective and impersonal. Is the part such in its character, and so circumstanced in its position, exposure, method of operation and the like, that in the ordinary course of human affairs danger may reasonably be anticipated from its use unfenced, not only to the prudent, alert and skilled operative intent upon his task, but also to the careless and inattentive worker whose inadvertent or indolent conduct may expose him to risk of injury or death from the unguarded part ? " Lord Jamieson had also said in *Mackay* v. *Ailsa Shipbuilding Co. Ltd.*, 1945 S.C. 414 at p. 418: " The question whether or not danger exists is primarily one of fact and to a large extent one of degree, and in some cases it may be difficult to determine whether a given machine, or part of a machine, does or does not fall within the definition of ' dangerous ' . . . " The court held in *Mackay's* case that the obligation to fence under s. 14 (1) was absolute and that commercial impossibility was no defence (approving and applying *Miller* v. *William Boothman & Sons Ltd.* [1944] K.B. 337).

[51] But not as a defence in a criminal prosecution—see *Simpson* v. *Hardie & Smith Ltd.*, 1968 S.L.T. 261; *cf. Mitchell* v. *N.B. Rubber Co.*, 1945 S.C.(J.) 69.

[52] In *Barnes* v. *Southhook Potteries Ltd.* (O.H.) 1946 S.L.T. 295 (based on s. 14 (1) of the Factories Act 1937) it was held that an employee's contributory negligence disentitled him from succeeding in his action based upon his employers' breach of the statutory duty. This case has now been nullified by the Law Reform (Contributory Negligence) Act 1945. The court will now apportion the blame and award accordingly.

[53] See *Kelly* v. *Steel Co. of Scotland* (1957) 73 Sh.Ct.Rep. 54; *Dobson* v. *Colville's Ltd.*, 1958 S.L.T. (Notes) 30 (obligation to fence part of a moving machine); *Finnie* v. *John Laird & Son Ltd.*, 1967 S.L.T. 243 (the obligation to fence a machine when " in motion or in use "; questions under ss. 16 and 20 also).

[54] (O.H.) 1963 S.L.T. (Notes) 63.

held that a fork lift truck was not machinery requiring to be fenced in terms of section 14 (1) of the 1961 Act. When it comes to matters of procedure and practice in cases based upon alleged breaches of statutory duty under sections 12, 13 and 14, the reported cases seem to indicate that there is no hard and fast rule of practice. The court will look at the pleadings and take into account the circumstances of each individual case, before deciding whether to allow a proof before answer or a jury trial.[55]

Section 15 contains certain provisions relating to unfenced machinery. These provisions may be classified as guide lines to an occupier/employer in enabling him to determine whether any part of machinery is in such a position or is of such construction as to be as safe as it would be if securely fenced (as mentioned previously in Part II of the statute). No account is to be taken of any person carrying out an examination, lubrication or adjustment of part of machinery in motion, if this can only be done whilst the machine is in motion; and in the case of transmission machinery used in a continuous process, specified in ministerial regulations,[56] a similar principle applies. It is very clearly specified by section 15 (2) that the person concerned must be a male person over eighteen years of age. Section 16 requires that all fencing or other safeguards provided in terms of Part II of the statute must be of substantial construction and be constantly maintained and kept in position whilst the parts required to be fenced or safeguarded are in motion or use (except where examination, lubrication or adjustment is necessary). The important phrase in this section is " in motion or use." [57] The section is to be read along with sections 12, 13, 14 and 15. It highlights the fact that fencing, etc., is applicable to a working machine, the only exceptions being those introduced by section 15 and referred to again in section 16 (namely, examination, lubrication and adjustment). The phrase " in motion or use " was considered by the House of Lords in *Richard Thomas & Baldwins Ltd.* v. *Cummings* [58] and was held to mean in motion or in use for the purpose for which the parts were intended and not for repair purposes. Moreover, if the machinery was power-driven the section and the phrase did not cover the situation where the machine was moved by hand operation. It must be made clear, once again, that the section applies to working machinery installed in a factory for purposes of the manufacturing process and not to any machine which is made in the factory as a product of that process.[59]

---

[55] See, in illustration, *Neil* v. *Alexander Cowan & Sons Ltd.* (O.H.) 1961 S.L.T. (Notes) 52 (proof before answer allowed); *Gardner* v. *Henry Bruce & Sons Ltd.* (O.H.) 1967 S.L.T. (Notes) 64 (proof allowed); *Swan* v. *Jute Industries Ltd.* (O.H.) 1968 S.L.T. (Notes) 8 and *Gault* v. *James Templeton & Co.* (O.H.) 1968 S.L.T. (Notes) 37 (pursuer's case suitable for jury trial in both of these actions).

[56] See the Operations at Unfenced Machinery Regulations 1938 and 1946 (S.R. & O. 1938 No. 641 and S.R. & O. 1946 No. 156); and Samuels, *Factory Law* (7th ed.), pp. 54–57, for a detailed note upon these Regulations.

[57] See *Finnie* v. *John Laird & Son Ltd.*, 1967 S.L.T. 243; and *McLean* v. *Glenroberts Wood Wool Industries Ltd.* (O.H.), 1969 S.L.T.(Notes) 29.

[58] [1955] A.C. 321 (see also *Finnie* v. *John Laird & Son Ltd.*, 1967 S.L.T. 243).

[59] *Parvin* v. *Morton Machine Co.*, 1952 S.C.(H.L.) 9; [1952] A.C. 515; 1952 S.L.T. 201.

Section 17 [60] introduces certain specific safety requirements for machines to be driven by mechanical power and widens the protection to purchasers and hirers of such machinery by imposing a heavy penalty upon sellers of such machinery or those who hire out such machinery (or their agents) within the United Kingdom. Subsection (1) requires certain specified parts of the machine to be sunk, encased or otherwise effectively guarded to prevent danger and certain other parts (*e.g.*, spur and toothed or friction gearing, not requiring frequent adjustment) to be completely encased, unless safe by position. The Minister is given powers in section 17 (3) to extend the subsection (2) provisions to other machinery or plant. The jurisdiction of the court, in the matter of a prosecution under section 17 (2) and (3), is determined by the location of the machine or machinery and plant.[61] The section does not govern any machine constructed before July 30, 1937, and any regulations made under section 17 (3) do not apply to any machinery or plant constructed before the making of such regulations.[62] Sections 18 and 19 deal respectively with dangerous substances and self-acting machines.

Section 20, relating to the cleaning of machinery by women and young persons, is important. It provides that a woman or young person shall not clean any part of a prime mover or of any transmission machinery whilst these are in motion, nor indeed clean any part of any machine if such cleaning would expose the woman or young person to risk of injury from any moving part of the particular machine or from any adjacent machinery. The machinery in question is, of course, that installed and working within the factory process.[63] The section is applicable only to women and young persons and does not apply to adult male employees.[64] If an adult male worker is involved in a cleaning process the liability situation would, therefore, seem to be governed by the common law (safe system of work, etc.), and any other section of the Factories Act 1961 (or kindred Regulations) which was relevant to the particular situation.

Section 21 prevents a young person from working at a dangerous machine—duly prescribed as such by ministerial regulations [65]—unless he has been fully instructed as to the dangers arising thereanent and the precautions to be observed and (a) he has received a sufficient training in the work at the machine or (b) he is working under the supervision of a knowledgeable and experienced person. The obligation under this section rests fairly and squarely upon the employer. The section imposes no

---

[60] For some very interesting points arising from s. 17, see Samuels, *op. cit.*, pp. 59–61 (notes).

[61] s. 17 (4).

[62] s. 17 (5).

[63] *Parvin* v. *Morton Machine Co.*, 1952 S.C.(H.L.) 9; [1952] A.C. 515; 1952 S.L.T. 201.

[64] See *Murray* v. *Donald MacDonald (Antartex) Ltd.* (O.H.), 1968 S.L.T. 10 (a reference to s. 20 in a case involving an adult workman was irrelevant), in which the earlier case of *Finnie* v. *John Laird & Son Ltd.*, 1967 S.L.T. 243 was considered.

[65] See the Dangerous Machines (Training of Young Persons) Order 1954 (S.I. 1954 No. 921).

special duty upon a young person which could be pleaded by an employer in any civil action in damages brought by the young person.[66]

The next six sections (*i.e.*, ss. 22–27 inclusive) deal with hoists and lifts, chains, ropes, lifting tackle and cranes. Section 22 might be called a general section which requires every hoist or lift to be of " good mechanical construction, sound material and adequate strength " and to be maintained properly. Regular examination (and appropriate notifications and reports) is required every six months.[67] Substantial enclosures with gates (with locking devices or suitable alternative devices for older lifts) must be provided.[68] The maximum working load which can safely be carried must be conspicuously marked on every lift (or hoist) and no load greater than that load is to be carried.[69]

It will be appreciated that the obligations which are imposed by this section are absolute, except the subsection (6) provisions relating to lifts, etc., constructed or reconstructed before July 30, 1937. In the important Scottish case of *Millar* v. *Galashiels Gas Co.*[70] an employee was killed because of a failure in the automatic braking mechanism of a lift and no explanation could be given for the failure nor could it have been detected or suspected prior to the accident. The employers were held liable for a breach of the statutory duty imposed by section 22 (1),[71] that duty being absolute. The word " maintained," which appears in section 22 (1), has been held to refer to and to mean the continuance of a state of working efficiency.[72] This is a higher obligation than the layman or man in the street would understand or expect from the phrase " properly maintained " and the point is, therefore, extremely important.

The Hoists Exemption Order 1938 (S.R. & O. 1938 No. 489) and the Hoists Exemption (Amendment) Order 1945 (S.R. & O. 1946 No. 1947) must be read along with the provisions contained in the 1961 Act.[73]

Section 23 spells out the requirements which apply to passenger-carrying lifts and hoists. Section 24 deals with teagle openings and doorways, whilst section 25 includes certain supplementary provisions.

Section 26 contains quite extensive provisions relating to chains, ropes and lifting tackle. Such equipment is not to be used unless it is " of good construction, sound material, adequate strength and free from patent defect." [74] A table showing the safe working load of all such equipment is to be kept in the factory storeroom and in other prominent places within

---

[66] *M'Cafferty* v. *Brown*, 1950 S.C. 300; 1950 S.L.T. 356.
[67] s. 22 (2).
[68] s. 22 (4), (5), (6) and (7).
[69] s. 22 (8).
[70] 1949 S.C.(H.L.) 31; [1949] A.C. 275; 1949 S.L.T. 223.
[71] This case was, of course, based upon the Factories Act 1937, s. 22 (1), but that numbering remains the same in the Factories Act 1961.
[72] Per Lord MacDermott in the English case of *Blakely* v. *C. & H. Clothing Co.* [1958] 1 All E.R. 297; [1958] 1 W.L.R. 378.
[73] See for example, *Thomson* v. *Irving*, 1961 S.L.T. 14 in which it was held (i) that the lift in question was exempted and (ii) that it was not reasonably practicable in the circumstances to protect the lift by an enclosure and gate in terms of a condition attached to the exemption.
[74] s. 26 (1) (*a*).

the factory premises. If any lifting tackle—including a multiple sling—has its safe working load marked on it, this is sufficient.[75] The safe working load must not be exceeded.[76] Regular examination of existing equipment and the testing of new equipment is required[77]; and chains and lifting tackle (except rope slings) must be annealed at least once every fourteen months or six months, depending upon size in some cases and usage in others.[78] Equipment which is not in regular use need be annealed only when necessary. A register containing the prescribed particulars must be kept for all chains, ropes or lifting tackle (excepting fibre rope slings). " Lifting tackle " is defined by subsection (3).

In the comparatively recent case of *Milne* v. *C. F. Wilson & Co. (1932) Ltd.*,[79] Lord Cameron (in the Outer House) held that adequacy of strength might be judged quite relevantly by referring to the use to which any chain or rope or lifting tackle was put. The employers, in this case, had argued that " of adequate strength " meant sufficient to carry the load for which the lifting tackle had been designed; an argument which his lordship could not accept. In the earlier case of *Reilly* v. *Wm. Beardmore & Co.*[80] the First Division held that there was a continuing obligation upon the employer or factory occupier to consider whether a rope had reached or passed its safe and useful working life and was of " adequate strength."

Cranes and other lifting machines are dealt with by section 27. This is indeed a very important section and its eight subsections require careful study. Section 27 (9) defines a " lifting machine." All parts and working gear must be " of good construction, sound material, adequate strength and free from patent defect, and shall be properly maintained." Examination, safe working loads, adequately strong rails with even running surfaces for travelling cranes, testing and warning systems for overhead travelling cranes are all provided for in this comprehensive section. Lord Wheatley held in *McNeill* v. *Dickson & Mann Ltd.*[81] that the plea of latent defect was not a valid defence to an action brought under the corresponding section[82] of the 1937 Act; the statutory requirement as to absence of patent defect did not qualify the earlier statutory requirement of "good construction, sound material, and adequate strength." Section 27 (7) and its predecessor (s. 24 (7) of the 1937 Act) have provided at least three cases of some interest, namely: *Ward* v. *Coltness Iron Co. Ltd.*[83]; *Hunter* v. *Glenfield & Kennedy*[84]; and *William Hamilton & Co. Ltd.* v. *W. G.*

[75] s. 26 (2).
[76] s. 26 (1) (*c*).
[77] s. 26 (1) (*d*) and (*e*).
[78] s. 26 (1) (*f*).
[79] 1960 S.L.T. 162.
[80] 1947 S.C. 275; 1947 S.L.T. 147; 1947 S.N. 46 (see particularly the opinion of the late Lord President Cooper).
[81] 1957 S.C. 345; 1957 S.L.T. 364 (a case in the Outer House).
[82] Factories Act 1937, s. 24.
[83] 1944 S.C. 318; 1944 S.L.T. 405; 1944 S.N. 26.
[84] 1947 S.C. 536; 1947 S.L.T. 337; 1947 S.N. 103.

Anderson & Co. Ltd.[85]   In *Ward's* case—where the employee of a firm of
contractors suffered injury during the construction of factory premises—
it was held (1) that pursuer had stated a relevant case under the statute in
relation to the building and the definition of " factory " contained in the
Act [86] and (2) that the fact that he was not an employee of the occupier
was immaterial because the legislation was designed to cover all persons
who were employed or working on or near the wheel-track of an overhead
travelling crane, in any place where he would be liable to be struck by the
crane.   In *Hunter's* case the First Division held that there was a clear
breach of the statutory duty,[87] whilst in *Hamilton's* case—a case based
upon the relevancy of an indemnity clause which referred to a claim " at
common law " whereas in fact there had been a breach of a statutory duty
—the First Division held the action to be relevant.   In the course of his
judgment, Lord President Cooper said that a claim based upon a breach of
the Factories Act or any other statute was accurately described as a claim
at common law.   " Statutory negligence " was nonetheless negligence.   It
inferred, continued his lordship, that breach of duty which underlay every
common law action for *culpa* . . . the right to recover damages is not
created by the statute but by the common law.   If his lordship is right then
all statute law might be regarded as being an addendum to the common
law. This view is not necessarily true of certain fields of law where new
and specialised legislation is introduced (*e.g.*, the Road Traffic Acts) but
it may be accepted in the case of employer's liability extended onwards
from the common law by legislation setting up statutory duties and obligations designed to protect industrial workers.

Section 28 deals with floors, steps, stairs, passages and gangways.
These must be of sound construction and properly maintained and—so
far as is reasonably practicable [88]—be kept free from any obstruction and
from any substance likely to cause persons to slip.[89]   The qualification as
to reasonable practicability is vital.   It means in effect that the risk of
injury must be balanced against the steps which should be taken to
eliminate that risk.   Substantial hand-rails, including lower rails as
necessary, are to be provided and maintained for open sides to any stair-
case.   All ladders must be soundly constructed and properly maintained,
as provided by section 28 (5).   This is an absolute obligation and it is not
a sufficient answer for a defender to aver and prove that he took all

[85]   1953 S.C. 129; 1953 S.L.T. 77.
[86]   Factories Act 1937, ss. 24 (7), 149 and 151 (1).
[87]   See particularly Lord President Cooper's opinion.
[88]   This phrase occurs again and again in industrial legislation and provides—in the
writer's opinion—a defence lifeline for employers, in the appropriate circumstances.
The legal position is discussed in this chapter.
[89]   It is interesting to note that the section of the 1937 Act (in fact, s. 25) corresponding to
s. 28 contained no requirement *re* freedom from obstruction or substances likely to
cause persons to slip.   The Factories Act 1959, s. 4, was the first statute to introduce
this requirement and, of course, the consolidating Act of 1961 retained it.   See also
the recent English case of *Williams* v. *Painter Bros.* (1968) V K.I.R. 487 (C.A.) where
the duty imposed under s. 28 (1) and a possible defence in special circumstances are
considered.

practical steps to see that a ladder was in good repair and in an efficient state.[90] The duty is clear and unequivocal.

Section 28 has been a fruitful source of litigation in recent years. In *Fern* v. *Dundee Corporation* [91] Lord Hunter made several helpful observations [92] upon the meaning of the words " reasonably practicable " and the onus of proving that a precaution was reasonably practicable. In his view, if a precaution is practicable it must be taken unless, in the whole circumstances, this would be unreasonable. In this particular case, defenders were held liable in damages, where pursuer slipped on a patch of oil in an omnibus depot and suffered injury. In *Drummond* v. *Harland Engineering Co. Ltd.*[93] it was held that an angle iron, part of a machine which was a fixture in the factory and which was in its normal place in the premises, was not an " obstruction " within the meaning of section 28 (1) and accordingly the pursuer's action was dismissed as irrelevant. However, in *Jenkins* v. *Allied Ironfounders Ltd.*[94] it was held that a gate or fin, which had been part of a casting, was an " obstruction " on the floor of a foundry. It would seem from *Hall* v. *Fairfield Shipbuilding & Engineering Co. Ltd.*[95] that the causal link between the alleged obstruction and the resultant injury to pursuer must be clearly proved—in a civil action—before pursuer will succeed. In this case the House (reversing the Second Division of the Court of Session) held there was no evidence to show that the employer's failure to prohibit the throwing of scraps of metal on the floor had caused the accident. Lord Reid and Lord Morris both dissented and indeed the former, in a powerful speech,[96] agreed with the unanimous opinion of the Second Division.

There have been conflicting opinions stated upon the onus of proving that it is " reasonably practicable " to keep all floors, steps, stairs, passages and gangways free from any obstruction and from any substance likely to cause persons to slip. Lord Kissen in *Donno* v. *British Railways Board* [97] expressed his opinion that the onus of proof in such a case lay upon the pursuer. Lord Avonside has disagreed [98] and has said that, in his view, the onus is upon defenders. This latter view supports the attitude of the English courts. However, in *Nimmo* v. *Alexander Cowan & Sons Ltd.*[99]

---

[90] See *Cole* v. *Blackstone & Co.* [1943] K.B. 615.
[91] (O.H.) 1964 S.L.T. 294 (based upon the 1937 Act, s. 25 (1), and the 1959 Act, s. 4, now replaced by s. 28 (1)).
[92] *Ibid.* p. 296.
[93] (O.H.) 1963 S.L.T. 115.
[94] (O.H.) 1968 S.L.T. (Notes) 68. The First Division (*dissenting* Lord Cameron) has now *reversed* the Lord Ordinary's finding and assoilzied defenders—see 1969 S.L.T. 185 (the pursuer having failed to discharge the onus of proof accepted by him on the pleadings and consequently no onus passed to the defenders.)
[95] (H.L.) 1964 S.L.T. 97; 1964 S.C. (H.L.) 72; followed in *Jenkins* v. *Allied Ironfounders Ltd.*, 1969 S.L.T. 185.
[96] *Ibid.* pp. 99–100.
[97] (O.H.) 1964 S.L.T. (Notes) 108.
[98] See *Duncan* v. *Smith & Phillips* (O.H.) 1965 S.L.T. (Notes) 16.
[99] (H.L.) 1967 S.L.T. 277; [1968] A.C. 107; a case concerned with s. 29 (1) but raising the same question of onus of proof. The Court of Appeal in England has applied *Nimmo* in the recent case of *Garner* v. *John Thompson* (*Wolverhampton*) *Ltd.* VI K.I.R. 1.

the House of Lords has ruled—by the narrow majority of three to two (Lord Reid's dissenting opinion being a very forceful one)—that the onus of proof that a precaution is not " reasonably practicable " lies upon the defenders, who are seeking to avoid responsibility.   The actual method of proof, in trying to establish the facts, may be a proof before answer (where there are difficulties about the onus of proof)[1] or a jury trial (where there are no such difficulties).[2]

Section 28 (4) states that " All openings in floors shall be securely fenced, except in so far as the nature of the work renders such fencing impracticable."   Lord Mackintosh observed in *Buchan* v. *Robert Hutchison & Co. Ltd.*[3] that the subsection places upon the occupiers/employers and not upon the workmen the burden of proving the applicability of the exception contained in the subsection.   In *Sullivan* v. *Hall Russell & Co. Ltd.*[4] it has been held that the earth surface of an open-air yard was not a floor within the meaning of the Factories Acts, whilst in *Johnston* v. *Colvilles Ltd.*[5] it was held that the word " floor " in section 28 (4) means the ordinary floor of the factory which was used as a means of access and it did not include the floor of a furnace (in course of construction and exempt from the statutory provisions, in this instance).

Safe means of access to every place of work must, so far as is reasonably practicable, be provided and maintained and every such place of work must be made and kept safe for any person working[5a] there, so far as is reasonably practicable, according to the terms of section 29.   It is clear from the wording of the section that an absolute duty is not being imposed upon the employer/occupier.[6]   Section 29 is, in a sense, a general section —in contrast with section 28—because it does not define or specify those parts of a factory which constitute the " means of access." [7]   If pursuer cannot lay his case upon a breach of section 28, he will immediately consider the relevancy of section 29.   It will be noted at once that the mandatory tone of the first limb of section 28 is departed from in section 29 —and that safe means of access and a safe working place shall—so far as is reasonably practicable—be provided, maintained, made or so kept safe. The question of the burden of proof in relation to the phrase " reasonably

---

1 See *Duncan* v. *Smith & Phillips, cit. supra.*
2 *Jack* v. *Guardbridge Paper Co.* (O.H.) 1968 S.L.T. (Notes) 8.
3 (O.H.) 1953 S.L.T. 306; this case being based on s. 25 (3) of the 1937 Act (the predecessor of s. 28 (4)).
4 (O.H.) 1964 S.L.T. 192.
5 (O.H.) 1966 S.L.T. 30.
5a The section relates to workmen employed in the factory premises.   In *Flannigan* v. *British Dyewood Co.* (O.H.) 1969 S.L.T. (Notes) 33, it has been held that occupiers of a factory have no statutory duty under the Act towards a fireman who is fighting a fire in the factory.   Nevertheless, they do owe a common law duty to avert an outbreak of fire and there was no voluntary assumption of risk by pursuer so as to relieve them of that duty.
6 " ' Occupier ' plainly means the person who runs the factory . . . who regulates and controls the work that is done there " (*per* Lord MacLaren in *Ramsay* v. *Mackie* (1904) 7 F. at p. 109).
7 See *Nisbet* v. *J. W. Ward Ltd.* (O.H.) 1968 S.L.T. (Notes) 73 (pursuer injured by falling over scrap in his path of access to his work and relevantly averred a breach of s. 29 (1)).

practicable " has been mentioned earlier.[8] The word " safe," used in section 29 (1), has been held, in England, to mean safe for all contingencies which may be reasonably foreseen.[9] Several interesting Scottish cases have arisen upon the interpretation of and the duty created by section 29 (and its forerunner, section 26 of the 1937 Act). In *Rose* v. *Colvilles Ltd.*,[10] where a workman was injured by hot slag on his way to the lavatory and sued his employers at common law and under statute (formerly section 26 (1) of the 1937 Act; now section 29), it was held that the statutory case was irrelevant because defenders were bound to provide and maintain a safe means of access only at places where the workman had to work. A roadway in a factory has been held to be a " means of access " within the meaning of the section, whilst a pursuer was working there.[11] Again, where a workman was injured by the condition of a floor over which he had to pass in working between a chute and a mixer it was held that a statutory breach had been relevantly averred.[12] A pursuer is entitled to put forward in his pleadings various means which might have been taken as reasonably practicable precautions and his case is not necessarily irrelevant because one suggestion is weak.[13] The wet surface of a platform is not a safe means of access for a workman who is wearing gumboots in the course of his employment.[14]

The use of the word " maintained " in the section means that the duty imposed is a continuing one.[15] If a pursuer falls and injures himself (or herself) because a floor is wet and slippery then there is a failure to " maintain " a safe means of access as required by the section.[16] The statutory duty may be higher than the common law duty, but defenders may still escape liability if they are able to show that it was not " reasonably practicable " for them to take certain additional steps referred to in the course of pleadings.[17]

The phrase " safe means of access " may not merely relate to the ordinary type of factory building. The definition section (s. 175) of the 1961 Act must be read along with section 29, *e.g.*, there must be a " safe means of access " to a place of work upon a vessel which was undergoing repair in a dry dock.[18] The duty to provide a safe access means that the

---

[8] See also the English case of *McCarthy* v. *Coldair* [1951] 2 T.L.R. 1226.

[9] *McCarthy* v. *Coldair, cit. supra.* See also the Scottish case of *Hill* v. *J. O. Buchanan & Co. Ltd.* (O.H.) 1965 S.L.T. (Notes) 24. In the recent English case of *Garner* v. *John Thompson (Wolverhampton)* VI K.I.R. 1 (*The Times*, November 28, 1968) the Court of Appeal has held that the mere slipping of a ladder is sufficient evidence that it was an unsafe means of access (in terms of s. 29 (1)) and plaintiff was entitled to succeed.

[10] (O.H.) 1950 S.L.T.(Notes) 72.

[11] *Fraser* v. *Mechans Ltd.* (O.H.) 1953 S.L.T.(Notes) 14.

[12] *Rolland* v. *United Glass Bottle Manufacturing Co. Ltd.* (O.H.) 1959 S.L.T.(Notes) 10.

[13] *Donnelly* v. *Colvilles Ltd.* (First Division) December 5, 1950; [1950] C.L.Y. 4819. But see the earlier notes in this chapter upon the onus of proof.

[14] *Johnstone* v. *Clyde Paper Co. Ltd.* (Second Division) March 9, 1951; [1951] C.L.Y. 4000.

[15] *Alison* v. *Henry Bruce & Sons Ltd.*, 1951 S.L.T. 399.

[16] *Ross* v. *W. & M. Duncan Ltd.* (O.H.) 1959 S.L.T.(Notes) 14.

[17] *Waters* v. *Rolls-Royce Ltd.*, 1960 S.L.T.(Notes) 91.

[18] *Gardiner* v. *The Admiralty* (H.L.) 1964 S.L.T. 194 (ss. 26 (1) and 151 (1) of the 1937 Act). The House of Lords reversing the First Division and holding that pursuer's averments were relevant in this case.

access is safe when used with reasonable care and caution by a workman.[19]
Section 29 (2) does not extend to a place where there is a secure foothold
in all normal circumstances but from which a workman may be thrown
off as a result of some abnormal occurrence such as an explosion.[20] The
phrase " has to work " which is contained in section 29 (2) requires that
it must be established either that the workman was ordered to work at the
place or that it was the only practicable place where he could have performed the particular operation.[21] The most important case in recent
years upon the application of section 29 (2) (formerly section 26 (2) of the
1937 Act) is of course *McWilliams* v. *Sir William Arrol & Co. Ltd.*[22] in
which the House of Lords held that the employers were in breach of both
their common law and statutory duties but the appellant (whose husband
had been killed and in respect of whose death she had brought the action)
had failed to establish the causal link between the breach of duty and the
resultant injury and accordingly she could not succeed in her action. It
was shown in evidence that even if the safety belts had been provided the
employees were in the habit of not using them. The House also considered
regulation 97 of the Buildings (Safety, Health and Welfare) Regulations
1948 (S.I. 1948 No. 1145)—under which employers have a duty to provide
safety belts to persons " who elect to use them " and held that employers
generally were not under a duty to exhort their employees to wear safety
belts.

Where cases are brought upon an alleged breach of section 29 the
Scottish courts will decide whether to allow a proof before answer or a
jury trial. If some difficult points of law are to be considered, a proof
before answer will normally be ordered.[23] If the issues can be decided
from an examination of facts and circumstances then a jury trial will be
allowed.[24]

The next ten sections (30–39 inclusive) of the Act deal with technical
matters such as: dangerous fumes, explosive or inflammable dust, steam
boilers (construction, maintenance, examination and use, etc.), steam
receivers and containers, air receivers and water-sealed gasholders.

The fire precautions (adopted from the 1959 Act and expanded) laid
down by the 1961 Act are extensive and are to be found in sections 40 to
52 both inclusive.[25] Certain powers and duties are conferred upon local

---

[19] *Brown* v. *Redpath Brown & Co. Ltd.*, 1963 S.L.T. 219.
[20] *Tinto* v. *Stewarts & Lloyds Ltd.* (O.H.) 1962 S.L.T. 314.
[21] *Davies* v. *John G. Stein & Co.*, 1965 S.L.T.(Notes) 43.
[22] 1962 S.C.(H.L.) 70; 1962 S.L.T. 121; [1962] 1 All E.R. 623 (H.L.); [1962] 1 W.L.R.
295 (the House applying *Wardlaw* v. *Bonnington Castings*, 1956 S.C.(H.L.) 26; 1956
S.L.T. 135; and *sub nom. Bonnington Castings* v. *Wardlaw* in [1956] A.C. 613; [1956]
2 W.L.R. 707; [1956] 1 All E.R. 615 (H.L.); *disapproving* certain dicta in *Roberts* v.
Dorman Long & Co. [1953] 1 W.L.R. 942; [1953] 2 All E.R. 428, and considering
certain dicta in *Qualcast (Wolverhampton) Ltd.* v. *Haynes* [1959] A.C. 743; [1959]
2 W.L.R. 312; [1959] 2 All E.R. 38; 1959 S.L.T.(News) 205).
[23] See, for example, *Cumming* v. *British Railways Board*, 1968 S.L.T.(Notes) 8.
[24] *Jack* v. *Guardbridge Paper Co.* (O.H.) 1968 S.L.T.(Notes) 8.
[25] The matter of fire precautions (and the need for regular inspections) was highlighted
in the recent Fatal Accidents Inquiry into the factory disaster at certain premises in
James Watt Street, Glasgow. The jury returned its verdict on February 6, 1969 (after

authorities and fire authorities in connection with this preventive legislation. A tightening up of this legislation seems to be necessary.

Section 53 gives the Minister power to make special safety regulations for the prevention of accidents. This section replaces section 38 of the 1937 Act and, of course, a multitude of regulations has been made under these two sections—as well as under powers conferred in the 1901 Act—by means of the Minister's delegated legislative powers (by Statutory Rule and Order and thereafter by Statutory Instrument).[26] Sections 54 and 55 confer upon the court (in Scotland a sheriff court; in England a magistrate's court) power to make orders as regards dangerous conditions and practices and safety of factory premises.

Examples of the special codes of safety regulations are numerous. Perhaps those most commonly known or giving rise to most litigation are broadly the following: (1) the Building (Safety, Health and Welfare) Regulations 1948 (S.I. 1948 No. 1145) [27] and the Construction (General Provisions) Regulations 1961 (S.I. 1961 No. 1580) [28]; (2) the Shipbuilding Regulations 1931 (S.R. & O. 1931 No. 133),[29] brought up to date and

---

a nine-day hearing) and attributed blame to the occupiers/employers. It appeared from the evidence that more regular inspections by H.M. Inspectorate and by the fire authorities is necessary in the industrial cities. It was hinted that H.M. Inspectorate might have been negligent—but the Sheriff-Principal pointed out that the power given to H.M. Inspectorate was a discretionary power to bring such prosecutions as they considered necessary and he did not think that civil liability attached to them. The Inspectorate tend to use their best endeavours (by persuasion, etc.) to ensure compliance and only bring a prosecution as a last resort.

[26] These are collected and published by H.M.S.O. For some examples see Redgrave's *Factories Acts* (21st ed., 1966) (Butterworths).

[27] See for example the following cases: *Harkness* v. *Oxy-Acetylene Welding Co.*, 1963 S.L.T. 205 (reg. 5 imposes an absolute duty); *Cowan* v. *Glasgow Corporation* (O.H.) 1964 S.L.T. 134; *Armstrong* v. *James Miller & Partners Ltd.* (O.H.) 1964 S.L.T.(Notes) 42; *Aitken* v. *John R. Bryson Ltd.* (O.H.) 1966 S.L.T. 234; *Allen* v. *Darlington Insulating Co.*, 1966 S.L.T.(Sh.Ct.) 59; *Price* v. *Claudgen Ltd.* (H.L.) 1967 S.L.T. 78, followed in *Lawson* v. *J. S. Harvey & Co.*, 1968 S.L.T.(Sh.Ct.) 24; and *O'Donnell* v. *Cochran & Co. (Annan) Ltd.* 1968 S.L.T.(Notes) 76 (reg. 2—"repair ").
   The House of Lords has just expressed the view in *Boyle* v. *Kodak Ltd.* (see the *Times Law Report* of May 1, 1969) that, where statutory regulations for safety at work impose an absolute duty upon both employers and employees, the employers must instruct even skilled men about the statutory requirements. If the employer cannot show that he did everything reasonably to be expected to ensure compliance with the regulations, he may not escape liability for injury to the employee, even where the employer had not been negligent at common law (*per* Lord Reid; stressing that, although absolute duties might be imposed upon employers, they were entitled to plead in defence any breach of duty by an employee; this being confirmed by *Ross* v. *Associated Portland Cement Manufacturers Ltd.* [1964] 1 W.L.R. 768). Boyle's appeal was allowed by the House and blame was apportioned equally regarding the breach of reg. 29 (4) of the 1948 Regulations.

[28] See, for example: *Byrne* v. *Trucson Ltd.* (O.H.) 1966 S.L.T.(Notes) 42; *Davies* v. *A. C. D. Bridge Co.* (O.H.) 1966 S.L.T. 339 (reg. 49 imposed an absolute duty); *McMullen* v. *Alexander Findlay & Co.* (O.H.) 1966 S.L.T. 146; *Ritchie* v. *James H. Russell Ltd.*, 1966 S.L.T. 244; *O'Donnell* v. *Murdoch McKenzie & Co. Ltd.* (H.L.) 1967 S.L.T. 229 (The House *reversing* the Second Division on reg. 7 (2), but Lord Guest and Lord Pearson *dissenting*); and *Martin* v. *Holland & Hannen & Cubitts (Scotland) Ltd.* (O.H.) 1967 S.L.T.(Notes) 117.

[29] See, for example, *Gaitens* v. *Blythswood Shipbuilding Co.* (O.H.) 1948 S.L.T.(Notes) 49; *Kilty* v. *Fairfield Shipbuilding and Engineering Co.*, 1954 S.L.T.(Notes) 7; *Blair* v. *Scott's Shipbuilding and Engineering Co. Ltd.* (O.H.) 1960 S.L.T.(Notes) 21. (Safety of access was a question of fact and jury trial allowed.) These Regulations did not apply to a berth in a public wet dock—*Bowman* v. *Ellerman Lines Ltd.* (O.H.) 1953 S.L.T. 271.

replaced by the Shipbuilding and Shiprepairing Regulations 1960 (S.I. 1960 No. 1932) [30]; (3) the Docks Regulations 1934 (S.R. & O. 1934 No. 279) [31]; (4) the Grinding of Metals (Miscellaneous Industries) Regulations, 1925 (S.R. & O. 1925 No. 904) [32]; (5) the Iron & Steel Foundries Regulations 1953 (S.I. 1953 No. 1464) [33]; and (6) the Woodworking Machinery Regulations 1922 (S.R. & O. 1922 No. 1196) [34]; and the Construction (Working Places) Regulations 1966 (S.I. 1966 No. 94). [35]

PART III—Welfare (General Provisions)

This part of the Act comprises sections 57 to 62 both inclusive. Section 57 requires an adequate supply of wholesome drinking water to be provided and maintained at suitable points conveniently accessible to all persons employed in the factory premises. Section 58, dealing with washing facilities, is rather important. It refers to the provision of " adequate and suitable " washing facilities, which is to include a supply of clean running hot and cold or warm water as well as soap and clean towels (or other suitable means of cleaning or drying). [36] These facilities are to be conveniently accessible and kept in a clean and orderly condition. The Minister has certain powers to make regulations, which may alter or modify or exempt from the terms of subsection (1). [37]

Two Scottish cases should be noted on this point. In Reid v. Westfield Paper Co., [38] which was brought under the corresponding section of the

30 McCormick v. Fairfield Shipbuilding and Engineering Co. Ltd. (O.H.) 1964 S.L.T. (Notes) 34 (a proof before answer allowed in this case); and Graham v. Greenock Dockyard Co. (O.H.) 1964 S.L.T. 61 (reg. 17 (1) applied also to a staging in course of construction or dismantling).
31 Stewart's Ex. v. Clyde Navigation Trustees, 1946 S.C. 317; 1946 S.L.T. 302 (reg. 43—failure to employ a signaller); Leeson v. J. & H. Gardner & Co. Ltd. (O.H.) 1947 S.L.T. 264 (reg. 9); Grant v. Sun Shipping Co., 1948 S.C.(H.L.) 73; 1949 S.L.T. 25; [1948] A.C. 549; [1948] 2 All E.R. 238 (H.L.) (regs. 12, 37 and 45—liability of shipowners and ship repairers); Reid v. James Spencer & Co., 1967 S.L.T.(Notes) 98 (reg. 15—beams used as hatch covers to be maintained so as to be removable by normal method); Harcus v. Rose Line Ltd. (O.H.) 1967 S.L.T.(Notes) 52 (reg. 27—duties of inspection and maintenance, and patent defects).
32 Quinn v. Cameron & Roberton Ltd., 1957 S.L.T. 143; 1957 S.C. (H.L.) 22; [1958] A.C. 9; [1957] 1 All E.R. 760 (H.L.) (reversing the First Division of the Court of Session and approving Wardlaw v. Bonnington Castings, 1956 S.C.(H.L.) 26; 1956 S.L.T. 135; and sub nom. Bonnington Castings v. Wardlaw in [1956] A.C. 613; [1956] 2 W.L.R. 707; [1956] 1 All E.R. 615 (H.L.)); Davie v. Scottish Enamelling Co. Ltd. (O.H.) 1962 S.C. 582 (reg. 13 is peremptory).
33 Smith v. James Dickie & Co. (Drop Forgings) Ltd. (O.H.) 1961 S.L.T.(Notes) 32 (reg. 8 (1) (c)—the meaning of " pouring molten metal "); Marshall v. Babcock & Wilcox Ltd., 1961 S.L.T. 259 (reg. 8 (1) (c)—" suitable goggles "; the duty imposed was not absolute); and contrast Baxter v. Carron Co. (O.H.) 1965 S.L.T.(Notes) 89 (goggles which did not fit properly were not suitable in terms of reg. 8 (1) (c)).
34 Gray v. Steel & Perris, 1953 S.L.T.(Sh.Ct.) 73; (1953) 69 Sh.Ct.Rep. 302 (reg. 9 (b)—did not apply here as pursuer was not " employed at a woodworking machine ").
35 See H.M. Inspector of Factories v. The Cementation Co. Ltd., 1968 S.L.T.(Sh.Ct.) 75 (reg. 6 (2)).
36 s. 58 (1). The subsection is mandatory.
37 See, for example, the Washing Facilities (Running Water) Exemption Regulations 1960 (S.I. 1960 No. 1029).
38 1957 S.C. 218; 1957 S.L.T. 184. See also the earlier sheriff court case of Porter v J. Fraser & Son Ltd. (1956) 72 Sh.Ct.Rep. 181, in which pursuer had failed to prove a breach of the statutory regulation and also failed to prove a breach of the employer's common law duty to provide a safe system of working.

1937 Act (*viz.*, s. 42), the pursuer contracted dermatitis whilst in the defenders' employment. Defenders pleaded that the duty to provide " adequate and suitable washing facilities " was a welfare provision and therefore any failure in that duty could not give rise to an action for damages. The court rejected that view, holding that any breach of this duty could give rise to an action for damages. In *Gardiner* v. *Motherwell Machinery Co. Ltd.*,[39] the pursuer recovered damages for a failure to provide adequate washing facilities. He had contracted dermatitis in working conditions likely to cause it and accordingly there was a prima facie presumption that the disease had been caused by those conditions.

Section 59 deals with accommodation for clothing, which again must be " adequate and suitable." It has been held in Scotland that any breach of this duty could give rise to an action for damages.[40] The risk of theft must be taken into account.[41] Sections 60 and 61 deal respectively with sitting facilities and first-aid.[42] Section 62 gives the Minister powers to make special welfare regulations under this part of the Act. There are in existence a substantial number of such regulations (dating from 1948 and referring back to the 1937 Act) in *inter alia* the building, pottery, iron and steel, shipbuilding and shiprepairing and railway industries.

PART IV—Health, Safety and Welfare (Special Provisions and Regulations)

This Part comprises sections 63 to 79 and deals with the special provisions and regulations relating to the health, safety and welfare of employees. It is not proposed to examine each individual section in detail, but alternatively to select for brief consideration and comment those sections which seem to give rise to most litigation or which form the more common grounds of claim against employers.

Section 63 deals specifically with the removal of dust or fumes likely to be injurious or offensive.[43] All practicable measures must be taken to prevent the inhalation of dust or fume or other impurity and to prevent a build-up of fumes or dust. Exhaust appliances are to be provided, if the nature of the factory process makes these things practicable, so as to prevent fumes and other impurities from entering the air of the workroom.[44] The general duty imposed by this section may be superseded by regulations

---

[39] 1961 S.C. (H.L.) 1; 1962 S.L.T. 2. The House of Lords on this occasion *reversing* the First Division of the Court of Session.

[40] *Barr* v. *Cruickshank & Co.* (1958) 74 Sh.Ct.Rep. 218; 1959 S.L.T.(Sh.Ct.) 9.

[41] *McCarthy* v. *Daily Mirror* [1949] 1 All E.R. 841.

[42] See G. H. L. Fridman, *The Modern Law of Employment* (1963) (and cumulative supplement). Chap. 16 at pp. 212–223 in particular, for a useful note on these matters. Several statutory instruments have also been issued on the subject of first-aid.

[43] See *Carmichael* v. *Cockburn & Co.*, 1955 S.C. 487; 1956 S.L.T. 241; also *Balfour* v. *William Beardmore & Co.*, 1956 S.L.T. 205.

[44] If dust, etc., does not emanate from one identifiable and concentrated source, there is no definite obligation to instal exhaust fans, etc.—*vide M'Leod* v. *Rolls-Royce Ltd.* (1956) 72 Sh.Ct.Rep. 214.

made by the Minister under section 76 of the Act.[45] The onus of proof in civil actions for damages brought under the section rests apparently upon pursuer—he must show, on a balance of probabilities, that his injuries resulted from defender's breach of duty. It is not enough for pursuer to show that he suffered a type of injury against which the section was designed to protect him and other employees and that his injury was possibly caused by a breach of the statutory duty.[46]

Sections 64 and 66–71 deal variously with meals in dangerous trades, shuttle threading by mouth, prohibition against white phosphorus, humid factories, underground rooms, basement bakehouses and laundries respectively. Section 65 is concerned with protection of the eyes in certain processes and enables the Minister to specify by regulations any process which involves special risk of injury to the eyes (from particles or fragments thrown off) and, accordingly, suitable goggles or effective screens shall be provided,[47] in accordance with any directions given in the regulations.[48] The statutory duty under section 65 is owed to the occupier/employer's own employees carrying out the particular manufacturing process,[49] but not to the employees of an independent contractor engaged by the occupier/employer to do other work—e.g., repairing the walls, etc., of the factory.[50] It has been held in *Kerr* v. *Cook* [51] that a pursuer, injured by an allegedly defective pick, might relevantly aver, in a claim based on common law negligence, that his employers had failed to make frequent and regular inspections without averring specifically at what intervals of time such inspections should have been made. An employer is not bound or obliged by a so-called " duty of exhortation " towards his employees in relation to the wearing of goggles. It is enough that he provides them and issues clear instructions about their use.[52]

---

[45] See *Ashwood* v. *Steel Co. of Scotland*, 1957 S.C. 17; 1957 S.L.T. 244; and, in England, *Franklin* v. *Gramophone Co.* [1948] 1 K.B. 542 (such regulations do not necessarily displace the common law duty of care owed by an employer to his employees; this depends upon a true construction of the regulations).

[46] *Wardlaw* v. *Bonnington Castings*, 1956 S.C.(H.L.) 26; and *sub nom. Bonnington Castings* v. *Wardlaw* [1956] A.C. 613; [1956] 2 W.L.R. 707; [1956] 1 All E.R. 615 (H.L.).

[47] *i.e.*, at the bench; or the employee must be clearly instructed about their use—*Finch* v. *Telegraph Construction Co.* [1949] 1 All E.R. 452; [1949] W.N. 57; and the employee must prove he would have worn them—*Nolan* v. *Dental Manufacturing Co.* [1958] 1 W.L.R. 936; [1958] 2 All E.R. 449. " Suitable " means well adapted for the process and the wearer.

[48] See the Protection of Eyes Regulations 1938 (S.R. & O. 1938 No. 654) (made under the 1937 Act); and *Hunter* v. *Singer Manufacturing Co.*, 1953 S.L.T.(Notes) 85 (cutting of metal) and *Leighton* v. *Harland & Wolff*, 1953 S.L.T.(Notes) 36 (fettling). It has been held, in England, in *Nolan* v. *Dental Manufacturing Co.* [1958] 1 W.L.R. 936; [1958] 2 All E.R. 449 that plaintiff (pursuer) must prove that if goggles had been provided he would have worn them.

[49] *Kerr* v. *Cook* (O.H.) 1953 S.L.T.(Notes) 23 (brought under F.A. 1937, s. 49).

[50] See *Whalley* v. *Briggs Motor Bodies* [1954] 1 W.L.R. 840; [1954] 2 All E.R. 193.

[51] (O.H.) 1953 S.L.T.(Notes) 23; see also *Szuca* v. *Balfour, Beatty & Co.*, 1953 S.L.T. (Notes) 6.

[52] *Wilson* v. *British Railways Board* (O.H.) 1964 S.L.T.(Notes) 102. (Lord Johnston quoting from Lord Radcliffe's opinion in *Qualcast (Wolverhampton) Ltd.* v. *Haynes* [1959] A.C. 743; [1959] 2 W.L.R. 510, [1959] 2 All E.R. 38; approved by Lord Reid in *McWilliams* v. *Sir Wm. Arrol & Co. Ltd.*, 1962 S.C.(H.L.) 70; 1962 S.L.T. 121 (H.L.); [1962] 1 W.L.R. 295.) But an employee is not guilty of contributory negligence because his goggles slipped without his knowledge or because he did not attempt to obtain better goggles—see *Brown* v. *Bonnington Castings Ltd.* (O.H.) 1969 S.L.T.(Notes) 24.

Section 72 is concerned with the question of lifting heavy weights and indeed subsection (1) provides that a person shall not be employed to lift, carry or move any load so heavy as to be likely to cause him injury. The Minister is given power by subsection (2) to make special regulations applying maximum weights and these may relate to persons generally or to a class of persons or to persons employed in any class or description of factory or in any process. He has already done so for certain textiles, jute and pottery.[53]

Sections 73, 74 and 75 prohibit the employment of female young persons in certain processes, of women and young persons in certain lead manufacturing processes and in processes involving the use of lead compounds. Section 76 gives powers to the Minister to make special regulations for the safety and health of all employees or any class of employees. Such powers have been used extensively and sets of regulations have been promulgated for a wide variety of industries.[54] Certain supplementary provisions appear in sections 77, 78 and 79, but these do not require detailed examination.

PART V—Notification of Accidents and Industrial Diseases

This Part of the Act comprises sections 80 to 85 and is very important.

Where an accident [55] in a factory—(a) causes the loss of life of an employee or (b) the disablement of an employee for more than three days, written notice of the accident (in prescribed [56] form, etc.) must be sent forthwith to the inspector for the district,[57] unless the accident is governed by the Explosives Act 1875 or the Petroleum (Consolidation) Act 1928.

Where an accident causing disablement is notified and thereafter the death of the disabled employee occurs, notice in writing of the death must be sent by the factory occupier to the inspector for the district as soon as he (the occupier) becomes aware of it.[58] Where the occupier of the factory is not the actual employer of the deceased or disabled employee, there is imposed upon the actual employer a statutory duty to notify the occupier [59] of the accident, failure in that duty constituting an offence with liability to a fine not exceeding ten pounds. The Dangerous Occurrences (Notification) Regulations 1947 [60] must be read along with section 80. The Minister is given power (as in previous statutes) to extend the notification of accidents provisions to dangerous occurrences. Section 82 is devoted to the notification of industrial diseases by medical practitioners. The

---

[53] S.R. & O. 1926 No. 1463 (woollen and worsted textiles); S.I. 1948 No. 1696 (jute) (see Part II); and S.I. 1950 No. 65 (reg. 6, paras. 6 and 7).

[54] See, in illustration, the *Scottish Current Law Statutes*, volume for 1961 (" General Note " to s. 76 of the Factories Act 1961); also the annual lists of statutory instruments; and particularly Redgrave's *Factories Acts* (21st ed., 1966), Part II.

[55] For the meaning of "accident" see *Fenton* v. *Thorley* [1903] A.C. 443, where the word was given its ordinary sense of an unlooked-for mishap or occurrence.

[56] " Prescribed " is defined in s. 176 (1) as meaning " prescribed by order of the Minister."

[57] s. 80 (1).

[58] s. 80 (2).

[59] s. 80 (3).

[60] S.R. & O. 1947 No. 31.

factory occupier also has certain obligations to notify the inspector for the district and the appointed factory doctor.

Section 83 deals with the procedure to be followed (in England and Wales) where a coroner's inquest is held following upon a death from accident or disease notified under Part V of the Act. The same procedure will apply *mutatis mutandis* to a fatal accident inquiry in Scotland held under the Fatal Accidents Inquiry (Scotland) Act 1895.

Section 84 gives power to the Minister to direct formal investigations into industrial accidents and diseases.[61] Section 85 sets out the duties of the appointed factory doctor *vis-à-vis* the investigation of and report upon certain cases of death or injury or disease referred to him by the Minister or by the district inspector or notified to him as a disease.

PART VI—Employment of Women and Young Persons

This is a very comprehensive part of the Act and runs from section 86 to section 119. Section 86 sets forth the general conditions relating to the employment of women and young persons, *i.e.*, the hours and periods of employment. Section 87 specifies the weekly hours of work of young persons under 16 years of age. Section 88 provides for the exhibition of notices within the factory premises containing information about the period of employment for each workday and the intervals allowed for meals or rest. Overtime employment is covered by section 89 and this is a very extensive section; many regulations having been made by ministerial order [62] in numerous trades from 1938 onwards. The supplementary provisions are enforced by sections 91, 92, 93 [63] and 95. Annual holidays are to be permitted on certain specified days.[64] Exceptions to the general rules mentioned in Part VI are allowed by sections 99 to 113 inclusive, whilst the " shift system " (authorised by the Minister and revoked [65] by him, if and when necessary) is fully recognised by section 97. Notices and registers, etc., relating to exceptions are required by section 115, the notices in question having to be served upon the inspector for the district and to be posted within the factory premises. Section 116 regulates the employment of young persons in certain occupations (carrying, collecting or delivering goods wholly or mainly outside of a factory or at a dock, wharf, quay or warehouse). Certain exemptions are also permitted by ministerial order, under section 117, in the interest of efficiency of industry

---

61 S. 84 (10) prevents duplication of the formal investigation procedure under the fatal accidents inquiry procedure in Scotland, unless the Lord Advocate directs that the fatal accidents inquiry be held also.

62 All issued as S.R. & O.s or S.I.s. See also Redgrave, *op. cit.*, Part III and Appendix for information on further Acts and orders relating to the employment of women, young persons and children and others in factories.

63 See *Macdonald* v. *McKechnie's Rolls Ltd.*, 1956 S.L.T. 305 (F.A. 1937, ss. 77 and 93 (1) —now F.A. 1961, ss. 93 and 111. The phrase " on two days other than Saturday " in any week included Sunday. No offence had been committed).

64 In England, Christmas Day, Good Friday and Bank holidays. In Scotland, six week-days (in the burghs, two of these days being burgh holidays fixed by the town council) as fixed by the occupier and notified by him (subject to the position in the burghs).

65 *Ibid.* s. 98.

and transport. Certificates of fitness for employment of young persons are required by section 118, and power is given to H.M. Inspectors by section 119 to serve notice upon factory occupiers requiring them to discontinue employing young persons (where such employment is prejudicial to their health or the health of their co-workers) which must be done unless a satisfactory examination and certificate are obtained from the appointed factory doctor.

PART VII—Special Applications and Extensions

This part, comprising sections 120 to 132, is highly technical and governs such things as tenement factories; institutions carried on for charitable or reformatory purposes; docks, wharves, quays, warehouses and ships; works of building and engineering construction; and lead processes carried on in places other than factories. A detailed consideration of these sections is inappropriate here.

PART VIII—Homework

Sections 133 and 134 make up this part of the Act. The former section deals with the keeping of lists of outworkers in certain trades (as prescribed by ministerial regulation) and the communication of such information to H.M. Factory Inspectorate and to the appropriate local authority.[66]

PART IX—Wages

Section 135 (1) requires the factory occupier, in the case of textile factories,[67] to supply to pieceworkers employed by him particulars of the rate of wages applicable to work to be done and also particulars of the work to which that rate is to be applied. The subsection then goes on to spell out the methods by which the various particulars are to be communicated to the workers concerned. The Minister has wide powers under section 135 (5) to make regulations under this heading and thereby apply this section to any class of factories other than textile factories, with such modifications as may be necessary in the circumstances; and similarly, he may apply the provisions (modified as aforesaid) to any class of persons employed as outworkers and to their employers. Section 136 prohibits deductions from wages contracted to be paid.

PART X—Notices, Returns, Records, Duties of Persons Employed and Application of Weights and Measures Acts

This part consists of sections 137 to 144 and stresses the need for a proper channel of communication between factory occupiers, H.M. Inspectorate and the local authorities. The new occupier of a factory

---

[66] In Scotland, this is either the county council or the town council of the burgh. Where a local authority receives a list which shows that an outworker (or outworkers) is employed outwith its own jurisdiction it must notify the appropriate local authority within whose jurisdiction the place of employment is situated.
[67] Defined in s. 135 (6).

(whether the factory itself is newly built or not) is obliged to notify the district inspector and to tell him whether mechanical power is being used.[68] The period of notice required is normally not less than one month where mechanical power is to be used,[69] but certain exceptions are permitted.[70]

Section 138 requires that certain notices (prescribed in section 138 (1)) and the prescribed abstract of the Act shall be kept posted at the principal entrances of the factory (or at such other places as may be directed by an inspector).

Each factory occupier is required to keep a " general register " for the factory [71] and to attach to it the certificate from the fire authority.[72] The information which the general register must contain is fully set forth in section 140 (1). Records are normally preserved for a minimum period of two years,[73] but annual returns must be made to H.M. Chief Inspector of persons employed in the factory, as directed by the Minister, such returns containing *inter alia* the particulars mentioned in section 142 (1).

Section 143 is most important and stipulates that no person employed in a factory (or in such other place as is governed by the Act) shall wilfully interfere with or misuse any means, appliance, convenience, etc., provided for securing the health, safety or welfare of the persons employed in the factory; and where such means or appliance for securing health or safety are provided then each employee shall use them.[74] Furthermore, no factory employee shall wilfully and without reasonable cause do anything likely to endanger himself or others.[75] The wilful interference or misuse to which the section refers relates to some meddling with appliances or equipment, which is likely to cause danger.[76] Whether a safety device or appliance is " provided " is a question which requires the facts of each individual case to be carefully examined.[77] Section 144 covers weights and measures and instruments used in connection with the ascertainment of wages.

PART XI—Administration

The administrative provisions are contained in sections 145 to 154 and relate *inter alia* to such matters as the appointment and duties of inspectors [78] and their powers [79]; the power of fire authority officers to

---

[68] s. 137 (1) and (3).
[69] s. 137 (2).
[70] s. 137 (3).
[71] s. 140 (1).
[72] s. 140 (2).
[73] s. 141.
[74] s. 143 (1).
[75] s. 143 (2).
[76] *George* v. *Glasgow Coal Co.* [1909] A.C. 123; *Charles* v. *Smith & Sons* [1954] 1 W.L.R. 451; [1954] 1 All E.R. 499.
[77] *Carr* v. *Decca Gramophone Co.* [1947] K.B. 728; *Beal* v. *Gomme* (1949) 65 T.L.R. 543 (both cases involving the Woodworking Machinery Regulations 1922, under which the duty to fence is not absolute but is met by compliance with the regulations themselves).
[78] s. 145.
[79] s. 146.

enter upon premises [80]; the power of inspectors to conduct proceedings [81] in the magistrates' courts in England and Wales and the courts of summary jurisdiction in Scotland; appointed factory doctors (their method of appointment, duties and powers) [82]; and the duties of medical officers of health and local authority inspectors. [83]

PART XII—Offences, Penalties and Legal Proceedings

This part comprises sections 155 to 171. Section 155, dealing specifically with offences, provides that where any contravention of the provisions of the Act (or relevant regulation) occurs in or in connection with or in relation to a factory, the occupier or, where appropriate and relevant, the owner of the factory shall—subject to what is said in the remaining sections of Part XII—be guilty of an offence. [84] Any contravention by an employed person of any of the provisions of Part X (or of a regulation expressly imposing a duty upon him) also constitutes an offence, [85] but liability may attach to the owner or occupier if it is proved that he failed to take all reasonable steps to prevent the contravention of the Part X provisions (or the duty expressly imposed by regulation). A director, manager, secretary or other officer of a company may be jointly guilty of an offence along with his company and he may be punished accordingly. [86] The term " occupier " is not defined in the Act, but the definition given in the old Scottish case of *Ramsay* v. *Mackie* [87] has long been adopted as a basic guide. Yet it is not always easy to identify the occupier and the circumstances may have to be looked at very carefully. Some of the fairly recent English cases [88] illustrate the difficulty.

Section 156 stipulates the amount of the fines for offences under the Act for which no express penalty is otherwise provided. In ordinary circumstances the maximum fine for an employed person is £15 and in other cases the maximum is £60. [89] If, however, the contravention was likely to cause the death of, or bodily injury to, any person then the amount of the fines becomes £75 and £300 respectively, in lieu of the lower figures just mentioned previously. [90] Expenses may also be awarded against the accused. [91]

---

[80] s. 148.
[81] s. 149.
[82] s. 151.
[83] s. 153.
[84] s. 155 (1).
[85] s. 155 (2).
[86] s. 155 (5).
[87] (1904) 7 F. 196. The " occupier " is " the person who runs the factory, who regulates and controls the work that is done there." In ordinary circumstances he is the employer.
[88] See, for example, *Turner* v. *Courtaulds Ltd.* [1937] 1 All E.R. 467; *Smith* v. *Cammell Laird & Co. Ltd.* [1940] A.C. 242; 56 T.L.R. 164; and *Wilkinson* v. *Rea Ltd.* [1941] 1 K.B. 688, followed in *Bryers* v. *Canadian Pacific Steamships* [1956] 3 W.L.R. 776; [1956] 3 All E.R. 560 (C.A.).
[89] s. 156 (1).
[90] s. 156 (2).
[91] s. 182 (7).

Section 157 is interesting because it authorises the court, in addition to or in substitution of a fine, to order the convicted occupier or owner—within a specified time limit [92]—to take such steps as may be specified by the court for remedying those matters in respect of which the contravention has occurred. Any failure to comply with the order results in a fine of £10 per day for each day of such non-compliance. The case of *Perdikou* v. *Glasgow Corporation*,[93] establishes that where an order is made under section 157, the sentence for the original offence should not be deferred; the order should specify the remedial measures which should be taken and any continued failure by accused to comply with the order (*i.e.,* a continuation of the original offence) requires the bringing of a further charge or complaint against him, if he is to be punished. A parent may be fined if his child (a " young person," to use the terminology of the Act) is employed in any factory in contravention of the provisions of the Act.[94]

Section 161 enables a person charged with an offence under the Act and provided the offence is committed in England or Wales, to exempt himself from liability by adopting a special procedure to bring the actual offender before the court. This procedure is incompetent and quite inapplicable in Scots law. The position in Scots law is clearly set forth in section 161 (3)—*viz.*: " . . . a person charged with an offence . . . who proves to the satisfaction of the court that he has used all due diligence to enforce the execution of this Act . . . and that the offence was due to the act or default of some other person who committed it without his consent, connivance or wilful default, shall be acquitted of the offence."

Sometimes the owner or hirer of machinery may be liable instead of the factory occupier.[95] All proceedings in respect of offences under the Act are to be tried by summary procedure [96] and it is competent to take summary proceedings against any person liable to a penalty for non-compliance with the Act (or relevant orders or regulations) within a period of three months from the holding of a fatal accidents inquiry in Scotland, where it appears from the proceedings at the inquiry that certain provisions of the Act (or any relevant orders or regulations) were not complied with by that person.[97]

Section 169 gives to the sheriff in Scotland (and the county court judge in England) power to set aside or modify the terms of any agreement (" as the . . . sheriff considers just and equitable in the circumstances of the case ") between the owner and occupier of premises which are being let, either in whole or in part, as a factory and by the terms of that original agreement the occupier or the owner is prevented from carrying out

[92] Which may be extended upon application to the court.
[93] 1951 S.C.(J.) 149; 1952 S.L.T. 18.
[94] s. 158.
[95] s. 163; and see *Whalley* v. *Briggs Motor Bodies* [1954] 1 W.L.R. 840; [1954] 2 All E.R. 193.
[96] s. 164 (1).
[97] s. 164 (4).

structural or other alterations in order to comply with the provisions of the Act or with any standards or requirements imposed by it (or with the terms of any regulation or order made under the Act). The sheriff shall hear the parties and any witnesses whom they desire to call.

The sheriff has a similar power by section 170 to apportion between an owner and an occupier of premises let as a factory the expenses of structural or other alterations to the premises in order to comply with the provisions of or standards imposed by the Act, etc.

PART XIII—Application of Act

This part contains the general application of the Act (s. 172); its application to the Crown, in respect of factories owned or occupied by the Crown and to building operations and works of engineering construction undertaken by or on behalf of the Crown (s. 173); and the consequential amendments to the Mines and Quarries Act 1954 (s. 174).

PART XIV—Interpretation and General

The meaning of the expression " factory " is to be found in section 175 (1) and this definition is also contained in the standard reference works on factory law.[98] Subsection (2) of section 175 also contains a very substantial list of specified premises or of premises wherein certain specified trades, occupations, processes or others are carried on, even although such premises do not fall within the subsection (1) definition.

The premises in question may be a factory, even although only one man is employed there.[99] Prison workshops do not, however, come within the scope of the Act, as such premises are not places where persons are employed.[99] The court will always look carefully at the circumstances.[1] The phrase " adapting for sale " used in purpose (c) of section 175 (1)

---

[98] See Samuels, *Factory Law* (7th ed.), pp. 285–287; also Redgrave's *Factories Acts* (21st ed., 1966). As this definition is of vital importance, s. 175 (1) is quoted in full, *viz.*:
" 175.—(1) Subject to the provisions of this section, the expression ' factory ' means any premises in which, or within the close or curtilage or precincts of which, persons are employed in manual labour in any process for or incidental to any of the following purposes, namely:—
    (a) the making of any article or of part of any article; or
    (b) the altering, repairing, ornamenting, finishing, cleaning, or washing or the breaking up or demolition of any article; or
    (c) the adapting for sale of any article;
    (d) the slaughtering of cattle, sheep, swine, goats, horses, asses or mules; or
    (e) the confinement of such animals as aforesaid while awaiting slaughter at other premises, in a case where the place of confinement is available in connection with those other premises, is not maintained primarily for agricultural purposes within the meaning of the Agriculture Act 1947 or, as the case may be, the Agriculture (Scotland) Act 1948, and does not form part of the premises used for the holding of a market in respect of such animals;
being premises in which, or within the close or curtilage or precincts of which, the work is carried on by way of trade or for purposes of gain and to or over which the employer of the persons employed therein has the right of access or control."
[99] *Pullin* v. *Prison Commissioners* [1957] 3 All E.R. 470; [1957] 1 W.L.R. 1186. For a very valuable set of Notes (including cases) on s. 175 see Samuels, *op. cit.*, pp. 287–297.
[1] See *Waddell's Curator Bonis* v. *Alexander Lindsay Ltd.* (O.H.) 1960 S.L.T. 189 (fitting shop where repairs were in progress; both defenders liable); also *Stirling* v. *James Hemphill Ltd.* (O.H.) 1966 S.L.T.(Notes) 79. (Lorry being cleaned in a repair depot; proof before answer allowed).

(and in earlier factory statutes) has merited the attention of the courts for many years—as in *Henderson* v. *Glasgow Corporation*,[2] where the process of separating saleable parts of refuse from unsaleable parts was held to be an adapting for sale.

The general interpretation section (s. 176) then follows.[3] References to " the Minister " have, until the year 1968 in United Kingdom politics and government, meant the Minister of Labour. However, since mid-1968, the Ministry of Labour has been restyled the Department of Employment and Productivity. It is symptomatic of the modern way of life that new and more up-to-date terminology should be applied, where possible, to older traditional institutions. (The sales experts would call it " good marketing technique.") This does not necessarily improve the efficiency of the institution—but creates the impression in the mind of the public (or electorate, if that is the target) that things are being rearranged, after careful thought, to meet the new technological age.

The general application of the Act to Scotland can be found in section 182. The Act itself came into force on April 1, 1962.[4] It is likely that further modifications and reforms will take place within the next five years. In the meantime the 1961 Act must be read along with certain consequential amendments and developments which have been introduced by subsequent statutes in the industrial field—most noticeably the Offices, Shops and Railway Premises Act 1963 and the Redundancy Payments Act 1965, both of which are dealt with in subsequent sections of this chapter.

(2) *Mines and Quarries*

The Mines and Quarries Act 1954 [5] is the relatively modern consolidating statute governing mines and quarries. It supersedes the Coal Mines Act 1911, the Metalliferous Mines Regulation Act 1872 and the Quarries Act 1894, which were the basic statutes previously applying to the industries of mining and quarrying. It will be recalled that on January 1, 1947,[6] the coal-mines passed out of the ownership of the great coal-masters (or their nominee companies, operating behind the shield of limited liability) into public ownership. A tightening-up of safety, health and welfare regulations and provisions was necessary and again the well accepted pattern of the Factories Acts was used. The Act is complementary to the ordinary common law duties of care owed by an employer to his workmen and, moreover, does not in any way supplant these common law duties. Nor does compliance with or observance of the new " general duty " introduced by section 1 of the Act free and relieve the employer/mine-owner from any other specific statutory duty which is

---

[2] (1900) 2 F. 1137.
[3] For " Notes " hereon, see Samuels, *op. cit.*, pp. 300–302.
[4] s. 185 (2).
[5] 2 & 3 Eliz. 2, c. 70. The Mines and Quarries (Tips) Act 1969 (c. 10) is dealt with at the end of this section.
[6] By the Coal Industry Nationalisation Act 1946.

imposed upon him elsewhere—either by the Act itself or by any regulation or order made by virtue of it.

The Act has fifteen main parts with five Schedules and contains 195 sections. An exhaustive examination of each part and section will not be undertaken in this work. It will suffice if the more important sections are commented upon and any relevant cases (mainly Scottish) noted.[7]

Part I (comprising s. 1) introduces into mines and quarries legislation a new concept of " general duties " upon mine and quarry owners requiring them to make such financial and other provisions and to take such other steps as may be necessary to ensure that the mine or quarry is worked in accordance with the provisions of the Act and any relevant orders and regulations; and, in particular, to give written instructions to those persons to whom the owner delegates his statutory responsibilities (copies of these instructions being sent to the inspector for the district and to the manager of the mine or quarry). Section 193, by which the common rights of an employee against his employer and the duties of an owner under any other section of the Act are expressly preserved, falls to be read along with section 1. It had been argued previously before the courts that detailed statutory provisions might override the common law, but this view has been decisively rejected.[8] The most famous case prior to the 1954 Act was perhaps *English* v. *Wilsons & Clyde Coal Co. Ltd.*[9] in which it was held that the provision of a " safe system of working " was a common law obligation of the mine-owner and liability or responsibility therefor could not be delegated, not even by the appointment of a qualified mine-manager. That position is retained and underlined by section 193 of the 1954 Act.

Part II (ss. 2–21) deals with the management and control of mines, including *inter alia* the appointment, duties, powers and qualifications of managers and under-managers.

Safety, health and welfare in mines is specifically dealt with in Part III (ss. 22–97), which is, understandably, the most substantial and important part of the Act. Such matters, *inter alia*, as provisions for securing safe ingress and egress; safety precautions in shafts and entrances; roads; support; ventilation; lighting; lamps and contraband; fire precautions; first aid; medical examinations; and general welfare provisions are all included therein. It will not be possible to attempt an exhaustive examination of each section in Part III but it will be necessary—in view of certain interesting decisions by the courts in Scotland and in England—to look at some of the statutory provisions which give rise to most litigation.

Sections 22 to 27 deal with such matters as—the provision of shafts and

---

[7] For a very valuable guide to the Act see *The Mines and Quarries Act 1954* by J. R. Pickering (Butterworths) (1957), reprinted from Butterworths' Annotated Legislation Service.

[8] See particularly *Matuszczyk* v. *National Coal Board*, 1953 S.C. 8; 1953 S.L.T. 39 (the Lord President dissenting); which was approved in *National Coal Board* v. *England* [1954] A.C. 403; [1954] 1 All E.R. 546.

[9] 1937 S.C.(H.L.) 46; 1937 S.L.T. 523; [1938] A.C. 57; [1937] 3 All E.R. 628.

outlets in coal mines, and other types of mine therein specified; communications between shafts and outlets; a limitation upon the number of persons employed at mines with single exits and in shafts and outlets or their insets; the application of any of the Part III provisions by special regulations to any other type of mine; and the powers of an inspector to require the provision of additional ways out from the working faces in coal mines.

Section 28 deals specifically with the provision of winding and haulage apparatus at every shaft and unwalkable outlet so as to provide ingress and egress for persons employed below ground. All apparatus provided in pursuance of the section is to be properly maintained and, when not in use, kept constantly available for use.[10]

Section 29 says that regulations may impose upon mine-owners special requirements regarding the provision and maintenance of prescribed machinery, etc., in the event of winding or haulage apparatus failing to function.

Section 30 lays down that every mine shaft and staple-pit shall—save in so far as the natural conditions of the strata make this unnecessary— be made secure and be kept secure. It is a defence in any prosecution hereunder to prove that no insecure part was in use or was the site of any operations in progress by driving or extending the shaft or staple-pit. The leading case of M'Mullan v. Lochgelly Iron and Coal Co.[11] illustrates that a complete and continuing security is required against all the known geological hazards inherent in mining operations. It has been decided,[12] fairly recently, that the obligation imposed by section 30 (1) is not merely one of keeping the walls of the shaft secure but also of providing against dangers arising in the airspace of the shaft (e.g., by introducing scaffolding, which may collapse and fall upon workmen below).

Section 31 specifies the safety precautions to be taken in respect of the surface entrance to every mine shaft and other entrance thereto (whether above or below ground) and every entrance to every staple-pit. An efficient enclosure or barrier (designed and constructed so as to prevent anyone from falling down the shaft or coming into contact with any moving part of the winding apparatus) is to be provided and be properly maintained. Additional requirements are contained or referred to in subsections (2) to (5) inclusive. The provisions in subsection (2) regarding removable or openable barriers and enclosures are most important indeed, as the security to be provided is against accidental mishap.

---

[10] s. 28 (3). The word " maintained " is not defined in the Act, nor does the statute adopt the definition of " maintain " which is used in s. 152 (1) of the Factories Act 1937 (now s. 176 of the Factories Act 1961) although it might be reasonable to assume that the 1937 Act definition should be followed in all industrial safety legislation. Mr. Pickering, however, argues that as all penal legislation should be interpreted leniently where possible it would be reasonable to substitute the word " serving " (or "serviced," presumably) and that the injured employee would have the burden of proving the failure to service the equipment properly (see The Mines and Quarries Act 1954, p. 63).
[11] 1933 S.C.(H.L.) 64; (1933) S.N. 61; [1934] A.C. 1.
[12] Coll v. Cementation Co. Ltd. and the National Coal Board, 1963 S.L.T. 105.

Sections 32 and 33 contain certain additional safety precautions relating to the fall of articles down shafts, etc., and the entrances to unfit parts of mines respectively.

Roads are governed by sections 34 to 41 inclusive. Section 34 is a general section introducing general provisions regarding the maintenance and construction of roads. The duty of complying with the statutory provisions is placed upon the manager (a term which includes the acting manager). Broadly, these provisions are to ensure that every length of road (made after the commencement of the Act) is so made and maintained as to avoid sudden changes of direction, height, width and gradient (unless safety dictates otherwise or it is unnecessary to do so); and also that every such length of road (whether new or old) is kept free from obstructions and the floor thereof shall be kept in good repair and in such a condition that any persons or animals using that length of road may do so with safety and reasonable convenience. The words " working place " occurring in the section have been held to mean the " ordinary place where a miner is set to work by his employers." [13] It would seem that the duty to keep the floor in good repair and free from obstructions which would constitute a danger to safe passage is an absolute and continuing one.[14] The term " obstruction " used in the section seems to be used in the wide sense of any form of hazard or danger, which prevents the use of the road with safety and reasonable convenience.[15] It has been held fairly recently [16] that the statutory obligation is complied with if a clear passage of adequate width has been left in the roadway. The pleadings may show that there was no established breach of duty by the mine manager, and that an obstructed passageway existed and this would be sufficient to defeat a pursuer's case.[17] Lord Strachan has taken the view, in a recent case,[17] that section 34 (1) (b) does not impose an absolute obligation upon the National Coal Board. The section specifically mentions the mine manager and says nothing about the owner. The owner's civil liability by the 1954 Act is created in terms of section 159 but, of course, he is also vicariously liable at common law, qua employer, for the wrongful actings of his employees. The defence of " impracticability," available under section 157, may be invoked on behalf of an owner, whenever that defence is relevant.[18] A rope forming part of a haulage system has been held not to be an " obstruction " within the meaning of section 34 (1) (b).[19] It is always open to a pursuer to aver that accidents similar to his own had occurred on the particular road, because such an averment is relevant to show the condition in which the defenders kept

[13] See *M'Mullan* v. *Lochgelly Iron and Coal Co. Ltd.*, *cit. supra*, *per* Lords Thankerton and Macmillan.
[14] But see subsequent footnote on *Kerr* v. *National Coal Board*, 1968 S.L.T. 49.
[15] See *Rafferty* v. *National Coal Board* (O.H.) 1961 S.L.T.(Notes) 41 (metal plate under a loader constituting an obstruction).
[16] *Wilson* v. *National Coal Board* (O.H.) 1966 S.L.T. 221.
[17] *Kerr* v. *National Coal Board*, 1968 S.L.T. 49.
[18] See *Jack* v. *National Coal Board*, 1964 S.L.T.(Sh.Ct.) 62.
[19] *King* v. *National Coal Board*, (O.H.) 1968 S.L.T.(Notes) 6.

the road.[20] Height and width of travelling roads is specified by section 35, whilst the following section prohibits the use of vehicles and conveyors in roads not affording free movement and is, in fact, an addition to the 1911 Act pattern.   New and very extensive transport rules are contained in section 37 and these rules apply to all mines.   It is the mine manager's duty to ensure that such transport rules are carried out and—where duties are imposed by the rules on other persons—that these latter rules are properly enforced.[21] Section 39 sets forth the provisions for securing the safety of foot-passengers in transport roads [21a]—and constitutes a considerable widening of the 1911 Act provisions.   Certain exemptions from subsections (1) (a) and (1) (b) of section 39 are permitted by the Coal and other Mines (Shafts, Outlets and Roads) Regulations 1956 [22]; the Miscellaneous Mines (General) Regulations 1956 [23] and the Coal and other Mines (Transport Roads) Regulations 1956.[24] Section 40 deals with the provision of refuge holes and section 41 with safety measures relating to the use of vehicles.   The latter section was considered in *Brandreth* v. *John G. Stein & Co. Ltd.*[25] wherein it was held that it must be read as a whole and that the duty imposed was not absolute.

The safety provisions for the operation of winding and rope haulage apparatus and conveyors are contained in sections 42 to 47 inclusive. Section 42 requires the appointment of competent male persons (21 years of age and over) to operate mechanical or gravity-operated winding apparatus or rope haulage apparatus which is being used for the carrying of persons.   It is the manager's duty to make these appointments.   So long as anyone is below ground a competent operator (appointed under section 42 (1)) must be in attendance.[26] When persons are not carried by the apparatus, section 43 is applicable and here the age limit drops, in the case of rope haulage apparatus, to eighteen years minimum.[27] Supervision of conveyors along a working face in a mine is governed by section 44.[28] Signalling—that is to say, the effective means of transmitting audible and visible signals from entrances to shafts and outlets (at distances in excess of 50 feet)—must be provided and maintained in shafts and outlets,

---

20 *Fairgrieve* v. *National Coal Board* (O.H.) 1951 S.L.T.(Notes) 39.   If a pursuer's averments of a breach of s. 34 (1) (b) are of doubtful relevancy then a proof before answer should be allowed—*Walters* v. *National Coal Board*, 1961 S.L.T.(Notes) 82.   If an action is based on s. 34 (1) (a) instead of s. 34 (1) (b) it will fail—see *Lister* v. *National Coal Board* [1969] 3 W.L.R. 439 (C.A.).

21 See *Harrison* v. *National Coal Board* [1951] A.C. 639 (H.L.); (1951) 1 All E.R. 1102 (H.L.).

21a See *Pullar* v. *National Coal Board*, (O.H.) 1969 S.L.T. (Notes) 62.

22 S.I. 1956 No. 1762 (see reg. 45).

23 S.I. 1956 No. 1778 (see reg. 23).

24 S.I. 1956 No. 1941 (initially to operate for 5 years from January 1, 1957 (date of commencement of the 1954 Act)).

25 (O.H.) 1966 S.L.T.(Notes) 87.

26 s. 42 (2).

27 s. 43 (2).

28 See *McAully* v. *National Coal Board*, 1967 S.L.T.(Sh.Ct.) 54, in which the sheriff held that the " operation " referred to in the section was a continuing process and accordingly the constant attendance of a competent male person (18 years and over) was implied.

in terms of section 45, as extended by special regulations.[29] The obligation imposed by this section (which replaces section 41 of the 1911 Act) is a continuing one.[30] Signalling in roads is regulated by section 46, whilst the application of all five sections, numbers 42 to 46, may be excluded or modified at any time by special regulations.[31]

The " support " provisions in the statute are to be found mainly in sections 48, 49, 51, 52 and 54. Section 50 gives power to make support regulations for types of mine other than those covered by the Act, whilst section 53 explains the duties of deputies in regard to support.

Section 48 places upon the mine manager a duty to take—with respect to every road and working place in the mine—such steps by way of controlling movement of strata in the mine and supporting the roof and sides of the road or working place as may be necessary for keeping the road or working place secure. An important proviso is added—the section does not apply to a road or part road which is provided with an enclosure or barrier, in terms of section 33. Section 48 (2) makes it the manager's duty to take such steps as may be necessary for securing that he is at all material times in possession of all information relevant for determining the nature and extent of any steps which it is requisite for him to take to discharge efficiently the duty imposed upon him by section 48 (1). This section extends the earlier provisions of section 49 of the 1911 Act. Because of technological advances in mining and mining engineering the study of strata movements is considerably improved and this section highlights the importance of managers being in possession of the fullest scientific and technical information and being ready to take steps to control strata movements and support the roof and sides of roads and working places. The duty appears prima facie to be an absolute duty, but perhaps this depends upon a careful construction and interpretation of the word " secure " in section 48 (1). This has been interpreted as meaning " security from all the known geological hazards inherent in mining operations." [32] However in Sinclair v. National Coal Board [33] it seems that the duty under section 48 (1) is not an absolute duty, but that it places upon the manager the obligation of exercising care and skill of the highest degree. In the earlier case of Elliot v. National Coal Board [34] it

---

[29] See, for example, the Coal and Other Mines (Shafts, Outlets and Roads) Regulations 1956 (S.I. 1956 No. 1762), Parts V, VI and X; and the Metalliferous Mines (General) Regulations 1956 (S.I. 1956 No. 1778), Part V.

[30] Close v. National Coal Board (O.H.) 1951 S.C. 578; 1952 S.L.T. 33.

[31] Within the powers conferred by s. 47; and utilising s. 141.

[32] Marshall v. Gotham Co. Ltd. [1954] A.C. 360; [1954] 1 All E.R. 937, per Lord Tucker at pp. 374–375 and p. 943 respectively; a dictum which was applied in Jackson v. The National Coal Board [1955] 1 All E.R. 145.

[33] 1963 S.L.T. 296 (in which the opinions in Brown v. National Coal Board [1962] A.C. 574 were considered). This was a case in which the sole averment of fault by pursuer was that he was injured at the working place by a fall of stone from the roof. A proof before answer was allowed.

[34] (O.H.) 1957 S.L.T. 193; 1956 S.C. 484 (based upon the Coal Mines Act 1911, s. 49). Compare and contrast the cases of: Mullen v. National Coal Board, 1957 S.L.T. 313; 1957 S.C. 202 (which followed Walsh v. N.C.B. [1956] 1 Q.B. 511), where the deceased miner had been engaged on repair work and was appointed for such purposes and

was held, after proof, that the face of the working place was excluded from the scope of section 49 of the 1911 Act but the defenders were liable for the failure of the shift deputy to require support for the opencast by a rance (he was responsible for examination of the working place).

The important case of *Grant* v. *National Coal Board* [35] illustrates that section 48 is designed to protect employees from consequences wider than a fall of roof or sides directly upon them. Here a miner was injured when a bogie ran into some stone which had fallen from the roof. The Inner House of the Court of Session had held the action (*i.e.*, based upon the 1911 Act, s. 49) to be irrelevant but the House of Lords, upholding the appeal, held that there was no ground for limiting the protection afforded by the section—here the cause of the accident was the employers' failure to make the roof of the travelling road secure. It has also been held [36] that the " roof " of a working place is not necessarily co-extensive with the pavement for the purposes of the section. Moreover, the manager may be in breach of his duty under section 48 (1)—and so render his employers liable in a civil action—although it was not foreseeable as more than a possibility that a fall of blaes would injure an employee.[37] An interesting situation arose in the comparatively recent case of *O'Hanlon* v. *John G. Stein & Co.*[38] where a repairer in a clay mine was injured by an accidental fall of clay from the side of a road, after shot-firing. The manager knew that shot-firing was going to take place and that a state of insecurity might exist, but he took no steps to support the sides of the road. Defenders argued that it was contrary to good mining practice to erect supports for the whole area and that, in the manager's opinion, it was better to take down anything loose than prop it up. The House of Lords (affirming the First Division) held that there had been a breach of section 48 (1). However, it has been held quite recently in an Outer House case that section 48 (1) does not apply to a situation where a miner was injured by a fall of coal while the coal was being deliberately brought down by the miner.[39]

It is necessary to read along with section 48 (and at the time, its predecessor, section 49 of the 1911 Act) the Coal Mines (Support of Roof and Sides) General Regulations 1947 [40] and any relevant cases.[41]

accordingly the exception to s. 49 applied and defenders were not liable; and *Burns* v. *The National Coal Board*, 1958 S.L.T. 34; 1957 S.C. 239, a case again involving repair work, in which defenders were assoilzied. Lord Justice-Clerk Thomson took the view that the work was not repair work (and in this he disagreed with his three colleagues on the Second Division bench) but defenders had discharged the onus of showing that it had not been reasonably practicable to avoid or prevent the breach of s. 49.

[35] 1956 S.L.T. 155; 1956 S.C.(H.L.) 48; [1956] A.C. 649; [1956] 2 W.L.R. 752; [1956] 1 All E.R. 682 (which, in fact, was based on s. 49 of the 1911 Act).

[36] *Dick* v. *National Coal Board* (O.H.) 1960 S.L.T.(Notes) 70.

[37] *Field* v. *National Coal Board* (O.H.) 1963 S.L.T.(Notes) 54.

[38] (H.L.) 1965 S.L.T. 125.

[39] *Anderson* v. *National Coal Board* (O.H.) 1968 S.L.T.(Notes) 69.

[40] S.R. & O. 1947 No. 973.

[41] See, for example, *Paterson* v. *National Coal Board* (O.H.) 1953 S.L.T.(Notes) 57, brought under reg. 9 (2), which applied where a miner was injured by a piece of metal which flew off a prop supporting a roof; and *Mazs* v. *National Coal Board*, 1958 S.C. 6; 1958 S.L.T. 43, where it was held that the latter part of reg. 2 (1) did not impose a continuing obligation.

Section 49 covers " systematic support "[42] in coal, shale and fireclay mines; section 50 deals with power to require systematic support in other mines; and section 51 with the supply of materials for support. The duty under section 51, to see that a sufficient supply of support materials is constantly and readily available, is an absolute one[43] and it is placed upon the manager of the mine. The duties relating to withdrawal to a place of safety and reporting forthwith to an official of the mine are also absolute and any breach of either duty by a workman renders him liable to a criminal prosecution.[44]

Sections 52, 53 and 54 deal respectively with withdrawal of support, duties of deputies in relation to support and provisions as to support rules.

Ventilation is governed by sections 55 to 60 inclusive. All six of these sections are important. Section 55 is a very substantial extension of the old section 29 provisions of the 1911 Act and it imposes upon the manager a general duty of taking such steps as are necessary for securing constant and adequate ventilation below ground for the purposes of: (a) diluting gases that are inflammable or noxious, so as to render them harmless and remove them; and (b) providing air which contains a sufficiency of oxygen. Section 55 (2) goes on to stipulate what is meant by " adequate " ventilation in certain cases. There is no statutory duty to ventilate (i) in any part of a mine which is stopped off, (ii) in any waste,[45] or (iii) in any other prescribed part of a mine. Subsection (5) of section 55 deals with a situation where ventilation is interrupted or ceases to be adequate for the purposes specified in section 55 (1). It does not seem to cover the situation of stopping ventilation machinery for maintenance purposes.[46] In the event of such maintenance being required an immediate replacement of the existing machinery by alternative machinery—without any diminution of the ventilation level—would seem to be necessary. Section 56 governs the avoidance of danger from gas in waste, whilst section 57 gives an inspector power to require an improvement in ventilation, in the interests of the safety or health of the employees. Section 58 gives the provisions as to the means of ventilation. Section 59 deals with the leakage of air between airways and section 60 with the provision of barometers and other measuring instruments.

Lighting, lamps and contraband are covered by sections 61 to 67 inclusive. Suitable and sufficient lighting must be provided both above ground and below ground (whether that lighting is natural or artificial) and it is the manager's duty to see to this. All apparatus installed for the

---

[42] Defined in subs. (5) as meaning " provision and maintenance of support in accordance with a system specified in rules to be made by the manager of the mine, being a system consistent with the proper control of movement of the strata in the mine."
[43] *Hamilton* v. *Niblock* [1956] N.I. 109.
[44] Under s. 152 (3) and perhaps s. 90 (1), subject always to the s. 157 defence. Persons in charge are liable under s. 152 (1)—with the defences available under ss. 156 and 157.
[45] See *Kirby* v. *National Coal Board*, 1959 S.L.T. 7 (based on s. 29 (1) of the 1911 Act) (affirming Lord Guthrie in the Outer House).
[46] *McCarthy* v. *Lewis* [1957] 1 All E.R. 556.

production of artificial lighting must be properly maintained.[47] Permitted
lights are dealt with in some detail by section 62 (read along with the Coal
Mines (Lighting and Contraband) General Regulations). Sections 63, 64
and 65 relate to safety-lamps and the making of regulations *re* safety-lamps
and lighting apparatus. Offences are specified by section 65—and the
criminal liability hereunder is a personal one. The National Coal Board
or other mine-owner is not vicariously liable in respect of that contravention, in accordance with the wording of section 152 (1).

Section 66 is the section which prevents the taking below ground or
the possession below ground of smoking materials (cigar, cigarette, pipe
or other contrivance or any match or mechanical lighter) in a safety-lamp
mine or in a safety-lamp part of a mine. The possession or carrying
below of " contraband " is an offence.[48] The section imposes a duty
upon the manager of a safety-lamp mine or a mine containing a safety-
lamp part to make arrangements—and ensure that they are efficiently
carried out—for searching (i) all persons employed below ground in that
mine or the safety-lamp part thereof; and (ii) such persons mentioned in
clause (i) hereof as may be selected in accordance with a system approved
by an inspector. Also, the manager must arrange for the searching of
any articles which they have with them. Possession of " contraband "
by a person who is about to go below ground is an offence and that
" contraband " itself may be confiscated.[49] The searcher himself must
have given to the two other persons the opportunity of searching him—
and, if so searched, must be found to be free of any " contraband." [50]
The purposes of this subsection is twofold—(a) to prevent the intentional
and malicious " planting " of contraband by X upon Y and (b) to avoid
the allegation by Y that contraband was planted upon him by X.

If any person refuses to be searched, or refuses to allow any article
which he has with him to be searched, he is guilty of an offence.[51] If the
refusal in question occurs before he goes below ground then he is not to
be allowed to go below ground; but if it occurs when he is in the mine he
is not to be allowed to remain on that occasion.

It is the manager's responsibility [52] to see that notices, warning persons
of their liability to prosecution for contravention of the " contraband "
regulations, are conspicuously displayed at or near the points of search.

Section 67 is an ancillary provision dealing with the prohibition of
articles producing flames or sparks (*i.e.*, unprotected flames or sparks) in
safety-lamp mines. However, certain exceptions are allowed—(i) if an
article is permitted by the Act or by regulation thereunder, (ii) if an article
is taken and used in a specified class of mine (or part thereof) and is

[47] *Ibid.* s. 61.
[48] s. 66 (1).
[49] s. 66 (3) and (4).
[50] s. 66 (5).
[51] s. 66 (6).
[52] s. 66 (7).

permitted by order of the Minister and (iii) if an article is authorised by an inspector.

Fire precautions and dust precautions occupy sections 70 to 74 inclusive, whilst section 75 (1) introduces a new statutory requirement by imposing upon every mine-owner and mine manager the duty (a) of taking such steps as necessary to secure that he is in possession of all information indicating or tending to indicate the presence or absence—in the vicinity of any workings carried on or proposed—of (i) disused workings; (ii) rock or stratum likely to contain water; (iii) peat, moss, sand, gravel, etc., likely to flow when wet; and (b) of taking necessary steps to substantiate such information (whether in discharge of his statutory duty or not). Section 75 (2) imposes a duty upon the owner and the manager of (a) furnishing particulars to the other of such information under section 75 (1) (*a*) as comes into his possession and (b) notifying the other of steps taken in discharge of the statutory duty under section 75 (1) (*b*) and of any conclusions reached thereafter. The purpose of section 75 (read along with sections 76 to 80 all of which are important) was to prevent a recurrence of the Knockshinnoch Castle Colliery disaster (on September 7, 1950) when thirteen lives were lost because of an inrush of moss into the workings. The total death roll might have been 116, but 103 persons miraculously survived after being trapped below ground for two days. Where inflammable gas is present in an excessive concentration or where a danger is constituted by inflammable gas (whether or not in excessive concentration) or otherwise, then workmen in the particular section of the mine affected (the " affected area ") must be withdrawn immediately and shall not be allowed to re-enter until the area is free from all danger.[53] The interpretation of section 77 has given rise to some difficulty, as has the onus of proof with special reference to that section. In these circumstances it has been held,[54] that a proof before answer rather than a jury trial was the most satisfactory method of dealing with the case.

Machinery and apparatus is governed by sections 81 to 85 inclusive. The wording used is generally reminiscent of factory legislation draftsmanship as it speaks of machinery being " of good construction, suitable material, adequate strength and free from patent defect and shall be properly maintained." [55] The only recognisable difference in drafting seems to be that the factory legislation speaks of " sound material " whilst the 1954 Act speaks of " suitable material." Perhaps the draftsman regarded the two adjectives as synonymous in the legal sense in which he employed them, although upon a strict literal interpretation this would not be so. So far, there is no authority which points to any real difference between the obligation of the factory occupier and that of the mine owner. It will be recalled from *Reilly* v. *Beardmore & Co.*[56] that the Court of

[53] See s. 79.
[54] *McNeil* v. *National Coal Board* (O.H.) 1965 S.L.T.(Notes) 52.
[55] s. 81 (1).
[56] 1947 S.C. 275; 1947 S.L.T. 147; 1947 S.N. 46 (before the First Division); based on s. 23 (1) (*a*) of the Factories Act 1937.

Session held that there was a continuing obligation upon an occupier to consider whether a chain, rope or lifting tackle had reached or passed its safe working life. They rejected the argument that the initial supply of a chain or rope, etc., of good construction, sound material, adequate strength, etc., was sufficient compliance with the subsection and they also rejected the argument that the breaking of a rope was *per se* proof of non-compliance with the statutory provision. Section 81 (1) which is in the following terms:

" 81.—(1) All parts and working gear, whether fixed or movable, including the anchoring and fixing appliances, of all machinery and apparatus used as, or forming, part of the equipment of a mine, and all foundations in or to which any such appliances are anchored or fixed shall be of good construction, suitable material, adequate strength and free from patent defect, and shall be properly maintained."

has been considered in some detail, over the past ten years, in four cases at least in which the standard of efficiency and the duty imposed have been examined by the Court of Session. These four cases are as follows— *Hamilton* v. *National Coal Board* [57]; *McDonald* v. *National Coal Board* [58]; *Chalmers* v. *National Coal Board* [59]; and *Sonka* v. *National Coal Board*.[60] *Hamilton* is, for obvious reasons, the most important case. Here the House of Lords, reversing the Second Division of the Court of Session and allowing the pursuer's appeal (and thereby agreeing with the *dissenting* opinion of the Lord Justice-Clerk) held that section 81 (1) imposed an absolute obligation. In the course of his speech Viscount Simonds said " the employer warrants that the machine or other equipment which he is obliged to maintain will never be out of order." He relied upon Lord Russell of Killowen's interpretation of " maintain " contained in *Smith* v. *Cammell Laird & Co. Ltd.*[61] and also the decision of the House in *Millar* v. *Galashiels Gas Co.*[62] Lord Keith of Avonholm saw the last five words of the subsection as " imposing an absolute obligation to keep the equipment in question at all times in a sound state of repair and fit for use." In *McDonald's* case Lord Kilbrandon, in the Outer House, followed *Hamilton's* case and approved issues for jury trial where the pursuer based his case upon section 81 (1), alleging that a broken waterpipe which resulted in a wet surface and thereby caused him to slip and suffer injury was a breach of the subsection, the defenders having failed to maintain the apparatus properly. Lord Strachan, in the case of *Chalmers*, again followed *Hamilton's* case and held the Board liable for a failure in the absolute obligation of keeping the equipment at all times in a sound state

---

[57] 1960 S.C.(H.L.) 1; 1960 S.L.T. 24 (H.L.); (formerly reported 1959 S.L.T. 255 *re* the hearing before the Second Division of the Court of Session).
[58] (O.H.) 1961 S.L.T.(Notes) 5.
[59] (O.H.) 1963 S.L.T. 358.
[60] 1965 S.L.T.(Notes) 64.
[61] [1940] A.C. 242.
[62] 1949 S.C.(H.L.) 31; 1949 S.L.T. 223; [1949] A.C. 275.

of repair and fit for use.[63] Lord Avonside did likewise in *Sonka's* case, where an engine switch attendant was injured when the engine was torn from its moorings because of the strain on a haulage rope. Furthermore, his lordship took the view that where the pursuer averred that certain fixed appliances were not of good construction as required by section 81 (1) he did not require to make further specification, as the duty imposed was absolute. The fencing of dangerous machinery is specifically governed by section 82. The obligation is absolute, except when the machine is exposed for examination or adjustment.[64] There is imposed upon the mine manager the specific duty of ensuring that the fencing which is provided is properly maintained and is kept in position (subject to the exceptions mentioned). Those cases, relating to the fencing of machinery, which have been cited in the previous section on factory legislation are all equally relevant to this part of the 1954 Act.[65]

Section 89, dealing with penalisation of any failure to observe safety directions says—

" A person employed at a mine who contravenes—

(*a*) any transport or support rules having effect with respect to the mine; or

(*b*) any directions given to him by or on behalf of the owner or manager of the mine or any rule made by the manager of the mine for regulating the conduct either of all persons employed thereat or any class of persons so employed to which that person belongs, being directions given, or a rule made, for the purpose of securing compliance with this Act, orders made thereunder or regulations or any transport or support rules having effect with respect to the mine or of securing the safety or health of that person or any other person employed at the mine;

shall be guilty of an offence."

Regulation 2 (1) of the Coal and Other Mines (General Duties and Conduct) Regulations [66] requires persons employed at mines of coal, stratified ironstone, shale and fireclay to obey instructions given by

---

[63] Phraseology which is identical with that used by Lord Keith of Avonholm in *Hamilton's* case, *supra*.

[64] S. 82 (2), giving effect to the case of *Sharp* v. *Coltness Iron Co. Ltd.*, 1937 S.C.(H.L.) 68; 1937 S.L.T. 589; 1937 S.N. 95; [1937] 3 All E.R. 593; and [1938] A.C. 90.

[65] See, particularly, *Nicholls* v. *Austin (Leyton) Ltd.* [1946] A.C. 493; [1946] 2 All E.R. 92; *Carroll* v *Andrew Barclay & Sons Ltd.*, 1947 S.C. 411; 1947 S.L.T. 223; 1947 S.N. 75; [1948] 2 All E.R. 386; *John Summers and Sons Ltd.* v. *Frost* [1955] A.C. 740; [1955] 1 All E.R. 870; [1955] 2 W.L.R. 825, and *Boryk* v. *National Coal Board*, 1959 S.C. 1. It would appear that the test as to whether a machine part is " dangerous " or not is a test of " reasonable foreseeability "—see Lord Reid's speech in *John Summers & Sons Ltd.*, *supra*; and *Mitchell* v. *North British Rubber Co.*, 1945 S.C.(J.) 69, 73. There is of course, a distinction between fencing the access to a machine and fencing the dangerous parts of a machine itself—and the former is not enough, *vide Sharp* v. *Coltness Iron Co. Ltd.*, 1937 S.C.(H.L.) 68; 1937 S.L.T. 589; 1937 3 All E.R. 593; [1938] A.C. 90. As for the test of '' secure fencing '' see *Burns* v. *Joseph Terry & Sons Ltd.* [1950] 2 All E.R. 987 (C.A.); [1951] 1 K.B. 454; approved by the House of Lords in *John Summers and Sons Ltd.* v. *Frost*, *supra*.

[66] S.I. 1956 No. 1761.

persons upon whom duties are laid by any regulation. Section 89 is widely drawn and no vicarious criminal liability attaches under it to the management of the mine. An interesting decision in a case where a workman refused to obey a direction given to him by a person in charge was that of *McNicol* v. *Burns*,[67] where it was held, in the circumstances, that a " direction " had been given in terms of regulation 23. As he (the workman) had disobeyed that direction he had been rightly convicted. Section 90 deals specifically with the penalisation of negligent acts or omissions and the unauthorised removal of articles.[68]

Parts IV (ss. 98–107) and V (ss. 108–115) [69] deal respectively with the management and control of quarries and with safety, health and welfare in quarries. Part VI (ss. 116–122) covers the notification and investigation of accidents and diseases, whilst Part VII (s. 123) deals with the inspections of mines and quarries on behalf of the workers therein employed.

Employment of women and young persons is governed by Part VIII (ss. 124–132) [70] and, in the case of the employment of young persons in Scotland, the various Children and Young Persons (Scotland) Acts and the Education (Scotland) Acts must be read along with this part of the Act. There is an absolute prohibition against the employment of female labour below ground at a mine.[71] Records and returns, etc., appear in Part IX (ss. 133–140); regulations and the relevant procedures thereanent, in Part X (ss. 141–143); and offences and penalties in Part XIV (ss. 152–167), whilst Part XV is a miscellaneous and general part (comprising ss. 168–195). There are five Schedules attached.

H.M. Inspectorate of Mines is specifically governed by Part XI, which states *inter alia* the methods of appointment of inspectors and their duties [72] together with their general powers.[73]

Part XIII (s. 151) is extremely important and imposes upon the owner of every abandoned mine—or every mine which has not been worked for a period of twelve months—the duty of securing that the surface entrance to every shaft or outlet is provided with an efficient enclosure, barrier, plug or other device in order to prevent any person from accidentally falling down the shaft or accidentally entering the outlet.[74] He must also see that each device which is provided is properly maintained.[74] These provisions do not apply to mines—other than coal mines and mines of

---

[67] 1956 S.L.T. 289, brought under the 1911 Act, ss. 86, 90 and 101 (3) and reg. 23 of the Coal Mines (General) Regulations 1913 (S.R. & O. 1913 No. 748).

[68] See *Alford* v. *National Coal Board*, 1952 S.L.T. 204; [1952] 1 All E.R. 754 (H.L.); [1952] 1 T.L.R. 687 (reversing a decision of the First Division in part) held that a breach of the relevant regulation makes the offender liable to criminal prosecution that the offender and his employers become liable in a civil action in damages and the defence of *volenti non fit injuria* is not available to defenders (Lord Reid *dubitans*).

[69] A case based upon a breach of s. 108 has recently been held suitable for jury trial— *vide O'Donnell* v. *Craigmuschat Quarry Ltd.*, 1968 S.L.T.(Notes) 40.

[70] S. 126, specifying the periods of employment of females and young male persons under 16, is very important. For young male persons over 16—see s. 127.

[71] s. 124.

[72] s. 144.

[73] s. 145.

[74] s. 151 (1).

stratified ironstone, shale or fireclay—which have not been worked prior to August 9, 1872. Section 151 (2) then goes on to specify certain " statutory nuisances " (shafts or outlets of mines not provided with properly maintained devices, as mentioned in section 151 (1) and quarries —whether used or not—not provided with proper barriers and which constitute dangers to the public), which, in their application to Scotland,[75] require a reference to Part II of the Public Health (Scotland) Act 1897 and particularly to section 16 paragraph (1) thereof.

As mentioned above, Part XIV (ss. 152–167) relates to offences, penalties and proceedings for any contravention of the Act or of any regulation made thereunder or of any requirement indicated by notice from an inspector or of any special condition stipulated by the Minister or by an inspector. Liability generally attaches to the following persons —(1) the owner, (2) any person to whom the statutory duties were delegated under section 1 (if the matter lies within the scope of his duties), (3) the manager (in the case of a quarry, every manager within whose jurisdiction the matter falls), (4) the acting manager (in a quarry, every acting manager within whose jurisdiction the matter falls) and (5) every under-manager and acting under-manager (in mines only). If the area of liability is widened by any regulation or order made under the Act, then those additional persons or classes of persons will be liable, in addition to those officials (including the owner) above mentioned.

Certain general defences to criminal proceedings are available to the owner, his delegate and to the manager or acting manager (mine or quarry) but excepting always the case where the statute imposes an absolute duty and an express liability for failure therein—namely (a) if he can prove that it was impracticable to avoid or prevent the contravention [76]; and (b) where a duty or prohibition is expressly imposed upon another person or upon a class to which that person belongs or upon all persons and the provision is contravened, if he (the owner, etc.) can prove that he used all diligence to secure compliance with the particular provision.[77] Moreover, the manager and acting manager of a mine or quarry are not liable for any contravention of a statutory provision which imposes a duty expressly upon the owner nor are they liable for any contravention of sections 3 and 101 of the Act.[78] The under-manager or acting under-manager of a mine has available to him the same general defences as are mentioned above, but, in addition, he may plead in his own defence that he used his " best endeavours " [79] or that his jurisdiction was limited.[80]

Where an action for civil damages is brought and this is based upon alleged breaches of statutory duties and obligations, it is open to the defender to plead, in his own defence, that it was impracticable to avoid or

[75] See s. 151 (5) of the 1954 Act.
[76] s. 157.
[77] s. 156.
[78] s. 152 (4).
[79] Vide s. 6 (4).
[80] s. 158.

prevent the contravention—unless the duty imposed is absolute and con-travention results in immediate responsibility or answerability for an offence. The owner himself cannot evade his own vicarious liability by trying to shelter behind his employee (*i.e.*, by pointing to a duty imposed upon the employee) or by trying to argue that the employee was appointed by someone other than him [81] (*i.e.*, the owner).

The monetary penalties are specified in section 155 (1). If, however, the contravention in question was (a) likely to cause the death of, or serious bodily injury to, an employee at the particular mine or quarry or a dangerous accident, or (b) likely to endanger the safety of any person, the court may impose upon the convicted person—in addition to or in substi-tution for a fine—imprisonment for a term not exceeding three months.[82]

Criminal proceedings may be taken summarily or on indictment, unless a specific provision is made as to the method of prosecution.[83] Where a prosecution is contemplated in respect of a breach of regulations made under sections 17 (1) and 20 (1) of the Act, proceedings must be brought within three months from the date when sufficient evidence exists, in Scotland, to justify a report to the Lord Advocate with a view to prosecution being considered.[84]

The 1954 Act is undoubtedly an improvement upon earlier legislation from the viewpoint of the identification of and placing of duties, responsi-bilities and liabilities. Yet, the accident rate in mines and quarries still gives cause for much public concern.[85] Although much re-organisation of the coal industry has taken place since its nationalisation, it is essential that the health, welfare and safety requirements should be kept under constant review. Balanced against the need for continual review is the undeniable fact that the mining industry has always had, and seemingly will always have, a very high degree of risk attached to it.

The most recent statute concerning mines and quarries is the Mines and Quarries (Tips) Act 1969.[86] This enactment is the legislative result of the Aberfan disaster which almost wiped out a whole generation of schoolchildren in the Welsh village of Aberfan and shocked the whole British nation into a swift realisation of the latent dangers from coal-tips.

Part I of the Act is designed to provide for the security of tips associated with mines and quarries and is consolidated with the Mines and Quarries Act 1954.[87] This Part is to be brought into effect upon a day to be appointed by statutory instrument by the Minister of Power.[87a] Section 2 defines " tip " and distinguishes between " active tips " and " closed

---

[81] *Vide* s. 159.
[82] s. 155 (2).
[83] s. 163 (1).
[84] s. 163 (4) and (6).
[85] See the Annual Reports of H.M. Chief Inspectors of Mines, published by H.M.S.O.
[86] 1969, c. 10.
[87] The combined legislation to be known as the " Mines and Quarries Acts 1954 and 1969."
[87a] See now the Mines and Quarries (Tips) Act, 1969 (Commencement No. 1) Order 1969 (No. 804 (c. 17)), which brings Part I into operation on 30th June, 1969.

tips," but applies the legislation to both types. The owner's duties and manager's duties are contained in sections 3 and 4 and penalties in section 9. The Minister of Power is given powers to make regulations by sections 1 (security of tips), 5 (tipping rules), 6 (plans and sections of tips and under-strata), 7 (plans of abandoned mines) and 8 (keeping of geological maps of areas in which tips are situated).

Part II of the Act is designed to prevent public danger from the instability of tips not governed by Part I. So far as Scotland is concerned, this Part is to come into force on a day to be appointed by statutory instrument by the Secretary of State for Scotland.[87b] Wide powers are given to local authorities to ensure that disused tips do not constitute a danger and these powers include powers of inspection [88] and the service of notices requiring remedial operations [89] or the carrying out of remedial operations by the local authority itself.[90] The court is given powers, by section 19, to make contribution orders for the expenses of remedial operations. H.M. Treasury may—through the appropriate Minister—make grants, under section 25 of the Act, for operations, exploratory tests and works of reinstatement carried out by local authorities. Miscellaneous provisions and meanings of terms—in relation to local authorities in Scotland and to Scotland generally—may be found in sections 34 and 35. The Act received the Royal Assent on March 27, 1969.

The test of this recent legislation will be the same as that which applies already to factories, mines, offices, etc., namely—how effective is the machinery for enforcement of the statutory provisions ? If that test receives an ineffectual or meaningless answer, then the legislation itself is worthless or, on another view, is mere legislative hypocrisy.

(3) Offices, Shops and Railway Premises

Legislation affecting shops has, in the past, been spread over the Public Health Acts and the various Public Health (Scotland) Acts as well as other statutes formerly named Shops Acts and ultimately consolidated by the Shops Act 1950.[90a] However, following upon the Gowers Committee Report,[90b] regarding which the then Labour Government and subsequent Labour and Conservative Governments displayed little interest, Mr. Richard Marsh, M.P., presented a Private Member's Bill in 1960 upon offices, which became the Offices Act 1960. That Act never became an operative statute and it was replaced by the Offices, Shops and Railway Premises Act 1963,[90c] which adopts many of the Gowers Committee's

---

[87b] See now the Mines and Quarries (Tips) Act, 1969 (Commencement No. 3) Order 1969 (No. 870 (c. 21)), which brings Part II into operation, as regards Scotland, on 30th June. 1969.

[88] *Ibid.* ss. 13 and 18.

[89] *Ibid.* s. 14. See now the Disused Mine and Quarry Tips (Prescribed Forms) (Scotland) Regulations 1969 (No. 1127), operative on 26th August, 1969.

[90] *Ibid.* s. 17.

[90a] 14 Geo. 6, c. 28.

[90b] 1949 Cmd. 7664.

[90c] 1963, c. 41.

recommendations. It is a form of protective legislation—following closely the pattern of and the legal phraseology of the Factories Act 1961 [90d]—which now extends into the non-industrial or commercial field. The " white-collar " employee now receives a measure of statutory protection which is broadly comparable with that accorded to his " blue-collar " colleague. The 1963 Act can give rise to criminal prosecutions and consequential penalties as well as to actions in civil damages.

Section 91 (2) provides that the Act shall come into operation upon such day or days as the Minister [90e] may by order appoint. In fact, two such orders have been issued,[91] the first of these containing in itself two extensive Schedules giving operative effect to numerous sections of the Act. The Act applies, with certain important modifications, to Scotland but not to Northern Ireland. It is binding upon the Crown in terms of section 83, but it will be noted that the extent to which it is so binding is limited.

The first three sections explain the " scope of the Act." The general provisions relating to the health, safety and welfare of employees are contained in sections 4–27 inclusive, whilst " fire precautions " receive extensive coverage in sections 28–41. Notification of accidents is governed by section 48 and the " enforcement " provisions appear in sections 52–62 inclusive. Offences, penalties and legal proceedings are dealt with in sections 63–73 inclusive, whilst certain general provisions are covered by sections 79–86. The interpretation section is section 90 and commencement, etc., may be found in section 91. Two Schedules are attached to the Act. It is necessary to look at the main groups of sections, with particular reference to Scotland and Scots law, but an exhaustive and clinical dissection of the statute, section by section, would be out of place herein.[92]

Section 1 (1) applies the 1963 Act to " office premises, shop premises and railway premises, being (in each case) premises in the case of which persons are employed to work therein." The three subsections immediately following then proceed to define, *inter alia*, the three types of premises mentioned, whilst section 1 (5) deals with the particular case of canteen premises and, broadly, for purposes of the Act, these are identified with the main class or type of premises in conjunction with which they are used. As the language used in this Act and the Factories Act 1961 is virtually the same there is a presumption that interpretations upon the latter will

---

[90d] 9 & 10 Eliz. 2, c. 34.
[90e] Then the Minister of Labour. The Ministry of Labour changed its name, in 1968, to the Department of Employment and Productivity.
[91] See the Offices, Shops and Railway Premises Act 1963 (Commencement No. 1) Order 1964 (S.I. 1964 No. 191); and the Offices, Shops and Railway Premises (Commencement No. 2) Order 1964 (S.I. 1964 No. 1045).
[92] Reference should be made to the *Encyclopedia of Factories, Shops and Offices* (Sweet & Maxwell) (1962, and annual supplementary services to date), Vol. 2; also to *The Offices, Shops and Railway Premises Act 1963* by Harry Samuels and N. Stewart-Pearson (Chas. Knight & Co. Ltd.) (1963); and a book of similar title by Ian Fife and E. Anthony Machin (Butterworths) (1963).

apply equally to the former [93] and also that the case law upon one statute shall be equally helpful to the court when considering the other.[94]

Section 2 excepts from the operation of the Act premises in which only the relatives (being husband, wife, parent, grandparent, son, daughter, grandchild, brother or sister) of the employer work and premises in which outworkers work. Section 3 excepts also from the scope of the Act those premises wherein not more than 21 man-hours per week are worked.

The general provisions governing the health, safety and welfare of employees are perhaps the most important provisions in the statute. These are grouped within sections 4 to 27 inclusive. Section 4 deals with cleanliness—imposing an obligation that all premises to which the Act applies and all furniture, furnishings and fittings therein shall be kept in a clean state. No dirt or refuse is to be allowed to accumulate [95] and floors and steps are to be kept clean. It is made quite clear from subsection (4) that the specification of floors and steps in subsection (2) is not intended to—and indeed shall not—limit or restrict the general obligation imposed by section 4 (1). The Minister may make regulations concerning cleanliness by virtue of section 4 (3). Some doubts have been raised from time to time as to whether a general health provision in a protective statute gives rise to an action in civil damages and whether this is also so in the case of a welfare provision. Most of the cases have turned on problems of construction of the various Factories Acts (the latest one being the consolidating statute of 1961) and the more popular view seems to be that breach of the health provision does give a right to bring such an action whilst breach of a welfare provision—which can be identified simply as a welfare provision—would not give such a right, unless that latter provision were wide enough to include certain elements of health and/or safety.[96]

Section 5 relates to overcrowding, and subsection (2) thereof gives the formula for calculating square footage area and cubic capacity. Effectively, this means that each employee is entitled to 40 square feet of floor area and to 400 cubic feet of space. Section 6 governs temperature, and subsection (1) says " effective provision shall be made for securing and maintaining a reasonable temperature in every room. . . . " Subsection (2) is more specific and states that where a substantial part of the work done in a room does not involve severe physical effort, then a reasonable temperature (after the first hour) would be not less than 16 degrees

[93] See *Hamilton* v. *National Coal Board*, 1960 S.C.(H.L.) 1; 1960 S.L.T. 24; [1960] A.C. 633; [1960] 2 W.L.R. 313; [1960] 1 All E.R. 76.
[94] See, for example, *M'Ewan* v. *Perth Corporation* (1905) 7 F. 714 (a partly open yard with a shed in one part and used for storing road-mending materials, held not to be a " warehouse "); and *Golder* v. *Thomas Johnston's (Bakers) Ltd.*, 1950 S.L.T.(Sh.Ct.) 50 (a case based on the Tenancy of Shops (Scotland) Act 1949, in which the phrase " carrying on," used in a statute, was held to involve a measure of permanency).
[95] s. 4 (2).
[96] See, for example, *Nicholson* v. *Atlas Steel Foundry and Engineering Co. Ltd.*, 1957 S.L.T. 186; 1957 S.C.(H.L.) 44; [1957] 1 All E.R. 776 (H.L.); [1957] 1 W.L.R. 613; *Carroll* v. *North British Locomotive Co. Ltd.*, 1957 S.L.T.(Sh.Ct.) 2; 73 Sh.Ct.Rep. 25; and *Reid* v. *Westfield Paper Co. Ltd.*, 1957 S.C. 218; 1957 S.L.T. 184.

Centigrade (60·8 degrees Fahrenheit). Subsection (3) contains certain exceptions and must be read along with subsection (6). Subsection (4) requires a thermometer to be provided on each floor so that the temperature in any room on that floor which comes within the operation of section 6 (1) may be readily determined. Subsection (5) gives the Minister power to make regulations prescribing a standard of reasonable temperature which may vary the standard prescribed in subsection (2), and conformity with these regulations shall be obligatory and a sufficient compliance with the section 6 (1) provisions.[97] It should be noted that the phrase " not reasonably practicable " appears in subsection (3) of section 6 in relation to the excepted premises. What has been said in the earlier section of this chapter in respect of factories applies equally here, as does the very difficult question of the burden of proof. Any failure by an employer to comply with subsection (3) makes him guilty of an offence and liable to a criminal prosecution.

" Effective and suitable provision " must be made, according to the wording of section 7, for securing and maintaining the ventilation of every room comprised in the premises to which the Act applies. A similar provision regarding lighting is contained in section 8, although, understandably, a provision is added herein requiring that all glazed windows and skylights used for lighting premises shall be kept clean (on both sides) and free from obstruction, so far as reasonably practicable. Whitewashing or shading to mitigate glare or heat is, however, permissible.[98] All apparatus used for producing artificial lighting must be properly maintained.[99]

Sanitary conveniences are required by section 9 to be provided at premises governed by the Act. Subsection (1) speaks of " suitable and sufficient sanitary conveniences " being " conveniently accessible to the persons employed to work in the premises." Such conveniences are to be kept clean, properly maintained and effectively lit and ventilated.[1] The Minister may make regulations under subsection (3) as to what is suitable and sufficient provision for the purposes of section 9 (1).[2]

Suitable and sufficient washing facilities must also be provided at places conveniently accessible for the employees.[3] Such places must be effectively lit and be kept clean and in orderly condition, and all apparatus used for washing or drying must also be kept clean and be properly

97 See, for example, the Offices, Shops and Railway Premises Act 1963 (Exemption No. 1) Order 1964 (S.I. 1964 No. 964) re, inter alia, the s. 6 provisions in relation to offices at building sites.
98 s. 8 (3).
99 s. 8 (4). Once again, there is no definition of " maintained " in the 1963 Act. It is accordingly necessary to refer to s. 176 (1) of the Factories Act for guidance. There the meaning is " maintained in an efficient state, in efficient working order and in good repair." The obligation imposed by the subsection would appear to be absolute— cf. Millar v. Galashiels Gas Co. Ltd., 1949 S.C.(H.L.) 31; 1949 S.L.T. 223; [1949] 1 All E.R. 319; (1949) 65 T.L.R. 76; [1949] A.C. 275.
1 s. 9 (2).
2 See now the Sanitary Conveniences Regulations 1964 (S.I. 1964 No. 966), which came into operation on January 1, 1966.
3 s. 10 (1); subs. (5) must be read along with subs. (1).

maintained.[4] The Minister has power [5] to make regulations [6] determining what is suitable and sufficient provision for the purposes of section 10 (1). It will be recalled from the case of *Reid* v. *The Westfield Paper Co. Ltd.*[7] that a civil action in damages was permitted at the instance of a pursuer who contracted dermatitis because of the defender's breach of certain health provisions in the Factories Acts (basically, at that time, the 1937 Act). It is submitted that a similar action could be relevantly brought upon a breach of section 10.

Section 11 provides for an adequate supply of wholesome drinking water at suitable places, conveniently accessible for employees. By subsection (2) it is laid down that where the water is not piped it must be contained in suitable vessels and be renewed at least daily. Moreover, all " practicable steps " must be taken to preserve the water and the vessels from contamination. This reference to " practicable steps " obviously imposes a higher duty of care than is intended in the more usual phrase " so far as is reasonably practicable."

Section 12 deals with accommodation for clothing. It is comparable with section 59 of the Factories Act 1961 and, accordingly, a civil action in damages may lie for a breach by the employer.[8]

Sitting facilities and eating facilities must be provided in accordance with the requirements contained in sections 13, 14 and 15. It should be noted that the " eating facilities " relate only to shop premises in which the employees eat their meals.[9] Breach of the section 13 (1) and (2) provisions makes the employer guilty of an offence and liable to a criminal prosecution.[10]

Section 16 applies to floors, passages, stairs, steps and gangways in premises falling within the application of the Act. The drafting language of the earlier Factories Acts is now more closely followed, for example— subsection (1) requires such floors, etc., to be of sound construction and properly maintained and, so far as is reasonably practicable, to be kept free from obstruction and from any substance likely to cause persons to slip. The provision of hand-rails for open-sided staircases and the secure

---

[4] s. 10 (2).

[5] s. 10 (3) and (4).

[6] See now the Washing Facilities Regulations 1964 (S.I. 1964 No. 965), which came into operation on January 1, 1966. It should also be noted that the Offices, Shops and Railway Premises Act 1963 (Exemption No. 1) Order 1964 (S.I. 1964 No. 964), *re* building site offices, and the Offices, Shops and Railway Premises Act 1963 (Exemption No. 2) Order 1964 (S.I. 1964 No. 1231), *re* railway signal boxes, contain certain exemptions from, *inter alia*, the s. 10 provisions.

[7] 1957 S.C. 218; 1957 S.L.T. 184.

[8] See *McCarthy* v. *Daily Mirror Newspapers Ltd.* [1949] 1 All E.R. 801 (C.A.); and *Barr* v. *Cruickshank & Co. Ltd.* (1958) 74 Sh.Ct.Rep. 218; 1959 S.L.T.(Sh.Ct.) 9; both cases were based upon a breach of the Factories Act 1937, s. 43 (1) (now replaced by s. 59 (1) of the 1961 Act), and both raised the interesting question as to whether an occupier/employer was under a duty to keep the clothing safe (from theft, etc.), but it was held that this was not so, although the risk of theft might be an element to be considered in determining whether or not accommodation which was provided was suitable.

[9] s. 15.

[10] s. 13 (3).

fencing of openings in floors are both called for by subsections (2), (3) and (4). Fuel storage premises are specially catered for by subsection (5). The cases which have already been considered in relation to the Factories Acts are equally relevant here,[11] when the interpretation of phrases and words is being considered. It will be noted that the phrase " so far as is reasonably practicable " qualifies the obligation imposed in section 16 (1), whilst the secure fencing requirements relating to openings in floors and contained in section 16 (4) are qualified by the words " except in so far as the nature of the work renders such fencing impracticable." The latter defence is more definite and less open to argument than the former.

Section 17 (1) requires that every dangerous part of any machinery used as, or forming, part of the equipment of premises to which the Act applies " shall be securely fenced unless it is in such a position or of such construction as to be as safe to every person working in the premises as it would be if securely fenced." Subsection (2) permits as an alternative the provision of a device which automatically prevents the operator from coming into contact with a dangerous part of the machine. Subsection (3) of section 17 provides that—in determining (for purposes of subsection (1)) whether a moving part of any machinery is in such a position or of such construction as to be as safe as if securely fenced, no account shall be taken of any person carrying out—whilst the part is in motion—an examination thereof or any lubrication or adjustment shown by the examination to be immediately necessary, if the examination, lubrication or adjustment can only be carried out while the part is in motion.

All fencing provided in accordance with the requirements of section 17 (1) and (2) shall be of substantial construction, be properly maintained and be kept in position while the parts required to be fenced are in motion or use, except when such parts are exposed necessarily for examination

---

11 See, for example, *Millar* v. *Galashiels Gas Co.,* 1949 S.C.(H.L.) 31; 1949 S.L.T. 223; [1949] 1 All E.R. 319; (1949) 65 T.L.R. 76; [1949] A.C. 275 (the words " properly maintained " connote an absolute obligation); *Braham* v. *J. Lyons & Co. Ltd.* [1962] 3 All E.R. 281 (in which Lord Denning M.R. explains the qualification of an absolute obligation by the words " so far as is reasonably practicable "); *McWilliams* v. *Sir Wm. Arrol & Co. Ltd.,* 1962 S.C.(H.L.) 70; 1962 S.L.T. 121 (H.L.); [1962] 1 All E.R. 623 (H.L.); [1962] 1 W.L.R. 295 (in which a factory occupier was held responsible for the failure of an independent contractor to take reasonable steps); *Harris* v. *Rugby Portland Cement Co. Ltd.* [1955] 2 All E.R. 500; [1955] 1 W.L.R. 648 (in which the words " special circumstances " were considered and held to mean something was likely to happen again and again and against which some permanent protection was necessary); *Drummond* v. *Harland Engineering Co.* (O.H.) 1963 S.L.T. 115; 1963 S.C. 162 (a vertical angle iron projecting ½in. above the floor of a foundry and situated at the corner of a plate supporting a moulding machine was not an " obstruction " but was part of the machine, itself a fixture); *Hall* v. *Fairfield Shipbuilding & Engineering Co.,* 1964 S.L.T. 94; 1964 S.C.(H.L.) 72 (a short length of metal rod which had fallen from a bench was held by the Lord Ordinary and the Second Division to be a " substance " likely to cause persons to slip, within the meaning of the Factories Act 1937, s. 25 (1) (now s. 28 (1) in the 1961 Act), and the words " likely to cause persons to slip " qualified only the word " substance " and did not limit the area to be kept free. The House of Lords held, however, that there was no evidence to establish that the employers' failure to prohibit metal clippings from being thrown on to the floor had caused the accident and accordingly defenders' appeal was allowed).

and for any lubrication or adjustment shown by that examination to be immediately necessary.[12]

Subsection (5) stipulates that subsection (3) and the exception mentioned in subsection (4) shall only apply where the examination, lubrication or adjustment in question is carried out by such persons who have attained the age of eighteen as may be specified in regulations made by the Minister and where all such other conditions so specified are complied with. This whole section is, very obviously, modelled upon sections 14, 15 and 16 of the Factories Act 1961. Accordingly, the cases [13] which are relevant to these three sections will be equally relevant to section 17. It is clear from the wording of section 17 (1) that an absolute obligation is being imposed in relation to " secure fencing " of dangerous parts of machinery. The same is true of the subsection (4) provisions regarding substantial construction, proper maintenance [14] and the keeping of fencing or guards in position whilst machinery is in motion or in use (except in the last-mentioned case where examination, etc., is immediately necessary). The purpose of fencing is to prevent workers from coming into contact with the machine.[15]

Section 18 is designed to protect young persons (*i.e.*, under eighteen years of age) from danger in cleaning machinery—the danger arising from any moving part of the machine which he is cleaning [16] or any moving part of an adjacent machine. Section 19 (1) deals with the training and supervision of persons working at dangerous machines, whilst subsection (2) of that section enables the Minister to apply section 19 by order [17] to such machines as he considers to be of such a dangerous character that persons ought not to work thereat unless the section 19 (1) requirements are complied with. No age limitation is imposed in this section and

---

[12] s. 17 (4).

[13] On subs. (1)—see, for example, *Close* v. *Steel Company of Wales Ltd.* [1961] 2 All E.R. 953 (H.L.); [1962] A.C. 367; [1961] 3 W.L.R. 319 (the reasonably foreseeable cause of injury to anyone acting in a way in which a human being may be expected to act in circumstances which may be reasonably expected to occur); *Mitchell* v. *North British Rubber Co.*, 1945 J.C. 69; 1946 S.L.T. 129 (the foreseeability test also includes reasonably foreseeable inadvertence and indolence). The question as to what part of a machine is a dangerous part is one of fact, but it is also one of degree—see *Lauder* v. *Barr and Stroud*, 1927 S.C.(J.) 21 (on the facts before the court, the complaint was found " not proven "). In *John Summers & Sons Ltd.* v. *Frost* [1955] 1 All E.R. 870 (H.L.); [1955] A.C. 740; [1955] 2 W.L.R. 825 the House of Lords reviewed the cases and earlier interpretations of " dangerous machinery " and adopted the observation above-mentioned from *Mitchell's* case, read along with an observation from *Walker* v. *Bletchley Flettons Ltd.* [1937] 1 All E.R. 170. In *Dobson* v. *Colvilles Ltd.*, 1958 S.l.T.(Notes) 30, a coke distributing machine moving about on rails was held to be " machinery." *Parvin* v. *Morton Machine Co. Ltd.*, 1952 S.L.T. 201; [1952] 1 All E.R. 670 (H.L.) (deciding that machinery which is a product of a factory process is not within the terms of the statutory provisions *re* fencing) would seem to be very much in point where certain machinery was offered for sale in a shop (or showroom, part of that shop), but machinery which was located in or used as equipment for an office or any railway premises would come within the statutory provisions.

[14] See particularly *Millar* v. *Galashiels Gas Co. Ltd.*, *cit. supra.*

[15] *Carroll* v. *Andrew Barclay & Sons Ltd.*, 1948 S.L.T. 464; 1948 S.C.(H.L.) 100; [1948] 2 All E.R. 386 (H.L.); [1948] A.C. 477.

[16] See *Taylor* v. (*Mark*) *Dawson & Son Ltd.* [1911] 1 K.B. 145.

[17] See now the Prescribed Dangerous Machines Order 1964 (S.I. 1964 No. 971), which came into operation on August 1, 1964.

therefore it applies to employees of all ages, unlike the earlier corresponding section 21 of the Factories Act 1961, which applied only to persons under eighteen years. It will be noted that the wording of section 19 (1) places no duty or obligation upon the employee himself.[18]

Section 20 (1) empowers the Minister to make special regulations for securing the health and safety of employees working in premises governed by the Act. Section 20 (3) is more specific and points to such special regulations dealing with such matters as, inter alia,—(a) regulating or prohibiting the use of any machinery, plant, equipment, etc., or the use of any process, (b) imposing requirements regarding the construction, installation, examination, repair, etc., of machinery, etc., and the safeguarding of dangerous parts thereof, (c) prohibiting the sale or letting on hire for use in premises to which the Act applies in Great Britain of any machinery, etc., which does not comply with the regulations made, and (d) incidental, supplementary or consequential matters. Anyone who contravenes any provisions in the said regulations is " guilty of an offence " [19] and liable to a criminal prosecution.[20] As yet, no special regulations have been made, but the intention seems to be to enable a code of special regulations to be issued in due course which will correspond broadly with the Dangerous Trades Regulations issued under the statutory authority of section 76 of the Factories Act 1961. It may be assumed, however, that any code to be issued under section 20 will not be as extensive as the Dangerous Trades Regulations.

Section 21 empowers the Minister to make special regulations controlling noise and vibrations, and any person contravening such regulations is guilty of an offence.[21]

The sheriff is empowered, by section 22, upon a summary application being made to him by the authority responsible for enforcement of the Act to prohibit—either absolutely or subject to certain conditions being fulfilled—certain dangerous practices and conditions within the premises. An interim order may be made [22] and at least three clear days' notice of the intention to make an application must be given to the occupier [23] of the premises. The jurisdiction of the sheriff court is tested by the location of the premises.[24]

Fairly extensive " first-aid " provisions are contained in sections 24–26. In fact, section 24 contains the general provisions,[25] while section 25 relates to premises located inside but not forming part of a factory [26]

---

[18] Vide M'Cafferty v. Brown (O.H.) 1950 S.C. 300; 1950 S.L.T. 356.
[19] s. 20 (4).
[20] Jurisdiction of the particular court is determined according to the location of the machinery, etc., at the time—s. 20 (6).
[21] s. 21 (3).
[22] s. 22 (2).
[23] This term is not defined in the Act—but see Ramsay v. Mackie (1904) 7 F. 106, per Lord MacLaren at p. 109.
[24] s. 22 (3).
[25] See now the Offices, Shops and Railway Premises First Aid Order 1964 (S.I. 1964 No. 970).
[26] See the Offices and Shops in Factories (First-Aid) Regulations 1964 (S.I. 1964 No. 1321).

(to which, of course, the Factories Act 1961 would have applied, had the premises been part of the factory) and section 26 to office premises at building sites.[27]

Section 27 (1) and (2) stipulates as follows—

" (1) A person who, in premises to which this Act applies, wilfully and without reasonable cause does anything likely to endanger the health or safety of persons employed to wo r therein shall be guilty of an offence.

" (2) A person who, in premises to which this Act applies, wilfully interferes with, wilfully misuses or without reasonable excuse removes any equipment, appliance, facilities or other thing provided there in pursuance of this Act or regulations thereunder shall be guilty of an offence."

Subsection (3) merely preserves the powers contained in sections 20 and 21, but makes it clear that these two sections are not limited by section 27. This section of the 1963 Act corresponds broadly with section 143 of the Factories Act 1961.[28] It will be seen that subsection (2) of section 27 says " A person who . . . wilfully interferes with, wilfully misuses or without reasonable excuse removes any equipment . . . shall be guilty of an offence." Section 143 (1) of the Factories Act 1961 uses the phrase " wilfully interfere with or misuse." [29] It is submitted that the wording of section 27 (2) is quite clear, viz.: any wilful interference with or any wilful misuse of or any removal (without reasonable excuse) of any equipment, etc., constitutes an offence. Any one of the three actings will suffice to make the doer liable to prosecution.

Sections 28–41 inclusive contain a fairly extensive code of fire precautions (comparable with sections 40–52 of the Factories Act 1961). The " fire certificate " requirements are specified in section 29 and must be read along with the Offices, Shops and Railway Premises Act 1963 (Modification of Section 29) Regulations 1964.[30] A right of appeal lies to the sheriff, against matters arising out of sections 29 and 30,[31] and, in fact, section 31 (1) stipulates the grounds of grievance upon which such an appeal may be brought. The sheriff may also, upon a summary application being made to him at the instance of the fire authority, make an order [32] prohibiting the employment of persons in the premises until such steps have been taken which—in the sheriff's opinion—are necessary to

[27] See now the Offices at Building Operations, etc., (First-Aid) Regulations 1964 (S.I. 1964 No. 1322).
[28] In *Charles* v. *S. Smith & Sons Ltd.* [1954] 1 All E.R. 499 Hilbery J. considered the phrase " wilfully and without reasonable cause " contained in s. 143 (2) but did not state with any exactitude what he thought it meant. It would seem that s. 27 (1) was intended to mean that any deliberate act done perversely (*i.e.*, without any justifiable excuse) endangering the health or safety of any persons would lead to a criminal prosecution.
[29] Hilbery J. in *Charles* v. *S. Smith & Sons Ltd.*, *cit. supra*, treated the word " or " as conjunctive and not disjunctive.
[30] S.I. 1964 No. 761.
[31] Which deals with the maintenance of means of escape in case of fire and inspection by the appropriate authority.
[32] *Vide* s. 32.

remedy dangerous conditions in regard to the means of escape in case of fire. The Minister is empowered [33] to make regulations regarding means of escape in case of fire.

Fire-fighting equipment must be provided and maintained and be so placed as to be readily available for use.[34] The appropriate authority responsible for the enforcement of the fire provisions is specifically dealt with in section 39 and the duty of that appropriate authority (if not concerned with buildings) to consult the authority responsible for buildings is—as regards Scotland—explained in section 41 (2).

Notification of accidents is provided for in section 48 [35] of the Act. Where an accident occurs in any premises to which the Act applies and (a) causes loss of life to an employee or (b) disables any such person for more than three days, notice [36] of the accident must be sent to the appropriate authority by the occupier of the premises. If a person who is disabled in an accident (notified as above) subsequently dies, then notice of the death must be sent by the occupier.[37] If the employer of the person killed or disabled is not the occupier of the premises and he fails to notify the occupier immediately, then he is guilty of an offence and liable to a fine not exceeding ten pounds.[38] The Minister is empowered by section 48 (4) to make regulations and to give either or both of the directions contained in that subsection. Subsection (5) defines the " appropriate authority." The word " accident " has its ordinary meaning of an unlooked-for mishap or an untoward event which is not expected or designed by the victim.[39]

Section 49 relates to the giving of certain information to the appropriate authority in prescribed form [40] by an employer. Any failure to comply with the obligation makes the employer guilty of a criminal offence and liable to a fine not exceeding twenty pounds. Proceedings in respect of this offence may be commenced at any time within twelve months from the time when the offence was committed.[41] This section corresponds to section 137 of the Factories Act 1961.

Section 50 gives the Minister powers to make regulations prescribing certain steps by which all employees working in premises governed by the Act are to be kept informed of the effect of the Act and any regulations made under it, including the posting of abstracts of the Act (or abstracts of parts of it) within the premises or the issue of books or explanatory leaflets (prepared under the auspices of the Ministry) to the employees. A person who contravenes the section is guilty of an offence. A set of

---

[33] By s. 35.
[34] See s. 38.
[35] This section is comparable with s. 80 of the Factories Act 1961.
[36] In such form as may be prescribed by the Minister. See the Offices, Shops and Railway Premises Forms Order 1964 (S.I. 1964 No. 605), cl. 5 and Sched. 4.
[37] s. 48 (2).
[38] s. 48 (3).
[39] See *Fenton* v. *Thorley & Co. Ltd.* [1903] A.C. 443 *per* Lord Macnaghten; and *Trim Joint District School Board of Management* v. *Kelly* [1914] A.C. 667; 30 T.L.R. 452.
[40] See the Notification of Employment of Persons Order 1964 (S.I. 1964 No. 533).
[41] s. 49 (4).

Regulations [42] was, in fact, made on February 25, 1965, and came into operation on June 1, 1965.

The enforcement provisions are to be found in sections 52–62 inclusive. Section 52 specifies the authorities responsible. These are (i) for sections 4–27 and 46–50, the local authorities or H.M. Inspectors of Factories or H.M. Inspectors of Mines and Quarries; and (ii) for sections 28–38, the fire authorities in most cases (but H.M. Inspectors of Factories for Crown premises or local authority premises and for offices within factory premises); and H.M. Inspector of Mines and Quarries for offices, fuel storage premises, etc., at mines and quarries. Section 52 (7) says quite specifically, so far as Scotland is concerned, that nothing in the section charging any authority with the enforcement of the Act or regulations thereunder is to be construed as authorising that authority to institute proceedings for any offence. This means that the prosecution of such offences, normally by summary procedure in the sheriff court, will remain in the hands of the procurator-fiscal in that court (*i.e.*, prosecution at the instance of the Crown). Yet the local authority's inspectors can institute certain provisions in terms of section 71, hereinafter mentioned.

Section 53 (1) specifies the powers available to inspectors appointed by the local authority and those appointed by the Minister (including factory inspectors), whilst subsection (2) makes it an offence punishable with a fine not exceeding twenty pounds for a person who fails to comply with any requirement imposed by an inspector or who prevents (or attempts to prevent) any person from appearing before an inspector or from answering any question which the inspector has a right to ask and to require an answer or who obstructs an inspector. This section corresponds to section 146 of the Factories Act 1961. The subsequent section of the 1963 Act explains the powers available to an inspector authorised by the Minister of Power. Every inspector must produce, if required, documentary evidence of his authority.[43] Officers of the appropriate fire brigade have the like powers as conferred by section 53 upon factory inspectors.[44] Local authorities (including the Greater London Council) may be required by regulations to discharge their duties in a uniform manner.[45] Local authorities and fire authorities must make an annual report to the Minister.[46] Section 62 extends to Scotland only (and corresponds to section 61 for England and Wales) and deals with the exercise and performance by the Minister of the powers of Scottish local authorities who are in default. In conducting any local inquiry under section 62 (1), regard must be had to the specific provisions contained in

---

[42] See the Information for Employees Regulations 1965 (S.I. 1965 No. 307). The Schedule attached thereto is extremely helpful in illustrating the information which is to be provided for all employees.

[43] s. 55.

[44] s. 56.

[45] s. 57.

[46] s. 60. See also the Offices, Shops and Railway Premises Annual Reports Order 1964 (S.I. 1964 No. 1247).

section 355, subss. (3) to (9) inclusive, of the Local Government (Scotland) Act 1947.[47]

Offences, penalties and legal proceedings are covered by sections 63 to 73 inclusive. From section 63 (1) it is clear that the occupier is basically responsible for complying with the Act's provisions and he is guilty of an offence for any failure to do so. However, some other person (or persons) may be made responsible along with the occupier or in lieu of the occupier. In the former case both (or all) are guilty of an offence, whilst in the latter case that other person (or persons) is guilty of an offence.[48] Offences by corporate bodies are dealt with in section 65 and it is very evident that any director or officer of the company may also be guilty of the offence, if that offence is proved to have been committed with the consent or connivance of, or to be attributable to any neglect on the part of, such director or officer. In the case of a nationalised industry, "director" means a member of the Board responsible for the administration of that nationalised industry.[49] Section 64 provides a penalty, which may be said to be a "general penalty," for those cases in which no specific penalty is provided by the Board. This penalty is a fine not exceeding £60, plus £15 per day for every day upon which the offence is continued after conviction of the offender.

Section 66 allows for the person who actually commits a contravention of the Act (or of any regulations made thereunder) being prosecuted along with the person who is primarily responsible for conforming with the provisions of the Act or being prosecuted alone. In either case the actual offender is liable to the same punishment, upon conviction, as the said other person is so liable. There seems to be no difficulty about the workability of this section in Scotland. It would be possible to regard both persons as wrongdoers and charge them jointly or, as the section says, charge the actual wrongdoer alone. It might well be decided to charge the person made primarily responsible by the Act and not trouble about the actual wrongdoer.

Section 67 provides that it shall be a defence for a person charged with a contravention of a provision of the Act or of regulations thereunder to prove that he used all due diligence to secure compliance with that provision.[49a] Broadly, the section corresponds to section 161 of the Factories Act, but it is more straightforward than the latter section, because it does not refer to an additional right to bring the actual offender before the court (a procedure for which there is no equivalent or counterpart in Scottish criminal practice—as this proceeding is quite alien to Scots criminal law). Accordingly, the section 67 defence is available to the person primarily responsible and for the actual wrongdoer—irrespective of

---

[47] 10 & 11 Geo. 6, c. 43.
[48] See s. 63 (1), paras. (b) and (c).
[49] s. 65 (2).
[49a] The section 67 defence is not available where an employer fails in his special obligation or duty imposed by the Act, e.g. a duty of supervision—see *J. H. Dewhurst* v. *Coventry Corporation*, [1969] 3 W.L.R. 249.

whether one person is involved or two persons are involved. The section may be pleaded only as a defence to a criminal prosecution—it is not a relevant defence in a civil action.[50] The burden of proof upon an accused is presumably not quite so high as that which rests upon the procurator-fiscal. The English courts seem to accept the "reasonable probability" test in relation to this defence.[51] The reference to proof that the accused "used all due diligence to secure compliance . . ." means that this raises immediately the question which is clearly one of fact—did accused, as a matter of fact, use all due diligence ?[52] It is essential that active steps should be taken to comply with the provisions of a statute of this kind.[53] Knowledge and consent on the part of the employer play an important part in deciding the question of the liability of the employer for the act of an employee which is done in contravention of a statutory provision. It would seem that there is a difference of view between the English courts and the Scottish courts upon this question. The tendency in England would seem to be to attach liability to the employer, although he has no knowledge of, or did not consent to, the particular operation. In Scotland, it seems that no liability attaches to the employer in such cases, as is clearly indicated in *Melville's* case [54] (a prosecution brought, unsuccessfully, under the Factory and Workshop Act 1878) and in *Duke's* case [54] (a prosecution brought, unsuccessfully, under the Factory and Workshop Act 1901).

Falsification of documents, false statements, entries, etc., and the removal or defacement of documents posted or displayed in premises governed by the Act, are all dealt with in sections 68 and 69. The terminology used in section 68 is essentially English legal terminology and in substitution therefor the Scottish common law of falsehood, fraud and wilful imposition will be applicable.[55]

Prosecution of offences is dealt with in section 70. It is categorically stated in subsection (1) that all offences shall be triable summarily, although power is given to the sheriff—upon the application of either party —to have the evidence noted and preserved.[56] A factory inspector (duly authorised by the Minister) may prosecute or conduct proceedings before

---

[50] See *Yelland* v. *Powell Duffryn Associated Collieries Ltd.* [1941] 1 All E.R. 278; [1941] 1 K.B. 154 (C.A.); *Riddell* v. *Reid*, 1942 S.C.(H.L.) 51; 1943 S.L.T. 51; [1943] A.C. 1; [1942] 2 All E.R. 161 (H.L.); and *Gallagher* v. *Dorman, Long & Co. Ltd.* [1947] 2 All E.R. 38 (C.A.).

[51] *Vide R.* v. *Carr-Briant* [1943] K.B. 607 (C.A.); [1943] 2 All E.R. 156; and *R.* v. *Dunbar* [1958] 1 Q.B. 1 (C.C.A.); [1957] 3 All E.R. 737.

[52] *R. C. Hammett Ltd.* v. *Crabb* [1931] All E.R. 70.

[53] *Rogers* v. *Barlow & Sons* (1906) 94 L.T. 519.

[54] See and compare the Scottish cases of *Robinson* v. *Melville* (1890) 17 R.(J.) 62; and *Paterson* v. *Duke* (1904) 6 F.(J.) 53, with the following English cases, *viz., Prior* v. *Slaithwaite Spinning Co.* [1898] 1 Q.B. 881; and *Rogers* v. *Barlow & Sons* (1906) 94 L.T. 519; and compare also *Ward* v. *W. H. Smith & Sons Ltd.* [1913] 3 K.B. 154; (1913) 109 L.T. 439.

[55] See *The Criminal Law of Scotland* by Sir J. H. A. Macdonald (5th ed.; eds. Jas. Walker & D. J. Stevenson), Greens (1948), mainly at pp. 52–66; and Gerald H. Gordon, *The Criminal Law of Scotland,* Greens (1967), principally Chap. 18 (pp. 537-577).

[56] s. 70 (2).

the sheriff, although that inspector is not an advocate or solicitor.[57] Moreover, the fact that he instituted the prosecution or conducted the proceedings does not disbar or prevent the inspector from giving evidence as a witness in any prosecution for an offence under the Act, notwithstanding any rule of law (evidence or practice) in Scotland.[58] Local authorities' inspectors in Scotland are given special powers, by section 71, to institute proceedings in certain cases—notably by summary application under section 22 (to enforce sections 4 to 21) and by similar application under section 32, for an order putting down dangerous conditions in regard to means of escape in case of fire.

The sheriff may set aside or modify agreements and apportion expenses between the parties in relation to structural alterations and others to the premises covered by the Act.

Certain necessary amendments to sections 123 (1), 124 (1) and 125 (1) of the Factories Act 1961 are made by sections 74 [59] and 75 of the 1963 Act, whilst certain amendments to the Public Health Act 1936 are made by the subsequent section 76.

The Minister is required by section 79 to lay before Parliament annually a report of his proceedings under the Act and generally about the operation of the Act. To date, the Minister has issued four such annual reports.[60] A comment upon the last report is contained in the final paragraph of this section.

The provisions relating to the making of regulations and orders appear in section 80, whilst methods of service of notices and expenses and receipts are dealt with in the next two sections. The 1963 Act does apply to the Crown and its specific application is set forth in section 83. Certain exclusions are stipulated for in sections 84, 85 and 86. Section 90 [61] is the interpretation section and it is fairly extensive. Section 91 is the final section. Two short Schedules are annexed, the first of these setting out the procedure for making special regulations.

The latest annual report [62] issued by the Minister [63] shows that employers and employees (or, more correctly perhaps, occupiers and employees) were becoming aware of (i) the responsibilities and (ii) the statutory provisions designed to improve working conditions created by the Act,[64] although few employees were making complaints and when they did so they preferred to remain anonymous. Non-registration of premises still, however, remained a widespread problem.[65] Inspection

[57] s. 70 (3).
[58] s. 70 (4).
[59] See the Offices in Electrical Stations (First-Aid) Regulations 1964 (S.I. 1964 No. 1323).
[60] For the years ended 1964, 1965, 1966 and 1967 respectively (House of Commons papers; published by H.M.S.O.).
[61] Amended to a certain extent as regards the subs. (1) definition of " local authority " by the London Government Act 1963, s. 51 (1).
[62] For year ended December 31, 1967 (published October 14, 1968).
[63] Now the Secretary of State for Employment and Productivity (since 1968).
[64] Annual Report for 1967, pp. 9 and 10.
[65] *Ibid.* p. 11. See Table 6 for the Statistical Summary.

of premises did not reveal any widespread evidence of bad conditions, although there were numerous minor contraventions of the statutory provisions, mainly in the private sector.[66] Railway premises were being improved. The numerical space standards of the Act came into force on August 1, 1967, for all premises.[67] A fairly substantial number of prosecutions were taken under the "dangerous machinery" sections,[68] but—taking the United Kingdom as a whole—the total does not give too much cause for concern, in the writer's view. It is difficult to say from that section of the 1967 Annual Report, which relates to fire provisions,[69] whether the measures taken in all inspected premises were fully satisfactory. Certainly it is apparent that a considerable number of premises were inspected, but it may be that the inspecting authorities must be given wider powers to require that every possible step to minimise loss of human life must be taken. The report upon accidents [70] is very interesting. It is apparent here that the pattern of accidents—looking to primary cause and nature of injury—has not varied significantly in the annual reports so far issued, although there is no doubt that some anxiety must be felt at the overall figure for reported accidents. This is recorded at 19,903 for the year 1967. It would seem that the picture here is comparable with those in factories and mines and quarries. The graph line seems to continue to rise. These are matters about which industry and commerce cannot afford to be complacent. Every establishment should be encouraged to employ a properly qualified Fire and Accidents Prevention Officer.

Each Annual Report has always contained [71] a most useful list of statutory instruments which are in force and which must be read along with the main Act.

(4) Agriculture

For many years the only source of protection available to an agricultural employee, who suffered injury within the scope of his employment, was the general common law, in which, of course, developing custom—sometimes peculiar to the main agricultural areas—had played a major part. It was only in 1952 and 1956 that firm legislative provisions, designed to protect the safety, health and welfare of the agricultural employee, went on the Statute Book. The first statute was the Agriculture (Poisonous Substances) Act 1952 [72] and the second, and more important, the Agriculture (Safety, Health and Welfare Provisions) Act 1956.[73] The 1956 Act gives specific powers to the Minister [74] to make regulations,[75]

---

[66] Ibid. p. 13.
[67] See pp. 14 and 15 on the space problem in offices and shops.
[68] Ibid. pp. 18 and 19.
[69] Ibid. Chap. III, pp. 21–24; and Table 5.
[70] Ibid. Chap. IV, pp. 25–29; and Tables 7 and 8.
[71] Ibid. Table 2.
[72] 15 & 16 Geo. 6 and 1 Eliz. 2, c. 60.
[73] 4 & 5 Eliz. 2, c. 49.
[74] In Scotland, the responsible Minister is the Secretary of State for Scotland.
[75] 1956 Act, s. 18.

which may, as necessary, restrict the application of the Factories Act 1961 (previously the main Act was the 1937 Act, as amended in 1948 and 1959) to places or premises which would otherwise have been governed by that Act or earlier legislation. The pattern of the 1956 Act and of the regulations made thereunder follows that of the factories legislation and accordingly only brief references to the main provisions will be made.[76] The 1956 Act provides the framework and foundation of the legislation while the numerous sets of regulations constitute the bricks and mortar. Examples of such regulations are—the Agriculture (Lifting of Heavy Weights) Regulations 1959 [77]; the Agriculture (First-Aid) Regulations.[78] The sanitary authorities may require an agricultural unit to be provided with suitable and sufficient sanitary conveniences.[79] The Minister (*i.e.*, the Secretary of State for Scotland, as regards Scotland) may require suitable and sufficient washing facilities to be provided for an agricultural unit. First-aid appliances, etc., must also be provided.[80] It is an offence for an employer to fail to provide any of the facilities mentioned above.[81] Protection against the use of poisonous substances was provided for initially in the Agriculture (Poisonous Substances) Act 1952 [82] to all employees subjected to the risk of poisoning arising from their working in agriculture, wherein use of poisonous substances [83] is being made or where such employees are working on land upon which such poisonous substances are being used or have been used in agriculture.[84] Section 1 (1) of the 1952 Act gives the Minister power to make regulations and, in fact, several issues of regulations were made between 1956 and 1962, although these have been replaced by the Agriculture (Poisonous Substances) Regulations 1963.[83] Contravention of any regulations made under the 1952 Act is made an offence punishable by a fine not exceeding fifty pounds and if the contravention is continued after conviction the penalty is a maximum fine of ten pounds per day during the continuation.[85] The defence that some other person committed the offence and that the accused used " all due diligence " to secure compliance with the particular provision and did not consent to or connive at or be guilty of any wilful default in relation to the Act or default of that other person [86] is available.

General provisions regarding safety are provided for by section 1 of

---

[76] For a more extensive account of the provisions relating to the health and welfare of agricultural employees see G. H. L. Fridman, *The Modern Law of Employment* (1963) and second supplement (1967) at pp. 262–268; and for those provisions concerning safety—*op. cit.* pp. 357–360.

[77] S.I. 1959 No. 2120.

[78] S.I. 1957 No. 940.

[79] 1956 Act, s. 3.

[80] *Ibid.* s. 6; see also the Agriculture (First-Aid) Regulations 1957 (S.I. 1957 No. 940).

[81] *Ibid.* ss. 5 and 6.

[82] 15 & 16 Geo. 6 & 1 Eliz. 2, c. 60.

[83] See the Agriculture (Poisonous Substances) Act 1952, s. 9; and, in particular, the Agriculture (Poisonous Substances) Regulations 1963 (S.I. 1963 No. 845).

[84] Employees under an ordinary contract of employment, and apprentices, are covered —1952 Act, s. 10 (1).

[85] 1952 Act, s. 4 (1) and (2).

[86] *Ibid.* s. 5.

the Agriculture (Safety, Health and Welfare Provisions) Act 1956 [87] and powers are given to make regulations regarding safety,[88] which may deal with particular and specific matters.[89] Any contravention is made an offence.[90] Regulations for the protection of children may be made under section 7 of the Act and, in fact, the Agriculture (Avoidance of Accidents to Children) Regulations 1958 [91] have been issued. Regulations may also be made, under section 8, for the notification of accidents and for the keeping of records. It is an offence [92] for any person to falsify an entry in any register, etc., or to make wilful use of a false entry.

Inspectors may be appointed to ensure that the provisions of the 1952 Act and 1956 Act are being properly carried out. The powers are broadly the same.[93] The sanitary authorities (burgh councils and town councils in Scotland) may require that certain conveniences and facilities be provided and that certain essential steps be carried out—with reference to maintenance and cleansing.[94] Inspectors, authorised by the sanitary authorities, may enter any land—at all reasonable hours—to check upon facilities to be provided and whether or not the terms of any notices issued are being complied with properly.[95] All offences committed under the 1952 and 1956 Acts are dealt with by summary procedure. The Crown is bound by the 1952 Act and partially bound by the 1956 Act.[96]

Wages and holidays in agricultural service are dealt with separately in an earlier chapter.[97]

(5) Merchant Shipping

The law of merchant shipping, though based to a certain extent on the common law, is mainly a creature of statute law [98] and was substantially codified by the Merchant Shipping Act 1894. The " master " [99] is the person having command or charge of a ship. That term does not include a pilot. A " seaman " [1] is the term applied to every person employed or engaged in any capacity on board a ship, but it does not include a master, pilot or indentured sea apprentice. It has been held to include a labourer

---

[87] 4 & 5 Eliz. 2, c. 49.
[88] Several sets of regulations have been issued—see, in illustration Fridman, *op. cit.* p. 357 and n. 3.
[89] 1956 Act, s. 1 (3), paras. (*a*)–(*b*) inclusive.
[90] *Ibid.* s. 1 (6).
[91] S.I. 1958 No. 366.
[92] *Ibid.* s. 12.
[93] Agriculture (Poisonous Substances) Act 1952, s. 3, and the Agriculture (Safety, Health and Welfare Provisions) Act 1956, s. 10.
[94] 1956 Act, s. 3. It is an offence to fail to comply—ss. 3 and 5.
[95] *Ibid.* s. 11.
[96] 1952 Act, s. 7, and the 1956 Act, s. 22.
[97] *Supra*, Chap. 8.
[98] For the early statute law see Fraser, *Master and Servant* (3rd ed., 1882) at Chap. XI. Reference should also be made to Green's *Encyclopaedia of the Laws of Scotland*, Vol. 13, paras. 630–681. The main reference work is Temperley's *Merchant Shipping Acts* (6th ed., 1963) (Stevens).
[99] 57 & 58 Vict., c. 60—see particularly Part II which deals with masters and seamen; and also the Merchant Shipping Act 1906 (6 Edw. 7, c. 48).
[1] *Ibid.* s. 742.

employed on board to discharge cargo.[2] A seaman is not entitled to be ranked as " A.B." (able-bodied seaman) unless he has served three years before the mast, or one year in a trading vessel in addition to two years on a decked fishing vessel.[3] It is a very serious offence for any seaman to make false representations in order to obtain an A.B. rating.[4]

The government department which has overall responsibility for merchant shipping was formerly the Board of Trade and is now the Ministry of Transport. It exercises control over the local Marine Boards and Mercantile Marine offices at the principal seaports.[5] The local superintendent has the duty of maintaining registers of seamen, supervising their engagement and discharge and arranging apprenticeships amongst other things.[6] The main registry offices (i.e., the general register and record office) is in London.[7]

Masters and officers of foreign-going ships or home trade passenger ships must be certificated by the Minister of Transport, as required by sections 92 to 102 of the main Act, as amended—with special reference to section 92 of the main Act—by the Merchant Shipping Act 1967.[8] Licences are also granted to certain persons by the Minister of Transport enabling them to engage or supply seamen for merchant ships in the United Kingdom.[9]

As regards the contract made with seamen, the position is that every master of a ship (excluding coasters under 80 registered tons) must enter into a written agreement with the crew, in a form approved by the Minister of Transport and the master must sign that agreement before any seaman does so.[10] The agreement (commonly known as the " ship's articles ") contains the usual terms and conditions applicable to this type of contractual relationship.[11] It must be observed that an oral engagement or hiring of a seaman is still possible—and perfectly valid. The signing of the written agreement—prior to sailing date—is a statutory requirement which has to be fulfilled before the ship puts to sea.[12] The written agreement, which each seaman is required to sign, must be so signed in the presence of the superintendent, who has the duty of explaining the agreement to the

---

[2] *Burns* v. *Allan* (1895) 3 S.L.T. 212.
[3] 1894 Act, s. 126, as amended by the 1906 Act, s. 58.
[4] 1906 Act, s. 58 (2).
[5] 1894 Act, ss. 244–250, as amended by the 1906 Act, s. 85 and Sched. II. For general control of the Minister of Transport, see the 1894 Act, s. 713, and the 1906 Act, s. 74.
[6] *Ibid.* s. 247; and the 1906 Act, ss. 36–49.
[7] Particulars of all seamen serving on ships governed by the Merchant Shipping Acts are available there.
[8] 1967, c. 26.
[9] ss. 110–111.
[10] ss. 113–114. (For apprenticeship agreements see ss. 105–109 and 168). Temperley. *op. cit.* pp. 78–82.
[11] Principally, duration and nature of voyage, number of the crew and boarding times, capacity of employment and wages of each seaman joining the ship, as well as a scale of provisions and the discipline regulations. As to the stipulation of wages in the ship's articles—see *Thompson* v. *H. & W. Nelson Ltd.* [1913] 2 K.B. 523.
[12] *Thomson* v. *Hart* (1890) 18 R.(J.) 3; 2 White 539; *Burns* v. *Allan, cit. supra.* A seaman may be said to " belong " to a ship, although the ship's articles have not yet been signed by him—see *Vickerson* v. *Crowe* [1914] 1 K.B. 462.

seaman and of attesting the signature of each seaman. The agreement may relate to a single voyage or it may be a " running agreement." [13] In the case of home trade ships the agreement may relate to service in a particular ship or in two or more ships of the same owning line. A copy of the agreement must be posted in the ship and it is therefore a public document which proves itself, no further proof being necessary.[14] Alterations to the document are permitted but the strict procedures for attestation contained in the main Act must be observed.[15] A stipulation which is not contained in the Ministry of Transport form may be made in the agreement itself but such a stipulation must not be contrary to law,[16] nor inconsistent with any statutory provision.[17]

Wages,[18] in the case of merchant seamen, are payable in one of two ways—either (i) by time or (ii) by voyage, and generally at an agreed rate. No seaman can be compelled to sign away his right to wages in the event of loss of the ship, nor can he be required to forgo or waive any right which he has or acquires to salvage,[19] except where the ship itself is specifically engaged in salvage services. The English case of *Cutter* v. *Powell* [20] provides an interesting illustration of the type of condition which may be inserted in a wages agreement. Here the seaman was to receive a lump sum as wages " provided he proceeds, continues, and does his duty as second mate in the said ship from hence to the port of Liverpool." Unfortunately, he died during the voyage and it was held that no wages were due. Wages run from the date upon which duty is commenced or from the date stipulated in the agreement, whichever is earlier in time.[21] Overtime may be served and the rules regulating this are basically the same as were mentioned earlier in the case of the ordinary contract of service.[22]

The seaman of a foreign-going ship [23] who is discharged in the United Kingdom, before a superintendent, must normally receive his wages from or through the superintendent and he (the seaman) will sign a release of all claims arising out of the engagement or voyage.[24] The same procedure may be adopted in the case of seamen from a home trade ship.[25] A statement of account of wages must be delivered and the superintendent is charged with the duty of adjudicating upon and arranging the settlement

---

[13] s. 115. See Temperley, *op. cit.* pp. 82–84.
[14] s. 123.
[15] s. 122. Special arrangements apply to the case of Lascar seamen—see s. 125; and Temperley, pp. 91–92.
[16] 1906 Act, s. 114 (3).
[17] *Mercantile Steamship Co.* v. *Hall* [1909] 2 K.B. 423, *per* Pickford J. at p. 428.
[18] See initially, the 1894 Act, ss. 131–139. Seamen's rights in relation to wages are governed by ss. 155–163.
[19] s. 156. See also *The Wilhelm Tell* [1892] P. 337.
[20] (1795) 2 Smith's Leading Cases 1; 6 T.R. 320.
[21] s. 155.
[22] *Supra*, Chap. 8 (wages, etc.).
[23] For definition see s. 742.
[24] s. 136. A specified claim or demand may always be excluded from the release—1906 Act, s. 60.
[25] s. 742 contains the definition.

of any dispute regarding the amount of the wages.[26] Advance of wages (not exceeding one month's wages in amount) may be made [27] and allotment of sums of money (not exceeding one-half of the wages) may be made to a near relative or a savings bank, as defined in the Act.[28] Should a seaman's wife desert her husband—or otherwise forfeit her right of support by him—then the allotment arrangements will fall to be cancelled.[29] A seaman's wages are not subject to arrestment.[30]

Forfeiture of wages (either wholly or partially) may take place where there is a breach of the discipline regulations [31] by the seaman. The most common examples are—absence without leave, desertion, wilful disobedience and wilful damage. Such forfeiture does not prejudice the owner or master in bringing the customary action for breach of contract.[32]

Fining procedures, involving deductions from wages, are also provided for by the statute.[33] Actual loss of wages may also take place, without any blame for that loss attaching to the seaman himself—e.g., wreck or loss of the ship or unseaworthiness occurring in a foreign port—and he will be entitled to recover wages until such time as the engagement is terminated. Where, however, a seaman neglects to carry out work properly ordered or unlawfully refuses to work, he is not entitled to any wages payment.

Payment of wages during illness is similar to the position under the ordinary service contract. In the general case no deduction falls to be made.[34] Should it happen that a seaman is incapable of carrying out his ordinary duties because of illness which is proved to have been brought about by his own default or his own wilful act then wages for the period of incapacity are forfeited.[35] The owner is under no obligation to pay for medical or surgical assistance in such a case.[35]

An action may be brought by a seaman for the recovery of his wages.[36] In such a case the court may rescind the service contract upon such terms as it considers to be just and equitable.[37] In addition, the seaman has a

---

[26] ss. 134 (*b*), 137, 138—(s. 137 being amended by the Merchant Shipping Act 1950, s. 2 (and Sched. II, para. 10)).

[27] An owner may be bound to the bona fide holder of an advance note, even if the voyage should subsequently be cancelled—see *Walker* v. *Lord Advocate* (1920) 2 Lloyd's Rep. 32.

[28] See ss. 140–142. and 144 (repealed by the 1906 Act and replaced by s. 62 thereof). For arrangement of allotments through savings banks see ss. 145–154. These sections were amended in several respects by the 1906 Act (ss. 61–65) and by the Merchant Shipping (Seamen's Allotment) Act 1911 (particularly s. 1).

[29] s. 143.

[30] s. 163. See also *M'Ritchie* v. *Milne* (1886) 3 Sh.Ct.Rep. 176; and Temperley—pp. 112 and 113.

[31] The " general offences against discipline " are specified in the 1894 Act, s. 225, as modified by the Merchant Shipping Act 1906, s. 44; and the Criminal Justice Act 1948, s. 1 (2) (*re* the abolition of imprisonment with hard labour).

[32] s. 226; see also *Sharp* v. *Rettie* (1884) 11 R. 745.

[33] See particularly the 1894 Act, s. 227; and the 1906 Act, s. 44.

[34] 1906 Act, s. 34.

[35] s. 160; read along with the 1906 Act, s. 34.

[36] 1894 Act, ss. 164–166; and *Bain* v. *Ormiston*, 1928 S.C. 764.

[37] s. 168.

lien [38] on the ship, which security is quite independent of the statute law and which he cannot be compelled to give up by any agreement purporting to do so.[39] Liability for payment of wages rests upon the owner and the master, both of whom are personally liable.[40] The master's rights and remedies for wages and disbursements, etc., are contained in section 167 of the main Act.[41]

It should also be pointed out that a seaman may be justified in leaving the ship where, because of fault on the part of the owners, the voyage could not be completed.[42]

It will be appreciated that the safety, health and welfare of the crew are of the utmost importance and that conditions on board ship, particularly from the viewpoint of members of the crew, have been improved substantially since the turn of the century. There is a clear and implied undertaking in every sea service contract or sea apprenticeship indenture that the owner will use all reasonable means at his disposal to make the ship seaworthy. Medical stores must be carried, together with suitable supplies of water and provisions for the crew.[43] The owner or master may insist upon the medical examination of any crew member before he is allowed to sail.[44] The ship may—if carrying more than one hundred passengers and being a foreign-going ship or an emigrant ship—be required to carry a qualified medical practitioner.[45] Should a seaman suffer illness or injury for some reason connected with his service in the ship, the owners are liable for the expense of medical services and maintenance and, if the illness or injury proves to be fatal, for the expenses of burial. The common law places upon the ship's master a duty of obtaining, so far as possible, all necessary medical help (including surgical help) and should he fail in that duty he is liable in damages for his failure in that duty.[46]

The disciplinary powers which the 1894 Act gives to the ship's master are an extension of his common law powers. He may use all necessary and reasonable methods to protect the lives of those on board and preserve the safety of the ship, including corporal punishment. However, he must not exceed what is necessary and reasonable, otherwise he may be liable to a personal action in damages. The main offences and penalties are

---

[38] The lien is a common law lien. However, there is such maritime lien for necessaries supplied to a Scottish ship in a Scottish port—see *Clydesdale Bank* v. *Walker & Bain*, 1926 S.C. 72. In *Currie* v. *McKnight* (1897) 24 R. (H.L.) 1—after considerable doubt had been expressed as to whether the law of maritime lien recognised in England applied to Scotland—it was decided that in maritime cases which exclusively belonged to the jurisdiction of the Admiralty Courts in Scotland and England the law was neither English nor Scottish but British law and therefore one and the same code.

[39] s. 156; and Temperley, pp. 107–108.

[40] See *The Salacia* (1862) 32 L.J.P.M. & A. 41, *per* Dr. Lushington at p. 42.

[41] The notes at pp. 115–118 of Temperley are most helpful in relation to s. 167.

[42] See *O'Neil* v. *Armstrong, Mitchell & Co.* [1895] 2 Q.B. 418; *Lang* v. *St. Enoch Shipping Co.*, 1908 S.C. 103; and *Caine* v. *Palace Shipping Co.* [1907] A.C. 386.

[43] ss. 200, 201 and 202; and supplementary orders and statutory instruments; see Temperley, pp. 135–138.

[44] s. 203; and the Merchant Shipping (International Labour Conventions) Act 1925, s. 3.

[45] ss. 209 and 303, the latter section dealing specifically with emigrant ships.

[46] *Taylor* v. *Hill* (1900) 7 S.L.T. 318.

contained in sections 220–228.[47] Where the offence in question is that of desertion this involves a complete abandonment of the ship and the firm intention of not returning. If there exists an *animus revertendi* there is not a full desertion and the whole wages would not be forfeited; only those for the period of absence. The intention to desert completely and quit the ship for good must be inferred from all the circumstances of the case.

Discharge is—in the case of those who have served on a foreign-going ship—always arranged through the superintendent. The master is obliged to give to every seaman a discharge certificate which specifies the period of service and the time and place of discharge.[48] Should he fail to do so it is not competent for a seaman to bring a civil action for damages against the master [49] or against the owner.[50] Moreover, where discharge occurs before a superintendent the master must give a report as to the seaman's conduct, character and qualifications or, alternatively, state that he declines to give an opinion thereon. A copy of any report so made must be given to the seaman.[51]

Should a seaman or a sea apprentice die on board a British ship during a voyage which is to terminate in the United Kingdom, the master must take charge of the deceased's effects and he may sell these by auction, entering the appropriate particulars in the log-book.[52] The Minister of Transport or the appropriate superintendent must be given an account of the deceased seaman's property (or apprentice's property) by the master,[53] where the death occurs during the voyage. If, on the other hand, death occurs in a foreign port and effects are found in that port it is the duty of the British consular officer (or customs officer) to dispose of these and to account to the Minister of Transport.[54] Section 174 of the Act provides that the Minister of Transport may, where a seaman or apprentice is lost with his ship, recover from the owners the wages accrued in favour of the deceased; and there is a presumption that a ship has been lost with all hands if it has not been heard of for twelve months. If death occurs in the United Kingdom the owner or master must account for any wages or effects to those who are administering the estate.[55] Administration by the Minister of Transport is governed by sections 175–180 of the main Act, as extended in 1906.

The court is given a special power by section 168—during the course of any proceedings relating to any dispute between the owners (or master)

---

47 See Temperley, pp. 146–154.
48 s. 128; see also the 1906 Act, s. 31 (discharge abroad) and s. 65 (2) (withholding of certificate by the Minister).
49 *Vallance* v. *Falle* (1884) 13 Q.B.D. 109.
50 *Downie* v. *Connell*, 1910 S.C. 781; 47 S.L.R. 666.
51 s. 129.
52 s. 169. This provision does not relate to death on wrecks—see *Stephens* v. *Duncan* (1862) 1 M. 146, and s. 174.
53 s. 170; as extended by the 1906 Act, ss. 29 and 59.
54 ss. 172 and 173 (extended by the 1906 Act, s. 29, to British ships whose voyages terminate abroad).
55 s. 175. See also the 1906 Act, s. 29, *re* the British ship terminating a voyage abroad.

of a ship and any seaman or apprentice—to rescind the contract upon any terms which it considers to be just and equitable.

The common law rule that an employee who continues to work in the face of a known danger may not generally be entitled to claim damages against his employer if he suffers injury at work does not appear to have been applied to seamen serving on board ship.[56] The seaman might conceivably undertake responsibility for his own injury at known dangerous work, but it would have to be proved very clearly indeed that he was both *sciens* and *volens*. In any case the safety regulations at sea are such that no seaman could ever be forced to accept personal responsibility in such cases.

The Merchant Shipping (International Labour Convention) Act 1925[57] stipulates that no person under eighteen years of age may be employed as a stoker or trimmer on a British ship registered in the United Kingdom.

There has followed the 1894 and 1906 Acts a considerable body of legislation right down to the present day,[58] which is detailed and specialistic. However, conditions in the shipping industry have been giving cause for concern for some years past and these were highlighted in the nation-wide seamen's strike in 1966. The Minister of Labour[59] appointed a Court of Inquiry on May 26, 1966, under the chairmanship of the Rt. Hon. Lord Pearson, with the following terms of reference:

" To inquire into:

1.   the immediate causes and circumstances of the dispute;
2.   the terms and conditions of service of seamen, taking into account the national interest, technological change and the need for an efficient and competitive shipping industry;
3.   relations between shipowners, officers and seamen;
4.   the law, including the Merchant Shipping Act 1894, relevant to paragraphs 2 and 3 above;

and to report."

The Court of Inquiry issued its First Report in June 1966[60] and made certain recommendations therein.[61] The Final Report[62] was laid before Parliament in February 1967 and it is a fairly substantial document. The specific proposals for revision of the Merchant Shipping Acts are contained in Part II (paras. 154–443) of the Final Report. The most important, in relation to this work, are the proposals governing engagement of seamen (including the Articles of Agreement),[63] termination and formalities

---

[56]   See *Rothwell* v. *Hutchison* (1886) 13 R. 463.
[57]   15 & 16 Geo. 5, c. 42.
[58]   See Temperley, *op. cit.*—Part Two (p. 471 *et seq.*); and supplements.
[59]   Now the Secretary of State for Employment and Productivity (since 1968).
[60]   Cmnd. 3025 (1966).
[61]   See paras. 43, 44 and 45 of the First Report (pp. 17 and 18).
[62]   Cmnd. 3211 (1967).
[63]   Cmnd. 3211 (1967), paras. 225–245.

of discharge,[64] discipline [65] and wages and allotments.[66] The summary [67] of the principal recommendations is most helpful, but it is the general section of the Part II proposals which point the way to new marker buoys in merchant shipping law and industrial relations.

Briefly, the main points from that general section are:

    (a) a newly-drafted Act. Presumably this means a single consolidating statute, in modern form;

    (b) amendment, as required, by Regulations and Orders issued by the Board of Trade;

    (c) many matters should be left to contractual arrangements and industrial negotiations;

    (d) less use of the criminal law and more use of the law of contract;

    (e) where criminal sanctions are still required, they should be imposed, in most cases, upon the employers rather than upon the master.

At the time of writing, no new consolidating statute has, as yet, appeared on the Statute Book. It is anticipated, however, that the new Merchant Shipping Act will emerge in 1970.

(6) *Local Employment, Industrial Organisation and Industrial Training*

(i) *Local Employment Acts.* The main statutes are those of 1960 [68] and 1963,[69] as amended and extended by the Industrial Development Act 1966.[70] The purpose behind these Acts is to deal with the changing emphasis in industrial life and industrial areas from dependence upon the " heavy " industries such as shipbuilding and engineering to the development of and need for " light " industries, particularly in the engineering and general manufacturing fields. That changing emphasis has, of course, resulted in certain areas—particularly in the North East of England and in Wales and Scotland—becoming " depressed areas " in which the incidence of unemployment is usually much higher than the national average figure for unemployment. These two statutes replace earlier post-war legislation relating to distribution of industry.[71] The government department having responsibility in these matters is the Board of Trade.[72] Loans or grants can be made to industrial concerns (or " undertakings ") in any development district, after consultation with an advisory committee appointed by the Board and upon the obtaining of Treasury approval, subject to such terms and conditions, including repayment,[73] as may be

---

64 *Ibid.* paras. 246–267; and 268–280.
65 *Ibid.* paras. 281–341.
66 *Ibid.* paras. 345–390.
67 para. 444 (pp. 122–127).
68 8 & 9 Eliz. 2, c. 18.
69 1963, c. 19.
70 1966, c. 34 (which is a fairly substantial statute dealing, *inter alia*, with investment grants and powers in respect of development areas).
71 See the Distribution of Industry Acts 1945 and 1950.
72 1960 Act, Part I.
73 *Ibid.* s. 3 (as amended by the 1963 Act in respect of grants made after April 3); and s. 4.

attached by the Board of Trade. To facilitate the practical development of these areas referred to above, new Industrial Estates Management Corporations were set up by the 1960 Act—one each for Scotland, England and Wales—which took over the assets, responsibilities and liabilities of the former Industrial Estates companies.[74]

Since 1960 other statutes have been passed which deal with specialist items of industrial expansion and employment—notably the North Atlantic Shipping Act 1961 [75]; the Fort William Pulp and Paper Mills Act 1963 [76]; the Shipbuilding Credit Act 1964 [77]; the Control of Office and Industrial Development Act 1965 [78]; the Industrial Reorganisation Corporation Act 1966 [79]; the Shipbuilding Industry Act 1967 [80]; the Industrial Expansion Act 1968 [81]; and the Highlands and Islands (Development) (Scotland) Acts 1965 and 1968 [82] with regard to the development and promotion of business activities and other activities, contributing to the economic or social expansion of the Highlands and Islands, as controlled by the Highlands and Islands Development Board.

(ii) *Industrial organisation and training.* By a statute of 1947—namely, the Industrial Organisation and Development Act 1947 [83]—private industry was enabled to obtain financial assistance for modernisation and reorganisation, through the aegis of a development council established within any particular industry [84] by the Secretary of State for Scotland or by other government departments concerned in England and Wales. Several of such councils have been created.[85] Levies may be imposed to meet the expenses of the councils.[86]

Another important statute is the Employment and Training Act 1948,[87] which is designed to assist persons to obtain and train for employment in accordance with their own wishes and to encourage and develop employment in particular areas as required to maintain the economic life of the communities involved. The Act continues the system of employment exchanges (originally called " labour exchanges " or by other more popular and less technical terms). Training courses may be provided through the aegis of the Ministry of Labour (now the Department of Employment and Productivity) for those persons who are above school

[74] *Ibid.* ss. 8–12.
[75] 9 & 10 Eliz. 2, c. 53; authorising the Minister of Transport to advance on loan to Cunard White Star Limited a sum of £18 million for the building of a large ocean liner for the North Atlantic shipping trade.
[76] 1963, c. 15.
[77] 1964, c. 7.
[78] 1965, c. 33 (which, *inter alia*, modifies the exemptions contained in s. 19 of the Local Employment Act 1960 as regards Scotland).
[79] 1966. c. 50.
[80] 1967, c. 40; amended *re* s. 7 by the Shipbuilding Industry Act 1969 (c. 6).
[81] 1968, c. 32.
[82] 1965, c. 46, and 1968, c. 51.
[83] 10 & 11 Geo. 6, c. 40.
[84] The functions of such a council are specified in the First Schedule to the Act.
[85] Notably in the furniture, clothing, jewellery and silverware trades or industries.
[86] 1947 Act, s. 4.
[87] 11 & 12 Geo. 6, c. 46.

age,[88] whether or not they are in employment at the time.[89] The Act also makes provision for a Youth Employment Service,[90] with a National Council and, in the case of Scotland, an Advisory Committee on Youth Employment to advise the council on matters relating to Scotland [91]; that Advisory Committee being appointed in terms of paragraph 3 of the First Schedule (Part I) to the Act.

The most recent statute of importance in the field of industrial training and employment is the Industrial Training Act 1964,[92] which makes further provision for industrial and commercial training and raises the limit on contributions out of the National Insurance Fund towards the expenses of the Minister of Labour [93] in providing training courses. The Act formally gives powers to the Minister to establish industrial training boards [94] and specifies,[95] at some length, the functions of an industrial training board. These boards may appoint committees [96] (including joint committees where more than one board is involved) and delegate to such committees some or all of the functions conferred upon the boards themselves.

In order to finance its expenses and outgoings an industrial training board may, from time to time, and in accordance with an order made by the Minister impose a levy upon employers in the industry other than those (if any) who are exempted by the levy order or the industrial training order.[97] Grants and loans to the industrial training boards are governed by section 5, and these grants or loans may either be made by the Minister (now the Secretary of State) out of moneys provided by Parliament [98] or approval may be given by the Minister to loans or overdrafts obtained

---

88 See the Education (Scotland) Act 1946, s. 32, and subsequent legislation.
89 See *ibid.* s. 3; and s. 4 (the secondment or attachment of training officers from the Ministry).
90 *Ibid.* Part II. S. 9 deals with the appointment of Youth Employment Committees.
91 See s. 8 and Sched. 1 (Part II—*re* constitution and functions).
92 1964, c. 16.
93 Now the Secretary of State for Employment and Productivity.
94 *Ibid.* s. 1.
95 *Ibid.* s. 2, which must be read along with s. 7.
96 *Ibid.* s. 3 (1).
97 The operative section is s. 4, which reads as follows:
   " 4.—(1) For the purpose of raising money towards meeting its expenses an industrial training board shall from time to time impose, in accordance with an order made by the Minister (in this section referred to as a levy order), a levy on employers in the industry, other than such (if any) as may be exempted by the levy order or the industrial training order.
   (2) A levy order shall give effect to proposals submitted to and approved by the Minister under section 7 of this Act, and such proposals may provide for the amendment of a previous levy order and may make different provision in relation to different classes or descriptions of employer.
   (3) A levy order may contain provisions as to the evidence by which a person's liability to the levy or his discharge of that liability may be established and as to the time at which any amount payable by any person by way of the levy shall become due and recoverable by the industrial training board, and shall give any person assessed to the levy a right of appeal to an appeal tribunal constituted under this Act.
   (4) The power to make a levy order shall be exercisable by statutory instrument, which shall be subject to annulment in pursuance of a resolution of either House of Parliament."
98 *Ibid.* s. 5 (1).

from elsewhere,[99] subject to the giving of valid security. The powers enabling the Minister (or those duly authorised by him) to obtain information from employers concerned in a particular industry for which a training board has been established and to require those same employers to keep records and make returns are set forth at some length in section 6. Proper accounts and records must be maintained and an annual Statement of Account (in a form approved by the Minister) must be submitted by every training board.[1]

Section 7 is one of the more important of the statutory provisions— dealing therein with proposals for the exercise of the board's functions and for levies. Every industrial training board is required from time to time, and whenever directed by the Minister, to submit for approval:

(a) proposals for the exercise of those functions conferred by section 2 of the Act; and for the establishment of committees under section 3 (to whom certain functions or all functions may be delegated); and

(b) proposals for the raising and collection of a levy.[2]

Failure to comply with the order of the Minister may result in the board being declared to be in default[3] and the board members must then vacate their offices and will be replaced by new members.[4] If the initial proposals are unsatisfactory the Minister may, under section 7 (2), require a fresh submission to be made.

Industrial training orders may be amended or revoked in accordance with the provisions set forth in section 9. Where an accident happens to an insured person[5] attending a course or availing himself of any other facility provided by a training board then the relevant sections numbers 7, 8 and 9 (formerly sections 8, 9 and 10 of the 1946 Act) of the National Insurance (Industrial Injuries) Act 1965 will apply (since these sections make provision for certain accidents arising out of and in the course of an insured's person's employment), subject to the modifications specified in section 10[6] of the 1964 Act.

The Central Training Council is established by section 11, with the declared duty of advising the Minister upon the exercise of his functions under the Act and on any other matter relating to industrial or commercial training.[7] The actual composition of the Council in section 11 (2) and the total possible membership thereof is thirty-three persons (including the chairman). Appeal tribunals to determine appeals from persons assessed to any levy imposed by the Act could be created by regulations made by the Minister, under the provisions of section 12. These matters are now

---

[99] *Ibid.* s. 5 (2).
[1] *Ibid.* s. 8. These accounts must be audited by qualified persons (which includes a Scottish firm whose partners are qualified for appointment)—s. 8 (2).
[2] *Ibid.* s. 7 (1).
[3] *Ibid.* s. 7 (2).
[4] *Ibid.* s. 7 (3).
[5] Now within the meaning of the National Insurance (Industrial Injuries) Act 1965.
[6] *Vide* s. 10 of the 1964 Act, subss. (2), (3) and (4).
[7] *Vide* s. 11 (1).

dealt with by the Industrial Tribunals and certain case decisions are referred to hereafter.

The cotton industry is specially provided for,[8] as is training for employment overseas.[9] The paid chairman of an industrial training board constituted under the 1964 Act, or of a committee appointed under that Act or a paid deputy chairman of such a board is disqualified from membership of the House of Commons.[10] The education authorities in Scotland in relation to facilities for further education may provide facilities for vocational and industrial training.[11] The Act received the Royal Assent on March 12, 1964, and came into force on that day.

Initially there was a substantial build-up of cases [12] coming before the Industrial Tribunals, but now the volume of appeals is tapering off as the various training boards appreciate the impact and meaning of the early decisions. A selection of the Scottish appeals [13] follows immediately hereafter and reference has been made, on occasion, to decisions in England which appear to be of interest and importance. The following Scottish decisions are considered to be helpful, viz.: (1) *Robert Nixon and Sons (Saltcoats) Limited* v. *The Construction Industry Training Board*,[14] where a small part of the appellant company's business was within the construction industry but the main part was not. It was held that the company was not liable to assessment to levy; (2) *Hallside Nail Company Ltd.* v. *The Engineering Industry Board*.[15] The company sold its undertaking on August 6, 1965, and changed its name. It was held liable to pay the levy imposed under the Industrial Training Levy (Engineering) Order 1965 (effective June 30, 1965), although the assessment would be amended in view of the change of name; (3) *Clydesdale Excavating and Construction Company Limited* v. *The Construction Industry Training Board*,[16] where certain activities of the appellant company were outwith the scope of the industry whilst others were within it, but as the appellants had failed to show that they were not within the industry they were liable to levy; (4) *Neilson Hollands Limited* v. *The Construction Industry Training Board*,[17] wherein it was held that a small builder engaged mostly in repair work but who did some building, chimney-sweeping and gardening, was engaged within the construction industry; (5) *Extol Engineering (Scotland) Limited* v. *The Construction Industry Training Board* [18]—the erection of signs on a building (defined in the Industrial Training (Construction Board) Order 1964) is an activity within the construction industry; (6)

---

[8] *Vide* s. 13.   [9] s. 14.
[10] House of Commons Disqualification Act 1957, Sched. 1, Part III, as amended by s. 15 of the Industrial Training Act 1964.
[11] Education (Scotland) Act 1962, s. 1, read along with the Industrial Training Act 1964, s. 16.
[12] See, for example, K.I.R., Vol. I.
[13] The Chairman of the Industrial Tribunal for Scotland is Mr. Robert Reid, Q.C.
[14] (January 6, 1966). I K.I.R. 75.
[15] (July 28, 1966). I K.I.R. 501.   [16] (June 6, 1966). I K.I.R. 359.
[17] (December 6, 1965). I K.I.R. 249. See also *John Rutherford and Sons Ltd.* v. *The Engineering Industry Training Board*, I K.I.R. 500.
[18] (December 20, 1965) I K.I.R. 72.

J. Grindlay and Company Limited v. *The Engineering Industry Training Board* [19]—cleaning of steel pipes and girders for manufacturers and painting and spraying of metal thereon are all activities of the engineering industry. *Whiteinch Galvanizing Company Limited* v. *The Engineering Industry Training Board* [20]—galvanizing is an activity within the industry; but the manufacture of fire-proof doors, mainly of wood, is not,[21] nor is the recovery of non-ferrous scrap metal [22]; (7) *J. Bisset & Sons Ltd. (In Liquidation)* v. *The Engineering Industry Training Board* [23]—a company in liquidation is liable to pay any levy assessed upon it after commencement of the liquidation and no reduction can be made. A holding company with a large number of interests in other subsidiary companies is also liable to levy.[24] In deciding whether an establishment is wholly or mainly engaged in an activity within a specific industry one must look at the time spent by and wages paid to employees in respect of each activity (and not to sales, turnover or profitability).[25] (8) In *Alexander Jack & Sons Ltd.* v. *The Engineering Industry Training Board*,[26] the appellants sought a reduction in the amount of levy on the plea that they were engaged in assessable activities for a part only of the first levy period, but their claim was disallowed. (9) The manufacture of fibreglass canoes at an inland factory (no access to sea or river) had been held, in England, not to be an activity within the shipbuilding industry.[27] (10) Where an assessment to levy had been made upon a company and that company's undertaking had been sold before the end of the " first levy period " to another company (the appellants), from whom the training board was now seeking payment, the tribunal has held that there is no liability upon the purchasers to pay the levy.[28] Wages or salary paid to company directors should be included as " emoluments " in any return made by a company in relation to assessment for levy.[29] It is vital to note that a training board does not have the power to extend the time limit for an appeal against an assessment to levy where that time limit has expired and, furthermore, an Industrial Tribunal cannot extend the time limit either, even although all interested parties purport to consent to such an extension.[30]

(7) *National Insurance (Industrial Injuries)*

The National Insurance (Industrial Injuries) Scheme is the present-day

[19] (July 27, 1966) I K.I.R. 501.
[20] (September 20, 1966) I K.I.R. 794.
[21] *Watson Brothers (Fire Protection Engineers) Ltd.*, I K.I.R. 501.
[22] *McLeod and Sons*, I K.I.R. 501.
[23] (January 23, 1967) II K.I.R. 509. Nor was a reduction in levy allowable.
[24] *Solar Industries Ltd.* v. *The Engineering Industry Training Board*, II K.I.R. 895.
[25] *H. Churchill & Sons Ltd.* v. *The Engineering Industry Training Board*, II K.I.R. 687.
[26] II K.I.R. 509.
[27] *Streamlyte Mouldings (Marine) Ltd.* v. *The Shipbuilding Industry Training Board*, III K.I.R. 481.
[28] *Tangye and Shelley Limited* v. *The Engineering Industry Training Board*, IV K.I.R. 289.
[29] See *Oak Filling Station Company (Hollinwood) Limited* v. *The Road Transport Industry Training Board*, V K.I.R. 26
[30] *T .& J. Shaw Limited* v. *Road Transport Industry Training Board*, V K.I.R. 145.

successor to the older Workmen's Compensation Scheme which was governed by statutes ranging from 1897 to 1925.[31] A huge volume of case-law was built around these statutes,[32] quite unintended by and unexpected to the legislators of the time, but caused by the persistent pressures of the insurance companies. At that time an employer was liable to pay compensation—subject however to certain qualifications imposed by statute—where personal injury by accident arising " out of and in the course of the employment " was caused to a workman.[33] These statutes applied to certain kinds of workmen only—those employed in dangerous forms of employment, namely, factories, mines and quarries, railways and engineering and certain building construction works and constituted the first statutory attempt to alleviate the hardships in which injured workmen found themselves. Although the common law had evolved and developed a general duty of care [34] towards employees it was very often difficult for a workman to succeed in a common law action because of the defences of contributory negligence, common employment and *volenti non fit injuria,* all of which operated in the employer's favour against the workman. What the statutes did was to impose a personal liability upon the employer to pay. The statutory claim was a " last chance " effort by the workman and the sum which he received was never substantial. The Workmen's Compensation Scheme was replaced in 1948 by a new National Insurance (Industrial Injuries) Scheme [35] which received statutory authorisation in the National Insurance (Industrial Injuries) Act 1946.[36] That Act was amended from time to time on many occasions and the whole operative statutes were consolidated by the National Insurance (Industrial Injuries) Act 1965.[37] There is little text-book material upon the 1946 legislation [38] and amending statutes, but

---

[31] The following were the statutes, which had applied, *viz.*: The Workmen's Compensation Act 1897 (60 & 61 Vict. c. 37); followed by others in 1900, 1906 (a consolidating Act), 1909, 1911, 1918, 1919, 1923 and the consolidating Act of 1925 (15 & 16 Geo. 5, c. 84), with subsequent amendments in 1926, 1927, 1930, 1931, 1934, 1938, 1940, 1941, 1943 and 1945.

[32] See the *Workmen's Compensation Cases 1907–1947* (published by Butterworths of London).

[33] See the 1925 Act, s. 1 (1).

[34] See *supra* Part A of this chapter.

[35] For a valuable note on the background to the National Insurance (Industrial Injuries) Act 1946 see Potter, D. and Stansfeld, D. H., *National Insurance (Industrial Injuries)* (2nd ed., 1950—Butterworth, London)—General Introduction, Part I.

[36] 9 & 10 Geo. 6, c. 67.

[37] 1965, c. 52 (which became effective on September 6, 1965), which has also been amended —see the National Insurance (Industrial Injuries) (Amendment) Act 1967 (c. 25); and the Industrial Injuries and Diseases (Old Cases) Act 1967 (c. 34), which continues workmen's compensation in certain cases and introduces schemes for supplementation of workmen's compensation; the National Insurance, etc., Act 1969 (c. 4) and the National Insurance Act, 1969 (c. 44), which increases rates of contributions and certain rates of benefits obtainable.

[38] See Potter and Stansfeld, *op. cit.,* which is the main reference work but which is now very much dated; see also the very useful work by Vester (Horatio) and Cartwright (Hilary Ann) *Industrial Industries* (1961) which covers the statute law from 1946 to 1960 (this is a short two-volume work—the second volume containing summaries of decisions relevant to the main text in volume one); also *The Modern Law of Employment* by G.H.L. Fridman (Stevens; 1963) with Second Supplement to December 31, 1966, at Chap. 39 and as brought down to 1966 in the supplement; also *The Law of Master and*

once again a large number of decisions—mainly by the Insurance Commissioner—have been built around that legislation and are being built around the 1965 Act and its own amending legislation. It is proposed to examine the broad scope of the 1965 Act, along with those decisions—preferably since 1965, but not necessarily restricted to that period—which are considered to be important. Certain statutory instruments issued prior to and subsequent to 1965 may have to be referred to from time to time.

Subsection (1) of section 1 lays down the basic statutory position of insured persons, *viz.*: " Subject to the provisions of this Act, all persons employed in insurable employment shall be insured in manner provided by this Act against personal injury . . . by accident arising out of and in the course of such employment." The insurable employments are specified in Part I of Schedule 1 and the excepted employments are contained in Part II thereof. Part I comprises thirteen types of " insurable employment," of which the first example is the most general in its application—namely, " Employment in Great Britain under any contract of service or apprenticeship, whether written or oral, and whether expressed or implied. . . ." The remaining examples relate to employment on board ship, in various stated capacities; as a pilot on board ship; as lifeboat crew; employment on board aircraft (again in certain stated capacities); employment in Great Britain with a public or local authority; employment in plying for hire with any vehicle or vessel (in Scotland, a contract of letting to hire) for payment of a fixed sum as remuneration or a share of earnings or otherwise; and finally employment as a member or trainee member of any fire brigade, rescue brigade, first-aid party or salvage party at a factory, mine or works as may be prescribed, or of any similar organisation as may be prescribed.

The test of the " contract of service " has been discussed earlier [39] and it was again applied, for insurance purposes, in *A.E.U.* v. *Minister of Pensions and National Insurance*.[40] In this case it was held that a trade union sick steward was employed under a contract of service, although the union itself did not have a right expressly to control the steward as to the way in which he did his work. It has arisen once again in the quite recent case of *Readymixed Concrete (South East)* v. *Minister of Pensions and National Insurance*,[41] wherein the person in question was held to be an independent contractor. It was observed however that a contract of service exists if three conditions are fulfilled, *viz.*: (i) the employee agrees

---

Servant by F. R. Batt (5th ed. by Dr. G. J. Webber), Chaps. XIII and XIV, both of which are extremely valuable, particularly in respect of those decisions arising before the Commissioner, up to the year 1965; and, Gloag and Henderson, *Introduction to the Law of Scotland* (7th ed., 1968) Chap. XXI, pp. 247–252.

[39] *Supra*, Chaps. 2 and 3.
[40] [1963] 1 W.L.R. 441, *per* Megaw J. at p. 454: " . . . a contract is a contract of service if it provides for employment of one person by another person."
[41] [1968] 2 W.L.R. 775; and see also [1968] 1 All E.R. 433; *sub nom. Readymixed Concrete (South East)* v. *Minister of Pensions and National Insurance; Minister of Social Security* v. *Greenham Ready Mixed Concrete; Minister of Social Security* v. *Ready Mixed Concrete (South East)*.

in consideration of a wage or other remuneration to provide his own work and skill in the performance of some service for the employer; (ii) he agrees, expressly or impliedly, to be subject to the control of the other as master (or employer); and (iii) the remaining provisions of the contract are consistent with its being a contract of service.

The "excepted employments" are listed in Part II of Schedule 1 and are nine in number or groups, being closely related to the Part I list. There are certain additions to the pattern—namely, employment in the service of the husband or wife of the employed person,[42] employment in certain other specified "family relationships"[43] and certain subsidiary employments prescribed by the Treasury[44] and certain part-time employments.[45] The Act applies to the Crown,[46] subject to such modifications as may be made by Order in Council, but it does not apply to employment in the naval, military or air force services or other prescribed employments under the Crown, all of which are classified as "excepted employments." Special regulations may be made in relation to mariners or airmen.[47] The Act also applies to members of a police force within the meaning of the Police Act 1964 or the Police (Scotland) Act 1956 and persons employed in any other prescribed employment, being employment in respect of which benefits are payable under the Police Pensions Act 1948, subject to such modifications as may be prescribed.[48]

Any insured person who suffers personal injury[49] caused by an accident arising out of and in the course of his employment[50] is entitled to certain benefits as specified in the Act and dealt with hereafter. An insured person who contracts any prescribed disease or any prescribed personal injury not so caused by accident but being a disease or injury attributable to the nature of the employment[51] is also entitled to certain benefits. The terms "personal injury"[52] and "accident" are not defined in the 1965 Act, nor were they defined in the earlier legislation. The important element is the injury—arising "by accident," i.e., in the ordinary sense of something quite unlooked for, or quite unexpected and not foreseen.[53] Where it is being alleged that a disease constituted the real ground of claim it must be shown (a) to have arisen "by accident"—i.e., immediately as distinct from being a protracted development occurring over

---

[42] See Sched. 1, Part II, para. 6.
[43] Ibid. para. 7 (employment in a private dwelling-house and not employment for the purposes of any trade or business carried on there).
[44] Ibid. paras. 8 and 9.
[45] See S.I. 1948 No. 1457 (Part II of Sched. 1); S.I. 1950 No. 1468.
[46] s. 74.
[47] s. 75.
[48] s. 77. See the Police (Scotland) Act 1967 (c. 77) s. 52 and Schedule 4.
[49] i.e., physical or physiological injury to the living body of a human being.
[50] s. 1 (1).
[51] s. 56 (1).
[52] Interpreted as meaning "injury to the living body of a human being "—R.(I) 7/56.
[53] C.I. 257/49; C.I. 123/49; and Stewart v. Wilsons & Clyde Coal Co. (1902) 5 F. 120; 7 S.L.T. 99, per Lord M'Laren, viz.: "If a workman in the reasonable performance of his duties sustains a physiological injury as the result of the work he is engaged in . . . this is an accidental injury in the sense of the statute."

many years which is ultimately responsible for the employee's disablement and inability to work [54]; and (b) to be causally connected with some external occurrence.[55] Even suicide might be regarded, in the appropriate circumstances, as being the result of an " accident," but the interval between the original injury and the resulting suicide should not be over-long, otherwise the causal link has become very tenuous indeed and it may not be possible to prove that it does in fact exist.[56] Several cases (particularly during the earlier days of workmen's compensation) have been based upon situations where one person assaults another person, both being fellow-employees, or an employee is assaulted by a stranger whilst the former is carrying out his normal duties. These cases will come within the " accident " classification so long as the injured person is carrying out his normal duties (i.e., the scope of employment test) [57] or the risk is incidental to the employment or the injured person was acting upon instructions given to him by his employer when the assault occurred.[58] However, the wording of section 10 of the 1965 Act [59] is now most important in relation to any accident arising within the course of employ-ment which is in fact caused by another person's misconduct.[60] The section is in the following terms, viz.:

" 10. An accident happening after 19th December 1961 shall be treated for the purposes of this Act, where it would not apart from this section be so treated, as arising out of a person's employment if—

(a) the accident arises in the course of the employment; and

(b) the accident either is caused by another person's misconduct, skylarking or negligence, or by steps taken in consequence of any such misconduct, skylarking or negligence, or by the behaviour or presence of an animal (including a bird, fish or insect), or is caused by or consists in the insured person being struck by any object or by lightning; and

(c) the insured person did not directly or indirectly induce or contribute to the happening of the accident by his conduct outside the employment or by any act not incidental to the employment."

It will be seen immediately that the section also covers any injury suffered at work although the accident was not connected with the work itself.[61]

[54] See Batt, op. cit., pp. 499–500.
[55] Batt, op. cit., p. 501 and n. (2) thereof, for many examples.
[56] Batt, op. cit., pp. 501–502 and examples cited thereat.
[57] St. Helens Colliery Co. v. Hewitson [1924] A.C. 59 (per Lord Atkinson at p. 71).
[58] The cases are numerous—see, in illustration of the rule: Trim Joint District School Board of Management v. Kelly [1914] A.C. 667; 30 T.L.R. 452; 7 B.W.C.C. 274 and Smith v. Stepney Corporation (1929) 22 B.W.C.C. 451 (lavatory attendant assaulted by a customer).
[59] Which re-enacts s. 2 of the Family Allowances and National Insurance Act 1961.
[60] " Skylarking " is now included within the operation of s. 10—see para. (b) thereof.
[61] See s. 10, para. (b), which, after referring to misconduct, skylarking or negligence, goes on to mention an accident caused by the behaviour or presence of an animal (including a bird, fish or insect) or where the insured person is struck by any object or

Many of the earlier cases upon these matters which arose in the days of Workmen's Compensation must now be disregarded, as they have been overtaken by the new statutory provisions.

Sandwiched between section 6 (which contains the general presumption before-mentioned) and section 10 are three very important sections which attempt to clarify the old law. Section 7 provides that an accident shall be deemed to arise out of and in the course of an insured person's employment, notwithstanding his contravening any statutory or other regulation applicable to the employment or any order of his employer or even his acting without instructions, if—(a) the accident would have been deemed so to have arisen had the act not been done in contravention or without instructions and (b) the act was so done for the purposes of and in connection with the employer's business.

Section 8 deals with the case of the insured person suffering an accident whilst travelling as a passenger in his employer's transport to or from his place of work—and with the express or implied permission of his employer. In such a case the accident is deemed to arise out of and in the course of employment, notwithstanding that the insured person was under no obligation so to travel, if—(a) the accident would have been deemed so to have arisen had he been under such an obligation; and (b) at the time of the accident the vehicle (i) is being operated by or on behalf of the employer or some other person by whom it is provided in pursuance of arrangements made with the employer; and (ii) it is not being operated in the ordinary course of a public transport service.

The accident happening in the course of an emergency is governed by section 9. Where it happens in or about premises at which the insured person is employed for the time being for purposes of his employer's trade or business then it shall be deemed to arise out of and in the course of his employment if it so happens while he is taking steps, upon an actual or supposed emergency at the premises, to rescue, succour or protect persons who are, or are thought to be or possibly to be, injured or imperilled, or to avert or minimise serious damage to property.

The benefits obtainable under the Act are three in number, viz.:

 (a) Injury benefit.[62]
 (b) Disablement benefit (or disablement pension or disablement gratuity).[63]
 (c) Death Benefit.[64]

Injury benefit is payable for a period of 156 days, beginning with the day of the accident, subject however to the customary " three days waiting time." [65] All rates of benefit payable under the Act are fully set forth in

---

by lightning. The insured person must not have contributed to the accident (either directly or indirectly) by his conduct outside of the employment or by any act not incidental to the employment (for the terms of this final sentence see para. (c) of s. 10).

[62] s. 11. See also the National Insurance Act, 1969 (c. 44) re increase in benefit.

[63] s. 12. See also the National Insurance Act, 1969 (c. 44) re increase in benefit.

[64] s. 19 (payable to a widow upon the terms and conditions stated herein); and s. 20 (payable to a widower upon the terms and conditions stated therein).

[65] See s. 11 (1) as to the condition to be fulfilled to enable this period to be counted.

Schedule 3 (containing twelve paragraphs and covering benefits and supplementary payments and allowances which may be payable in the appropriate circumstances). These rates are, of course, subject to variation from time to time.

Before a claim for disablement benefit is dealt with it is necessary that there should be an assessment of the disablement in terms of section 12 and Schedule 4 to the Act, read along with the National Insurance (Industrial Injuries) (Benefit) Regulations 1964.[66] If the degree of assessment is less than 20 per cent. the payment is a once-for-all " disablement gratuity." If more than 19 per cent. (in fact, 20 per cent. and above) the benefit becomes a " disablement pension " payable as indicated in the third paragraph of Schedule 3 to the Act. It should be noted that certain supplements or additional allowances may be obtained in accordance with the terms of sections 13 to 18 of the 1965 Act read along with Schedule 3, viz.:

(a) by section 13 and paragraph 4 of Schedule 3—an increase of disablement pension by reason of unemployability;

(b) by section 14 and paragraph 5, an increase of pension in cases of special hardship;

(c) by section 15 and paragraph 6, an increase of pension where constant attendance is needed;

(d) by section 16 an increase of disablement benefit during hospital treatment;

(e) by section 17 and paragraph 7 of Schedule 3 an increase of injury benefit or disablement pension in respect of children;

(f) by section 18 and paragraph 8, an increase of injury benefit or disablement pension in respect of adult dependants.

Industrial death benefit is payable to the persons stipulated in section 19 (widow), section 20 (widower), section 21 (children of deceased's family), section 22 (parents), section 23 (relatives) and section 24 (women having care of deceased's children).

The obligations of employers are stipulated in section 26, viz.:

(a) to make reports of accidents in respect of which benefit may be payable (in such form as may be prescribed);

(b) to furnish any information required for the determination of claims or of questions arising in connection with claims or awards (to the prescribed person);

(c) to take such other steps as may be prescribed to facilitate the giving notice of accidents, the making of claims and the determination of claims and of questions arising as above.

Part III (ss. 35–55) relates to the matter of determination of questions and claims. The Secretary of State (formerly the Minister) has, subject

---

[66] S.I. 1964 No. 504. The Second Schedule gives the table of prescribed degrees of disablement from 1 per cent. to 100 per cent. The Third Schedule gives the scale of disablement gratuities (ranging from £38 (1 per cent.) to £380 (19 per cent.)).

to the provisions contained in Part III, the right to determine any of the following questions [67]:

(a) whether a person is or was employed in insurable employment;

(b) whether a person so employed or his employer is or was exempt from payment of contributions as provided in Part II of Schedule 2 to the Act;

(c) who is or was liable for payment of contributions as the employer of any insured person;

(d) at what rate contributions are or were payable by or in respect of any person or class of persons;

(e) whether any employment is or was one in respect of which contributions are or were payable in accordance with regulations under section 2 (2) of the Act;

(f) whether an increase of disablement pension in respect of the need of constant attendance is to be granted or renewed and, if so, for what period and of what amount;

(g) how the limitations under Schedule 5 to the Act on the benefit payable in respect of any death are to be applied in the circumstances of any case.

An appeal or a reference to the Court of Session on a question of law arising from any of the questions contained in paragraphs (a) to (e) above is permitted by subsection (3) of section 35, in the same way as was authorised by section 65 of the National Insurance Act 1965.[68]

Disablement questions [69] are determined [70] by a medical board or a medical appeal tribunal, as appointed by the Minister.[71] The appeals and references procedure from board to tribunal is set forth in section 39. Appeals and references from any decision [72] of a medical appeal tribunal, upon the ground that the decision is erroneous in point of law, lie to the Industrial Injuries Commissioner [73] and may be taken or made by (i) the claimant or (ii) an association of employed persons of which the claimant

---

[67] See s. 35 (1).

[68] 1965, c. 51.

[69] The two disablement questions (see s. 37) are:
    (a) whether the relevant accident has resulted in a loss of faculty;
    (b) at what degree the extent of disablement resulting from a loss of faculty is to be assessed, and what period is to be taken into account by the assessment.

[70] See particularly ss. 37, 39 and 40; with which must be read the National Insurance (Industrial Injuries) (Determination of Claims and Questions) Amendment Regulations 1967 (No. 153), commencing February 20, 1967, and amending S.I. 1948 No. 1299.

[71] See s. 38 for the constitution of each.

[72] Any decision given after September 27, 1959.

[73] See s. 42; and illustrated, in Scotland, by Decisions Nos. R. (I.) 7/65; R. (I.) 9/65; and generally, by Decisions Nos. R. (I.) 3/66; R. (I.) 12/66; R. (I.) 14/66; R. (I.) 16/66 was subsequently *quashed* by the House of Lords *sub nom. R.* v. *Amalgamated Engineering Union ex p. Dowling* (Lord Hodson's speech is most instructive); also Decisions Nos. R. (I.) 17/66; R. (I.) 6/67; R. (I.) 7/67; R. (I.) 3/68; and R. (I.) 4/68; R. (I.) 5/68 and R. (I.) 10/68 (in each case the Commissioner held that the decision of the Medical Appeal Tribunal was not erroneous in law); and R. (I.) 11/68 (a decision in which the Medical Appeal Tribunal's finding was held to be erroneous in law; the opinions of the Chief Commissioner and the two Commissioners who sat with him being extremely interesting). See also R. (I.) 14/68, (the decision of the Commissioner being quashed by the Court of Appeal *sub nom. R.* v. *Deputy Industrial Injuries Commissioner ex p. Thomas Howarth*).

was a member at the time of the accident or (iii) the Secretary of State, but upon the conditions contained in subsection (2) of section 42 (the main one being that leave of the tribunal or of the commissioner is required). The Medical Appeal Tribunal may itself refer [74] any question of law which arises in a case before it to the Commissioner for his decision.

The determination of claims and questions by the insurance officers, by local appeal tribunals [75] or by the Commissioner (*i.e.*, the Industrial Injuries Commissioner) can be found in sections 44 to 49, both inclusive. The procedure relating to the insurance officers is explained in section 44.[76] An appeal lies from a decision of the insurance officer to a local appeal tribunal.[77] Moreover, within a period of three months (or other prescribed period), an appeal may be taken to the Industrial Injuries Commissioner [78] from any decision of a local appeal tribunal, at the instance of:

(a) an insurance officer;

(b) a claimant or beneficiary or a person whose right to benefit is or may be (under Schedule 5) affected by the decision appealed against; or

(c) an association of employed persons of which the claimant or beneficiary or, in a case relating to death benefit, the deceased was a member at the time of the relevant accident.[79]

Part V (ss. 59–70) covers matters of finance, administration and legal proceedings. For example, section 59 continues the control and management of the Industrial Injuries Fund in the hands of the Secretary of State, whilst sections 62,[79a] 63 and 64 deal respectively with the Industrial Injuries Advisory Council, local advisory committees and inspectors. Methods of payment of contributions are governed by section 67 and here the procedure is equated with that under the National Insurance Act 1965. The same device is adopted in respect of legal proceedings by a reference back to sections 93 (offences and penalties), 94 (prosecutions) and 96 (civil proceedings for recovery of sums due) of the National Insurance Act 1965, as extended by sections 69 and 70 of the Industrial Injuries Act 1965. Offences under section 93 (1) are prosecuted summarily and the maximum penalty is a fine of one hundred pounds or a term of imprisonment of three months. Certain offences against regulations carry a lighter penalty (usually a fine of ten pounds) under subsection (2) of section 93 and the appropriate regulations. Proceedings in Scotland are brought in the ordinary way—through the Crown Office (the Lord Advocate bearing the primary responsibility) and the procurator-fiscal's office of the sheriff court in which the prosecution is being brought.

[74] s. 42 (3).
[75] Constituted under s. 51 of the Act.
[76] Read along with s. 48 (2) (*b*) of the National Insurance Act 1965.
[77] s. 45.
[78] For the provisions governing the appointment and payment of the Industrial Injuries Commissioner, Deputy Commissioners, assessors and others, see ss. 52 and 53.
[79] s. 46 (1) (2).
[79a] Amended by the National Insurance, etc., Act 1969 (c. 4), s. 3 (1) *re* regulations made under s. 3 (2) of that Act.

The interpretation section is section 86. The Act applies to Scotland without modification and it came into force on the same day as the National Insurance Act 1965.[80]

The decisions of the Industrial Injuries Commissioner are published by H.M. Stationery Office.[81] It is not considered necessary, in view of the 1965 consolidating legislation, to attempt an exhaustive catalogue and examination of those decisions prior to 1965, but it will certainly be necessary to look at certain decisions arising during and since 1965 for guidance upon some very important points which have been considered, whether by the Commissioner or by the courts of law. For example, (i) it has been held that where an accident happens during an extended break in employment, it does not arise out of and in the course of insurable employment [82]; (2) although deceased's death may be clearly caused by his employment it is necessary to show that there was personal injury " by accident " [83]; (3) the accident has been held to arise out of and in the course of insurable employment where a fireman was playing volleyball during a waiting period (which was, in fact, used as a recreational period within the daily routine of employment) [84]; (4) where an accident happens during a journey preparatory to performance of work which a home help was employed to do, this is not an accident which arises out of and in the course of employment [85]; (5) where an accident happens during a short break in employment (in this case, an interval for smoking in the corridor, as permitted by the employer), this does not mean that the accident is not an industrial accident arising out of and in the course of employment [86]; (6) if an accident happens when claimant is using a legitimate means of access to his place of work (e.g., by a beaten path, which was not a public road or a right of way) and his employers have knowledge of the position, then it (the accident) arises out of and in the course of employment [87]; (7) in a case [88] based on the Industrial Injuries and Diseases (Old Cases) Act 1967, where a former coal miner disabled by pneumoconiosis during his working life died from lung cancer, it was held as follows: (a) failure to diagnose

[80] See s. 88 (3) of the Industrial Injuries Act 1965. The operative date was, in fact, September 6, 1965 (see the National Insurance Act 1965 (Commencement) Order 1965 (No. 1650)).

[81] In fact, four volumes of decisions have now been issued, the last two volumes preceding the 1965 legislation and dealing with the years 1957–60 (Vol. III) and 1961–64 (Vol. IV). Since then the decisions have been published separately, the next bound volume probably being available in 1970 for the years 1965–68.

[82] Decision R. (I.) 4/66 (the Court of Appeal in England subsequently heard an application for an order of certiorari to quash the Commissioner's decision but dismissed it—see R. v. Industrial Injuries Commissioner, ex p. Amalgamated Engineering Union (No. 2) [1966] 1 All E.R. 97; [1966] 2 W.L.R. 97.

[83] Decision R. (I.) 7/66; R. (I.) 8/66.

[84] Decision R. (I.) 13/66. It was not necessary to prove that the employee was carrying out specific instructions or doing something expressly stipulated by the contract of employment; and claimant's accident was not automatically and as a matter of law taken outwith the statute because his superior officers had not ordered him directly to play volleyball.

[85] Decision R. (I.) 2/67.

[86] Decisions R. (I.) 3/67; R. (I.) 4/67.

[87] Decision R. (I.) 5/67 (a railway shunter injured on way to work); see also R. (I.) 1/68.

[88] Decision R. (I.) 9/67.

cancer earlier was due to its masking by pneumoconiosis, (b) had it been possible to operate it was probable that deceased would have lived longer, (c) pneumoconiosis was not the primary cause of death but it contributed to or precipitated death by making treatment impossible and (d) death was the result of pneumoconiosis (which is a prescribed disease); (8) if an accident happens to the claimant when he is attending a day-release class at a Technical College with the permission of his employers this is an accident arising out of and in the course of employment [89]; (9) if claimant is late in making a claim he has to show good cause for his delay and if he does so his claim will not be rejected because of the time lag [90]; (10) it has been held recently that a myocardial infarction resulting from an effort at work constitutes a personal injury by accident arising out of and in the course of his employment [91]; (11) if claimant suffers an injury whilst waiting for a repair being done to a vehicle driven by him within his employment his action is incidental to his employment and the accident has been held to arise out of and in the course of that employment.[92]

The Industrial Injuries Commissioner has no jurisdiction to entertain an application for leave to appeal against an exercise of the discretionary power given to the Medical Appeal Tribunal under section 40 (4) of the National Insurance (Industrial Injuries) Act 1965.[93]

(8) *Compulsory Insurance*

As the typescript draft of this volume was going into proof the Employers' Liability (Compulsory Insurance) Bill was approaching the Statute Book. Its object is to ensure that employees who have been awarded damages for injuries sustained in their employment are not deprived of their rights—as happened previously where certain employers had failed to insure against this liability and had proved to be " men of straw." The new Act [94] received the Royal Assent on October 22, 1969 but is yet to be brought into operation by statutory instrument. It imposes upon certain employers (those exempted are specified in section 3) a new statutory duty of compulsory insurance against bodily injury or disease sustained by employees (excepting those specified in section 2 (2)) and arising out of and in the course of their employment in Great Britain. The penalty for failure to insure is specified in section 5. Additional regulations may be made by the Secretary of State [95] in terms of section 6.[96]

[89] Decision R. (I.) 2/68.
[90] Decision R. (I.) 9/68 (a Scottish decision by H. A. Shewan Q.C., the Scottish Commissioner).
[91] R. (I.) 12/68. A case in which two eminent cardiologists nominated by the Royal College of Physicians gave evidence by means of reports which linked physical effort with myocardial infarction (see the Appendix to this decision).
[92] R. (I.) 13/68.   [93] R. (I.) 15/68.
[94] Employers' Liability (Compulsory Insurance) Act 1969 (c. 57). The text is contained in Appendix 3 to this volume.
[95] *i.e.* for Employment and Productivity.
[96] Any such regulations may affect section 1 (1) and 1 (2) as well as sections 1 (3), 2 (2) para. (b), 3 (1) para. (c) and 4 (1) and (2).

CHAPTER 12

THE LIABILITY OF THE EMPLOYER TO THIRD PARTIES

(a) *Liability for the Delictual Acts of Employees*

The ground of delictual liability was formerly generally accepted as being based upon the maxim *qui facit per alium facit per se*, although this view was never entirely satisfactory. Sometimes the brocard *respondeat superior* was used. The older view tied liability very closely to the agency concept within the field of contract, but as the law developed and industrial and commercial life became more complicated a new ground of liability had to be found. In modern times " the scope of employment " test has replaced the older concepts or bases of vicarious liability. Most of the modern text writers deal with this delictual liability of the employer for the wrongful acts of his employees under the general heading of " vicarious liability " or the " doctrine of vicarious liability." This doctrine or principle is not wholly modern but had its place in the writings of George Joseph Bell[1] in Scotland and in the works of the early English jurists.[2] The employer is responsible for any injury or loss caused to a third party by the wrongful (*i.e.*, in the civil sense) acts or negligent actings or omissions of his employees, so long as they were acting within the scope or course of the employment.[3] The employer escapes liability if he can show that the employee was not, in fact, an employee at the time[4] or, alternatively, that the particular act complained of was not within the scope of the employee's employment, although that employee was, to all intents and purposes, and in all other respects, an employee at the particular time or that the act complained of was not incidental to the employment so as to create a liability upon the employer.

Where the claim by pursuer against the employer is being rested upon the employer and employee relationship, the pursuer (*i.e.*, the third party involved) is generally required to establish three main points, *viz.*:

(1) that the act of the employee was the proximate cause of the loss or injury;

(2) that the wrongdoer (*i.e.*, the employee) was at the particular time

---

[1] See his *Principles*, § 547.

[2] The most famous book in English law was Baty's *Vicarious Liability* (1916); but see now the recent and interesting book by Mr. P. S. Atiyah, *Vicarious Liability in the Law of Torts* (Butterworths, 1967).

[3] See, in illustration, *John Young & Co.* (*Kelvinhaugh*) *Ltd.* v. *O'Donnell* (H.L.) 1958 S.L.T.(Notes) 46; *Kilgower* v. *National Coal Board*, 1958 S.L.T.(Notes) 48; *Baxter* v. *Colvilles Ltd.*, 1959 S.L.T. 325; and *Kirby* v. *National Coal Board*, 1959 S.L.T. 7; 1958 S.C. 514. The third party concerned may be the wife of the driver of the vehicle— vide *Webb* v. *Inglis* (O.H.) 1958 S.L.T.(Notes) 8.

[4] See *Docherty* v. *Ancell Motor Co.* (1963) 79 Sh.Ct.Rep. 50 (where employers failed to prove that their employee had been acting outwith the scope of his employment).

acting on behalf of and in the furtherance of the employer's interests; and

(3) that the employer and employee relationship did apply between the wrongdoer and the defender (*i.e.*, the employer).

The employee remains liable, of course, for his own wrongful acts and he may be made a joint defender in the civil proceedings taken by the injured third party. There may be cases in which a rule of absolute or strict liability applies to create a legal liability upon the employer without proof of fault on the employee's part, *e.g.*, in cases of the *Rylands* v. *Fletcher* [5] type or in those cases where the edict *nautae, caupones, stabularii,* etc., applies; or again where dangerous animals are kept.[6] It is not appropriate to elaborate upon the *Rylands* v. *Fletcher* doctrine at this point, nor indeed to consider whether, if at all, it applies in Scots law. Much guidance on these points will be obtained from the Thirteenth Report of the Law Reform Committee for Scotland [7] and from the dissenting view of Professor T. B. Smith therein contained, as well as from other text writers.[8]

The liability of an employer to a third party for the negligence of his employees is undoubtedly greater than that of an employer for contractors engaged by him. In the latter case the employer's liability is not strictly a liability *qua* employer but it may be nevertheless vicarious as, for example, the owner or occupier of heritable property or alternatively, it is based upon an express statutory liability. In the case of the true employer and employee relationship, the employer is the person who directs the performance of the work and exercises a complete control over the employee. This " doctrine of control " has been exceedingly popular for many years as the test of liability, although, for some time now attempts have been made to formulate a new test. So far, these attempts have not been fully successful in replacing the " control " test.[9] It is now necessary to examine, in a little more detail, the three requirements which have been stipulated above as being necessary to support the pursuer's case.

(1) The question of " proximate cause," mentioned above as the first requirement, is part of the general law of delict or reparation [10] and the rules thereof apply with equal force here. Any defences which would have been available to the employer under the general law of delict may be pleaded relevantly here also; *e.g.*, contributory negligence of the pursuer will perhaps excuse the employer completely or will substantially reduce his (the employer's) ultimate liability in damages to the pursuer, depending upon the facts and circumstances. Prior to the passing of the Law Reform

---

[5] (1866) L.R. 1 Ex. 265; (1868) L.R. 3 H.L.
[6] See D. M. Walker, *The Law of Delict in Scotland*, pp. 641–651.
[7] Cmnd. 2348 (1964).
[8] See D. M. Walker, *op. cit.*, particularly pp. 980–986.
[9] See *supra*, Chap. 3.
[10] See Glegg, *Reparation* (4th ed.) Chap. 2, p. 37 *et seq.*, and D. M. Walker, *op. cit.*, p. 219 *et seq.*

(Contributory Negligence) Act 1945, a defence plea of contributory negligence would, if successful, have excused the employer completely from liability.

The general tests of negligence [11] and foreseeability [12] and the rules of remoteness of damage and of injury,[13] which also apply within the general law of delict, must again be applied to the field of employer's liability. Proof or jury trial may be authorised by the court, depending upon the circumstances and the pleadings of the parties.[14]

(2) The second requirement of " scope of employment " is perhaps on occasion regarded more as a defence available to the employer rather than as a primary ground of liability. This is because the employer is not normally liable for the wrongful acts (i.e., delictual acts) of or the negligence of his employees whilst they are acting outwith the scope of their employment. The separate question of criminal acts committed by employees and the employer's probable liability therefore is considered hereafter.[15] The particular question as to whether or not the act of the employee was done within the scope of his employment is one of fact and the answer to that question will determine the employer's liability or non-liability, as a question of law. A selection of some earlier cases and, more usefully, some of the more recent cases will serve to illustrate the attitude of the courts in determining the question of scope of employment.[16]

Nevertheless, there must be a reasonable latitude allowed to the employee. His duties must not be scrutinised with meticulous exactitude [17]

---

[11] See for example *Johnston* v. *National Coal Board* (O.H.) 1960 S.L.T.(Notes) 84 (driver guilty of negligence when he lost control of vehicle, because a fly had entered one of his eyes); and *Waugh* v. *James K. Allan Ltd.*, 1964 S.L.T. 269; [1964] 2 Lloyd's Rep. 1 (H.L.) (driver dying of a coronary attack at the wheel not proved guilty of negligence) (H.L. affirming the First Division).

[12] *Hughes* v. *Lord Advocate*, 1963 S.C.(H.L.) 31; 1963 S.L.T. 150; [1963] A.C. 837; [1963] 1 All E.R. 705 (H.L.) (Post Office employees who left a lamp in such a position that it could be knocked into a manhole were bound to have foreseen an accident of the type which occurred).

[13] See D. M. Walker, *Delict* (" remoteness of damage " and " remoteness of injury ").

[14] See *Roberts* v. *Logan*, 1966 S.L.T. 77 (proof before answer allowed); and *Winchester* v. *Ramsay* (O.H.) 1966 S.L.T. 97 (proof before answer again the appropriate mode of inquiry).

[15] See *infra*, Chap. 22.

[16] See particularly *Gallagher* v. *Burrell & Son* (1883) 11 R. 53 (the culpable bargee); *Martin* v. *Ward* (1887) 14 R. 814 (the employee taking over from a drunken driver—no part of his duties to drive); *Beard* v. *London General Omnibus Co.* [1900] 2 Q.B. 530 (the 'bus conductor who drove the 'bus when his driver was ill—no part of his duties and no implied authority—the 'bus company was *not* liable); and, more recently, the following cases: *Peebles* v. *Cowan & Co.* (O.H.) 1915, 1 S.L.T. 363 (driver giving " lifts "—employers not liable); similarly, *Dowd* v. *Fletcher*, 1936 S.N. 118; and again *Togher* v. *Gilbert McClung Ltd.* (O.H.) 1962 S.L.T.(Notes) 31; the English cases of interest here are *Twine* v. *Bean's Express* [1946] 1 All E.R. 202; 62 T.L.R. 458 (C.A.); *Conway* v. *George Wimpey & Co.* [1951] 1 All E.R. 363; [1951] 2 K.B. 266 (C.A.); and *Young* v. *Edward Box* [1951] 1 T.L.R. 789 (C.A.) (the foreman's " ostensible " authority in this last-mentioned case being sufficient to create a liability upon his employers); *Ilkiw* v. *Samuels* [1963] 2 All E.R. 879 (C.A.) (the negligent lorry driver who allowed an incompetent workman—not an employee of defendants—to drive the firm's lorry and so rendered them liable).

[17] In *Beddie* v. *B.T.C.*, 1958 S.L.T.(Sh.Ct.) 42; 74 Sh.Ct.Rep. 130, the sheriff-substitute (A. Hamilton) observed that the primary duty of an engine-driver is to see that the track is clear by signal; he is entitled to assume it is clear of physical obstruction, unless he has warning to the contrary (and quoting the opinion of the L.J.-C. in the unreported case of *Shevlin* v. *L.M.S. Ry.*).

in order to discover whether or not the particular act was properly undertaken—that is to say, within the so-called " strict scope " of employment. There are occasions when an employee may do more than is strictly and even reasonably required of him. The attitude of the law must then be a reasonable one; namely, this—if the employee's actings are in the general line of duty and for the benefit and interest of his employer, the responsibility must rest upon the employer.[18] It is perhaps, in these modern times, no longer fashionable to talk about the particular act being done for the " benefit of the employer." The better test seems to be to inquire whether the act in question was strictly relevant to the scope of employment or whether it was incidentally or peripherally relevant to the employee's duties. In both cases it may then be regarded as arising out of the employment or as part of the duties of the employee engaged in that particular employment. In any other case the act is so unconnected with or remote from the ambit or scope of the employee's duties that it cannot be regarded as part thereof, with the result that the employer will normally escape liability.

If the particular act is done by the employee for his own ends then the whole responsibility for the consequences lies upon him and not upon the employer. It very often happens that an employee who is driving motor transport belonging to his employer deviates from the route which he normally takes, for some purpose which is purely personal to him or again, having completed certain delivery tasks instructed by his employer, he takes out a motor-van or lorry on a ploy of his own. Who is responsible in these two cases—the employee alone or the employer also ? It seems that if the employee is engaged upon the employer's business—even although he might deviate for his own personal reasons—the employer will still be liable.[19] The second example seems to be a separate circumstance not strictly relating to the law of employment—the employee is

---

[18] See the English cases of *Limpus* v. *London General Omnibus Co.* (1862) 1 H. & C. 526; and *Ward* v. *General Omnibus Co.* (1873) 42 L.J.C.P. 265. If the act was done within the scope of employment then it will surely be a question for the jury to say, as a matter of fact, in whose interest and for what purpose the act was done; and the Scottish cases of *Avery* v. *New Park School* (O.H.) 1949 S.L.T.(Notes) 7; *Henderson* v. *Edinburgh Corporation* (O.H.) 1950 S.L.T.(Notes) 63; *Hutchison* v. *Dumfries County Council*, 1949 S.L.T.(Notes) 10; and *Bell* v. *Blackwood Morton & Sons Ltd.*, 1960 S.C. 11; 1960 S.L.T. 145.

[19] The following are the most important English and Scottish cases on " deviation," *viz.*: *Joel* v. *Morrison* (1834) 6 C. & P. 501; *Storey* v. *Ashton* (1869) L.R. 4 Q.B. 476 (the leading English case); and the recent Scottish cases of *Williams* v. *A. & W. Hemphill Ltd.* (H.L.) 1966 S.L.T. 259 (where the House of Lords considered it to be a question of degree as to how far the particular deviation could be regarded as constituting a separate journey). In the instant case, the House of Lords held pursuer entitled to recover as the driver was still within the course of employment although he had deviated quite considerably from the authorised route. " Deviation distance " evaluations are quite unsound. The test is " course of employment " and in that case the employer is clearly liable; *Stewart's (Edinburgh) Holdings Ltd.* v. *Lord Advocate*, 1966 S.L.T. (Sh.Ct.) 86 (Army driver who deviated from route but not exclusively for his own business rendered his employers liable in reparation: *Crook* v. *Derbyshire Stone Ltd.* [1956] 1 W.L.R. 432 not followed). In the earlier Scottish case of *Wallace* v. *Morrison & Co. Ltd.* (O.H.) 1929 S.L.T. 73 the employer was again held liable in the circumstances (the Lord Ordinary (Constable) observing that the question was whether the deviation took him (*i.e.*, employee) out of the course of his employment or, in other words, broke for the time being the relationship of service).

here " borrowing " the transport for his own purposes [20]; that is to say he is making use of it without any authority so to do and, accordingly, no liability will attach to the employer. Of course, the act complained of by pursuer need not be some particular act of service within the scope of the employee's duties to create a liability in the employer. It is good enough as has been pointed out above—if the act is merely incidental to the employment.[21]

The employer may expressly forbid the doing of a particular act or he may forbid its performance in a particular manner. Does disobedience by the employee to these instructions enable the employer to escape liability ? [22] The answer seems to be that it does not necessarily excuse the employer. It seems to be the case that the employer is liable even although he had expressly forbidden the employee to do the particular act, so long as the act which was done was within the scope of the employment. For example, an employee who drives in such a way as to annoy or endanger vehicles of a rival concern will make his own employer liable, even although his employer had expressly forbidden him to race with other vehicles of that other concern, or indeed of any concern.[23]

The question of express prohibitions has been considered fairly recently and mainly in England in *Twine* v. *Bean's Express Ltd.*[24] and *Conway* v. *Geo. Wimpey & Co. Ltd.*[25] In the former case, express orders were displayed in the van prohibiting " lifts " to third parties. The driver gave a lift to a third party, who was killed because of the driver's negligence. It was held that the employers were not liable, on the ground that the employee was acting outwith the scope of his employment by bringing within the class of persons to whom the employer owed a duty of care a person who was carried on the van against express instructions. *Conway's* case took the same view—although, here, lifts were frequently given, in spite of a prohibition against this, but the defendants had no knowledge that this practice was in operation. In both of these English cases, the third party who was carried on the vehicle had been regarded as a trespasser. Denning L.J. (as he then was) discussed this point in *Young* v. *Edward Box & Co. Ltd.*[26] but he did not think that it was conclusive. Young was an employee of the defendants, responsible (under his contract) for getting to and from the site of his work. On Sunday evenings, the

---

20 The now famous phrase " on a frolic of his own," first used by Baron Parke in *Joel* v. *Morrison* (1834) 6 C. & P. 501 at p. 503, is often quoted by judges in subsequent cases both in England and in Scotland.

21 See *Ruddiman* v. *Smith* (1889) 60 L.T. 708; and the Scottish case of *Mulholland* v. *Wm. Reid & Leys Ltd.*, 1958 S.C. 290; 1958 S.L.T. 285.

22 See *Twine* v. *Bean's Express Ltd.* [1946] 1 All E.R. 202; *Conway* v. *Geo. Wimpey & Co. Ltd.* [1951] 2 K.B. 266; [1951] 1 All E.R. 363; and *Young* v. *Edward Box & Co. Ltd.* [1951] 1 T.L.R. 789—particularly *per* Denning L.J. (as he then was) at p. 794; *Ilkiw* v. *Samuels* [1963] 2 All E.R. 879 (C.A.).

23 *Limpus* v. *London General Omnibus Co.* (1862) 1 H. & C. 526; *London County Council* v. *Cattermoles (Garages) Ltd.* [1953] 2 All E.R. 582, considered in the later Scottish case of *Mulholland* v. *Wm. Reid & Leys Ltd.* 1958 S.C. 290; 1958 S.L.T. 285.

24 [1946] 1 All E.R. 202; see also Tony Weir's *Casebook on Tort*, pp. 186–188.

25 [1951] 2 K.B. 266; [1951] 1 All E.R. 363.

26 [1951] 1 T.L.R. 789 at p. 794; See also Weir's *Casebook*, pp. 189–190.

plaintiff and his fellow-workmen were given lifts on defendants' vehicles, because of pressure on public transport. The plaintiff's foreman and the driver concurred in this practice. Two judges of the Court of Appeal held that the right to sanction a ride on the lorry was within the ostensible authority of the foreman and that in relying upon that authority the plaintiff became a licensee. Denning L.J. said " the liability of the owner does not depend on whether the passenger was a trespasser or not; it depends on whether the driver was acting within the scope of his employment. . . . "

It seems that the employer might escape liability if he could show that he not only expressly forbade the particular act but also that the act in question was for the exclusive benefit or convenience of the employees themselves.[27] The employee, as a general agent, is presumed to be vested with all the powers proper to his tasks.[28] However, an employer is entitled to lay down limits within which the employee is to perform his duties and if the prohibitions applied by the employer extend to things which are outwith the normal scope of such duties then there is no liability upon the employer.[29]

It is sometimes argued that the employer is *not* liable for any wilful and illegal (in the sense of unlawful but not necessarily criminal) act done by the employee.[30] It has already been observed that the employer may be liable for the wilful act of his employee and he may also be liable in a civil action, if the offence is a criminal one, so long as it was committed in the course of the employment.[31] Railway and omnibus company employees and shipping company employees have a presumed authority to use force against persons who misconduct themselves upon the railway, etc., property or who, for example, attempt to travel without a ticket. If unnecessary violence is used or if the employees use force improperly then the companies or railways board, as employers, will be liable.[32]

---

[27] See *Rand* v. *Craig* [1919] 1 Ch. 1 (carters employed to dump rubbish on a dump provided by their employers but instead they dumped it on appellant's ground—to earn more money by shifting more rubbish per day; the employers were held *not* liable in the circumstances).

[28] See *Limpus* v. *London General Omnibus Co.* (1862) 1 H. & C. 526, *per* Willes J. at p. 539.

[29] See *Duke of Roxburgh* v. *Waldie* (1822) 1 S. 344; (1825) 1 W.S. 1; *Docherty* v. *Glasgow Tramway Co.* (1894) 32 S.L.R. 353; *Limpus* v. *London General Omnibus Co.*, cit. *supra*; *Stevens* v. *Woodward* (1881) 6 Q.B.D. 318, *per* Grove J. at p. 320.

[30] See *Hanlon* v. *Glasgow & S.W. Ry.* (1899) 1 F. 559; *Wardrope* v. *Duke of Hamilton* (1876) 3 R. 876; and *Duke of Roxburgh* v. *Waldie*, cit. *supra*.

[31] *Bayley* v. *Manchester S. and L. Ry.* (1873) L.R. 8 C.P. 148; *Bryce* v. *Glasgow Tramway Co.* (1898) 6 S.L.T. 49; *Wood* v. *N.B. Ry.* (1899) 1 F. 562; but *cf. Gillespie* v. *Hunter* (1898) 25 R. 916 (the barman arguing politics with a customer and forcibly ejecting him—no action against the proprietors). See also *Baillie* v. *Corporation of Edinburgh and Dickie* (1906) 14 S.L.T. 344; *Hynds* v. *Singer Sewing Machine Co. Ltd.*, 1909, 2 S.L.T. 127; *Knight* v. *Inverness District Board of Control*, 1920, 2 S.L.T. 157; but see *Jardine* v. *Lang*, 1911, 2 S.L.T. 494 (employer not liable as employee acting outwith scope of his authority), and similarly *Lurie* v. *N.B. Ry.*, 1917, 2 S.L.T. 59.

[32] *Highland Ry.* v. *Menzies* (1878) 5 R. 887; *Apthorpe* v. *Edinburgh Tramways Co.* (1882) 10 R. 344; *Lowe* v. *Great Northern Ry.* (1893) 62 L.J.Q.B. 524; *Seymour* v. *Greenwood* (1861) 6 H. & N. 359; *Hanlon* v. *Glasgow and South-Western Ry.* (1899) 1 F. 559; *Bayley* v. *Manchester S. and L. Ry.* (1873) L.R. 8 C.P. 148 and *Maxwell* v. *Caledonian*

Any personal and spiteful act by an employee against a passenger does not necessarily create a liability upon the employer.[33]

A statutory power to apprehend may be conferred (usually upon railway companies and the like) and any misuse of that power by employees would render the employer liable. The pursuer, who is pleading misuse of the power or authority vested in the employers, must establish (a) that a power to apprehend was conferred for the particular offence and (b) that the employee who did arrest him was an employee duly authorised by the employers to execute the statutory right.[34]   But if there is no statutory power to make the particular arrest the employers cannot be made liable. The particular abuse or misuse of the power must be very clearly set forth —for example by an assault, excessive violence, or other illegal use of the power conferred by law.   Another English case illustrating the unusual act falling within the scope of employment is *Poland* v. *John Parr & Sons*[35] where a carter, employed by the defendants, was walking home after work, behind a lorry being driven by one of his employers. Seeing a young man climbing upon the lorry and thinking that he was stealing or about to steal sugar, the carter struck him so that the youth fell and was injured. The employers were held liable. The opinion was expressed that if the carter's act had been so excessive as to take it outwith the scope of authorised acts then his employers would not have been liable. It is the emergency which justifies the act. Whether there is an emergency or not is a question of fact.[36]

An employer is also responsible for any slander or defamation uttered by an employee within the scope of employment or incidental to that employment.[37] It was formerly required that the particular slander or defamation had to be shown to be for the employer's benefit before liability attached,[38] but as in the fraud cases—this point is no longer essential to liability.

Ry. (1898) 25 R. 550; 5 S.L.T. 300; also *Wood* v. *N.B. Ry.* (1899) 1 F. 562; 6 S.L.T. 323; *Coutts* v. *David MacBrayne Ltd.,* 1910 S.C. 386; 1910, 1 S.L.T. 144; *Cumming* v. *Great North of Scotland Ry.,* 1916, 1 S.L.T. 181; *Stevenson* v. *Glasgow Corporation,* 1922 S.L.T. 185.

[33] *Power* v. *Central S.M.T. Co.,* 1949 S.C. 376; 1949 S.L.T. 302 (conductress deliberately and spitefully " belling " the 'bus to proceed whilst passenger in act of alighting).

[34] See *Lundie* v. *MacBrayne* (1894) 21 R. 1085 (following *Moore* v. *Metropolitan Ry.* (1872) 8 Q.B. 36).

[35] [1927] 1 K.B. 236.

[36] See *Gwilliam* v. *Twist* [1895] 2 Q.B. 84; *Beard* v. *London General Omnibus Co.* [1900] 2 Q.B. 530; but *cf. Ricketts* v. *Thos. Tilling Ltd.* [1915] 1 K.B. 644 (employers liable for a driver's negligence in allowing an unauthorised person to drive the vehicle).

[37] See *Eprile* v. *Caledonian Ry.* (1898) 6 S.L.T. 65; *Cameron* v. *Yeats* (1899) 1 F. 456; 6 S.L.T. 329; *Ellis* v. *National Free Labour Association* (1905) 7 F. 629; 13 S.L.T. 70; *Agnew* v. *British Legal Life Assurance Co. Ltd.* (1906) 8 F. 422; 13 S.L.T. 742; *Handasyde* v. *Hepworth & Son Ltd.* (1907) 15 S.L.T. 180; *Nicklas* v. *The New Popular Cafe Co.* (1908) 15 S.L.T. 735; *Finburgh* v. *Moss' Empires* (1908) 16 S.L.T. 116; 1908 S.C. 928; *Cumming* v. *Great North of Scotland Ry.,* 1916, 1 S.L.T. 181; *Lurie* v. *N.B. Ry.,* 1917, 2 S.L.T. 59; *Mandelston* v. *N.B. Ry.,* 1917 S.C. 442; 1917, 1 S.L.T. 244; *Jardine* v. *N.B. Ry.,* 1923 S.L.T. 55; *Neville* v. *C. & A. Modes,* 1945 S.C. 175; 1945 S.L.T. 189 (shop assistant making charge of theft against a customer); *Cameron* v. *Young's Express Deliveries Ltd.,* 1950 S.L.T.(Sh.Ct.) 40; (1950) 66 Sh.Ct.Rep. 182.

[38] *Finburgh* v. *Moss' Empires,* cit. supra.

The employer is liable for any fraud or embezzlement committed by the employee in the course of his employment, just as he is for any other wrongful act. The ground of liability is that the employee is acting in a particular capacity with reference to certain kinds of acts and accordingly the employer must be liable for the way in which these acts are carried out by the employee.[39]

(3) The third and final requirement, if the employer is to be held responsible, is that the relationship of employer and employee must apply. The existence of a contract of service is sufficient proof, but if this is denied on the record then the pursuer has the onus of proving that the relationship does in fact exist.

Some difficulties might be apparent where two persons are entitled to give orders to an employee at the time of the wrongful or negligent act. This is not so much the case of the superior and inferior employee (the superior employee is not legally liable for the wrongful acts of the junior employee) as the case where the employee is virtually serving two employers. The question to be answered is this—who was the employer at the particular time when the wrongful or negligent act took place ? That person is the person who is responsible. Two different tests have been suggested in answer to this question, viz.:

(a) who selected the employee, who pays him and who can dismiss him ?; or

(b) who has the right to control the employee as to the way in which he must perform his duties ?

The former test is certainly important as regards determining such questions as breach of contract or lawful or unlawful dismissal. However as regards liability in negligence there seems to be little doubt that the " control test " is still meantime accepted as being the primary one.[40] This view has obtained from the earlier part of the nineteenth century [41] right down to the present time. It was tested again in the comparatively

---

[39] See *Lloyd* v. *Grace Smith & Co.* [1912] A.C. 716; also *United Africa Co.* v. *Saka Owade* [1955] A.C. 130; and *Uxbridge Permanent Benefit Building Society* v. *Pickard* [1939] 2 K.B. 248; [1939] 2 All E.R. 344 (C.A.). The older approach of the law on this point was that the employer was not liable unless the fraud was committed in the course of employment and for the employer's benefit (see *Robb* v. *Gow Brothers & Gemmell* (1905) 8 F. 90; 13 S.L.T. 609), but the latter requirement is no longer considered to be necessary for liability to attach.

[40] See *Cairns* v. *Clyde Navigation Trs.* (1898) 25 R. 1021; *Connelly* v. *Clyde Navigation Trs.* (1902) 5 F. 8; *Anderson* v. *Glasgow Tramway Co.* (1893) 21 R. 318; *Ballantyne & Co.* v. *Paton & Hendry*, 1912 S.C. 246; 1911, 2 S.L.T. 510; and *Ainslie* v. *Leith Dock Commissioners*, 1919 S.C. 676; 1919, 2 S.L.T. 180 (following *Cairns*, *supra*, and *M'Cartan* v. *Belfast Harbour Commissioners* [1911] 2 I.R. 143 but *distinguishing Donovan* v. *Laing Wharton*, etc., hereafter cited); *Johnson* v. *Lindsay* [1891] A.C. 371; *Donovan* v. *Laing Wharton & Down Construction Syndicate* [1893] 1 Q.B. 629; and see the earlier cases of *Murray* v. *Currie*, 1870 L.R. 6 C.P. 24 and *Rourke* v. *White Moss Colliery Co.* (1877) 2 C.P.D. 205.

[41] See *Dalyell* v. *Tyrer* (1858) El.Bl. & El. 899 and *Fenton* v. *Dublin Steam Packet Co.* (1838) 8 A. & E. 835; and in particular the following well-known English cases: *Quarman* v. *Burnett* (1840) 6 M. & W. 499; *Jones* v. *Liverpool Corporation* (1885) 14 Q.B.D. 890, and *Jones* v. *Scullard* [1898] 2 Q.B. 565, where the issue raised was the liability of the owner of a vehicle as against the hirer; the " control test " was still held to apply. For an interesting article by Professor Otto Kahn-Freund, criticising the " control " test see 14 M.L.R. 505.

recent and leading English case of *Mersey Docks and Harbour Board* v. *Coggins & Griffiths (Liverpool) Ltd.*,[42] a case in which *Donovan* v. *Laing Wharton and Down Construction Syndicate* [43] was carefully considered and distinguished. In the *Mersey Docks* case the facts were, briefly, that the Harbour Board let a mobile crane (with driver) to a firm of stevedores. The Board employed the driver, paid him and had the power to dismiss him. The conditions of hire stipulated that the driver was to be regarded as a servant of the hirers (the Stevedoring Company). The stevedores controlled the movement of cargo but had no authority to instruct the driver how to work his crane. The Harbour Board were held liable for the crane driver's negligence as they " controlled " the way in which the work should be done.

The general principles relating to the transference or loan of employees from one employer to another were very carefully considered and discussed in England in *Chowdhary* v. *Gillot*.[44] The facts in this case were that the plaintiff left his car with the second defendants (the Daimler Co. Ltd.) for repairs and asked an employee of the company to drive him to the station. Gillot, another employee of the company, was instructed to drive the plaintiff and his wife. During the journey the car collided with a lorry driven by Jones, the third defendant. It was held that Gillot remained an employee of the Daimler company and did not come under the control of the plaintiff whilst driving the car. Mr. Justice Streatfeild's five propositions in that case are indeed most helpful and are as follows, *viz.*:

(1) Where transfer is in issue, the presumption is against such transfer.
(2) The burden of proof is upon the general employer to show that control has passed.
(3) The general employer must prove that there is such a transference as passes the right to control the employee concerned in the manner of execution of the act in question.
(4) Whether such a transference has taken place is always a question of fact.
(5) There cannot be such a transference without the employee's consent.

The " control test " has come up for consideration time and time again in the " hospital cases." It may be thought, not without some justification perhaps, that the control test has been pushed too far in these cases and that it has been allowed to obscure the real test of the basic contractual relationship between the parties; this relationship being determined by a careful examination of the position of both parties under the contract rather than by the element of control. If it is clear that the contract discloses an employer/employee relationship, the employer will then be liable vicariously for any delictual acts of the employee. If,

---

[42] [1947] A.C. 1; [1946] 2 All E.R. 345 (H.L.) and 62 T.L.R. 533.
[43] [1893] 1 Q.B. 629.
[44] [1947] 2 All E.R. 541.

however, the contract is not identified as an employment contract, then prima facie liability does not rest upon the board of management or any other body engaging the other party to the contract, and a third party suffering injury or loss must, initially and perhaps finally, look to the second party (*i.e.*, the person engaged to do the particular work governed by the contract) for recovery in respect of his loss or injury. From any logical standpoint, it is a patent exaggeration and oversimplification to say, in any case, that a board of management of any hospital group " controls " its qualified medical staff. As the " hospital cases " are generally relevant to the ordinary application of the " control test " they have been discussed elsewhere.[45] It must be conceded, however—and the earlier cases such as *Donovan* and *Mersey Docks* seem to illustrate this point quite clearly—that where there is some actual mechanical or physical operation involved, the correct test to apply seems to be the " control " test. In other cases, the " organisational " test may be valid.[46]

The leading Scottish case upon employment or service *pro hac vice* is *Malley* v. *L.M.S. Railway Co.*[47] where an engine and crew were lent to a steelworks for shunting duties. The engine crew were in actual charge of the operations and because of their negligence the pursuer was injured. It was held that the railway company as general employers were liable vicariously. There was no liability upon the steelworks company. The opinion of the Lord Justice-Clerk (L.J.-C. Cooper, as he then was) is most helpful. His lordship observed that the onus of proof is upon the party seeking to establish the transfer and also that the terms of an agreement between the two employers is always important and may be conclusive. The employee himself must always be a party to any transfer arrangement, whether it is the actual transfer of the employee himself or the transfer of the use and benefit of his services.

It is obvious from the pattern of cases quoted in this section that much litigation is brought against the corporate employer—whether it be one of the large nationalised industries or a large industrial or commercial concern. Yet the common law (and statutory elaborations thereof) duty does not change in the field of civil liability. The matter is a little more complicated in the case of a penal sanction being imposed. It is not possible to imprison the large corporation—the simple solution is to

---

[45] *Supra*, Chap. 3. But note that a resident *medical* officer in a hospital is not guilty of negligence if he fails to diagnose the *mental* condition of a patient—*vide McHardy* v. *Dundee General Hospitals Board* (O.H.) 1960 S.L.T.(Notes) 19.

[46] The " organisational " test is referred to in Chap. 3, *supra*.

[47] 1944 S.C. 129; 1945 S.L.T. 313; 1944 S.N. 6; see also the earlier cases of *Elliott* v. *Beattie*, 1926 S.L.T. 588 (Lord Fleming at p. 589); *Fulton's Tutor* v. *Mason & Sons Ltd.*, 1927 S.L.T. 428; *M'Intosh* v. *Cameron*, 1929 S.C. 44; 1929 S.L.T. 22; and *Bowie* v. *Shenkin*, 1934 S.C. 459; 1934 S.L.T. 374 (applying *M'Cartan* v. *Belfast Harbour Commissioners* [1911] 2 I.R. 143 and Lord Dunedin's tests; the opinion of the L.J.-C. (Craigie Aitchison) is most helpful); and the more recent cases of *Brogan* v. *William Allan Smith & Co.* (O.H.) 1965 S.L.T.(Notes) 36; and *McGregor* v. *J. S. Duthie & Sons & Co. Ltd.*, 1966 S.L.T.(Notes) 26 (pursuer had discharged the *onus* of proof that the driver was in the *pro hac vice* employment of defenders).

impose a large fine upon it and, if appropriate, imprison its leading officers.

Difficulties were encountered under the older law, when civil actions in damages were brought against police officers or, sometimes by elaborate procedure (mostly in England and Wales), against the Crown in special cases. Unless, in the former case, it could be shown that a police constable was acting upon the direct and specific instructions of his chief constable,[48] the action became a personal action in reparation against the constable himself. This was of little assistance to a litigant seeking substantial damages. The law has been clarified, as regards Scotland, by the Police (Scotland) Act 1967 [49] and, as regards England and Wales, by the Police Act 1964 (c. 48). The relevant section of the 1967 Act is section 39 (1) which says:

" 39.—(1) The chief constable of a police force shall be liable in reparation in respect of any wrongful act or omission on the part of any constable under his general direction in the performance of his functions in like manner as a master is so liable in respect of a wrongful act or omission on the part of his servant in the course of the servant's employment."

The police authority is made liable in payment of damages and expenses or of any approved settlement sum in terms of subsection (2). The position is therefore broadly the same in Scotland and England as regards the vicarious responsibility of chief constables.

The position regarding litigation against the Crown has been clarified and improved by the Crown Proceedings Act 1947.[50] Indeed, the outstanding feature of this statute is that it creates a delictual liability in the Crown for the wrongful acts or omissions of its employees (be they servants or agents) in the same way as the ordinary employer is liable for the wrongful acts or omissions of his employees.[51] There are special provisions relating to the armed forces [52] and a special saving clause in respect of acts done under the prerogative or statutory powers.[53] Civil proceedings

---

[48] See, for example, *Adamson* v. *Martin*, 1916 S.C. 319; 1916, 1 S.L.T. 53 (pursuers' action irrelevant as he failed to aver and prove that direct instructions had been given by the chief constable).

[49] 1967, c. 77, which received the Royal Assent on July 27, 1967, and came into operation on October 27, 1967, except for s. 39 (liability for wrongful acts of constables). S. 39 is to be brought into force on such date as the Secretary of State for Scotland by order appoints (the order may be retrospective but not beyond June 10, 1964). Meantime, the operative statutory provision is to be found in the Police (Scotland) Act 1956, s. 23A (1)–(4) and the Police Act 1964, Sched. 7, para. 14. As regards the position of a police constable himself, the recent case of *Robertson and Another* v. *Bell and Others* (O.H.) 1969 S.L.T. 119 is also of interest because Lord Fraser (allowing an inquiry against the chief constable) has expressed the view that (i) a chief constable may owe a duty of care to his officers though the master and servant relationship does not apply, and (ii) a police committee has no such duty by statute or at common law. (The S.L.T. report indicates that a reclaiming motion has been enrolled.)

[50] 10 & 11 Geo. 6, c. 44 (Part V contains the relevant particulars regarding the application of the Act to Scotland).

[51] *Ibid*. s. 2. (See also s. 4 (3) regarding the Law Reform (Contributory Negligence) Act 1945, which now binds the Crown.)

[52] *Ibid*. s. 10.

[53] *Ibid*. s. 11.

against the Crown in Scotland may be brought either in the Court of Session or the sheriff court,[54] and, if in the latter court, the case must be remitted to the Court of Session upon a certificate from the Lord Advocate to the effect that an important question of law is involved or that the case is a test case likely to establish a new precedent for future cases or for other reasons which show that the case is more suitable for hearing by the Court of Session.

A special duty may, as we have already indicated, rest upon an employer not essentially *qua* employer but as owner or proprietor of property. The point is well illustrated by the case of *Wyngrove's Curator Bonis* v. *Scottish Omnibuses Ltd.*,[55] where the House of Lords (reversing the Second Division of the Court of Session and assoilzing defenders) observed that an omnibus proprietor must take all precautions for the safety of his passengers which a reasonable and careful person would take, but he is entitled nevertheless in discharging that duty to have regard to his own experience and that of others as to what precautions are necessary, and to weigh the additional precautions to meet very exceptional circumstances against the general inconvenience. In the instant case the passenger/pursuer had fallen from the rear platform of a " Bristol Lodeka " omnibus. It was shown in evidence that the statistics for the previous six years, involving 600 buses of this design, revealed no similar accidents to passengers.

Another special case involving the ownership of property or materials and possible duty towards third parties arises where, for example, an employee of X is permitted to use equipment which is owned by Y and, because of some defect, injury is caused to X's employee. Who is responsible for that injury ? Is it X's employer *qua* employer or is it Y *qua* owner of the defective equipment ? Again, the property upon which the third party employee is working may be dangerous or some dangerous operation may be under way upon that property and the third party employee suffers injury. Who is responsible ? These problems are illustrated by the following cases: (i) *Oliver* v. *Saddler & Co.*,[56] an employee of X was killed by a defect in stevedoring plant (slings, in fact) owned by Y but which X's employees were allowed to use. No formal or informal hiring contract existed. The House of Lords, reversing the first Division of the Court of Session, held the stevedoring firm, owners of the plant, liable to the deceased in respect of a duty upon them to inspect the plant. No opportunity was given to the deceased or his fellow porters to test the slings. The later case of *Carlin* v. *Clan Line Steamers Ltd.*[57] (defective ship's tackle causing injury to a stevedore) followed the same

---

[54] *Ibid.* s. 44.
[55] (H.L.) 1966 S.L.T. 273.
[56] 1929 S.C.(H.L.) 94; 1929 S.L.T. 307; [1929] A.C. 584 (in which *Caledonian Ry.* v. *Warwick* (1897) 25 R.(H.L.) 1 was *distinguished*): The speeches of Viscount Dunedin and Lord Atkin are most instructive. This case pointed the way to *Donoghue* v. *Stevenson* which came some two years later.
[57] (O.H.) 1937 S.L.T. 190.

pattern; (ii) in *Eccles* v. *Cross and M'Ilwham*,[58] defective electric light plant had been installed in premises and the owner of these premises had retained control over the operations. The employee of another tradesman working on the premises died from injuries suffered because of the faulty installation. Who was to blame—owner or contractor? The First Division upon a reclaiming motion from an interlocutor of Lord Stevenson, and after reviewing the authorities in detail, held (a) that the contractor responsible for the installation owed a duty of care to the injured employee but the alleged breach of duty was not so proximate to the injury, in the circumstances of this case, as to involve liability and (b) that the averments of negligence on the owner's part should go to a proof before answer; (iii) in *Thos. W. Ward Ltd.* v. *Revie & Co.*[59] a contractor was carrying out a dangerous operation upon premises and in the course thereof an employee of the owner of the premises was injured. That employee and the contractor's foreman were both aware of the danger. Certain precautions were taken by the foreman but these were not sufficient. The employee continued with his work. The First Division held that the foreman was guilty of negligence, for which his employers (*i.e.*, contractors) were liable. Contributory negligence by the injured employee had not been established (in the absence of proof that he, the injured employee, knew or ought to have known that the precautions taken were insufficient); and (iv) in *Christie* v. *James Scott & Co. (Electrical Engineers) Ltd.*[60] Lord Kilbrandon held that an employee of contractor X working upon premises was relevantly blamed for causing injury to an employee of contractor Y working upon the same premises, by extinguishing a light in the vicinity of an unguarded pit.[60a]

(b) *Liability for the Contractual Acts of Employees*

Basically, each employee is the general agent of his employer and the test of the latter's liability is that the employee must be acting within the scope of his employment when the particular contractual act is performed. The employee may also be a special agent (normally an *ad hoc* appointment) and here the scope of his authority is the main criterion for fixing the employer's liability.

The normal ability to act as an agent arises either from (i) the employee's

---

[58] 1938 S.C. 697; 1938 S.L.T. 502. The opinion of Lord President Normand is important. The second-named defenders (owners) had pleaded (plea No. 4) that having entrusted the work to independent contractors they were under no liability for the employee's death and should be assoilzied. The Lord Ordinary held the action against the first-named defenders irrelevant; repelled the second defenders' plea-in-law No. 4 and allowed a proof before answer. The First Division recalled the Lord Ordinary's interlocutor so far as it repelled the fourth plea-in-law for the second defenders and *quoad ultra* adhered.

[59] 1944 S.C. 325; 1945 S.L.T. 49. Lord Moncrieff's opinion and his observations upon *Davies* v. *Mann* (1842) 10 M. & W. 546 make delightful reading.

[60] (O.H.) 1961 S.L.T.(Notes) 5.

[60a] The Industrial Injuries (Independent Contractors) Bill proposes that a superior contractor shall owe to every sub-contractor and to every employee of a sub-contractor a duty of care in respect of his personal safety, as though he were an employee of the superior contractor.

own position as representing his employer in dealings with third parties, when he is presumed to have a certain authority (*e.g.*, shop-managers, works-managers and the like); or (ii) from the fact that the employer has held him out as an agent with the authority to make certain contracts (*e.g.*, the domestic or personal employee).

The employer's liability may well be different in the cases of the general and the special agency. In the former case the liability upon the employer is usually wider and it is more likely to arise in broad terms than usually happens in the case of the special agent, where the authority is more clearly defined.[61]

The case of *Morrison* v. *Statter* [62] illustrates that any acting outwith the general scope of employment is a special agency and the agent's capacity to bind his employer is strictly tested by reference to the private instructions upon which the authority tests. Some of the earlier " railway cases " follow the same line in assessing the liability of the employer (principal).[63] It seems that whether or not the employee has an implied or presumed authority to bind his employer is a question which requires the closest examination of the facts and circumstances in each particular case. In the " holding-out " cases, the presumed authority is limited of course by the extent of the holding-out. The test then becomes one of ascertaining whether the employee's conduct was such as to create in the mind of the third party an understanding that the employee was indeed a general agent. Should there be a change made in the employee's authority there is an onus upon the employer to show that such change was notified to the third party involved in the transaction.

The principle of ratification [64] from the general law of agency applies equally to the employer and employee relationship, so that a contractual liability in the employer for acts done by his employee, and which acts were quite unauthorised at the time, may be created subsequently and be referable back to the date of their commission. The actual termination of the employer and employee relationship does not necessarily prevent the third party from proceeding against the employer. It is a question of circumstances whether the third party had notice of a withdrawal of authority or ought to have been on his guard against the possibility of a cancellation of the agent's authority, *e.g.*, by the death or insolvency of his employer. These are facts which ought to have been commonly known to the ordinary prudent man of business. The legal effect of a termination

---

[61] See *Brady* v. *Todd* (1861) 9 C.B.(N.S.) 592; *Howard* v. *Sheward* (1866) L.R. 2 C.P. 148 on the question of the giving of warranties by general and special agents.

[62] (1885) 12 R. 1152; 22 S.L.R. 770 (head shepherd on a farm having a general duty of supervising under-shepherds had no authority—without special instructions—to buy sheep for the farm).

[63] See *Montgomery* v. *N.B. Ry.* (1878) 5 R. 796; and see also *Walker* v. *Great Western Ry.* (1867) L.R. 2 Ex. 228; and again *Langan* v. *Great Western Ry.* (1873) 30 L.T.(N.S.) 173, where the likelihood of different grades of employee binding their employers was considered.

[64] See Gloag, *Contract* (2nd ed.), p. 143 *et seq.*; Bowstead, *Agency* (13th ed.), p. 34 *et seq.*; and Gloag and Henderson, *Introduction to the Law of Scotland* (7th ed.), p. 262.

is that there now rests upon the employer (as principal) the onus of showing that the third party had no reasonable cause for supposing that the employee's authority still continued in force.

Whenever an employee contracts as such without any authority whatsoever—either specific or implied—then he binds himself personally on the contract and he becomes personally liable thereunder. There is no liability whatsoever upon the employer in such a case, because there is not the slightest vestige of authority in the employee who is not an agent at all in such circumstances.

(c) *Liability for the Criminal Acts of Employees*

Any order or instruction given by an employer to his employee to do something which amounts to a criminal offence involves both of these parties in criminal liability. In Scots law, both are " art and part " in the offence. If the employee is merely an " innocent agent " then he himself escapes liability and it is the master alone who is answerable for the crime. In the case of a common law offence, the prosecution will require to prove the master's (*i.e.*, employer's) participation in the offence before a conviction will be obtained against him. The nature of the offence will be a very important matter to be considered in the first place. For example, an indictment for reckless driving or driving whilst under the influence of drink or drugs would not normally involve the employer, *qua* employer, in any criminal liability, although it would most certainly usually involve him in a civil action for damages in respect of his position as employer.

The liability under statute law may be quite different and so far as the employer is concerned he may be made absolutely liable *qua* employer (and that liability may attach to him as a principal or it may also attach to him vicariously as the employer of the particular employee or agent who committed the statutory breach which is averred) or as the owner or occupier or proprietor of particular premises which are themselves occupied and used for a particular purpose and which are also governed by special statutes.[65] There may be a " saving clause " to the advantage of the employer in certain statutes which will enable him to report that the particular breach was caused by a definite and identifiable person and that he (the employer) had no knowledge of the breach and indeed had used all due diligence to see that the statutory requirements were fully met.

---

[65] See, for example, the Factories Act 1961; the Mines and Quarries Act 1954; the Offices, Shops and Railway Premises Act 1963; and the statutes relating to licensing and to weights and measures; and see also the cases (which are a selection only) of: *Greenhill* v. *Stirling* (1885) 12 R.(J.) 37; *Galloway* v. *Weber* (1889) 16 R.(J.) 46; *Lindsay* v. *Dempster*, 1912 S.C.(J.) 110; *Robertson* v. *Gray*, 1945 J.C. 113 (weights and measures); *Ferguson* v. *Campbell*, 1946 J.C. 28; 1946 S.L.T. 58 (Licensing Acts) and *Shields* v. *Little*, 1954 S.L.T. 146; 1954 J.C. 25 (trafficking in exciseable liquor); and also—from the aspect of vicarious criminality under statute—the older cases of *Burnette* v. *Mackenna*, 1917 J.C. 20; 1916, 2 S.L.T. 293; *Auld* v. *Devlin*, 1918 J.C. 41; 1918, 1 S.L.T. 33; *Davidson* v. *Alexander*, 1927 S.N. 91; *Bean* v. *Sinclair*, 1930 J.C. 31; 1930 S.L.T. 423; and, most importantly, *Hall* v. *Begg*, 1928 J.C. 29; 1928 S.L.T. 336.

English procedure enables that other person to be brought before the court. Scottish procedure does not permit this to be done but the defence referred to above is a good defence (if it is established) to a prosecution in Scotland. However, the liability which is imposed by the statute may be an absolute liability upon the employer, to which there will be no defence. The breach of the statutory provision will create an immediate liability upon the employer.

In each case of statutory liability the primary task is one of construction of the particular statutory provision in order to ascertain (a) the reason for the obligation and (b) the capacity in which that obligation is being imposed by the legislature. Knowledge on the part of an employer may be vital in fixing an additional liability or even the primary liability upon him, as the prosecution would require, in the ordinary case, to prove this knowledge on the part of the employer.[66] If, on the other hand, the wording of the statute is clearly absolute, giving knowledge or acquiescence no place in the offence, the test of liability is—as mentioned in the preceding paragraph—the factual commission of the particular act which is expressly forbidden by the statute itself.

The common law doctrine of vicarious liability—so well known in the field of delict or civil wrongs—does not have an identical application within the field of common law crime. Vicarious criminal liability can, however, arise under statute law, as does general criminal liability.

The impact of the criminal law upon the relationship of employer and employee is important and it has been examined in more detail in a later chapter.[67]

---

[66] See particularly *Mens Rea in Statutory Offences* by J. Ll. J. Edwards (Macmillan, 1955), where the question of statutory liability is examined at some length.
[67] *Infra*, Chap. 22.

CHAPTER 13

THE LIABILITY OF THE EMPLOYEE TO THIRD PARTIES

(a) *In Delict*

When the employee himself has committed some wrongful act (*i.e.*, in the "civil" sense) or is guilty of some negligence, this makes him liable as a wrongdoer to a third party who has suffered injury or loss arising from that act or negligence. The fact that the employer has had to pay the claim made by the third party or is by the existing law, under the doctrine of vicarious liability, required, *qua* employer, to meet the loss does not excuse the offending employee from his personal responsibility. Indeed the real primary responsibility lies with the employee. It is the social and economic policies of a developed society which place the financial burden upon the employer. Perhaps it is only fair and reasonable that it should do so. If the wrongful act is done by both employer and employee together, then each is a contributing party with a shared primary responsibility. The employer may have his legal claim to a contribution [1] from the employee or, in the true case of vicarious liability, he may have a right of indemnity [2] against the employee. Whether it is good policy for an employer to enforce either of these rights is quite another matter, principally because (i) such enforcement is not calculated to improve the industrial relations in any particular establishment (the simple remedy is to get rid of the careless or incompetent employee); and (ii) if it becomes widespread local knowledge that a particular employer is in the habit of enforcing his rights of indemnity or contribution, recruitment of a suitable labour force for the particular establishment will become a very difficult task indeed.[3]

Procedurally, the pursuer might raise his action of damages against both employer and employee, jointly and severally, and enforce his decree against one or other or both. If he takes a decree against the employer only and tries to enforce it, but is unsuccessful, he cannot then initiate a

---

[1] See particularly the Law Reform (Miscellaneous Provisions) (Scotland) Act 1940, s. 3.

[2] See the leading English case of *Lister* v. *Romford Ice and Cold Storage Co. Ltd.* [1957] A.C. 555; [1957] 1 All E.R. 125; [1957] 2 W.L.R. 158, which presumably has clarified for English lawyers a point of principle which seems to have been accepted as good law in Scotland since the early 19th century. The House of Lords devoted much thought and legal argument to what has become known as the "implied term" with reference to indemnity and insurance in the employer/employee relationship, but eventually they decided against its implied incorporation into the contract of employment.

[3] It is understood that the insurance companies have agreed not to enforce their rights in cases of the *Lister* type. This particular case was responsible for the flashing of so many warning signals in the law of employment that an Interdepartmental Committee was set up immediately and its Report was issued in 1959. See the article by Gerald Gardiner (now Lord Gardiner L.C.) in (1959) 22 M.L.R. 652.

fresh action in respect of the same wrong against the employee. In practice the pursuer will almost always go against the employer and that will be an end of the matter. The incidence of employer's liability insurance in modern commercial and industrial practice simplifies the choice which the pursuer may have to make in deciding whom to sue, but the fact that there is an insurance policy in existence must never be regarded as creating any presumptive liability on the employer's part.[4]

The indemnity principle in Scots law seems to be founded upon the authority of the old case of *Anderson* v. *Brownlee*,[5] upon the reasoning that as the employer was and is bound at common law to relieve and indemnify the employee for any loss to him from conformation with orders, so the employee has a reciprocal obligation to indemnify the employer—whether the loss be a direct loss to the employer or a payment of damages or compensation to a third party. The English law appears to have taken the same view, but it has needed a long passage of time for the same conclusion to be evidenced in an outstanding common law case; this gap is now very clearly filled by the *Lister* case.[2] The right of an innocent tortfeasor in England to obtain contribution from the actual wrongdoer seems to be founded upon the exception to the rule in the old case of *Merryweather* v. *Nixan*[6] and the principle of contribution amongst joint wrongdoers in England was statutorily recognised by the Law Reform (Married Women and Tortfeasors) Act 1935.[7]

(b) *In Contract*

So long as an employee keeps within the limits of his mandate or authority he is not liable (unless in the special case of the master of a ship, for furnishings supplied to the ship) for contracts entered into by him on his employer's behalf. Yet an employee, like any other agent, who deals with the other party as though he (the employee) were a principal and does not disclose the fact that he is only an employee, will be liable personally upon the contractual obligation. So also if an employee, in contracting in his employer's name, goes beyond the scope of his authority or commission, then he will be liable personally to anyone dealing with him in the bona fide belief that he is acting within his employer's authority.[8] In any case in which an employee is acting as the special agent of his employer it becomes necessary to prove the special authority vested in him, and the employer's contractual liability rests upon the relevant

---

[4] Indeed, Viscount Simonds said in the course of his speech in *Davie* v. *New Merton Board Mills Ltd.* [1959] A.C. 604; [1959] 1 All E.R. 346; [1959] 2 W.L.R. 331: " It is not the function of a court of law to fasten upon the fortuitous circumstance of insurance to impose a greater burden on the employer than would otherwise lie upon him." However, the Employers' Liability (Compulsory Insurance) Bill, which is now before the House of Lords, proposes compulsory insurance in relation to an employer's own employees, but does not extend to third parties so as to create any special protection for them. See Appendix 3 to this volume, which contains the text of the new Act.
[5] (1822) 1 S. 442; see also *Clydesdale Bank* v. *Beatson* (1882) 10 R. 88.
[6] (1799) 8 T.R. 186; and see Winfield (8th ed.), pp. 647–649; Salmond (14th ed.), pp. 635–639.
[7] 25 & 26 Geo. 5, c. 30.
[8] Bell's *Commentaries*, i. 540; Gloag, *Contract* (2nd ed.); Bowstead, *Agency* (13th ed.).

exercise of that special authority. Such matters are governed by the general law of agency.

(c) *In Criminal Law*

Basically, an employee is answerable for any criminal act which he commits and which affects a third party. Primarily, that liability is personal and the employee himself becomes liable to a criminal prosecution. However, there may be cases in which an instruction has been given by an employer to his employee to do something which amounts to a criminal offence. Both employer and employee then become involved in criminal liability—the employer as instigator and the employee as perpetrator— and, of course, in Scotland both are liable as " art and part " in the offence. If the employee is merely an " innocent agent," then he escapes liability and it is the employer alone who has to answer for the crime. The prosecution will, in the case of the common law offences, require to prove the employer's participation in any offence committed by an employee before a conviction will be obtained against the employer. This will mean that the nature of the offence must be considered initially and carefully. For example, an indictment for reckless or drunken-driving taken against an employee does not prima facie involve the employer, *qua* employer, in any criminal liability. It will most certainly involve the employer, however, in a civil action in damages at the instance of the injured party (or his dependants) where the employee is acting within the scope of his employment at the time when the accident happens. The delictual principle of vicarious liability normally applies to this latter situation.

Liability under statute law may, however, be quite different. An employer may be made absolutely liable *qua* employer, or owner or occupier of particular premises occupied and used for a particular purpose, for the wrongful, including criminal, acts of his employees and the employees themselves may be made liable to prosecution for breaches of certain statutory provisions. Examples of this type of liability arise under, *inter alia*, the Factories Act 1961, the Mines and Quarries Act 1954, the Licensing (Scotland) Acts and the Weights and Measures Acts. There may be a " saving clause " to the employer which would enable him to escape prosecution. This device has been referred to in the preceding chapter. In each case of statutory liability the primary task is—as we have mentioned previously—an interpretation of the statutory provision in order to ascertain (i) the reason for the obligation and (ii) the capacity in which that obligation is being imposed by the legislature. As has been indicated above, the question of knowledge on the employer's part may be vital, because the prosecution must establish this knowledge before a conviction can be obtained.[9] The doctrine of vicarious liability, so well known in the field of delict, does not have quite the same application in the field of criminal law, but the " scope of employment " test may be

---

[9] See particularly *Mens Rea in Statutory Offences* (1955) by J. Ll. J. Edwards, where the question of statutory liability is very exhaustively examined. See also Chap. 12, *supra*.

very relevant indeed. Whilst an employee may clearly be liable to prosecution in the ordinary case, the relationship of employer and employee may raise a statutory liability (either as an alternative to or along with a common law liability) of which notice would have to be taken by the prosecuting authorities.

The general application of the criminal law to the employer and employee relationship is examined later herein.[10]

[10] *Infra*, Chap. 22.

CHAPTER 14

RIGHTS AND REMEDIES OF THE EMPLOYER AGAINST THIRD PARTIES

THE following remedies (whether actual or notional) must be considered:

    (i)   an action for inducing a breach of contract;

    (ii) an action for harbouring an employee;

    (iii) an action for injury to an employee (?).

(i) *Action for Inducing a Breach of Contract*

There is a long tradition in the common law of Scotland that if any person, knowingly and intentionally, induces an employee to commit a breach of his contract, *e.g.*, by deserting the employment, so that the employer suffers loss, such a person becomes liable to an action of damages at the instance of the employer.[1] It seems that the third party's act, by which he induces the breach, may be an act of any kind which results in a breach causing loss, *e.g.*, it may be the revealing of trade secrets or of confidential information,[2] and that it is not restricted to the most common case of X inducing Y to leave Z's employment in breach of the contract of employment between Y and Z.

The third party who is to be made liable must have had notice of the contract infringed, otherwise he cannot be said to have committed any wrongful act. Even knowledge of the existing relationship between the employer and his employee will not be enough—if such knowledge does not justify an inference of wilfully and intentionally inducing the breach. Obviously, a mere giving of advice, without injurious motive or wilful intention against the employer, will not involve liability to the employer.

The particular contract, the breach of which has been alleged, must be one which is enforceable; if, for example, it is void, there can be no contractual right arising to the employer and there is no question of his having a remedy for breach—because the contract itself is a nullity.[3]

Note on grounds of action against third parties who interfere with the contractual relationship: There must be considered briefly the development of the grounds of action against third parties who interfere with the employer and employee relationship. This is a matter of very considerable

---

[1] See *Dickson* v. *Taylor* (1816) 1 Mur. 141; *Rutherford* v. *Boak* (1836) 14 S. 732; *Couper & Sons* v. *Macfarlane* (1879) 6 R. 683; and *Exchange Telegraph Co.* v. *Giulianotti,* 1959 S.C. 19; (O.H.) 1959 S.L.T. 293 (*per* Lord Guest).

[2] *Rutherford* v. *Boak, supra; Kerr* v. *D. Roxburgh* (1822) 3 Mur. 126; *Roxburgh* v. *McArthur* (1841) 3 D. 556.

[3] *Sykes* v. *Dixon* (1839) 9 A. & E. 693; *Hartley* v. *Cummings* (1847) 5 C.B.(M.G. & S.) 247; *De Francesco* v. *Barnum* (1890) 45 Ch.D. 430.

interest and importance and not a little complexity. These grounds seem to fall into two basic categories, *viz.*:

(a) where the acts in question are unlawful acts; and

(b) where the said acts are lawful but are procured by unlawful means.

The older authorities which must be examined initially on this topic are mainly drawn from English law but, nevertheless, there are one or two important Scottish authorities. The early leading cases hereon are as follows: *Lumley* v. *Gye* [4]; *Bowen* v. *Hall* [5]; *Mogul SS. Co.* v. *McGregor Gow & Co.* [6]; *Temperton* v. *Russell* [7]; *Flood* v. *Jackson* [8] (appealed to the House of Lords as *Allen* v. *Flood* [9]); and *Quinn* v. *Leathem*.[10]

In *Lumley* v. *Gye* [4] the ground of action was that defendant had " maliciously intending to injure plaintiff . . . enticed and procured (Miss) Wagner to break her contract with plaintiff." The action was held to be competent.[11] Coleridge J. dissented, taking the following points: (i) the damage was too remote, (ii) the motive was too elusive in character to be a test of legal action, and (iii) the action of damages for enticing an employee was an exception to the general rule, applying only to labourers in husbandry or one of the classes of menial employees to which the Statute of Labourers had applied.

In *Bowen* v. *Hall*,[5] the decision in *Lumley's* case was considered and approved. Again, defendant and another person had knowingly induced a breach of a five-year contract in plaintiff's favour.[12] The three conditions laid down in the judgment of Brett L.J. (as he then was) are interesting as the foundation for an action where these conditions were fulfilled, *viz.*: (a) the defendant's act must be wrongful in law and in fact; (b) the breach of contract should be a natural and probable consequence of the act of persuasion; and (c) the breach should cause injury to the plaintiff—but such injury must not be too remote.

In *Mogul SS. Co.* v. *McGregor Gow & Co.*[6] no allegation of procuring a breach was made. The position was that certain traders in the China tea trade combined to keep their competitors out of the market, by offering rebates to customers who dealt exclusively with them and by reducing freights, as well as by threatening to cease employing their own agents who also acted for other traders outside the combination. The action was in damages, founded upon an illegal combination or alternatively, standing the combination, that it made use of unlawful means. The action was unsuccessful—the court holding that, in spite of any loss to plaintiffs,

[4] (1853) 2 E. & B. 216.
[5] (1881) 6 Q.B.D. 333.
[6] (1889) 23 Q.B.D. 598; [1892] A.C. 25.
[7] [1893] Q.B. 715.
[8] [1895] 2 Q.B. 21.
[9] [1898] A.C. 1.
[10] [1901] A.C. 495 (reported as *Leathem* v. *Craig* [1899] 2 I.R. 667).
[11] See *per* Crompton J. at p. 224.
[12] See *per* Brett L.J. (as he then was) (later to become Lord Esher) at p. 337, delivering the majority judgment of the court.

the object of the combination was to secure and protect the trade of the defendants. No violence, intimidation, fraud, misrepresentations or procurement of a breach of contract had occurred. No right of the plaintiffs had been violated.[13] Both the Court of Appeal and the House of Lords held that the defendants had not exceeded the legal limits of competition in the course of trade.

Temperton v. *Russell* [13a] is interesting as it was an action taken by a manufacturer against the members of a joint committee of three trade unions. Two grounds of action were relied upon: (a) that defendants unlawfully and maliciously procured certain persons to break contracts which they had entered into with the plaintiff, and (b) that they did maliciously conspire to induce certain persons not to enter into contracts with plaintiff. The court held that defendants were actuated in what they did, not by any spite or malice against plaintiff personally, but by a desire to injure him in his business by forcing him not to do something which he had a legal right to do and to compel him to comply with the unions' requirements; accordingly, they had then induced certain persons to break their contracts with plaintiff and they knew about the existence of these contracts; and, moreover, the plaintiff had sustained loss from the breaches of contract. On the second ground of action the facts proved to the court's satisfaction were—the same desire of defendants, their acting in combination, their success in inducing breaches of contract and a consequent loss to plaintiff. The malicious purpose, successful inducement of breaches of contract and consequent loss, taken together, were held to found a good ground of action against those persons acting in combination.[14]

The foregoing cases seem to indicate that two basic conditions must be fulfilled before the action in damages for procuring a breach will succeed, *viz.*: (a) loss must be caused to the party claiming damages and (b) the procuring of the breach must be " malicious," in the sense of an intention to cause injury to pursuer or to his business interests—and must be coupled with some unlawful act, whether of the inducer himself or of one of the parties to the contract which is broken.

The important question of the meaning and effect of " malice " was discussed, at great length, in *Flood* v. *Jackson* [15] which went to the House of Lords under the name of *Allen* v. *Flood*.[16] Briefly, the facts were—two shipwrights, Flood and Taylor, were employed by Glengall Iron Co. to repair a ship. The boilermakers employed by the company objected to Flood and Taylor being employed on this work, claiming that these two men had invaded their province by carrying out iron-work in another yard (" demarcation " at an early stage). Allen, the trade union delegate of

---

[13] See dictum of Bowen L.J. in the Court of Appeal—23 Q.B.D. at p. 613 (criticised by Lord Herschell in *Allen* v. *Flood* [1898] A.C. 1 at p. 139).
[13a] [1893] Q.B. 715.
[14] See *per* Lopes L.J. at p. 731 of the report.
[15] [1895] 2 Q.B. 21.
[16] [1898] A.C. 1.

the boilermakers, persuaded the company to dismiss Flood and Taylor, threatening that if it did not do so the boilermakers would be called out on strike or would come out on strike. There was, of course, no breach of contract between the company and its employees, as the company could discharge Flood and Taylor at any time. The jury found that Allen had " maliciously induced " the company to dispense with the services of plaintiffs and had " maliciously induced " the company not to engage plaintiffs. " Maliciously " in this case meant that there was a deliberate intention to punish plaintiffs or to injure them in their trade or to obtain some benefit to the boilermakers at the expense of the shipwrights. The House of Lords held, however, there was no ground upon which an action could be maintained. The company had committed no legal wrong against plaintiffs and presumably there was nothing wrongful in Allen persuading or inducing the company to do exactly what they had a legal right to do at any time. A strong argument was put forward that a special right existed in every person to exercise his trade or to dispose of his labour, free from molestation or interference and that any such interference was actionable unless done with just cause or excuse. But this was rejected as a so-called special right. Before any action could be taken there had to be a wrongful act and, moreover, an act which is otherwise lawful cannot be made unlawful (*i.e.*, wrongful) because it is prompted by a bad motive. Malice *per se* is not actionable.

Quinn v. *Leathem* [17] took the development a stage further. This case involved the elements of (i) threats and (ii) conspiracy. The court made no attempt to define " legal threats " or " illegal threats." It was, however, found as a matter of fact that defendants had acted in combination and with a common purpose to injure plaintiff in his business by preventing the free action of those dealing with him and with the effect of actually injuring him and that this was done without just cause or excuse. The acts in question were not proved to have resulted in any breach of contract through which plaintiff suffered loss, but they caused others to refuse to deal with plaintiff and in this way pecuniary damage was caused to plaintiff. The action, based upon these facts, was sustained.[18] Although *Quinn's* case lies clearly upon the foundation of an illegal conspiracy it was suggested that the means employed—*viz.*, coercion by threats—were in themselves sufficient to attach liability to defendants. This point was to come before the courts again some sixty years later in the now famous case of *Rookes* v. *Barnard* [19] and once again a decision of the House of Lords was to perturb the trade union world.

---

[17] [1901] A.C. 495 (reported as *Leathem* v. *Craig* in [1899] 2 I.R. 667).

[18] This case seems to approve, therefore, the second ground of action in *Temperton* v. *Russell*.

[19] [1964] A.C. 1129 (H.L.); [1964] 1 All E.R. 367; [1964] 2 W.L.R. 269; [1964] 1 Lloyd's Rep. 28.
See *infra* Chap. 17 for the trade union situation.

There are, accordingly, two types of case to be met with, *viz.*:

(i)   where the action is based upon a wrongful act (done either by one or more persons, but with no acting in concert); and

(ii) where the action is based upon a lawful or unlawful act done by unlawful means, including therein an illegal combination.

It seems that *Lumley, Bowen* and *Allen* v. *Flood* fall into the first category: whilst *Mogul SS. Co.* and *Quinn* v. *Leathem* fall into the second category. It also appears that *Temperton* v. *Russell* overlaps both. The former category apparently requires a violation of some right, based on contract or otherwise, done knowingly and intentionally and resulting in some loss. The latter, based upon illegal conspiracy, apparently requires a combination of persons with the object of causing injury to another, followed by some act or acts done in furtherance of that purpose and also pecuniary loss arising therefrom.

Scots law has not developed the law of " conspiracy " to the same extent as English law. Instead, it has chosen to regard conspiracy as a form of " attempt " in the criminal sense or as a form of " fraud " or undue influence or coercion by a plurality of persons in the civil sense, leaving the common law remedies to be applied. Nevertheless, there is one older Scottish civil case of " conspiracy " which must be examined at this point, *viz.*: *Scottish Co-operative Society* v. *Glasgow Fleshers Association*.[20] Here it was alleged that the defenders had entered into an illegal combination to induce, and had induced, the salesmen at Yorkhill Quay in Glasgow to insert in their conditions of sale provisions under which bids from the pursuers were not to be received; that such conditions were illegal and that the pursuers had sustained injury because of the refusal of salesmen to accept bids from them. It was held that the conditions excluding the pursuers' bids were not illegal, and, as regards a conspiracy to induce salesmen to insert conditions refusing bids, the defenders had merely done what was legitimate for their own protection, under conditions of trade competition. The case was said to be clearly governed by the precedent of *Mogul SS. Co.* v. *McGregor Gow & Co.*[21] This very important point of protection of trade in business interests was to appear again in the most important Scottish case of *Crofter Hand Woven Harris Tweed Co.* v. *Veitch*[22] which went to the House of Lords. This case is classified in the Scottish reports and digests as a case on " restraint of trade " and might be thought to be of very little importance except in the field of contract. This would be quite a false picture, because the House of Lords decision—which, by this very case, is an outstanding one in the field of labour law—did much to clarify both " conspiracy " and " intimidation " as torts in the whole common law world. Its importance for Scots law—in the special fields of delict and the law of employment— must not be overlooked and indeed the case itself is examined in more

[20] (1893) 35 S.L.R. 645.
[21] (1889) 23 Q.B.D. 598; [1892] A.C. 25.
[22] 1942 S.C.(H.L.) 1; 1943 S.L.T. 2 (H.L.); [1942] A.C. 435; [1942] 1 All E.R. 142.

detail later on in a succeeding chapter,[23] where the trade union position is considered in some detail.

" Conspiracy " in English law is throughout most reports and text-books referred to but perhaps not very clearly defined, thus—" that which is lawful when done by one person or several persons acting individually may be unlawful when done by a number of persons acting in combination." Moreover, conspiracy was an offence [24] punishable in the English criminal courts and at the same time it could give rise to a civil action in damages. This civil action in damages has now become generally known in English law as the tort of conspiracy. It is important to realise that the illegal conspiracy has two branches, viz.: (a) its whole object may be unlawful, or (b) its object may be quite lawful, but the method or means of attaining that object may be unlawful—for example, by the use of violence or threats or other forms of intimidation or fraud.

So far as Scotland is concerned, it has been said that " where an act would not be unlawful if done by one person it does not become unlawful or criminal when two or more persons combine to do it." [25] The conspiracy may be charged as a criminal act in Scotland,[26] as well as the particular criminal acts themselves, but such criminal proceedings for conspiracy alone have never been popular in Scotland.

It seems that civil liability in Scotland arising from a combination which is not criminal could only be attached to the persons concerned where the acts done or the methods used by the combination would be wrongful if done by a single individual.[27]

Intimidation (which is itself another form of delict—giving rise to civil proceedings for damages—very like conspiracy, and often arising perhaps from the same set of circumstances, and the importance of which was stressed by the House of Lords in *Rookes* v. *Barnard*,[28] although in this particular instance the action was taken by a dismissed employee against certain union officials as individual defenders in the action) is expressly forbidden by the Conspiracy and Protection of Property Act 1875, s. 7. But it seems, from *Allen* v. *Flood*,[29] that molestation and obstruction may not be actionable, unless either is effected by unlawful means.[30]

The trade unions have been involved to a very considerable extent in these matters relating to conspiracy, coercion and intimidation, with

---

[23] *Infra*, Chap. 17.
[24] See Russell, *Crime*; Kenny, *Outlines of Criminal Law* (19th ea.).
[25] *Couper & Sons* v. *Macfarlane* (1879) 6 R. 683, *per* Lord Gifford at p. 697.
[26] See Alison, i. 369; Hume, i. 170. But see Macdonald, *The Criminal Law of Scotland* (introductory section).
[27] The House of Lords apparently overruled this view in *Quinn* v. *Leathem* [1901] A.C. 495. The law was amended *re* trade disputes by the Trade Disputes Act 1906, s. 1.
[28] [1964] A.C. 1129; [1964] 1 All E.R. 367; [1964] 2 W.L.R. 269; [1964] 1 Lloyd's Rep. 28, applied later—following after the Trade Disputes Act 1965—in *Morgan* v. *Fry* [1967] 3 W.L.R. 65; [1967] 2 All E.R. 386 (but see Chap. 17 *infra*, dealing with trade union matters and with *Morgan* v. *Fry* on appeal).
[29] *Cit. supra.*
[30] See also *Mogul SS. Co.* and *Scottish Co-operative Society* cases cited above.

the tendency in earlier times for the courts to find against the trade unions. However, in 1906, by the Trade Disputes Act of that year, the trade unions gained a general immunity in actions of delict (or tort)[31] and, with special reference to trade disputes,[32] an immunity was set up protecting them from any proceedings against the unions themselves arising therefrom and, of course, protecting simultaneously the substantial union funds. These matters are more fully discussed in a later chapter of this volume.[33]

The employer may sue any third party who induces his employees to disclose confidential information[34] or he may obtain an interdict (injunction, in England) against any rival firm which employs his workmen and which obtains certain advantages from their specialised skills.[35]

Unjustifiable encouragement to break contracts must be distinguished clearly from (i) cases where a person is induced to stop working, without a breach of contract and there is no use of unlawful means[36] and from (ii) cases where the defenders neither knew nor ought to have known about the alleged wrongful act—see *British Industrial Plastics Ltd.* v. *Ferguson*,[37] where the plaintiff's employee made a leaving agreement with them and promised not to interest himself in the manufacture or sale of certain chemicals (used in the plaintiff's secret processes) before a certain date. Some three months later the employee went to the defendants and offered them a process for which their patent agent made application for a patent. The plaintiffs began an action of breach of contract against their former employee and against the defendants for inducing the breach. It was held that there was no ground of action against the company as they had *no* knowledge (either actual or constructive) of the breach.

Wrongful interference was also lacking in the well-known case of *D. C. Thomson & Co. Ltd.* v. *Deakin*,[38] where plaintiffs required their employees to sign an undertaking (known in the trade union world— and utilising a most expressive American term—as a " yellow-dog " contract). Several employees had broken this undertaking and they dismissed *one* such employee. He subsequently appealed to the union for help. The union called out its members on strike and asked other unions for assistance. Certain employees of another (*i.e.*, a third party) company which supplied paper to the plaintiffs said that they were unwilling to handle paper destined for the plaintiffs. This supplying company then told the plaintiffs they would not be able to make deliveries of paper as required by the supply contract. The plaintiffs then took injunction proceedings (interdict would have been the equivalent in Scotland) against the union

---

31 See Trade Disputes Act 1906, s. 4.
32 *Ibid.* s. 3.
33 *Infra*, Chap. 17.
34 *Bents Brewery Co. Ltd.* v. *Hogan* [1945] 2 All E.R. 570.
35 *Hivac Ltd.* v. *Park Royal Scientific Instruments Ltd.* [1946] 1 Ch. 169; [1946] 1 All E.R. 350.
36 *i.e., Allen* v. *Flood* [1898] A.C. 1.
37 [1940] 1 All E.R. 479.
38 [1952] Ch. 646; [1952] 2 All E.R. 361.

officials [39] to restrain them from causing or procuring breaches of contract between the supplying company and plaintiffs. The court was of the opinion that had the defendants had actual knowledge of the contract and had they attempted by wrongful acts to make it impossible to perform (that is to say, by direct interference), an action would have lain. But this had not been so, on the evidence, so the injunction was refused. Jenkins L.J. held [40] that actionable interference with contractual relations should be confined to cases where it is clearly shown:

(a) that the person charged with actionable interference knew of the existence of the contract and intended to procure its breach;

(b) that that person did definitely and unequivocally persuade, induce or procure the employees to break their contract, with intent;

(c) that the employees so persuaded . . . did break their contracts of employment; and

(d) that the breach of contract forming the alleged subjects of interference resulted as a consequence of the breaches of the contracts of employment.

The question of inducing the breach of a " commercial contract " (including within that framework any inter-union controversy relating to negotiation and representation during an industrial dispute) must be distinguished carefully from that of inducing the breach of a contract of employment (or labour contract). The latter is evidenced by *Rookes* v. *Barnard* [41] and the former by two recent cases, one English and one Scottish, *viz.*: *J. T. Stratford & Son Ltd.* v. *Lindley*,[42] which went to the House of Lords and concerned the inducement of breaches of barge-hiring contracts which would have resulted in heavy financial loss to the appellants. The House restored the interlocutory injunction which had been granted at first instance, but which had been subsequently discharged by the Court of Appeal. It was held also that the respondents could not shelter behind the statutory protection created by the Trade Disputes Act 1906 because the dispute which arose here was not a trade dispute within the meaning of section 5 (3) of that statute. It was merely an inter-union controversy. The Scottish case of *Square Grip Reinforcement Co.* v.

---

[39] In Scottish procedure the action against an unregistered trade union may be taken in the sheriff court or the Court of Session. In the former court the trade union is sued or may sue in its " descriptive " name alone (Sheriff Courts (Scotland) Act 1913, Sched. 11). In the latter court the names of responsible officials or representatives— duly authorised by the rules or by any resolution passed at a meeting of the union— should be added (see *Renton Football Club* v. *M'Dowell* (1891) 18 R. 670). Defenders are entitled to know who are the responsible officers bringing the action (*Pagan and Osborne* v. *Haig*, 1910 S.C. 341, *per* Lord Dundas at p. 350). For a valuable note on Scottish procedure and a commentary upon some of the difficulties of English procedure, see Citrine, *Trade Union Law* (3rd ed.), pp. 191–194.

[40] *Ibid.* pp. 696 and 379 respectively.

[41] [1964] A.C. 1129; [1964] 1 All E.R. 367; [1964] 2 W.L.R. 269; [1964] 1 Lloyd's Rep. 28 and reading along with that case the statutory provisions of the Trade Disputes Acts 1906 and 1965 in so far as these relate to inducement to break contracts of employment.

[42] [1964] 3 All E.R. 102; [1965] A.C. 269; see also *Emerald Construction Co. Ltd.* v. *Lowthian* [1966] 1 W.L.R. 691.

MacDonald[43] is interesting because it raised the question of sections 3 and 5 (3) of the Trade Disputes Act 1906[44] and section 1 of the Trade Disputes Act 1965[45] in relation to inducement of the breach of a commercial contract. The company pursuer had refused to negotiate through a trade union but preferred direct negotiation with their employees. However, a large number of these employees—being dissatisfied with pay and conditions—had joined a trade union. A strike was called because the company would not recognise the trade union. Because of the actings of certain officials and members of the union, who attended at building sites and induced workers there to refuse to off-load transport carrying materials supplied by the company to contractors, who were substantial customers, these contractors were forced into breaking their commercial contracts with the company. The company now sought suspension and interdict (corresponding to the English " interlocutory injunction ") against the union officials and union members as individuals. This was granted and continued, it being held (i) that there was a trade dispute, within the meaning of the Trade Disputes Act 1906, between the employees and the company and accordingly the 1906 Act applied and (2) that section 3 of the Act afforded no protection to the employees (and union members) because the contract in question was a commercial contract and not a contract of employment. The methods by which these breaches of contract are induced—be it by conspiracy or intimidation or some other form of unlawful acting—are more fully discussed in the later chapter[46] on the subject of the trade unions.

It is, however, evident from both of these cases that any inducement of breach of contract, coupled with knowledge of the contract and the clear intention to break, it will create a prima facie liability on the part of the contract-breaker. Where the interdict (or injunction) procedure is being used it seems that the courts will not inquire too deeply at that stage whether the methods used were lawful or unlawful. In view of the modern use of the injunction or interdict in labour disputes it may be necessary to modify one's views on the *D. C. Thomson & Co. Ltd.* v. *Deakin* judgment, where the court refused to attach liability because the means utilised for procuring the breach were not, in themselves, unlawful.[47]

Justification is said to be a defence to any proceedings based upon inducement of breach of contract, but it is extremely difficult to identify the scope of this defence. There is no clear-cut formula to which reference can be made to enable a defender or his legal advisers to decide at once whether to use justification as a defence. Accordingly, only after a consideration of all the facts and circumstances of the particular case in hand can a decision be reached and advice be given. It has been argued,

[43] (O.H.) 1968 S.L.T. 65.
[44] 6 Edw. 7, c. 47.
[45] 1965, c. 48.
[46] Chap. 17, *infra*.
[47] See Winfield, *Tort* (8th ed.), p. 543.

in England, that a person whose contractual interests (in a contract between himself and X) are likely to be prejudicially affected by the conclusion of a subsequent contract between X and Y, is entitled to protect himself by inducing X to break that subsequent contract [48]; and also it would appear that any action taken—without violence or threats or other unlawful means—in the interests of public decency and morality—would be justified—see *Stott* v. *Gamble* [49] and *Brimelow* v. *Casson.* [50] The giving of bona fide advice, whether by lawyers or medical men or other professional men, which might well result in a breach of contract would not be such as to render these persons responsible for any " inducement of breach," because they have a duty—not just wholly a moral duty—to protect the interests and the health of their clients. It must be pointed out, however, that there are conflicting views [51] upon this question of pressures of moral duties or social duties amounting to justification for any interference by A in a contractual relationship between B and C.   Whilst regard must be had to the possible defence of justification in cases of this type, it is by no means certain that it is always available to the defender. Nor should the mistake be made of equating justification in this type of action with justification or privilege in the defamation actions.

(ii) *Action for Harbouring an Employee*

It is equally well established at common law that if any person harbours or continues to employ a deserting employee, after notice of the facts, then he becomes liable to the employer who has been deserted by that employee. [52]   The test of liability is the third party's continuation of the employment of the employee, after he has become aware of the fact that the employee is in desertion from his previous employment. Such an action would then be a deliberate interference with the primary relationship and accordingly some protection must be given to the primary employer provided he has suffered loss. [53] The deserting employee is, of course, also liable to the primary employer for the breach of his own contract of employment. This type of action might be tried in such circumstances as those disclosed in the English case of *Hivac Ltd.* v. *Park Royal Scientific Instruments Ltd.*, [54] but it is submitted that the more logical proceeding to take in such a case is an application for interdict in

---

[48] *Smithies* v. *National Association of Operative Plasterers* [1909] 1 K.B. 310, *per* Buckley L.J. at p. 337.

[49] [1916] 2 K.B. 504.

[50] [1924] 1 Ch. 302.

[51] See particularly *South Wales Miners' Federation* v. *Glamorgan Coal Co.* [1905] A.C. 239—*per* Lord Halsbury L.C. at p. 245; Lord James at p. 249; and compare the view of Lord Lindley at p. 255.

[52] *Dickson* v. *Taylor, cit. supra*; *Blake* v. *Lanyon* (1795) 6 T.R. 221; *Sykes* v. *Dixon, Hartley* v. *Cummings* and *De Francesco* v. *Barnum, cit. supra*; *Pilkington* v. *Scott* (1846) 15 M. & W. 657; *Rose Street Foundry Co.* v. *Lewis*, 1917 S.C. 341; and *Cave* v. *Trench* [1949] C.L.Y. 1397; also *Bell's Principles*, 2033.

[53] *Jones Bros.* (*Hunstanton*) v. *Stevens* [1954] 3 All E.R. 677; [1955] 1 Q.B. 275; and *D. C. Thomson Ltd.* v. *Deakin* [1952] Ch. 646, 649 *per* Jenkins L.J.

[54] [1946] Ch. 169.

Scotland (injunction, in England) and thereafter to pursue a claim for damages, if such a claim can be substantiated.

This type of action is probably nowadays more a matter of historical interest than one of practical applicability. Indeed the Law Reform Committee [55] has recommended that it be abolished.[56] Doubtless the simple action for damages would be quite sufficient, based upon the contractual interference by the third party, who would be the defender in the action.

(iii) *Injury to the Employee by a Third Party* (?)

Scots law does not permit any action at the instance of an employer against a third party who has caused injury to the employee, thereby, of course, resulting in loss and inconvenience to the employer. English law tends to allow such an action upon the basis of a deprivation of services in which the employer is said to have a quasi right of property; and this action is restricted in England to a relationship which is a domestic or family one involving personal services to the employer (or parent). Hence, the action is said to be based upon a loss of those services— *per quod servitium amisit*.[57]

This type of action was attempted in Scotland in *Allan* v. *Barclay*,[58] but the Lord Ordinary held it incompetent, apparently upon the ground of remoteness of damage; and the Inner House expressed serious doubts as to its competency. The same type of action was again tried in Scotland many years later in *Reavis* v. *Clan Line Steamers* [59] but was again regarded as incompetent. English law seems to be the same in principle as Scots law but—as we have said above—it allows an exception in the case of menial employees, employed as part of the domestic staff, basing damages upon the action *per quod servitium amisit*,[60] which has just been mentioned. This matter was only recently exhaustively examined by the Law Reform Committee for Scotland. Their Report [61] concludes unanimously that any possible alterations in the law would produce worse results than any supposed defect or unfairness and, therefore, for the reasons explained [62] by them, they recommended that no legislation was necessary. It is perhaps interesting to observe that all the bodies which tendered evidence to the Committee—with one specific exception—favoured the retention of the *status quo*.[63] That is how matters still stand.

---

[55] *i.e.*, for England and Wales.
[56] See the Eleventh Report (Cmnd. 2017: 1963), para. 23.
[57] See particularly *Inland Revenue Commissioners* v. *Hambrook* and *Receiver for the Metropolitan Police District* v. *Croydon Corporation*, cited below at note 60.
[58] (1864) 2 M. 873.
[59] 1925 S.C. 725; and see also *Young* v. *Ormiston*, 1936 S.L.T. 79.
[60] See *Inland Revenue Commissioners* v. *Hambrook* [1956] 2 Q.B. 641; and *Receiver for the Metropolitan Police District* v. *Croydon Corporation and Another* [1957] 2 Q.B. 154.
[61] Eleventh Report of the Law Reform Committee for Scotland (Cmnd. 1997) (1963).
[62] *Ibid.* pp. 4 and 5.
[63] *Ibid.* p. 2.

CHAPTER 15

RIGHTS AND REMEDIES OF THE EMPLOYEE AGAINST THIRD PARTIES

IT has been pointed out in the preceding chapter than an employer has, in Scotland, no right of action in damages against any third party who causes loss to the employer because of some wrong done to an employee. In support of this statement the cases of *Allan* v. *Barclay*[1] and *Reavis* v. *Clan Line Steamers*[2] have been cited and reference was also made to the Eleventh Report[3] of the Law Reform Committee for Scotland. The principle of law established in *Allan* v. *Barclay* is that a wrongdoer " cannot be held bound to have surmised the secondary injuries done to all holding relations with the individual, whether that of a master or any other." The only recognised exception to this principle is the special cause of action arising in favour of a near relative of a deceased person whose death was caused by the fault of a third party. This exception is clearly established in the well-known case of *Eisten* v. *North British Railway Company*[4] although Lord President Inglis described it as a " peculiarity in our system."[5]

Presumably the reason for the *Allan* v. *Barclay* principle gaining such a general acceptance is that the loss or damage incurred is too remote, in the circumstances, or, alternatively, a third party who becomes involved in a contractual relationship between an employer and an employee— but without any other special ground of liability arising in respect of either party as an individual—could not possibly have foreseen all the ramifications which would occur from his initial wrongful act. Theoretically, if one accepts that the business interests of the employer and the employee are one and the same, then there is no reason why either should not be able to sue the offending third party who has caused loss to the " business " (which affects and supports the well-being of employer and employees). However, leaving aside the questions of remoteness and foreseeability, there is little doubt that from the practical point of view the law is correct in its present form. Otherwise the incidence of liability would become intolerable, the whole legal process might be reduced to absurdity and Lord Kilbrandon's reference to " Bingo sessions "[6] might have a wider application than his lordship initially had in mind. It might

---

[1] (1864) 2 M. 873.
[2] 1925 S.C. 725.
[3] Cmnd. 1997.
[4] (1870) 8 M. 980; and see D. M. Walker, *The Law of Delict in Scotland* at pp. 725–726.
[5] *Ibid.* at p. 984.
[6] *Other People's Law* (Hamlyn Lectures 1966) at pp. 52–53.

be thought that if a third party caused loss to a firm or company by any injury to a partner or director thereof, the firm or company might have a cause of action for what amounts, in a sense, to the " organisation " or " management " content or element in the whole business structure. But this is not so—the law meantime gives no such right of action.[7]

Although what has been said above has reference mainly to the employer/management side of industry and commerce, it is equally true to say that Scots law does not allow an employee who suffers loss by reason of the death of or an injury to his employer to bring an action in damages against the third party responsible for that death or injury. The *Allan* v. *Barclay* principle applies with equal force to that situation as it does to the employer's situation; indeed, perhaps it applies more strongly in the case of the employee, because there is no obligation upon an employer to give services to an employee, with the result that the employee's argument is considerably weakened. Moreover, the business—as an economic asset or an economic liability—is the responsibility of the employer himself. Undoubtedly he possesses certain rights of property in his business which he is quite well able to protect, be it under the umbrella of property law or patent law or otherwise, but he cannot do so against any third party upon the basis of a damages claim for the injury or death of an employee which occasions loss to him. The same is true of the employee who may also have certain property rights to be protected—for example, in respect of inventions patented by him and coupled with licence agreements to his employers—but again the contractual relationship of employer/employee does not give grounds for an action arising from the death of or injury to the employer. It is understood that English law takes a similar view of the employee's position.[8]

However, quite apart from the inability of the employee to sue a third party in respect of injury or death to the employer, it is always possible for an employee to take proceedings against and claim damages from any third party who successfully (a) induces the employer to break the contract of employment with that employee[9] or (b) induces an employer either not to engage the pursuer as an employee or to discharge the pursuer as an employee. Now these matters are never easy to prove and perhaps it is much more difficult to bring a successful action under the second heading

---

[7] See *Gibson and Others* v. *Glasgow Corporation,* 1963 S.L.T.(Notes) 16 (partnership).

[8] See, for example, *Earl* v. *Lubbock* [1905] 1 K.B. 253; *Cavalier* v. *Pope* [1906] A.C. 428; *Cattle* v. *Stockton Waterworks Co.* [1907] 2 K.B. 141; and *Dickson* v. *Reuter's Telegraph Co.* (1877) 3 C.P.D. 1.

[9] See *Read* v. *Friendly Society of Operative Stonemasons, etc.* [1902] 2 K.B. 733, a case in which an apprentice brought proceedings, successfully, against a trade union which had induced his master to dismiss him, in breach of the indenture (or articles) of apprenticeship. The union based its case on the argument that this particular apprenticeship was a breach of the union rules, because plaintiff was too old to serve an apprenticeship. It is clear from the later cases of *Conway* v. *Wade* [1909] A.C. 506 at p. 510 and *Rookes* v. *Barnard* [1964] A.C. 1129 (particularly the speech of Lord Devlin at p. 1214) that mere belief of the third party that he is acting in his own interests is no answer to the pursuer's claim and there is certainly much less chance of a valid defence where threats are used to back up the inducement or persuasion.

than it is under the first. Such proceedings taken at the instance of the employee correspond to the remedies available to the employer against any third party who persuades, entices, induces or procures the employee to break his contract of employment. It is often difficult to draw the line between advice and genuine complaints to an employer, by which the employer is more or less manoeuvred, if not forced, into the position of having to get rid of an employee, and threats made by the defender against the employer. The former methods would not give any right of action to the employee—but the latter might if intimidation, coercion or duress could be established.[10]

The third party who is sued by the employee may rely upon these same defences which are available to him in any action brought by the employer, namely—(i) the statutory defences established by the Trade Disputes Act 1906,[11] as amended or extended by the Trade Disputes Act 1965 [12]; and (ii) the common law defence of " justification," which has been explained in the preceding chapter [13] and which need not be repeated here.

The 1906 Act above-mentioned amends the law of conspiracy [14] in relation to trade disputes [15] and permits peaceful picketing whilst a trade dispute is actually in contemplation or in progress.[16] But the main defences are contained in sections 3 and 4 (1), viz.: section 3—" An act done by a person in contemplation or furtherance of a trade dispute shall not be actionable on the ground only that it induces some other person to break a contract of employment or that it is an interference with the trade, business, or employment of some other person, or with the right of some other person to dispose of his capital or his labour as he wills "; and section 4 (1)—" An action against a trade union, whether of workmen or masters, or against any members or officials thereof on behalf of themselves and all other members of the trade union in respect of any tortious act

---

[10] See particularly *Allen* v. *Flood* [1898] A.C. 1, where the plaintiffs sued trade union officials who had advised the employing company to dismiss them, which was done in proper dismissal form. There was no direct evidence of intimidation or conspiracy or coercion, although there was undoubtedly malice against the plaintiffs. Apart from this malicious intent (which, by itself, was not enough to enable plaintiffs to succeed), there was no wrongful acting which, in the view of the House of Lords, could attach liability to the trade union officials. See also the English cases of *Valentine* v. *Hyde* [1919] 2 Ch. 129 (where plaintiff succeeded) and *Hodges* v. *Webb* [1920] 2 Ch. 80, and compare these two cases with the views expressed on " just cause " in the Scottish case of *Crofter Hand-Woven Harris Tweed Co.* v. *Veitch* [1942] A.C. 435, *per* Lord Wright at p. 478 and Lord Porter at p. 496; and 1942 S.C.(H.L.) 1 *et seq.* and 1943 S.L.T. 2 *et seq.* (H.L.) for the speeches in full.
[11] 6 Edw. 7, c. 47.
[12] 1965, c. 48.
[13] *Supra*, Chap. 14.
[14] As contained in s. 3 of the Conspiracy and Protection of Property Act 1875 (38 & 39 Vict., c. 86).
[15] Defined in s. 5 (3) of the 1906 Act (with reference to that Act and the Conspiracy and Protection of Property Act 1875) as " any dispute between employers and workmen, or between workmen and workmen, which is connected with the employment or non-employment or the terms of the employment, or with the conditions of labour, of any person." It should be noted that the expression " workmen " as used in both the 1875 and 1906 Acts means " all persons employed in trade or industry, whether or not in the employment of the employer with whom a trade dispute arises."
[16] *Ibid.* s. 2 (" in contemplation or furtherance of a trade dispute ").

alleged to have been committed by or on behalf of the trade union, shall not be entertained by any court." The section 4 (1) provision is a general exemption from liability in delict (or tort, in England) and it is not limited to the trade dispute situation. It does not, of course, prevent proceedings being taken against trade union officials as individuals so as to attach personal liability in delict actions.[17] Historically, this exemption from delictual or tort liability is traceable back to the first great trade union case—*Taff Vale Railway Company* v. *The Amalgamated Society of Railway Servants* [18] which cost the trade union many thousands of pounds in damages and legal costs. Thereafter political pressures were brought to bear upon the government of the day and after certain political bargaining and dealing the 1906 Act went on the Statute Book. For some years past many right-wing politicians and other writers on politics, sociology and government have advocated a withdrawal of this exemption and a return to the *Taff Vale* days when it was possible to attach the very substantial trade union funds. The Donovan Commission [19] has, as expected, made recommendations [20] upon section 4 (1) and these are being eagerly studied by trade unionists, politicians and the legal profession.

Section 3 is the main section of the 1906 Act which is normally relied upon during labour disputes and it refers specifically to the act done in contemplation or furtherance of a trade dispute, which " shall not be actionable on the ground only that it induces some other person to break a contract of employment, or that it is an interference with the trade, business, or employment of some other person, or with the right of some other person to dispose of his capital and his labour as he wills." There is no doubt that this section was not intended to give legal approval or sanction to any form of (unlawful) industrial pressure such as coercion, intimidation, fraud or personal violence against employees or fellow-employees. That section would not have changed the decision in *Quinn* v. *Leathem*,[21] on its particular facts, but it must be remembered that a substantial development has taken place with regard to " legitimate trade interests "—illustrated by the leading case of *Crofter Hand Woven Harris Tweed Co.* v. *Veitch* [22]—and counsel for defenders would make much of cases of the *Crofter Harris* pattern in legal debate. The most famous case in recent years in which section 3 was invoked is, of course, *Rookes* v. *Barnard and Others*.[23] The plaintiff, in this case, who was employed as a draughtsman at London Airport, resigned from his union. The union had an understanding with B.O.A.C., plaintiff's employers, that certain

---

[17] See *Huntley* v. *Thornton* [1957] 1 W.L.R. 321.

[18] [1901] A.C. 426; 17 T.L.R. 698.

[19] The Royal Commission on the Trade Unions and Employers' Associations (Report published by H.M.S.O. 1968); Cmnd. 3623.

[20] *Infra*, Chap. 17.

[21] [1901] A.C. 1.

[22] [1942] S.C.(H.L.) 1; 1943 S.L.T. 2; [1942] A.C. 435; [1942] 1 All E.R. 142.

[23] (At first instance see [1961] 2 All E.R. 825; and in the Court of Appeal [1962]   All E.R. 579). See now [1964] A.C. 1129; [1964] 1 All E.R. 367; [1964] 2 W.L.R. 269; [1964] 1 Lloyd's Rep. 28.

sections in that establishment should be staffed only with union members. The union tried to get Rookes to rejoin—but without success. Thereafter the employers were informed that if Rookes was not removed from his present position a strike would be called. Plaintiff was dismissed with notice, in terms of his contract of service. He sued the officials of the union for damages for wrongfully inducing a breach. Defendants relied upon sections 1 and 3 of the 1906 Act. Sachs J. (at first instance) held that the threat to strike (there was an agreement between B.O.A.C. and the union stipulating for no strike action before negotiation) was an unlawful act and so section 1 was not available as a defence. Similarly section 3 was not available either as the act itself was unlawful. But, on appeal, the Court of Appeal held that the protection afforded by section 3 extends to threats to break or to a breach of one's own contract of service. The test is this—was the conduct of the defendants actionable ? If it was actionable (*e.g.*, by introducing intimidation) then the protection would be lost. The House of Lords [24] overturned the Court of Appeal's decision, taking the view that the conduct of the defendants amounted to intimidation. The question of protection under section 3 of the Trade Disputes Act 1906 was, in their view, irrelevant. In any case both sides admitted that there did exist a " trade dispute " in the sense of the 1906 Act. The House reached its decision upon an examination of the way in which the defendants conducted matters. They were satisfied that this amounted to intimidation and, accordingly, they upheld the appeal. The case was sent back to the lower court for a reassessment of the damages to be awarded. Before this rehearing on damages took place, the union and Mr. Rookes reached agreement on an extra-judicial basis. It is understood that the union paid the sum of £4,000 agreed damages and also undertook to pay the legal expenses of the action. This case caused as much consternation in trade union circles as the *Taff Vale Railway* case had done more than sixty years earlier. Leading trade unionists took the view that their bargaining powers and their rights to organise strikes were now under severe attack from the courts. Political pressures were again brought to bear on the Government, and the Trade Disputes Act 1965 [25] went on the Statute Book. This statute allegedly protects trade union officials during trade dispute negotiations where breaches of contracts of employment occur and even where threats are used within reason, but it does not give a *carte blanche* to union officials to adopt any form of pressure, inducement, intimidation or other unlawful act to achieve their objects. Should they do so then they run the risk of being made personally liable in a damages action based upon their unlawful conduct. The *Rookes* v. *Barnard* case and subsequent cases,[26] as well as the Trade Disputes Acts 1906 and 1965,

---

[24] See [1964] A.C. 1129; [1964] 2 W.L.R. 269; [1964] 1 All E.R. 367; [1964] 1 Lloyd's Rep. 28.

[25] 1965, c. 48.

[26] See also *Morgan* v. *Fry* [1967] 3 W.L.R. 65; [1967] 2 All E.R. 386; and on appeal; discussed in Chap. 17, *infra*.

are more fully discussed elsewhere in this book [27] where the field of trade union law is considered in some detail.

The statutory protection created by section 3—which opens the protective umbrella of " trade dispute "—is not available where a trade union is pursuing a grudge against an employee or against an employer,[28] nor is it available where there is merely a possibility of a trade dispute, unless a strike is indeed imminent.[29] Finally, the Acts of 1906 and 1965 create a protection in relation to the inducement of the breach of a contract of employment alone—not any other form of contract, be it a commercial contract or other type.[30] This is not to say that a genuine " trade dispute " may not exist, in accordance with the definition contained in section 5 (3) of the 1906 Act, from a consideration of all the facts and circumstances of the particular case. It may well do—but section 3 will afford no protection to defenders if the contract whose breach is sought to be induced is not a contract of employment. Moreover, even where the statutory protection is invoked—and relevantly so—the courts may still choose to sidestep that defence and, at the invitation of pursuer's counsel, concentrate upon the methods adopted by defenders which may amount to conspiracy or unlawful restraint, intimidation, coercion or other unlawful acting, which would entitle the pursuer to the remedy which he seeks.[31]

---

[27] *Infra*, Chap. 17.
[28] *Huntley* v. *Thornton* [1957] 1 W.L.R. 321, at p. 350 *per* Harman J.; and *J. T. Stratford & Son Ltd.* v. *Lindley* [1965] A.C. 269, at p. 341.
[29] *John Milligan & Co. Ltd.* v. *Ayr Harbour Trustees*, 1915 S.C. 937.
[30] See *J. T. Stratford & Son Ltd.* v. *Lindley, cit. supra*; and *Square Grip Reinforcement Co. Ltd.* v. *MacDonald* (O.H.) 1968 S.L.T. 65.
[31] *Rookes* v. *Barnard, cit. supra*; *Morgan* v. *Fry, cit. supra*.

CHAPTER 16

THE REMEDIES OF THE EMPLOYER AGAINST HIS EMPLOYEE (AND VICE VERSA) FOR CONTRACTUAL BREACH

(a) *The Employer's Remedies upon his Employee's Breach of Contract*

BASICALLY, the general rule of contract law applies where there is a breach. The aggrieved party (*i.e.*, the employer in this instance) will be in a position to claim damages. Moreover, he may be able to terminate the relationship and regard the initial obligation as no longer binding upon him. This will depend upon the circumstances, however. The situation involving breach may arise before the actual commencement of the service. For example, either side may indicate that he has no intention of going ahead with performance upon the due date. To the English lawyer this is an " anticipatory breach." The party not at fault may sue on the breach at once, if he elects to do so, rather than wait until the effective commencement date of the agreement.[1]

A much more difficult case is whether there can be a breach of contract, after the service relationship has been terminated (quite apart from the " restraint of trade " cases). This matter came up for consideration in the important Scottish case of *Liverpool Victoria Friendly Society* v. *Houston*[2] where the court granted interdict against the defender (who was a former employee of pursuers) prohibiting the circulation of information, which was obtained during the employment, to third parties and concerning pursuer's business affairs. A nominal sum in name of damages was awarded in this instance, as pursuers could not prove actual loss. The decision was based upon breach of contract—namely, a breach of faith by an employee; loyalty is the primary obligation of any employee. Confidential information had been used unlawfully. It seems that English law is the same on this point of breach of fidelity and loyalty.[3] The principle of post-service breach is, therefore, fully recognised and it is not just restricted to restraint of trade cases.

The rights and remedies available to an employer, upon breach of any contract of service with an employee, may be summarised as follows, *viz.*:

(1) a claim of damages;
(2) a right to withhold or refuse to pay wages;
(3) specific implement;
(4) interdict.

---

[1] See *Hochster* v. *De la Tour* (1853) 2 E. & B. 678, *per* Lord Campbell C.J. at p. 689; also *Frost* v. *Knight* (1872) L.R. 7 Ex. 111; *Johnstone* v. *Milling* (1886) 16 Q.B.D. 460.
[2] (1900) 3 F. 42.
[3] See *Merryweather* v. *Moore* [1892] 2 Ch. 518; *Lamb* v. *Evans* [1893] 1 Ch. 218; *Robb* v. *Green* [1895] 2 Q.B. 315; and *Barr* v. *Craven* (1903) 20 T.L.R. 51.

Each remedy must be examined briefly in order to assess its usefulness and its suitability in modern law and practice.

(1) *Employer's Claim of Damages*

The claim may rest upon the breach of an express term or of an implied obligation in the contract.[4] Generally, the employer will have to prove his loss and the usual principles of contract law relating to the assessment of damages will apply—even although the basis of the claim is pitched no higher than that of trouble and inconvenience caused to the employer.[5]

(2) *Employer Withholding or Refusing to Pay Wages*

The employee who breaks his contract is generally held to have forfeited his claim to wages for the period after termination and perhaps also, in certain cases, for the prior period.[6] The early view of the common law was that the employee ought to be punished for desertion or misconduct and as a result he forfeited his wages. This is certainly not the position today in the sense of imposing some punishment geared to his breach of contract. If the misconduct is, in fact, criminal then it is punished separately (not by the employer) in the criminal courts as an offence or an attempted offence of a particular kind.

Earlier statute law [7] had fortified the employer's position by enabling him to have criminal proceedings taken against an offending or deserting employee. Meanwhile the common law was moving towards the " freedom of contract " theory, although as shall be seen later the bargaining power was scarcely evenly balanced between employer and employee.

There has already been considered the question of accrual and apportionment of wages.[8] Wages of service do not necessarily accrue *de die in diem*. The employee will normally be entitled to claim all wages which have become due prior to the termination,[9] but his claim is for those wages which have accrued and which are outstanding at the date of termination. Where the employee is paid monthly or quarterly, or even half-yearly and is properly dismissed during the month, quarter or half-year, then it seems that the wages for the whole period are forfeited. English law appears to follow a similar rule.[10]

---

4 *Clerk* v. *Murchison* (1799) Mor. 9186; *Cameron* v. *Gibb* (1867) 3 S.L.R. 282; *Murray* v. *Macfarlane* (1886) 2 Sh.Ct.Rep. 6; *Cooper* v. *McEwan* (1893) 9 Sh.Ct.Rep. 311; *Gunn* v. *Goodall* (1835) 13 S. 1142.

5 *Webster & Co.* v. *Crammond Iron Co.* (1875) 2 R. 752.

6 See *Taylor* v. *Guthrie* (1798) Hume 382; *Elder* v. *Bennet* (1802) Hume 386; *Silvie* v. *Stewart* (1830) 8 S. 1010; *Wilson* v. *Simson* (1844) 6 D. 1256; *Gibson* v. *McNaughton* (1861) 23 D. 358; *Cooper* v. *McEwan, cit. supra*; and *Cobban* v. *Lawson* (1868) 6 S.L.R. 60.

7 See the earlier Master and Servant Acts, as noted by Lord Fraser; also the Employers and Workmen Act 1875, *re* defaulting apprentices (this Act being still in force).

8 See *supra* Chap. 8.

9 *Gibson* v. *McNaughton* (1861) 23 D. 358; and *Hoey* v. *McEwan and Auld* (1867) 5 M. 814.

10 *Ridgway* v. *Hungerford Market Co.* (1835) 3 A. & E. 171; *Lilley* v. *Elwin* (1848) 11 Q.B. (A. & E.) 742; *Button* v. *Thompson* (1869) L.R. 4 C.P. 330.

An interesting feature of the Employers and Workmen Act 1875 [11] is that, in determining what is an equitable amount in all the circumstances, the court has power to adjust and set-off all claims for wages, damages and otherwise and irrespective of whether these claims are liquidated or unliquidated.

(3) Specific Implement

The old Scottish common law permitted a summary petition in the sheriff court, either that of the defender's domicile or of the actual place of work,[12] for the apprehension of an employee or apprentice who had deserted his service and this might be enforced, if necessary, by imprisonment.[13] Before imprisonment was competent there had to be desertion of the service. Otherwise, the court might order the employee to enter upon the service, that is to say, by issuing a decree *ad factum praestandum*, enforceable as any decree of this type.[14] This old procedure was inaugurated by a complaint to the police and thereafter punishment was at the discretion of the court. The employer could still have his action of damages in breach of contract [15] or he might attempt to enforce a penalty clause in the agreement. As Mr. Umpherston points out [16] there is no legal principle which sanctions the enforcement of a contract, which is purely a civil contract, in this way and, moreover, this procedure was quite contrary to the recognised rule that a civil obligation could not be enforced by summary imprisonment. Perhaps not surprisingly, the procedure under discussion was limited to the humbler classes of employees, notably labourers and artisans.

It is mainly to statute law, however, that one must attribute the improvement in the status of the employee and the development of the modern view that both parties are essentially free and equal in the service relationship [17]; that their duties under the service contract are reciprocal; and, that their rights are virtually identical. The main statutes which effected this change were:

   (1) The Act 4 Geo. 4, c. 34,

   (2) The Master and Servant Act 1867,[18]

   (3) The Employers and Workmen Act 1875 [19] and

   (4) The Conspiracy and Protection of Property Act 1875.[20]

---

[11] See particularly s. 3 (38 & 39 Vict., c. 90).
[12] *McDougall* v. *Stewart* (1833) 11 S. 795.
[13] See Umpherston, *op. cit.*, pp. 132–136 and in particular the list of cases cited in n. 4 to p. 132.
[14] *Tulk* v. *Anderson* (1843) 5 D. 1096.
[15] *Anderson* v. *Moon* (1836) 14 S. 863.
[16] *Op. cit.*, p. 134 and n. 3 thereto.
[17] This statement is of course, in reality, an over-simplification of the position, because no single individual employee has the same bargaining power as his employer.
[18] 30 & 31 Vict., c. 141 (no longer in force).
[19] 38 & 39 Vict., c. 90 (still in force).
[20] 38 & 39 Vict., c. 86 (a most important statute in relation to industrial conflict).

The first of these statutes introduced a summary procedure for complaints against an employee or apprentice, based upon failure to perform or upon misconduct, and allowed imprisonment as a punishment.

The 1867 Act, which allowed adjustment of claims between employer and employee, retained imprisonment as a penalty—which could only be enforced where there was refusal or failure by the employee or apprentice to implement a decree of the court.

The Conspiracy and Protection of Property Act 1875 repealed the foregoing statutes and dispensed with imprisonment on the previous wider basis of enforcement—although it was retained in the case of employees in specialised undertakings,[21] whose breach of contract was likely to cause injury to life, person or property. Now, of course, the punishment was awarded by a criminal court (not by a civil court) for what was in essence a criminal offence. An examination of the Employers and Workmen Act 1875 [22] reveals that it does retain the penalty of imprisonment for those apprentices who fail to comply with an order to perform their duties, but this award of imprisonment is a penalty for disobedience to an order of the court. It is no longer in essence a criminal proceeding.[23]

(4) *Interdict*

No court of law in Scotland will grant an interdict against an employee or an employer by which performance or implement of a contract of employment is ordered.[24] The correct remedy is usually a claim of damages. Obviously, to put the parties back into a relationship which has previously been characterised by an absence of mutual trust and mutual respect would only add insult to injury. Although the general rule which has just been stated is basically true in relation to the employment situation nevertheless it may be possible to identify an obligation or undertaking which is contained in the main employment contract and which can be enforced by interdict—for example, any breach, and possibly any repeated breach, of a clause in restraint of trade (even after normal termination of the relationship) or, again, the employee's duty to respect the confidential nature of his employer's business (any breach thereof evidencing a lack of good faith and an absence of loyalty).[25] The English cases [26] (in which the corresponding remedy is termed an " injunction ") are also helpful as illustrating the attitude of the English courts to this point of breach of faith. However, the use of the injunction in England in the employment cases, and in the circumstances which are under discussion here, appears to be limited to the enforcement of an obligation (either express or implied)

---

[21] For example, gas and water undertakings.
[22] See particularly s. 6.
[23] *Ibid.* s. 9.
[24] The same principle is basically true of English law, where the equitable remedy of injunction would be sought.
[25] See *Liverpool Victoria Friendly Society* v. *Houston* (1900) 3 F. 42.
[26] See particularly *Hivac Ltd.* v. *Park Royal Scientific Instruments Ltd.* [1946] 1 Ch. 169.

which is of a negative character.[27] The Scottish courts would on this point, as in the restraint of trade cases, tend perhaps to take a broader view of what is reasonable and equitable in the circumstances, looking to the restriction imposed upon one party and the particular interest of the other party in having that restriction enforced; but there is little, if any, real Scottish authority upon the point.

(b) *The Employee's Remedies upon his Employer's Breach of Contract*

The remedies available to an employee are:

(1) a claim of damages (or perhaps a *quantum meruit*),

(2) a lien or right of retention.

(1) *Damages*

The employee's claim of damages is allowed upon exactly the same principles as that of his employer. In practice, this claim will most often be made for wrongous dismissal [28] and the sum payable will be technically a sum of damages in this case [29] although it may be equivalent to a sum which represents the wages for the unexpired period of the contract or, where the contractual term is indefinite, a sum representing an amount which the employee was prevented from earning. The ordinary rule of contract law that the employee " must minimise the loss " applies equally here,[30] but he is not obliged to take just any kind of employment at all— as this might prejudicially affect his position.[31] Interdict is not a competent remedy.[32]

The cases on wrongful dismissal are relatively numerous and most of them indicate the court's practice of endeavouring to compensate the employee for the loss which he has suffered.[33] At the same time regard will be paid to any presumptions governing the accepted length of time of an engagement to serve—*e.g.*, the agricultural worker, such as a grieve or farm overseer, who is presumed to be hired for a year and if he is improperly dismissed the court may, in the appropriate circumstances, award a year's wages.[34] Where an employee is bringing an action of

---

[27] See Macdonnell, *Master and Servant*, p. 199; Smith, *Master and Servant*, p. 126; Fraser, *op. cit.*, p. 112; and Umpherston, *op. cit.*, pp. 137 and 138 and relevant footnotes.

[28] The older Scottish legal terminology is used on this occasion, but in future it is hoped that no exception will be taken to the modern and more common " wrongful dismissal," even allowing that the expression is borrowed from south of the Tweed.

[29] *Cameron* v. *Fletcher* (1872) 10 M. 301.

[30] *Stuart* v. *Richardson* (1806) Hume 390; *Rae* v. *Leith Glasswork Co.* (1750) Mor. 13, 989; *Hoey* v. *McEwan* (1867) 5 M. 814; *Ross* v. *Pender* (1874) 1 R. 352; *London* v. *Brand* (1894) 11 Sh.Ct.Rep. 317.

[31] *Gunn* v. *Ramsay* (1801) Hume 384; *Ross* v. *Pender, cit. supra*, and *Ross* v. *McFarlane* (1894) 21 R. 396.

[32] *Murray* v. *Dunbarton County Council*, 1935 S.L.T. 239; 1935 S.N. 47.

[33] *Batchelor* v. *M'Gilvray* (1831) 9 S. 549; *Craig* v. *Graham* (1844) 6 D. 684; *Todd* v. *Arrol & Co.* (1881) 18 S.L.R. 673; *Campbell* v. *Mackenzie* (1887) 24 S.L.R. 354; *Wilson* v. *Anthony*, 1958 S.L.T.(Sh.Ct.) 13; (1957) 73 Sh.Ct.Rep. 298; and *Palmer* v. *Inverness Hospitals Board of Management* (O.H.) 1963 S.L.T. 124.

[34] *Finlayson* v. *M'Kenzie* (1829) 7 S. 717; *Cameron* v. *Fletcher* (1872) 10 M. 301 (it was made clear in this case that the correct form of claim lies in damages and not for wages).

damages for wrongful dismissal it is irrelevant for him to aver loss of benefits of prestige and publicity.[35] Indeed it is virtually impossible to quantify these two elements in any case. The Crown employee has, of course, no right of action based upon wrongful dismissal, nor has he any formal right of action even where the particular office held by him is abolished.[36] The Contracts of Employment Act [37] made no change in the Crown employee's position.

The employee may often complain that his employer is actuated by " malice " in dismissing him and where wrongful dismissal is pleaded it is not unusual to find averments of malice added. Two cases will perhaps illustrate this point: (a) In *Brown* v. *Edinburgh Magistrates* [38] an Edinburgh police officer brought an action of damages for wrongful dismissal against the magistrates and the chief constable. He averred " improper and malicious motives " of the chief constable. The First Division held (1) that there was no relevant case against the magistrates or the chief constable (the latter had the power to dismiss this officer at pleasure) and (2) (reversing the Lord Ordinary) that pursuer was not entitled to an issue for " wrongous and malicious " dismissal. He had suffered no wrong, therefore, motive was irrelevant. Lord Kinnear's opinion [39] is most helpful. After citing the definitions of " malice " by Bowen L.J. in *Mogul Steamship Co.* v. *M'Gregor, Gow & Co.*[40] and Bailey J. in *Bromage* v. *Prosser* [41] his lordship relied upon the House of Lords judgment in *Allen* v. *Flood* [42] and the views expressed in that case on the whole question of " malice." Lord Kinnear also referred to the illustration by Lord Watson in *Allen's* case, drawn from the field of master and servant [43]; (b) in *Macallister* v. *Argyll County Council* [44] a schoolteacher sued the education authority for wrongful dismissal again averring malice. It was held (1) that as her appointment was made at the pleasure of the education authority her averment of malice was irrelevant; and (2) that she was not entitled to be informed of the complaints made against her. Both of these cases illustrate clearly that motive by itself is generally irrelevant—a bad motive cannot convert an otherwise lawful act into an unlawful act so as to give rise to damages. The main test must remain the lawfulness or otherwise of the act done by the defender. There is always, of course, great difficulty to be encountered in trying to prove—as a pure matter of evidence—an improper motive by defender. It may sometimes be possible to take proceedings on the ground of defamation or on some other ground

---

[35] *Dodwell* v. *Highland Industrial Caterers Ltd.* (O.H.) 1952 S.L.T.(Notes) 57.
[36] *Hay* v. *Officers of State* (1832) 11 S. 196 (clerk to the Judge Advocate dismissed upon the abolition of that office).
[37] 1963, c. 49.
[38] 1907 S.C. 256; 14 S.L.T. 610.
[39] 1907 S.C. 268–271.
[40] (1889) L.R. 23 Q.B.D. 598 at p. 612.
[41] (1825) 4 B. & C. 247 at p. 255.
[42] [1898] A.C. 1.
[43] *Ibid.* at p. 100.
[44] 1948 S.C.L.Y., para. 4266 (Oban Sheriff Court; May 13, 1948).

(*e.g.*, intimidation), if an action based upon wrongful dismissal is unlikely to succeed. These points should not be overlooked.

It is always open to the court to award a larger sum than mere wages, where it is satisfied that the circumstances justify such an increase.[45] If the sum sued for truly represents an amount which is, in fact, compensation in lieu of notice then basically this is a compensation claim and not a damages claim,[46] although the method of dismissal provides the test as to whether the action is taken on the basis of damages or of payment of wages. As a practical matter, the claim for payment may relate to the same amount of hard cash, although in theory it might be thought that a claim which was based in damages might be more fruitful than one based in compensation.

Reference must be made to the contract itself to ascertain whether some provision is made for the settlement of disputes arising upon dismissal [47] (for example, by reference to a named arbiter or arbiters). If so, this machinery would have to be set in motion in the first instance as being binding upon the parties. Should this machinery fail completely then normal resort might be had to the courts. If an award were made by an arbiter or arbiters appointed, then it would only be possible, in the general case, to query this award where the arbiter had acted in some irregular or illegal way, *e.g.*, by exceeding his powers or jurisdiction or by a complete misinterpretation of the reference.

The *quantum meruit* award or payment in the field of employer and employee relationships is a very difficult one indeed to establish [48] and will rarely if ever arise for consideration. In almost all cases the matter will be disposed of as a damages claim. However, the *quantum meruit* claim does arise in relation to independent contractors where variations in contract specifications do arise from time to time.[49]

(2) *Lien or Right of Retention*

Again, the general principles of contract law apply. All that need be said is that whilst the employer has a right of lien over an employee's wages for non-implement of his contractual obligations, the employee may, in certain circumstances, also have a right of retention over property belonging to his employer which he is holding in possession. If, however, the property of the employer is in his custody purely as an employee then in theory his possession is truly that of the employer.[50] The employee's position is stronger, *vis-à-vis* retention, when he is more properly an agent rather than an employee.[51] The matter is never an easy one to

---

[45] *Cameron* v. *Fletcher, cit. supra*; *Maw* v. *Jones* (1890) 25 Q.B.D. 107.
[46] *Morrison* v. *Abernethy School Board* (1876) 3 R. 945.
[47] *Finlay* v. *Royal Liver Friendly Society* (1901) 4 F. 34.
[48] See Gloag, *Contract* (2nd ed.), p. 292.
[49] See Gloag, *op. cit.*, p. 358; and D. M. Walker, *Damages*, p. 412.
[50] *Clift* v. *Portobello Pier Co.* (1877) 4 R. 462; and *Gladstone* v. *McCallum* (1896) 23 R. 783; and *Barnton Hotel Co. Ltd.* v. *Cook* (1899) 1 F. 1190.
[51] See *Dickson* v. *Nicholson* (1855) 17 D. 1011, *per* Lord Ivory at p. 1014.

decide; it hinges mainly upon the authority and position of the employee in relation to third parties.

Seamen were in a special position at common law so far as a lien for their wages was concerned. However, references to the Merchant Shipping Acts and to the leading authorities on British shipping law will confirm the statutory liens [52] which were set up in favour of the master of a ship in respect of (a) his wages and (b) any disbursements or liabilities made or incurred by him on account of the ship; and also that in favour of the seamen for their wages. A detailed consideration of these statutory maritime liens is outwith the scope of this work.

[52] See particularly the Merchant Shipping Act 1894, s. 167.

CHAPTER 17

(I) TRADE UNIONS AND ASSOCIATIONS; AND (II) CONCILIATION AND ARBITRATION AND THE SETTLEMENT OF INDUSTRIAL DISPUTES BY STATUTORY MACHINERY

(I) TRADE UNIONS AND ASSOCIATIONS

PART A—Historical Introduction, Definition, Objects and Registration

(1) *Historical Introduction*

The origin of the modern trade union is often said to be the small craft organisation which developed in the early eighteenth century, following upon the decay of the medieval system of wage-fixing. Sidney and Beatrice Webb do not subscribe to that view,[1] nor does Henry Pelling.[2]

Historically, a most significant date in England was the year of the Black Death (1348). From that time onwards, because of shortages of skilled labour, the craftsmen and journeymen began to help each other in negotiating for improved conditions of work, notably in agriculture. Prior to 1348, various Ordinances of Conspirators had been directed against collaboration by workers.[3] After 1348, there appeared numerous Statutes of Labourers, notably, in England, those of 1349, 1350, 1351 and others[4] down to those of 1512 and 1514 (during Henry VIII's reign). The Statute of Artificers in 1562 (*i.e.*, in the reign of Elizabeth I) overhauled the regulation of wages by the state and indeed extended that regulation. A long series of statutes which were concerned with various trades[5] followed from 1603 (the Union of the Crowns) to the end of the eighteenth century and, very importantly, those statutes of 1755 and 1756 gave the justices of the peace power to fix piecework rates.

Scotland, too, had its early statutes against combinations, notably in 1411 and 1413 (5 & 7 James 1), 1426 and 1547 (5 Mary). The statute of 1411 dealt with " fees of craftsmen and the price of their work " and the 1547 statute with " the price of craftsmen's work." The late Sheriff J. R. Philip has pointed out, in a most interesting article[6] on early labour law in Scotland, that in its earliest form the regulation of craftsmen's

---

1 *The History of Trade Unionism* (1920), pp. 13–15.
2 *A History of British Trade Unionism* (Pelican Books; 1963), pp. 18 and 19.
3 In 1292 (20 Ed. 1); 1300 (28 Ed. 1); and 1305 (33 Ed. 1).
4 In the reigns of Richard II, Henry IV and Henry VI.
5 In 1662 (for the silk trade); 1720 and 1721 (tailoring); 1720 (the woollen trade); 1748 and 1749 (the hat trade), as illustrative of this development.
6 " Early Labour Law in Scotland," 1934 J.R. (Vol. xlvi), pp. 121–132.

wages was dealt with by the town councils of the burghs under the authority conferred upon them by two Acts of 1426 (James 1, cc. 3 and 4). In a sense, the town councils acted as a middle-ages " prices and incomes board " because they performed a double task, *viz.*: seeing and pricing the materials and labour of the workmen and thereafter pricing the completed work (*i.e.*, piecework pricing)—under the first statute of 1426—and —under the second statute of 1426—regulating wages in those other trades wherein a computation of wages could not be undertaken upon a piece-work basis. It will be appreciated that this legislation was " craft " legislation and it was to be replaced in 1617 and 1661 by " general " legislation. It is interesting to note that the 1661 statute, in relation to its wage-fixing provisions, remained in force until 1813,[7] when it was then replaced by a new statute. Measures were also taken against combinations of workmen in Scotland at common law as well as under statute law. Mr. Burnett in his early work on the criminal law in Scotland [8] says that " a combination to alter the price of labour is indictable at common law." The older authorities of *Hunter's* case [9] and *Sprot's* case [10] should also be consulted on this point.

In all of the early statutes the justices of the peace in England and Scotland were given the task of enforcing wage rates and of fixing and imposing penalties upon workmen who refused to work at the wage rates so fixed. In Scotland the procedure was that of summary jurisdiction and essentially it was administered by the justices of the counties.[11] The justices, at quarter sessions (held in February and August each year for this particular purpose) were to fix the " ordinary hire and wages of labourers, workmen and servants " and had the power to imprison or punish in some other form those who did not accept and work for the wages stipulated by them.[12] The justices could also give decree in favour of a servant against any employer who was not paying or had refused to pay the appointed wages. The Act of 1641 enabled the amount of wages, mainly in coal-mining and salt-mining, to be fixed at a stipulated maximum. The purpose behind this " maximum-wage legislation " was to prevent any unscrupulous employer from enticing away colliers and salters, who were elsewhere employed, by offering them higher wages. This type of legislation also effectively prevented any voluntary negotiating or bargaining (whether individual or collective) between workmen and their employers —not so much in specific terms but as a practical result, because the employer was bound by the maximum stipulated wage and could not go beyond it.[13]

Various reasons have been advanced for the decay of this system of

[7] 53 Geo. 3, c. 40.
[8] *Criminal Law of Scotland* (1811) at p. 237.
[9] (1837) 1 Swinton 550.
[10] (1844) 2 Broun 179.
[11] See J. R. Philip, " Early Labour Law in Scotland," *cit. supra.*
[12] Act of 1617 (c. 8) as extended in 1661 (c. 38).
[13] See Philip, *loc. cit.*, p. 128.

wage-fixing and regulation. The most popular of these seem to be the following—(i) the whole procedure was discretionary and therefore unsatisfactory, (ii) the administration was local and accordingly it lacked the power and co-ordinating control of a central authority, (iii) the popular philosophy was " laissez-faire " and (iv) the advent of the Industrial Revolution rendered the whole system anachronistic and too limited and parochial to deal with the new problems of a new era.

The next important milestone was the year 1799 when the first Combination Act was passed. This statute made all combinations of workmen, acting together to regulate their conditions of work, illegal. The consolidating Act of 1800 then followed and it was designed specifically " to prevent unlawful combinations of workmen." However, it did introduce certain machinery for arbitration. These restrictive and limiting statutes displeased the Benthamite School [14] of social reformers, and pressures were brought to bear for the reform of the law. Finally, in 1824, the Combination Laws Repeal Act swept away the old Combination Acts. However, because of threats of widespread industrial unrest the 1824 statute was amended in 1825 by a " tightening-up " measure. Combinations were now limited to those for determining wages prices and hours of work, although the common law combination had still to be examined carefully in relation to the statutes. Picketing was made illegal and remained so until the Molestation of Workmen Act 1859. The more liberal attitude to associations of workmen after the legislation of 1824 and 1825 provided a great impetus for the trade union movement. It must not be imagined, however, that the development was simple, logical and readily accepted by employers and the state. It was none of these things and indeed the trade unions had a long and bitter struggle to achieve legal recognition. This is undoubtedly a fascinating field of study for lawyers, historians, political scientists and sociologists but it is outwith the terms of reference of this volume. It would be most helpful, in Scotland, if research could be done into the legal history and historical development of the trade unions north of the Tweed. The historical aspects, mainly concerned with England and Wales, are well covered in several popular books and others to which reference should be made.[15]

[14] Notably Joseph Hume, Francis Place and J. R. McCulloch, in addition to Jeremy Bentham himself.

[15] See G. D. H. Cole and R. Postgate, *The Common People* (2nd ed., 1946); Cole, *Short History of the British Working Class Movement* (revised ed., 1948); Henry Pelling, *A History of British Trade Unionism* (1963); and Clegg, Fox and Thompson, *History of British Trade Unions since 1889* (Vol. 1, 1964; others to follow). So far as Scotland is concerned the following may give some guidance, *viz.*: *The Social and Industrial History of Scotland* (From the Union to the Present Time) by James Mac-Kinnon (Longmans Green, 1921), p. 158 *et seq.* (the Scottish Trade Union Movement); and relevant sections in *The Early English Trade Unions* by A. Aspinall (Batchwork Press, 1949); also references in *The State and The Trade Unions* by D. F. Macdonald (Macmillan & Co., 1960); and in G. D. H. Cole's *Short History of the British Working Class Movement*, *supra*, and Cole and Postgate, *The Common People*, *supra*. The most penetrating contribution on the Scottish trade union development is from the pen of the late the Rt. Hon. Tom Johnston, P.C., M.P., in his *History of The Working Classes in Scotland* (first published in 1920 by Forward Publishing Co.,

However, for purposes of this chapter, it is essential to confine our attention to the post-1825 period.

The first great milestone was the Trade Union Act 1871 [16] although there had been interesting developments at common law and by statute law between 1825 and 1871. Ostensibly, the 1824 Act above-mentioned had removed all criminal liability of trade unions in relation to wage fixing or alterations in hours of work, etc., whilst the 1825 Act, although following the spirit of the 1824 legislation, introduced the new offences of intimidation, threats and obstruction and molestation. These offences applied both to individuals and combinations.

The association or combination in restraint of trade, for a bona fide trade purpose, ceased after 1825 to be a statutory offence. At common law, the more authoritative view seems to have been that such an association or combination was not illegal, in the criminal sense.[17] The common law conspiracy in restraint of trade was certainly void and unenforceable but it never seems to have been truly a common law offence after 1825. There appears to be a general agreement amongst most writers on trade union law that two aspects of the common law limited the activities of the trade unions, namely: (i) the doctrine of restraint of trade (which vitiated the contracts and trusts of a trade union); and (ii) the criminal offence of conspiracy (a weapon which enabled trade union leaders and members to be imprisoned, after conviction). The " conspiracy " is defined as " an agreement of two or more persons to do an unlawful act, or to do a lawful act by unlawful means." If the object or means of achieving it were unlawful then an offence had been committed and all participants could be punished.

A Royal Commission was appointed in 1867 to inquire into the position of the trade unions and, following upon its report, the Trade Union Act 1871 was passed. This statute had the following objects: (a) to modify the criminal law of conspiracy, (b) to extend the protection of the law to the property, contracts and trusts of a trade union and (c) to encourage trade unions to register and so bring themselves under the umbrella of the law. The consequences of the Act did not quite measure up to expectations. There were perforations in the umbrella. The severity of the common law was modified subsequently by later statutes. Section 2 of the 1871 Act purported to modify the law of conspiracy. Members of a union were not to be liable to prosecution for criminal conspiracy because the union's purposes were in restraint of trade. It has been doubted whether this section was necessary or whether it changed

---

Glasgow), Chap. XIII. The standard work on the historical legal development of trade unionism in England and Wales is R. Y. Hedges and A. Winterbottom, *The Legal History of Trade Unionism* (Longmans Green, 1930), although understandably it terminates between the two Great Wars (*i.e.*, 40 years ago). *The Law Relating to Trade Combinations* by Dr. A. L. Haslam (Allen & Unwin, 1931) is also a helpful work, particularly Chaps. II, V and VII thereof.

[16] 34 & 35 Vict., c. 31.

[17] See *Mogul Steamship Co.* v. *McGregor Gow & Co.* (1889) 23 Q.B.D. 598, *per* Fry L.J. at p. 631 (this case later went to the House of Lords—see [1892] A.C. 25).

the law.[18] Section 3 extends the protection of the law to the trusts, property and agreements of a trade union. These arrangements are no longer to be void or voidable because the objects are in restraint of trade. Section 4 makes certain agreements not directly enforceable in the courts although they remain lawful.[19]

Registration may be sought, if the members so desire.[20] Certain conditions must be fulfilled, viz.: written rules are required which, inter alia, set out the union's objects, make provision for its management and officers and for the investment and safe-keeping of its funds.[21] A trade union governed by the statute must have a registered office [22] and it must also make annual returns to the Registrar of Friendly Societies setting out its property, income, expenditure and so forth.[23] Section 23 defined a trade union thus: " The term ' trade union ' means such combination, whether temporary or permanent, for regulating the relations between workmen and masters, or between workmen and workmen, or between masters and masters, or for imposing restrictive conditions on the conduct of any trade or business, as would, if this Act had not been passed, have been deemed to have been an unlawful combination by reason of some one or more of its purposes being in restraint of trade." Some unexpected consequences were to result from this definition. For example, it was soon appreciated that there were certain defects, thus: (i) the phrase " such combinations as would have been unlawful if this Act had not been passed " meant that the statute was limited to those unions which were unlawful combinations. Accordingly, to be able to register, a trade union had to satisfy the Registrar that its rules were in restraint of trade. A union which had avoided common law illegality was unable to register under the 1871 Act; (ii) the intended modification of criminal conspiracy meant virtually nothing in practice. Although a strike could not be a criminal conspiracy in restraint of trade it usually remained a conspiracy

---

[18] *Mogul Steamship Co.* v. *McGregor Gow & Co.* [1892] A.C. 25.
[19] This is a most important section. Certain writers take the view that the trade union leaders themselves preferred s. 4 in that form to leave them freedom to bargain and not to be subject to judicial pressures. Others, however, take the view that s. 4 was framed in its existing form in order to continue the theory of unlawful restraint of trade and to deprive the unions of free contractual powers (*e.g.*, the view of Lord James in *Yorkshire Miners' Association* v. *Howden* [1905] A.C. at p. 275 that s. 4 was a " remarkable relic of prejudice.") See also the comments on s. 4 by Prof K. W. Wedderburn in *The Worker and the Law* (Penguin Books 1965), pp. 224 and 225 in particular, which explains the attitudes of the unions at that time. The " collective agreement," as known today in British industrial relations, is unenforceable under s. 4 (4) of the 1871 Act. This point came up for consideration and decision in the recent case of *Ford Motor Co. Ltd.* v. *Amalgamated Union of Engineering and Foundry Workers* [1969] 1 W.L.R. 339 and *The Times* report of March 6, 1969, in which it has been held by Mr. Justice Geoffrey Lane (see particularly his conclusion at p. 356 of the report) that a collective agreement is not a form of agreement which can be enforced in a court of law. (Many of the earlier interesting cases are referred to in the course of the judgment.) The agreements in question (*i.e.*, under s. 4) are usually concerned with penalties, subscriptions, benefits and conditions of employment.
[20] 1871 Act, s. 6.
[21] *Ibid.* Sched. I.
[22] *Ibid.* s. 15.
[23] *Ibid.* s. 16.

to coerce and was open to prosecution on that ground [24]; (iii) the Act gave no protection against civil conspiracy, which enabled employers to bring actions in delict or tort to recover damages for loss occasioned to them during strike action. A good example of that type of action was *Quinn* v. *Leathem*,[25] in which the jury awarded £250 damages to Leathem and that award was upheld by the House of Lords in dismissing Quinn's appeal.

Prior to 1871 it seems that there was no machinery for enforcing a decree or judgment against a trade union itself or indeed against any unincorporated association, whether based in England or in Scotland. The 1871 Act changed this position because it authorised proceedings against the trustees of a union in any matter " touching or concerning " any right or claim to the union's property.[26] Almost contemporaneously, a reorganisation of the courts was undertaken in England and Wales by the Judicature Acts 1873–1875 and as a result of improved procedures the " representative action " came into being. This allowed proceedings to be taken against office-bearers or other representatives of a body or society or institution which did not have corporate status. In Scotland the " descriptive action " became a feature of civil process [27] and by this means a court action could be brought against an unregistered union in its descriptive name, with the names of the principal office-bearers written into the process (*i.e.*, calling them as parties in the action).

The judges were also to cause some dissatisfaction in the ranks of the trade unionists. In *Taff Vale Railway Co.* v. *The Amalgamated Society of Railway Servants* [28] the House of Lords held, *inter alia*, that a registered trade union could be sued in its registered name. A trade union which was registered under the Act of 1871 had acquired a sufficient corporate existence to permit of its being sued in its registered name. This case was to prove a landmark in trade union history and reference must be made to it again in this chapter. It contributed much to the then current view of leading trade unionists that the 1871 Act was an outstanding piece of oppressive legislation. This was perhaps underlined in the subsequent case of *Osborne* v. *The Amalgamated Society of Railway Servants* [29] in which the House of Lords held that the " specified objects " definition contained in section 23 of the Trade Union Act 1871, as amended by section 16 of the 1876 Act,[30] was exhaustive and did not permit the collection of funds for political purposes. Any such collection and distribution was *ultra vires* and unlawful. This decision required a statutory provision

---

[24] See *R.* v. *Bunn* (1872) 12 Cox 316 (sentences of 12 months hard labour imposed).
[25] [1901] A.C. 495.
[26] 1871 Act, s. 9.
[27] See the Sheriff Courts (Scotland) Acts 1907 and 1913 and the Rules of the Court of Session.
[28] [i901] A.C. 426.
[29] [1910] A.C. 89; 26 T.L.R. 177 (the first *Osborne* case).
[30] The Trade Union Act 1871 (Amendment) Act 1876.

to change the law and this was done, in fact, by the Trade Union Act 1913.[31]

The next important stage in the chronicle of development was the Conspiracy and Protection of Property Act 1875.[32] This Act made an agreement by two or more persons to do or procure acts in contemplation or furtherance of a trade dispute not indictable as a conspiracy unless the acts themselves were punishable as a crime.[33] This provision removed the danger of " criminal conspiracy." The Act of 1876 [34] above-mentioned made a number of minor alterations in the law and modified the definition of a trade union so as to include unions which were not unlawful at common law,[35] but did not amend the proviso contained in section 23 of the 1871 Act. The Trade Disputes Act 1906 [36] was an important measure. The intention of the statute was to correct the balance after the *Taff Vale* case and to give greater protection to the trade unions. Four points should be noted initially about that statute, *viz.*: (1) It apparently did away with the possibility of any action for damages for civil conspiracy during or as a result of a trade dispute.[37] Later events did not justify this view, but it seemed at the time that the statutory provision was sufficient assurance, *viz.*—any act done pursuant to an agreement in contemplation or further-ance of a trade dispute was not to be actionable unless the act itself, if done without the agreement or combination would be actionable: (2) All persons acting in the course or furtherance of a trade dispute were granted immunity from liability for procuring breaches of contracts of employ-ment. The " lightning strike," called in breach of the employees' contracts of employment became an instrument of trade union tactics [38]—in the sense that the strike was supported by the union and to that extent was often said to be " official." This loose terminology which is to be found almost daily in the national press is very often confusing, and sometimes wholly misleading. It is possible for the so-called " official strike " to be illegal and for the so-called " unofficial strike " to be perfectly legal. This difficulty is referred to again in this chapter: (3) The most important provision in the statute was probably the substantial degree of immunity granted to trade unions against proceedings for delicts (torts, in England) committed on their behalf. The union funds were no longer to be avail-able to satisfy an award of civil damages in delict or tort actions against the trade union itself (or in any descriptive or representative action) whether in relation to defamation, negligence, strike activity or other-wise [39]: and (4) a " trade dispute " was defined as " a dispute between employers and workmen, or workmen and workmen, connected with the

---

[31] 2 & 3 Geo. 5, c. 30.
[32] 38 & 39 Vict., c. 86.
[33] *Ibid.* s. 3.
[34] 39 & 40 Vict., c. 22.
[35] *Ibid.* s. 16.
[36] 6 Edw. 7, c. 47.
[37] See s. 1 (amending s. 3 of the Conspiracy and Protection of Property Act 1875).
[38] See s. 3.
[39] See s. 4.

employment or terms of employment or conditions of labour of any person." [40]

Before passing to the next statute it is necessary to recall the political history of the opening decade of the twentieth century. The Labour Party had been formed in 1906 [41] and it looked to the unions for financial and political (i.e., electoral) support. The Osborne case [42] was to dash its financial hopes for some three years. This case was an interesting example of the application of the *ultra vires* doctrine of company law to registered trade unions. The same principle was subsequently applied to unregistered trade unions in the Scottish case of Wilson v. *Scottish Typographical Association*.[43] The forces of labour were now marshalled against the Osborne decision and as a result of these pressures the Trade Union Act 1913 [44] was passed. This statute made the definition of a trade union more flexible [45] and it authorised political activities and certain political objects. A separate union fund was to be established and administered for such purposes and rules were required to be prepared in respect of such activities, including a provision in the said rules that any member who did not wish to contribute to the political fund should be exempted from so doing. Furthermore, there must be no unjust discrimination against non-contributors [46]—a point which was to be raised in another leading case some thirty-seven years later. Any person who considers himself to be aggrieved by a breach of the Political Fund Rules has a right of complaint to the Registrar of Friendly Societies [47] who can make an order to remedy the grievance. This order has the same weight as an interlocutor or a decree of the sheriff court in Scotland or an order of the county court in England.

After the close of the First World War developments were mainly of a social and political nature. There was much industrial unrest.[48] In 1919 there occurred a police strike which was quickly followed by a statutory measure, viz., the Police Act 1919, prohibiting members of the police force from joining a trade union. The Act established the Police Federation and granted to chief constables the power to permit those police officers who had been members of a trade union before joining the police to continue their membership, but there must be no conflict of interest which prevented the proper performance of their duties as police officers. In the following year a major strike took place in the mining

[40] s. 5 (3).
[41] Its outstanding predecessor was the Independent Labour Party (which had brought national fame to James Keir Hardie).
[42] [1909] 1 Ch. 163 (C.A.); on appeal to the House of Lords *sub nom. Amalgamated Society of Railway Servants* v. *Osborne* [1910] A.C. 87; 26 T.L.R. 177, which overruled *Steele* v. *South Wales Miners' Federation* [1907] 1 K.B. 361.
[3] 1912 S.C. 534; 1912, 1 S.L.T. 203.
[44] 2 & 3 Geo. 5, c. 30.
[45] *Ibid.* ss. 1 and 2.
[46] *Ibid.* s. 3.
[47] s. 3 (2).
[48] See G. D. H. Cole, *Short History of the British Working Class Movement, op. cit.,* Chap. VII, p. 372 *et seq.* and Chap. VIII, p. 380 *et seq.*

industry. The Government quickly passed the Emergency Powers Act 1920, by which it took powers to proclaim a state of emergency if it appeared that essential services to the community were threatened by industrial action or any intended industrial action.[49] Regulations could be made under the statute to procure the continuance of essential public services. Whilst nothing was done to amend or restrict or limit the right to strike, or the right to persuade others peacefully to strike, nevertheless any breach of a regulation issued was made punishable by fine or imprisonment or both.[50] However, there followed the General Strike in 1926, to which the Conservative Government of 1927 reacted by placing the Trade Disputes and Trade Unions Act 1927 [51] on the Statute Book. This Act made two types of strike or lock-out illegal,[52] viz.: (a) a strike or lock-out which had any object other than that of furthering a dispute within the trade or industry in which the strikers were employed (that is to say, the " sympathetic strike " was outlawed); and (b) a strike or lock-out designed or calculated to coerce the government, either directly or indirectly by inflicting hardship on the community. Strikes having political or quasi-political objects were declared illegal, therefore, and in addition, certain restrictions were placed upon the right to picket.[53] Furthermore, the rules governing political funds were changed—and " contracting in " was substituted for " contracting out." [54] The emphasis of the political fund contribution was now altered and the union member was required to indicate his willingness to contribute.

Section 6 prohibited local authorities and other public bodies from making it a condition of employment with them that any person should or should not be a member of a trade union. The trade unions were bitterly opposed to the 1927 Act, mainly because the " sympathetic strike " was outlawed. When the Labour Party came to power in 1945 it was a foregone conclusion that the 1927 Act would be repealed. This was duly done by the Trade Disputes and Trade Unions Act 1946 [55] which restored the status quo (i.e., the position prior to 1927). One of the outstanding cases raising the issue of " the spirit of the 1913 Act in relation to the political fund rules " was Birch v. The National Union of Railwaymen.[56] This union had a rule which made any non-contributor to the political fund ineligible for any office involving control of the political fund. Branch chairmen had, by virtue of their offices, control of, inter alia, the political fund. Plaintiff, a branch chairman but a non-contributor to the fund, was removed accordingly from his office. He brought an action for a declaration (in Scotland, for a declarator) that

[49] 1920 Act, s. 1, amended by the Emergency Powers Act 1964. See also K. W. Wedderburn, Cases and Materials on Labour Law (Cambridge U.P., 1967) pp. 386–388.
[50] Ibid. s. 2.
[51] 17 & 18 Geo. 5, c. 22.
[52] s. 1 (a) (i) and (b) (i); and 1 (a) (ii) and (b) (ii) respectively.
[53] s. 3.
[54] s. 4.
[55] 9 & 10 Geo. 6, c. 52.
[56] [1950] Ch. 602.

he had been unlawfully removed from office. It was held [57] that the rule discriminated against non-contributors, in a manner contrary to the spirit of the 1913 Act and accordingly the fund was unlawful.

Legislation dealing with amalgamation, etc., has also appeared from time to time,[58] but the latest statute affecting trade unions is the Trade Disputes Act 1965 [59] which ostensibly corrected the difficult and doubtful position in which the unions found themselves after the decision of the House of Lords in *Rookes* v. *Barnard and Others*.[60] Now, almost exactly one hundred years after the Royal Commission of 1867 made possible the Trade Union Act of 1871—another Royal Commission has, within the past year, issued its own Report.[61] For the sake of brevity, the Royal Commission will be referred to throughout this chapter as the " Donovan Commission " and its Report as the " Donovan Report." Since the Donovan Report was issued the Government has issued the appropriate White Paper,[62] but this has not been received with universal acclaim.[63] Both the Donovan Report and the White Paper will be considered and commented upon as necessary throughout the course of this chapter. It has been clearly indicated that new legislation is necessary and that a new Industrial Relations Act can be expected some time during the next twelve months. Further talks and discussions between and among the Government and both sides of industry (and including the C.B.I. and T.U.C.) must, however, take place first. In the meantime, the new Commission on Industrial Relations [64] has been set up as a Royal Commission but presumably it will be reconstituted as a statutory body when the new Industrial Relations Act is enacted.

The non-enforceability (or, as some politicians might term it, the extra-judicial sanctity) of the collective agreement has just been confirmed in *Ford Motor Co. Ltd.* v. *Amalgamated Union of Engineering and Foundry Workers and Others*,[65] before Mr. Justice Geoffrey Lane in the Queen's

---

[57] By Danckwerts J.
[58] Trade Union (Amalgamation) Act 1917 (7 & 8 Geo. 5, c. 24) and the Trade Union (Amalgamations, etc.) Act 1964 (c. 24).
[59] 1965, c. 48.
[60] [1964] A.C. 1129; [1964] 1 All E.R. 367; [1964] 2 W.L.R. 269; [1964] 1 Lloyd's Rep. 28 (H.L.).
[61] Report of the Royal Commission on Trade Unions and Employers' Associations (Cmnd. 3623, 1968). Several interesting Research Papers were issued from time to time by the Commission's order and these may be referred to later herein. See also the Interim Statement published in November 1968 by the T.U.C. General Council and titled " Action on Donovan."
[62] " In Place of Strife " (A Policy for Industrial Relations) (Cmnd. 3888) (presented January 1969).
[63] In the House of Commons Debate on the White Paper some strong criticisms were voiced and when the division was called the resulting vote against the motion moved by Mrs. Barbara Castle (Secretary of State for Employment and Productivity) was (approximately) 100. It is understood that there is a clear division of opinion within the Parliamentary Labour Party. Subsequently, in June 1969, the Government and the T.U.C. reached an agreement by which the proposed primary Bill to deal with unofficial strikes (employing penal sanctions) would be dropped and the T.U.C. undertook to extend its participation in the bargaining field.
[64] It began its functions on March 3, 1969, under the chairmanship of the Rt. Hon. George Woodcock, C.B.E., former General Secretary of the Trades Union Congress.
[65] See law report of March 6, 1969, in *The Times* newspaper of March 7, 1969; this case is now reported in [1969] 1 W.L.R. 339.

Bench Division. There are today three disturbing and explosive elements in the field of industrial relations in Great Britain, *viz.*—(i) the " wildcat strike," (ii) the demarcation dispute and (iii) the recognition dispute. The Donovan Commission and the Government both firmly believe that the new attitude to collective bargaining which they advocate —and the Commission on Industrial Relations is expected to make a substantial contribution to this development—will help to change existing attitudes to strikes and inter-union disputes as well as to improve the approach of management to industrial relations, whether plant-wide or nation-wide. Only time (and infinite patience) will tell.

(2) *Definition of a Trade Union* [66]

Section 23 of the Trade Union Act 1871 gave the first statutory definition of a trade union. Originally this section applied only to un-lawful combinations, but section 16 of the amending Act of 1876 repealed that definition (except for the proviso) [67] and re-enacted it in a form applicable to both lawful and unlawful (combinations or) trade unions. Section 16 is as follows: "The term 'trade union' means any com-bination, whether temporary or permanent, for regulating the relations between workmen and masters, or between workmen and workmen, or between masters and masters, or for imposing restrictive conditions on the conduct of any trade or business, whether such combination would or would not, if the principal Act had not been passed, have been deemed to have been an unlawful combination by reason of some one or more of its purposes being in restraint of trade." The *Osborne* decision [68] held that definition to be restrictive. The Trade Union Act 1913 expanded the definition in the following ways: (i) it distinguished between principal and subordinate objects of a union and defined a trade union as any combination the principal objects of which are one or more of the statutory objects (s. 2 (1)); (ii) it defined statutory objects as the objects mentioned in the earlier Acts and added the words " and also the provision of benefits to members " (s. 1 (2)); (iii) it authorised (subject to the Act's provisions *re* political objects) the expenditure of the funds of a trade union on any other lawful object for the time being authorised by its constitution (s. 1 (1)); (iv) it provided that a combination having any objects which

---

[66] The major reference book on *Trade Union Law* is Citrine (N.A.) (now 3rd ed., 1967, by Professor M. A. Hickling) (published by Stevens & Sons). This work is extremely valuable because there is a liberal citation of and reference to Scottish cases and authorities. The most readable and recent monograph, which is also a useful text-book, is Professor Cyril Grunfeld's *Modern Trade Union Law* (Sweet & Maxwell, 1966). References will be made from time to time to both of these works. Green's *Encyclopaedia of the Laws of Scotland* (3rd ed., 1933), Vol. 14 (paras. 1182–1336) (and supplements) also contains a helpful section on trade unions.

[67] The proviso reads: " Provided that this Act shall not affect—
   1. Any agreement between partners as to their own business;
   2. Any agreement between an employer and those employed by him as to such employment;
   3. Any agreement in consideration of the sale of the goodwill of a business or of instruction in any profession, trade or handicraft."

[68] *Cit. supra.*

were not " statutory objects " should not for that reason cease to be a trade union, provided always that the principal objects were statutory objects (s. 1 (1)); and (v) it declared that registered and certified trade unions should be deemed to be trade unions so long as they were so registered or certified.

The 1913 Act, s. 2, definition of a trade union is as follows: " The expression ' trade union ' for the purpose of the Trade Union Acts 1871 to 1906, and this Act, means any combination, whether temporary or permanent, the principal objects of which are under its constitution statutory objects: Provided that any combination which is for the time being registered as a trade union shall be deemed to be a trade union as defined by this Act so long as it continues to be so registered." [69] The " statutory objects " are defined in section 1 (2) as " the objects mentioned in section sixteen of the Trade Union Act Amendment Act 1876, namely, the regulation of the relations between workmen and masters, or between workmen and workmen, or between masters and masters, or the imposing of restrictive conditions on the conduct of any trade or business, and also the provision of benefits to members." The statutory definition is therefore to be found partly in the 1871 Act (proviso to s. 23), partly in the 1876 Act (s. 16) and partly in the 1913 Act (ss. 1 (1) and (2) and 2 (1)).[70]

A trade union is basically a combination of two or more persons, but it never seems to have been decided by the Scottish courts or the English courts what the meaning of the term " combination " as used in the statutory definition is in their view.

(3) The Objects of a Trade Union

These may be either principal objects or subsidiary objects. The principal objects are limited to one or more statutory objects.[71] Should it happen that none of the principal objects is, in fact, a statutory object then the association or combination in question is not a trade union. In order to ascertain what the principal objects of a combination are, the court or the Registrar of Friendly Societies is not specifically restricted to the " objects clause " of the rulebook. The constitution must be read as a whole. If the union is to come within the statutory definition then one or more of its principal objects must be concerned with any of the following purposes, viz.: (i) the regulation of relations between workmen [72] and masters, workmen and workmen or masters and masters and (ii) the imposing of restrictive conditions upon the conduct of any trade or business. The provision of benefits to members is an additional optional

---

[69] s. 2 (1).

[70] See also the Societies (Miscellaneous Provisions) Act 1940, s. 6, which must be read along with the other definition sections.

[71] Vide the 1913 Act, s. 2 (1). An incorporated company cannot, however, act as a trade union, even if it takes over the assets and liabilities of an association which was a trade union—see Aberdeen Master Masons' Incorporation Ltd. v. Smith, 1908 S.C. 669.

[72] " Workmen " is defined in the Trade Disputes Act 1906, s. 5 (3), as " all persons employed in trade or industry." It is thought that the Registrar interprets this fairly widely to mean " persons in gainful occupations."

principal object.[73] The Trade Union Act 1871 had authorised benevolent objects as ancillary objects, but it will be appreciated that if the sole principal object of an association is the provision of benefits to members then it is not a trade union within the meaning of the Trade Union Acts.

There are certain points about the subordinate (or subsidiary) objects which must be noted, namely: (1) it is not relevant to the question of whether an association is or is not a trade union as to what subordinate object or objects are contained in its rules; but if a statutory object (as explained above) is subordinate the association in question is not a trade union; and (2) a trade union may pursue any lawful subordinate object it so wishes, subject always to the provisions of section 1 (1) of the 1913 Act and the additional provisions in that statute regarding political objects. No trade union may have an object which is unlawful nor one which is contrary to the Restrictive Practices Acts.[74] The word " unlawful " in this context means unlawful for a trade union and it does not include objects which are classified as unlawful for the sole reason that they are in restraint of trade. It is perfectly lawful for a trade union to have restrictive practices.[75] But if any purpose is unlawful the registration of the union is void,[76] and the Registrar would be able to cancel the registration. When an original application for registration is made the Registrar has the task of scrutinising the rules to see that there is nothing unlawful therein, otherwise he would refuse to complete the registration process. If any challenge is to be made that any object of a trade union is *ultra vires* then it would seem that such a challenge can only be made upon one or more of three main grounds, *viz*.: (i) that the object in question was not authorised by the constitution, (ii) that the object is unlawful for a trade union or (iii) that the object was and is a political object under section 3 of the 1913 Act but the union had failed to comply with the provisions of the 1913 Act relating specially to political objects. If it were necessary to restrain a trade union from applying its funds upon any alleged *ultra vires* object the normal procedure would be by interdict in Scotland (or injunction, in England). It may be possible to trace and recover moneys which have been expended upon an *ultra vires* object and it is also possible that trustees who are involved, or members of the executive council, would be held personally liable to make good any resulting deficiencies.

A trade union is not necessarily a permanent institution,[77] nor need it be so. The *ad hoc* strike committee, having as its principal object(s) one or more of the statutory objects, is essentially a trade union, within the definition of the Trade Union Acts. Accordingly, the legal status of being a " trade union " will attach to an association only so long as its

---

[73] See the Trade Union Act 1913, s. 1 (2).
[74] See s. 10 of the Monopolies and Restrictive Practices (Inquiry and Control) Act 1948 and s. 24 of the Restrictive Trade Practices Act 1956 and subsequent legislation.
[75] Trade Union Act 1871, s. 3.
[76] 1871 Act, s. 6.
[77] See the 1913 Act, s. 2 (1).

principal objects are statutory objects and subject always to the following qualifications, as appropriate: (a) a registered trade union is deemed to be a trade union so long as it is so registered and (b) a certificate by the Registrar is conclusive so long as it remains in force.

(4) *Registration of a Trade Union* [78]

In order to register under the Trade Union Acts, a union is required to comply with the following provisions:

(1) It must have a set of written rules.

(2) Seven or more members of the union must subscribe two printed copies of the rules of the union and also sign an application for registration.[79] These papers, together with a list of the titles and names of the officers of the union must be sent to the Chief Registrar of Friendly Societies in London, if the union is being registered in England and Wales or to the Assistant Registrar in Edinburgh if the union is being registered in Scotland. The signatories to the application must be members of the union but they need not be officers of the union nor members of its executive (or management) committee.

(3) Notice must be given to the appropriate Registrar of the situation of the registered office.[80] The provisions contained in the Acts have not been complied with until such notification is made.

(4) If the union has been in operation for more than one year before the date of the application there must be deposited with the application a general statement [81] of the receipts, funds, effects and expenditure of such union in the same form and showing the same particulars as if it were an annual general statement as required by section 16 of the 1871 Act.

Upon receipt of an application for registration under the Trade Union Acts it is the duty of the Registrar concerned to do the following things:

(i) He must not register the union unless all the provisions above explained have been complied with by the union in question.

(ii) He must not register an association or combination as a trade union unless, in his opinion and having regard to the constitution, the principal objects are statutory objects. In forming his opinion the Registrar is entitled to look not only at the rulebook but also at the practices of the union in order to ascertain the principal objects.

(iii) He should satisfy himself that none of the purposes is unlawful— because registration would then be void.

---

[78] For detailed information upon registration requirements and procedures see Citrine, *op. cit.*
[79] See ss. 6, 13 and 14 of the Trade Union Act 1871.
[80] 1871 Act, s. 15. The requirement is mandatory.
[81] *Ibid.* s. 13, para. (4).

iv) He must not register a trade union which has a name identical with or closely resembling that of another union which is already registered, so that the public may be misled or deceived.[82]

(v) If the union is operating at the time of the application the Registrar should refuse to register it if he has reason to believe that the applicants have not been authorised by the union to make the application. He may require to verify the position with the union itself before completing the registration procedure, and

(vi) Upon being satisfied about the foregoing requirements the union must be registered and a certificate of registration must be issued.

If any person considers himself to be aggrieved by the refusal of the Registrar to effect registration he has a right of appeal [83] to the Court of Session or to the High Court of Justice, as the case may be.

The certificate of registration which the Registrar issues is conclusive evidence that the regulations regarding registration have been complied with and that the combination is a trade union, although *per se* it is not conclusive on the subject of the validity of the rules themselves—because that is the task of the courts of law. In addition, a court of law has the right to ignore the certificate and inquire *ex proprio motu* whether any of the union's purposes is unlawful. The Registrar has the right to withdraw the certificate if any alteration is made to the constitution of the union whereby the principal objects cease to be statutory objects or if they are not statutory objects in any event. The certificate may also be withdrawn or cancelled [84] in any of the following circumstances: (1) at the request of the union itself or (2) by the Registrar himself if—the certificate was obtained by fraud or error or the union has (after due notice given to it) violated the provisions of the Acts or the union has now ceased to exist. The Registrar must give two months' notice to the union concerned of his intention to withdraw or cancel the certificate of registration and must specify the grounds for so doing. When the withdrawal becomes effective the union reverts to its former status of an unregistered union. An unregistered trade union has always the right to apply for certification under section 2 (3) of the Trade Union Act 1913, but in this case it is not required to complete the full registration procedure required by the Acts and of course it is then classified as a " certified trade union," in contrast with the registered trade union which follows the full registration procedure.

Any appeal regarding the grant or withdrawal of a certificate of

---

[82] *Ibid.* s. 13, para. (3). See also *National Society of Operative Printers' Assistants* v. *Smith and Others* (*The Times*, April 8, 1910) where members of an unregistered trade union proposing to call themselves " The National Association of Operative Printers " were restrained by injunction from doing so, on the application of the National Society of Operative Printers' Assistants.

[83] Trade Union Act 1913, s. 2 (4).

[84] See the Trade Union Act (1871) Amendment Act 1876, s. 8.

registration also lies to the Court of Session or the High Court of Justice.[85] Whilst the Registrar's certificate remains in force it is conclusive for all purposes that the combination is a trade union.[86]

Where a trade union has one or more principal objects which are statutory objects, but it has not applied for registration or certification within the Trade Union Acts, it remains an unregistered and uncertified union and it is subject to no special statutory provision regarding its form or its organisation, unless it wishes to establish a political fund. In that case it must comply with the provisions of the Trade Union Act 1913.[87] Most of the larger trade unions are registered but many of the smaller ones are not, although the modern tendency is for mergers and amalgamations with the bigger unions. If a trade union is not registered it has in theory no legal personality whatsoever and it remains essentially in the eyes of the law a mere voluntary association of the members themselves.

PART B—Organisation and Powers of Trade Unions

(1) Property

Trade unions do not have sufficient legal personality to hold property, whether heritable or moveable, in the union names. Such property can however be vested in or held by trustees for the benefit of the members, subject always to the general law of trusts, whether statute law [88] and/or common law. The trust must not infringe the rules against accumulations and perpetuities. The ordinary machinery for preservation and administration of trust property is available to members and trustees of the union. A registered trade union can hold an unlimited amount of moveable property through its trustees and it can sell, exchange, grant heritable securities over or let heritable property without any need for inquiry by the purchaser, etc., into the authority of the trustees. The trustees themselves can grant a good discharge.[89] All heritable property and moveable property belonging to a registered trade union must be vested in the trustees for the time being and be held by them for and on behalf of the members.[90] Property which belongs to a trade union branch should be held by the trustees of the branch or alternatively by the trustees of the union itself.

---

[85] See the Trade Union Act 1913, s. 2 (4), and the Rules of Court in Scotland (in England, the Supreme Court Rules). A period of two months from the date of the Registrar's decision is allowed for the appeal to be intimated.

[86] 1913 Act, s. 2 (5).

[87] See particularly ss. 3, 4, 5 and 6; and the notes *infra* in this chapter regarding political objects.

[88] See the Trusts (Scotland) Acts 1921–1961 and the Trustee Investments Act 1961.

[89] Trade Union Act 1871, s. 7.

[90] It should be noted that the Law Reform (Miscellaneous Provisions) (Scotland) Act 1968 (c. 70) removed a restriction upon the extent of land which trade unions registered in Scotland may purchase. The English case of *N.U.R.* v. *Registrar of Friendly Societies* (1967) 111 S.J. 926 and *sub nom. N.U.R.* v. *Registry of Friendly Societies* [1968] 1 W.L.R. 69; [1968] 1 All E.R. 5 and *The Times* of November 17, 1967 (raising the importance of s. 8 of the Trade Union Act 1871), illustrates that property must be vested in names of trustees and that no other form of registration is valid.

As regards the trustees, the rules should make provision for their appointment and removal,[91] but they need not be members of the union. Provision can be made, so far as England and Wales are concerned, for the appointment of the Public Trustee but this must be provided for in the rules. When a trustee of a registered trade union dies or is removed from office the trust property vests in the remaining trustees for the same purposes and interests as previously. Stocks and securities must, however, be transferred to the names of the new trustees.[92] If a trustee or former trustee of a branch or union is absent from Great Britain or becomes bankrupt or executes a trust deed for his creditors or becomes a lunatic or is deceased, etc., the Registrar may, on the application in writing of the secretary and three members of the branch or union and upon submission of satisfactory proof, direct the transfer of stock into the names of any other persons as trustees for the branch or the union. The transfer must be made by the surviving or continuing trustees and if there be none (or if they are unable to do so or refuse to do so) and the Registrar so directs, then this can be done by a special procedure.[93] A trustee is liable for all moneys received by him on account of his trade union but he is not liable generally as a trustee for deficiencies occurring in the union's funds. He is liable, however, for any loss caused by any distribution of or intromission with union property contrary to the rules of the union and it is no excuse for him to say that he was acting on the instructions of the governing body of the union, the liability in question being a personal liability.

Every treasurer or other officer of a registered trade union must render to the trustees of the union and its members, at a meeting of the union and at the times provided by the rules or when required to do so, a proper account of all moneys received and paid by him since his last account and of all balances in his hands and of all investments of the union.[94] The trustees must have the accounts audited by an auditor, being a fit and proper person. The trustees can proceed against any officer or treasurer of the union for balances, securities or other funds held by him on behalf of the registered trade union.

(2) Members and Officers

Admission to membership of a trade union should be governed by the rules. Thereafter every member is bound by the contract contained in the rules [95] and his membership is subject to the terms of that contract. In the absence of a provision to the contrary in the rules, a member may terminate his membership by giving notice to the secretary. Thereupon he ceases to be a member and can only be readmitted by re-election, unless the rules provide otherwise. A member cannot be expelled unless

---

[91] Trade Union Act 1871, s. 14 and Sched. 1.
[92] Ibid. s. 8.
[93] See reg. 20 of the Trade Union Regulations 1876 and Form R annexed thereto.
[94] Trade Union Act 1871, s. 11.
[95] See Wedderburn, Casebook, op. cit., Chap. 5, section B, p. 564 et seq.

the rules give power for this to be done.[96] If membership is obtained by misrepresentation, the contract can be rescinded in the same way as any other contract. In Scotland, a minor who is sixteen years or over would seem to be free to join a trade union or combination provided there is nothing in the rules to the contrary, but he might not necessarily be bound by the contract contained in the rules unless that contract taken as a whole is for his benefit.

A police officer is prohibited from being a member of a trade union [97] and any police officer who contravenes this provision is disqualified from being a member of the police force, although if he is a member of a union when he joins the police force he may continue his membership with the consent of his chief constable.

There is nothing in the Trade Union Acts which limits the liability of members of a union. In theory, it would seem that the liability of members for the debts of a trade union (including a damages award in contract) is unlimited. If a court decree is obtained against a registered trade union in its registered name (or perhaps also against its trustee or authorised officers), diligence can only be instructed against the funds and property of the union.

Every registered trade union must have a committee of management, trustees, a treasurer and a secretary. The offices of treasurer and secretary can be combined in one holder. There are no statutory requirements affecting the officers of an unregistered trade union but, obviously, if it is to function efficiently and effectively it must have officers corresponding to those of a registered trade union. The rights, duties and powers of all officers should be laid down in the union rules and, within the scope of his authority, it is the duty of every trade union officer to protect the interests of the members.

A trade union can only act by and through its officers, who are its agents. If a union is a registered union it is probably correct to regard it as a principal and its officers as its agents. If the union is unregistered, its members, or more probably its committee of management or other executive body, would seem to be the principal. In the fields of contract and agency, the general law of principal and agent applies to the relationship between a union and its officers, but subject always to the limitations contained in section 4 (4) of the Trade Union Act 1871. When an officer contracts on behalf of a union within the scope of his authority (whether real or ostensible) he binds the union. If he exceeds his authority he will be personally liable upon the contract, unless the union should subsequently adopt and ratify his actions. The same principal and agent relationship

---

[96] Any member who claims that he has been wrongfully expelled may seek a declarator (in England, a declaration) to this effect and/or claim damages. In *Martin* v. *Amalgamated Society of Painters and Decorators, The Times,* July 10, 1967; [1968] 7 C.L. 449 the widow of a member who was wrongfully expelled recovered £1,392 damages in respect thereof.

[97] See the Police Act 1919 and subsequent legislation concerning the police, particularly the Police (Scotland) Act 1956, as amended by the Police Act 1964 (c. 48), the statute law being now consolidated in the Police (Scotland) Act 1967.

applies within the field of delict, subject always to the limitations upon the jurisdiction of the courts imposed by the Trade Union Acts (and including the Trade Disputes Acts 1906 and 1965) both in relation to the personal liability of the officers and the liability of the union itself and its members as principals. Prima facie, the position seems to be that an officer of a union can be presumed to have only that authority to do or sanction acts which the union itself may lawfully do, and if any officer should exceed any authority conferred upon him by the rules or should he act in contravention of the rules in some other respect the trade union will not be liable. In the absence of evidence to the contrary, a branch should not be assumed to be an agent for the union itself, but where the union has authorised or ordered or ratified the actings of a branch or its officers it will be liable therefor. The trade union has always imputed to it a knowledge of those matters which are within the actual knowledge of its agents—being matters which it is the duty of these agents to communicate to the principal (*i.e.*, the union itself).

The Race Relations Act 1968 [98] lays down important provisions *vis-à-vis* membership of trade unions and employers' and trade organisations. Section 4 provides as follows:

" 4.—(1) It shall be unlawful for an organisation to which this section applies or any person concerned with the affairs of such an organisation—

> (*a*) to discriminate against a person who is not a member of the organisation by refusing or deliberately omitting to admit him to membership of the organisation on the like terms as other persons applying for membership;
>
> (*b*) to discriminate against a member of the organisation by refusing or deliberately omitting to accord him the same benefits as are accorded to other members thereof, or to take the like action on his behalf as is taken on behalf of other members, or by expelling him from the organisation.

(2) This section applies to organisations of employers or workers or other organisations concerned with the carrying on of trades, businesses, professions or occupations."

The meaning of the verb " discriminate " for purposes of the 1968 Act may be found in section 1 thereof and is extremely important.

(3) *The Rules*

The rules constitute a contract between the members and, in the case of a registered trade union, between each member and the union. Some writers seem to regard this contract as a simple two-party contract between each member and his trade union. Professor Grunfeld,[99] on the other hand, regards the contract in question as a multi-lateral contract involving

---

[98] 1968, c. 71.
[99] See his *Modern Trade Union Law, op. cit.* at p. 38.

all members and the union and he quotes the two under-noted cases [1] in support of his argument. It may be that from the viewpoint of modern labour relations Professor Grunfeld's view is to be preferred.

The powers of the union, its officers and committees and the rights and obligations of its members must all be found within that contract, whether expressly or by implication. Any acting outside of the rules is an *ultra vires* acting. The rules must indicate the objects and purposes of the union; and the activities are confined to these specified objects and activities. If the union is lawful at common law, its rules can be enforced in the same way as any other lawful contract. If a union is unlawful at common law it may well be that many of its rules may in practice fall under section 4 of the Trade Union Act 1871 and therefore not be directly enforceable, nor be enforceable by an award of damages. In an important sense, therefore, the wheel has turned full circle, because the unions themselves are now able to avoid their legal responsibilities and liabilities by pleading common law illegality, with the result that a member or the representative of a member may be deprived [2] of a remedy before the courts because of the section 4 classification adopted in the 1871 Act. It would perhaps be agreed that collective agreements which fall, of course, within paragraph 4 of section 4 are a special category and in any case the recommendations of the Donovan Report and the White Paper ought to be given a trial. But there seems to be no valid reason as to why the remaining categories of agreements in section 4 should not be made enforceable in the courts of law. This anachronistic myth of restraint of trade and common law illegality—which give an undeserved protection by outlawing the law—should be swept away. It is against all principles of natural and social justice. In any event any breach of the rules can be stopped by interdict and the court may be asked to interpret the rules by means of a petition for declarator. So far as possible the rules—and particularly those relating to membership—are given their literal meaning by the courts of law and the interests of both individual members on the one side and the trade union itself on the other must receive an equal recognition.[3] There should be no question of bias or discrimination. As

---

[1] *Bonsor* v. *Musicians' Union* [1956] A.C. 104; [1955] 3 W.L.R. 788; [1955] 3 All E.R. 518, and *Faramus* v. *Film Artistes' Association* [1964] A.C. 925; [1964] 2 W.L.R. 126; [1964] 1 All E.R. 25. For notes on these cases and excerpts from the speeches see Wedderburn's *Casebook* at p. 643 *et seq.* and p. 573 *et seq.* respectively.

[2] This is illustrated most recently in Scotland in *Briggs* v. *National Union of Mineworkers*, 1969 S.L.T. 165 where Lord Kissen, in the Outer House and dismissing the action as incompetent, took a wide interpretation of s. 4 (3) (*a*). His lordship was somewhat critical of Lord Fraser's opinion (Lord Fraser having allowed a proof before answer in the earlier case) in the prior case of *McGahie* v. *Union of Shop, Distributive and Allied Workers*, 1966 S.L.T. 74 (a case raising questions of application of funds, an agreement for " benefit " and the Law Reform (Limitation of Actions) Act 1954, s. 6 (1) (*a*), in relation to s. 4 of the Trade Union Act 1871). For a commentary on *McGahie*, see Citrine, *op. cit.*, particularly at pp. 128 and 129. See also Wedderburn, *Cases and Materials on Labour Law, op. cit.*, for illustrations of other decisions within s. 4 of the 1871 Act.

[3] See particularly *Martin* v. *Scottish T. & G.W.U.*, 1952 S.L.T. 224; [1952] W.N. 142; [1952] 1 T.L.R. 677; [1952] 1 All E.R. 691 (H.L.); (the House of Lords affirming the First Division of the Court of Session). In this case, appellant's temporary membership

indicated above, a trade union is a voluntary association which should be left free to deal with its own affairs and with its conditions of membership.

The rules must give power to levy contributions, because there is no statutory power to do so.[4] An unauthorised levy is *ultra vires* and will be restrained by an interdict in Scotland. If the union is lawful at common law it seems that a contractual obligation to pay contributions can be enforced; but, if it is unlawful at common law the obligation cannot be enforced either directly or by an award of damages. The political fund rules are quite a separate matter and are governed by the Trade Union Act 1913.[5] The unregistered trade union need not have rules in writing or in any particular form, because there are no statutory requirements governing their form and content—except that if the association is properly classified as a trade union its principal objects must be one or more of the statutory objects [6] and if it wishes to have a political fund it must comply with the special requirements of the 1913 Act. In practice, written rules are always used.

The registered trade union will have printed rules which should take account *inter alia* of the following matters—the union's name, place of meeting for business, objects and purposes for which its funds are to be applied, conditions for qualifying for benefit, fines and forfeitures, procedure for making, altering, amending, or rescinding the rules, appointment and removal of trustees, treasurer, general committee of management and other officers, investment of funds and periodical audits, inspection of books, dissolution, and the special rules protecting members who do not contribute to the political fund.[7]

If a trade union is primarily registered in England and wishes to expand its activities into Scotland, then it must send copies of its rules (with amendments noted) to the Assistant Registrar in Scotland. The same procedure must be followed if a Scottish-based trade union wishes to expand its activities to England and Wales, and notification must then be

of the union was revoked following a resolution of the general executive council. Appellant sought a declarator that he had been validly admitted and also a reduction of the resolution. It was held, however, that he had not been validly admitted to membership—as the officials had no authority to admit M. or anyone else to temporary membership. Accordingly, they had acted *ultra vires* and their act was invalid; *Faramus* v. *Film Artistes' Association* [1964] A.C. 925; [1964] 2 W.L.R. 126; [1964] 1 All E.R. 25; and *Boulting* v. *Assocn. of Cinematograph, Television and Allied Technicians* [1963] 2 Q.B. 606; [1963] 2 W.L.R. 529; [1963] 1 All E.R. 716 (C.A.) (in this last-mentioned case—on a true construction of the rule in question—the managing directors were eligible for membership because they were employees of the company and there was nothing *ultra vires* or unlawful in this).

[4] In the case of *Haggarty* v. *Scottish Transport and General Workers' Union*, 1955 S.C. 109, H. averred that he had been admitted to membership during the war and—on the basis of the *condictio indebiti* remedy (which is an equitable remedy)—sought recovery of the entry fee and weekly contributions, on the ground that the union had acted *ultra vires* in admitting him and that he had never been a member. The union admitted acting *ultra vires* but pleaded that pursuer had enjoyed all the rights and advantages of membership. The court held that the *condictio indebiti* remedy should be available to pursuer but there must be an inquiry as to whether retention of the money by the union was equitable and accordingly the case was remitted for proof.

[5] *Ibid.* ss. 3–6.

[6] *Ibid.* s. 2 (1).

[7] See the Trade Union Act 1913 and *Birch* v. *N.U.R.* [1950] Ch. 602.

made to the Chief Registrar in London. Any proposed change in the union's name must be approved by a two-thirds majority of all the members. Notice of such change, in writing, and signed by seven members and the secretary must be lodged with the Registrar, together with a form of statutory declaration which the secretary is required to sign. Every trade union is required to have a registered office.[8] It should also have " a place of meeting for the business of the trade union." [9] It is not necessary that the registered office and the place of meeting should be at the same address, although obviously this is most convenient.

The rules should specify with care the whole objects of the union,[10] preferably in a comprehensive single clause. The funds of a trade union may be applied in furtherance of any lawful object or purpose authorised by the constitution, although the rules need not expressly provide for such expenditure. Any special purpose which is not governed directly or indirectly by the objects clause must be mentioned specifically in order to give it legal effect.[11] A union can be restrained by interdict from applying its funds for any purpose not authorised by its constitution and rules or indeed if it applies any funds or proposes to apply any funds for an unlawful purpose. The provision of benefits is a secondary or optional principal object for a union and, of course, it is not obligatory. The rules must set out the full machinery for the collection of contributions and payment of benefits.[12]

The position regarding fines and forfeitures is exceedingly important. If the rulebook does not authorise fines and forfeitures the union itself will have no disciplinary power.[13] A power to expel a member is only exercisable in the circumstances specified in the rules and in accordance with any conditions laid down therein.[14] Any expulsion for which there is no power in the rules, or which is based upon a wrong construction of the rules, will be invalidated.[15] *Lee* v. *Showmen's Guild of Great*

---

[8] 1871 Act, s. 15.
[9] *Ibid*. Sched. I, para. 1.
[10] *Ibid*. para. 2.
[11] *e.g.*, publishing a newspaper, making charitable gifts, etc.
[12] *e.g.*, accident or sick benefit, loss of tools compensation, strike pay, superannuation, etc.
[13] In *Fraser* v. *United Society of Boilermakers*, 1963 S.L.T.(Sh.Ct.) 17; 79 Sh.Ct.Rep. 132, F. brought an action in the sheriff court for declarator that fines imposed upon him for defying a ban on overtime were *ultra vires*. Defenders contended, *inter alia*, that the action was in substance an action of reduction and therefore incompetent in the sheriff court and, furthermore, the court had no power to interfere as the imposition of the fines was within the rules. It was held (1) that the action was competent, but (2) that no breach of the rules had been relevantly averred by pursuer and the action must be dismissed.
[14] The rules should be free from ambiguity. If, for example, a member, by reason of his own carelessness, allows his subscriptions to run into arrears over a substantial period of time then the union generally has a justifiable reason for expelling him. But if the arrears accumulate because of the refusal of union branch treasurers to accept subscriptions (*i.e.*, an unsubtle method of putting pressure on X to leave) this is not a good ground for invoking the rulebook—see *Connell* v. *National Union of Distributive Workers (Glasgow)*, *The Times*, January 28, 1928.
[15] See *Abbott* v. *Sullivan* [1952] 1 K.B. 189 (in the Court of Appeal); and *Lee* v. *Showmen's Guild of Great Britain* [1952] 2 Q.B. 329; [1952] 1 All E.R. 1175; [1952] 1 T.L.R. 1115. In *Silvester* v. *National Union of Printing, Bookbinding and Paper Workers* (1966) 1 K.I.R. 679, disciplinary action was taken against S. following his refusal to work

Britain [16] is an important illustration of an area committee placing a wrong construction upon a union rule, fining a member and thereafter expelling him. The Court of Appeal held the Committee's decisions to be wrong in law, *ultra vires* the rules and therefore quite void. A disciplinary function is quasi-judicial and it normally requires a special domestic tribunal to exercise it. The discipline rules should be unambiguous and always reasonable so that every union member can understand them. The courts have, for some years past, been concerned with applying the principle of " natural justice." This principle means that no person should have any punishment imposed upon him without having the opportunity of being heard in his own defence [16a]; and it has been applied in several of the trade union cases—see, for example, *Annamunthodo* v. *Oilfields' Workers' Trade Union*,[17] and the recent Scottish case of *Walker* v. *Amalgamated Union of Engineers and Foundry Workers*.[18]

If no provision for alteration or amendment of the rules is contained in the rulebook, then the unanimous consent of all the members might well be needed to enable the appropriate alterations to be made.

As a trade union cannot act in person it requires to appoint as its principal agent a committee of management (or its executive council or committee). The Trade Union Acts place no special duty upon this committee. It should be noted that a minor cannot be a member of this committee. The rules must make provision for the appointment and removal of the trustees of a registered union and the rules can give supplementary powers to the trustees to those conferred in the trade union statutes. These statutes require all property to be vested in the trustees, who must control the funds and property of the union. The trustees can

overtime. The construction of the rule required consideration of the point as to whether such a refusal was " detrimental to the union's interests " (which was the basis of the union case). It was held in the circumstances that the disciplinary action was *ultra vires* and void and the declarations sought by plaintiff were granted by Mr. Justice Goff in the Chancery Division.

Moreover, lacking powers of expulsion, a union cannot dissolve itself, and then reconstitute itself, phoenix-like, but refusing to admit to membership the particular individual it was anxious to be rid of in the first place—see *Gardner* v. *McClintock* (1904) 11 S.L.T. 654.

[16] *Cit. supra.*

[16a] But there is no basic right to legal representation before a domestic tribunal—*per* Lyell J. in *Pett* v. *Greyhound Racing Association (No. 2)* [1969] 2 All E.R. 221 at p. 231.

[17] [1961] A.C. 945; [1961] 3 W.L.R. 650. The principle has also been applied in the ordinary case of employment—see *Palmer* v. *Inverness Hospitals Board of Management*, 1963 S.L.T. 124; 1963 S.C. 311. Other interesting cases on " natural justice " in relation to the unions are *Taylor* v. *National Union of Seamen* [1967] 1 W.L.R. 532; [1967] 1 All E.R. 767; and *Hiles* v. *Amalgamated Society of Woodworkers* [1967] 3 W.L.R. 896; [1967] 3 All E.R. 70; there was no flouting of the principle in the earlier case of *Evans* v. *National Union of Printing, Bookbinding and Paper Workers* [1965] 2 W.L.R. 579; [1965] Ch. 712; [1965] 1 All E.R. 353 (for an instructive and lengthy excerpt from the opinion of Mr. Justice Ungoed-Thomas, see Wedderburn's *Casebook* at pp. 633–639).

In the Scottish case of *Milton* v. *Nicolson* (O.H.) 1965 S.L.T. 319, it was held that where the executive council of a trade union has power to dismiss an officer as an administrative act and it is not acting as a tribunal in so doing, the court cannot interfere with that administrative decision. Pursuer's action was, therefore, irrelevant.

[18] [1969] 2 C.L. 703 (Outer House: December 12, 1968) (following *Pett* v. *Greyhound Racing Association* [1968] 2 W.L.R. 1471; [1968] 2 All E.R. 545 (C.A.)) and now reported, 1969 S.L.T. 150.

also bring and defend legal actions on behalf of the union, as well as call upon the treasurer and others to account and have the accounts audited. Moreover, they have all the general powers and duties of trustees by statute and at common law. Anyone who is a minor cannot act as a trustee of a union registered in Scotland.

A treasurer should also be appointed and the same person may act as secretary. He cannot, however, also be a trustee. It is his duty to account and deliver to the trustees any property belonging to the union. As he is the union's chief finance officer the rules should define his duties. He must also be not less than twenty-one years of age.[19] A secretary should also be appointed [20] and he may also be the treasurer.

The Trade Union Acts do not contain any special requirements regarding investments. Unless the rules make provision otherwise, trustee securities would be meant and implied.[21] The rules may give wider powers of investment than the statutes dealing with trust law. Accounts should be audited annually as the union is required to make an annual return (audited) to the Registrar. Books of account must be kept and be available for inspection at all reasonable times—as specified in the rules—not only to members but to all others having an interest in the funds. Inspection may be carried out by a member or other interested party himself or by his authorised agent.

Voting is also an important matter which should be provided for specially in the rules. Voting rights and procedures to be adopted at elections ought to be covered and these will be protected by the courts.[22] If the rules are silent in this matter then the voting rights are governed by the common law.[23] Where the rules provide for a ballot without qualification, it is essential that the identity of each voter must be kept secret. Postal ballots may also be required but these are costly and administratively onerous, with the result that it is only the larger unions which use them.

(4) *Political Activities* [24]

Professor Grunfeld has pointed out [25] that the modern law regulating the political activities of British trade unions is based upon three important principles or basic policies, *viz.*: (i) that trade unions should be free to express themselves through their own institutions and any political

---

[19] Trade Union Act (1871) Amendment Act 1876, s. 9.

[20] Trade Union Act 1871, s. 16.

[21] See Trusts (Scotland) Acts 1921 and 1961 and Trustee Investments Act 1961.

[22] See *Watson* v. *Smith* [1941] 2 All E.R. 725, where an injunction to restrain an irregular election was granted together with an award of damages against the secretary and members of the executive council of a trade union. See also *Byrne* v. *Foulkes and Others* [1961] C.L.Y. 8921 and *The Times*, June 29 and July 4, 1961; also *All Those in Favour* by C. H. Rolph (André Deutsch), an interesting account of the E.T.U. trial.

[23] Normally by a show of hands, except that a poll may be demanded—if this is not excluded by the rules.

[24] For details of the statutory requirements, see Citrine, *op. cit.*; and also Vester (H.) and Gardner (A. H.), *Trade Union Law and Practice* (Sweet & Maxwell, 1958).

[25] See *Modern Trade Union Law, op. cit.*, at p. 255.

institutions and to give financial support to these institutions; (ii) that a trade union member should not be coerced into supporting financially any political organisation if he does not wish to do so; and (iii) that the industrial power of the trade unions should not be used directly for purely political ends. These principles owe their existence to the constant pressures from within the trade union movement itself towards recognition of their bargaining status, as well as to other pressures from outside the movement which demanded a limitation upon the activities of the trade unions, in the political and industrial fields. The case of *Osborne* v. *Amalgamated Society of Railway Servants*,[26] which had decided that trade unions were not entitled to conduct political activities or to collect funds from their members for political purposes was, as we have mentioned earlier, a bitter disappointment to the unions.[27] That decision was reversed by the Trade Union Act 1913 which expanded the definition of a trade union, as explained above. Section 1 (1) states that " the fact that a combination has under its constitution objects or powers other than statutory objects . . . shall not prevent the combination from being a trade union " and authorises a union to apply its funds (subject to the Act's provisions regarding political activities) for any legal purpose authorised by the constitution. If a union decides to expend money on specified political activities it must do so exclusively out of a " political fund " [28] and it must have special rules protecting the non-contributing members. Moreover, if it is anxious to establish a political fund a ballot must be taken which requires that a majority of the members must be in favour of such.[28] The two important conditions precedent to the establishment of a political fund [29] are, as just mentioned, namely—(i) the specified political objects must be approved by a ballot vote held under rules approved by the Registrar and (ii) members who do not wish to contribute to the fund must be catered for by the rules and their interests within the union must be protected. The political activities which are affected by the Act are as follows:

(1) the payment of any expenses incurred directly or indirectly

[26] [1909] 1 Ch. 163 (C.A.); on appeal *sub nom. Amalgamated Society of Railway Servants* v. *Osborne* [1910] A.C. 87 (the first *Osborne* case) and 26 T.L.R. 177.

[27] Trade unions had established parliamentary candidates' funds since 1873 and the Royal Commission on Labour (1894) noted that unions had expended funds on parliamentary representation as one of their main purposes. In *Steele* v. *South Wales Miners' Federation* [1907] 1 K.B. at pp. 367–368 expenditure of funds on political objects was regarded as being within the law, but the *Osborne* case (which overruled *Steele*) was to draw a very clear boundary line which outlawed political objects. Thereafter the unions were limited to " friendly society activities " and statutory industrial objects. Their hopes of continuing to build up a strong parliamentary representation were halted temporarily and again they felt this decision to be another example of judicial prejudice against the trade union movement.

[28] 1913 Act, s. 3 (1).

[29] The Trade Union Act 1913 does not, of course, prevent the political fund itself being used for other purposes, political or non-political, than the special political objects listed in s. 3 (3) of the statute. Before such expenditure could be incurred validly, it would be necessary to verify the position from the political fund rules (which may place an absolute restriction upon the use of moneys for political objects only, but if no such limitation could be found therein then expenditure would seem to be justified upon any general or non-political object authorised by the union rulebook).

by a candidate or prospective candidate for election to Parliament or any public office [30] (before, during and after the election);

(2) the holding of any meeting or the distribution of any literature or documents in support of such candidate or prospective candidate;

(3) the maintenance of any person who is a member of Parliament or who holds a public office;

(4) in connection with the registration of electors or the selection of a candidate for Parliament or any public office; and

(5) the holding of political meetings of any kind or the distribution of political literature or documents of any kind (unless in furtherance of the statutory objects).[31]

The rules relating to the holding of the ballot must be approved [32] by the Registrar and it is essential that every member must have an equal right and a fair opportunity of voting. Any member who claims exemption from the political fund contribution must not be excluded from any benefits of the union nor should he be placed under any disability or disadvantage as compared with other members by reason of being so exempt.[33] If any member considers himself aggrieved by a breach of any of the political fund rules he has the special remedy of complaining to the Registrar who hears both the complaining member and the trade union. If the Registrar is satisfied that there is a statutory breach he will make an order remedying it—and this order may be recorded and enforced as if it were an order of the sheriff in Scotland or a county court in England. The order is conclusive and is not itself subject to appeal or recourse to the courts and no declarator can be sought from the courts that the order is erroneous. An appeal to the courts is only possible where the Registrar has exceeded his jurisdiction or where the rules themselves do not comply with the requirements of the 1913 Act or any of the other trade union statutes. The right of complaint to the Registrar conferred by the 1913 Act [34] is limited to the political fund rules and is not a general right of complaint upon any other matter. Examples of the particular right of complaint might be—(1) any attempted move to spend the union's general funds upon political activities, (2) any refusal to exempt from the political fund contribution a member who has given written intimation of his wish to " contract out " of the fund, and (3) any victimisation of a member who maintains his refusal to participate in contributing to the political fund.

It is interesting to note from an examination of the 1913 Act that no special penalties are provided for any failure to observe its provisions. It is likely that if a registered union failed to comply with any statutory

---

[30] " Public office " means the office of a member of any county, county borough (burgh. in Scotland), district or parish council or other public body raising money by means of a rate.

[31] Trade Union Act 1913, s. 3 (3).

[32] This is an administrative matter only.

[33] See *Birch* v. *N.U.R.* [1950] Ch. 602. (The N.U.R. was thought to have revised its rulebook immediately after that decision.)

[34] *Ibid.* s. 3 (2).

provision then the operative sanction would be a withdrawal or cancellation of its registration. Any political fund which was administered outwith the ambit of the 1913 Act would then be an illegal fund. The form of notice which should be given by a union member who does not wish to contribute to the political fund may be found in section 5 (1) [35] of the 1913 Act.

(5) *Disciplinary Powers of Trade Unions*

A trade union has no inherent right to fine, suspend or expel a member or to act in a quasi-judicial manner, because the common law provides for all legal *personae* (or *quasi-personae juridicae*) having a right of recourse to the courts.[36] It is possible for a trade union to acquire limited disciplinary powers by its constitution and rules, which are regarded as providing an administrative basis between a union and its members.[37] Where disciplinary powers are taken this will involve the creation of a domestic tribunal (very often a special committee designated the " discipline committee " or sometimes a general committee such as the executive committee).[38] A court of law always has jurisdiction over these domestic tribunals, based upon two apparently conflicting principles which have been developed over the years, *viz.*: (i) that the courts will not permit any persons to oust the jurisdiction of the courts by any agreement or contract and (ii) that freedom of contract should not be unduly limited.[39] Accordingly, the law tries to hold a balance between these two principles and any attempt by a domestic tribunal to oust the court's jurisdiction will result in the rules governing that domestic tribunal being treated as invalid.[40] It may be, however, that a union's rules merely create an arbitration procedure within the union framework which allows for inter-member disputes or any dispute between a member and the union to be referred to a domestic tribunal as a preliminary procedure before any subsequent proceedings are brought to the courts. An agreement of that type will be upheld—including the primary reference to a domestic tribunal,[41] before resort is made to the courts. Where an application or petition is made subsequently to the court, it is not the court's function to act as a court of appeal from the tribunal. On the other hand it is the court's

---

[35] Read along with the Schedule to the Act, which contains a Form of Exemption Notice.
[36] *Scott* v. *Avery* (1856) 5 H.L.C. 811.
[37] In *Nisbet* v. *Scottish National Operative Plasterers' Union,* 1951 S.L.T. 257; 1951 S.C. 350 it was held that the national organiser of a trade union—who averred that his appointment was made in terms of the union's rules and minutes—seeking a declarator of wrongous dismissal and damages for such, had failed to aver relevantly any probative contract in relation to his appointment and his action was dismissed (in such circumstances as these the rules do not form the basis of an enforceable contractual right against the union) (applying *Beattie* v. *E. & F. Beattie* [1938] Ch. 708).
[38] The nomenclature is immaterial. What is vital is the exercise of the disciplinary function.
[39] See Vester (H.) and Gardner (A. H.), *Trade Union Law and Practice* (Sweet & Maxwell, 1958), Chap. 21 (pp. 172–174).
[40] See *Lee* v. *Showmen's Guild* [1952] 2 Q.B. 329; [1952] 1 All E.R. 1175; [1952] 1 T.L.R. 1115.
[41] *Whyte* v. *Kuzych* [1951] A.C. 585; [1951] 2 T.L.R. 277; [1951] 2 All E.R. 435.

task to inquire into the following questions—(1) whether the union does possess valid disciplinary powers [42] and (2), if so, whether such powers have been validly exercised. The member who brings proceedings before the court generally bases his case upon a wrongful expulsion and a breach of contract. That is a right which he possesses by the common law and no agreement or contract which attempts to limit or exclude that right will be upheld by the courts. Nor can any disciplinary tribunal or other executive committee reserve the sole right to interpret the rules, because that is the function of a court of law.

The registered trade union's rules must provide for the fines and forfeitures which may be imposed upon any member,[43] including suspension of membership or expulsion therefrom. The unregistered trade union should also provide for disciplinary powers if it intends to exercise these, because otherwise it will have no powers to discipline its members. The disciplinary powers may be expressed in the rulebook or may arise by implication from the language of the rulebook. It is recommended, therefore, that the drafting ought to be reasonably precise.[44]

If the rules contain a power of amendment the union can acquire disciplinary powers to whatever extent is required by a valid amendment. If the rules do not contain power to alter or amend, it is only possible to acquire disciplinary powers by the unanimous consent of all members in support of a special resolution or motion which proposes such powers.

The relevant domestic tribunal or committee responsible for exercising disciplinary powers must always have regard to the following principles or tenets, namely—(1) it must act in accordance with the rules, (2) it must act in good faith for the benefit of the union and its members, (3) it must act according to the principles of " natural justice," [45] which apply to every inquiry held by a disciplinary body, and (4) the facts before the tribunal should be reasonably capable of supporting its decision.

A party who claims to be aggrieved by the tribunal's decision has the following remedies: (i) petition for a declarator in Scotland (or a declaration in England) which defines his rights. The Court of Session (in

---

[42] A general expulsion rule which is framed, for example, as follows: " The General Executive Committee shall have power to expel a member for conduct prejudicial to the interests of the union " is obviously very wide and basically ambiguous. The courts have tended to take a reasonable view and have refused to operate the general expulsion where a trade union—angered at the action of a member who has taken court proceedings to stop union expenditure of funds on unauthorised objects—has tried to take its revenge on the member by expelling him. The most famous example of this was, of course, *Osborne* v. *A.S.R.S.* [1911] 1 Ch. 540 (the second *Osborne* case). An example from Scotland is *McDowall* v. *McGhee*, 1913, 2 S.L.T. 238.

Professor Grunfeld points out (*Modern Trade Union Law*, pp. 182–185) some of the difficulties which can arise when expulsion is resorted to and illustrates his arguments by citation of *Kelly* v. *N.A.T.S.O.P.A.* (1915) 31 T.L.R. 632; *Wolstenholme* v. *Amalgamated Musicians' Union* [1920] 2 Ch. 388; and *Evans* v. *National Union of Printing, Bookbinding and Paper Workers* [1938] 4 All E.R. 51.

[43] Trade Union Act 1871, Sched. I.

[44] For example, a clause reading " power to deal with disputes between members " would not give, by implication, a right to expel any member of the union.

[45] See the case of *Annamunthodo* v. *Oilfields' Workers' Trade Union* [1961] A.C. 945; [1961] 3 W.L.R. 650; see also the other cases on " natural justice," which have been cited above at notes 17 and 18.

England, the High Court of Justice) has jurisdiction and power to grant such a declarator to any party having an interest in the subject-matter of the rules. It is thought that a sheriff court (or county court) might also grant such a remedy, but only as an ancillary to the main claim, which is usually one of damages; (ii) apply for an interdict to restrain the union and its officers and employees from acting in breach of pursuer's rights. This is a discretionary remedy which the Court of Session or the sheriff court (as the case may be) will grant when it is right and equitable so to do. Certain types of contract or agreement cannot, however, be enforced by the courts, no matter what form of proceeding is attempted [46]; (iii) bring an action for damages for wrongful expulsion, as such a step taken by the union is a breach of the contract contained in the rules. Damages, if awarded, would be payable out of the union's funds.[47] There seems to be no good reason why a damages action of this type (*i.e.*, based on a contractual breach) could not be brought against an unregistered trade union,[48] as well as against a registered trade union.

In all disciplinary procedures, the provisions of the rulebook must be strictly adhered to by the union and by the tribunal concerned with the operation of such procedures. No such tribunal can delegate its functions unless it is specifically authorised to do so by the rules or unless the power to delegate arises or appears to be competent by necessary implication from an examination of the language of the rulebook.[49] Moreover, the principles of "natural justice" will apply, and even if an exclusion clause were written into the rulebook, by which any member would be deprived ostensibly of the benefit of such principles, it is considered that the courts would disregard it and would give a decision against a union where it had obviously paid no attention to the " natural justice " principles.[50] It

[46] Trade Union Act 1871, s. 4. This section has been invoked and operated so as to prevent an executrix from recovering, by court action, funeral benefit nominated to her by the deceased member—see *M'Laren* v. *National Union of Dock Labourers*, 1918 S.C. 834; as well as to prevent personal representatives from suing for arrears of superannuation benefit which had accrued to the date of the member's death—see *Miller* v. *A.E.U.* [1938] Ch. 669; and *Love* v. *Amalgamated Soc. of Lithographic Printers*, 1912 S.C. 1078.

[47] See *Bonsor* v. *Musicians' Union* [1956] A.C. 104; [1955] 3 W.L.R. 788; [1955] 3 All E.R. 518 (reversing [1954] 1 Ch. 479), which overruled *Kelly* v. *N.A.T.S.O.P.A.* (1915) 84 L.J.K.B. 2236 (in the Court of Appeal).

[48] Mr. Citrine was of opinion in his *Trade Union Law* (2nd ed.) that *Bonsor's* case was no authority for the proposition that a member of an unregistered trade union could recover damages against the union. However, the learned editor of the third edition (Prof. Hickling) takes perhaps a more cautious view and points out the procedural obstacles which face the plaintiff in England who proposes to sue an unregistered union, whilst explaining the more advantageous position in which a Scottish pursuer would find himself (3rd ed. at pp. 298 and 299). The procedural position in Scotland is that all trade unions, whether registered or unregistered, can sue and be sued, in the appropriate circumstances, by using the descriptive name of the union itself.

[49] See *Bonsor* v. *Musicians' Union*, *cit. supra*, where it was held that, upon a true construction of the union's rules, the power to exclude a member who was in arrears with his subscriptions was given only to a branch committee and the purported exercise of the power by a branch secretary was *ultra vires* and ineffective.

[50] There are at least three important elements contained in these principles, *viz.*: (a) that the member knows the charge he has to answer, (b) that he is given a proper opportunity of answering it and a fair hearing and (c) that the decision arrived at by the tribunal is an honest one.

is the judge's task, as a matter of law, to decide whether a power of expulsion has been exercised in accordance with these principles.[51]   A domestic tribunal is not bound to follow a strictly judicial procedure—for example, it may accept evidence which might well be technically inadmissible in a court of law [52] and it is not bound by the evidential doctrine of " corroboration " in Scotland.[53]   Furthermore, it should never prejudge the issue [54] and it must arrive at an honest decision, in good faith and without bias; otherwise its decision will be invalid.[55]   In the absence of fraud or personal malice or bias, the court will not interfere with the tribunal's decision.[56]   The onus of proving *mala fides* rests upon the trade union member who alleges it.[57]

(6) *Amalgamation and Dissolution of Trade Unions*

Amalgamation.[58]   The question of amalgamation of trade unions first appeared in the Trade Union Act (1871) Amendment Act 1876,[59] s. 12. By that section any two or more trade unions might, upon the consent of not less than two-thirds of the members of each (or every) trade union concerned, amalgamate together as one trade union, without the need for any dissolution or division of funds of the unions involved; and no creditor of a union which was participating in the amalgamation was to be prejudiced by such amalgamation.   Section 12 was amended by the Trade Union (Amalgamation) Act 1917,[60] s. 1.   The first subsection of that section repealed the " two-thirds requirement " in the 1876 Act and substituted the following " if in the case of each or every such trade union, on a ballot being taken, the votes of at least fifty per cent. of the members entitled to vote thereat are recorded, and of the votes recorded those in favour of the proposal exceed by twenty per cent. or more the votes against the proposal."   The second subsection of section 1 declared that section 12 of the 1876 Act applied to the amalgamation of one or more registered trade unions with one or more unregistered trade unions.

The next statutory change came in 1940 with the Societies (Miscellaneous Provisions) Act 1940,[61] s. 6, which provided for the amalgamation and transfer of engagements of trade unions.   Such transfer could be effected by a special resolution of the union wishing to transfer its engagements and that resolution had to be placed before a general meeting of the union (or meetings of delegates) and be carried by not less than two-thirds of the members (or delegates) present and entitled to vote at that

[51] *Russell* v. *Duke of Norfolk* [1949] 1 All E.R. 109 at p. 117 *per* Tucker L.J.
[52] *Maclean* v. *The Workers' Union* [1929] 1 Ch. 602 at pp. 620–621 *per* Maugham J.
[53] For details of this doctrine, see Walker (A. G.) and Walker (N. M. L.), *The Law of Evidence in Scotland* (Hodge, 1964).
[54] *Whyte* v. *Kuzych* [1951] A.C. *per* Simon L.C. at pp. 595–596.
[55] *Dawkins* v. *Antrobus* (1881) 17 Ch.D. at p. 630.
[56] *Ross* v. *Electrical Trades Union* (1937) 81 S.J. 650.
[57] *Dawkins* v. *Antrobus* (1881) 17 Ch.D. 615.
[58] See Citrine, *op. cit.*, Chap. 7, p. 453 *et seq.*
[59] 39 & 40 Vict., c. 22.
[60] 7 & 8 Geo. 5, c. 24.
[61] 3 & 4 Geo. 6, c. 19.

meeting. No transfer under section 6 could become effective, unless or until—(a) the consent of not less than two-thirds of the members of the transferring union had been obtained (either in writing or at meetings called for the purpose) or that consent had been dispensed with by the Chief Registrar, after hearing the union and any other persons whom he considered entitled to be heard; and (b) notice of the transfer had been registered. The vesting provisions were set out in section 6 (3). It was provided there that property held for the benefit of any amalgamating or transferring union (or branch) should vest in the appropriate trustees without any conveyance or assignation upon registration of the notice of amalgamation or transfer or upon the appointment of the appropriate trustees, whichever was the later. Where it was intended that the trustees of the amalgamated union or of the union undertaking to fulfil the engagements were not to be or would not be the appropriate trustees in respect of any property to be vested under the section 6 provisions, then the instrument of amalgamation or transfer must have designated the persons who were or would be the appropriate trustees in relation to that property.

The most recent statutory enactment on amalgamations and transfer of engagements is the Trade Union (Amalgamations, etc.) Act 1964 [62] which repealed (i) sections 11, 12 and 13 of the 1876 Act, (ii) the whole of the 1917 Act above-mentioned, and (iii) section 6 of the Societies (Miscellaneous Provisions) Act 1940. The 1964 Act has to be read along with the Trade Union Acts 1871 to 1913, but it must be noted that the modern law on amalgamations and transfer of engagements is contained therein. The first five sections deal specifically with—(a) the conditions necessary for amalgamation and such transfer [63]; (b) the manner of voting upon, and the majority required for, the resolution approving an instrument of amalgamation or transfer [64]; (c) power to alter the rules of the transferee union for purposes of such transfer [65]; (d) complaints to the Registrar as regards the passing of the resolution relating to the instrument of amalgamation or transfer [66]; and (e) the disposal of property, upon amalgamation or transfer.[67] The important feature in subsections (1) and (2) of section 1 of the 1964 Act is the specification of the conditions which are necessary before amalgamation or transfer can be undertaken, and it is a specific requirement of section 1 (3) that all members must be notified of the details of the instrument of amalgamation or transfer or must be given sufficient information to enable them to reach a reasonable judgment of the position for themselves. If copies of the instrument are not circulated, members must be told where full copies may be consulted by those who receive the notice. It is no longer necessary for the rule-books to allow for and permit amalgamation or transfer, as section 2 (1)

[62] 1964, c. 24 (see, for repeals, Sched. 3 thereto).
[63] *Ibid.* s. 1.
[64] *Ibid.* s. 2.
[65] *Ibid.* s. 3.
[66] *Ibid.* s. 4.
[67] *Ibid.* s. 5.

makes it clear that amalgamation or transfer can be carried through at any time, provided the procedural steps, etc., contained in the 1964 Act are followed. Voting arrangements may be made under section 2 (2) or alternatively under certain provisions to be contained in the union rule-book. A simple majority of the votes cast is now sufficient to carry the resolution,[68] notwithstanding any other provisions in the union rulebook, but, by the proviso to section 2 (3), the voting provisions which are contained in that subsection itself do not apply to any trade union which has specifically and expressly provided in its own rules that subsection (3) is not to apply to that particular union.

Section 4 sets out four grounds of complaint to the Registrar as regards the passing of the resolution and any complaining member may base his case upon any one or more of such grounds. The section explains the " complaint " procedure, including the powers of the Registrar in relation to it.[69] Although the validity of the resolution approving the instrument of amalgamation or transfer cannot normally be questioned in any legal proceedings,[70] except proceedings before the Registrar under section 4 (or proceedings arising therefrom), nevertheless by subsection (8) the Registrar may, if he thinks fit, at the request of the complainer or of the trade union, state a case for the opinion of the Court of Session in Scotland (or the High Court in England) on any question of law arising in the proceedings. The decision of that court upon any case stated shall be final.

Section 6 extends the requirements relating to the change of name of a trade union and provides for the registration of such change with the Registrar where a registered trade union is concerned. Again, there must be no possible confusion of names (*i.e.*, the provisions of section 13 (3) of the Trade Union Act 1871 must be observed). Section 7 gives the Minister (now the Secretary of State for Employment and Productivity) power to make regulations (dealing, for example, with applications, registration of documents, inspection of documents and fees), including regulations dealing with a situation where a Northern Ireland trade union is involved in amalgamation or transfer or is not so involved. Section 8 gives the Registrar the power to delegate to an Assistant Registrar. Section 9 is the interpretation section. The Act received the Royal Assent on March 25, 1964, and came into operation on July 1, 1964.[71]

An amalgamated union cannot, however, attempt to cure an omission in its rulebook by endeavouring to carry a resolution which purports to correct the omission—see *Braithwaite* v. *Electrical, Electronic and Tele-communication Union—Plumbing Trades Union* [71a] where plaintiff, who

---

[68] *Ibid.* s. 2 (3).
[69] *Ibid.* subss. (3), (4) and (5) of s. 4 in particular, together with Schedule 1 to the Act (which is a fairly lengthy procedural Schedule).
[70] *Ibid.* section 4 (7).
[71] See the Trade Union (Amalgamations, etc.) Act 1964 (Commencement) Order 1964 (S.I. 1964 No. 878) (dated June 15, 1964).
[71a] (1969) 113 S.J. 305 (C.A.); [1969] 2 All E.R. 859 (C.A.).

had been expelled by the executive council of his trade union, subsequently intimated an appeal, per the rules procedure, but before the appeal was heard, plaintiff's trade union amalgamated with another. The rules of the amalgamated union made no provision for appeals pending and a resolution was passed which purported to correct the omission in the rulebook. It was held, however, that the resolution was void and that plaintiff was entitled to interlocutory injunctions restraining the amalgamated union from acting upon the expulsion decision.

Dissolution.[72] The Trade Union Act (1871) Amendment Act 1876 provided for dissolution in section 14 thereof, as follows:

" 14. The rules of every trade union shall provide for the manner of dissolving the same, and notice of every dissolution of a trade union under the hand of the secretary and seven members of the same shall be sent within fourteen days thereafter to the central office herein-before mentioned, or, in the case of trade unions registered and doing business exclusively in Scotland or Ireland, to the assistant registrar for Scotland or Ireland respectively, and shall be registered by them: Provided, that the rules of any trade union registered before the passing of this Act shall not be invalidated by the absence of a provision for dissolution."

This section appears to apply to registered trade unions only and not to unregistered trade unions.[73] Accordingly, there is no statutory provision requiring an unregistered trade union to have a dissolution rule. Such a body does not have an inherent power to dissolve itself, in the absence of an agreement by all of its members.[74] Accordingly, it is of great practical advantage to frame a rule which governs the procedure for and at dissolution. Failing such a rule, or failing the agreement of all members, it will be necessary to petition the court for authority to dissolve the association and distribute its funds.

(7) *Trades Union Congress and Inter-Union Rivalry*

Membership of the Trades Union Congress is entirely a voluntary matter and is open to both registered and unregistered trade unions. The T.U.C. regards itself as being above or outwith the realm of party politics,[75] and it has successfully followed this line by scrupulously underlining its firm adherence to the following tenets, *viz.*: (i) membership of a particular political party has never been made a condition for membership of a particular trade union, (ii) no trade union joining the T.U.C. is

---

[72] See Citrine, *op. cit.*, p. 364 *et seq.*
[73] Citrine, *op. cit.*, p. 364.
[74] *Free Church of Scotland* v. *Overtoun* [1904] A.C. 515; (1904) 7 F.(H.L.) 1.
[75] The Rt. Hon. George Woodcock, former General Secretary of the T.U.C. and a public figure of some considerable eminence, would always have regarded, as a matter of public interest generally, the important role which Congress had to play in giving advice to or criticising, when necessary, any proposed actings by H.M. Government upon any matter of policy, whether economic, social or otherwise. The Scottish T.U.C. is the national body in Scotland.

required to affiliate to the Labour Party and (iii) the constitution of the T.U.C. does not itself include party-political objects as defined in the Trade Union Act 1913, s. 3 (3), nor indeed are the funds of Congress utilised for any such object or purpose.[76]

Congress is, from the legal viewpoint, a large voluntary unincorporated association. It is not clear whether it forms a " trade union " within the meaning of the Trade Union Acts—and no help on this point is obtained from a study of its own constitution. Professor Grunfeld sees it [77] as not being a trade union in the legal sense, but he explains that the constitution of Congress is, in fact, a multilateral inter-union agreement comparable with other multilateral union agreements, such as the Bridlington Agreement.

The T.U.C. also keeps a watchful eye upon inter-union rivalry and the " poaching " of members. In an attempt to regulate conduct of this kind—which could destroy public faith in the trade union movement—the T.U.C. prepared a set of rules governing inter-union competition and the transfer of members from one affiliated union to another. These rules were first incorporated in the Hull Agreement of 1924 and subsequently replaced by the Bridlington Agreement of 1939, both agreements being directed towards the peaceful settlement of any inter-union disputes. Congress has a Disputes Committee which, in terms of the Bridlington Agreement, may deal with any matter brought before it in any of the following ways, viz.: (1) affirm the complaining union's right to organise workers within any particular plant or section or grade or class, (2) state that certain workers have been wrongly enrolled in the defending union and require that they be retransferred or that their membership be cancelled and (3) if appropriate, add a rider requiring further consultations. Any award issued by the Disputes Committee is not legally binding upon the parties concerned, although it is generally accepted that each party is under a moral obligation to accept it. In any case, the only sanction which seems possible would be disaffiliation or suspension from Congress.

One of the recent and distressing examples of inter-union rivalry has been the " recognition dispute " in the British Steel Industry.[78] Normally a recognition dispute involves a union, fighting for recognition, in a conflict with an employer. In the British Steel Corporation case, however, the conflict vis-à-vis recognition is an inter-union conflict between blue-collar unions and white-collar unions. Congress has issued a statement

---

[76] See Grunfeld, op. cit., pp. 215 and 216.

[77] Op. cit. at p. 220 (sections (1) to (3) of Chap. 11 are extremely helpful on the role of the T.U.C.). Much helpful assistance on these matters and recommendations for improvement may be found in the Donovan Commission's Research Paper No. 5 entitled " Trade Union Structure and Government " by John Hughes, particularly Part 1 (paras. 49–54 and 69–73) and Part 2 (paras. 201–204).

[78] A second example is that at Vickers-Armstrong (where demarcation was also a major issue) and the Report (March 1969) of the Court of Inquiry headed by Sir Jack Scamp has been outspokenly critical of both sides for their attitudes to industrial relations in the plant.

in support of the former but the crux of the matter is that it is powerless to take any real steps to bring about a settlement. It is a deliberative body without enforcement powers. Of course the notion or suggestion that Congress should be given clearly defined statutory powers in these matters would not be generally welcomed in the hierarchies of the trade union movement, although the rank-and-file might well take a majority view that it was essential to give the T.U.C. some powers of regulation and control, no matter in what legislative or other agreed form these were so granted.[79]

PART C—Conspiracy,[80] Intimidation and Trade Disputes

Understandably, a section dealing with trade disputes and intimidation etc., is of some importance in relation to the industrial relations scene. Two important facts must be borne in mind, viz.: (i) delictual (or tortious) acts may be committed by union officials and members outwith the ambit of a trade dispute and (ii) such acts are very often committed by union officials and members within the ambit of a trade dispute, that is to say, in contemplation or in furtherance of a trade dispute. Intimidation and conspiracy [81] are often met with in the area of labour disputes. The bargaining power of management is balanced by the right of employees to withdraw their labour. The strike weapon is probably the only real and effective weapon which employees possess and most active trade unionists would support that view. When labour is withdrawn or withheld or is about to be withdrawn the legal question of major importance is this—how far may X go in his interference with Y's business ? The answer seems to be that so long as X does not exceed the limitations which the law has established and is able to enforce and is not otherwise guilty of some unlawful conduct, then he has not committed any legal wrong against Y.[82] No action based upon a delict (or tort), which is alleged to have been committed by or on behalf of a trade union, can be brought either against the union itself or against its officers or members acting in their capacity as representatives of the union.[83] This protection has been

---

[79] For a valuable study of the problem of trade union recognition, see the Donovan Commission's Research Paper No. 6, " Trade Union Growth and Recognition " by George Sayers Bain (particularly Chap. V, paras. 154–242, on the " recognition " problem).

[80] See Grunfeld, op. cit., Chap. 21, pp. 405–441.

[81] Basically, these are delicts in Scotland (or torts in England)—see D. M. Walker, Delict, at pp. 926 et seq. and 932 et seq. respectively. An element of criminality may also arise in each case—much depends upon how the participants conduct themselves; Professor J. J. Gow tends to regard " conspiracy " as an " English delict " (see The Mercantile, etc., Law of Scotland (Greens, 1964), at pp. 763 and 764.

[82] Crofter Hand-Woven Harris Tweed Co. v. Veitch [1942] A.C. at p. 463 per Lord Wright. This case is also reported at 1942 S.C.(H.L.) 1; and 1943 S.L.T. 2.

[83] Trade Disputes Act 1906, s. 4; and this protection also extends to any proposed injunction or interdict proceedings—see Torquay Hotel Co. v. Cousins [1969] 2 W.L.R. 289 (C.A.); [1969] 1 All E.R. 522 (C.A.), particularly the opinion of Lord Denning M.R. (taking the same view as Atkin L.J. and Scrutton L.J. in Ware & De Freville Ltd. v. Motor Trade Association [1921] 3 K.B. 40; 37 T.L.R. 213). This case is not to go on appeal to H.L., as leave to appeal was refused.

much criticised for some years past and it will be necessary to return to the point when the Donovan Commission Report [84] and the recent White Paper [85] are being examined and compared. It does not, however, prevent the officers and members of a union from being proceeded against in a *personal* action even although they were acting ostensibly on behalf of the union.[86] The civil wrongs which cause most attention and difficulty in labour disputes are intimidation, inducement of breach of contract and conspiracy. The first two of these may be committed by one person or by a plurality of persons. Conspiracy may only be committed by a plurality of persons. Intimidation and conspiracy may, as has been mentioned earlier, also involve the operation of the criminal law.[87] Inducement of breach of contract, whilst not *per se* involving the criminal law, might give rise to criminal proceedings depending upon the methods used by X to effect his purpose (for example, some form of bribery, etc.). When the particular act which X has done is being considered it is also necessary to apply the test established by the Trade Disputes Act 1906,[88] and maintained by the Trade Disputes Act 1965,[89] namely—was the act done " in contemplation or furtherance of a trade dispute " or was it not so done ?

(1) *Intimidation* [90]

If X threatens Y with some harm in order to force Y to do something which X wishes done or to force Y to abstain from doing something in accordance with X's wishes, and as a result Y suffers some loss or damage, Y has a good cause of action against X based upon the civil wrong of intimidation. A similar action lies at Y's instance if, instead of threatening Y himself, X threatens a third party, Z, who happens to be a customer of Y or is otherwise involved in some business relationship with Y, so that any interference with that relationship will cause loss or damage to Y. Intimidation has been defined as " any menacing action or language the influence of which no man of ordinary firmness or strength of mind can reasonably be expected to resist, if used or employed with intent to destroy the freedom of will in another, and to compel him, through fear of such menaces, to do that which it is not his will to do." [91] In *Giblan's* case [92] an ex-official of a union owed the union money which he had

---

[84] Report of the Royal Commission on Trade Unions and Employers' Associations (Cmnd. 3623) (1968).
[85] " In Place of Strife " (A Policy for Industrial Relations) (Cmnd. 3888) (January 1969).
[86] See *Vacher & Son* v. *London Society of Compositors* [1913] A.C. 107; and *Bussy* v. *The Amalgamated Society of Railway Servants* (1908) 24 T.L.R. 437.
[87] See Gerald H. Gordon, *The Criminal Law of Scotland* (Greens, 1967), p. 184 *et seq.*
[88] 6 Edw. 7, c. 47.
[89] 1965, c. 48.
[90] See D. M. Walker, *op. cit.*, p. 932 *et seq.*
[91] See *Quinn* v. *Leathem* [1901] A.C. 495, where L., a master-butcher in Belfast, was held to have a good cause of action against Q. and others who compelled M., a customer of L., to cease trading with L. by threatening to call out M.'s employees on strike, in order to force L. to dismiss his non-union employees. It will be noted that this case antedated the Trade Disputes Act 1906.
[92] *Giblan* v. *National Amalgamated Labourers' Union* [1903] 2 K.B. 618; see also *Pratt* v. *B.M.A.* [1919] 1 K.B. 244.

misappropriated. In order to compel repayment the union procured his dismissal from several employments by threatening his employers with a strike. He was held to have a good cause of action against them.

When intimidation is being considered it is often said to be essential to distinguish the threat from the warning. So that this does not amount to a meaningless exercise in semantics, the criterion is relied upon that any notification to an employer which shows an intention to do a lawful act (whether on behalf of an individual or a group of persons) is not unlawful.[93] It has been argued that intimidation may be acceptable or justifiable in certain circumstances, for example, in the protection of legitimate trade interests.[94] This point is examined later in the context of legitimate trade interests.[95]

(2) Inducement of Breach of Contract

If X knowingly induces Y to break his contract with Z, and Z thereby suffers loss or damage, X is prima facie liable in damages to Z[96]—for example, where a miners' trade union ordered its members to stay out in breach of contract in order to keep up the price of coal, this was held to be actionable.[97] A questionnaire seeking information about a company which was confidential to the company was held to be an inducement of breach of contract.[98] Justification is thought to be a valid defence to an action based upon inducement of breach, e.g., where a parent persuades his daughter to break her engagement to a scoundrel. The only example in England of this plea being accepted as a defence was *Brimelow* v. *Casson*.[99] In any case based upon alleged inducement of breach the court will look at (i) the nature of the contract, (ii) the position of parties, (iii) the grounds for breach, (iv) the means employed to induce or procure the breach, (v) the relationship between the inducer and the contract-breaker and (vi), very importantly, the object or purpose of the person who

---

[93] *Wolstenholme* v. *Arriss* [1920] 2 Ch. 403; *Allen* v. *Flood* [1898] A C. 1; *White* v. *Riley* [1921] 1 Ch. 1; and *Davies* v. *Thomas* [1920] 2 Ch. 189; and *Morgan* v. *Fry* [1968] 3 W.L.R. 506 (C.A.) (in which the Court of Appeal applied *Allen* v. *Flood* and *White* v. *Riley* and distinguished *Rookes* v. *Barnard and Others*), in which it was held (i) that the strike notice was of proper length and not unlawful; (ii) as the notice was lawful there was no intimidation; and (iii) defendants' honest belief that they were acting in the true interests of union A negatived any allegation of conspiracy. *Morgan* v. *Fry* is also reported in V K.I.R. 275.

[94] See *Read* v. *Friendly Society of Operative Stonemasons* [1902] 2 K.B. at p. 737 and *Ware & De Freville Ltd.* v. *Motor Trade Association* [1921] 3 K.B. at p. 60.

[95] For two early Scottish cases on so-called " black-lists " see *Keith* v. *Lauder* (1905) 8 F. 356; 13 S.L.T. 650; 43 S.L.R. 230 and *MacKenzie* v. *Iron Trades Employers' Insurance Association Ltd.*, 1910 S.C. 79; 1909, 2 S.L.T. 366; 47 S.L.R. 103 (for a commentary on *MacKenzie*, see Citrine, *op. cit.*, pp. 61 and 62), and see, in particular, the opinion of the Lord President (Dunedin).

[96] But it must be established that defender did in fact cause and incite or induce employees of pursuer to break their contracts—see the early case of *Couper & Sons* v. *Macfarlane* (1879) 6 R. 683; 16 S.L.R. 379. See also Chap. 14, section (i), *supra*.

[97] *South Wales Miners' Federation* v. *Glamorgan Coal Co.* [1905] A.C. 239.

[98] *Bents Brewery Co. Ltd.* v. *Hogan* [1945] 2 All E.R. 570.

[99] [1924] 1 Ch. 302, where a theatrical manager paid his chorus girls such low wages that they were driven to immorality.

induced or procured the breach.[1] Any prior contractual rights inconsistent with the pursuer's contract may justify the procurement of a breach.[2] It is no justification at common law that a breach of contract was induced for the purpose of advancing the legitimate interests of the union or its members—*South Wales Miners' Federation* v. *Glamorgan Coal Co.*[3]

If there is no justification, a good cause of action will lie.[4] This is well illustrated by the case of *Smithies* v. *National Association of Operative Plasterers*,[5] where a trade union sanctioned a strike in ignorance of notice conditions in the contracts of employment and continued to make payment of strike pay after becoming aware of the contracts, with the result that the employers were held to have a good cause of action against the union. Moreover, it was no justification for the union inducing the breach to show that the employers had intended to evade a settlement of the dispute by arbitration. In all these matters of breach of contract the vital question is—what is meant by " unlawful interference " (and when does it exist) ? There seems to be an actionable interference by any third party who, knowing of the existence of a contract between Y and Z and with the intention of causing a breach (or preventing due performance), persuades, induces or procures employees of Y or Z, upon whose services either relies for due performance, to break the contracts of employment.[6] A breach of the contract between Y and Z must result because the breach itself is an integral part of the cause of action. A mere agreement (or conspiracy) to induce a breach is probably not good enough to found an action.[7] Procurement of breach occurs where the wrongdoer (*i.e.*, defender in the subsequent action), with knowledge of the contract, takes some positive step which is designed to facilitate the breach of contract.[8] It would appear that there is no real distinction between persuading a man to break his contract by placing physical restraint upon him to prevent his performing it or making performance impossible by hiding tools or machinery or depriving him of the services of his employees in breach of their employment contracts. Where an action is based upon inducement of breach the following facts must be shown—(i) knowledge of the existence of the contract and an intention to procure its breach, (ii) a definite and unequivocal persuasion or inducement of the employees to break their contracts of employment, (iii) breaches of the contracts of employment and

---

1 *South Wales Miners' Federation* v. *Glamorgan Coal Co.*, *cit. supra*. For the facts, see [1903] 2 K.B. at p. 545 *et seq.* (in the Court of Appeal).
2 *Smithies* v. *National Association of Operative Plasterers* [1909] 1 K.B. 310.
3 *Cit. supra.*
4 *Read* v. *Friendly Society of Operative Stonemasons* [1902] 2 K.B. 732, where a builder indentured an apprentice aged 25 in breach of a union rule agreed by the employers in the trade. The builder broke the indenture after pressures by the union. The plaintiff was held entitled to succeed against the union—and it was immaterial that the union had acted in good faith and in the best interests of the union. (Note that since the Trade Disputes Act 1906, s. 4, a delictual action can no longer be brought against the union itself—only against the officers and members in their personal capacities.)
5 *Cit. supra.*
6 By departing without notice or by refusing to perform their contracts.
7 *De Jetley* v. *Greenwood* [1936] 1 All E.R. 863.
8 *British Motor Trade Association* v. *Salvadori* [1949] Ch. 556.

(iv) breach of the main contract following the breaches of the service contracts. Exhortations to " stop supplying Y " or " treat Z as black " during a trade dispute are not, by themselves, unlawful acts.[9]

(3) *Conspiracy*

The definition of conspiracy is " an agreement of two or more persons to do an unlawful act or to do a lawful act by unlawful means." [10] The criminal act of conspiracy is constituted by a mere agreement but the civil wrong of conspiracy is incomplete unless the conspirators follow up their agreement with definite acts causing loss or damage to pursuers.[11] Pursuers must establish that the agreement between defenders is designed to effect an unlawful purpose and results in loss and damage to them. In the leading case of *Sorrell* v. *Smith* [12] the principle seems to be established that if the unlawful combination is intended to injure a man in his trade, that is an unlawful purpose, but if the real purpose is to defend or protect trade interests, this is not an unlawful purpose although damage is caused to another person (*i.e.,* pursuer). Motive is not necessarily relevant or conclusive in the case of an individual who is acting against pursuer—the test must always be whether the particular act is an unlawful act or is a lawful act carried out by unlawful means. In the case of a combination of persons motive is always material and relevant,[13] because it very often enables the intention to be identified and indeed the main purpose of the combined exercise. The court has the task of carefully examining the facts in each case in order to decide between lawful acts on the one hand and conspiratorial acts on the other. The latter pattern is illustrated by the well-known cases of *Temperton* v. *Russell* [14] (an example of the secondary boycott), *Quinn* v. *Leathem* [15] and *Conway* v. *Wade.*[16] The former pattern (*i.e.,* lawful acts) is illustrated by—*Mogul SS. Co.* v. *MacGregor Gow & Co.,*[17] *Allen* v. *Flood,*[18] *Sorrell* v. *Smith* [19] and *Scala Ballroom* (*Wolverhampton*) v. *Ratcliffe.*[20]

The policy of operating a " closed shop " has been challenged in

---

[9] *D. C. Thomson & Co. Ltd.* v. *Deakin* [1952] Ch. 646 *per* Jenkins L.J.
[10] *Mulcahy* v. *R.* (1868) L.R. 3 H.L. 306.
[11] *Crofter Hand-Woven Harris Tweed Co.* v. *Veitch* [1942] A.C. 435 *per* Lord Wright; see also the speech of Viscount Simon L.C.
[12] [1925] A.C. 700—in which reference was made to the well-known " trilogy " of cases— *Mogul SS. Co.* v. *MacGregor Gow & Co.* [1892] A.C. 25; *Allen* v. *Flood* [1898] A.C. 1; and *Quinn* v. *Leathem* [1901] A.C. 495; and see comments on " conspiracy " and defendants' honest belief in their interests negativing conspiracy in *Morgan* v. *Fry* [1968] 3 W.L.R. 506 (C.A.); V K.I.R. 275.
[13] Where there is a combination of persons acting against pursuer it is unnecessary to aver malice, and so long as the pursuer's averments disclose an actionable wrong, that is sufficient for him to succeed—*Hewitt* v. *Edinburgh and District Operative Lath-splitters', etc., Association* (1906) 14 S.L.T. 489 (O.H.).
[14] [1893] 1 Q.B. 715.
[15] [1901] A.C. 495.
[16] [1909] A.C. 506.
[17] [1892] A.C. 25.
[18] [1898] A.C. 1; see also *Lyons* v. *Wilkins* [1896] 1 Ch. 811; [1899] 1 Ch. 255.
[19] [1925] A.C. 700.
[20] [1958] 1 W.L.R. 1057.

several cases, but it is accepted [21] throughout the field of industrial relations that it is a perfectly legitimate operation for a trade union and employers in the particular industry to conduct. In *Reynolds* v. *Shipping Federation* [22] an action by a trade union member against an association of ship-owners who adopted a closed shop policy in favour of another trade union failed upon the basis of an alleged conspiracy. It is also clear from the speeches in the House of Lords in the leading case of *Crofter Hand-Woven Harris Tweed Co.* v. *Veitch* [23] that the adoption of a closed shop policy may be perfectly legitimate. In this particular instance the purpose of the combination was the legitimate promotion of the interests of the persons who were combining.

(4) Civil Wrongs Committed during a " Trade Dispute "

The statutory definition of a " trade dispute " and the protections created by statute law are to be found mainly in the Trade Disputes Act 1906 [24] and the Trade Disputes Act 1965.[25] Section 5 (3) of the 1906 Act states that—" the expression ' trade dispute ' means any dispute between employers and workmen, or between workmen and workmen, which is connected with the employment or non-employment or the terms of the employment, or with the conditions of labour, of any person "; and the expression " workmen " means " all persons employed in trade or industry, whether or not in the employment of the employer with whom a trade dispute arises." The meaning of " trade " in modern legislation dealing with conditions of employment and collective bargaining was considered by the House of Lords in *N.A.L.G.O.* v. *Bolton Corporation.*[26] The reference to " trade dispute " requires some factual assessment of what amounts to a dispute situation.[27] It seems that the necessary element or ingredient has to be something definite and of substance beyond the stage of a mere personal quarrel or some form of ordinary agitation.[28] A dispute between employers is not a trade dispute even although employees or their trade union take sides therein.[29] A dispute between trade unions is a " trade dispute " notwithstanding the fact that employees are not themselves identified with it.[30] If workmen themselves are in disagreement over membership of a particular trade union, that is also a " trade dispute." [31]

---

21 The Donovan Report accepts the continued existence of the " closed shop."
22 [1924] 1 Ch. 28 at p. 39 in particular.
23 [1942] A.C. 435; 1942 S.C.(H.L.) 1; and 1943 S.L.T. 2.
24 6 Edw. 7, c. 47, s. 5 (3).
25 1965, c. 48, s. 1 (1) to be read along with the 1906 Act and the definition section in the latter statute.
26 [1943] A.C. 166.
27 A recent case illustrating facts which did not amount to a genuine " trade dispute " situation is *Torquay Hotel Co.* v. *Cousins, cit. supra.*
28 See *Conway* v. *Wade* [1909] A.C. 506; see also *Huntley* v. *Thornton* [1957] 1 W.L.R. 321.
29 *Larkin* v. *Long* [1915] A.C. 814; see also *Esplanade Pharmacy* v. *Larkin* [1957] I.R. 285.
30 *Dallimore* v. *Williams* (1912) 29 T.L.R. 67; and 30 T.L.R. 432.
31 *White* v. *Riley* [1921] 1 Ch. 1; *Gaskell* v. *Lancashire and Cheshire Miners' Federation* (1912) 28 T.L.R. 518.

Inducing a breach of contract during a trade dispute. An action in damages can always be brought against any person who induces a breach of contract, quite apart from the trade dispute situation. It was believed by the unions (and many of their advisers) for many years that no proceedings could be taken where the act complained of was done " in contemplation or furtherance of a trade dispute." The Trade Disputes Act 1906, s. 3, had provided that " an act done by a person in contemplation or furtherance of a trade dispute shall not be actionable on the ground only that it induces some other person to break a contract of employment or that it is an interference with the trade, business or employment of some other person, or with the right of some other person to dispose of his capital or his labour as he wills." Certainly the 1906 Act gave officers and members of a union a reasonably wide scope of action, but it did not give them a *carte blanche* to do exactly as they pleased, and injunctions have been granted in England, and interdicts in Scotland, against trade union officials restraining them from acts which are not in furtherance of a trade dispute within the meaning of the 1906 Act.[32] Their actions might give rise to proceedings upon some other ground, *e.g.*, defamation, breach of statutory duty or coercion,[33] although the magical formula of " trade dispute " seemed to cover a multitude of sins. However, the now famous case of *Rookes* v. *Barnard and Others* [34] was to shatter many illusions and we must return to it again, in some detail, in the course of this chapter.

It must be observed immediately that it is the inducing of a breach of a contract of employment only which falls within section 3. No other form of contract acquires the statutory protection.[35] The statutory

---

[32] But such injunction or interdict cannot be granted against the trade union itself (in view of the s. 4 (1) protection)—see *Torquay Hotel Co.* v. *Cousins* [1969] 2 W.L.R. 289 (C.A.); and [1969] 1 All E.R. 522 (C.A.).

[33] *Dallimore* v. *Williams, cit. supra*; *Milligan* v. *Ayr Harbour Trustees*, 1915 S.C. at p. 953; and *Valentine* v. *Hyde* [1919] 2 Ch. 129.

[34] [1964] A.C. 1129; [1964] 1 All E.R. 367; [1964] 2 W.L.R. 269; [1964] 1 Lloyd's Rep. 28 (H.L.). The speech of Lord Reid is of outstanding importance. Lord Devlin's speech is also important and is indeed noteworthy for his excursus on the law of damages. In the course of his speech Lord Reid said: " Section 3 deals with two classes of acts done by individuals, and, by virtue of section 1, the immunity given by section 3 to individuals must also extend to combinations or conspiracies. The classes of acts permitted (if done in contemplation or furtherance of a trade dispute) are (1) inducing a breach of a contract of employment and (2) interfering with a person's trade, business or employment or right to dispose of his capital or labour as he wills. The facts in this case fall within the second class." And somewhat later on, " In my judgment, it is clear that section 3 does not protect inducement of breach of contract where that is brought about by intimidation or other illegal means and the section must be given a similar construction with regard to interference with trade, business or employment. So, in my opinion, the section does not apply to this case because the interference here was brought about by unlawful intimidation. I would therefore allow this appeal." It was, of course, Lord Devlin who first used the references to " the first limb " and " the second limb " of s. 3 (which Lord Reid had identified as above) and this terminology has been adopted in later cases and academic writings.

[35] *Brimelow* v. *Casson* [1924] 1 Ch. 302; *J. T. Stratford & Son* v. *Lindley* [1965] A.C. 269; [1964] 3 W.L.R. 541; [1964] 3 All E.R. 102; [1964] 2 Lloyd's Rep. 133, and *Square Grip Reinforcement Co.* v. *MacDonald* (O.H.) 1968 S.L.T. 65. The recent White Paper " In Place of Strife " proposes to extend the inducement of breach to commercial contracts as well as to contracts of employment.

immunity does not apply to the actual breach of the contract itself—and any person who commits that breach is prima facie liable in damages for breach of contract. But that is quite a separate matter from the delict (or tort) of inducement of breach of contract giving rise to civil damages in a reparation action. It is interesting to note that section 3 did not protect an employee who broke his own contract of employment in the course of inducing a breach of employment contracts. The Trade Disputes Act 1965 [36] has changed the law in this respect—and reference will be made later herein to this statute.

The act done " in contemplation " means something which is done in the expectation of or with a view to a dispute which is imminent. An act done " in furtherance " is one which is done in support of either side during the existence of a trade dispute.[37] Motive is always a material factor. The parties who are acting together may be doing so under the cloak or shield of a trade dispute—whereas in reality they are pursuing a grudge or some spiteful act against another's business interests, an action which will not receive any statutory or common law protection.[38] The important element in relation to the act done " in contemplation " is the imminence of the dispute—e.g., the imminence of a strike,[39] and the scope of " trade dispute " is wide.[40]

Strikes [41] *and lock-outs.* These are convenient terms in the field of industrial relations. They are not strictly legal terminology. A strike is defined as the " cessation of work by a body of persons employed acting in combination, or a concerted refusal or a refusal under a common understanding of any number of persons employed to continue to work for an employer in consequence of a dispute, done as a means of compelling their employer or any person or body of persons employed, to accept or not to accept terms or conditions of or affecting employment."

A lock-out is defined as the " closing of a place of employment or the suspension of work, or the refusal of an employer to continue to employ any number of persons employed by him, in consequence of a dispute, done with a view to compelling those persons or to aid another employer in compelling persons employed by him to accept terms or conditions of or affecting employment."

At common law, the strike is not *per se* unlawful. It is always legitimate so long as there is no unlawful purpose or no accomplishment of a lawful purpose by any unlawful means.[42] The legality of a strike depends

---

[36] 1965, c. 48, s. 1 (1) (see para. (*a*) therein).
[37] *Conway* v. *Wade* [1909] A.C. 506 (see the speeches therein).
[38] See *Huntley* v. *Thornton* [1957] 1 W.L.R. 321 at p. 350.
[39] *Milligan* v. *Ayr Harbour Trustees, cit. supra.*
[40] See *Fowler* v. *Kibble* [1922] 1 Ch. 140 (acts done to preserve industrial peace by keeping out non-union labour); and *Dallimore* v. *Williams, cit. supra* (acts done to prevent union members carrying out contracts below union rates).
[41] Professor Grunfeld gives many useful examples of direct action in *Modern Trade Union Law* at Chap. 22 (pp. 455–459).
[42] *Gozney* v. *Bristol Trade and Provident Society* [1909] 1 K.B. at p. 922.

always upon the means employed by the strikers and upon the objects of the strike.[43] Any cessation of work in breach of a contract of employment or in breach of an agreement upon disputes procedures (*e.g.*, striking without giving fair or agreed warning notice to employers) is unlawful, unless of course where the time limit of an agreement has expired.[44] A good example of the unlawful strike is the " lightning " strike (sometimes called, in more picturesque language, the "wildcat" strike) because illegal means are used—*viz.*, the breaking of agreements with the employers concerned without notice or warning to them. Such an acting together, employing illegal means or having in view unlawful objects, would make the strike an unlawful conspiracy at common law. In order to give some bargaining protection to unions and their officials, statute law creates the following immunities: (i) no proceedings in delict (or tort) can be taken against a trade union itself [45]; (ii) the participants in a strike or lock-out, acting in combination and in contemplation or furtherance of a trade dispute, are protected from criminal proceedings in respect of any act done pursuant to the combination which would not be punishable if done by a person acting alone [46]; (iii) the participants in a strike or lock-out, acting in combination and in contemplation or furtherance of a trade dispute are protected from civil proceedings in respect of any act done pursuant to the combination which would not be actionable if done by a person acting alone [47]; and (iv) any person acting in contemplation or furtherance of a trade dispute who procures a breach of a contract or contracts of employment, provided always that his actions are not otherwise unlawful at common law and not contrary to the Trade Disputes Act, s. 3, as amended by the Trade Disputes Act 1965,[48] s. 1 (1). The latter subsection reads as follows:

" 1.—(1) An act done after the passing of this Act by a person in contemplation or furtherance of a trade dispute (within the meaning

---

[43] See *Farrer* v. *Close* (1869) L.R. 4 Q.B. at p. 612.

[44] *Russell* v. *Amalgamated Society of Carpenters and Joiners* [1912] A.C. at p. 435; and see also the recent Scottish case of *Cummings* v. *Charles Connell & Co. (Shipbuilders) Ltd.*, 1969 S.L.T. 25, in which a contract of employment undertook to guarantee employment for a period of 18 months and expressly provided that the withholding of employment or withdrawal of labour due to a strike or lock-out was excluded. The defenders terminated pursuer's contract during a trade dispute and he based his case upon a breach of contract. Defenders tried to rely upon an implied term that a strike or lock-out would not constitute a breach but their plea was rejected. Defenders' action was a breach of contract in the circumstances of the express clause in the contract. (The dictum of Lord McLaren in *William Morton and Co.* v. *Muir Brothers and Co.*, 1907 S.C. 1211 at p. 1224 was applied.)

[45] Trade Disputes Act 1906, s. 4.

[46] Conspiracy and Protection of Property Act 1875, s. 3.

[47] Trade Disputes Act 1906, s. 1 (which adds a new paragraph to the 1875 Act, s. 3). (Note 46.)

[48] 1965, c. 48. This statute was passed by Parliament after pressure from the trade unions as a result of the House of Lords decision in *Rookes* v. *Barnard and Others* [1964] A.C. 1129; [1964] 2 W.L.R. 269; [1964] 1 All E.R. 367 (H.L.); [1964] 1 Lloyd's Rep. 28 (H.L.). This case caused considerable anxiety to trade unionists because they believed (i) that it severely limited their right to strike and (ii) that it rendered union officials liable to heavy damages in a personal capacity even during the existence of a trade dispute. For Prof. Wedderburn's views, see *The Worker and the Law* (Penguin Books) and his articles in the *Modern Law Review*.

of the Trade Disputes Act 1906) shall not be actionable in tort on the ground only that it consists in his threatening—

    (a)   that a contract of employment (whether one to which he is a party or not) will be broken, or

    (b)   that he will induce another to break a contract of employment to which that other is a party;

or be capable of giving rise to an action of reparation on the ground only that it so consists."

The case of *Rookes* v. *Barnard and Others* [49] (decided the year before the Trade Disputes Act 1965) showed that the delict or tort of intimidation was an established delict or tort [50] and that it comprehended not only threats of criminal or delictual (or tortious) acts but also threats of breaches of contracts. It was obvious from that case that the Trade Disputes Act 1906, s. 3,[51] did not protect any person who induces a breach of contract by intimidation or by some other tortious or delictual means; and a similar construction must be placed upon any case where there is interference with trade, business or employment. The House of Lords was quite satisfied about the following points: (1) the defendants had used intimidation; (2) the Trade Disputes Act 1906, s. 1, afforded no defence to them—because even if the tort (or delict) had been committed by an individual it would still have been actionable; (3) the Trade Disputes Act, s. 3, afforded no protection either, as unlawful intimidation had been used (Lord Evershed *dubitante*); and (4) there was no case for exemplary damages. [52]

It is an unlawful act for any person or combination to maintain strikers who are taking part in an unlawful strike, provided that there is knowledge on the part of the person or combination that the particular strike is unlawful.

There has been much debate and argument about the validity of a so-called " general strike " [53] and the nice legal point is whether a strike which is intended to coerce the Government is illegal. The Trade Disputes and Trade Unions Act 1927 had made such a strike illegal, but that Act was repealed by the Trade Disputes and Trade Unions Act 1946.[54] It

---

[49] [1964] A.C. 1129; [1964] 2 W.L.R. 269; [1964] 1 All E.R. 367 (H.L.); [1964] 1 Lloyd's Rep. 28 (H.L.).

[50] Certainly it is a nominate tort in English law. Whether or not it is a specific delict in Scotland may be a fine academic point—but the criterion in all cases of this type is the behaviour of the defenders and if defenders' conduct amounts to intimidation in a form not now protected by the Trade Disputes Act 1965 there seems to be no reason why the Scottish courts would not grant the remedy of civil damages in a delictual action.

[51] The case was concerned with the " second limb " of s. 3, as explained by Lords Reid and Devlin.

[52] This last point *re* exemplary damages is very important in English law (see Lord Devlin's speech).

[53] The only example is the General Strike of 1926. It is interesting to note that Mr. Justice Astbury held the General Strike of 1926 to be illegal in *National Sailors' and Firemen's Union* v. *Reed* [1926] Ch. 536, but he adduced no identifiable authority for that view.

[54] 9 & 10 Geo. 6, c. 52.

would seem not unreasonable to apply the test of coercion of the Government—and if the general strike in question was intended to do that, then it will be illegal.

In order to protect the community during emergencies created by strikes and other industrial unrest the Emergency Powers Act 1920 was passed. If it appears to the Crown that any action has been taken or is threatened by any person or body of persons . . . to be calculated, by interfering with the supply and distribution of food, water, fuel or light . . . to deprive the community, or any substantial part of the community, of the essentials of life, a state of emergency may be proclaimed.[55] That proclamation cannot remain in force for more than a month. Regulations may confer upon a Secretary of State, government department or other person acting on behalf of the Crown such powers and duties as may be necessary for (i) the preservation of the peace, (ii) securing and regulating the supply and distribution of food, water, fuel and light and other necessities, (iii) maintaining the means of transport and locomotion and (iv) for any other purpose essential to the public safety and life of the community. These regulations must be laid before Parliament and usually it requires a resolution of both Houses for them to be continued in force. Offences against such regulations are often dealt with by summary jurisdiction—i.e., in Scotland, before the sheriff's summary court.

Any person participating in a strike may be disqualified from receiving unemployment benefit or other benefits and assistance grants.[56]

In addition to what has been said about essential services in relation to the Emergency Powers Act 1920, it must also be noted that in the gas, water and electricity supply industries certain actions involving stoppage of work are subject to the criminal law and the strikers may be prosecuted.[57] Prosecutions may also be brought under the Conspiracy and Protection of Property Act 1875, s. 5, where any person wilfully and maliciously breaks a contract of service or of hiring, knowing or having reasonable cause to believe that the probable consequences of his so doing—either alone or in combination with others—will be to endanger human life or cause serious bodily injury or expose valuable property (heritable or moveable) to destruction or serious damage. The maximum penalty is £20 or a term of imprisonment not exceeding three months.

Statutory Intimidation.[58] This matter is governed by section 7 of the Conspiracy and Protection of Property Act 1875 as follows:

" 7. Every person who, with a view to compel any other person to abstain from doing or to do any act which such other person has a

---

[55] *Ibid.* s. 1 (1).
[56] See the National Insurance Act 1965, s. 22. The White Paper " In Place of Strife " indicates that consultations are to take place as to whether this disqualification is to be removed (presumably in the new Industrial Relations Bill or an amending statute).
[57] See the Conspiracy and Protection of Property Act 1875, s. 4, and the Electricity Supply Act 1919.
[58] See the Conspiracy and Protection of Property Act 1875 (38 & 39 Vict., c. 86), s. 7, as amended by the Trade Disputes Act 1906, s. 2 (2).

legal right to do or abstain from doing, wrongfully and without legal authority,—

1. Uses violence to or intimidates such other person or his wife or children, or injures his property; or,

2. Persistently follows such other person about from place to place; or,

3. Hides any tools, clothes, or other property owned or used by such other person, or deprives him of or hinders him in the use thereof; or,

4. Watches or besets the house or other place where such other person resides, or works, or carries on business, or happens to be, or the approach to such house or place; or

5. Follows such other person with two or more other persons in a disorderly manner in or through any street or road,

shall, on conviction thereof by a court of summary jurisdiction, or on indictment as herein-after mentioned, be liable either to pay a penalty not exceeding twenty pounds, or to be imprisoned for a term not exceeding three months, with or without hard labour." [59]

The original final paragraph of section 7 was repealed by section 2 (2) of the Trade Disputes Act 1906. It must be noted immediately that section 2 (1) of the 1906 Act contains the relevant statutory provision on " peaceful picketing " as follows:

" 2.—(1) It shall be lawful for one or more persons, acting on their own behalf or on behalf of a trade union or of an individual employer or firm in contemplation or furtherance of a trade dispute, to attend at or near a house or place where a person resides or works or carries on business or happens to be, if they so attend merely for the purpose of peacefully obtaining or communicating information, or of peacefully persuading any person to work or abstain from working."

The conduct of the persons involved and the whole circumstances must be considered carefully—for example in *Bernard Sunley & Sons* v. *Henry* [60] it was held, in England, that six of the defendants had gone beyond lawful picketing and they would be enjoined by the court from such further behaviour.

A member of a group using violence or committing an act of injury may be convicted with other members of the group even although he took no active part in the particular violent conduct or the infliction of injury. [61] The " following " is an offence even if it is done in an orderly fashion and

---

[59] Hard labour is no longer competent as a mode of punishment.
[60] (1967) 117 New L.J. 184; [1967] C.L.Y. 3982.
[61] See *Young* v. *Peek* (1912) 29 T.L.R. 31.

without the accompaniment of violence.[62] Furthermore, a member of a group which is following in a disorderly manner may be guilty of an offence even although he himself does nothing disorderly, unless he can show that he was there purely by accident or for a lawful purpose (for example, attempting to induce the marchers to desist).[63] " Peaceful picketing " is always permissible.[64]

Statutory breaches of employment contracts.[65] Reference has been made in the previous section of this chapter to the operation of sections 4 and 5 of the Conspiracy and Protection of Property Act 1875, because the factual situations mentioned in these two sections generally arise out of a situation which itself involves intimidation in some form or another, including the statutory form established by section 7 of the 1875 Act. However, it is more correct to identify the situations arising from sections 4 and 5 as " statutory breaches of contract " and any breach of these two sections could result in the imposition of a monetary penalty not exceeding twenty pounds or a term of imprisonment not exceeding three months upon any employee who is convicted of a breach of contract under either section. Section 4 is concerned with employees in the gas or water industry (extended subsequently to the electricity industry by the Electricity Supply Act 1919) employed by a municipal authority or other company employer or contractor who is under a statutory duty, or who has assumed the duty, of supplying gas or water or electricity to any city, borough, town or place or part thereof, who break their service contracts. The employer must post at the gasworks, etc., a printed copy of section 4 and is subject to penalties if he should fail to do so.

Section 5 involves breaches of service contracts which are likely to result in danger to human life, serious bodily injury or serious damage to valuable property. Examples of such might be employees in the hospital service, ambulance service and fire services.

It should perhaps also be pointed out that where a master, being legally liable to provide for his servant or apprentice necessary food, clothing, medical aid, or lodging, wilfully and without lawful excuse refuses or neglects to do so whereby the health of the servant or apprentice is or is likely to be seriously or permanently injured, he (the master) is liable on summary conviction to a penalty not exceeding twenty pounds or fo a term of imprisonment not exceeding six months.[66]

---

[62] *Wilson* v. *Renton*, 1910 S.C.(J.) 32; 1910, 1 S.L.T. 30; 6 Adam 166; and (1909) 47 S.L.R. 209. This is an interesting case because objections were taken to the relevancy of the complaint on three grounds, *viz.*: (i) it did not specify the particular subsection(s) of s. 7 alleged to have been contravened; (ii) that in view of s. 2 (1) of the 1906 Act an express charge of intimidation should have been included; and (iii) that whereas the charges were alternative the prayer was general. All of these objections were *repelled* and furthermore, in a stated case on appeal to the Second Division of the Court of Session, it was held that the facts proved justified the conviction.
[63] *McKinlay* v. *Hart* (1897) 25 R.(J.) 7.
[64] Trade Disputes Act 1906, s. 2.
[65] See the Conspiracy and Protection of Property Act 1875, ss. 4 and 5.
[66] *Ibid.* s. 6.

PART D—Trade Union Involvement in Collective Bargaining and Agreements

Mention was made in an earlier chapter [67] of the importance of voluntary collective bargaining in British industrial relations. It is in this area of bargaining where the real power of the trade unions lies and it has been made clear for many years by leading figures in the trade union movement that unions must retain this freedom to bargain, free from the shackles of legal or judicial process. That freedom was built into the Trade Union Act 1871 [68] and has been zealously guarded ever since.

The outcome of each bargaining process, in whatever industry negotiations are taking place and by whatever machinery these negotiations are being conducted,[69] is normally the conclusion of a " collective agreement." Basically, this is a bilateral agreement concluded between management on the one side and a union or a group of unions on the other, but it is " collective " in the sense that it affects the working terms and conditions of thousands of blue-collar (and also white-collar) employees who are members of the negotiating union. Two very obvious questions arise immediately for consideration in this situation of collective bargaining, viz.: (a) what legal rights (if any) accrue to each of the main parties to the collective agreement ? and (b) what legal rights (if any) does an individual employee/member of a trade union acquire from the negotiated collective agreement which has been concluded by his own union, ostensibly on behalf of the union members ? The answers to these questions are not precise and well defined. In the case of question (a) above, the general rule as to the enforceability or, more correctly, the non-enforceability of a collective agreement can be ascertained from section 4 (4) of the Trade Union Act 1871, which says " Nothing in this Act shall enable any court to entertain any legal proceeding instituted with the object of directly enforcing or recovering damages for the breach of any of the following agreements namely,

1. . . . .

4. Any agreement made between one trade union and another; or . . . . But nothing in this section shall be deemed to constitute any of the above-mentioned agreements unlawful."

The collective agreement between the employers' association or confederation and the employees' trade union is, accordingly, a lawful agreement but it is one which cannot be enforced in the courts of law.[70]

---

[67] Chap. 8, *supra*; and further commentary herein.

[68] See s. 4 thereof.

[69] For valuable studies in voluntary bargaining, see the *Industrial Relations Handbook* (H.M.S.O.) (1961), Chaps. II, III, IV and V; also *An Introduction to the Study of Industrial Relations* by J. Henry Richardson (1954), Chap. 15; and *The System of Industrial Relations in Great Britain* (eds. Allan Flanders and H. A. Clegg), Chap. V.

[70] See now the judgment of Mr. Justice Geoffrey Lane in the Queen's Bench Division in *Ford Motor Co. Ltd.* v. *Amalgamated Union of Engineering and Foundry Workers* [1969] 1 W.L.R. 339. A selection of earlier cases in which reference was made to agreements falling within s. 4 of the Trade Union Act 1871 may be found in Professor Wedderburn's *Cases and Materials on Labour Law, op. cit.*, although the issue had never effectively and directly been raised until the *Ford Motor Co.* case.

Therefore, it is a contract (if it is permissible to use that term in its widest sense, at this stage) or agreement which cannot give rise to an action in damages for any alleged breach thereof, nor to any application or petition for specific implement. It has been suggested that the parties might refer any matters in dispute between them to civil arbitration, in Scotland or England as appropriate, because it is said that this is not a judicial process. With respect, this point is probably entirely academic—and indeed it is submitted that the medium of civil arbitration is meantime unsuitable for references of this kind, even if the procedure itself were to be regarded as relevant. It is believed that parties to a collective agreement would prefer to make use of their own disputes procedures where the bargaining arrangements had broken down and, failing that, to resort to the statutory procedures available under the Conciliation Act 1896 and the Industrial Courts Act 1919.[71] However, it must not be thought that section 4 (4) above-mentioned prevents all and every kind of contractual agreement from being considered and, where necessary, enforced by the courts. The following are some of the cases which illustrate the modifications to section 4 (4), viz.: (i) section 4 (4) does not prohibit an action in damages for breach of contract between a single employer and a workers' trade union. Loss or damage would require to be shown, in accordance with the general principles of the law of contract. The growth of the nationalised industries and statutory corporations has resulted in the classification of these bodies as " single employers " so that it does become possible that more damages actions, based on contract, could be brought against these corporations; (ii) section 4 (4) does not cover unions which are lawful at common law. Section 3 of the Trade Union Act 1871 states that " The purposes of any trade union shall not, by reason merely that they are in restraint of trade, be unlawful so as to render void or voidable any agreement or trust." If the only taint of illegality is restraint of trade, any such agreement will be valid and enforceable. If a trade union's purposes are not illegal at common law, then its agreements and trusts are enforceable without any assistance from section 3 and, moreover, section 4 does not affect their agreements either. Where however section 3 is relevant in relation to a particular trade union it must be read along with section 4; (iii) the lack of legal status of a trade union placed certain procedural limitations upon damages actions for breaches of contract, particularly in England—where it seems that in the case of a registered trade union an action could not be brought by an employees' trade union in its registered name (even though it were lawful at common law) although it seems that such an action could have been competently brought in Scotland, so long as it is not an agreement caught by section 4 (4). The unregistered trade union does not have enough legal personality in English law to bring or defend actions and accordingly use was made of the " representative action " in England, i.e., utilising the office-bearers and trustees as representative of the union. So far as Scotland is concerned, it seems that the

---

[71] These two statutes are considered in the second part of this chapter.

registered trade union can sue and be sued in its registered name and, in addition, the unregistered trade union can sue or be sued using its " descriptive name " and adding a number of responsible officials or representatives both in the sheriff court and the Court of Session.[72] The Donovan Report [73] recommended that the trade unions be given corporate legal personality [74] but the recent White Paper [75] which follows on from the Report does not accept that recommendation but states quite clearly [76] that the Government accepts the view of the T.U.C. and others in the trade union movement that the granting of corporate personality to the trade unions is unsuited to their constitutions and their functions.

As regards question (b) above—the rights (if any) which an individual employee/member of a union acquires from a negotiated collective agreement—the general effect of a collective agreement between an employers' federation and a workers' association or trade union is, in fact, wider than is at first suggested by an examination of section 4 (4) of the Trade Union Act 1871. The individual employee is always concerned with the difficult questions as to whether he has a right to rely upon the terms and conditions of employment contained in a negotiated collective agreement and whether he can enforce these terms and conditions. Two basic limitations must be noted in relation to bargaining negotiations between trade unions and groups of employers. First, a trade union does not act as an agent of its members in this situation, but as a principal.[77] Secondly, it is extremely doubtful whether the union member—who is in the position of a third party—can acquire any rights under the collective agreement at the negotiation stage. In the English law of contract the basic rule seems (at the moment) to be that a third party cannot acquire any rights or be subject to any obligations from a contract entered into between X and Y and to which the third party himself does not consent. In Scots law, by operation of the *jus quaesitum tertio* rule, it is possible for a third party to acquire certain rights under a contract although he is not a signatory thereto, but the facts and circumstances must be such that the third party has a right, in view of his own relationship with one or other of the main parties, which he can pursue. At the same time, regard must be given to established practice in the field of industrial relations. Therefore, looking to the fact that a collective agreement is not basically an enforceable contract [78] at all at the instance of either of the two sides involved it would be incorrect to expect that any right or obligation might arise directly

---

[72] See the Sheriff Courts (Scotland) Acts 1907 (Sched. 1, rule 11) and 1913; also *Renton Football Club* v. *McDowell* (1891) 18 R. 670; *Crieff Musical Association* v. *Neil* (1901) 17 Sh.Ct.Rep. 185; and *International Tailors, etc.* v. *Goldberg* (1902) 19 Sh.Ct.Rep. 312.

[73] Report of the Royal Commission on Trade Unions and Employers' Associations (Cmnd. 3623) (1968).

[74] *Ibid.* para. 782 (pp. 209–210).

[75] " In Place of Strife " (A Policy for Industrial Relations) (Cmnd. 3888) (January 1969).

[76] *Ibid.* para. 111 (p. 33).

[77] *Holland* v. *London Society of Compositors* (1924) 40 T.L.R. 440.

[78] See now the recent and interesting decision in *Ford Motor Co. Ltd.* v. *Amalgamated Union of Engineering and Foundry Workers* [1969] 1 W.L.R. 339.

from it and be enforceable by an individual employee who was trying to trace his right through his own trade union. However, although it is not possible for a worker to claim that his trade union was acting as his agent in negotiating a collective agreement it may be possible for him to show that the terms and conditions of that collective agreement have become incorporated into his own contract of employment. These incorporated terms may be of two kinds, *viz.*: (1) conditions of engagement or (2) terms of employment. The former provide conditions under which an employer may or may not engage labour, *e.g.*, that apprenticeships shall not commence before the age of eighteen years or that all persons entering the employment of a particular employer or group of employers must be members of a particular trade union. It is unlikely, however, that conditions of engagement of that type would become part of an individual contract of employment. Terms of employment (*i.e.*, type (2) above-mentioned) relate to those conditions which govern an employee once he has entered upon his employment and would normally mean such things as wages, hours of work, rest periods, overtime working, holidays, etc. It is usual for those terms to become expressly incorporated into individual contracts of employment, whilst it is always possible, of course, for such terms to be implied into the employment relationship between the individual employee and his own employer. Accordingly, any term which is so incorporated directly or impliedly into the contract of employment can be enforced by the employee. Such a term may also be implied by virtue of certain statutory provisions, *e.g.*, as contained in the Road Haulage Wages Act 1938 or the House of Commons Resolution on Fair Wages 1946 or the Wages Councils Act 1959. It is not necessary to incorporate these terms *ad longum* in employment contracts. It is very often sufficient to use such phrases as " employees will be taken on at union rates " or " under union conditions." [79] To return to the basic question of an individual employee being able to enforce any term or condition in a collective agreement, the answer now seems to be reasonably clear—namely, that the individual workman can only claim to be able to do so where such term or condition has become incorporated into his own individual contract of employment by any of the methods above-mentioned.

PART E—Recommendations of the Donovan Commission and the recent White Paper " In Place of Strife "

(1) *The Donovan Report* [80]

The Royal Commission was appointed in April 1965 and its Report was subsequently presented to Parliament in June 1968. The Report is a very substantial document running to approximately 300 pages of text

---

[79] See *Industrial Relations Handbook*, Chap. II (collective bargaining and the development of joint negotiation, etc.).

[80] Report of the Royal Commission on Trade Unions and Employers' Associations (Cmnd. 3623) (1968).

and the Research Papers [81] also make a substantial contribution to knowledge in the industrial relations field.   The Report makes many recommendations [82] but, in broad conspectus, it may be said to take a very careful, conservative, middle-of-the-road approach following or being impressed by the official T.U.C. standpoint that a new attitude to and development of the system of voluntary collective bargaining in Great Britain is the best way of dealing with industrial relations problems. If anyone expected startling new proposals or a closer involvement of the law with industrial relations then he will be sadly disappointed by the Report.   However, it is inopportune, if not irrelevant, to make an exhaustive critical examination of the conclusions and recommendations therein, in the course of a work of this type.   What will be important to management and workers alike, as well as to the lawyer whose task it is to advise them, will of course be the final form in which the proposed new Industrial Relations Act emerges.   It seems that this new statute will not now appear until the spring of 1970 or even later.

It may be permissible and useful to mention some of the recommendations and conclusions which, in the writer's opinion, seem to be most important.   These are:

(1) Boards of companies should review industrial relations within their own undertakings.

(2) An Industrial Relations Act should be passed as soon as is possible.

(3) An Industrial Relations Commission should be established,[83] with a full-time chairman.

(4) Problems of trade union recognition should be dealt with by the new Commission.

(5) Compulsory unilateral arbitration by the Industrial Court should be available in industries or undertakings (certified by the Secretary of State on the advice of the new Commission) that it can contribute to the growth or maintenance of sound collective bargaining machinery.

(6) The proposals for the reform of collective bargaining are fundamental to solving the problem of unofficial strikes and other unofficial action.

(7) It is recommended (by a majority) that legislation to establish statutory machinery safeguarding employees against unfair dismissal should be passed at an early date.

(8) The existing Industrial Tribunals should be re-named " Labour Tribunals " and their jurisdiction be extended.[84]

---

[81] Eleven such papers have been published by H.M.S.O. and each is instructive and helpful in understanding the industrial relations system and trade union structures.

[82] A summary of the main conclusions and recommendations is conveniently set out in Chap. XVI (pp. 261–277) of the Report itself.

[83] The new Commission on Industrial Relations came into formal existence on March 3, 1969, with The Rt. Hon. George Woodcock, C.B.E., as full-time chairman.   It functions meantime as a Royal Commission, but doubtless it will be re-defined in the new Act.

[84] See Chap. X of the Report for recommendations.

(9) **The** proposal to prohibit the closed shop is rejected.[85]

(10) There is scope for many more mergers between unions.

(11) More use should be made of the check-off for collecting union subscriptions.

(12) A codification of the law in England and Scotland is recommended for the future.[86]

(13) A majority recommend the repeal of section 4 of the Trade Union Act 1871, and

(14) The immunity conferred by section 4 of the Trade Disputes Act 1906 in respect of tort (delict) should be confined to torts (delicts) committed in contemplation or furtherance of a trade dispute.

The Report was thereafter considered by the Government and in due course there appeared [87] the White Paper " In Place of Strife " which reflects the official attitude of the Government to the problems of industrial relations and sets out its policy in respect thereof.   However, there were indications from the trade union movement itself that many of the proposals and recommendations in the White Paper were unacceptable to the unions and there were also indications of differing views within the Parliamentary Labour Party.   No Labour Government can afford to alienate the affections of the unions and hope to be re-elected with a reasonable majority—or perhaps, more simply, hope to be re-elected. Although an early or primary Bill was expected in May 1969, dealing with unofficial strikes and introducing sanctions against those who disrupted ordinary and regular industrial procedures, in fact, the Government— being inevitably in a major dilemma—delayed introducing legislation. Finally, in June 1969, an arrangement or agreement was arrived at with the T.U.C. which passed the initiative back to Congress.   It is understood that Congress itself is to develop special supervisory and conciliatory procedures which will enable it to participate actively in the course of any industrial dispute—and particularly one which originates from an unofficial stoppage.   The only effective sanction which Congress can meantime impose against any trade union (which is unable to control or discipline its members) is, presumably, disaffiliation.   Trade unionists are understood to view that sanction as a very serious matter indeed.

It is necessary to look briefly at the White Paper.

(2) *The White Paper " In Place of Strife "* [88]

As was mentioned above, the White Paper is the policy statement on industrial relations made by the present Government after having studied the Donovan Report.   It must be noted that the White Paper does not examine or consider in detail those recommendations of a strictly legal nature which were dealt with by the Donovan Commission.   It is made

---

[85] Chap. XI explains the safeguards which should be made available to workers.

[86] See Chap. XIV.

[87] In January 1969 (Cmnd. 3888).

[88] " In Place of Strife " (A Policy for Industrial Relations) (Cmnd. 3888) (January 1969).

clear that these matters will be considered and discussed before possible inclusion in the new Industrial Relations Bill.[89] There are several important points made in the White Paper which link up with the Donovan Report and which must now be mentioned, *viz.*:

(a) The Government proposes to establish[90] a Commission on Industrial Relations.

(b) The Government proposes to modify section 4 (4) of the Trade Union Act 1871 so that agreements between trade unions and employers' associations will be equated with those agreements between trade unions and individual employers. Such agreements are to be made legally binding only if there is an express written provision to this effect *in gremio* of the agreement.[91]

(c) The Government proposes to include a provision in the new Bill to enable trade unions to obtain from employers certain sorts of information that are needed for negotiations.

(d) The Government favours experiments for worker-participation in management (which will include experiments *re* workers' representatives on boards of undertakings).

(e) The Government looks to the unions—with T.U.C. guidance—to co-operate in using the new opportunities that will be created to extend their role and membership, without wasting energies and resources in unnecessary competition.

(f) The new Bill will give statutory support to Article 1 of the International Labour Convention on the Right to Organise and on Collective Bargaining (No. 98).

(g) The Government proposes that the Secretary of State for Employment and Productivity should be empowered to require an employer by Order to recognise and negotiate with a union (following upon a recommendation by the C.I.R.). If an employer then fails to recognise the union it will be possible for the union unilaterally to take him to arbitration before the Industrial Court, whose award will be legally binding.[92]

(h) A review of the Wages Council system is promised. The T.U.C., the C.B.I. and the Wages Councils are to be consulted.

(i) The new Bill will provide for loans and grants to trade unions by the C.I.R.—which is further than the Donovan Commission was prepared to go.[93]

(j) the Government rejects the view of a majority of the Royal Commission that the protection given by section 3 of the Trade Disputes Act 1906 and by the Trade Disputes Act 1965 in relation

[89] *Ibid.* p. 37. The preliminary Bill against " wildcat " strikes has been abandoned (June 1969), as explained above.

[90] It began its existence on March 3, 1969, with The Rt. Hon. George Woodcock, C.B.E., as full-time chairman. See pp. 13 and 14 of the White Paper for a note of the functions proposed for the C.I.R.

[91] *Ibid.* pp. 15 and 16.

[92] *Ibid.* p. 19.

[93] *Ibid.* pp. 23 and 24.

to inducement of breach of a contract of employment should be limited to registered trade unions (and those acting on their behalf), *i.e.*, that unofficial strike leaders could be sued by employers for inducing strikers to break their contracts. This recommendation would have a seriously harmful effect.

(k) The new Bill may give the Secretary of State a discretionary power to secure a " conciliation pause " in unconstitutional strikes and in strikes where adequate joint discussions have not taken place.[94] The period would be twenty-eight days. Financial penalties would be imposed for failure to comply with the Order issued by the Secretary of State.

(l) Although the Royal Commission rejected the obligatory strike ballot, the Government proposed to insert in the new Bill a discretionary power to the Secretary of State to require the union (or unions) concerned to hold a ballot on the question of strike action. That ballot will be conducted by the union according to its own rules.[95]

(m) The Government accepts the recommendation of the Royal Commission that the inducement of breach of a commercial contract in the circumstances of a trade dispute should be protected in the same way as inducement of breach of a contract of employment. The sympathetic strike is not to be outlawed, but the Secretary of State may require a strike ballot in relation to an official sympathetic strike or a conciliation pause in relation to an unconstitutional sympathetic strike.[96]

(n) Safeguards against unfair dismissal or arbitrary dismissal are to be introduced into the new Bill. A clear definition clause will be required.[97]

(o) A revision of the Contracts of Employment Act 1963 is promised in order to safeguard employees, particularly in the interests of the long-service employees.[98]

(p) Trade unions will be required to register with a new Registrar of Trade Union and Employers' Associations. The matters to be contained in the rules will be specified in the Bill. Financial penalties will be imposed for failure to register.[99]

(q) The Government rejects the recommendation of the Royal Commission that the unions be given corporate status.[1]

(r) The new Bill will provide for the removal of the immunity created

---

[94] *Ibid.* pp. 28 and 29. The unions are against this proposal.
[95] *Ibid.* pp. 29 and 30. The unions are opposed to this. In view of the agreement made with the T.U.C. in June 1969, this proposal and the preceding one will doubtless be abandoned. It is difficult to say, at this moment, how much (if anything) of the White Paper remains acceptable to the unions.
[96] *Ibid.* p. 30. But see, *supra*, regarding the arrangement with the T.U.C.
[97] See the suggestion in para. 104 (p. 31).
[98] *Ibid.* para. 105 (p. 31).
[99] See para. 109 (pp. 32 and 33).
[1] *Ibid.* para. 111 (p. 33).

by section 4 of the Trade Disputes Act 1906, except in the circumstances of a trade dispute.[2]

(s) The Government accepts the assessment of the Royal Commission
that the closed shop be retained but that safeguards for individual
members of a union be introduced and that references to the
Industrial Board be available.[3] The Board may award damages
or order admission or reinstatement.

A summary of the proposals for inclusion in the Industrial Relations
Act can be found in Appendix 1 to the White Paper. Tables of statistics
(United Kingdom tables and a comparative table [4]) will be found in
Appendix 2.

(II) Conciliation and Arbitration and the Settlement of Industrial Disputes by Statutory Machinery

Collective bargaining processes can break down or fail to operate in two
differing situations, viz.: (a) in the actual negotiation of a new agreement
on wages and other conditions of employment; and (b) where there is an
alleged failure by one side to carry out the terms of an existing negotiated
agreement. It appears that there are, at the present time, four methods
of settling disputes by the use of certain statutory provisions and processes
which are to be found in the following Acts, namely:

    (i) the Conciliation Act 1896;

    (ii) the Industrial Courts Act 1919;

    (iii) section 8 of the Terms and Conditions of Employment Act 1959
        (known as the " claims procedure "); and

    (iv) the Employers and Workmen Act 1875.

Each must be considered briefly.

    (i) *The Conciliation Act 1896*.[5] By this statute the Minister [6] has
certain powers where any difference is existing or is apprehended between
employers and workmen or between different classes of workmen. These
powers enable the Secretary of State to do the following things:

    (a) without any request from the parties the Secretary of State may—
        (1) inquire into the causes and circumstances of the dispute and
        (2) take steps to bring the parties round the table in an attempt
        to conclude an amicable settlement.

    (b) Upon the application of either side, he may appoint a single
        conciliator or a board of conciliation, but only after he has con-
        sidered the adequacy of all means available for voluntary concilia-
        tion within the district or within the trade and has also considered

---

[2] *Ibid.* para. 113 (p. 33).

[3] *Ibid.* paras. 117 and 118 (p. 34).

[4] *Ibid.* p. 38.

[5] 59 & 60 Vict., c. 30.

[6] Formerly the President of the Board of Trade, thereafter the Minister of Labour and, since 1968, the Secretary of State for Employment and Productivity.

the circumstances of the dispute. It is the conciliator's task to inquire into the causes of the dispute and to try to bring about a satisfactory settlement.

(c) Upon the application of both sides, he may appoint an arbitrator.[7]

When a settlement has been effected by conciliation or arbitration, a memorandum of the terms must be drawn up and signed by the parties. A copy of that memorandum is sent to the Secretary of State. No party can be bound or obliged to go to industrial arbitration under the 1896 Act and any award made thereunder is not legally binding upon the parties. In practice, however, any award is almost always observed by both sides.

(ii) *The Industrial Courts Act 1919.*[8] The Industrial Court is not a part of the juridical system but it is, nevertheless, a permanent tribunal which consists of members representing employers, members representing workmen and independent members. One or more women members must also be appointed. The President is one of the independent members. All members are appointed by the Secretary of State for Employment and Productivity [9] and hold office for such term as may be fixed by the Secretary of State at the time of appointment. The court may sit in divisions and it is the President's duty to decide which members shall deal with a particular matter referred to the court as well as to decide upon the membership of the divisions. The chairman of the division must be an independent member.

The 1919 Act also provides for a single arbitrator or board of arbitrators, which are *ad hoc* appointments.

The main function of the Industrial Court is to settle trade disputes. Section 8 defines a trade dispute as " any dispute or difference between employers and workmen or between workmen and workmen connected with the employment or non-employment, or the terms of the employment or with the conditions of labour of any person." This definition is substantially the same as that contained in the Trade Disputes Acts 1906 and 1965. The Secretary of State has the following powers where a trade dispute exists or is apprehended, namely: (1) after either party has reported the dispute to him, the Secretary of State considers and takes expedient steps towards a settlement [10]; (2) if he thinks fit,[11] and if both parties consent, refer the matter for settlement to the Industrial Court or refer to one or more arbitrators appointed by himself or refer the matter to a board of arbitration. This board must consist of one or more persons nominated by employers with an equal number nominated by workmen, together with an independent chairman nominated by the Secretary of

---

[7] This is the term used in s. 2 (1) of the Act. In Scotland, the term " arbiter " is more commonly and correctly used in general arbitration matters.
[8] 9 & 10 Geo. 5, c. 69.
[9] Formerly the Minister of Labour.
[10] *Ibid.* s. 2 (1).
[11] *Ibid.* s. 2 (2).

State [12]; (3) refer to the Industrial Court for advice on any matter relating to or arising out of a trade dispute or any other matter which in his opinion ought to be referred to the court [13]; (4) where voluntary arrangements exist for the settlement of disputes in any trade or industry, made in pursuance of an agreement between organisations of employers and organisations of workmen, representative respectively of substantial proportions of employers and workmen in that trade or industry, the Secretary of State must not refer a matter for settlement or advice unless with the consent of both parties to the dispute and unless and until there has been a failure to obtain a settlement by means of these voluntary arrangements [14]; (5) under Part II of the Act the Secretary of State may—whether the dispute is reported to him or not—inquire into the causes and circumstances and, if he thinks fit, refer any matters thereanent to a Court of Inquiry for investigation and report.[15] This Court of Inquiry consists [16] of such persons as the Secretary of State wishes to appoint and may even consist of one person (very often a judge of the High Court in England or of the Court of Session in Scotland [17]). A Court of Inquiry may, if authorised under rules issued by the Secretary of State, require any person who has knowledge of the subject-matter to furnish particulars in writing or under oath. The report which is ultimately issued by the Court of Inquiry must be laid before both Houses of Parliament.

There are three methods available under the 1919 Act in relation to industrial arbitration, namely: (i) by the Industrial Court itself, (ii) by a single arbitrator and (iii) by a board of arbitrators. In the case of method (i) the parties to the dispute enter into an agreement to refer and agree the terms of reference, *i.e.*, they will state concisely the matter which the Industrial Court is required to decide. If the parties cannot agree the terms of reference the court will look at all correspondence passing between the parties themselves and including the statements reporting the dispute—these items together forming the terms of reference. The court's procedure is governed by the Industrial Court (Procedure) Rules 1920.[18] Whilst it is not bound by the strict rules of evidence the court does normally follow the method of presentation and conduct of a case as in a court of law, although it cannot order the production of documents nor compel the attendance of witnesses. Assessors may sit to give advice on technical matters but they are in no way answerable or responsible for the court's decision. After hearing the evidence (much of which is presented in written form by the parties, who should then be in attendance)

---

[12] Panels of suitable persons must be constituted by the Secretary of State and must contain women members.
[13] *Ibid.* s. 2 (3).
[14] *Ibid.* s. 2 (4).
[15] *Ibid.* s. 4 (1).
[16] *Ibid.* s. 4 (2).
[17] Lord Cameron has presided over several Courts of Inquiry.
[18] See *The Industrial Court: Practice and Procedure* (1923) by Sir William Mackenzie (afterwards Lord Amulree) at Appendix II. This is a very useful monograph on the work of the court.

the court makes its award or decision. This award must not go beyond the terms of reference, nor should it be inconsistent with the provisions of any existing statutory enactments. The award is communicated in writing to both parties. If any interpretation of the award is necessary, then either the Secretary of State or either party to the award may ask for an interpretation.

As regards method (ii) (arbitration by a single arbitrator) the Secretary of State may make rules regulating the procedure for this type of arbitration. After the award is made the arbitrator is *functus officio*. Moreover, he may not amend his award, even to correct an obvious slip or clerical error. Nor can an interpretation be obtained, unless both parties agree.

Method (iii) is the board of arbitrators. In order to facilitate the establishment of such boards of arbitrators the Secretary of State is required to set up panels of suitable persons (including women) to serve upon these boards. In practice, one employer and one employee are very often chosen from these panels to serve along with an independent chairman. If a greater number than three members is required it is always essential to have an exactly similar representation from both sides of industry. The Secretary of State may make rules regarding the procedure of these arbitration boards. What has been said above regarding the non-correction and interpretation of awards by a single arbitrator applies with equal force to the awards by boards of arbitration.

Parties engaged in arbitration before the court do not pay any fees. Single arbitrators and chairmen of the boards are paid fees on a recognised scale.

The effects of an award in relation to arbitration under the 1919 Act are interesting. No award by the Industrial Court or by a single arbitrator or by a board of arbitrators can be enforced by any action or proceedings in the courts of law, nor can any criminal consequences follow upon a refusal or neglect to obey any such award or decision. If the parties accept an award or act upon it this may well become a term of the contract of employment and accordingly an action may follow upon any breach of that contract.

(iii) *The " claims procedure " under section 8 of the Terms and Conditions of Employment Act 1959.* Section 8 of the Terms and Conditions of Employment Act 1959 [19] sets out a special procedure for the settlement of claims as to recognised terms or conditions of employment. A claim may be reported to the Secretary of State—(a) that terms or conditions of employment are established in any trade or industry, or section thereof, either generally or in any district, which have been settled by an agreement

---

[19] 7 & 8 Eliz. 2, c. 26. (The whole Act has been repealed except for the s. 8 provisions.) It must be kept in mind that the jurisdiction of the Industrial Court in relation to the " claims procedure " has been extended by the Redundancy Payments Act 1965, ss. 11 and 12, which bring within the court's sphere of operations redundancy agreements under s. 12 and redundancy schemes exempted by ministerial order from the 1965 Act (see s. 11) and transferable to the Industrial Court.

or award; and (b) that the parties to the agreement or award are or represent employers' organisations and workers' organisations (or associations
thereof) and represent a substantial proportion of employers and workers
in the trade, industry or section to which the agreement or award relates;
and (c) that, as respects any worker of the relevant description an employer
engaged in the trade, industry or section (or district, if appropriate),
whether represented or not, is not observing the terms or conditions (*i.e.*,
the " recognised terms or conditions "). When that is done the Secretary
of State may take any steps which seem expedient to settle, or secure the
use of appropriate machinery to settle, the claim and shall—if the claim
is not otherwise settled—refer it to the Industrial Court. Section 8 does
not cover [20] the case of workmen whose wages or minimum wages (meaning " remuneration " in the wider sense as used in the statute) are fixed by
some other statutory enactment or the case where some other statutory
provision is made for the settlement of questions relating to such remuneration or minimum remuneration and no claim can be reported in respect of
terms and conditions so fixed.[21]

Once a reference has been made to the Industrial Court under the
" claims procedure " explained above, the court shall—upon being
satisfied that the claim is well-founded and unless it is also satisfied that
the terms and conditions being observed by the employer are not less
favourable than the recognised terms or conditions—make an award
requiring the employer to observe the recognised terms or conditions in
respect of the workers concerned.[22] The award which the Industrial
Court makes under section 8 has the effect of an implied term of the
contract of employment and becomes operative upon a date determined
by the court.[23] The award which is made under this section ceases to be
operative or effective when a new agreement or award comes into force
which varies or abrogates the " recognised terms or conditions." Section 8
equates the activities of public authorities and local authorities with the
carrying on of a trade or industry.

(iv) *The Employers and Workmen Act 1875.*[24] Under section 4 of the
Act a court of summary jurisdiction has power to hear disputes between
an employer and a workman. After hearing the dispute the court may
order payment of any sum which it finds to be due either as wages or
damages. The court's jurisdiction is restricted, however, as are its powers,
in the following respects: (a) the court has no jurisdiction where the amount
of the claim exceeds £10; (b) it may not make an order for the payment of

---

[20] See the proviso thereto.
[21] The Donovan Report (and the White Paper promises consultation on this) recommends
that the s. 8 provisions be applied to those industries governed by the Wages Councils
Acts.
[22] See s. 8 (3).
[23] But the date must not be earlier than the date on which, in the court's opinion, the
employer was first informed of the claim giving rise to the award by the organisation
or association which reported the claim to the Secretary of State.
[24] 38 & 39 Vict., c. 90.

any sum exceeding £10, exclusive of expenses; and (c) it may not require security to an amount exceeding £10 from any defender or his cautioner. Moreover, any dispute between a master and an apprentice may also be heard by a court of summary jurisdiction.[25] In this instance the court has similar powers to those above explained, but it may also exercise the following additional powers: (1) order an apprentice to perform his duties under his indenture, failing which, imprison him, (2) rescind the indenture, or (3) order any cautioner in the deed of indenture to pay damages not exceeding the limit (if any) specified in the indenture deed or take from him a sum by way of caution or an undertaking that the apprentice will duly perform his contract.[26]

Section 14 deals specifically with the application of the Act to Scotland and gives, as expected, the Scottish equivalents of the English terminological references. So far as Scotland is concerned, a reference to a " county court " means the ordinary sheriff court, whilst a reference to " the court of summary jurisdiction " means the sheriff's small debt court. The judicial officers responsible for carrying out the terms and provisions of the statute are indeed the sheriffs.

It will be observed that the industrial arbitration procedures available under the Conciliation Act 1896 and the Industrial Courts Act 1919 are not compulsory procedures. There is a certain measure of compulsion about the " claims procedure " under section 8 of the Terms and Conditions of Employment Act 1959, but this should not be confused with compulsory arbitration which may be introduced by the state during an emergency— for example, during a period of war in which Great Britain is an active participant—when the preservation of industrial peace is absolutely vital for the country's safety and security.[27] Mobility of labour is also extremely important and necessary during a crisis and this means that the requisite delegated legislative authority must be given to the appropriate government department (the old Ministry of Labour and National Service during the Second World War) to issue Essential Works Orders and thereafter carry out the requisite operations and movements thereunder. The rank and file of the Labour Party and the trade unions have a healthy disrespect for compulsory arbitration and would resist it *per ardua ad mortem*.

---

[25] *Ibid.* s. 6.

[26] *Ibid.* s. 7.

[27] This has occurred during the First and Second World Wars and the aftermath of the latter and is illustrated by the Conditions of Employment and National Arbitration Order 1940 (S.R. & O. 1940 No. 1305) and the Industrial Disputes Order 1951 (this Order being revoked by S.I. 1958 No. 1796). An account of these Orders and of the war-time procedures may be found in Chap. VIII of the *Industrial Relations Handbook*, particularly at pp. 143–146. See also Research Paper No. 8 issued by the Donovan Commission and study No. 2 thereof (by Dr. W. E. J. McCarthy) entitled " Compulsory Arbitration in Britain: The Work of the Industrial Disputes Tribunal."

DISSOLUTION OF THE RELATIONSHIP OF EMPLOYER AND EMPLOYEE

CHAPTER 18

TERMINATION OF THE RELATIONSHIP OF EMPLOYER AND EMPLOYEE BY NOTICE

THE requirement of notice as a preliminary to termination of the employer-and-employee relationship was not, so far as the common law was concerned, a part of every contract of service. Its use was general and, of course, it was and still is a mutual obligation.[1] Yet it must be noted that whenever a mutual desire to terminate the contract becomes apparent, effect can be given to it at once by the parties themselves without any resort to formal notice procedures. This was the common law position prior to the passing of the Contracts of Employment Act 1963 [2] and it is still the position as regards those contracts which do not fall within the ambit of the Act.[3] What the Act does in relation to termination by the mutual agreement of parties is to preserve their right to do so [4] but nevertheless it is made quite clear that any contractual provision for cutting short the statutory notice shall be of no effect and the statutory notice will prevail. Not only may either party waive his right to notice upon any occasion, but either party may alternatively accept a payment in lieu of notice. This latter provision is intended to preserve the common law rule whereby an employer may always pay to the employee the correct amount of wages or salary related to the notice period and get rid of him immediately. It also seems to permit an employer to receive from an employee a sum of money which is presumably equivalent to a " damages " claim, if the employee leaves without due notice and so causes loss to the employer. This last-mentioned point seems to be underlining the common law approach to breach and resultant damages but it is not apparently giving to an employee a legislative right to " buy himself out of his contract," although the practical result at the end of the day is virtually the same. We must refer to this matter again, somewhat later. It will also be necessary to examine in some detail the main provisions of the 1963 Act so far as these change, alter or create notice procedures.

The requirements as to notice may be express or implied. The latter is decided by reference to either local custom [5] or the custom of the trade,[6] but not apparently to the custom of the particular establishment, though this last-mentioned illustration of custom is far from clear.

---

[1] *Renwick* v. *Gordon*, 10 S.L.R.(Sh.Ct.Rep.) 321.
[2] 1963, c. 49.
[3] See particularly s. 1 (1) and (2) as regards the *minimal* period of employment and s. 6.
[4] s. 1 (3).
[5] *Morrison* v. *Allardyce* (1823) 2 S. 387.
[6] *Hamilton* v. *Outram* (1855) 17 D. 798; *McLean* v. *McFarlane* (1863) 4 Irv. 351.

The objects of giving notice are said to be twofold: (a) it prevents a tacit relocation which would otherwise be inferred or (b) it fixes a due termination to a contract of employment during pleasure.[7] If neither object is to be achieved, then the requirement as to notice seems to be without value.[8]

Instead of giving notice and permitting the employee to " work his notice " the employer may pay him the wages (including board wages, if appropriate) due in lieu of notice and dismiss him instantly. Such action by the employer does not amount to a breach of contract in the ordinary case.[9]

The common law did not seem to give a corresponding or converse right in favour of the employee by which he might " dismiss himself on the spot " by giving to his employer a payment of money which represented the unexpired portion of the notice period which he must work. Mr. Umpherston suggests that he might break his contract deliberately and then be liable in damages; and it seems that this practical method was not uncommon. The employer kept the initiative, because he had the right to accept or refuse a damages payment tendered to him in settlement or if the employee skipped off without payment, the employer could sue for breach of contract and, if appropriate, offset any " lying-time " and other credits against the damages claim. The employee possessed no legal right at common law to claim or demand a cancellation of the contract by paying a sum of money equivalent to the unexpired notice period. The Contracts of Employment Act 1963 [10] preserves, as mentioned above, the right to terminate a contract of employment at the mutual pleasure of parties and allows them to waive any notice period or to accept a payment in lieu thereof. This latter provision allows the employee to receive an immediate payment in place of notice or an employer to accept a sum by way of damages. What the Act does not do—as has already been indicated—is to give an employee a statutory right to pay over money in lieu of notice and so " buy himself out." The legal position of the employee who is anxious to leave before his notice expires seems to be this—if he chooses to depart before expiry of the notice period this is a technical breach of contract and the correct procedure for the employer (if he elects to follow that procedure) is to sue the employee for damages based upon breach of contract.

The giving of the notice need not be formal—it may be in writing or be given orally or it may be inferred from the actings of the parties. However, it must be timeous and it must be definite. The requirement of notice will not be lightly inferred.[11] If the giving of notice is to be

[7] *Morrison* v. *Abernethy School Board* (1876) 3 R. 945; *Robson* v. *Overend* (1878) 6 R. 213.
[8] *Wallace* v. *Wishart* (1800) Hume 383; *Brenan* v. *Campbell's Trs.* (1898) 25 R. 423; but see *Lennox* v. *Allan & Son* (1880) 8 R. 38 for dicta which seem to be in conflict with the objects of notice (see opinions of L.J.-C. Moncreiff and Lord Young).
[9] *Morrison* v. *Abernethy School Board* (1876) 3 R. 945; *Robson* v. *Overend* (1878) 6 R. 213; and *Hastie* v. *McMurtrie* (1889) 16 R. 715.
[10] See s. 1 (3).
[11] See *MacLean* v. *Fyfe*, February 4, 1813, F.C.

inferred from the actings of parties, then this becomes a question of fact to be decided by the jury.[12] The question of timeous notice of dismissal was raised in respect of a shepherd who occupied a house as part of his wages in the case of *Stewart* v. *Robertson*.[13]

The length of notice required to be given is usually expressed in the contract between the parties. If not so, then it is determined by the equity of the case and, in any event, it must be reasonable. In the case of *Stevenson* v. *North British Railway Co.*,[14] concerning a shipping agent, it was held that the agent was entitled to a year's notice because the contract was one of yearly service. The employee's right to warning is said to rest on " equity and custom." [15] Agricultural and domestic employees, hired by the year or half-year, were thought to be entitled to forty clear days' notice and similarly for all employees (*e.g.*, foresters, gamekeepers, gardeners, farm managers, etc.) hired termly by the year or half-year.[16] The forty days' period of notice above mentioned was to be counted from the date at which *de facto* the term of the employment was due to expire.[17] But, of course, the Removal Terms (Scotland) Act 1886 [18] altered the law as stated in *Cameron* v. *Scott* [19] by requiring the warning to be given forty days before May 15 and November 11 although the actual date of cessation of the tenancy or employment was May 28 or November 28. However, in the later case of *Stewart* v. *Robertson* [20] it seems that forty days' notice before these last mentioned days is sufficient. The Rent Act 1957 and subsequent legislation have made some further changes with regard to the giving of notice in the case of property held on lease.[21] However, the employment occupancy is in no way affected or protected by the statute. Moreover, neither the Rent Act 1957 nor the Rent Act 1965 makes any alteration in the customary notice referred to above which applies to the agricultural and domestic employees. There is no doubt that the employer, seeking to recover possession of a dwelling-house occupied by an employee is likely to be confronted with the problem as to whether the employee's occupation is *qua* tenant or *qua* employee. If the former, then the general law of landlord and tenant will apply to the situation; whilst if the latter, the employer is in a better

[12] *Anderson* v. *Wishart* (1818) 1 Mur. 429, *per* L.C.C. Adam at p. 438.

[13] 1937 S.C. 701; 1937 S.L.T. 465.

[14] (1905) 7 F. 1106; 13 S.L.T. 267.

[15] See L.J.-C. Moncreiff in *Cameron* v. *Scott* (1870) 9 M. 233; and Lord Gifford in *Lennox* v. *Allen & Son* (1880) 8 R. 38 at p. 40.

[16] *Ross* v. *Pender* (1874) 1 R. 352; *Armstrong* v. *Bainbridge* (1847) 9 D. 1198; *McLean* v. *Fyfe*, February 4, 1813, F.C.; *Anderson* v. *Wishart* (1818) 1 Mur. 429, *per* L.C.C. Adam at p. 438. See the comments on the custom of 40 days' notice for agricultural and domestic employees in the case of *Lennox* v. *Allan & Son, cit. supra*, particularly *per* the L.J.-C. and Lord Gifford—where that notice applies to a special class of servant and is based wholly upon custom.

[17] This is applying the analogy of the leasehold tenant who is to remove at Whitsunday or Martinmas—see *Cameron* v. *Scott* (1870) 9 M. 233; 8 S.L.R. 181.

[18] Amended in 1890.

[19] *Cit. supra.*

[20] 1937 S.C. 701; 1937 S.L.T. 465.

[21] See particularly s. 16 and paras. 28, 29 and 30 of Sched. 6 to the 1957 Act; and the Rent Act 1965 (c. 75), s. 16, which is important.

position and can usually recover possession without any judicial process of law.[22]

Otherwise, the length of notice may be settled by local custom or custom of the trade or perhaps even by the regulations of the particular establishment,[23] though this last mentioned method seems to be very doubtful. Where custom is pleaded it must be proved.[24] Quite often, particulars as to the length of notice required and other general conditions and regulations affecting the employment may be exhibited in the factory or works or be contained in a written or printed form which the workmen must sign or which must be brought to the attention of the employees in some other way.[25] This practice does indeed receive a formal recognition by the Contracts of Employment Act 1963.[26] Failing determination of the length of notice by any of the methods hereinbefore mentioned, the rule is that the length of notice must be reasonable in the circumstances.[27] This means that the employee is to receive an adequate opportunity of looking for another situation or the employer a similar opportunity of recruiting a replacement employee.[28] The modern Scottish cases maintain this same principle of the test of reasonableness, viz.: a period of four weeks was considered reasonable in the case of a clerk of works [29]; and a similar period was also thought to be reasonable in the case of the assistant manageress of an hotel.[30] The English cases follow the same pattern: e.g., three months was reasonable notice for a clerk [31] or commercial traveller [32]; twelve months for the editor of a major newspaper [33]; three months for the editor of a minor newspaper [34]; six months was reasonable for a sub-editor [35] and foreign correspondent,[36] whilst an ordinary journalist might reasonably expect one month's notice.

22 See *MacGregor* v. *Dunnet*, 1949 S.C. 510; 1949 S.L.T. 412.
23 *Hamilton* v. *Outram* (1855) 17 D. 798, *per* L.J.-C. Hope at p. 801.
24 *Moult* v. *Halliday* [1898] 1 Q.B. 125.
25 See *Fosdick* v. *N.B. Ry.* (1850) 13 D. 281; *Anderson* v. *Moon* (1837) 15 S. 412; *Cowden-beath Coal Co.* v. *Drylie* (1886) 3 Sh.Ct.Rep. 3; *Wright* v. *Howard Baker & Co.* (1893) 21 R. 25.
26 1963, c. 49, s. 4 (5).
27 *Davies* v. *City of Glasgow Friendly Society*, 1935 S.C. 224.
28 Some of the older cases giving some helpful guidance on what is reasonable: See *Campbell* v. *Fyfe* (1851) 13 D. 1041; *Eddy* v. *Glasgow Echo Co.* (1895) 11 Sh.Ct.Rep. 345 (15 days insufficient for a newspaper editor); *Morrison* v. *Abernethy School Board* (1876) 3 R. 945 (3 months for parish schoolmaster); *Forsyth* v. *Heathery Knowe Coal Co.* (1880) 7 R. 887 (3 months for colliery manager); *Mollison* v. *Baillie* (1885) 22 S.L.R. 595 (3 months for an estate factor); *Hawkins* v. *Thomson Dickie & Co.* (1897) 14 Sh.Ct.Rep. 159 (3 months for ship's husband); *Lawrie* v. *Airdrie Model Lodging House Co.* (1902) 19 Sh.Ct.Rep. 108 (3 months for model house manager); *Vibert* v. *Eastern Telegraph Co.* (1883) 1 C. & E. 17 (one month for Telegraph Co. clerk on £135 per annum); and *Byrne* v. *Schott* (1883) 1 C. & E. 17 (one month for shop manager on £250 p.a.); also *Manbert* v. *Kemp & Son* (1884) 1 Sh.Ct.Rep. 18 (one month for managing dressmaker on £250 p.a.).
29 *Currie* v. *Glasgow Central Stores Limited* (1905) 13 S.L.T. 88.
30 *Wilson* v. *Anthony* (1958) S.L.T.(Sh.Ct.) 13; (1957) 73 Sh.Ct.Rep. 298.
31 *Foxall* v. *International Land Credit Co.* (1867) 16 L.T. 637.
32 *Metzner* v. *Bolton* (1854) 9 Ex. 518; 23 L.J.Ex. 130; 23 L.T.(o.s.) 22.; *Grundon* v. *Master & Co.* (1885) 1 T.L.R. 105.
33 *Grundy* v. *Sun Printing & Publishing Association* (1916) 33 T.L.R 77.
34 *Baker* v. *Maudeville* (1896) 13 T.L.R. 71.
35 *Chamberlain* v. *Bennett* (1892) 8 T.L.R. 234.
36 *Lowe* v. *Walter* (1892) 8 T.L.R. 358.

The chief officer of an ocean-going passenger liner might, however, require twelve months' notice.[37]

Since the passing of the Contracts of Employment Act 1963 [38] there has been introduced for the first time [39] into British law the general concept of statutory notice intended to protect workpeople. It is essential to look now at the relevant sections of the Act in order to identify the changes which have been made. Although the Act was hailed by certain sections of the press as the " worker's charter " this view must honestly be regarded as typical journalistic exaggeration. The main changes, relating to notice, introduced by the statute are these:

(1) The employer is required to give notice, as follows, where the employee has been continuously employed for twenty-six weeks or more under a contract of employment—

(a) not less than one week, if the period of continuous employment is less than two years;

(b) not less than two weeks, if the period of continuous employment is two years or more but less than five years;

(c) not less than four weeks, if the said period of continuous employment is five years or more.[40]

(2) The employee is required to give not less than one week's notice, where he has been continuously employed for twenty-six weeks or more.[41]

(3) The employer is prevented from stipulating for shorter periods of notice than those contained in the Act in any agreement with an employee, who has been continuously employed for twenty-six weeks or more.[42] Nevertheless the right of either party to waive the notice required or to accept a payment in lieu thereof is preserved.[43] The method of calculation or computation of the employee's period of employment and the question of whether or not it is continuous are to be decided by reference to Schedule 1 to the Act, which comprises an extensive set of regulations spread over eleven paragraphs. That Schedule (and in particular paragraph 7, which relates to industrial disputes after the 1963 Act came into force and paragraph 10, which relates to a change of employer) was duly amended by the Redundancy Payments Act 1965.[44] That Schedule adopts a normal working week of twenty-one hours or more (para. 3) and goes on to deal with illness and incapacity and cessation for other

---

[37] *Savage* v. *British India Steam Navigation Co.* (1930) 46 T.L.R. 294.

[38] 1963, c. 49 (generally effective from July 6, 1964).

[39] Excepting, of course, the special case of dock workers, governed by an earlier scheme.

[40] *Ibid.* s. 1 (1). " Two years " and " five years " are to be calculated as 104 weeks and 260 weeks (Sched. 1, para. 1 (1)). It has been held by the Industrial Tribunal (in England) that it is sufficient if the 104 weeks' period is completed at the expiry of the notice—it need not have been completed when the notice was given—see *Hambling* v. *Marsden Builders Ltd.* [1966] I.T.R. 494.

[41] *Ibid.* s. 1 (2).

[42] *Ibid.* s. 1 (3).

[43] *Ibid.* s. 1 (3).

[44] 1965, c. 62; see particularly ss. 37 and 48 (7) thereof respectively. Reference should also be made generally to Dix on *Contracts of Employment* (3rd ed., 1968 by the author, now Judge Dorothy Knight Waddy, Q.C.); and specifically as regards Sched. 1, paras. 7, 10 and 10A to the notes at pp. 86, 88 and 89 respectively of Dix.

reasons (para. 5) which do not break the continuity of employment. Paragraphs 6, 7 and 8 govern the position in relation to industrial disputes. Any absence because of a strike or lock-out before the Act came into force counts as a period of employment, under paragraph 6. Furthermore, by paragraph 7 (as amended by section 37 of the Redundancy Payments Act 1965) the continuity of employment is not broken if the employee takes part in a strike but nevertheless any week of absence arising from that strike does not count in the computation of the period of employment. In other words the " blank " weeks are not counted and it takes that much longer to make up the employment period, although there is no prejudice to the continuity of employment. Nor is the continuity broken if the employee is locked-out by the employer (para. 8). Reinstatement in civilian employment is governed by paragraph 9, while—very importantly—the question of change of employer is regulated by paragraph 10 (as amended by section 48 (7) of the said 1965 Act), and the new paragraph 10A. " Strike " and " lock-out " are defined by paragraph 11.

(4) Section 1 of the 1963 Act does not affect in any way the common law right of either party to treat the contract as terminable without notice because of the conduct of the other party.[45] This means that the employer's common law right of summary dismissal of an employee upon justifiable grounds is fully preserved. At the same time, the employee's right to terminate upon justifiable grounds (e.g., ill conduct of or immoral conduct towards an employee by an employer) is also preserved.

(5) Where notice is given by an employer or employee in accordance with section 1 of the 1963 Act, the liability of the employer during the period of notice and the rights arising in favour of the employee within that period are determined by Schedule 2 to the Act, which contains seven paragraphs dealing basically with employment for which there are normal working hours and employment for which there are no such normal working hours. The Schedule takes account of termination of the employment during the notice period by providing, in paragraph 6, that if an employer breaks the contract of employment then all payments made after the breach shall go towards mitigating the damages which the employee will recover, on the basis of loss of earnings for the balance of the notice period. If the employee is himself in breach, within the notice period, no further payments fall to be made to him under the Schedule, in respect of the balance of the notice period. Schedule 2 was subsequently amended by the Redundancy Payments Act 1965, s. 39 (which added two new sub-paragraphs (4A) and (4B) to sub-paragraph (4) of paragraph 2), and by section 40 (4) which introduces a consequential amendment to section 2 and Schedule 2 to the 1963 Act. This Schedule and the preceding one are, with respect, very loosely drafted and seem to leave a great deal to the good sense of management and employees.

[45] See s. 1 (6).

Failing their agreement the Industrial Tribunals, or the court, will adjudicate upon the matter. In a sense this " makeshift " legislation follows the pattern which industry seems to prefer—namely, that both sides will try by voluntary negotiation to reach a settlement and when they fail to do so the legal machinery—regarded as the last resort solution—will be utilised. British industry and the British trade unions are not enthusiastic about a Labour Code enforced by Labour Courts. In terms of Schedule 2 one must first ascertain whether the situation is one governed by " normal working hours " and thereafter it is necessary to determine the rate of remuneration during the notice period. This latter exercise is one which requires a distinction to be drawn between the " time-basis " employee (where remuneration is paid at a constant rate) and the pieceworker. The alternative situation is that of the employee who does not have normal working hours (see para. 3). Absence due to a strike is governed by paragraph 5 and no payment is due if the employee is absent before the formal termination of his contract of employment. Schedule 2 to the 1963 Act has—in its meaning and ascertainment of " normal working hours "— become very important since the Redundancy Payments Act 1965 came into force, because Schedule 1, para. 5 (1) of the 1965 Act is to be read along with Schedule 2 in making certain redundancy payment calculations under the later Act.

(6) It is recognised by subsection (3) of section 2 of the 1963 Act that the parties themselves may contract out of the main provision of section 2 and of the relevant Schedule 2 provided that the notice to be given by the employee to terminate the contract is at least one week more than the statutory periods provided by section 1 (1) of the Act. The employee will have to decide whether the new substituted contractual basis of settlement during a notice period is more beneficial to him than the statutory protection in section 2 and Schedule 2. A clear express contractual provision which is intended to exclude section 2 should preferably be adopted by the parties—if they so intend and agree—rather than allow matters to rest upon the basis of custom of trade. If that custom is long established and judicially noticed then no doubt section 2 will be regarded as excluded, but something less than this weight of evidence will—in the absence of an express contractual term—be insufficient to supersede the operation of section 2 and Schedule 2.

(7) Finally, section 3 of the Act deals with the measure of damages in proceedings against employers. Where an employer fails to give the notice required by section 1 of the Act the rights conferred by section 2 (and Schedule 2) are to be taken into account [46] in assessing his liability for breach of contract. This section virtually prevents an award of double damages and at the same time points to the pursuer mitigating his own

---

[46] See the meaning of " taken into account " as stated by Devlin J. in *Flowers* v. *George Wimpey & Co. Ltd.* [1956] 1 Q.B. 73 at p. 87; [1955] 3 All E.R. 165 at p. 172. His lordship stated that the phrase meant an accurate calculation in the book-keeping sense.

loss—that is to say, he (pursuer) cannot expect to receive unrestricted damages.

The section 1 provisions, as well as sections 2 and 3, do not apply to registered dock workers (separately governed by a statute of 1946),[47] masters or seamen on seagoing British ships (80 gross registered tons or more), apprentices to the Sea Service in terms of section 108 of the Merchant Shipping Act 1894 and skippers or seamen of fishing boats registered under section 373 of the said Act of 1894.[48] Nor do sections 1, 2 and 3 (and section 4 also for that matter) apply in relation to any employment for any period when an employee is engaged in work wholly or mainly outside Great Britain, unless he ordinarily works in Great Britain and the work outside is for the same employer.[49] The interpretation section [50] makes it clear that an " employee " under the Act means " an individual who has entered into or works under a contract with an employer, whether the contract be for manual labour, clerical work or otherwise, be expressed or implied, oral or in writing, and whether it be a contract of service or of apprenticeship. . . ." This means that the statute—in accordance with modern tendencies in industrial legislation—applies both to white-collar workers and blue-collar workers.

Where insufficient notice is given this cannot operate to avoid the principle of tacit relocation, because such notice is completely worthless and might as well not have been given at all.[51] Where employment is during mutual pleasure and insufficient notice is given the employee's claim is for wages (and board wages, if appropriate) in lieu of notice, not damages. It is argued that an employee who accepts wages and departs quietly on dismissal without notice at the termination of his contract waives any claim he may have based upon inadequate notice.[52] But waiver of any such claim must not be readily inferred. Although an employee must leave quietly (even although unjustifiably dismissed) he is under no duty to intimate a claim for damages or compensation. It is quite useless for an employer to plead acquiescence by the employee and attempt to support that plea by saying that the employee left without protest or intimation of a claim.[53]

Tacit relocation. By reference to the law of leases, the Institutional Writers define [54] tacit relocation as a presumption in the mind of both parties to continue the lease, by mutual consent, upon the same terms and conditions as previously. This same principle is applied to the employer

[47] The Dock Workers (Regulation of Employment) Act 1946.
[48] 1963 Act, s. 6.
[49] *Ibid.* s. 9.
[50] s. 8.
[51] See *Anderson* v. *Wishart, cit. supra*; *Ross* v. *Pender*; and *Campbell* v. *Fyfe, cit. supra.*
[52] *Baird* v. *Don* (1779) 5 B.S. 514; but see M. 9182.
[53] *Ross* v. *Pender, cit. supra.*
[54] See Stair ii, 9, 22; Bank 2, 9, 33; Erskine II, 6, 35; Bell's *Principles*, s. 1265 (see also *Neilson* v. *Mossend Iron Co. Ltd.* (1886) 13 R.(H.L.) 50, *per* Lord Watson at p. 54).

and employee relationship and it sets up an implied contract to continue that relationship.[55]

If either party relies upon a different agreement then the implied contract would be inapplicable,[56] whilst a reference to new terms, not contained in the original agreement, would mean that the party who alleges the existence of these new terms would have to prove them.[57] This presumption of tacit relocation may also be based upon a lack of due notice or timeous warning of the termination of the contract being given. That is to say, the operative date for the giving of effective notice has passed and parties still continue to stand in the relationship of employer and employee.[58] However, the principle of tacit relocation cannot be applied to those contracts which do not require any form of notice or other warning to bring them to a conclusion.[59] The *Lennox* case [59] appears to indicate that there are three important elements in relation to the probable application of the tacit relocation principle, where there has been a lack of notice, namely: (a) a written contract, (b) an employee of the artisan class and (c) an unusual duration. As regards (a), the form of the original contract may be in writing or oral; the particular form does not affect tacit relocation. In the case of element (b), the rule seems to be that the doctrine only applies in those cases where warning is necessary,[60] as indicated above. So far as element (c) is concerned, it would appear that tacit relocation may follow upon a contract for any length of time, but not when the duration of the contract or any of the other conditions are of an unusual character in the class of employment, in which case the contract will conclude at the time mentioned without need for any notice.[61]

The legal effect of tacit relocation is that all the stipulations and conditions of the original contract remain in force, so far as these are not inconsistent with any implied term of the renewed contract.[62] But where employment is continued at different wages, or in a different character, it cannot be ascribed to tacit relocation.[63] The duration of the renewed contract may differ from that of the original one, though generally it will be the same, *e.g.*, the agricultural or domestic employee engaged for a year or for six months will, by tacit relocation, continue for a further year or for six months, as the case may be.[64] Tacit relocation is essentially

---

[55] See *Stanley Ltd.* v. *Hanway*, 1911, 2 S.L.T. 2; 48 S.L.R. 757 and the observations of the Lord President therein.

[56] *Sutherland's Trustees* v. *Miller's Tr.* (1888) 16 R. 10.

[57] *Tait* v. *McIntosh* (1841) 13 Sc.Jur. 180.

[58] See Erskine II, 6, 36; Bell's *Principles*, s. 173; *Baird* v. *Don* (1779) M. 9182; *Kelly* v. *Cowan's Exrs.* (1891) 7 Sh.Ct.Rep. 109; *Morrison* v. *Allardyce* (1823) 2 S. 387.

[59] *Lennox* v. *Allan & Son* (1880) 8 R. 38; *Brenan* v. *Campbell's Trs.* (1898) 25 R. 423; the opinion of L.J.-C. Moncreiff in *Lennox's* case (see particularly p. 40 of the report) is most instructive.

[60] Umpherston, p. 88 and cases there cited (nn. 3–12).

[61] *Brenan* v. *Campbell's Trs.* (1898) 25 R. 423; *Lennox* v. *Allan & Son* (1880) 8 R. 38; see also the opinion of Lord Robertson in *MacLean* v. *Fyfe*, February 4, 1813, F.C.

[62] *Neilson* v. *Mossend Iron Co.* (1886) 13 R.(H.L.) 50, *per* Lord Watson at p. 54.

[63] *Murray* v. *McGilchrist* (1863) 4 Irv. 461.

[64] *Kelly* v. *Cowan's Exrs.* (1891) 7 Sh.Ct.Rep. 109.

based upon custom and the extension of the particular contract will involve the application of a time addition which is customary for the particular type or character of service.

Tacit relocation can, of course, only apply where the parties to the new implied contract are the same as those who entered into the original agreement.   There can be no tacit relocation with a new employer.[65]

It has already been observed and explained, in the course of this chapter, that the Contracts of Employment Act 1963 introduced a statutory minimal protection to employees in relation to notice, but nevertheless the common law position was and is maintained in relation to contracts made between the parties which provide for notice in excess of the statutory minima and in relation to contracts which are not governed by section 1. The former group is by far the more important and the Scottish and English cases will still be helpful in giving some guidance as to how the test of reasonable notice is to be arrived at and applied between the parties.

In 1965 the important new principle of compensation for displaced workers was introduced by the Redundancy Payments Act.[66]   The payments are limited in amount and must not be thought of as equating the industrial worker with the " golden handshake " given to leaders of industry who are moved out of high-ranking appointments.   The basic intention is to tide the worker over until he is retrained for another job or, in the case of the more elderly employee, until he qualifies for his pension rights.   It is perhaps more appropriate to consider these redundancy payments as part of the law of wages or as an adjunct thereto and accordingly this whole question has been examined in some detail in the earlier chapter dealing with wages.[67]

---

[65] *Taylor* v. *Thomson* (1901) 9 S.L.T. (No. 313) 373; (1902) 10 S.L.T. 195; *Houston* v. *Calico Printers' Association* (1903) 10 S.L.T. 532.

[66] 1965, c. 62.

[67] *Supra,* Chap. 8.

CHAPTER 19

TERMINATION OF THE RELATIONSHIP OF EMPLOYER AND EMPLOYEE OTHER THAN BY NOTICE

WE have already considered the question of the normal duration of the contract of employment and the normal manner in which it is terminated.[1] However, it may well happen, and very often does, that the relationship is terminated in a manner other than that contemplated originally by the parties, *e.g.*, death, illness or other unforeseen event. Sometimes the happening may amount to a breach of contract by one or other party. Sometimes neither may be at fault. Although the general law of contract applies it is necessary to examine certain of these methods which are most commonly met with in the area of employment and, accordingly, termination by death, insolvency, dissolution of firm or company, dismissal of employee, illness, marriage of employee, imprisonment of employee and termination by the court must now be considered. Before examining each of these in turn, termination by lapse of time and by consent must be noted.

(1) *Expiry of Time*

Where the parties have agreed expressly that the contractual relationship of employer and employee is to exist for a definite period of time, there is no doubt that the relationship continues in being for that time and the contract expires at the conclusion of the agreed period. The original contract may be replaced by a new written agreement or by an implied contract, set up by tacit relocation. Where the contract is not in express terms, the court will consider the presumed intention of the parties and, as aids to ascertaining this intention, they will also consider the custom of the particular trade or of the particular locality. Where notice has to be given to terminate a particular contract then this should always be done, otherwise (as explained in the preceding chapter) tacit relocation may apply to continue the contract for a further period corresponding with the original contract.

(2) *Consent*

The contract may also be terminated by the consent of the parties, whether expressly or impliedly from the manner in which they behave towards each other.[2] Where an employer is told that his employee intends to

---

[1] *Supra*, Chap. 18.
[2] *Ferguson* v. *McKenzie* (1815) Hume's Decis. 21; *Robinson* v. *Smith & Co.* (1800) Hume's Decis. 20.

leave and thereupon he (the employer) acts in such manner as to indicate an assent to the employee's departure then an implied consent to the termination has been given. Once the employee intimates his resignation and this is accepted by his employer, he may be dismissed and he has no claim for damages—even although he attempted to retract his resignation shortly after making it.[3]

(3) Death

The death of either party dissolves the contractual relationship of employer and employee. Death never operates as a breach of contract— it is a factual circumstance which prevents performance.[4] The executors of a deceased employee are able to recover from his employers the pro- portion of wages for the time he had served from the last payment of wages to the date of death.[5] Where the employee has been employed on piecework, then the employer's liability is to pay for so much of the work as has been done. Where the employee was in occupation of a dwelling- house (a " tied " house) by virtue of his employment, then upon his death the occupancy right terminates [6] and the employer may re-possess.[7]

Upon the employer's death the liability to pay wages does not neces- sarily cease and such wages become a competent charge against the estate; e.g., where a domestic or other employee is hired for a term he or she continues in the employment of the family until the following term or perhaps the next term after that if death occurred within the notice period and no notice of termination had been given.[8] Any prior dismissal of the employee would give him a right to claim wages from the estate (and also board wages, if appropriate).[9] However, the employee cannot then sit back and do nothing—he must seek another situation. Wages earned in his new situation are taken into account in computing the liability of his late employer's estate for outstanding wages and mainten- ance.[10] Should the domestic employee have been hired for a year, instead of half-yearly term, then it seems that she is able to claim maintenance until the end of that year, if the employer has died within the yearly period.[11] In all other cases, provided the hiring period is definite, the principle is still the same. When wages accrue periodically the employee becomes entitled to wages for the whole period current at death.[12]

It seems that if the representatives of a deceased employer make an offer to employ any employee until the completion of the term, at the

---

[3] *Peter* v. *Glasgow Millboard Co.* (1875) 13 S.L.R. 127.
[4] *Hoey* v. *M'Ewan and Auld* (1867) 5 M. 814.
[5] Erskine III, 3, 16; Bell's *Principles*, s. 179.
[6] See particularly *Dunbar's Trustees* v. *Bruce* (1900) 3 F. 137; *Aitchison* v. *Lothian* (1890) 18 R. 337.
[7] *Torrance* v. *Traill's Trustees* (1897) 24 R. 837.
[8] *Hoey* v. *M'Ewan and Auld, cit. supra, per* Lord Deas at p. 818.
[9] Bell's *Principles*, s. 186; Fraser, *Master and Servant*, p. 143; *Shepherd* v. *Meldrum* (1812) Hume 394.
[10] *Hoey* v. *M'Ewan and Auld, cit. supra; Kelly* v. *Cowan's Exrs.* (1891) 7 Sh.Ct.Rep. 109.
[11] *Muir* v. *M'Kenzie* (1829) 7 S. 717.
[12] See *Hoey* v. *M'Ewan and Auld, supra.*

same work and at the same rate of wages, this would be a good defence
to a claim for wages for the balance of the term.[13] This is perhaps another
application of the rule that the employee cannot sit back and do nothing.
In those cases where the employment is during pleasure, it would appear
that the death of the employer is equivalent to notice and, accordingly, if
the employee continues to serve the late employer's representatives or
successors then it may well be that a new contract is implied. The terms
of this new contract will fall to be deduced from the actings of parties.[14]

The common law gave to certain classes of employee, on the death of
their employer, a certain preference for wages, *viz.*, the executor was
entitled to pay them within the six months' period after death, without
constitution of the debt.[15] According to Mr. Bell,[16] the effect of this was
that if the employer died insolvent the employee's wages are privileged as
on his bankruptcy, the date of death being substituted for that of bankruptcy.

(4) *Employer's Insolvency and Sequestration* (*or Bankruptcy*)

The insolvency or sequestration (**bankruptcy**) of the employer terminates the contract of service, even though it is involuntary. The
ground of termination is that the fact of bankruptcy itself constitutes a
breach of the contract.[17] Consequently the employee is now entitled to a
claim in damages for the breach—it is not a claim for wages in respect of
the balance period of the contract.[18] In the case of a limited company,
there is authority for the principle that an order for its liquidation (or
winding up) amounts to constructive notice to all employees, with the
result that they may leave at once; they need not remain after notice,
unless the company as employer is able to pay full wages during the period
of notice.[19] Where the liquidation (or winding up) is voluntary it seems
that the resolution to liquidate has a similar effect, *i.e.*, it operates as
constructive notice.[20] As regards the operative date, the better opinion
seems to be that this is the date of publication of the *Gazette* notice and
not the date of the resolution itself.[21] The sum which the employee
receives is an amount representing wages in lieu of notice. English law
appears to regard the payment as damages as for wrongful dismissal. It
is always open to the liquidator and the employees to waive the notice, so
long as it is quite clear what their intentions are, *i.e.*, that there is an un-
mistakable consensus to waive the notice.[22] The liquidator may convert

---

[13] See opinions in *Ross* v. *M'Farlane* (1894) 21 R. 396.
[14] Umpherston, *Master and Servant*, p. 92.
[15] Stair, iii, 8, 64, 72; Erskine III, 9, 43; Bell's *Principles*, s. 1404; *Commentaries* ii, 149.
[16] *Principles*, s. 186.
[17] Bell's *Principles*, s. 185; *Puncheon* v. *Haig's Trs.* (1790) M. 13, 990; *Hoey* v. *M'Ewan and Auld* (1867) 5 M. 814, *per* Lord President (Inglis); *Day* v. *Tait* (1900) 8 S.L.T. 40.
[18] *Puncheon* v. *Haig's Trs., cit. supra*.
[19] *Day* v. *Tait, cit. supra*; *Chapman's Case* (1866) L.R. 1 Eq. 346; *MacDowall's Case* (1886) 32 Ch.D. 366; *Laing* v. *Gowans* (1902) 10 S.L.T. 461.
[20] The authority on this is mainly English—*vide Shirreff's Case* (1872) L.R. 14 Eq. 417; *Ex parte Schumann* (1887) L.R. 19 Ir. 240 is also helpful.
[21] *Vide Chapman's Case* (1866) L.R. 1 Eq. 346.
[22] *Per* Chitty J. in *MacDowall's* case, *cit. supra*.

the constructive notice into actual notice—and it appears that he might then be entitled to obtain from the employee his normal service until the notice period expires, so long as he can pay the correct rate of wages and make available the right type of work.[23]   It will be appreciated that the decisions point towards the ascertainment as a question of fact, in cases where the liquidator continues the business, whether the employees are working under a new contract or whether the employees are continuing to complete the period under the original contract, which is now defined by the constructive notice.[24]

When sequestration (bankruptcy) or liquidation arises, the employees have certain privileges or preferences in respect of wages, both at common law and by statute.   It is necessary to examine each.   At common law, a preference or privilege is given " for the term's wages, but not for board, which is not wages." [25]   This relates to wages for the term current at the employer's death or bankruptcy irrespective of whether the " term " be a year or half-year or some other period.[26]   Now, the important point is that this privilege seems to arise only in favour of the domestic and the agricultural employee.[27]   Perhaps the most interesting feature about it, however, is that it is not simply applicable to employees taken on at Whitsunday or Martinmas or to those engaged in regular employment.   It also covers casual employees (of the classes stipulated), taken on at irregular times and for short periods, so long as they are in employment at the date of death or bankruptcy.[28]   It may, of course, be a very difficult point to decide who is a domestic and who is an agricultural employee.   There is no hard and fast rule or precise formula for arriving at a decision.   Some of the older cases give some help in this matter.[29]   The court may tend to take a liberal view where the employee performs a dual task.[30]   The term for which the wages are preferred is that current at the date of death or bankruptcy as the case may be.   It has been held in the sheriff court that the term " bankruptcy " as used here does not necessarily mean or refer to either sequestration or notour bankruptcy but may mean insolvency and stoppage of payment.[31]   Accordingly, the privilege arising at that

---

[23] *Per* Lord Stormonth Darling in *Day* v. *Tait, cit. supra.*

[24] *Day* v. *Tait, cit. supra; MacDowall's* case, *cit. supra; Reid* v. *Explosives Co. Ltd.* (1887) 19 Q.B.D. 264; *Ex parte Harding* (1867) L.R. 3 Eq. 341.

[25] Bell's *Principles,* s. 186.

[26] Bell's *Principles,* ss. 186, 1404; Erskine III, 9, 43; *Crawford* v. *Hutton* (1680) Mor. 11, 832; Stair, iii, 8, 64, 72; Bell's Com. ii, 149; Bank 1, 2, 55.

[27] Bell's *Principles,* s. 1404; *Marshall* v. *Philip* (1828) 6 S. 515; Fraser, *Master and Servant,* p. 145.

[28] *Lockhart* v. *Paterson* (1804) Mor. (*voce* " Private Debt," App. ii).

[29] See *Melvil* v. *Barclay* (1779) Mor. 11, 853 (" servants kept for the purposes of the farm " were privileged); *White* v. *Christie* (1781) Mor. 11, 853 (servants on the farm were entitled to the privilege; others employed in the trade of wright were not); see also *Ridley* v. *Haigs Crs.* (1789) Mor. 11, 854 and *Marshall* v. *Philip, cit. supra; Maben* v. *Perkins* (1837) 15 S. 1087.

[30] *e.g.,* in *M'Lean* v. *Shireffs* (1832) 10 S. 217, where an employee was engaged as a gardener but also did some agricultural duties—the privilege was extended to him. The question of whether a gardener was a domestic employee or not was reserved. On this point the Lord President (Hope) was non-committal.

[31] *Watt* v. *Mackie's Trs.* (1885) 1 Sh.Ct.Rep. 219.

date is not lost by expiry of the term of employment before sequestration.[32]

The position by statute law must now be considered briefly. Initially the matter was dealt with by the Bankruptcy (Scotland) Act 1856, s. 122, and thereafter by the Bankruptcy (Scotland) Act 1875, s. 3, taken in conjunction with the Preferential Payments in Bankruptcy Act 1888 (which seems to have been basically an English Act, but may also have been applicable to Scotland [33]). Thereafter, it appears in the Bankruptcy (Scotland) Act 1913 and the Companies Act 1948. The relevant provisions of these statutes may be briefly summarised, viz.:

In the Bankruptcy (Scotland) Act 1913, the section which deals with preferential payments is section 118. A priority is created over all other debts in respect of:

(a) all poor or other local rates and land tax, property tax and income tax for a period of twelve months prior to the sequestration date;

(b) all wages or salary of any clerk or employee in respect of employment rendered to the bankrupt during four months before the date of the sequestration award, not exceeding £50 to any one clerk or employee; and

(c) all wages of any workman or labourer, not exceeding £25 to any one workman or labourer, whether payable for time or piece-work, in respect of services rendered to the bankrupt during two months before the said date of sequestration.[34]

In addition to the above, the National Insurance (Industrial Injuries) employers' contribution for a twelve months' period and also contributions as an employer or employee under the National Insurance Acts were to be regarded as preferential. All of the foregoing were to rank *pari passu* and were to be paid in full, unless the assets were insufficient to meet them, in which case they were to abate in equal proportions.

In the case of the company employer going into liquidation, the relevant section is section 319 of the Companies Act 1948, which follows broadly the pattern of section 118 of the Bankruptcy (Scotland) Act 1913. Briefly, section 319 creates a priority for payment of the following debts:

(a) rates and taxes (*e.g.*, local rates, land tax, income tax, profits tax, purchase tax); and

(b) all wages or salary of any clerk or employee during the four months prior to the relevant date (appointment of a provisional liquidator or of the winding-up order in a compulsory liquidation or winding-up; otherwise the date of the passing of the resolution for the winding-up) and all wages

---

[32] *Templeton & Son* v. *M'Kenna* (1896) 12 Sh.Ct.Rep. 99; *Ex parte Sanders* (1836) 2 Mont. & A. 684.

[33] See Umpherston, *Master and Servant*, pp. 100–101 and, in particular, the cases cited at nn. 5 and 6 to p. 100.

[34] S. 118 generally was extended by 11 & 12 Geo. 6, c. 64, s. 56 (*b*)—*viz.*, the National Service Act 1948 (on a question of compensation); s. 118 (1) was extended by 3 & 4 Geo. 6, c. 32, s. 8 (2), and 5 & 6 Geo. 6, c. 21, s. 20 (1) (4)—*viz.*, the Finance Act 1942 on a question of purchase tax; and 7 & 8 Geo. 6, c. 15, s. 21—*viz.*, the Reinstatement in Civil Employment Act 1944 as amended by 10 & 11 Geo. 6, c. 47, s. 115 (1), *viz.*, the Companies Act 1947.

of any workman or labourer in respect of services rendered for a like period.   In addition, any sum ordered to be paid under the Reinstatement in Civil Employment Act 1944 (and later legislation thereanent) or accrued holiday pay, national health insurance and industrial injuries insurance contributions of the employer (for the 12 months' period), workmen's compensation payments and so on, must also be given a preferential treatment but the limit applied is £200 for each claimant under paras. (a) to (g) of section 319 (1).[35]   All of these debts are again to rank *pari passu* and to be paid in full, unless the assets are insufficient, in which case they are to abate in equal proportions.   There is a special exception under section 319 (9) where the relevant date defined in section 264 (7) of the Companies Act 1919 occurred before the commencement of the 1948 Act.[36]

The definitions of the terms " clerks and shopmen and employees " and " workmen " contained in the 1875 Act and of the terms " clerk or servant," " labourer or workman " and " labourer in husbandry " contained in the 1888 Act had occasioned, particularly in the later statute, some consideration and litigation.[37]

This matter became of little or no importance with the passing of the Bankruptcy (Scotland) Act 1913, as section 118 (6) makes it clear that the Preferential Payments in Bankruptcy Act 1888 was not to apply to Scotland and, moreover, references to that Act or to section 3 of the Bankruptcy (Scotland) Act 1875, in any Act of Parliament, were, as regards Scotland, to be read and construed as references to section 118 of the 1913 Act.   There is authority in an old case [38] that the preference of the farm-servant's wages prevailed over the landlord's hypothec for rent.   The textwriters tended to favour this view.[39]   Mr. Umpherston explains [40] that the decisions in the sheriff court are contradictory and that there was no Court of Session judgment to give any help on the point, although there was a tendency to prefer such a type of debt as servant's wages.

(5) *Dissolution of Firm*

The position in Scots law [41] seems to be that where a contract of employment is entered into between a person and a firm, in the firm's name, the contract is with the firm and not with the individual partners.   Accordingly, a dissolution of the firm would involve the employees in no obligation towards the partners as such.   The foregoing statement cannot be accepted in absolute terms and falls to be qualified in certain respects as hereafter mentioned.

[35] Companies Act 1948, s. 319 (2).   The 1948 Act was considerably amended in many other respects by the Companies Act 1967 (c. 81).
[36] S. 319 was amended by 15 & 16 Geo. 6 & 1 Eliz. 2, c. 33 (the Finance Act 1952), s. 30; and also by 9 & 10 Eliz. 2, c. 46, s. 7 (the Companies (Floating Charges) (Scotland) Act 1961).
[37] See Umpherston, *Master and Servant*, pp. 101–102 and cases there cited.
[38] *M'Glashan* v. *Duke of Athole*, June 29, 1819, F.C.; Bell on *Leases*, 1, p. 411 n.
[39] Fraser, *Master and Servant*, pp. 148–150; Goudy on *Bankruptcy*, p. 563; Hunter on *Landlord and Tenant*, Vol. 2, p. 408, n. (4); Rankine on *Leases*, p. 358.
[40] p. 103 and n. 6 thereto.
[41] Umpherston, *op. cit.* p. 92.

If dissolution occurs because of the death of one partner, the contract does not in theory subsist against the remaining partners.[42] There is no legal breach of contract but a failure of performance (or frustration)— and the parties' rights are determined in the same way as upon the employer's death.[43] The firm may, of course, be dissolved for other reasons, e.g., retiral of elderly partners and the assumption of new and younger ones. This is not quite the same situation as arises upon the death of a partner. Certainly each case involves a technical dissolution of an existing firm and the creation of a new one (i.e., substituting one *persona* for another). But, if the alteration does not prevent the parties to the contract of employment from performing their respective duties to one another then the *delectus personae* element is not affected to any appreciable extent. Technically and theoretically, there may well be no real foundation for anyone leaving the employment and claiming damages [44] although it is argued that in certain circumstances the employee might be able to claim from the retiring partners a guarantee or indemnity against any loss arising from the changed situation.[45] In one case, [46] two new partners were taken on by the defender (Smith), whom the pursuer (Harkins) had agreed to serve for a period of five years as works manager, during the subsistence of the contract of service. The pursuer left the service and claimed the balance of salary for the remainder of the term, basing his claim upon the ground that the introduction of two new partners constituted a breach of contract. The court held that the defender had not committed any breach which would have allowed the pursuer to leave and claim damages. Had the defender left the business altogether or transferred it to the two new persons themselves then that would have been quite a different matter [47]; because the defender would then have been unable to perform the obligations which he had undertaken towards the pursuer. The legal point decided by the case just mentioned is that an artisan employee is not able to sue his employer in breach of contract upon the ground that his employer had assumed partners into the business.[48] Mr. Umpherston suggests [49] that probably the more correct ground for the decision would have been that, allowing that a technical breach had occurred, the employee was not entitled to leave the employment and claim damages. A great deal will depend upon the personal relationship between employees and their employers.

---

[42] *Hoey* v. *MacEwan and Auld* (1867) 5 M. 814; *Tasker* v. *Shepherd*, 6 H. & N. 575.
[43] *Hoey* v. *MacEwan and Auld, cit. supra.*
[44] See *Young* v. *Brown & Co.* (1785) 3 Pat.App. 42 (apprenticeship indenture); but compare *Brace* v. *Calder* [1895] 2 Q.B. 253; *cf. Robson* v. *Drummond* (1831) 2 B. & A. 303; and see also Lord McLaren's remarks in *Berlitz School of Languages* v. *Duchêne* (1903) 6 F. 181.
[45] *Ross* v. *M'Farlane* (1894) 21 R. 396; *Brace* v. *Calder* [1895] 2 Q.B. 253.
[46] *Harkins* v. *Smith*, March 11, 1841, F.C.
[47] See *Ross* v. *M'Farlane* (1894) 21 R. 396.
[48] See the Lord Ordinary's opinion: " Artisan servants . . . are not warranted by law in holding that their employers violate their contract . . . by the mere act of introducing a new partner."
[49] *Op. cit.* p. 94.

(6) *Employee's Dismissal* (*including Summary Dismissal*)

In this case the contractual relationship is being terminated by the employer before it runs its full course. It has always been accepted that the employer is entitled to dismiss an employee at any time upon payment of wages to the end of the term.[50] Mr. Umpherston takes the view [51] that the employee has a correlative right to leave at any time upon the payment of a sum equivalent to damages and that these rights taken together differentiate the employer and employee relationship from the master and slave relationship. The courts will certainly not order or enforce the specific implement of a personal contract between free parties.

Dismissal becomes unjustifiable when it occurs without payment of wages and without good cause. It is necessary, therefore, to look at the quality and character of the dismissal to decide whether it is lawful or not. It must be noted at once that in all those cases which we are considering under this heading wages will not have been paid for the unexpired portion of the term. Obviously, if this had been done, no question could arise as to the legality or otherwise of the dismissal. Where the parties have been involved in some heated argument or difference of opinion it may be very difficult to determine whether the employee was dismissed or whether he departed voluntarily. The question is one of fact.[52] The employer may, by his actings, allow an employee to stay on and thereafter attempt to dismiss him or replace him but then be unjustified in so doing.[53] If the contract itself contains specific conditions as to its termination then the sole test is compliance with the conditions contained in the agreement of parties.[54] No question of justifiability can arise and no reason needs to be given for the dismissal.[55] No action in damages for wrongful dismissal will lie in such a case. But the conditions stipulated in the agreement of parties do not conflict in any respect with the employer's right of dismissal for misconduct or other cause.[56]

Although dismissal may be justified it need not operate immediately. It may suit the employer (and the employee) to allow the employee to work to a time notice (quite apart from and not to be confused with the length of notice which would have operated had the contract been fully performed) and the employee will receive wages for the period during which he has worked.[57] There is, of course, no duty or obligation upon either side to make or accept this agreement. When dismissal (whether justifiable or not) operates, the employee is obliged to leave quietly. He has no right

---

[50] *Graham* v. *Thomson* (1822) 1 S. 287; *Mollison* v. *Baillie* (1885) 22 S.L.R. 595.
[51] *Op. cit.* p. 104.
[52] Umpherston, *op. cit.* p. 105 and cases cited at n. 1 thereof; also *Pepper* v. *Webb* (1969) VI K.I.R. 109.
[53] See *Campbell* v. *MacKenzie* (1887) 24 S.L.R. 354.
[54] *Pollock's Trs.* v. *Commercial Banking Co.* (1822) 1 S. 428; *Mitchell* v. *Smith*, (1836) 14 S. 358; *Mollison* v. *Baillie* (1885) 22 S.L.R. 595; *Barkley* v. *Prudential Assce. Co.* (1896) 13 Sh.Ct.Rep. 71; *Finlay* v. *Royal Liver Friendly Society* (1901) 4 F. 34.
[55] See *Taylor* v. *Smith*, 1909, 1 S.L.T. 453 (O.H.).
[56] See *Silvie* v. *Stewart* (1830) 8 S. 1010.
[57] *Thomson* v. *Stewart* (1888) 15 R. 806; *Scott* v. *M'Murdo* (1869) 6 S.L.R. 301.

to stay on, by relying upon an alleged illegal dismissal.[58] At the same time, if he is in occupation of a dwelling-house *qua* employee then he must relinquish this. He must also hand back or assign (where appropriate) to the employer any property or rights therein acquired during the employment.[59] When an employee is unlawfully dismissed he does not have to make a reservation of his claim or intimate to the employer that he does not acquiesce.[60] His claim against the employer is reserved by law, where he departs quietly in compliance with the obligation so to do.

The important question now to be considered is—whether the dismissal is justified or not ? The employer can dismiss summarily (that is to say, without paying wages for an unexpired period) an employee only when the latter has committed a breach of contract and then, of course, the dismissal is legal. If the dismissal is illegal, the employer himself is in breach of the contract.[61] Those actings which involve summary dismissal of the employee have been classified as " moral misconduct (either pecuniary or otherwise), wilful disobedience or habitual neglect." [62]

It is perhaps more convenient to examine them (as Mr. Umpherston does) [63] under the following divisions, *viz.*:

(a) Disobedience and want of respect;

(b) Dishonesty, drunkenness, insubordination and other misconduct; and

(c) Incompetence, general neglect and absence from work.

(a) *Disobedience and want of respect.* The best example of disobedience is the wilful and direct refusal by the employee to obey a peremptory and lawful order from the employer (or his authorised agent) or the deliberate carrying out by the employee of an act which is expressly forbidden by the employer (or his authorised agent). Such conduct inverts the position of the employee. Accordingly, this type of conduct justifies immediate dismissal.[64] The English courts take the view that wilful disobedience justifies dismissal provided the order given is a reasonable one.[65] The general circumstances, in cases other than the foregoing, must be looked at very carefully. It may be that dismissal was too harsh a step to take

---

[58] See *Ross* v. *Pender* (1874) 1 R. 352; *First Edinburgh, etc., Building Society* v. *Munro* (1884) 21 S.L.R. 291.

[59] See *Clift* v. *Portobello Pier Co.* (1877) 4 R. 462; also see *Hawick Heritable Investment Bank* v. *Huggan* (1902) 5 F. 75.

[60] *Ross* v. *Pender, supra; Baird* v. *Don* (1779) 5 B.S. 514, Mor. 9182; *Batchelor* v. *M'Gilvray* (1831) 9 S. 549.

[61] See *Finlayson* v. *M'Kenzie* (1829) 7 S. 717; *Batchelor* v. *M'Gilvray* (1831) 9 S. 549; and *Wilson* v. *Anthony*, 1958 S.L.T.(Sh.Ct.) 13; (1957) 73 Sh.Ct.Rep. 298.

[62] *Per* Parke J. in *Callo* v. *Brouncker* (1831) 4 C. & P. 518.

[63] *Op. cit.* p. 108. See also the valuable new work by Professor Alfred Avins on *Employees' Misconduct* (Law Book Co., Allahabad; 1968).

[64] *Wilson* v. *Simson* (1844) 6 D. 1256; *A.* v. *B.* (1853) 16 D. 269, 26 J. 129; *Hamilton* v. *M'Lean* (1824) 3 S. 268; *Cobban* v. *Lawson* (1868) 6 S.L.R. 60; *M'Kellar* v. *M'Farlane* (1852) 15 D. 246; *Trotters* v. *Briggs* (1897) 5 S.L.T. 17.

[65] See *Turner* v. *Mason* (1845) 14 M. & W. 112; see also *Reid* v. *Lindsay Crawford* (*Lady M.*) (1822) 1 Shaw's App. 124, where the employer was held entitled to dismiss a gardener who had been absent from his service without leave for four days.

and that a warning or reprimand from the employer was perfectly adequate.[66] In general, the court will tend not to interfere with the employer's discretion to dismiss, unless the employee was entitled to refuse to obey the particular order or unless the court was satisfied that the plea of disobedience was merely used as a pretext for getting rid of the employee or unless the employer's act was too harsh and oppressive in the circumstances.

An employer cannot lawfully dismiss an employee for refusing to obey an order which the employer has no right to give or which the employee was perfectly entitled to refuse to comply with in the circumstances (e.g., if personal danger is involved). Again, the employer may give the order in such a way that he shows little consideration for the employee, who is provoked into refusing. In such a case the employer is barred from founding upon the disobedience to the extent of instant dismissal,[67] but this case is an exceptional one. The corresponding duty upon an employee is to treat his employer (including his authorised representatives) with deference and respect, even in these modern times when respect for authority or seniority seems to be no longer a basic virtue. The ideal situation is to have mutual trust and mutual respect between employer and employee. The degree of deference owed by employees will vary according to the type or character of their employment, e.g., there is a world of difference between the domestic employee and, say, the highly qualified works manager of a large shipbuilding and engineering establishment. This means a distinction by skill and qualification—not by social class. Accordingly, the want of respect which will justify an employer in dismissing an employee is always a question of degree and circumstances. No employer need tolerate gross insolence.[68] Any combination of disobedience and disrespectful conduct, which amounts in fact to insolence, will justify dismissal.[69] It seems to be accepted that an employer will not be justified in dismissing an employee for one single act of disrespect, so long as it does not amount to gross insolence (what constitutes this being always a question of circumstances).[70] Continued disrespect will certainly enable the employer to exercise his discretion and dismiss the employee.

(b) *Dishonesty, drunkenness, insubordination and other misconduct.* Misconduct justifying dismissal (and its type and degree may be both

---

[66] See *per* L.J.-C. Moncreiff in *Thomson* v. *Stewart* (1888) 15 R. 806; see also *Thomson* v. *Douglas* (1807) Hume 392 (the gardener who was absent from his work on one occasion, without leave; this being his first fault, his employer was held not justified in dismissing him).

[67] *Greig* v. *Moir* (1892) 9 Sh.Ct.Rep. 341.

[68] *Dobbie* v. *Cross* (1895) 12 Sh.Ct.Rep. 246; *Pepper* v. *Webb, cit. supra.*

[69] *Elder* v. *Bennet* (1802) Hume 386; *Silvie* v. *Stewart* (1830) 8 S. 1010; *Callo* v. *Brouncker, supra*; *Stewart* v. *Crichton* (1847) 9 D. 1042; *Scott* v. *M'Murdo* (1869) 6 S.L.R. 301.

[70] See *Ridgway* v. *Hungerford Market Co.* (1835) 3 A. & E. 171 and *Edwards* v. *Levy* (1860) 2 F. & F. 94; also *Laws* v *London Chronicle (Indicator Newspapers) Limited* [1959] 1 W.L.R. 698—showing reluctance of the courts in these modern times, to regard a single act of disobedience as justifying dismissal.

difficult to decide upon and the conclusion be a very narrow one indeed) need not involve moral turpitude so long as it involves a failure in duty by the employee. If the misconduct is prior to the contract this cannot justify dismissal [71] for two very good reasons (i) because the duty cannot arise until the contract is made and (ii) there is no general duty of disclosure on the prospective employee apart from specific inquiries. Once the contract has been completed and employment entered upon, the misconduct may take place either during working hours or outwith them. [72] So far as domestic and personal (*i.e.*, family rather than purely business) employees are concerned, the accepted principle would seem to be that dismissal is justified by misconduct which interferes with the proper discharge of duties or which disturbs the harmony of the family home or which adversely affects the morals of the household. In the case of the employee engaged in a business or profession, the misconduct necessary to justify dismissal would be, again, such as interfered with the proper performance of duties or such as would be calculated to injure the business of the employer. It is important to note that it is quite enough for the conduct to be prejudicial, or be likely to be prejudicial, to the business reputation or business interests of the employer. [73]

Any act of dishonesty (*e.g.*, theft) or destruction of the employer's property justifies dismissal, whether or not the employee has been convicted by the appropriate criminal court. [74] The number of cases involving misconduct of a minor nature but nevertheless sufficient to justify dismissal is large, as can be expected. A selection of these is noted below. [75]

Drunkenness is quite a common ground for dismissal, particularly if it is an aggravated case (both as to the degree of drunkenness and the occasion upon which it occurred or either of these). Then there is no real difficulty in justifying dismissal. [76] It seems doubtful whether the employer can dismiss an employee for a single instance of drunkenness, unless it is aggravated by the occasion upon which it takes place. [77] Habitual drunkenness is most certainly a good ground for dismissing the personal or domestic employee and also for dismissing the business or

---

[71] Fraser, *Master and Servant*, p. 85; *Fletcher* v. *Knell* (1872) 42 L.J.Q.B. 55; *Andrews* v. *Garstin* (1861) 31 L.J.C.P. 15; and *K.* v. *Raschen* (1878) 38 L.T. 38.

[72] *Read* v. *Dunsmore* (1840) 9 C. & P. 588.

[73] *Pearce* v. *Foster* (1886) 17 Q.B.D. 536, per Lopes L.J.; *Lacy* v. *Osbaldiston* (1837) 8 C. & P. 80.

[74] *Maxwell* v. *Buchanan* (1776) Mor. 593, App.; *voce* Apprentice, 1; *Sharp* v. *Rettie* (1884) 11 R. 745 (averments of damage to ship's machinery caused by engineer's neglect of duty).

[75] *Malloch* v. *Duffy* (1882) 19 S.L.R. 697 (soliciting business from the employer's customers); *Wight* v. *Ewing* (1828) 4 Mur. 584 (cheating the customers); *Amor* v. *Fearon* (1839) 1 P. & D. 398 and (1839) 9 A. & E. 548 (employee claiming he was a partner); *Pearce* v. *Foster* (1886) 17 Q.B.D. 536 (Stock Exchange Clerk speculating); *Baillie* v. *Kell* (1838) 4 Bing. 638 (false entries in the books); *Horton* v. *M'Murtry* (1860) 5 H. & N. 667 (false statements to employer); *Boston Fishing Co.* v. *Ansell* (1888) 39 Ch.D. 339 (secret commissions); *Blenkarn* v. *Hodge's Distillery Co. Ltd.* (1867) 16 L.T. 608 (traveller supplying goods to a married woman who kept a brothel and from whom payment could not be recovered); *Bray* v. *Chandler* (1856) 18 C.B. 718 (agent receiving money, contrary to his express instructions).

[76] See *Edwards* v. *Mackie* (1848) 11 D. 67; *Watson* v. *Noble* (1885) 13 R. 347.

[77] See *per* Lord Mackenzie in *Wise* v. *Wilson* (1844) 1 C. & K. 662.

professional employee, where such inebriation occurs during working hours or if it causes irregularity in attendance or otherwise interferes with the proper performance of duties by the employee.

Any insubordination occasioned by an employee who is creating a disturbance or arguing with other employees seems also to form a good ground for dismissal.[78] The circumstances must be looked at carefully in such cases as these and the propriety of the act itself is very much a matter for the employer's discretion. There is no doubt that immorality is a valid ground for dismissing the personal (including family and domestic) employee.[79] It may also be so in the case of other employees. The employer does not seem to have any legal right to insist upon the medical examination of an employee whom he suspects to be pregnant.[80]

(c) *Incompetence, general neglect and absence from work.* There is always an implied term in the contract that the employee is (i) reasonably competent to discharge the duties which he undertakes and (ii) ready and willing to render the particular services. Should it turn out that the employee is incompetent or is guilty of a wilful refusal or omission to serve then the employer may dismiss him, as there has been a breach of contract on the employee's part.[81] If, however, the employer, knowing that the potential employee does not have the capacity of the particular job, nevertheless takes him on then he is debarred from dismissing him on the ground of incompetence.[82] It will be appreciated that the employee must show reasonable skill and reasonable diligence. His skill need not be that of the expert nor is he required to guarantee success to the employer in every facet of his task.[83]

Habitual neglect certainly justifies dismissal, as does a single case of gross neglect.[84] It has been held that a single act of forgetfulness or neglect, causing serious damage to valuable machinery, was a sufficient reason to justify immediate dismissal.[85]

Absence from work during recognised hours of employment, without leave or good excuse, also forms a good ground for dismissal. It may be necessary to decide what is meant by " recognised hours of employment." In the case of the personal employee no particular hours may be specified and, therefore, any unpermitted absence will require a sufficient reason. In other cases, the hours may be stipulated in the particular contract or agreement between the parties or may be decided by reference to a collective agreement whose terms are followed in practice or by reference to

---

[78] *Trotters* v. *Briggs* (1897) 5 S.L.T. 17; *Churchward* v. *Chambers* (1860) 2 F. & F. 229.
[79] See *Matheson* v. *Mackinnon* (1832) 10 S. 825; *De Grasbert* (1765) 16 Mor. 456; *Connors* v. *Justice* (1862) 13 Ir.C.L.R. 451; *Atkin* v. *Acton* (1830) 4 C. & P. 208; *Greig* v. *Sanderson* (1864) 2 M. 1278.
[80] *Latter* v. *Braddell* (1881) 50 L.J.(Q.B.) 448.
[81] *Sharp* v. *Rettie* (1884) 11 R. 745; *Cuckson* v. *Stones* (1858) 1 E. & E. 248; *Harmer* v. *Cornelius* (1858) 5 C.B.(N.S.) 236; *Searle* v. *Ridley* (1873) 28 L.T. 411.
[82] *Gunn* v. *Ramsay* (1801) Hume 384.
[83] *Dowling* v. *Henderson* (1890) 17 R. 921.
[84] *Campbell* v. *Price* (1831) 9 S. 264.
[85] *Baster* v. *London and County Printing Works* [1890] 1 Q.B. 901.

trade custom or local custom. It has been held, in the mining industry, that dismissal for absence may take place where a workman has undertaken to work so many days per fortnight and fails to complete the required number.[86] What particular absence justifies dismissal of the employee is entirely a matter of the circumstances, e.g., if a head gardener absents himself for four days then his dismissal is justified [87]; similarly, the apprentice who attends irregularly, is habitually late and wastes time whilst on errands for his employer, may also justifiably be dismissed.[88] The circumstances in question are (a) the nature of the employment to be given to the employer and (b) the trouble and inconvenience likely to be occasioned to the employer by the absence.

The employer is not, however, entitled to dismiss an employee because a member of the latter's family is suffering from an infectious disease.[89] Neither can he dismiss an employee merely because he is ill.[90] It may be, though, that the employer is within his rights in refusing to allow an employee to work where there is a danger of the spreading of disease.[91] If it can be shown that the employee was under a duty to stay away, then it would appear that the case is equated with the situation where the employee cannot work because of his own illness.[92]

It seems, as a matter of principle, that an employer is not entitled to dismiss a workman because he refuses to join the trade union to which his other employees belong. Should the trade union in question threaten to call out the other employees in an attempt to put pressure on the employer, this does not prima facie form any justification for the dismissal of the employee.[93] But what has been said here is of little assistance, in these modern times, to the employer, who is subjected to pressures from a trade union trying to enforce a " closed shop " in the particular establishment. Generally, such unions endeavour to negotiate an agreement with employers that union membership will be accepted. That agreement may well become implied into the contractual arrangements between the employer and his own employees with the result that the employees themselves must accept union membership. Any failure by them in so doing would normally result in the employer terminating their service engagement by giving the appropriate notice.

The question sometimes arises as to whether an employer is justified in dismissing an employee upon facts not known to him at the time of the

---

[86] *Cowdenbeath Coal Co.* v. *Drylie* (1886) 3 Sh.Ct.Rep. 3. See also *Morrison* v. *Galloway & Co.* (1890) 7 Sh.Ct.Rep. 65 (where miners agreed to take an " idle " day, which combination was held to be a breach of good faith and therefore justified the dismissal of one employee affected by the combination); see also *Bowes* v. *Press* [1894] 1 Q.B. 202 (miners refusing to go down the pit in a cage with a non-union employee—held to have committed a breach of contract by absenting themselves from work).

[87] *Craufurd* v. *Reid* (1822) 1 Sh.Ap. 124, reversing *Reid* v. *Lindsay* (1816) Hume 398.

[88] *Stewart* v. *Crichton* (1847) 9 D. 1042.

[89] *King* v. *Reid* (1878) 2 Guthrie's Sh.Ct. Cases 356.

[90] *Craig* v. *Graham* (1844) 6 D. 684.

[91] Fraser, *op. cit.* p. 330.

[92] Umpherston, *op. cit.* p. 120.

[93] See *Mennie* v. *Blair* (1842) 14 D. 359.

dismissal.[94]   Mr. Umpherston, disagreeing with the older authorities referred to by him, takes the view [95] that the real ground of dismissal is breach of contract by the employee and, accordingly, as soon as this breach comes to the knowledge of the employer he may determine the contract or elect to hold it at an end.   Termination from any other cause, in the meantime, does not bar the employer from his election.   However, if the employer had been aware of the employee's breach and continued to employ him, though subsequently dismissing him for some other cause, he has condoned the earlier breach but he must be able to justify the dismissal by those subsequent events which led up to it.[96]   So far as English law is concerned, Coleridge J. has said [97]: " Where the employee has been dismissed and the employer is sued for wages, the employer may avail himself of the misconduct of the employee as a defence, although he may not have dismissed him for that cause "; and Alderson B. has also said [98]: " If an employer discharge his employee and at the time of the discharge a good cause of discharge in fact exists, the employer is justified in discharging the employee although at the time of the discharge the employer did not know of the existence of that cause."   This rule was affirmed in *Boston Fishing Co.* v. *Ansell.*[99]

Where the cause of dismissal is obvious, the employer need give no reason or explanation for it.   In other cases, where an employee asks the cause of dismissal the older authorities tend to support the view that the employer is under a moral obligation to state it.[1] However, this moral right of the employee is not founded upon the contract itself and indeed it is quite unenforceable against the employer.[2] The employer may refuse to assign a reason—and if the employee subsequently sues him, then he (the employer) may always justify the dismissal in defence.[3]

It is appropriate to consider under this sub-heading the question of desertion.   There is no doubt that if an employee leaves his work *sine animo revertendi* and without lawful cause then he has committed a breach of his contract of employment.   The position of merchant seamen is special and is governed by statute law.[4]   Desertion here is something more than a mere temporary absence (which may well justify dismissal in certain cases) or absence through illness or other necessary cause, which

---

[94] See *Bentinck* v. *Macpherson* (1869) 6 S.L.R. 376; and also Lord Chief Commissioner Adam's charge to the jury in *Wight* v. *Ewing* (1828) 4 Mur. 584 at p. 592, which support the view that he is not so justified.

[95] *Op. cit.* p. 121.

[96] *Horton* v. *M'Murtry* (1860) 5 H. & N. 667, *per* Bramwell B. at p. 657; *Cussons* v. *Skinner* (1843) 11 M. & W. 161, *per* Lord Abinger C.B. at p. 169; and *Boston Fishing Co.* v. *Ansell* (1888) 39 Ch.D. 339, *per* Cotton L.J. at p. 358.

[97] See *Ridgeway* v. *Hungerford Market Co.* (1835) 3 A. & E. 171.

[98] In *Willets* v. *Green* (1850) 3 Car. & K. 59.

[99] (1888) 39 Ch.D. 339.

[1] See *Watson* v. *Burnet* (1862) 24 D. 494, *per* Lord Deas at p. 497.

[2] In *Mitchell* v. *Smith* (1836) 14 S. 358, directors of a bank—who dismissed their manager (engaged at pleasure)—were held not bound to justify their dismissal.

[3] See Bell's *Principles* 182.

[4] See particularly the Merchant Shipping Act 1894, ss. 221–224; and *O'Neil* v. *Rankin* (1873) 11 M. 538.

may terminate the contract because of failure of performance. The existence or absence of the *animus revertendi* will require to be deduced from the facts. Perhaps the absence may only be such as to justify dismissal without there being a complete desertion. It may be helpful to consider one or two cases to illustrate whether or not desertion has, in fact, occurred: in *Cooper* v. *M'Ewan* [5] the contract was for three years and the employers alone had power to terminate it at any time by notice. After two years' service the employee gave a month's notice and left. He was held to be in the position of a deserter. Again, in *Dumbarton Glass Co.* v. *Coatsworth* [6] an employee, who had entered into a seven years' contract, left before the completion of the term but was held not to be a deserter because a reduction in his wages had ended the old contract and substituted a new contract, during pleasure. Where an employee is entitled to quit his employment after giving notice of a certain length, it is desertion if he leaves on shorter notice, because the latter is equivalent to no notice at all.[7] These cases are now mainly of historical interest only and must not be overstressed. The law at that time enabled an employer to proceed against an employee and have him punished (if necessary by imprisonment) and at the same time have an order made against him for specific implement. Nowadays the correct remedy is a damages action. Should the employer himself commit a breach of contract which entitles the employee to hold the contract as terminated, it is then no desertion for the employee to leave the employment. Examples of such breach would be—an employer becoming bankrupt [8]; assigning his business to another [9]; treating his employees harshly and making their position unbearable [10]; or failing to pay the stipulated wages.[11] Another example would be where, by the act of the employer, the service became dangerous beyond the degree contemplated; if the employee left the employment, this would not amount to desertion.[12] Where an employee is dismissed illegally, he is not bound to return if a continuation of employment is offered, and indeed he is not liable whether as a deserter or as a contract-breaker if he refuses.

(7) *Dismissal procedures and protection against arbitrary dismissal*

In the field of British industrial relations there is very little use apparently made of formal dismissal procedures. Bargaining agreements refer normally to periods of notice but have little to say about dismissal procedures. These notice periods very often become implied into the service

---

[5] (1893) 9 Sh.Ct.Rep. 311.
[6] (1847) 9 D. 732.
[7] *Gibson* v. *M'Naughton* (1861) 23 D. 358.
[8] *Day* v. *Tait* (1900) 8 S.L.T. 40.
[9] *Ross* v. *M'Farlane* (1894) 21 R. 396.
[10] *Smart* v. *Gairns* (1794) Hume 18; *Reekie* v. *Norrie* (1842) 5 D. 368; *Gunn* v. *Goodall* (1835) 13 S. 1142.
[11] *Dumbarton Glass Co.* v. *Coatsworth, supra.*
[12] *O'Neil* v. *Armstrong, Mitchell & Co.* [1895] 2 Q.B. 70, 418; *Burton* v. *Pinkerton* (1867) L.R. 2 Ex. 340.

contract and are governed by the ordinary law of contract. Collective agreements themselves do not have any legal force in Great Britain.[13] It is true to say, however, that attention has been given for some years to the problem of redundancy, in view of the changing emphasis from heavy industries to light engineering industries, developing in many instances in the new industrial estates. The heavy industries have declined—notably perhaps on Clydeside, Tyneside and Merseyside—and workers laid off have had to seek other employment. The trade unions, conscious of the problems involved, adopted the method of voluntary arrangements with management and from the early practice of " last in; first out " there developed the more modern and sophisticated redundancy agreements. At the same time, the various British Governments—through the agency of their own Ministry of Labour [14]—sponsored research into the practices adopted by the leading British industrial companies.[15]

The purpose behind the Contracts of Employment Act 1963 [16] and the Redundancy Payments Act 1965 [17] was to provide certain minimal statutory protections for employees. It must be appreciated that these statutes are a first stage in the legislative protections and legislative sanctions which are being extended throughout the whole field of employment. Recently, H.M. Government has been concerned about the creation of effective safeguards against the arbitrary dismissal of employees and, in this connection, they accepted Recommendation No. 119 concerning Termination of Employment at the Initiative of the Employer, which had been adopted at the Forty-seventh (1963) Session of the International Labour Conference.[18] The underlying principle of that Recommendation is very important and is as follows: " . . . termination of employment should not take place unless there is a valid reason . . . connected with the capacity or conduct of the worker or based on the operational requirements of the undertaking, establishment or service." H.M. Government accepted what might be called the general clauses of Recommendation 119, including the principle that workers should not be dismissed without a valid reason (though accepted in practice in Great Britain, there is no statutory provision which protects the worker in this respect), and proposed to discuss with representatives of employers and trade unions the provision of procedures to give effective safeguards against arbitrary dismissal.[19] They had certain reservations about paragraph 18 of the Recommendation and proposed to exclude certain categories specified therein, including specifically the Civil Service.[20] In addition, merchant

---

13 See Flanders and Clegg, *The System of Industrial Relations in Great Britain* (1956, Basil Blackwell) at pp. 56–57; also Chap. 8, s. (6), and Chap. 17, Part D, *supra.*
14 Now the Department of Employment and Productivity (since 1968).
15 " Positive Employment Policies "—Ministry of Labour and National Service (1958).
16 1963, c. 49.
17 1965, c. 62.
18 See Cmnd. 2548 (December 1964) containing a statement of the proposed action by H.M. Government upon, *inter alia*, Recommendation No. 119. The actual text of, *inter alia*, Recommendation No. 119 was published in Cmnd. 2159.
19 Cmnd. 2548, p. 7.   20 *Ibid.* p. 8.

seamen and fishermen would be excluded as the terms of their employment were not appropriate to the application of the Recommendation.[20]

In April 1965, the National Joint Advisory Council (acting through the Ministry of Labour) set up a special committee to examine dismissals and dismissal procedures and to report. The committee's work was embodied in a Report on Dismissal Procedures.[21] Part I thereof contained an examination of the existing system, including internal and external procedures in the private sector and procedures in the public sector. Part II contains a comparison of the protection afforded in certain European countries and in the United States of America and in Sweden. Part III [22] is the discursive part of the Report and it relates to three major topics: (i) internal voluntary procedures, (ii) external voluntary procedures and (iii) statutory machinery, these matters being summed up in the final part.[23] Broadly, the committee makes the following points on:

(i) *Internal voluntary procedures*: The best way, in their view, of safeguarding against arbitrary dismissal in Great Britain was by the extension of satisfactory internal procedures.[24] These procedures should be encouraged by the Ministry of Labour, the C.B.I. and the T.U.C. (and its affiliated unions), as well as by individual managements.

(ii) *External voluntary procedures*: The committee considers these to be supplementary to internal procedures and therefore valuable. Accordingly, they recommend that all industries should be encouraged to develop voluntary procedures, external to the firm.

(iii) *Statutory machinery*: The committee stresses that all voluntary procedures should not be undermined by any statutory machinery, but that the latter should provide exemption for agreed voluntary procedures (whether internal or external) [25] by joint approach to the Minister of Labour.[26] The committee talks about an aggrieved worker (*i.e.*, aggrieved in relation to his dismissal) taking his case —if no exempted procedure applies—to a " statutory official," who—if he could not resolve the matter—might then refer the case to a tribunal (of three persons). This tribunal is to be of a different composition from the existing Industrial Tribunal and would seem to be given wide discretionary powers.[27] However, the committee has second thoughts and serious doubts about the efficacy of statutory machinery, which might (it says) [28] " bring a legalistic atmosphere into work-place relations and weaken the

---

[21] Published by H.M.S.O. in 1967.
[22] paras. 117–175.
[23] Part IV, paras. 176–195.
[24] Para. 183 specifies the features of an internal procedure which the committee feels to be indispensable.
[25] para. 192.
[26] Now, since 1968, the Secretary of State for Employment and Productivity.
[27] para. 193.
[28] para. 194.

authority of management . . . and it would raise difficult questions
as to what should be done about strikes over dismissals." Accordingly it indicates [29] that it might be advisable to consider the
Report from the Royal Commission on Trade Unions and Employers' Associations [30] to see what changes in the system of
industrial relations are recommended therein.

Perhaps it would not be unfair to say that whilst Parts I and II of the
Report on Dismissal Procedures contain much valuable information upon
practices here and elsewhere, Parts III and IV do not exactly set the heather
on fire.   There is hardly any original thinking contained in the proposals,
apart from the references to the statutory official and the (appellate)
tribunal.   It is implied that the civil servants will continue to make their
customary substantial contribution to the industrial scene (doubtless
seeing themselves as the " experts " who keep management, unions and
workers right) and it may be that a new grade of civil servant will be
created to man the new machinery.   There is poor comfort for the labour
lawyer in this Report.   Management and workers are to be kept well
away from the law, if the writer is reading correctly—through the lines
and between the lines.   An attempt has been made in an earlier chapter [31]
to show that the lawyer (who has also studied industrial relations) and the
industrial relations expert (who has a healthy respect for the law) can both
make a valuable contribution in restoring civilisation to the " industrial
jungle."

The latest consideration of dismissal and dismissal procedures was, of
course, undertaken by the Royal Commission [32] above-mentioned (for
brevity's sake, called hereafter the " Donovan Commission " and their
report, the " Donovan Report ").   The Commission expresses the view [33]
that it is urgently necessary for workers to be given better protection
against unfair dismissal but it confirms the earlier view that voluntary
procedures should be encouraged.   The arguments for and against
statutory machinery are carefully considered in the Report [34] and, with
the exception of two dissenting views,[35] the Commission favours the
establishment of statutory machinery and they recommend early legislation to this end.[36]   The lines upon which statutory machinery might be
established are next examined.[37]   It is pointed out immediately that such
legislation mentioned will have to give guidance as to the meaning of

[29] para. 195.
[30] Published, in fact, in June 1968 (Cmnd. 3623).   This Report is examined, in some detail,
in Chap. 17, *supra*.
[31] *Supra*, Chap. 17.
[32] *Supra*, note 30.   See, in particular, Chap. IX of the Donovan Report where safeguards
against unfair dismissal are considered.   The Report makes reference to Recommendation 119 and the Report of the committee set up by the National Joint Advisory
Council, to which reference has already been made.
[33] Donovan Report, para. 529.
[34] *Ibid.* paras. 533–544.
[35] By Sir George Pollock and Mr. John Thomson (see para. 567).
[36] *Ibid.* para. 544.
[37] *Ibid.* paras. 545–566.

" unfair dismissal." The Donovan Commission regards the stipulation of specific reasons which are not valid reasons for dismissal as the best way of dealing with this matter and they suggest that " dismissal by reason of trade union membership or activity or by reason of race, colour, sex, marital status, religious or political opinion, national extraction or social origin should be deemed to be unfair." [38] The Commission takes the view [39] that the Industrial Tribunals should be reconstituted as Labour Tribunals and would deal with, *inter alia*, such things as wrongful dismissal. Conciliation between the parties would be the first method in any inter-party disagreement.[40] The suggested remedies are reinstatement or compensation.[41] It is also suggested that the Labour Tribunal should —where a dismissal takes place for breach of a rule (*i.e.*, upon a disciplinary ground)—be able to consider, in the course of reaching its decision, not only the seriousness of the breach but the reasonableness of the rule.[42] This latter point is a judicial function, which is met by the fact that the chairman of the Labour Tribunal is legally qualified. It will be essential to retain the right of appeal to the Court of Session in Scotland (and the High Court of Justice in England) from the Labour Tribunal (in the same way as the present appellate machinery from the decisions of the Industrial Tribunal).

The courts of law have been concerned for some years past that in all cases where disciplinary and summary dismissal procedures are invoked or taken against employees, whether by their employers or by their trade unions, that these employees should be made aware of the nature of the complaint against them and should also be given an opportunity of stating their own case before a decision in the matter is taken. The principle of equity involved in this approach has come to be known as the doctrine of " natural justice." This doctrine or principle has been illustrated in a few common law cases within the field of employment, of which the Scottish decision of *Palmer* v. *Inverness Hospitals Board of Management* [43] is an outstanding example. There have been other cases of importance, particularly in the fields of public law and trade union law. The trade union cases are most relevant to the field of study with which this volume deals and, accordingly, are discussed in some detail in the appropriate chapter [44] hereof.

---

[38] *Ibid.* para. 545.

[39] Which is contrary to that taken by the committee's " Dismissal Procedures " Report (H.M.S.O. 1967), discussed earlier in this chapter.

[40] See paras. 548–550.

[41] *Ibid.* paras. 551–554.

[42] *Ibid.* para. 565.

[43] (O.H.) 1963 S.L.T. 124. A decision (also raising questions of administrative law) involving a doctor (or house officer) employed by the Hospitals Board, who was summarily dismissed without any apparently valid reason or explanation and whose side of the case was not heard by the appeals body concerned.

[44] *Supra*, Chap. 17.

(8) *The Race Relations Acts 1965 and 1968* [45]

The 1965 Act was the first statutory attempt in Great Britain to deal with the problem of racial discrimination. The Act had a limited scope, dealing only with such matters as the prohibition of racial discrimination in public places,[46] the prevention or imposition of restrictions on racial grounds upon the transfer of tenancies [47] and the penalisation of incitement to racial hatred.[48] Essentially, therefore, the statute was principally concerned with public order and preservation of the peace. Section 7 of the 1965 Act extended the Public Order Act 1936 by substituting a new section 5 which dealt not only with abusive or insulting words or behaviour but also with the distribution or display of written material which is threatening, abusive or insulting. The Race Relations Board and Local Conciliation Committees were formally established by the 1965 statute.[49]

The 1968 Act is a much more extensive and sophisticated piece of legislation, which replaces certain parts of the 1965 Act [50] but leaves the remainder unaffected.[51] The meaning of " discriminate " is given in section 1, as follows:

" 1.—(1) For the purposes of this Act a person discriminates against another if on the ground of colour, race or ethnic or national origins he treats that other, in any situation to which section 2, 3, 4 or 5 below applies, less favourably than he treats or would treat other persons, and in this Act references to discrimination are references to discrimination on any of those grounds.

(2) It is hereby declared that for those purposes segregating a person from other persons on any of those grounds is treating him less favourably than they are treated." [51a]

It is unlawful for any person concerned with the provision to the public (or a section thereof) of any goods, facilities or services to discriminate against any person seeking to obtain or use such goods, facilities or services by refusing or deliberately omitting to provide him with them or to provide them on the same terms as normally given to other members of the public.[52] Certain examples of facilities and services are given in the statute [53] of which—from the employer's viewpoint—the following are the most important, *viz.*: (a) facilities for education, instruction or training; and (b) the services of any business, profession or trade or local or other public authority.

---

[45] 1965, c. 73, and 1968, c. 71, respectively.
[46] 1965 Act, s. 1.
[47] *Ibid.* s. 5.
[48] *Ibid.* s. 6.
[49] *Ibid.* s. 2; and the Schedule to the Act.
[50] 1968 Act, s. 28 (8) (repealing ss. 1 to 4 and s. 8 (2) and the words of exception in s. 8 (3) and the Schedule).
[51] Ss. 5, 6 and 7 remain very important.
[51a] It will be noted that religion is not mentioned in the definition. Nevertheless, the definition remains very wide and general in sub-section (1).
[52] *Ibid.* s. 2 (1).   [53] *Ibid.* s. 2 (2).

Discrimination by employers is dealt with specifically in section 3 of the 1968 Act. It is unlawful for an employer to discriminate against any other person, who is seeking employment, by refusing or deliberately omitting to employ him on available work for which he is qualified or by refusing or deliberately omitting to offer or afford him the same terms and conditions of employment and opportunities for training and promotion as are available for other persons with the same qualifications working on the same type of work.[54] It is equally unlawful for an employer to discriminate against another person who is an employee by dismissing him in circumstances in which other persons employed on similar work by the employer would not be dismissed.[55] Discrimination by trade unions, employers' organisations or trade, business and professional organisations or bodies—in relation to membership, benefits, support or expulsion—is also made unlawful by the Act.[56] Certain exceptions or limitations in respect of small businesses are permitted in the case of employment.[57] A most important exception is allowed, in relation to sections 2 and 3 of the Act, where the employer acts in good faith for the purpose of securing or preserving a reasonable balance of persons of different racial groups employed in an undertaking or part of an undertaking.[58] All the circumstances must be taken into account in assessing whether a balance is reasonable.[59] The term " racial group " is defined [60] by section 8 (4) as meaning—" a group of persons defined by reference to colour, race or ethnic or national origins and for the purposes of that subsection persons wholly or mainly educated in Great Britain shall be treated as members of the same racial group." The reference to persons wholly or mainly educated in Great Britain (the test being the place of education rather than colour or race or national origin) is interesting but vague. It may not always be easy to apply nor is its meaning particularly clear. Presumably, education in Great Britain entitles the person in question to be included in a racial group which includes the British generally. Somehow or other the phraseology implies a certain supercilious attitude or academic superiority approach which would have been better left out of the statute. Fortunately, the Secretary of State is given power to repeal the exceptions contained in subsections (2) to (4) of section 8.

Employment for the purposes of a private household is not affected by sections 2 and 3 of the 1968 Act,[61] nor is employment out of Great Britain or on ships or aircraft (British or otherwise) operating out of Great Britain.[62] It is also made clear that section 3 does not render unlawful the selection of a person of a particular nationality or particular

[54] *Ibid.* s. 3 (1) (*a*) and (*b*).
[55] *Ibid.* s. 3 (1) (*c*).
[56] *Vide* s. 4.
[57] *Ibid.* s. 8 (1) (*a*) and (*b*).
[58] *Ibid.* s. 8 (2).
[59] *Ibid.* s. 8 (3).
[60] In relation to s. 8 (2).
[61] *Ibid.* s. 8 (6). There may still be " discrimination," however in terms of section 1.
[62] *Ibid.* s. 8 (7).

descent for employment requiring attributes especially possessed by persons of that nationality or descent.[63]

The liability of employers and principals is specifically dealt with by section 13. It is therein provided that anything done by a person in the course of his employment shall be treated, for purposes of the 1968 Act, as done by the employer also, irrespective of whether the employer knew or did not know or approved or did not approve of the thing done by the employee.[64] The same principle applies to the agent acting with authority (express or implied) on behalf of another.[65]   However, in relation to the act of an employee which results in proceedings being brought, in Scotland, under section 20 [66] it is a defence to the employer, against whom such proceedings are taken, to prove that he took such steps as were reasonably practicable to prevent the employee from doing in the course of his employment acts of the same description as that act.[67]

The Race Relations Board is continued in being and consists of a chairman and not more than eleven other members appointed by the Secretary of State.[68]   Conciliation Committees (operating on an area basis) are also to be constituted by the Board.[69]   The general provisions regarding investigation of complaints of discrimination by the Board or by a conciliation committee are contained in section 15, which is a most important procedural section.   In the course of an investigation the Board, or a conciliation committee, is required to form an opinion as to whether any person has done any act which is unlawful under Part I of the Act,[70] after inquiring into the facts; also, in the case of a complaint based upon discrimination against a person, to use their best endeavours to secure a settlement of any difference between the parties and to obtain a satisfactory written assurance against a repetition of the unlawful act or similar acts [71]; and, finally, in the case of any other complaint, to use their best endeavours to secure a satisfactory written assurance.[72]   Where the Board investigates a complaint and finds that the act is, in its opinion, unlawful under Part I of the Act and is unable to secure a settlement or obtain an assurance or the act in question was done in breach of an assurance, it is then required to determine whether or not to bring proceedings under section 19 (England and Wales) or section 20 (Scotland).[73]   Where the conciliation committee is investigating a complaint with any of the results just mentioned in the case of the Board, it is required to report to the Board and the Board itself

---

[63] s. 8 (11).
[64] *Ibid.* s. 13 (1).
[65] *Ibid.* s. 13 (2).
[66] s. 19 for England and Wales.
[67] s. 13 (3).
[68] Sched. 1 gives the particulars regarding the constitution of the Board and its conciliation committees.
[69] 1968 Act, s. 15 and Sched. 1.
[70] s. 15 (3) (*a*).
[71] *Ibid.* s. 15 (3) (*b*).
[72] *Ibid.* s. 15 (3) (*c*).
[73] *Ibid.* s. 15 (4).

must consider the report and then either investigate the complaint themselves or, without investigating, determine whether or not to bring proceedings under section 19 or 20 of the Act.[74] When the investigation [75]
by the Board or by a conciliation committee is completed a written
notification must be given to the parties and this should state:

    (a) whether or not they have been able to form an opinion regarding
        the complaint and, if so, what opinion;

    (b) whether or not they have secured a settlement and assurance or
        simply an assurance (in terms of section 15 (3));

    (c) what action, if any, they propose to take in the matter.[76]

Where the Board comes to a determination,[77] without investigation, it is
required to give written notification of this to the parties, stating also
what action, if any, it proposes to take.[78]

The investigation of complaints made to the Secretary of State for
Employment and Productivity, the Race Relations Board or to any
conciliation committee that an act has been done which is unlawful by
virtue of any provision of Part I of the Act and is an act of discrimination
with respect to employment, or to membership of, or services or facilities
provided by, an organisation of employers or workers or an act of aiding,
inducing or inciting the doing of such an act of discrimination, is regulated
by section 16 and Schedule 2.[79] The Board may itself investigate, or
refer for investigation, any unlawful conduct which comes to its notice,
although no formal complaint had been made to the Board or the Secretary of State for Employment and Productivity or to a conciliation committee or a complaint had, in fact, been made but was subsequently
withdrawn.[80] If the investigation relates to an act mentioned in section 16
of the Act, the procedural paragraphs of Part II of Schedule 3 apply to it,
whilst in the case of any other act the provisions of Part I of that Schedule
apply.[81]

Legal proceedings in Scotland in relation to contraventions of the Act
are provided for by section 20 of the Act. These proceedings are civil
proceedings brought at the instance of the Race Relations Board (following a determination under section 15 or Schedule 2 or 3 to the Act) and
may consist of an application or claim for: (a) an order in terms of
section 21; (b) for damages, as mentioned in section 22; (c) for such an
order and damages; and (d) for a declarator that the particular act is
unlawful by virtue of any provisions of Part I of the Act.[82] An application may also be made, in accordance with section 23, for revision of any

---

[74] *Ibid.* s. 15 (5).
[75] Under s. 15 (2) or (5).
[76] *Ibid.* s. 15 (6).
[77] Under s. 15 (5).
[78] *Ibid.* s. 15 (7).
[79] Sched. 2 is a very extensive procedural schedule containing 16 paragraphs (all of which
    are important), which may be amended or repealed by regulations made by the Secre-
    tary of State, under the authority given to him by s. 16 (2).
[80] *Ibid.* s. 17.
[81] *Ibid.* s. 17 (1).
[82] *Ibid.* s. 20 (1).

contract or any term thereof which is alleged to contravene any provision
of Part I of the Act.[83]   It is the function of the Secretary of State (for
Scotland) to appoint those sheriff courts which are to have jurisdiction to
deal with proceedings brought under the Act.[84]   The sheriff is assisted by
two assessors.[85]   An appeal lies to the Court of Session, whose decision
is to be final.[86]   Section 21 (2) must be read along with section 20, as
regards proceedings in Scotland and the order which the sheriff may
make, as he considers proper in the circumstances.   Damages may be
awarded in accordance with the provisions of section 22.   It is the duty
of the Race Relations Board to account to any person for any damages
recovered by it in respect of that person.[87]

Section 23 contains a most interesting provision in relation to contracts
and contractual terms.   It is provided therein that if any contract or
contractual term contravenes any provision of Part I of the Act, such
contract or term is not thereby void or unenforceable (*i.e.*, by reason only
of the contravention), but may be revised in accordance with the provisions
of subsections (2), (3) and (4).   The application is brought under section
20, as regards Scotland.

Section 25 [88] establishes the Community Relations Commission.   The
Act also binds the Crown [89] and applies in certain special ways to the
police [90] and public bodies.[91]   The Act received the Royal Assent on
October 25, 1968, and came into force after one month from that date.[92]

It is much too early to assess the importance or otherwise of the 1968
legislation, but it is refreshing to see that legal procedures arising out of
that statute involve references and applications to the ordinary courts of
law in Scotland and in England separately.[93]   Doubtless the reason for
this is that the rights and liberties of individual citizens within the framework of the British society are affected and can only be protected properly
and effectively by the courts, rather than by yet another quasi-judicial
administrative tribunal.   The writer anticipates that a body of case-law
will emerge in due course from the Part I provisions of the 1968 Act,
particularly sections 2, 3 and 4.[94]   It remains to be seen whether the
legislation will be interpreted reasonably and with common sense.

---

[83] *Ibid.* s. 20 (1).
[84] *Ibid.* s. 20 (2) and (3) (which may consist of a part or parts of sheriffdoms or two or
    more sheriffdoms).
[85] *Ibid.* s. 20 (7).   [86] *Ibid.* s. 20 (9).
[87] *Ibid.* s. 22 (3).
[88] Read along with Sched. 4.
[89] *Ibid.* s. 27 (1) and (3) (for Scotland).
[90] *Ibid.* s. 27 (4) to (8), in particular.
[91] See s. 27 (12) for the definition.
[92] See s. 29 (3).
[93] There being no further appeal to the House of Lords in either case.
[94] Ss. 2 and 3 being subject to the exceptions contained in s. 8.   The first case (taken in
    England) has been dismissed on a pure technicality.   It is also understood that another
    complaint—this time involving the medical profession—is pending in the Aberdeen-
    shire area.   The Race Relations Board has recently (November, 1969) come in for
    much public and parliamentary criticism over the case of the Scottish doctor in East-
    bourne who advertised for a " Scottish daily help " (see *The Glasgow Herald*, November
    20, 1969).   Modifications to the legislation are already being sought.

CHAPTER 20

TERMINATION OF THE RELATIONSHIP OF EMPLOYER AND EMPLOYEE UPON CERTAIN GENERAL GROUNDS

(1) *Illness*

Mere illness of the employer or employee does not terminate the contract of employment. Much depends upon the way in which the contract is framed, with special reference to its duration and the grounds upon which it can be terminated. The opening statement contained in this paragraph has to be qualified by saying that if the illness should prevent either party from properly fulfilling his duties and obligations under the contract then the contract may be ended because of failure in the performance thereof—without (except as hereinafter mentioned) involving the consequences of a breach of contract.[1] If the unforeseen illness on the employee's part be protracted or entail consequences inconsistent with the continuance of the relationship then, understandably, the contractual relationship may well cease. Obviously, if the illness is serious and lengthy there is very little doubt about impossibility of performance arising. If the illness is a brief one, this would not justify the employer terminating the relationship.[2] Where the question of impossibility of performance arises the whole circumstances of the case will have to be looked at—and particularly (a) the duration of the contract, (b) the nature of the business and (c) the services to be given. If the employer has to hire a substitute this could well be a matter of considerable importance.[3] One Scottish case which is of much value as a guide to this difficult question is *Westwood* v. *Scottish Motor Traction Co.*[4] In this instance, a transfer of business took place and the defenders agreed to pay a salary of £6 per week for three years under a contract of service which terminated on March 30, 1938. The employee pursuer was injured in an accident during the course of his employment and gave no services thereafter. Defenders paid full salary until December 4, 1936, thereafter £4 per week to May 14, 1937, and a sum of £2 for the week ending May 14, 1937, when all payments stopped. Pursuer claimed full salary for the period to March 30, 1938. It was held as follows: (1) an antecedent agreement referred to gave no higher rights than those of a simple service contract; (2) the pursuer was entitled to full salary until his contract terminated; (3) it was a question of circumstances in each case whether a contract of service was terminated by incapacity due to illness and no

[1] *Manson* v. *Downie* (1885) 12 R. 1103.
[2] *Craig* v. *Graham* (1844) 6 D. 684.
[3] *Manson* v. *Downie, cit. supra*; *White* v. *Baillie* (1794) Mor. 10, 147.
[4] 1938 S.N. 8 (an Outer House case).

notice of termination was necessary; (4) reasonable allowance must be made before a contract could legitimately be regarded as terminated in these circumstances; and (5) in this particular case the employers were not entitled to terminate the contract as at May 14, 1937.

Should it be that the employee's illness was caused by his own misconduct or fault it seems that his disability amounts to a breach of contract for which he is liable.[5] Lord Fraser says [6] (apparently in reliance upon American authority) that the law is the same when the disability—due to a cause preceding the contract—might have been foreseen but was in fact concealed, upon the reasoning that the employee had broken the condition that one who undertakes to give personal services must not render himself physically incapable of performing them. But, in an old English case where an employee became unable to perform his employment through illness contracted prior to but only developing after the contract was made, which he could not be expected to foresee and did not conceal when he entered into the contract, the court held that they were not entitled to go behind the occurrence of the illness and consider whether it was due to the employee's misconduct.[7] In the case where the contract does come to an end because of the unforeseen illness of the employee, and for which he is not blameworthy, his rights regarding wages are similar to those arising in the event of his death.

(2) *Marriage of an Employee*

Mr. Umpherston states [8] that if a female employee is married during the term her husband has a claim upon her society and services in preference to her employer. Nevertheless, should she leave the employment on that account she commits a breach of contract. The rule of law seems to be that the marriage of an employee has no effect upon the relationship of parties to the contract and it cannot liberate the employee from any obligations under it.[9] Where termination of the contract is desired by the employee, such may take place by relying upon the notice period specified by the parties or alternatively a new mutual agreement may be made which would enable the employee to go earlier or later, as suited the convenience of both parties.

Where a married woman becomes pregnant during the subsistence of a contract of employment, the position is probably closely allied to that of temporary illness. A reasonable absence to permit delivery of the child should be agreed between the parties. If the female employee becomes seriously ill at the birth of her child then the matter of continuance of the

---

5 *McEwan* v. *Malcolm* (1867) 5 S.L.R. 62.
6 *Op. cit.* pp. 318 and 319.
7 *K.* v. *Raschen* (1878) 38 L.T.(N.S.) 38.
8 *Op. cit.* p. 124.
9 See particularly *Watson* v. *Merrilees* (1848) 10 D. 370. But unpermitted absence due to pregnancy may break the continuity of employment and mean loss of wages or benefits under the Contracts of Employment Act 1963 and the Redundancy Payments Act 1965.

employment contract would have to be considered from the point of view of a failure to implement that contract. Finally, if the employee intended to terminate the employment because of her pregnancy and the impending delivery of her child, she would again rely upon the notice period in the contract or make a new agreement with her employer regarding her release. Pregnancy *per se* of the married female employee does not appear to be a good ground for terminating the contract of employment. The question of the pregnancy of an unmarried female employee is quite a different matter—as it raises immediately the right of an employer to dismiss for immorality. Nevertheless, the whole circumstances must be considered before that right of dismissal is exercised. The modern attitude to this factual situation would be more enlightened than that of the Victorian era. The reasonable employer might well continue the contract so as to enable the unmarried female to support her child. The exercise of a sensible discretion on the employer's part would very often be necessary, instead of a formal exercise of his right to dismiss the employee upon learning of her pregnancy.

(3) *Imprisonment of Employee*

When the employee is imprisoned he is quite obviously unable to perform his part of the contract. It is important to ascertain whether or not the imprisonment is due to the fault of the employee—and in this connection the position seems to be the same as an inability to perform the contract through illness. Where the imprisonment is lawful and the fault of the employee himself, he has disabled himself from performance and he is guilty of breach of contract. Conversely, if the imprisonment is wrongful—termination of the relationship may occur but the consequences of a breach of contract will not follow. Mr. Umpherston explains [10] that under the old law relating to imprisonment of employees for desertion, such imprisonment did not terminate the contract, because the employer had elected to punish the employee and retained him in employment rather than terminating the relationship for breach of contract. This type of imprisonment is now, of course, abolished in relation to the ordinary adult employee.[11]

(4) *Termination by the Court*

In terms of the Employers and Workmen Act 1875 [12] the sheriff court in Scotland has the power to rescind any contract where there is any proceeding before the court in relation to any dispute between an employer and a workman arising out of or incidental to their employment relationship. This termination may be ordered by the court upon such terms as to the apportionment of wages or other sums due under the contract, and as to the payment of wages or damages or other sums due, as the court

---

[10] *Op. cit.* p. 125.
[11] As regards apprentices, see the Employers and Workmen Act 1875.
[12] See ss. 3 and 4. The monetary value involved must not exceed £10.

itself thinks is just in all the circumstances.[12] The court has a similar jurisdiction over apprentices governed by the Act [13] and certain powers in the case of indentured apprentices, under section 6 of the Act. Section 6 gives the court (i) the same powers in the case of master and apprentice as it has in the ordinary case of employer and workman, where a dispute under the Act arises between a master and his apprentice (taking the indenture of apprenticeship as equivalent to the service contract) and (ii) the following additional powers:

(a) to make an order directing the apprentice to perform his duties under the apprenticeship;

(b) if it rescinds the indenture of apprenticeship, it may order the whole or any part of the premium paid to be repaid.

If the apprentice fails to perform his duties as ordered in paragraph (a) above, the court may—after a period of one month from the date of the order—order the apprentice to be imprisoned for a period not exceeding fourteen days. A cautioner (surety or guarantor in England) may be summoned before the court and may be ordered to pay damages, in addition to or in substitution for any order which the court is authorised to make against the apprentice, or may be accepted to give additional security in lieu of or in mitigation of punishment against the apprentice.[14] The application of the Act to Scotland is specifically dealt with by section 14, relating to interpretation and procedure. The Act relates to apprentices in respect of whom no premium is paid or the particular premium does not exceed £25.[15]

(5) Effects of Termination of Employment

When the employee's contract is terminated, whether lawfully or otherwise, he is obliged to leave quietly—silence not being regarded as acquiescence in the breach of contract by the employer.[16] The employee must also hand over to the employer all property belonging to the latter which was held during the subsistence of relationship.[17] If the employer had undertaken to provide clothes (e.g., livery to a chauffeur) these articles remain—in the absence of any special agreement to the contrary—the property of the employer.[18] Where the employee is occupying a dwelling-house or other premises qua employee then he must quit such subjects upon the termination of the employment relationship.[19] Normally the employee does not have the privileges of a tenant, nor is he entitled in the

---

[13] See s. 5.
[14] s. 7.
[15] s. 12.
[16] Ross v. Pender (1874) 1 R. 352.
[17] Clift v. Portobello Pier Co. (1877) 4 R. 462 (delivery of a licence; interesting questions raised re grant and assignation of licence).
[18] Shiells v. Dalyell (1825) 4 S. 136.
[19] It is important to verify that the occupancy is qua employee and not qua tenant. If the latter, the employee may not be required to remove immediately or indeed he may even be able to continue in occupation under a tenancy which is protected by the Rent Acts.

general case to any warning notice or notice to quit, which must be given or served in the case of the ordinary tenant. A summary application for his removal appears to be competent,[20] although in most cases it should not be necessary. If the employee refuses to leave of his own accord, it seems that the employer is entitled to turn him out and remove his effects from the premises without process of law.[21] It has been held in England that even where an employer wrongfully dismissed an employee (for which of course, he became liable in damages for breach of contract) who refused to leave the premises occupied by him, the employer might remove the furniture to another place and he was not liable for any subsequent damage to it or for any loss from the removal—upon the ground that when the employment ceased the employee had no right to retain possession of the premises and so he became a trespasser.[22] The opinion has been expressed that it is irrelevant whether the dismissal was effected by someone who had the power to dismiss. When the dismissal is made it is valid as an act in itself. But, of course, the actual event of dismissal raises the quite separate issue as to whether that dismissal is justifiable or wrongful. This is quite another matter and it has been dealt with elsewhere.[23]

[20] *Whyte* v. *School Board of Haddington* (1874) 1 R. 1124.
[21] See Fraser, *op. cit.* p. 332; *Scott* v. *McMurdo* (1869) 6 S.L.R. 301; Smith, *Master and Servant*, 3rd ed., p. 112; and *cf.* the old case of *Scougal* v. *Crawford*, 2 Mur. 110.
[22] *Per* Williams J. in *Lake* v. *Campbell* (1862) 5 L.T.(N.S.) 582.
[23] *Supra*, Chap. 19.

PART IV

MISCELLANEOUS MATTERS CONCERNING THE RELATIONSHIP OF EMPLOYER AND EMPLOYEE

THE CONTRACT (OR INDENTURE) OF APPRENTICESHIP AND THE RIGHTS, DUTIES AND OBLIGATIONS ARISING THEREFROM

In Scotland, the deed or instrument which constitutes an apprenticeship is an indenture. This deed is signed by the apprentice (who is usually a minor) and by his father as curator and administrator or by any other curator, should the father be deceased. If there be no curator it is quite competent for the minor apprentice to sign the indenture himself.[1] There is no difficulty about the intending apprentice who is *major sui juris*; he requires no co-signatory, as does the minor apprentice. The latter may, where appropriate, plead enorm lesion but if there is any fraud or other wilful misrepresentation on his part he will not be protected. The father or curator is guaranteeing that the apprentice will faithfully perform his tasks.[2] The obligations arising from the deed rest upon the apprentice and the master respectively and are part and parcel of the apprenticeship contract. Other cautioners assume a similar burden of undertaking that the apprentice will faithfully perform the tasks laid upon him and any failure in the performance of these tasks will enable the master to enforce the penalty clause against the cautioner concerned. Cautioners are bound normally as individuals and as such have the benefit of division. Moreover, the master may proceed against a cautioner without discussing the apprentice. If the cautioners are bound jointly and severally the benefit of division does not apply and each is liable *singuli in solidum*. Where a cautioner is called upon to pay any sum, whether under the deed or arising from the cautionary obligation created by the deed, he (the cautioner) has an action of relief against the apprentice.[3]

Before a master could proceed to recover damages or enforce a penalty the court would require to be satisfied that the master himself was not in breach of his own obligations under the deed, that is to say by some negligence or lack of supervision on his part which was the proximate cause of the loss.[4] It also seems that in the desertion cases a reasonable time must be allowed to a cautioner to persuade the apprentice to return to work. The master cannot enforce the penalty clause immediately.[5] Nor indeed

---

[1] Erskine, I, 7, 62.
[2] See *Stevenson* v. *Adair* (1872) 10 M. 919 where a minor, without his father's consent, signed an apprenticeship contract, to which a cautioner was also added. The *cautioner* would be clearly liable under the contract, in the event of the *minor* apprentice deserting the service.
[3] Erskine, III, 3, 65.
[4] See Fraser, *op. cit.* pp. 341–342, particularly in relation to embezzlement by apprentices who were not properly supervised.
[5] Fraser, *op. cit.* p. 341 and n. (*f*) for old cases thereon.

can he (the master) enforce the penalty clause where he himself has been guilty of some acquiescence in the actings of the apprentice.[6]

The undertaking to be given by the apprentice is one of lawful and faithful service to the master and he must not absent himself during business hours. The corresponding obligation undertaken by the master is to teach and instruct the apprentice in his trade.[7] Should an apprentice have a valid defence to an action of damages for breach of the apprenticeship contract raised against him by his master, it seems to be accepted that any cautioner in the apprenticeship indenture may plead the same defence.[8] It also appears that the cautioner cannot plead that the apprentice was a minor acting without curators—certainly where the cautioner knew or ought to have known this.

Formation of the contract. A written form of contract is essential for apprenticeship,[9] but it is not necessary for every essential of the apprenticeship to be set forth in the writing which constitutes the contract and which is relied upon to prove its existence.[10] The technical term given to the deed or instrument is of course an indenture. The doctrine of *rei interventus* applies to the improbative apprenticeship agreement,[11] as it does to other contracts in improbative form, and the conduct of parties will, therefore, be a major factor in deciding whether or not the parties are to be bound as if the contract had been made in proper form.[12] An oral agreement, even followed by *rei interventus*, is not good enough to set up the contract of apprenticeship in Scotland.[13] The parties should translate their oral agreement into one in written form (whether probative or not) before it will become a binding agreement. The Contracts of Employment Act 1963 [14] appears to apply in a limited way to the apprenticeship contract but it does not alter, and has not altered, the rules governing the formation of a contract of apprenticeship in Scots law— and, moreover, in any application to the Industrial Tribunal in Scotland concerning any apprenticeship matter it must be shown that those rules have been followed.[15]

The premium, that is to say, the consideration or *quid pro quo*, which is to be paid to the master, should be set forth clearly in the indenture.

---

6 See *Robertson* v. *Smith & Co.* (1800) Hume 20, where an apprentice, deserting for the second time, had occupied himself as a farm labourer for four years, with the full knowledge of his master. It was held that the latter had debarred himself from enforcing the penalty clause against the apprentice and/or his cautioner. See also *Ferguson* v. *Mackenzie* (1815) Hume 21.

7 *Frame* v. *Campbell* (1836) 14 S. 914, *per* Lord Jeffrey at p. 918; affirmed 1839 M'L. & R. 595. See also *Gardner* v. *Smith & Wardrobe* (1775) Mor. 593; *Lyle* v. *Service* (1863) 2 M. 115; and *Royce* v. *Greig*, 1909, 2 S.L.T. 298.

8 Fraser, p. 342.

9 *Murray* v. *McGilchrist* (1864) 4 Irv. 461; and *Grant* v. *Ramage and Ferguson* (1897) 25 R. 35.

10 *Gordon* v. *Cran & Co.* (1904) 12 S.L.T. 471; 42 S.L.R. 123.

11 See *Gow* v. *M'Ewan & Son* (1901) (O.H.) 8 S.L.T. 484.

12 *Neil* v. *Vashon* (1807) Hume 20.

13 *Murray* v. *McGilchrist, cit. supra*; and *Grant* v. *Ramage & Ferguson* (1897) 25 R. 35.

14 1963, c. 49, s. 8.

15 *Douglas* v. *J. H. Melville Co. Ltd.*, II K.I.R. 181.

The main reason for this seems to have been the concern of the Inland Revenue to see that the appropriate stamp duty was properly exigible and paid upon the instrument. At the same time, any sum paid over as caution or to be paid over as caution or guarantee or penalty in relation to failure in performance, whether that failure be on the part of the master or of the apprentice, should also be set forth clearly in the deed. Should the premium or other sums mentioned not be set forth in the instrument itself then it seems that payment thereof cannot be enforced against the apprentice or cautioner or master, as the case may be. In modern practice, it is becoming very unusual to stipulate for a premium,[16] other than a nominal sum, except possibly in relation to certain professions. This chapter is concerned mainly with industrial apprenticeships and to a lesser extent with " white collar " apprentices. The older statute law makes this distinction abundantly clear, but more recent statute law, dealing mainly with adult workers, tends to overlap the " white collar " and the " blue collar " employees. This is a process of unification and simplification which ought to be encouraged.

Duties of the apprentice. As in the case of the ordinary employee, the primary duty of the apprentice is to enter into his service and continue in it. Any failure to do so by an apprentice is a clear breach of contract [17] and would normally entitle his master to call upon the cautioner to instruct performance and, failing that, would enable the master to recover the sum stipulated as caution. At the same time, the master would probably regard the apprenticeship deed as at an end. Alternatively, he might avail himself of the summary procedure available under the Employers and Workmen Act 1875, thereby requiring the court to make an order for performance by the apprentice. Any subsequent failure by the apprentice to carry out that order is itself a contempt of court and imprisonment of the apprentice would follow. More is said later on about this statutory procedure.

The second duty of an apprentice is to be obedient and respectful to his master and to perform his tasks earnestly and diligently. This duty equates with a similar obligation upon employees generally. Accordingly, the apprentice who is a bad timekeeper, insolent, guilty of lies and prevarication may be dismissed from his apprenticeship and the cautioners under his indenture will be liable to pay up under the penalty clause.[18] It must be stressed that, in order to justify dismissal of an apprentice from his contract, there must be misconduct which is serious and recurrent. It will not suffice if the conduct complained of occurs upon one occasion

---

[16] Indeed, by the Wages Councils Act 1959, s. 12, an employer is prohibited, under certain circumstances, from exacting from an apprentice, who is governed by a wages regulation order, any sum in respect of premium.

[17] See *Stirling Gordon & Co.* v. *Calderhead's Exrs.* (1832) 11 S. 180 and *Gunn* v. *Goodall* (1835) 13 S. 1142.

[18] See *Stewart* v. *Crichton* (1847) 9 D. 1042.

only. In the old case of *Malloch* v. *Duffy* [19] the master was held entitled to dismiss an apprentice who solicited business from his customers.

The third duty of the apprentice is to keep regular hours of employment as fixed by the master and to follow his master from one town to another, so long as no needless trouble and expense is caused to the apprentice and there is no interference with his instruction in his trade.[20] He need not, however, follow his master out of the United Kingdom.[21] The practical thing to do in such an eventuality is to arrange for the indenture to be transferred to another master, always of course with the consent of the apprentice himself and his father or curator.[22]

The fourth duty is very close to that of the ordinary employee, namely, a duty or obligation to act morally and decently, so as to bring no ill reputation or scandal upon his master or his master's household. Repeated acts of drunkenness or acts which constituted serious thefts or serious misappropriations of his master's property would justify the dismissal of the apprentice, as would sexual immorality within his master's household or within the place of business. It is submitted that serious acts of the type mentioned would justify the master in instantly dismissing the apprentice. In those cases where the misconduct is not so serious there is an obligation upon the master to reprove his apprentice and call him to order and request him to behave himself. The apprenticeship contract is one which involves instruction in a trade.[23] This is its primary purpose. Dismissal of an apprentice and termination of the indenture are really " last resort " remedies. Every other possible course should be tried before the ultimate sanction is applied. Although payment of wages may be made to apprentices, generally at a rate negotiated between the trade unions and management, this is really an irrelevant factor in relation to the bad behaviour of the apprentice. In the case of the ordinary male employee of full age, it is a very simple matter for an employer to rid himself of a worthless employee —either by giving him notice or by paying him wages in lieu thereof—so that in the latter case he is sent off the premises at once. In the apprenticeship contract this dismissal procedure cannot be adopted by the master, by reason of the nature of the contract itself. Dismissal of an apprentice is, therefore, justified only where his repeatedly bad behaviour is such as to prevent his being properly instructed in his trade. In a sense the apprentice is failing to implement the contractual obligation upon him by preventing his own instruction and learning processes. Then, and then only, will the court be sympathetic to the master.

A deserting apprentice was liable to imprisonment at common law.[24]

---

19 (1882) 19 S.L.R. 697.
20 Fraser, *op. cit.* and the old cases there cited.
21 See *Eaton* v. *Western* (1882) 9 Q.B.D. 636.
22 *Edinburgh Glasshouse Co.* v. *Shaw* (1789) Mor. 597.
23 See *Peter* v. *Terrol* (1818) 2 Mur. 28—an apprentice is not bound to work for his master except in relation to his trade.
24 *M'Dermott* v. *Ramsay* (1876) 4 R. 217; and see also the earlier cases of *Stewart* v. *Stewart* (1832) 10 S. 674; (1833) 11 S. 628; *Bookless* v. *Normand* (1832) 11 S. 50; 5 J. 87; and *Cameron* v. *Murray & Hepburn* (1866) 4 M. 547; 38 J. 281.

It will be remembered that statute law takes a hand in the master-and-apprentice relationship for, by the Employers and Workmen Act 1875,[25] certain discretionary powers are given to the court where differences and disputes arise between master and apprentice. It is open to the court to order the apprentice to implement his contract, or it may rescind the indenture, or it may award damages as appropriate. This situation is in direct contrast with the general legal position affecting the ordinary employer and employee in which specific implement of a contract of service will not be ordered by the court. What the legislature intended to do in 1875 was no doubt to exercise a supra-paternal benevolent disciplinary authority over both parties although *ex facie* it might appear that the apprentice was more often at the receiving end of the governmental cane wielded by the parliamentary housemasters. However, at the end of the nineteenth century, it was recognised that the master, in the exercise of a quasi-parental authority, could administer moderate personal chastisement to his apprentice.[26] This was certainly so at a time when apprentices lodged in their master's household. It is considered to be of little importance today as a remedy available to the master, when other remedies and pressures are available. Not only that, but the changed attitude in modern times to any form of physical punishment, whether administered by parents, school-teachers or " old-fashioned " policemen or masters, would probably mean that anyone resorting to such form of chastisement today would probably find himself very quickly involved in a civil action for assault.

Duties of the master. The corresponding duties upon the master are as follows: first and primarily, it is the master's duty to teach and instruct the apprentice in his trade.[27] Any conduct by the apprentice which amounted to a refusal to be taught would enable the master to plead this in any proceedings taken against him by the apprentice based upon a complaint of lack of instruction. Such proceedings would normally have resulted in the rescission or cancellation of the indenture and an award of damages as for a breach of contract. If, of course, there is a legitimate ground of complaint against the master, then the apprentice will have his damages, as in the old case of *Lyle* v. *Service*,[28] where an apprentice baker was held to have a lawful complaint because the master had not fully instructed him in his trade. The master must not employ the apprentice upon any tasks which are not part of his learning process in his trade. Any master who, for example, employs his apprentice upon tasks which should be performed by a person whose duties are quite different from

[25] 38 & 39 Vict., c. 90, ss. 3 and 6.
[26] Erskine I, 7, 62; *Forbes* v. *Dickson* (1708) 4 Bro.Supp. 708; and *Wight* v. *Burns* (1884) 11 R. 217, *per* Lord Young. This right is retained by the ship's master over the sea apprentice (Merchant Shipping Act 1894) and it was always so in his case at common law—*Wight* v. *Burns, supra.*
[27] The master may require a senior apprentice to instruct a junior apprentice—see *Ballantyne & Co.* v. *Kerr*, November 21, 1811, F.C.
[28] (1863) 2 M. 115; see also the earlier case of *Gardner* v. *Smith and Wardrobe* (1775) Mor. 593 and the later case of *Royce* v. *Greig*, 1909, 2 S.L.T. 298.

those of the apprentice is in clear breach of his obligation towards his apprentice.[29]

The second duty of the master is to ensure that he is validly qualified to exercise his trade or profession. Should he not be so qualified, the apprentice will be able to claim release from his indenture.

The third obligation upon the master is not to assign the apprentice. Although it is agreed that *delectus personae* forms part of the apprenticeship contract, as it does in the case of the ordinary contract of service, nevertheless the master may delegate the duty or task of instruction to his foremen or senior employees, fully qualified and responsible, who will act in his room and place. This principle is designed to protect the apprentice. What is meant is that the assignation cannot be a unilateral act at the whim, discretion or decision of the master. There can be a valid transfer or assignation of the indenture but the consent of the apprentice and of his parent (or curator) must also be obtained. Such an instrument of transfer is theoretically and practically a tripartite agreement. Where an apprentice is serving a firm (*i.e.*, a partnership) any change in the constitution of the membership of that partnership by the retiral or death or resignation or assumption of a partner generally makes no difference to the indenture. The well-drawn indenture will make provision for all these eventualities. It is agreed, however, that where a complete dissolution of the firm is involved the indenture is broken by this failure on the master's part. Such failure in performance would normally give rise to an action in damages. The position is the same as that which arises within the ordinary contract of employment.[30] But a situation may arise in which—notwithstanding dissolution—the apprentice quite clearly continues to serve a partner who continues to carry on the business of the old firm, although the indenture was initially with the old firm. If all parties (including outgoing partners) agree to this voluntary arrangement it seems that the apprentice is now bound to the partner who carries on the business.[31]

The fourth duty upon the master is to treat his apprentice with reasonable care and moderation,[32] and this includes, theoretically, the right to inflict disciplinary corporal punishment, based upon the view that the master is *in loco parentis* to the apprentice. The master must provide reasonable board and lodging and medical care where the apprentice is resident in the household. This obligation—apart from what has been aid about a general duty of reasonable care and moderate treatment—is pidly falling into the realm of legal history. Statute law makes the master criminally liable if he wilfully and without lawful excuse refuses or neglects to provide any food, clothing, medical aid or lodging for an

---

[29] *Peter* v. *Terrol, cit. supra.*
[30] See *Hoey* v. *MacEwan and Auld* (1867) 5 M. 814.
[31] See *Pagan* v. *McKie* (1837) 10 J. 90.
[32] See *Learmouth* v. *Blackie* (1828) 6 S. 533 where a master tried, unreasonably, to enforce the penalty clause, but was held not entitled to do so.

apprentice, with the result that the apprentice's health is either permanently impaired or seriously impaired.[33]

The fifth obligation or duty upon the master is to behave morally towards his apprentice and to set him a good example. Any conduct by the master which is criminal, corrupt or immoral will enable the apprentice to obtain release from his indenture. Moreover, if a master attempted to insist upon the performance of certain duties which were in contravention of the express terms of the indenture or against the spirit of the general law or general custom, there is no doubt that the apprentice would not be bound to obey the instruction—see for example, *Phillips* v. *Innes* [34] where a barber's apprentice, bound by his indenture to work on weekdays and holidays, was held not bound to shave his master's customers on Sundays.

Any breach by the master of any term (whether express or implied) in the contract or of any of the foregoing obligations would enable the apprentice to claim release from his indenture and to claim damages. Of course, the general law relating to damages based upon breach of contract will apply,[35] and the apprentice will normally have to prove his actual loss and recover for that alone. It may be that the indenture stipulates a particular sum to be payable upon breach or failure in performance, and it then has to be decided whether that sum is a penalty or liquidated damages. The general rules of the common law—as evidenced in the leading case of *Clydebank Engineering Company* v. *Castaneda* [36] will be applied to ascertain the true legal position as to whether the stipulated sum is a penalty (which is not recoverable) or a genuine pre-estimate of the damages (which is recoverable). It may also be the case that the apprentice would be entitled to claim return of any premium which he had paid to the master, as originally required by the indenture. A claim for repayment of this premium would be in addition to the ordinary claim for damages.

The common law and statutory duties of care which rest upon employers generally in the field of employer's liability, reparation and civil damages apply with equal force to the master and apprentice situation as they do to the ordinary employer and employee situation. These general matters have been quite fully dealt with in an earlier chapter [37] and it is not necessary to repeat what has been said there. Special attention must be paid, of course, to statutory provisions which deal specifically with young persons. Historically, it is interesting to note that the old doctrine of common employment (abolished in 1948) was not excluded by the fact that an employee was an apprentice.

Termination. Summary dismissal does not figure to the same extent in the master and apprentice relationship as it does in the ordinary contract

---

[33] 38 & 39 Vict., c. 86, s. 6.
[34] (1837) 2 S. & M'L. 465.
[35] See Professor D. M. Walker's *Law of Damages in Scotland*, Chaps. 5, 6 and 7 (pp. 86 to 181 inclusive).
[36] (1904) 7 F.(H.L.) 77; 12 S.L.T. 498; [1905] A.C. 6.
[37] See Chap. 11, *supra.*

of employment. Indeed it is very doubtful whether the phrase " summary dismissal " can be relevantly used at all in the former relationship. No master can get rid of his apprentice at his own hand. He must satisfy the courts that there is a justifiable case for termination of the indenture. What is required, therefore, is a great deal of patience and understanding on the master's part coupled with a willingness to learn and to accept criticism during that learning period on the apprentice's part.

The death of the individual master will terminate the relationship. This position, involving the individual master, is not so common in modern times where it is more usual to find a plurality of masters, either in the form of a partnership or in the form of a corporate body. In the case of the partnership, the indenture will normally be drafted so that the contract is between X, Y and Z as partners and masters and A, as apprentice, and A will be bound and obliged to serve X, Y and Z and the survivors and survivor of them. Provision may also be made for the assumption of new partners (who must be acceptable as new masters to the apprentice himself and his curator) and it is thought that this matter could be adequately covered by the endorsement of a short minute of agreement upon the original indenture. It must be stated at once that an apprentice is not bound to continue to serve the trustees or executor of an individual master, nor is he bound to serve those who succeed to his master's business. He may, of course, decide to do so, but this situation is a new contractual relationship and requires the preparation of a new agreement or indenture. The old agreement falls because of the failure of performance arising from the master's death. The question of return of premium may arise, and an apprentice may, where appropriate, feel justified in asking the trustees or executors of his late master for the return or refund of a substantial proportion of the premium paid.[38] It seems, in principle, that such refund cannot be enforced because the master's death does not amount to an ordinary breach of contract. It is a special circumstance preventing performance. Nevertheless, it is quite possible that the trustees or executors would arrange to make an *ex gratia* refund upon an equitable basis, *e.g.*, where a very short time only had elapsed since the commencement of the apprenticeship. This point may be largely academic in modern times, where payment of premium is not usually insisted upon by masters. Where the apprentice himself dies no claim for a refund of a proportion of premium can be made.[39]

When the apprentice has entered upon and duly served throughout the whole period of his indenture and has fulfilled all the conditions therein, he is then entitled to a formal discharge of the indenture. This is normally carried out in practice by the endorsement of a short discharge upon the last page or reverse of the indenture itself.

It is always open to the master and apprentice to terminate the contract

[38] *Cutler* v. *Littleton* (1711) Mor. 583.
[39] See *Shephard* v. *Innes* (1760) Mor. 589.

by mutual consent. Where the contract is in written form its termination by mutual consent may be evidenced by a short minute of agreement. If the original contract was informal, but validated by *rei interventus*, it seems that an informal termination (*i.e.*, without writing) will suffice.[40]

The position regarding notice is not quite the same as that of ordinary employment. Indentures are usually for fixed periods and require no notice to be given. The informal agreement probably does require notice of termination and certainly if the agreement is based upon custom of trade the particular notice which is normal and usual within the trade should be given.[41]

Another possible ground of termination is illness of the apprentice. This is as difficult to determine as in the ordinary contract of service. The important question to be decided is the gravity of the illness. If it is of a temporary nature only, the apprentice is not excused from performing his obligations under the indenture, nor is the master. It may be, however, that the illness is such as to prevent a due and proper performance of the contract and the master would seem to be justified in that case in seeking to terminate the relationship. This would certainly be so where the illness was of a permanent nature (whether physical or mental) and it may also be so where the illness or incapacity was brought about by the apprentice's own misconduct. This right of the master to terminate, upon the ground of permanent disability, was particularly important in older days when the master was obliged, not only to teach the apprentice, but also to support and maintain him.[42] The latter obligation was obviously quite onerous from an economic viewpoint, whereas the former was not.

The sequestration of the master also terminates the apprenticeship, upon the theory that a legal incapacity has overtaken the master, thereby preventing his fulfilment of his contractual obligations. Nevertheless, the apprentice is apparently entitled to rank upon the sequestrated estate for a proportion of his apprenticeship premium or fee. This right to rank is of little consequence in modern times when an apprenticeship fee or premium is very seldom paid in any case.

Finally, it will be recalled that by the Employers and Workmen Act 1875,[43] a court of summary jurisdiction in Scotland (and in the case of master and apprentice the court in question is the Sheriff's Small Debt Court [44]) may, looking to all the circumstances and applying its discretion in the matter, rescind the indenture and make an order for the refund of all or part of the premium or apprenticeship fee (the premium itself not being in excess of £25 Sterling). The pecuniary jurisdictional limit of the court is restricted to a sum of £10. This sum is rapidly becoming unrealistic in modern times.

---

[40] Fraser, *op. cit.* p. 366 and n. 6.
[41] *Hamilton* v. *Outram* (1855) 17 D. 798; 27 J. 414.
[42] Fraser, *op. cit.* p. 368.
[43] 38 & 39 Vict., c. 90, ss. 3 and 6.
[44] Fraser, *op. cit.* p. 392.

Certain types of apprenticeship are regulated by special statutory rules and these types require strict compliance with the provisions and conditions contained in the appropriate statutes—as, for example, the Merchant Shipping Act 1894, s. 108,[45] and the Pilotage Act 1913, s. 17 (1) (c) and (d).

[45] As amended by the Finance Act 1949, s. 52 (10), Sched. VIII, Part V. See Temperley *The Merchant Shipping Acts* (6th ed., 1963)—being Vol. 11 in the *British Shipping Laws* Series.

CHAPTER 22

THE EMPLOYER AND EMPLOYEE RELATIONSHIP WITH PARTICULAR REFERENCE TO THE CRIMINAL LAW

ANY instruction by an employer to his employee to do something which amounts to a criminal offence would involve both parties in criminal liability, in the ordinary case—the employer being the instigator and the employee the perpetrator. In Scotland, both would be liable " art and part " in the offence. The employee might, however, escape liability if he could satisfy the court that he was an " innocent agent." The prosecution would normally require to establish the employer's participation in the case of common law offences before a conviction could be obtained against him. It may, therefore, be not unreasonable to suggest that, from the Scottish common law viewpoint, there is no such thing as vicarious criminal liability. Yet vicarious liability in civil actions will often clearly arise in cases involving tests of " scope of employment " and delegation (agency), where the circumstances themselves point to possible criminal prosecutions against defenders.

Liability upon an employer under statute law is quite a different matter. It may be that an employer is made absolutely liable *qua* employer or owner or occupier or licensee of premises occupied for a particular purpose or used for a particular purpose. Examples of statutory liability can be found in the Factories Act 1961,[1] the Mines and Quarries Act 1954,[2] the Contracts of Employment Act 1963,[3] the Offices, Shops and Railway Premises Act 1963 [4] and the various Licensing Acts, Food and Drugs Acts, Weights and Measures Acts, etc.[5] There may be a " saving clause " in certain statutes which would enable an employer to argue that the particular breach complained of was caused by a specific identifiable person and

---

[1] 9 & 10 Eliz. 2, c. 34.
[2] 2 & 3 Eliz. 2, c. 70.
[3] 1963, c. 49.
[4] 1963, c. 41.
[5] Prosecutions under the Licensing (Scotland) Acts are almost legion in number. The following selection (preceding the First World War) illustrate the earlier position *re* the employee's authority and the employer's resulting liability, *viz.*: *Greenhill* v. *Stirling* (1885) 12 R.(J.) 37; 5 Coup. 602; 22 S.L.R. 564; *Galloway* v. *Weber* (1889) 16 R.(J.) 46; 2 White 171; 26 S.L.R. 218; *Linton* v. *Stirling* (1893) 20 R.(J.) 71; 1 Adam 61; 1 S.L.T. 160; *Patrick* v. *Kirkhope* (1894) 21 R.(J.) 27; 1 Adam 360; 1 S.L.T. 468; *Hogg* v. *Davidson* (1901) 3 F.(J.) 49; 3 Adam 335; 8 S.L.T. 487; *Greig* v. *Macleod*, 1908 S.C.(J.) 14; 5 Adam 445; 15 S.L.T. 620; *Lindsay* v. *Dempster*, 1912 S.C.(J.) 110; 6 Adam 707; 1912, 2 S.L.T. 177. For a comment upon *Greig* v. *MacLeod* and the difficulty of identifying the application of vicarious *mens rea* in Scotland, see Gerald H. Gordon, *The Criminal Law of Scotland* (Greens, 1967) at p. 267 *et seq.*, where he also considers the cases of *Patrick* v. *Kirkhope* (1894) 1 Adam 360; and *Campbell* v. *Cameron* (1915) 7 Adam 697 (the other two cases quoted at p. 268 being probably strict statutory liability cases) and concludes that there is no real Scottish authority for the imposition of a doctrine or principle of vicarious *mens rea*.

that he (the employer) had no knowledge whatsoever of the breach, nor did he subsequently give any approval to or make any adoption or ratification of the particular act when it became known to him and, moreover, that he had done his best to ensure that the requirements of the particular statute were complied with by all concerned. But that plea is not relevant in the situation where an absolute and unqualified liability is imposed by a statute.

In all cases of statutory liability the primary task is one of construction of the particular provision in order to ascertain (i) the reason for the obligation which is imposed, (ii) the person or persons (be it employers, occupiers, owners, licensees and employees or others) upon whom that obligation is imposed and (iii) the nature of the obligation itself—that is to say, whether it is absolute or qualified in any respect or even whether it is merely indicative of what should be done, without imposing a particular duty of compliance. All of these points may well be vital where a complaint is brought against the employer. Moreover, the employer's knowledge [6] or lack of knowledge can—as indicated above—also be vital. If knowledge is essential or is to be imputed to the employer in a statutory offence then the prosecution has the task of establishing that knowledge or the imputation of that knowledge. *Mens rea* may be essential in the common law crimes and offences but it is not necessarily essential in statutory offences.[7]

The doctrine of vicarious liability [8]—which operates broadly across the whole field of delict—has a different application in the field of criminal law and sometimes it seems to be doubtful whether the relationship of employer and employee is really relevant at all in criminal liability. The matter is difficult and it is all too easy to identify X *qua* employer and Y *qua* employee and to base liability on the contract of service formula. The approach of the criminal law seems to be to attach liability to X because he is, factually and legally, the owner of the particular business or the occupier of the particular factory premises or the licensee of the particular public-house or the retailer of the particular articles (be these, milk, drugs, coal or others). The fact that Y is his servant or employee is not so important as the fact that Y is deputising for him in conducting the particular business and therefore the act of Y is, to all intents and purposes, the act of X himself. It is admitted, of course, that modern

---

[6] See Gordon, *op. cit.* pp. 227–279 (for comments on the position regarding motor insurance in particular, see the learned author's comments at pp. 279–280) and also at pp. 280–281.

[7] For a very valuable monograph on this question of the relationship of *mens rea* to statutory offences, see J. Ll. J. Edwards, *Mens Rea in Statutory Offences* (Macmillan & Co., 1955). See also Gordon, *op. cit.*, particularly at pp. 235–258 (*re mens rea* in statutory offences). So far as the English law of employment is concerned see Fridman, *Modern Law of Employment, op. cit.*, particularly at pp. 533–555 and also generally at pp. 602–616; and supplement to December 31, 1966.

[8] For an excellent and very helpful article, see " Vicarious Liability for Crime " by J. Neil Young in 1967 J.R. 1–28. See also Gordon, *op. cit.* at pp. 258–285 (vicarious responsibility for crime).

industrial legislation [9] does tend to place a specific duty or liability upon employees themselves, in addition to that which is placed upon employers/ occupiers or owners, and any failure by an employee to obey that duty or obligation may render him liable to a criminal prosecution.[10]

Perhaps the statement by the late Lord Justice-General Strathclyde that " the doctrine of vicarious responsibility has no place in our criminal jurisprudence " [11] is the most important basic statement on the non-application of the doctrine of vicarious liability to the field of criminal law. But the matter is not quite so basic or simple as his lordship's pronouncement might lead us to believe, because even he admitted that the Licensing Acts were an exception to his dictum. In modern times, there has been a considerable development of statutory liability and the result has been a widening of vicarious liability not only in the field of delict but also in the field of criminal law. Lord Clyde carried the application of the doctrine further into the trading field when he stated that if a trader is " allowed to carry on his trade only under certain conditions the trader is . . . answerable for any breach of these conditions committed in the course of his trade." [12] From the practical viewpoint, therefore, regard must be had to the existence of the doctrine because for the reasons above considered, the prosecution will have to consider the circumstances of each case involving the employer and his employee and relate their actings to the statutory provisions. The existence of a " contract of service " [13] may be relevant and the " control test " will again be applied.[14] It is not essential for any summons or complaint to specify that the act was the servant's act nor is it essential to identify the particular employee,[15] but the late Lord Cooper did say that it was preferable and prudent to identify the employee, in the interest of fair play to the accused.[16]

One of the major difficulties in relation to the contract of employment

---

[9] For example, the Factories Act 1961; the Mines and Quarries Act 1954; and the Offices, Shops and Railway Premises Act 1963, all above-mentioned.

[10] See *Wright* v. *Ford Motor Company Ltd.* [1966] 2 All E.R. 518. Conversely, see the case of *Graham* v. *Strathern*, 1927 J.C. 29; 1927 S.N. 41; 1927 S.L.T. 368; see also *Glasgow Corporation* v. *Strathern*, 1929 J.C. 5; 1928 S.N. 127; 1929 S.L.T. 139.

[11] See *Gair* v. *Brewster*, 1916, 1 S.L.T. 388; 53 S.L.R. 550; 1916 S.C.(J.) 36.

[12] *Bean* v. *Sinclair*, 1930 S.L.T. 423; 1930 J.C. 31. His lordship also quoted from Lord McLaren in *Hogg* v. *Davidson* (1901) 3 F.(J.) 49 in respect of the maxim *qui facit per alium facit per se* which Lord McLaren said did not strictly apply to criminal cases.

[13] Including, of course, the important question of " scope and course of employment "— see *Scottish Farmers Dairy Co. (Glasgow)* v. *MacKenna*; *City and Suburban Dairies* v. *MacKenna*, 1918 J.C. 105; 1918, 2 S.L.T. 155; *Lawson* v. *Macgregor*, 1924 J.C. 112; 1924 S.L.T. 609; 61 S.L.R. 550; *Davidson* v. *Alexander*, 1927 S.N. 91; *Linstead* v. *Simpson*, 1927 J.C. 101; 1927 S.L.T. 644; *Duguid* v. *Fraser*, 1942 J.C. 1; 1942 S.L.T. 51; *Napier* v. *H.M. Advocate*, 1944 J.C. 61; 1944 S.L.T. 287; *Robertson* v. *Gray*, 1945 J.C. 113; 1945 S.L.T. 256; *Ferguson* v. *Campbell*, 1946 J.C. 28; 1946 S.L.T. 58; and *Shields* v. *Little*, 1954 J.C. 25; 1954 S.L.T. 146.

[14] See *Soutar* v. *Hutton*, 1916, 1 S.L.T. 380; 53 S.L.R. 547; where a licensee was held responsible (and not the partnership which owned the public-house concerned) for the offence of the barman. A recent English case on the same point is *Goodfellow* v. *Johnson* [1965] 1 All E.R. 941.

[15] See *McKenna* v. *Burnette*, 1916, 2 S.L.T. 293; 54 S.L.R. 135; 1917 J.C. 20; and *Hall* v. *Begg*, 1928 S.L.T. 336; 1928 J.C. 29; 1928 S.N. 48; and *Wilson* v. *Brown*, 1947 J.C. 81; 1947 S.L.T. 276.

[16] See *John Pollock and Sons* v. *Robertson*, 1945 S.L.T. 33.

is the situation where knowledge of the employee is imputed to the employer in a case where there has been delegation of authority to the employee. There are several important English cases on this topic and not much Scottish authority. What can be said, however, seems to be this—that the Scottish courts are very reluctant indeed to impute knowledge—and hence an immediate criminal liability—upon the employer. The starting point of this development in England was probably *Emary* v. *Nolloth* [17] where the court refused to convict without proof of knowledge, but there had not been in any case a proper delegation of authority to the licensee's employee. The *Emary* finding was subsequently approved in Scotland in *Greig* v. *Macleod*. [18] However the outstanding English case is *Vane* v. *Yiannopoullos* [19] where the whole matter was exhaustively examined. The particular act complained of in this case was the serving of drinks by a waitress to two customers who were not having a meal (that being an unlawful act in terms of the particular licence and the statute). The licensee was in the basement premises at the time and he had no knowledge whatsoever of what had been done, nor had he ever authorised the doing of such an act by his waitresses. The information laid against the licensee was dismissed by the magistrate and the Divisional Court, the House of Lords upholding the finding. Much reliance is placed upon Lord Evershed's speech in this case, particularly on the question of " knowledge." His lordship said ". . . where the relevant regulation imports the word ' knowingly ' as the condition of liability on the part of the licensee or proprietor . . . ' knowledge,' [20] that is *mens rea* in a real sense, . . . should normally be established as a fact, if he is to be held liable under the statute." Most judges and textwriters would agree with that statement. His lordship went on, however, to deal with " delegation " and his views have not been accepted by his own judicial colleagues. [21] The views expressed in *Vane's* case were examined in Scotland in *Thornley* v. *Hunter* [22] and Lord Strachan thought that the opinion of Lord McLaren in *Greig* v. *Macleod* might require to be reviewed in relation to the recent English case. Yet *Greig's* case was a very clear contravention of section 59 of the Licensing (Scotland) Act 1903 and, moreover, the statutory provision clearly allowed for agency and delegation by a licence-holder. However, in the recent case of *Noble* v. *Heatly* [23] the High Court of

---

[17] [1903] 2 K.B. 264.

[18] (1907) 15 S.L.T. 620.

[19] [1965] A.C. 486; [1964] 3 W.L.R. 1218; [1964] 3 All E.R. 821; an offence under s. 22 (1) (*a*) of the Licensing Act 1961 (an English statute). This case was followed by the Divisional Court in England in *John Henshall (Quarries) Ltd.* v. *Harvey* [1965] 2 Q.B. 233.

[20] Which may be inferred also from the circumstances—see *Dryden* v. *Mackay*, 1924 S.L.T. 457; and *Thornley* v. *Hunter*, 1965 S.L.T. 206.

[21] See particularly the comments of Lord Parker C.J. in *Ross* v. *Moss and Others* [1965] 2 Q.B. 396; [1965] 3 W.L.R. 416; [1965] 3 All E.R. 145 who referred to the uncertainty arising from *Vane's* case on the question of " delegation."

[22] *Cit. supra.*

[23] 1967 S.L.T. 26 (an appeal by stated case from Edinburgh Burgh Court).

Justiciary [24] apparently rejects the theories upon imputed knowledge and delegation which have been developed in England and is highly critical of Lord McLaren for adopting dicta of Lord Alverstone in *Emary* v. *Nolloth* above-mentioned and for misapplying these dicta in other respects. The Scottish judges found the speeches in *Vane's* case very helpful on the question of the application of the word " knowingly " although rejecting the concepts of imputed knowledge and delegation. If " knowingly " is an essential part of the offence there must be personal knowledge on the accused's part.

Other statutory phrases causing some difficulty of interpretation in criminal law are " permitting " and " causing." [25] If, however, as we have indicated earlier herein, the particular statutory provision is absolute or strict then there may be little hope of arguing upon the wording of the section and only a sound plea in mitigation may help to alleviate the position.

The present state of the law upon vicarious criminal liability may be said to be unsatisfactory and it is to be hoped that Lord Evershed's plea for uniformity of expression in *Vane's* case will not go unheard. There must also be a clarification of the defences available to an employer— and, in this respect, the language of the new industrial legislation (*e.g.*, the Factories Act 1961) in its application to Scotland could be used with advantage.[26]

Criminal breaches of the contract of employment in relation to certain industries and particular situations, as governed by sections 4 and 5 of the Conspiracy and Protection of Property Act 1875, and also statutory intimidation under section 7 of that Act have already been dealt with in an earlier chapter.[27] Offences arising under the Employers and Workmen Act 1875, particularly in relation to the contract or indenture of apprenticeship,[28] have also been previously considered. In addition to the range of offences arising under the Licensing (Scotland) Acts, the Food and Drugs Acts, the Weights and Measures Acts and kindred statutes, it should be noticed that the Race Relations Act 1968 might well give rise to another group of vicarious criminal offences in the field of employment.

It is, however, in the field of trade union law that there is most speculation at the moment. The Donovan Commission [29] did not favour the use of criminal sanctions against workers. The present Labour Government was caught very neatly on the horns of a political and economic dilemma. It must maintain friendly relations with the rank-and-file of trade union

---

[24] On this occasion, consisting of a bench of five judges.

[25] See Edwards, *op. cit. passim*; and J. Neil Young's article in 1967 J.R. 1, particularly pp. 14–18; also Gordon, *op. cit.* at pp. 264–266 and pp. 276–279.

[26] Some of the earlier procedural difficulties caused by draftsmanship in English legal form can be gauged from *Dumfries and Maxwelltown Co-operative Society* v. *Williamson*, 1950 J.C. 76; 1950 S.L.T. 305. For a note upon statutory defences generally, see Gordon, *op. cit.* pp. 274–276.

[27] *Supra*, Chap. 17.

[28] *Supra*, Chap. 21.

[29] See Chap. 17, *supra*, for notes and comments on the Donovan Report.

members but it cannot permit the country to be held to ransom by widespread and unofficial strikes which are prejudicing economic recovery and growth. Accordingly, the Government began by pinning its faith on the White Paper [30] and it intimated that a short statute would be introduced, as soon as possible and prior to the major Industrial Relations Act envisaged by the Donovan Commission and the White Paper. This short statute was to have as its purpose the outlawing of unofficial strikes by introducing the proposed " conciliation pause " of twenty-eight days. Any breach of the statutory provisions was to involve the offender in payment of a penalty or fine. Should payment of that fine or penalty not be made the offender was not to be imprisoned but his goods, gear and effects might be poinded and sold (presumably at the instigation of an Industrial Board) to satisfy the penalty or fine. This proposed legislation met with strong opposition from the unions.[31] The choice before the Cabinet was unenviable—either (i) support the new Bill and run the risk of alienating the rank-and-file of the trade union movement or (ii) come to the country and seek the backing of a majority of the electorate in a political climate which was not particularly favourable. A political crisis was neatly averted —and the method aroused much criticism in certain sections of the press and from the Conservative Opposition—in June 1969, when an agreement was reached between the Government and Trades Union Congress. In return for the abandonment of the new short Bill to deal with unofficial strikes (which has been mentioned above) the T.U.C. are understood to have promised greater participation by Congress itself in industrial relations and the creation of new consultative procedures which would enable Congress to step into the scene of any industrial dispute (whether official or unofficial or also a demarcation dispute). Presumably Congress will have to develop a disciplinary machinery to give some force to the agreements which are made, probably using the threat of disaffiliation from Congress as the ultimate sanction against any trade union which fails to keep its agreement or its undertakings.

The question of " corporate responsibility," that is to say the responsibility of a corporate body for criminal offences—particularly an offence involving *mens rea*—is an extremely difficult one to answer. Where an offence is a statutory offence involving absolute or strict liability, it is usual to find in that part of the statute dealing with offences and penalties a specific penalty being imposed upon a corporate body for any breach of a statutory provision. The responsible officers may be, and often are, liable to be prosecuted and may be imprisoned. There seems to be little (if any) reported Scottish authority, as Gerald Gordon points out,[32] for a corporate body being prosecuted for an offence involving *mens rea* and, indeed, no reported Scottish examples of a corporate body being prosecuted for a common law offence.

[30] " In Place of Strife," Cmnd. 3888 (January 1969).
[31] Indeed the Scottish Trades Union Congress at its April 1969 Conference in Rothesay firmly rejected the Government's White Paper.
[32] *Op. cit.* pp. 283–285, for a very helpful note on corporate responsibility.

APPENDIX 1

Employer's Liability (Defective Equipment) Act 1969 (c. 37)

An Act to make further provision with respect to the liability of an
employer for injury to his employee which is attributable to any
defect in equipment provided by the employer for the purposes of
the employer's business; and for purposes connected with the matter
aforesaid. [25th July 1969]

Extension of employer's liability for defective equipment

1.—(1) Where after the commencement of this Act—

(*a*) an employee suffers personal injury in the course of his
employment in consequence of a defect in equipment provided
by his employer for the purposes of the employer's business;
and

(*b*) the defect is attributable wholly or partly to the fault of a
third party (whether identified or not),

the injury shall be deemed to be also attributable to negligence on the
part of the employer (whether or not he is liable in respect of the injury
apart from this subsection), but without prejudice to the law relating to
contributory negligence and to any remedy by way of contribution or in
contract or otherwise which is available to the employer in respect of the
injury.

(2) In so far as any agreement purports to exclude or limit any liability
of an employer arising under subsection (1) of this section, the agreement
shall be void.

(3) In this section—

" business " includes the activities carried on by any public body;

" employee " means a person who is employed by another person
under a contract of service or apprenticeship and is so employed for the purposes of a business carried on by that other
person, and " employer " shall be construed accordingly;

" equipment " includes any plant and machinery, vehicle, aircraft
and clothing;

" fault " means negligence, breach of statutory duty or other act
or omission which gives rise to liability in tort in England
and Wales or which is wrongful and gives rise to liability in
damages in Scotland; and

" personal injury " includes loss of life, any impairment of a
person's physical or mental condition and any disease.

(4) This section binds the Crown, and persons in the service of the
Crown shall accordingly be treated for the purposes of this section as

employees of the Crown if they would not be so treated apart from this subsection.

Short title, commencement and extent

2.—(1) This Act may be cited as the Employer's Liability (Defective Equipment) Act 1969.

(2) This Act shall come into force on the expiration of the period of three months beginning with the date on which it is passed.

(3) Nothing in the Government of Ireland Act 1920 shall prevent the Parliament of Northern Ireland from making laws for purposes similar to the purposes of section 1 of this Act.

(4) This Act, except the foregoing subsection, does not extend to Northern Ireland.

APPENDIX 2

Age of Majority (Scotland) Act 1969 (c. 39)

An Act to amend the law of Scotland relating to the age of majority; and for connected purposes. [25th July 1969]

Reduction of age of majority to 18

1.—(1) As from the date on which this Act comes into force a person shall attain majority on attaining the age of eighteen instead of on attaining the age of twenty-one; and a person shall attain majority on that date if he has then already attained the age of eighteen but not the age of twenty-one.

(2) The foregoing subsection applies for the purposes of any rule of law, and, in the absence of a definition or of any indication of a contrary intention, for the construction of " major ", " majority ", " full age ", " perfect age ", " complete age ", " lawful age ", " minor ", " minority ", " under age ", " less age " and similar expressions in—

(*a*) any statutory provision, whether passed or made before, on or after the date on which this Act comes into force; and

(*b*) any deed executed on or after that date other than a deed made in the exercise of a special power of appointment where the deed creating the power was executed before that date.

(3) In the statutory provisions specified in Schedule 1 to this Act, for any reference to the age of twenty-one years or twenty-five years there shall be substituted a reference to the age of eighteen years.

(4) This section does not affect the construction of any such expression as is referred to in subsection (2) of this section in any of the statutory provisions described in Schedule 2 to this Act.

(5) The Secretary of State may, by order made by statutory instrument, amend any provision in any local enactment passed on or before the date on which this Act comes into force by substituting a reference to the age of eighteen years for any reference therein to the age of twenty-one years; and any statutory instrument containing an order under this subsection shall be subject to annulment in pursuance of a resolution of either House of Parliament.

(6) Notwithstanding any rule of law, a testamentary instrument or codicil executed before the date on which this Act comes into force shall not be treated for the purposes of this section as made on or after that date by reason only that the instrument or codicil is confirmed by a codicil executed on or after that date.

(7) This section shall not affect the construction of any statutory provision where it is incorporated in and has effect as part of any deed the construction of which is not affected by this section.

(8) This section shall not prevent the making of an adoption order or provisional adoption order under the Adoption Act 1958 in respect of a person who has attained the age of eighteen if the application for the order was made before this Act comes into force, and in relation to any such case that Act shall have effect as if this section had not been enacted.

(9) Section 4 of the Entail Amendment (Scotland) Act 1875 (consent to disentail may be given at 21) is hereby repealed.

(10) In this section—

" statutory provision " means any enactment and any order, rule, regulation, byelaw or other instrument made in the exercise of a power conferred by any enactment; and

" deed " includes any disposition, contract, instrument or writing (not being a statutory provision), whether *inter vivos* or *mortis causa.*

Short title, interpretation, commencement and extent

2.—(1) This Act may be cited as the Age of Majority (Scotland) Act 1969.

(2) Except where the context otherwise requires, any reference in this Act to any enactment shall be construed as a reference to that enactment as amended, extended or applied by or under any other enactment.

(3) This Act shall come into force on such date as the Secretary of State may appoint by order made by statutory instrument.

(4) This Act shall extend to Scotland only.

SCHEDULES

Section 1 (3)   SCHEDULE 1

STATUTORY PROVISIONS AMENDED BY SUBSTITUTING
18 FOR 21 OR 25 YEARS

PART I

ENACTMENTS

	Short Title	*Section*	*Subject matter*
c. 6.	The Tutors Act 1474.		Nearest agnate over 25 to be tutor.
c. 12.	The Prescription Act 1617.		Prescription not to run during minority.
c. 6.	The Diligence Act 1621.		Right of person under 25 and of his successor to redeem comprised lands.
c. 4.	The Minority Act 1663.		Right of person under 21 to surplus of maills and duties from comprised lands.
c. 85.	The Oaths of Minors Act 1681.		Ratification of writ by oath of minor not to deprive him of right of reduction.
c. 120.	The Court of Session Act 1825.	Section 25.	Limitation of time for appeal to House of Lords.
c. 36.	The Entail Amendment Act 1848.	Sections 1, 2 and 3.	Power to disentail.
c. 22.	The Trade Union Act Amendment Act 1876.	Section 9.	Person under 21 but above 16 eligible as member of trade union but not of committee of management etc.

Short Title	Section	Subject matter
c. 25. The Friendly Societies Act 1896.	Section 36.	Person under 21 eligible as member of society and branches but not of committee etc.
c. 44. The Customs and Excise Act 1952.	Section 244 (2) (a).	Entry invalid unless made by person over 21.
c. 46. The Hypnotism Act 1952.	Section 3.	Persons under 21 not to be hypnotised at public entertainment.
c. 63. The Trustee Savings Banks Act 1954.	Section 23.	Payments to persons under 21.
c. 5. The Adoption Act 1958.	Section 57 (1).	Definition of " infant " by reference to age of 21.
c. 61. The Mental Health (Scotland) Act 1960.	Section 45 (4) (c).	Provision where nearest relative of patient is under 21.
	Section 47 (1).	Meaning of " nearest relative " of patient who has not attained the age of 21.
c. 57. The Trusts (Scotland) Act 1961.	Section 1 (2).	Person over age of pupillarity but under 21 incapable of assenting to variation of trust purposes etc.
c. 37. The Building Societies Act 1962.	Section 9.	Person under 21 eligible as member of building society but cannot vote or hold office.
	Section 47.	Receipt given to building society by person under 21 to be valid.
c. 2. The Betting, Gaming and Lotteries Act 1963.	Section 22 (1) and (3).	Offence of sending betting advertisements to persons under 21.
c. 12. The Industrial and Provident Societies Act 1965.	Section 20.	Person under 21 but above 16 eligible as member of society but not of committee etc.
c. 49. The Registration of Births, Deaths and Marriages (Scotland) Act 1965.	Section 43 (5), (6) and (7).	Application for change of name etc. by person over 16 and under 21.

PART II

REGULATIONS AND RULES

Title	Provision	Subject matter
1929 S.R. & O. 1048. The Trustee Savings Banks Regulations 1929.	Regulation 28 (2).	Payments to persons under 21.
1933 S.R. & O. 1149. The Savings Certificates Regulations 1933.	Regulation 2 (1) (a).	Persons entitled to purchase and hold certificates.
	Regulation 21 (2).	Persons under disability.
1946 S.R. & O. 1156. The North of Scotland Hydro-Electric Board (Borrowing and Stock) Regulations 1946.	Regulation 36 (1) and (2).	Stock held by persons under 21.
1949 S.I. 751. The Gas (Stock) Regulations 1949.	Regulation 19 (1) and (2).	Stock held by persons under 21.
1953 S.I. 42. The Local and Other Authorities (Scotland) (Transfer of Stock) Regulations 1953.	Regulation 12 (1) and (2).	Stock held by persons under 21.
1955 S.I. 1752. The South of Scotland Electricity Board (Borrowing and Stock) Regulations 1955.	Regulation 30 (1) and (2).	Stock held by persons under 21.
1956 S.I. 1657. The Premium Savings Bonds Regulations 1956.	Regulation 2 (1).	Persons entitled to purchase and hold bonds.
	Regulation 12 (2).	Persons under disability.

Title	Provision	Subject matter
1957 S.I. 2228. The Electricity (Stock) Regulations 1957.	Regulation 22 (1) and (2).	Stock held by persons under 21.
1963 S.I. 935. The Exchange of Securities (General) Rules 1963.	Rule 1 (1).	Definition of " minor ".
1965 S.I. 1420. The Government Stock Regulations 1965.	Regulation 14 (1), (2), (3) and (5).	Stock held by persons under 21.
1965 S.I. 1839. The Registration of Births, Still-births, Deaths and Marriages (Prescription of Forms) (Scotland) Regulations 1965.	Schedule 24.	Recording of change of name or surname.

Section 1 (4)   SCHEDULE 2

STATUTORY PROVISIONS UNAFFECTED BY SECTION 1

    1. The Regency Acts 1937 to 1953.

    2. The Representation of the People Acts (and any regulations, rules or other instruments thereunder) and section 50 of the Local Government (Scotland) Act 1947.

    3. Any statutory provision relating to income tax (including surtax), capital gains tax, corporation tax or estate duty.

APPENDIX 3

Employers' Liability (Compulsory Insurance) Act 1969 (c. 57)

An Act to require employers to insure against their liability for personal injury to their employees; and for purposes connected with the matter aforesaid.   [22nd October 1969]

Insurance against liability for employees

1.—(1) Except as otherwise provided by this Act, every employer carrying on any business in Great Britain shall insure, and maintain insurance, under one or more approved policies with an authorised insurer or insurers against liability for bodily injury or disease sustained by his employees, and arising out of and in the course of their employment in Great Britain in that business, but except in so far as regulations otherwise provide not including injury or disease suffered or contracted outside Great Britain.

(2) Regulations may provide that the amount for which an employer is required by this Act to insure and maintain insurance shall, either generally or in such cases or classes of case as may be prescribed by the regulations, be limited in such manner as may be so prescribed.

(3) For the purposes of this Act—

    (*a*) " approved policy " means a policy of insurance not subject to any conditions or exceptions prohibited for those purposes by regulations;

    (*b*) " authorised insurer " means a person or body of persons lawfully carrying on in Great Britain insurance business of any class relevant for the purposes of Part II of the Companies Act 1967 and issuing the policy or policies in the course thereof;

    (*c*) " business " includes a trade or profession, and includes any activity carried on by a body of persons, whether corporate or unincorporate;

    (*d*) except as otherwise provided by regulations, an employer not having a place of business in Great Britain shall be deemed not to carry on business there.

Employees to be covered

2.—(1) For the purposes of this Act the term " employee " means an individual who has entered into or works under a contract of service or apprenticeship with an employer whether by way of manual labour, clerical work or otherwise, whether such contract is expressed or implied, oral or in writing.

(2) This Act shall not require an employer to insure—

    (*a*) in respect of an employee of whom the employer is the husband, wife, father, mother, grandfather, grandmother, step-father, step-mother, son, daughter, grandson, granddaughter, stepson, stepdaughter, brother, sister, half-brother or half-sister; or

(b) except as otherwise provided by regulations, in respect of employees not ordinarily resident in Great Britain.

Employers exempted from insurance

3.—(1) This Act shall not require any insurance to be effected by—

(a) any such authority as is mentioned in subsection (2) below; or

(b) any body corporate established by or under any enactment for the carrying on of any industry or part of an industry, or of any undertaking, under national ownership or control; or

(c) in relation to any such cases as may be specified in the regulations, any employer exempted by regulations.

(2) The authorities referred to in subsection (1) (a) above are the Common Council of the City of London, the Greater London Council, the council of a London borough, the council of a county, county borough or country district in England or Wales, a county, town or district council in Scotland, any joint board or joint committee in England and Wales or joint committee in Scotland which is so constituted as to include among its members representatives of any such council, and any police authority.

Certificates of insurance

4.—(1) Provision may be made by regulations for securing that certificates of insurance in such form and containing such particulars as may be prescribed by the regulations, are issued by insurers to employers entering into contracts of insurance in accordance with the requirements of this Act and for the surrender in such circumstances as may be so prescribed of certificates so issued.

(2) Where a certificate of insurance is required to be issued to an employer in accordance with regulations under subsection (1) above, the employer (subject to any provision made by the regulations as to the surrender of the certificate) shall during the currency of the insurance and such further period (if any) as may be provided by regulations—

(a) comply with any regulations requiring him to display copies of the certificate of insurance for the information of his employees;

(b) produce the certificate of insurance or a copy thereof on demand to any inspector duly authorised by the Secretary of State for the purposes of this Act and produce or send the certificate or a copy thereof to such other persons, at such place and in such circumstances as may be prescribed by regulations;

(c) permit the policy of insurance or a copy thereof to be inspected by such persons and in such circumstances as may be so prescribed.

(3) A person who fails to comply with a requirement imposed by or under this section shall be liable on summary conviction to a fine not exceeding £50.

Penalty for failure to insure

5. An employer who on any day is not insured in accordance with this Act when required to be so shall be guilty of an offence and shall be liable on summary conviction to a fine not exceeding two hundred pounds; and where an offence under this section committed by a corporation has been committed with the consent or connivance of, or facilitated by any neglect on the part of, any director, manager, secretary or other officer of the corporation, he, as well as the corporation, shall be deemed to be guilty of that offence and shall be liable to be proceeded against and punished accordingly.

Regulations

6.—(1) The Secretary of State may by statutory instrument make regulations for any purpose for which regulations are authorised to be made by this Act, but any such statutory instrument shall be subject to annulment in pursuance of a resolution of either House of Parliament.

(2) Any regulations under this Act may make different provision for different cases or classes of case, and may contain such incidental and supplementary provisions as appear to the Secretary of State to be necessary or expedient for the purposes of the regulations.

Short title, extent and commencement

7.—(1) This Act may be cited as the Employers' Liability (Compulsory Insurance) Act 1969.

(2) This Act shall not extend to Northern Ireland.

(3) This Act shall come into force for any purpose on such date as the Secretary of State may by order contained in a statutory instrument appoint, and the purposes for which this Act is to come into force at any time may be defined by reference to the nature of an employer's business, or to that of an employee's work, or in any other way.

INDEX

PRINTED IN GREAT BRITAIN
BY
THE EASTERN PRESS LTD.
OF LONDON AND READING

WITHDRAWN

from

STIRLING UNIVERSITY LIBRARY